THE
LITTLE BROWN
ENCYCLOPEDIA
OF
ANIMALS

THE LITTLE BROWN ENCYCLOPEDIA OF ANIMALS

Little, Brown and Company

Contents

Introduction, 5

Fishes: The First Invertebrates, 6

Amphibians and Reptiles, 54

Birds, 122

Mammals, 176

Index, 252

A LITTLE, BROWN BOOK

This edition first published 2000

Copyright © 2000 Little, Brown and Company
Copyright © 1968, 1969, 1970, 1976 Phoebus Publishing
Company/BPC Publishing Ltd
Copyright © 1968 Macdonald & Co (Publishers) Ltd

All rights reserved. No part of this publication may be
reproduced, stored in a retrieval system, or transmitted,
in any form or by any means, without the prior permission
in writing of the publisher, nor be otherwise circulated in
any form of binding or cover other than that in which it is
published and without a similar condition including this
condition being imposed on the subsequent purchaser.

This book is adapted from *Encyclopedia of The Animal Kingdom*

ISBN 0-316-85691-6

Printed in Spain

Little, Brown and Company (UK)
Brettenham House
Lancaster Place
London WC2E 7EN

Introduction

The word 'animal' is often equated with mammals in every day usage, but the term includes a wide range of organisms from the single-celled protozoans to humans. This being so, it is worth restating the characteristics that distinguish animals from plants: animals cannot manufacture their own food, they have a sensitivity that is usually operative through special sense organs, are capable of locomotion, and have no cellulose cell walls.

It is usually stated that there are a million species of animals. More correctly, this should be at least a million known species. By 'known' is meant species that have been given a specific name and of which a description has been published in a recognised scientific journal. It is important to make this distinction because the truth is that there are not enough zoologists classifying animals to keep pace with the collection of new forms. In addition, there must be large numbers of species yet to be discovered, and estimates of the true number of animal species living today vary between three and ten million.

The great majority of the million usually referred to are insects, of which there are at least 750,000. If we ever reach the point where all the species of insects have been described and named the total will probably be nearer three million.

There must be few, if any, large animals yet to be discovered. Among mammals, small species are occasionally discovered, especially mice, shrews and bats.

Most of the species yet to be discovered, apart from insects, must comprise those of microscopic size, particularly Protozoa, as well as the parasitic species, such as the various kinds of so-called worms, like the threadworms and flatworms. There must also be a very large number of mites yet to be identified and described. Thus we have the anomaly that most of the most familiar animals, including those of large bulk and those upon which the human economy is based because they represent food, beasts of burden or sources of supply of raw materials, represent only a small minority in terms of numbers of species and populations.

The present day classification of animals emerged after a series of tentative attempts on the part of a number of authors to arrange the animals in orderly groups, but the real breakthrough came with the acceptance of Darwin's theory of natural selection and involved a long arrangement along evolutionary lines. The theory of evolution itself had been mooted long before Darwin's days, but his theory of how species arose gave the maximum publicity to an idea that had previously only a select few scholars.

Arrangement on an evolutionary basis meant that the classification was based mainly on the study of comparative anatomy. In practice, this meant putting the simplest, least organised animals at the top. The rest were arranged intermediately according to the degree of organisation of their bodily structures.

The most that can be done to represent the millions of species, and this is the purpose of this volume, is to give a skeletal representation in pictorial and textual form of the living members of this vast assemblage of organisms we refer to when we speak of the animal world.

In the following pages, a selection of animals known to be in existance today are detailed, representing the vertebrates and comprising of four sections: fishes, amphibians and reptiles, birds and mammals. With a few exceptions, most of the phyla are illustrated and the effect is to provide within two covers a brief outline of the scope of the animal world, its components arranged in their evolutionary sequence, so far as we know it.

Fishes: The First Vertebrates

It is an accepted convention to visualize the classification of the animal kingdom as starting with the Protozoa, the single-celled animals typified by the amoeba and ending with the mammals, which includes the human species. This resulted in a catch-phrase, less used today than formerly 'from amoeba to man'. When set down on paper in tabular form, such a classification gives the impression of a steady and continuous progression from the Protozoa, through the lower invertebrates and the higher invertebrates to the vertebrates. It must be nearer the truth to suppose that somewhere among the more organized echelons of the lower invertebrates there came a parting of the ways. One path led to the higher invertebrates, the other to the vertebrates. This bifurcation may have occurred at the level of the phylum Echinodermata (starfishes, sea-urchins and others). There is, however, a distinct gap here in our knowledge that can be bridged only by speculation based on fragmentary information, and it is not our purpose here to discuss these questions.

It is sufficient to note that the first true vertebrates were jawless fishes and that there is living today a form of pre-vertebrate, the lancelet, which embodies all that could be expected in the ancestral vertebrate. How it was evolved from an invertebrate stock is, however, still shrouded in mystery. That a form like the lancelet must have preceded the fishes seems reasonable.

The earliest fossils of fishes have been taken from rocks of the Ordovician period, 450 million years old. They are recognizable as being fishes, though they lacked jaws. Relatively few species of these jawless fishes have been discovered and fewer still have survived. From this ancestral stock, however, sprang two main lines of descent: the cartilaginous fishes typified by the sharks, skates and rays, which were almost entirely marine, and the bony fishes, represented by the more familiar fishes in our present-day rivers and lakes as well as many others in the sea. The bony fishes outnumber the cartilaginous fishes by more than thirty to one. The latter have, however, the distinction of having produced one of the largest of all animals, the whale shark, reportedly having a maximum length of 60 ft and a weight of 20 tons or more. This leviathan is outmatched only by the larger whales, particularly the blue whale. On the other hand, the bony fishes include the smallest of all vertebrates, a goby from the freshwaters of the Philippines which, fully grown, is under $\frac{1}{2}$ inch long.

The first primitive jawless fishes of the Ordovician period found an environment inhabited by invertebrates, in which the only animals rivalling them in size and agility were the cephalopod molluscs, represented by the ammonites and belemnites, the ancestors of modern squids, octopuses and cuttlefishes. It was near to being an empty ecological niche and they took full advantage of it to diversify. By the middle of the Devonian period, a little over 50 million years later, they had evolved many species and spread widely through both salt and fresh waters of the world, so much so that the Devonian period has become known as the Age of Fishes. The jawless fishes, which appeared first, soon began to decline in numbers, and are represented today only by the lampreys and hagfishes. The cartilaginous fishes fared better but in numbers of species are poorer today than in those distant times. It was the bony fishes, the last of the three groups to appear, that finally became dominant, as they still are.

It is worth noting, within the context of what has been said previously about evolutionary trends, the courses followed by the three groups. The jawless fishes threw off relatively few species and there were no startling variations in form. So far as we know their colours were mainly unobtrusive, if not positively drab. Much the same can be said of the cartilaginous fishes. They did achieve a change in shape so that they are basically of two forms, the typical fusiform shark and the flattened rays and skates. Apart from this, in these two groups, the one free-swimming, the other bottom-living, there is no great diversity in behaviour, exploitation of environment or colour. The bony fishes, especially those of today, combine a remarkable range of size, a great diversity of colour and bodily adornment and an exploitation of almost every kind of aquatic habitat.

The major groups of fishes are as follows:

Class Agnatha
 (lampreys and hagfishes)   45 species
Class Chondrichthyes
 (cartilaginous fishes,
 sharks and rays)   600 species
Class Osteichthyes (or
 Pisces) (bony fishes)   20,000 species

Lancelet

A semi-transparent, elongated marine animal usually under 2½ in. long, the lancelet is shaped rather like a fish; it swims like a fish, too, by sideways undulations of its flattened body, which is pointed at each end. But it lacks the paired fins of a fish and—for other reasons—cannot qualify as a vertebrate. The various species are widely distributed in the seas throughout the world. On the coast of Amoy, China, 35 tons of lancelets are harvested for food each year.

*Lancelets are found in tropical and temperate seas, generally close to the shore. Originally they were given the scientific name **Amphioxus**, which means 'sharp at both ends', but this has now been changed to **Branchiostoma** for reasons given at the end of this article, and amphioxus, the anglicised form of the scientific name, is now used as an alternative common name, especially in biological laboratories.*

Taking evasive action

Most of the time, the lancelet lies with its hind end buried in sand or gravel, the head pointing more or less vertically upwards above the surface. The beating of cilia around its mouth creates a current drawing water in through the mouth and thence through a sort of sieve, known as the branchial basket, in the front half of the body. The water passes through the sieve and out through a pore near the middle of the body, on the underside. When disturbed, the lancelet leaves the sand, zig-zags rapidly around in the water above and then dives back into the sand a few seconds later.

Curtains of food

The branchial basket is an elongated oval in shape with vertical slits on either side. It serves as a set of gills for taking oxygen from the water flowing through it, and also for capturing food. Along the floor of the basket is a groove known as the endostyle. This constantly secretes mucus that is carried up the internal sides of the branchial basket by the beating of cilia lining the walls, in a kind of curtain. This curtain of mucus contains many minute gaps through which water can flow through the gill slits and so to the outside. Food particles, such as diatoms, are, however, trapped on the inside of the mucus curtain which continues to be driven upwards by the cilia until it reaches another longitudinal groove in the roof of the basket. There another set of cilia drive the mucus backward into the stomach where it is digested.

Lopsided larvae

The lancelet lives 1–4 years, varying with the species. The eggs and sperm of the lancelet are released into the sea to be fertilised. About 8 hours after the egg is fertilised a ciliated embryo has been formed which swims about and then changes into an elongated, lopsided larva. This eventually develops into the adult. The lopsided larvae is $\frac{1}{3}$–$\frac{2}{3}$ in. long but sometimes it grows much larger than this and becomes sexually mature without changing into an adult. This process is called neoteny. These giant larvae of the lancelet were once regarded as a separate species and given the name *Amphioxides*.

Vertebrate/invertebrate?

In 1774 a strange little animal was picked up on the coast of Cornwall and sent, preserved in alcohol, to the celebrated Russian naturalist, Pallas. There seems to be no record of who picked it up or why it was sent right across Europe when there were many competent naturalists in Britain who might have examined it. At all events, Pallas described it in a footnote in a book he was publishing, giving a very brief description in Latin and naming the animal *Limax lanceolatus* under the impression that it was a slug. Half a century later, on December 21, 1831, Jonathan Couch, one of the leading English naturalists of that time, was walking along the shore near Polperro, in Cornwall, after a storm. It is the practice of some naturalists to go beachcombing after a storm to see what specimens may have been thrown ashore. Apparently Couch turned over a flat pebble lying on the sand about 50 feet from the ebbing tide and saw a tiny tail sticking out of the sand. He dug out the rest of the animal and was able to watch it in a sea-water aquarium and see how active it was. Couch sent the specimen to William Yarrell (the English zoologist) who in 1836 described it in a book *A History of British Fishes* as a fish of very low organisation to which he gave the name *Amphioxus*. He also recognised it as the same animal that Pallas had looked at. Previously, however, in 1834, the Italian naturalist Costa had published a description of the same animal collected from the shore at Naples and had given it the name *Branchiostoma lubricum*. This brief history accounts for the changing of the animal's name. It had become generally known as *Amphioxus* because Costa's description had been overlooked and was not brought to light until 45 years ago. The international rules of nomenclature state that the first name proposed for an animal must be the one used even if it has been overlooked for years. So the name given by Costa had to take precedence over Yarrell's *Amphioxus*.

The relationship of the lancelet with the rest of the animal kingdom remains one of the most interesting features of the animal. Amphioxus resembles the vertebrates in having a dorsal nerve cord lying above a stiffening rod, the notochord, and an arrangement of muscles along its tail much as in a fish. At the same time it lacks a backbone, jaws, or indeed any bone, and a brain as well as the eyes and other sense-organs associated with the brain. So it is not a vertebrate, yet comes very near to being one. The current view is that both amphioxus and the vertebrates evolved from the same ancestors as the sea-squirts or tunicates, which feed in much the same way as amphioxus but are anchored to a solid support when adult and look most unlike amphioxus. They do, however, have a free-swimming tadpole-like larva. If this were to become sexually mature without taking on the sessile adult form, like the 'amphioxides' larva, then we should have something like both the ancestral amphioxus and the ancestral vertebrate.

phylum	**Chordata**
subphylum	**Cephalochordata**
family	**Branchiostomidae**
genus & species	***Branchiostoma lanceolatum*** ***B. californiense*** others

Heads upwards, a pair of lancelets sift the water for food. The fish-like muscle blocks can be seen along the body. The squares showing through the skin of the belly are reproductive organs.

Lamprey

Lampreys look like eels and have sometimes been called lamprey eels or lamper eels. They are, however, jawless like the hagfish which is their nearest relative, and, like the hagfishes, lampreys are not true fishes but direct descendants of the jawless Ostracoderms. There are about 30 species, both marine and freshwater. Some are parasitic on fish, others are not. Lampreys live in temperate regions of northern and southern hemispheres. The sea lamprey, the best known, lives on both sides of the North Atlantic. Members of the genus **Lampetra** *are found in Europe and Asia as well as North America. In the southern hemisphere, species of* **Geotria** *and* **Mordacia** *are found off the coasts of Chile, Australia and New Zealand.* **Geotria** *has a large fleshy bag, of unknown function, almost hiding its mouth.*

Pump-like gills

The eel-like body of a lamprey has a slimy scaleless skin. Its fins are found along the centre-line of the body. There is a single nostril in the middle of the head, which leads behind into a blind sac. The eyes are well-developed. The head ends in front in a large funnel-like mouth with horny teeth lining the funnel, some of the teeth being on the muscular tongue protruding at the base of the funnel. Behind the head is a row of small circular gill openings running along each side of the body. Inside are seven pairs of gill pouches lined with blood-red gill-filaments which open into a tube that is blind at one end and opens into the back of the mouth in front. A lamprey can breathe by taking in water through its mouth to pass across the gills. More often, because the mouth is so much used as a sucker, a lamprey breathes by contracting muscles around the gill-pouches, driving the water out. As the muscles relax water is drawn in. This pumping action seems to be helped by movements of the sinuous latticework of cartilage, the branchial basket, surrounding the gill-pouches.

The lamprey feeds by pressing the circular edge of its mouth against the side of a fish which it finds by eyesight, not by smell as in the hagfish. It protrudes its tongue and punctures the fish's skin by rasping the teeth on it; the fish starts to bleed and the blood is sucked in by the lamprey. It sucks in a few fragments of flesh as well, but it feeds more on the blood than on the flesh. Not all adult lampreys feed in this way; some species do not feed as adults.

Lampreys barricade their nests

There are three species of lamprey in Europe. They are usually spoken of as the sea lamprey, river lamprey and brook lamprey. It is better to use the second's alternative name of lampern, because it also spends its adult life in the sea. The brook lamprey is also known as the pride. It lives all the time in freshwater. Those lampreys living in the sea enter rivers to spawn. The migration begins in winter and by spring the lampreys are in the rivers and building nests. They swim strongly and can make their way over rocks or up vertical walls, hauling themselves up with the sucker mouth. The male lamprey makes a nest by holding pebbles in its sucker mouth and moving them downstream to form a barricade. In a depression made upstream of this, the eggs will later be laid.

△ *The hooded larva of a brook lamprey.*
▽ *Lamprey skeleton showing branchial basket, which supports the gill pouches, and the viciously toothed, circular mouth cartilage, which serves instead of jaws.*
▽▽ *Powerful sucker of a brook lamprey.*

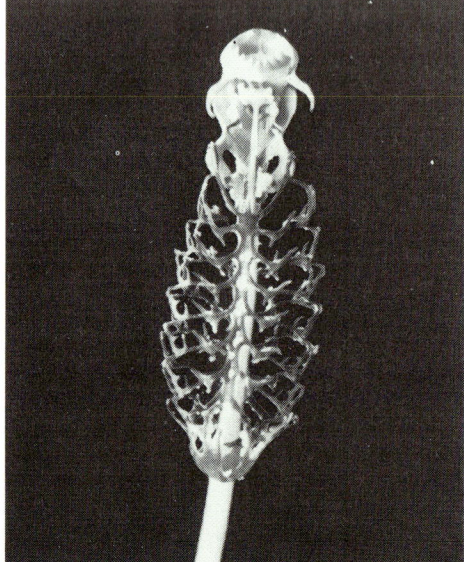

The females arrive later than the males and then help build the nest, the two sometimes combining to move large pebbles. After spawning the adults drift downriver to die. The eggs are $\frac{1}{25}$ in. diameter and they hatch 2 weeks later. The larva, or ammocoete, was once thought to be a different species. It is small and worm-like, and lives by burrowing in the sand or mud and coming out at night to feed on particles of plant and animal bodies. These are strained through fleshy tentacles (cirri) on a hood-like mouth and passed into the gullet where they are caught by sticky secretions on a special groove, the endostyle. This endostyle becomes the thyroid gland—the chemical controller of growth—in the adult.

After 3–5 years of larval life the ammocoete, now 4–5 in. long, changes into an adult lamprey. The hooded mouth becomes funnel-shaped, the cirri are replaced by horny teeth, the nostril moves from the front of the snout to the top of the head, the eye grows larger. The sea lamprey becomes silvery and goes down to the sea, as does the lampern, but the latter does not parasitize fishes. Instead it feeds on molluscs, crustaceans and worms. The pride or brook lamprey, which remains in rivers, does not feed when adult.

Surfeit of lampreys

It is often said that King John died of a surfeit of lampreys. It was, in fact, Henry I. It was King John who fined the men of Gloucester 40 marks because 'they did not pay him sufficient respect in the matter of lampreys'. American history is more recent and has to do with a surfeit of lampreys in the Great Lakes. Gradually, over the years, the lampreys made their way up the New York State Barge Canal and the Welland Canal and became firmly established in the Great Lakes. There they ruined a commercial fishery that had been yielding a yearly catch of 11 million pounds of lake trout and other fishes. A big research programme was set going to find ways of killing off the lampreys. Weirs were built to stop further migrations into the lakes, the lampreys were poisoned and electrocuted. Some success was achieved but now that a poison that kills the larvae has been discovered lampreys are being wiped out and the fisheries are recovering.

class	**Agnatha**
order	**Petromyzoniformes**
family	**Petromyzonidae**
genera & species	*Petromyzon marinus* sea lamprey *Lampetra fluviatilis* lampern *L. planeri* pride others

Maneater shark

A single species of heavy-bodied shark bears the ominous name of maneater, or great white shark. It grows to 20 ft long or more and is bluish-grey to slate grey above, shading to white below, with fins growing darker towards their edges. It also has a conspicuous black spot just behind where the pectoral fin joins the body. Its snout is pointed and overhangs an awesome, crescent-shaped mouth which is armed with a frightful array of triangular saw-edged teeth. In large individuals the largest teeth may be 3 in. high. The pectoral fins are large. The pelvic fins, and the second dorsal and the anal fins, which lie opposite each other, are small. The tail fin is nearly symmetrical instead of having the upper lobe larger as in most sharks. There is a large keel along the side of the tail in front of the tail fin.

The maneater belongs to the family of mackerel sharks, which includes the porbeagles and mako shark. These are similar to the maneater but smaller, up to 12 ft long being about the limit. They feed on fishes such as mackerel, herring, cod, whiting, hake and dogfish. They also provide sport for sea anglers because of the fight they put up when hooked. Most mackerel sharks are dangerous to man.

The maneater is found in all warm seas and occasionally strays into temperate seas. It lives in the open sea, coming inshore only when the shallow seas are near deep water. One maneater was caught at a depth of 4 200 ft off Cuba and other evidence also suggests the shark is a deepwater fish.

Not as big as was believed

Maneaters may be much maligned monsters. They are neither as big as is generally said nor as voracious. Very little is known about the habits of the maneater except what can be deduced from its shape and the contents of the stomachs of individuals caught and dissected. Its shape suggests it can swim rapidly, but from those hooked and landed with angling tackle it is fairly certain the maneater is not as swift as the smaller mako. Since young have been found in a female's body the species is presumed to bear its young alive. The maneater is said to be of uncertain temper, yet skin divers report it to be wary and even easily scared. It is probably less dangerous than the mako which is known to attack small boats as well as swimmers. The maneater's bad reputation probably rests on its large size and fearsome teeth, coupled with occasional attacks that look deliberate. On the first of these two points it is hard to speak with certainty. The largest maneater of which we have reliable information measured 36½ ft long, and this one was caught a century ago, off Port Fairey, Australia. Most of the others are between 20 and 25 ft. One that was 21 ft long weighed 7 100 lb; another 17 ft long weighed 2 800 lb. Maneaters have been said by authoritative writers to grow to over 40 ft but there is no solid evidence.

Nothing refused

Several books have been published in the last 10 years which give details of shark attacks. Two are devoted solely to the subject. They are: *Shark Attack* by V M Coppleson, an Australian doctor who has collected the case histories of injuries from sharks, and *Danger Shark!* by Jean Campbell Butler, whose narrative is based on the New Orleans Shark Conference of 1958, at which shark researchers pooled their findings. Putting the information from these and other sources together, there is the general impression that sharks, the maneater in particular, will try to eat anything that looks like food. As a result they snap at living animals, including bathers or people who have accidentally fallen into the sea, as well as corpses and carrion, even inanimate objects such as tin cans. The attacks on boats, as in the attack on the 14ft cod boat off Nova Scotia in 1953, by a maneater, which left some of its teeth in the timbers, are probably due to mistake rather than malice. Several times whole human corpses have been taken from sharks' stomachs but they proved to be of people who had been drowned.

Maneater or corpse swallower?

There are several instances of maneaters found to contain the intact bodies of other animals. These include a 100lb sea-lion, a 50lb seal, and sharks 6–7 ft long. While human beings have been badly bitten, usually producing frightful wounds, some of which have proved fatal, there is little evidence of limbs being severed, and less of a person being swallowed whole. Two things have also emerged from the studies so far made. The first is that sharks digest food very slowly and animal remains swallowed take days, even weeks, to be digested. The other, which seems linked with this but is learned more from sharks in captivity, is that sharks seem to eat little.

Extenuating circumstances

When one speaks of malice in relation to shark attack one is only reflecting the attitude of mariners to these beasts. As a class they are hated. There are many stories of captured sharks being treated with savagery, being disembowelled and then thrown back live into the sea. Yet in the economy of the sea they are scavengers rather than evil predators. Moreover, in areas where shark attack is heavy there is reason to suppose man has not been blameless. For example, in the region around Sydney Harbour, Australia, and again at Florida, blood from abattoirs seeps into the sea, and sharks are drawn by the smell of blood. In the Bay of Bengal, where human corpses are floated down the Ganges from the burning ghats, shark attack is again high.

None of these things lessens one's sympathy for victims of shark attack, nor lessens one's own fear of the sharks themselves, but they put the subject in perspective zoologically. One of the first scientific conclusions we are led to is that while sharks may be ferocious they seem not to be voracious, as they are so often described. In fact, because they will engulf almost anything they come across, sharks have at times aided the course of human justice.

Silent witness

The classic example of this concerned the United States brig *Nancy* which was captured on July 3, 1799 by HM Cutter *Sparrow* and taken to Port Royal, Jamaica, Britain and the United States then being at war, to be condemned as a prize. The captain of the *Nancy* produced papers at the trial which were, in fact, false and he was about to be discharged when another British warship put in at the port with papers found in a shark caught on August 30. They proved to be the ship's papers thrown overboard by the captain of the *Nancy*, when capture seemed inevitable. They led to the condemnation of the brig and her cargo.

class	**Selachii**
order	**Pleurotremata**
family	**Isuridae**
genus & species	***Carcharodon carcharias***

Maligned monster: the maneater shark's bad reputation stems from its large size and supposed voraciousness. Most maneaters measure between 20 and 25 ft and not 40 ft as often quoted. They seem to eat anything that looks like food which results in bathers, corpses, carrion and rubbish being taken.

Despite a sleek and shark-like appearance, sturgeons are slow-moving fish. Here two Volga sterlets cruise gently above the sandy bottom, searching for food. They have poor eyesight and locate their food mainly by touch, using the sensitive barbels seen on the underside of their long snouts.

Sturgeon

The sturgeon is best known as the fish that gives caviare, the luxury food which could soon be a thing of the past. Of greater interest is the fact that the two dozen species are relics of a primitive race of fishes. They are more or less halfway between the sharks and the bony fishes, having a skeleton partly of bone and partly of cartilage. They are shark-like in shape and in the way the hind end of the body turns upwards into the upper lobe of the tailfin. The snout is tapered in the young fish, long and broad in adults, and in front of the mouth, on the underside of the head, are four barbels. The body is scaleless except for five rows of large plate-like scales with sharp points running from behind the gill-covers to the tailfin.

The largest is the Russian sturgeon or beluga (not to be confused with the mammal beluga, the white whale), of the Caspian and Black Seas and the Volga, Don, Dnieper and other rivers of that region. It is up to 28 ft long and 3 210 lb weight. One that was 13 ft long and weighed 2 200 lb was known to be 75 years old. It yielded 400 lb of caviare. The Atlantic sturgeon, on both sides of the North Atlantic reaches 11 ft and 600 lb. The white sturgeon of the Pacific coast of North America usually weighs less than 300 lb, but there are records of 1 285, 1 800 and 1 900 lb. The sterlet of the rivers of the USSR is up to 3 ft long. The rest of the two dozen species of sturgeon are all found in temperate waters throughout the northern hemisphere.

Numbers down everywhere

Sturgeons are slow-moving fish, spending their time grubbing on the bottom for food. Some, however, make long migrations. Individuals tagged in North American waters have been found to travel 900 miles. Most species live in the sea and go back up the rivers to spawn. The largest, the beluga, from which half the world's supply of caviare comes, is entirely freshwater. Today all sturgeons are fewer in number than they were a century or two ago, partly from overfishing and partly from the pollution of rivers and to some extent because hydro-electric schemes have spoilt their spawning runs. In the 17th century a prosperous sturgeon fishery flourished in the New England States of America. In the mid-19th century they were still being caught, for their caviare and for a high quality lamp oil their flesh yielded. A century later the annual catch had fallen by 90%. Sturgeons were once abundant off the Atlantic coast of Europe. Now they are found mainly around the mouth of the Gironde river in western France, the Guadalquivir in Spain and in Lake Ladoga in the USSR. A few only are caught each year around the British Isles and adjacent seas. Around the Black Sea—Caspian area overfishing has brought the sturgeon yield to a low ebb and efforts have been made to establish hatcheries, to rear young sturgeon and so replenish the stock. It has been estimated that as many as 15 000 sturgeons have been caught in these seas and adjoining rivers in a day.

Rummages for food in the mud

The name of this fish in several European languages means the stirrer, from the way the sturgeon rummages among the mud for food. This it finds largely by touch, using its sensitive barbels. Sturgeon also have

A young sterlet barely drifts along, its sensitive barbels tracing food. As it grows the nose broadens and the fish may reach 3 ft in length.

taste-buds, which are normally on the tongue or inside the mouth in other fish, but in the sturgeon are on the outside of the mouth. These help in the selection of food. They protrude from the toothless mouth to suck in the food. Sturgeons are slow feeders and can survive several weeks without eating. In freshwater they eat insect larvae, worms, crayfish, snails and other small fishes. In the sea they take bivalve molluscs, shrimps and other small crustaceans, worms and more small fishes than are eaten in fresh water. The beluga feeds in winter mainly on flounder, mullet and gobies in the Black Sea, and on roach, herring and gobies in the Caspian.

When caviare hatches

Spawning takes place in depths of 18–20 ft. The eggs are blackish, $\frac{1}{10}$ in. diameter and sticky so they adhere to water plants and stones, or clump together in masses. A single female may lay 2–3 million in one season. These hatch in 3–7 days, the larvae being $\frac{1}{2}$ in. long but their first summer they may grow to 8 in.

Use for the swimbladder

Sturgeon have been fished for their flesh and their oil as well as for their caviare. They have also supplied isinglass. This is from the swimbladder and was first named by the Dutch in 1525. They called it *huisenblas* which became anglicized as isinglass. When prepared for use it looks like semitransparent plastic sheets, and it is almost pure gelatin. It is still used today for special cements and water-proofing materials, but its main use is in clearing white wines, an ounce of isinglass being enough to clarify up to 300 gallons.

Royal fish

In the days of Ancient Rome the fish, garlanded with flowers, was piped into the banquet carried by slaves similarly crowned with flowers. It was, however, Edward II of England who made it a royal fish. His decree ran: 'The King shall have the wreck of the sea throughout the realm, whales and great sturgeons, except in certain places privileged by the King.' Sturgeon have ascended English rivers including the Thames and at one time any caught above London Bridge belonged to the Lord Mayor of London. Henry I is said to have banned even that. Indeed, he forbade the eating of sturgeon at any table than his own. A royal fish indeed: and, in the 1950's, as Sir Alister Hardy recalls in his book *The Open Sea*: a sturgeon 'died in an excess of misplaced homage, and was covered with distinction, by burying itself in the condenser pipe of one of Her Majesty's aircraft-carriers: HMS *Glory*!' – a worthy burial.

class	**Pisces**
order	**Chondrostei**
family	**Acipensenidae**
genera & species	***Acipenser ruthenus*** sterlet *A. sturio* Atlantic sturgeon *A. transmontanus* white sturgeon ***Huso huso*** beluga others

The aptly named shovelnose sturgeon **Scaphirhynchus platorhynchus**; *the bizarre snout is used to dig snails, shrimps and other morsel from the gravel.*

△ *Suffering from exposure: waste eggs trapped in stream debris. Eggs are usually covered by sand.*

Pacific salmon

There are six species of salmon in the North Pacific, by contrast with the North Atlantic where there is only one species, called the Atlantic salmon. Except for the Japanese species, the masu, these range from about Kamchatka in Siberia to the American west coast as far south as California. Of these the chinook, also known as the tyee, quinnat, king, spring, Sacramento or Columbia River salmon, weighs 10–50 lb, with a maximum of 108 lb. The sockeye, red or blueback salmon weighs 5–7 lb, but may weigh up to $15\frac{1}{2}$ lb; the silver salmon or coho weighs 6–12 lb, going up to $26\frac{1}{2}$ lb; the chum, keta or dog salmon weighs 8–18 lb; but is sometimes as much as 30 lb, and the humpback or pink salmon which is 3–5 lb, may weigh up to 10 lb.

Drastic changes for spawning

Pacific salmon return to spawn in the same river in which they hatched, and when they do so they become brilliant red, and their heads turn pea green. The males grow long hooked snouts and their mouths become filled with sharp teeth. The females do not grow the hooked snout. Most of the returning salmon are 4–5 years old. The humpback matures the earliest at 2 years, the silver salmon at 3, but some of the sockeye and chinook may be as much as 8 years old.

The salmon return in early summer, even in late spring, or in autumn in the case of the chum. They stop feeding as their digestive organs deteriorate and head for the coast from their feeding grounds out in the Pacific. On reaching the mouth of a river they head upstream, except the chum which usually spawns near tidal waters. The silver salmon moves only a short distance upstream. The chinook, on the other hand, has been known to travel as much as 2 250 miles up rivers. One exception to this is a subspecies of the sockeye which is non-migratory. In contrast with the Atlantic salmon, however, Pacific salmon never survive the spawning run.

Mating ends in death

By the time the salmon near the spawning grounds, they are mere bags of bones housing the eggs or the sperms. The males often look the worse for wear as they fight with each other. The females look for a place in the sandy or gravelly shallows where the water is clear with plenty of oxygen. Then they start digging troughs (redds) in the river beds with their tails; each one lying on her side and flapping with her tail. When her trough is deep enough, she lies in it to spawn, her mate swimming over to her to shed his milt to fertilise the eggs. Each female lays several batches of eggs, to a total of 3–5 thousand, in different troughs, by the end of which time she is completely exhausted. With her tail fins worn to stubs, her skin blackening and with blotches of grey fungus attacking it, she dies. The males share the same fate, and the carcases of both drift downstream or are stranded at the edge.

Down to the sea as infants

Each batch of eggs becomes buried under sand as fresh redds are dug and the loosened sand is wafted over them. Thus protected, the orange-pink eggs hatch 8 weeks later. The alevins or young salmon remain under the gravel feeding on their yolk sacs for some weeks before wriggling to the surface as fry. They feed heavily on water fleas and other small animals and in the following spring are carried downstream by the current. The humpback and chum go to the sea as fry but the sockeye may go as fry or as 1–3 year fish, and the quinnat and coho go when 1–2 years old.

Finding their way home

There has always been a great interest in how salmon find their way back to the streams where they were hatched. The full story has not yet been pieced together but sufficient is now known to sketch in many of the details. There is evidence, for example, to show that the thyroid gland plays a part in the salmon's changing preference for water of varying salinity. When the coho was injected with a certain hormone it sought sea water. When the injections were stopped it sought fresh water. The opposite effect was found in the humpback. Probably other glands are involved, as well as the length of day and possibly the diet. The sense of smell may play a part, as it does in finding food. Temperatures also influence the fish, certainly once they have entered fresh water. When these are too low or too high the fish make no effort to surmount obstacles. There is some evidence also that celestial navigation, using the sun by day and the stars by night, as in migrating birds, keeps the salmon on their compass runs along the coast to the mouths of the rivers they came from.

Expert water-tasters

Of the different ways that salmon find their way back, one of the easier to test is the odour, or the taste of the water from which the fishes originated. Laboratory experiments have shown beyond doubt that fishes, including salmon, can recognize waters of only slightly different tastes; smell and taste are closely linked. This is not so very surprising since water-tasters dealing with the purification of drinking water are able to tell by tasting, in an almost uncanny way, where a particular glass of water came

△ *The remains. Reduced to blackened bags of bones after spawning, dead sockeye salmon are washed up at the river's edge.*

△ *On home ground. A pair of sockeye salmon, having swum from the Pacific Ocean up to the head waters of the river in which they hatched 4 or 5 years before, are now ready to spawn themselves – then die, starved and exhausted by their marathon journey on which they do not feed at all.*

from. These same tests show that the memory of a particular type of water persists for a long time in a fish, and that the younger the fish the longer the memory will probably be.

Controlled fishing

Many people living a long way from the Pacific are familiar with the Pacific salmon —in canned form. The salmon fishery is commercially highly valuable, with 2–10 million sockeye alone being caught and canned. The salmon are taken in gill nets, reef nets and purse seines on their way to the Fraser River in British Columbia. Unrestricted fishing could kill the industry, so by an agreement between Canada and the United States, 20% of each race of fish are allowed through to continue their journey to the spawning grounds. This is taken care of by a joint International Pacific Salmon Fisheries Commission, which also arranges for the catch to be divided equally between the two countries. There is co-operation also in providing concrete and steel fishways to assist the salmon up the rivers. The Pacific salmon fishery is therefore as near as it has so far been possible to an actual husbandry of a wild resource. Moreover, research is being carried out to produce strains of salmon that can tolerate less favourable rivers than they use at present, and to transplant fry which, when mature, will return to spawn in waters earmarked for cultivation.

class	**Pisces**
order	**Salmoniformes**
family	**Salmonidae**
genus & species	***Oncorhynchus gorbuscha*** *humpback* ***O. keta*** *chum* ***O. kisutch*** *silver salmon* ***O. masou*** *masu* ***O. nerka*** *sockeye* ***O. tshawytscha*** *chinook*

13

Trout

The European trout, of very variable colour, is known by three names. The brown trout is small, dark and non-migratory. It can weigh up to 17 lb 12 oz and lives in the smaller rivers and pools. The lake trout is larger and paler. It lives in larger rivers and lakes and it may be migratory. The sea trout, large, silvery up to 4½ ft long and weighing up to 30 lb, is distinctly migratory. All three belong to the same species.

The European brown trout and lake trout are greenish brown, the flanks being lighter than the back, and the belly yellowish. They are covered with many red and black spots, the latter surrounded by pale rings. There are spots even on the gill covers. These two and the sea trout resemble the salmon in shape and appearance except that the angle of the jaw reaches to well behind the eye and the adipose fin is tinged with orange.

The North American species are similar. The cut-throat trout has two red marks across the throat. The Dolly Varden is named for its conspicuous red spots, coloured like the cherry ribbons worn by the Dickens character. In the brook trout the pattern is more mottled but it also has red spots on the flanks. The rainbow trout has a reddish band along the flanks. The lake or mackinau trout lives in deep water, down to 400 ft. The golden trout lives in water 8 000 ft or more above sea level.

▷ *Like some figment of an angler's daydream, a big New Zealand rainbow trout jumps from its shoal for a flying titbit.*
▽ *Mixed bunch, with rainbow trout in front of brown. Because of aquarium glass, the red line on the rainbows' sides cannot be seen.*

Temperature important

Trout grow best in clear, aerated waters and although they are sometimes found in turbid waters it is only when the surface layers are well supplied with oxygen. They are readily affected by silt; it may spoil their spawning sites, reduce their food supply or act directly on the fishes themselves. Laboratory experiments have shown that particles in suspension in the water, at a level as low as 270 parts per million, abrade the gills or cause them to thicken. The rate of growth of trout varies in other ways as well, often to a remarkable extent, with the conditions of their surroundings. Temperature, for instance, is highly important, and an example can be seen at the time when they resume feeding after the winter fast. Normally, trout stop feeding in autumn and resume in spring, in about March when the water reaches a temperature of 2°C/36°F or more. In a mild winter they may begin feeding in December and continue until the first cold snap of the following autumn.

The rate of growth also varies from one river to another, or from river to sea. Trout living in small streams grow more slowly than those in large rivers, and those in large bodies of fresh water grow more slowly than those living in the sea. A trout in a small river will grow 2½, 5 and 8 in. in its first, second and third years respectively. Corresponding figures for a sea trout will be 3–5, 4–5 and 10–11 in.

Diet changes

The diet of trout varies with their age. Fry eat mainly aquatic larvae of insects, rarely the adults. Later they eat large numbers of winged insects, as well as water fleas and freshwater shrimps. When adult they eat mainly small fishes as well as shrimps, insect larvae and adults, especially the winged insects. Sea trout feed on sprats, young herring and sand eels and also on a large percentage of small crustaceans, including shrimps and prawns.

Correct place to spawn

Male trout begin to breed at two years, females at three, returning to do so to the place where they themselves were hatched. This homing has been verified experimentally, by transporting marked trout to other parts of a river system, then finding them later, back on their 'home ground'. Breeding usually takes place from October to February, the time varying from one locality to another. Spawning is normally in running water, trout living in lakes going into the feeder streams.

For spawning the female makes a 'redd' in gravelly shallows, digging a depression with flicks of her tail. As she lays her eggs, the male, in attendance on her, fertilises them, stationing himself beside her but slightly to the rear. It has been found that a successful redd is one with a current flowing downwards through the gravel. The eggs hatch in about 40 days. The fry are ½–1 in. long at hatching, and the yolk sac is absorbed in 4–6 weeks.

Surrounded by enemies

WE Frost and ME Brown, in their book *The Trout*, state that 94% of fry are lost during the first 3–4 months of their lives. After this the mortality drops to 20%. Eels are often said to kill trout and especially to ravage the spawning grounds, but there is no evidence of this. The chief enemies of trout are water shrew, mink, the common rat, and to some extent otters and herons. Another enemy of trout is larger trout. Well grown ones have sometimes been found to have another trout, 5–6 in. long, in their stomachs. The record for the brown trout comes from New Zealand, where the fish were introduced. In 1967 a 20lb trout had a foot-long trout in its stomach. In their cannibalism, therefore, trout vie with pike, always regarded as a traditional enemy, which, with few exceptions, take only medium to large sized trout.

There are two other contributors to trout depletion — apart from man. Numbers of other animals compete with it for food, and of these, which include several water birds, the eel is probably one of the worst, more so in rivers than in lakes. The other natural 'enemy' is lack of oxygen, especially during the winter. When the pools and lakes are frozen over, trout must rely on oxygen trapped under ice. This is replenished by oxygen given out by water plants. When, however, the ice is blanketed by snow, light does not penetrate, plants cannot 'work', and trout are asphyxiated.

Many species

The wide variation in size and colour of the European trout is brought out by the history of its species. In 1758 Linnaeus named three species: the Swedish river trout, the sea trout and the lake trout. Dr Albert Gunther, leading authority on fishes, wrote in 1880: 'We know of no other group of fishes which offers so many difficulties . . . to the distinction of species'. He recognized 10 species in the British Isles alone – the sea trout, sewin, phinnock, Galway sea trout, Orkney sea trout, river trout, great lake trout, gillaroo, Welsh blackfinned trout and Loch Leven trout. Thirty years later, C Tate Regan, Günther's successor, put forward strong arguments for treating these and all species and races in continental Europe as one very variable species.

class	**Pisces**
order	**Salmoniformes**
family	**Salmonidae**
genera & species	***Salmo aguabonita*** golden ***S. clarki*** cutthroat ***S. gairdneri*** rainbow ***S. trutta*** brown ***Salvelinus fontinalis*** brook ***S. malma*** Dolly Varden ***S. namaycush*** lake, others

Young brown trout, easily identified by the red spots on the side of its body, swims in clear river water; the clearer the water, the faster it grows.

Butterfly fish

It is virtually impossible to speak about butterfly fishes without confusion since the name is commonly used for different kinds of unrelated fishes. The same can be said of angelfishes. Attention is drawn to this on page 36, where butterfly fishes are described, together with their very close relatives, the marine angelfishes. Here we discuss this subject in order to deal with a freshwater fish that has been called a butterfly fish. At the same time this gives us the opportunity to contrast and compare it with the marine fishes, inhabitants of coral reefs especially, which are also called butterfly fishes. For our description of the habits of marine butterfly fishes we must refer to page 36. But here on the following pages we portray these fishes, belonging to the family Chaetodontidae, in a series of fascinating and beautiful photographs.

The one species of freshwater butterfly fish is sufficiently extraordinary to merit close attention on its own. Never more than 4 in. long, it lives in the rivers of tropical West Africa. Its head and body are boat-shaped, flattened above, bluntly rounded below. It is coloured grey-green to brownish-silver, marked with spots and streaks. The large mouth is directed upwards, and the nostrils are tubular. Another remarkable feature is its fins. The pectoral fins are large and wing-like.

Each pelvic fin has four very long filamentous rays not connected to each other, and the unpaired fins are large, transparent and supported by long rays.

For a long time the relationships of this fish, first discovered in 1876, have been in doubt, but it is now placed in a family on its own near that of the large South American fish, the arapaima. It has no relationship with the marine butterfly fishes of the family Chaetodontidae.

▽ *The freshwater butterfly fish is not related to marine butterfly fishes of the tropical seas.*

▽▽ *Four-eyed butterfly fish, so-called because of the false 'eye' markings at its tail end.*

▽ *Vividly-striped marine butterfly fishes are deep-bodied and flattened from side to side*

A fish that flies

This remarkable fish is reckoned to fly over the water, flapping its wings like a bat or a bird. The freshwater butterfly fish spends most of its time just below the surface of still or stagnant waters in the Congo and Niger basins, in the weedy backwaters and standing pools. But it is most renowned for its ability to leap out of water for distances up to 6 ft, its large pectoral fins being used, as are those of the true flying fishes, in gliding flight. It has also been credited with flapping these fins in true powered flight, as in bats and birds. By 1960, however, it had been generally agreed that this was not so.

Then came a remarkable sequel. PH Greenwood and KS Thomson investigated the anatomy of this fish. They found it had a most unusual shoulder girdle, the arrangement of bones to which the pectoral fins are attached. In fact, these two authors described it as unique among fishes. The bones were so thin that they had to be very careful not to damage them while dissecting them out. The whole of the shoulder girdle is broad and flattened to give support to a highly developed system of muscles, comparable with the large pectoral muscles that work the wings of birds. The two scientists also found that the fins could not be folded against the body, as is usual in fishes, but could be moved up and down. In brief, they concluded that, while it was still unproven whether or not the butterfly fish could make a powered flight, its shoulder girdle and muscles were such that it ought to be able to fly. The best that can be said is that the fish has been seen to beat its fins up and down when held in the hand. It has, however, been suggested that this is only used to give the butterfly fish a push-off from the water to become airborne.

Insect feeder

The food consists almost entirely of the small insects, such as flies, that fall on to the surface of the water.

Life history

Relatively little is known about the breeding, and such details as we have are from the few butterfly fishes that have bred in captivity. Numerous false matings have been seen, with the male riding on the back of the female, sometimes for hours at a time, holding her firmly with the long rays of the pelvic fins. Mating finally is effected by the two twisting their bodies together to bring the vents opposite each other. Fertilisation seems, however, not to be internal. As soon

▽▽ *Marine butterfly fishes* **Chaetodon** *live around coral reefs in shallow tropical seas.*

▽ *The butterfly fish* **Heniochus acuminatus** *lives in the warm seas around the Philippine Islands. It has a very deep body, most of the depth being due to a highly arched back.*

The freshwater butterfly fish **Pantodon buchholzi** *found in the waters of western Africa is one of the strangest of the so-called flying fishes. It spends most of its time swimming just under the surface and is capable of leaping out of the water for a distance of 6 or more feet.*

as they are laid the eggs float to the surface, and in 3 days these hatch. The fry remain at the surface feeding on the tiniest of the insects, such as springtails and aphides, which fall on them.

Flying or gliding

The ability to make either gliding or powered flights through the air is rare among fishes, although to be able to leap from the water is common enough. For years, scientists have argued among themselves whether or not the flying fishes of the oceans beat their wings when airborne. At present, evidence suggests that they do not. Similarly, it may be some years before we can be sure whether the West African butterfly fishes beat their wings or not. There is, however, one group of freshwater fishes that do beat their fins to achieve true flight through the air. These are the hatchet fishes of northern South America, found from the River Plate to Panama.

As so often happens, another confusion of names arises. We already have it over butterfly fishes, as we have seen. There are also two kinds of hatchet fishes. One is marine hatchet fish and the other is freshwater. Both are named for their shape, the body being flattened from side to side, so that it looks like the blade of a hatchet.

The freshwater hatchet fishes beat their pectoral fins rapidly when making a take-off run over the surface before becoming airborne, and they continue to beat their fins when airborne.

To make the confusion even more confounded, it may be mentioned that freshwater hatchet fishes do a butterfly-like dance during their courtship. Fortunately we can note the scientific names and there can be no doubt as to the animal referred to. Each animal has a binomial name of genus and species, rather like the surname and christian name used to identify humans.

class	**Pisces**
order	**Osteoglossiformes**
family	**Pantodontidae**
genus & species	***Pantodon buchholzi*** *freshwater butterfly fish*

Piranha

Few accounts of travel in South and Central America fail to contain some references to the piranha or piraya, the small but allegedly very ferocious fish that inhabits the rivers of this region. In some places it abounds in such vast numbers as to be a serious pest, making the infested streams either very hazardous or quite impossible for fording or bathing.

The name piranha applies loosely to about 18 species, of which only 4 seem to be dangerous to humans. All are members of the genus **Serrasalmus,** having a general similarity of appearance and habits. Some scientists, however, classify them differently. Most of the species average 8 in. in length but **Serrasalmus piraya,** of the River São Francisco in eastern Brazil, one of the most dangerous, may reach 2 ft. Most of them are olive-green or blue-black above and silvery or dark grey on flanks and belly. Some species have reddish or yellowish tinted fins. The colours seem to vary considerably from place to place and with age. For example, old specimens of the white piranha **Serrasalmus rhombeus,** found in the Amazon system and north-eastern South America, are often dark enough to be called black piranhas.

The body of the piranha is deep, short and rather compressed from side to side. A large bony crest on top of the skull supports a keel on the back, and a similar keel on the belly is strengthened by a firm

Red piranha (**Serrasalmus nattereri**); close-up of fish lurking among weeds.

row of enlarged scales bearing sharp, backwardly-directed points, so the deep and heavy forepart of the fish is provided with a cut-water above and below. There is a fleshy adipose fin on the back between the dorsal and tail fins. The tail is slender and muscular and together with the broad, tough, blade-like tail fin helps to drive the body through the water with great force. As in all really swift fish the scales are very small. The most striking feature is the mouth. The massive lower jaw has relatively huge muscles operating it. The teeth are large, flat and triangular with very sharp points. These points merely pierce the skin, the rest is done by the

◁ *The gates of hell? A piranha displays its razor-sharp teeth which can strip a carcase to the bone with ease.*
▷ *Red piranha—one of the smaller piranhas, popular with aquarium-owners.*

usual erratic spawning behaviour of most of the other members of its family. The male guards the eggs as well as the fry, when they hatch. These became free-swimming about 5 days after hatching.

Ferocity exaggerated?
The ferocity of the piranha has become almost legendary. Stories are told of a cow or a pig, falling into a river, being stripped to a skeleton in a few minutes. One of the most famous stories is that of a man, fording a stream on horseback, who was brought down and killed by a swarm of piranha. Later the bones of horse and rider were found, picked perfectly clean, the man's clothes undamaged. It is probable that a lot of the stories have been exaggerated. Some travellers now say that they have waded in or swam in rivers infested with piranha shoals and have never been attacked. Yet others say they have come on villages where hardly a native had not suffered the loss of a toe or finger. It is difficult to know what to believe but there must be some truth in the danger from these fish.

It is possible that the ferocity of the piranha may vary with the species and from place to place, and it may be that they are much more aggressive at the beginning of the rainy season when the males are guarding the eggs. This could also explain why it is that they will attack bathers at certain places in a river, where perhaps they have laid eggs, leaving others unmolested not far away. Nevertheless, those aquarists who keep these fishes admit to treating them with respect and taking extra care in feeding them, or when netting them to transfer them from one aquarium to another.

edges, which are literally razor-sharp. The teeth of the upper jaw are similar but much smaller and fit exactly into the spaces between the points of the lower ones when the mouth is closed. The jaws are so strong and the teeth so sharp that they can chop out a piece of flesh as neatly as a razor. The fact that there is a reliable record of a 100lb capybara reduced to a skeleton in less than a minute shows the efficiency of the teeth.

A few of the smaller species are kept in aquaria, the most popular seen in tropical fish stores and public aquaria being *Serrasalmus nattereri,* the red or common piranha, up to 1 ft long and coloured red on the underside and fins.

Some piranhas are found only in certain river systems, such as the Rio São Francisco, Rio Paraguay or Rio Orinoco, while others range over a wide area.

Water alive with fish
Piranha hunt in shoals, sometimes of several thousands, so in places the water seems to be alive with them. Smaller fishes form their staple diet, but any animal entering or falling into the water accidentally may be attacked. They often attack each other. It is said that they will instantly be attracted by blood in the water but apparently anything out of the ordinary will attract them.

Waterplant hatcheries
It is thought that piranha breed when the rainy season sets in about January or February. The female deposits her eggs on water plants or roots. On hatching, the fry stay attached to the vegetation in clusters until they have absorbed most of the yolk sac, and then become free-swimming. *Serrasalmus spilopleura* is one of the few species which has been seen breeding in an aquarium. The female deposited her eggs carefully on aquatic plants, which is unlike the

class	**Pisces**
order	**Cypriniformes**
family	**Serrasalmidae**
genus & species	*Serrasalmus nattereri* red or Natterer's piranha *S. piraya* piraya *S. rhombeus* white or spotted piranha *S. spilopleura* common piranha others

20

The electric eel, unrelated to the true eels, emits high-voltage discharges which stun or kill fishes or frogs, those dying near the eel being eaten.

Electric eel

The South American electric eel, which can kill a horse with an electric shock, is not even related to eels. It has less than 50 relatives, which include the gymnotid eels, and knife-fishes, all tropical American and probably generating electricity to a greater or lesser extent; but the most spectacular and notorious is the electric eel itself, which can discharge up to 550 volts when fully grown.

The electric eel has a cylindrical body, a uniform olive-brown, up to 6 ft long—the largest recorded 9½ ft—running to a pointed tail. It has no fins on the back, only very small paired fins behind the gills, and a long conspicuous anal fin running from the tip of the tail almost to the throat. Its eyes are very small. About ⅞ths of the body is tail, with the internal organs crowded into a small space behind the head. The tail contains the electric organs, made up of 5–6 thousand electroplates (elements) arranged like the cells in a dry battery. Moreover, there are three parts to the electric organ, two small batteries and the main battery. The electric eel is positive towards the head end, negative at the tail end, the reverse order to that of the electric catfish.

Poor gills, no lungs

The electric eel lives in waters poor in oxygen. It comes to the surface from time to time to gulp air. In its mouth are patches of superficial blood vessels which take up oxygen from the air gulped at the surface, so acting as auxiliary breathing organs.

It swims by undulating the long anal fin and is said to be able to swim forwards or backwards, up or down, with equal ease. So long as it is still its main electric organ at least is not working, but the small battery in the tail is working continuously. As soon as the eel starts to move it gives out electric impulses at the rate of 20–30 a second which later increases to 50 a second. These are used for direction-finding, it is now known, although they do not form an electric field, as in the Nile fish.

High-voltage jolts

It has been said that the second of the small batteries probably fires the larger battery, which gives out a series of 3–6 waves at intervals of 5/1000 of a second, each wave lasting 2/1000 of a second. These are the high-voltage discharges which stun or kill fishes or frogs, those dying near the eel being eaten. Larger animals coming into contact with a large electric eel are stunned. A stunned horse falls and is liable to be drowned. A man can stand the shock, but not repeatedly.

Unknown breeding places

Little is known of the breeding; there is no obvious difference between the sexes and the breeding places are unknown. The eels disappear from their usual haunts in the breeding season. When they return young eels 4–6 in. long come back with them, still guarded by the parents. Young eels are light brown with bands. Later they become marbled and finally olive-brown with the throat brilliant orange.

Millions of years ahead

Even more remarkable than the electric eel is the story of the first man to study its electrical discharge. From the beginning of the 16th century Spain had refused all non-Spaniards permission to visit her American colonies. In 1800, when rapid strides were being made in the study of electricity, the German naturalist, Baron Friedrich von Humboldt, applied for and was granted permission to visit South America. With a companion he arrived at the upper reaches of the Orinoco River and Calabozo, a town of exiles.

Von Humboldt took with him a large amount of scientific apparatus. Oxygen had only recently been recognized and von Humboldt took the latest apparatus in order to analyse the gases in the swim-bladders of fishes. He also took the latest electrical apparatus, only to find that Carlos del Pozo, resident in the town of exiles, had begun making similar apparatus thousands of miles from the centres of learning in Europe—a remarkable coincidence. And there also von Humboldt found large fishes that had developed their own electrical apparatus, but millions of years in advance of del Pozo and the European scientists.

This gifted German gave the world the first scientific accounts of the behaviour of the electric eel. He stood on one of these fishes and experienced a painful numbness. He also found that for the rest of the day he was afflicted with a violent pain in the knees and in the rest of his joints. Having studied the eel he made a remarkable prophecy: 'The discoveries that will be made on the electromotive apparatus of these fishes will extend to all the phenomena of muscular motion subject to volition. It will perhaps be found that in most animals every contraction of muscle fibre is preceded by a discharge from the nerve into the muscle.' He also predicted that electricity is the source of life and movement in all living things.

class	**Pisces**
order	**Cypriniformes**
family	**Gymnotidae**
genus & species	***Electrophorus electricus***

The South American electric eel lives in waters poor in oxygen. It comes to the surface from time to time to gulp air. In its mouth are patches of superficial blood vessels which take up oxygen from the air gulped at the surface, so helping with breathing.

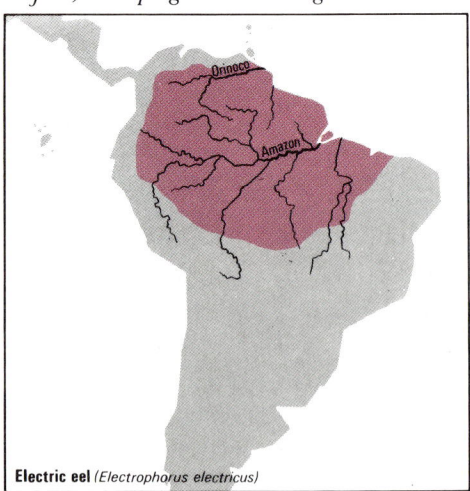

Electric eel (*Electrophorus electricus*)

Trunkfish

The trunkfishes are the nearest we have to fishes masquerading as turtles. They are also known as boxfishes and cofferfishes because their bodies are enclosed within bony boxes made up of 6-sided bony plates fitting closely into one another, leaving only the tail unarmoured. Inside, the backbone is short with only 14 vertebrae between the skull and the beginning of the tail, all joined in a compact manner.

A typical trunkfish has a more or less conical head, the face sloping down at a steep angle to the small mouth, which is armed with strong crushing teeth. The eyes are large and there is only a small opening from the gill chamber. The length of a trunkfish seldom exceeds 1 ft. The single dorsal fin and the anal fin are fairly large, as are the pectoral fins, but there are no pelvic fins. The fleshy, naked tail ending in a large fanlike tail fin projects backwards from the bony box and, except for the other fins, is the only part capable of movement. The box enclosing the body is flat on the undersurface and it may be 3-, 4- or 5-sided in cross section, and one or more of its edges may be armed with strong spines.

Trunkfishes live at or near the bottom of warm waters, especially in tropical seas, all round the world.

Geometrical fishes: a comparison between the fishes above and overleaf will show the 3- and 4-faced arrangements of trunkfish armour. These arrangements vary according to species and serve as a rough means of classification.

△ *Its transparent, fan-shaped fins beating rapidly, the cumbersome body of a smooth trunkfish moves slowly forwards. Unlike most fish, trunkfishes swim almost entirely by just a rapid beating of their fins.*
◁ *Passing beauty:* **Ostracion meleagris** *in the Hawaii reef. Like other trunkfishes, it can adopt a variety of colour schemes. The sexes and young of the same species are often quite differently patterned and coloured.*

23

Slow moving

Like tortoises on land, trunkfishes are slow moving, and for much the same reasons. The normal fish swims by strong side to side movements of the whole body and, more especially, by the muscular tail. A trunkfish can move its tail only to a small extent. Its swimming is like a small boat being propelled by a single oar sculling from the stern. The only difference is that the hydrodynamic principles are more complex in the fish because the tail is flexible. The main swimming force is produced by side to side movements of the dorsal and anal fins, aided by the pectoral fins. A trunkfish is the very opposite of being streamlined – in fact the flat faces must create considerable resistance to progress – and when swimming it moves its fins very rapidly, giving the impression of a great expenditure of energy with only a little gain in forward movement.

Confusion of colours

Rapid movement is not necessary for so heavily armoured a fish, which can also rely on its colour and colour changes for security, and on its ability to poison other fishes. A common trunkfish found in the seas on both sides of the tropical Atlantic is the cowfish, so named because it has two sharp, forward-pointing spines on the forehead, rather like the horns of a cow. It is pale green in colour, marked with blue spots and lines, but it can change this to yellow with blue spots or brown with a network of light blue markings, or even to pure white. The colours also differ between the sexes. The 4-sided blue trunkfish of the Indo-Pacific is an example. The females and the young fish are purplish blue with numerous small white spots scattered thickly and evenly over the whole body. The male is very different, being purplish blue with a pale blue network except for the flat upper surface, which is a brownish purple with small white dots with a brick-red border. Even the eyes differ: in the females and young fish they are blue, in the males they have a red border.

Emit poison

It has been suggested that the gaudy colours act as warning colours, advertising to possible enemies that trunkfishes do not depend entirely on their armour but have other undesirable qualities. We do not know yet exactly how it is used, but we do know that trunkfishes can give out a poison. When one of them is placed in an aquarium it is not long before the other fishes begin to show signs of distress, coming to the surface to gulp air, and dying soon afterwards. The only fishes not affected are tough characters such as moray eels, the large groupers, and other trunkfishes. The poison persists even after the trunkfish have been removed.

Search for food in corals

Trunkfishes live among the corals, which they search for food, biting off pieces of coral to digest the polyps. At the same time, in biting pieces from the coral, they expose worms and other small invertebrates sheltering in it. Some trunkfishes use their spout-like snouts to blow jets of water at the sandy bottom to uncover and dislodge worms, molluscs and small crustaceans, which they immediately snap up.

Dingleberries

The breeding habits of the cowfish of tropical American waters are probably typical of the whole family. It lays buoyant eggs, $\frac{1}{32}$ in. diameter, which hatch in 2–3 days. The larvae begin to develop the hard cover in about a week and they become somewhat rounded in shape, and it is only as the young fishes mature that the box-like edges to the body become sharply defined. During the early stages of life young trunkfishes shelter under clumps of floating seaweed. Their rounded shape has earned them, in the United States, the name of dingleberries. At this stage they seem to have rather cherubic faces, with their large eyes, small mouths and what look like puffed cheeks.

Regarded as delicacy

The heaviest mortality among trunkfishes is in the early stages, when eggs, larvae and young fishes are often eaten. Once they reach maturity their protective boxes, and in some species the poison they give out, deter predators. Also, being so slow, they lack the large muscles that make the flesh of other fishes attractive. Yet trunkfishes are eaten, even by human beings, and in some places are regarded as a delicacy. They are cooked in their own boxes, and some people of the South Pacific are said to 'roast them like chestnuts'. There are, nevertheless, other opinions, one of which is that what little flesh there is cannot be praised for its flavour, although the liver is proportionately quite large and oily.

class	**Pisces**
order	**Tetraodontiformes**
family	**Ostraciontidae**
genera & species	**Lactophrys bicaudalis** *large spotted trunkfish* **L. quadricornis** *cowfish* **Ostracion lentiginosus** *blue trunkfish* others

◁ *Always in shape, the complete covering of interlocking hexagonal plates of* **O. cornutus** *forms a rigid protective shield over the whole of the body except the flexible tail.*

Carp

Of the extensive carp family (Cyprinidae), this is the most widely distributed. Native of Japan, China and Central Asia, from Turkestan to the Black Sea and the Danube basin, it has been introduced into many European countries as well as the United States. It differs from other members of the family in its unusually long dorsal fin, with 17–22 branched rays, the strongly serrated third spine of the dorsal and anal fins, and in its four barbels, two at each corner of the slightly protrusible mouth. There are no teeth in the mouth, but there are throat-teeth. The colour of the wild form is olive to yellow-green on the back, greenish-yellow to bronze-yellow on the flanks, and underparts yellowish. The fins are grey-green to brown, sometimes slightly reddish.

Wild carp at home

Carp prefer shallow sunny waters with a muddy bottom and abundant water plants. They avoid clear, swift-flowing or cold waters. Wild carp are found in large rivers and, more commonly, in ponds. Their food is insect larvae, freshwater shrimps and other crustaceans, worms and snails, as well as some plant matter. The barbels, organs of touch, and the protrusible mouth are used for grubbing in the mud, much of which is swallowed and later ejected when the edible parts have been digested. In winter feeding ceases and the fish enter a resting period, a form of hibernation. In May to June carp move into shallow water to spawn, the eggs laid on the leaves of water plants. Each lays over 60 000 eggs/lb of her bodyweight. The larvae hatch out in 2–3 days, the adults return to deeper water, while the young fishes remain in shallow water, near the bank. They become sexually mature in 3–4 years. Small carp will be eaten by almost any fish significantly larger than themselves, including larger carp.

Domesticated varieties

As with many other domesticated animals, carp are found in a number of varieties, of two main types: leather carp and mirror carp. The first is scaleless, the second has large scales in two rows on each side of the body. Both can throw back to the original carp form. The shape of the body varies, from relatively slender to deep-bodied with a humpback. Some fish culturists claim these vary with the food, sparse feeding producing the slender forms, abundant feeding giving rise to humpbacks.

How old is a carp

Carp have probably been domesticated for many centuries, and have been carried all over the world for ornamental ponds, or for food. Surprisingly, therefore, in view of the familiarity that should have resulted from this, there is a conflict of opinion on important points—for instance, their longevity and maximum weights. Above all, there are serious discrepancies about when carp were introduced into Europe.

△ *Cyprinid fishes, for instance roach, tench and some carp, often show red forms which breed true to type. Aquarists take advantage, with results like these Japanese* **Hi-goi**, *golden carps.*

Gesner, the 16th-century Swiss naturalist, mentioned a carp 150 years old. Carp in the lakes of Fontainebleau, France, have been credited with ages of up to 400 years. Bingley, writing in 1805, records a carp in the pond in the garden of Emmanuel College, Cambridge, England, that had been an inhabitant more than 70 years. Tate Regan, authority on fishes in Britain in the first half of this century, was of the opinion that under artificial conditions a carp may attain 50 years but that 15 years would probably be the maximum in the wild state.

Perhaps one reason for the excessive claims is their hardiness when removed from water. This is also the reason why the fish could be spread over such a wide area by man. Wrapped in damp moss or water plants, it can survive transport over long distances. If Pennant is to be believed, this remark has the force of under-statement. In his *British Zoology* he tells of a carp wrapped in moss, with only its mouth exposed, placed in a net and hung in a cellar. It was fed with bread and milk and lived over a fortnight. It is only fair to add that it was 'often plunged in water'.

Carp usually grow to about 15 lb in the United States but in Europe a fish of over 60 lb and a length of 40 in. has been recorded. Claims have been made for 400 lb carp. Frederick II of Prussia is said to have caught one of 76 lb and a 140 lb carp is said to have

△ *Clarissa, the largest carp caught in Great Britain, was taken from Redmere Pool by R Walker in 1952. She was about 15 years old and weighed 44 lb. She lived in an aquarium until 1972.*

△ *The mirror carp is identified by rows of large scales along its back and sides.*

▽ *Some think carp found in Britain today came from carp cultivated in monastery stewponds.*

been caught at Frankfurt on Oder. There are several records of carp around 25 lb in Britain, but there is one for 44 lb taken by R Walker in 1952.

Historical uncertainty

The introduced form of the common carp was known to the Greeks and Romans, and has long been kept in ponds in parts of Europe. We know it is today found widely over England, the southern parts of Wales and in southern Scotland. The question remains: when was it first introduced into Britain?

Writers on the subject seem to have been fairly unanimous that all our carp must be regarded as descendants of fishes cultivated by the monks for centuries in their stewponds. Certainly, carp are still to be found in many of the surviving stewponds adjacent to ruins of monasteries and priories. That on its own is very little help in finding the date when they were first put there. Other than this, information comes from documentary evidence or guesswork, or a mixture of the two.

Eric Taverner, in his *Freshwater Fishes of the British Isles* (1957), suggested that carp were brought here from France and the Low Countries in the 14th century. Richard Fitter, writing in 1959, invokes an entry in *The Boke of St Albans* for dating their introduction prior to 1486. Emma Phipson, in *The Animal-Lore of Shakespeare's Time* (1883), speaks of Leonard Mascall, a Sussex gentleman, who has had the credit for importing the carp into England about the year 1514. She also points out that in the Privy Purse Expenses of Elizabeth of York, 1502, mention is made of a reward paid for the present of a carp. Izaak Walton, in *The Compleat Angler*, opined that the date was around 1530. Dr Albert Günther, celebrated authority on fishes in the last half of the 19th century, fixed the date at 1614.

The latest pronouncement is by Günther Sterba, in his *Freshwater Fishes of the World* (1962), that the carp reached England in 1512, Denmark in 1560, Prussia 1585, St Petersburg (Leningrad) 1729, and North America (California) 1872.

The dissolution of the monasteries began in 1535. A plan of a Benedictine monastery of the 12th century shows the site of a fishpond. Accepting the dates quoted here the fishponds of religious houses in England must have been stocked for at least two centuries with fish other than carp. Two of our seven authorities give dates about or after the dissolution of the monasteries, and three give dates only slightly before that event.

It is a romantic idea that English monks could supply themselves with carp to be eaten on fast days. But the evidence seems to be in favour of some other fish, probably the perch.

class	**Pisces**
order	**Cypriniformes**
family	**Cyprinidae**
genus & species	***Cyprinus carpio***

27

Swordtail

The swordtail is one of the more important as well as most popular of aquarium fishes, not only for its beauty but because it is a good subject for selective breeding. Swordtails are live-bearing tooth-carps, so they have the shape of that family. The dorsal fin is relatively large and so is the tailfin which is broad-based and rounded at the rear edge. The pelvic fins are at about the middle of the body. The females are up to 5 in., the males being up to $3\frac{1}{4}$ in. exclusive of the sword, which is formed from much elongated rays of the lower part of the tailfin. The outstanding feature of the swordtail is its colours.

Swordtails have been bred in so many colours and colour variations that a description of these in a small space would be impossible. What follows here can, however, be taken as a sort of standard colouring, the one most likely to be seen. The back is olive-green shading to greenish-yellow on the flanks and yellowish on the belly. The scales are edged with

brown so the whole body seems to be covered with a fine net. The fins are yellowish-green, the dorsal fin being ornamented with reddish blotches and streaks. From the tip of the snout to the base of the tailfin runs a rainbow band of colour made up of zigzag lines of carmine, green, cinnabar, purple or violet. The sword of the male is yellow at the base shading to orange, bordered with black above and below.

Swordtails live in the fresh waters of southern Mexico, British Honduras and Guatemala in Central America.

Bullying males

As is usual with popular aquarium fishes more is gleaned about their way of life from individuals kept in tanks than from those living in the wild. They live the usual uneventful lives of small fishes, most of their time being taken up with searching for food – or bullying each other. Their mouth is inclined slightly upward making it easy for them to take any food floating at the surface. They can also search on the bottom, the body held almost vertical with the head downward. They also snap at small swimming invertebrates. They are, in fact, omnivorous, taking anything small, both plant and animal, swimming or floating, and in the aquarium they spend much time grazing small algae growing on the glass or stones.

There seems to be a strong social hierarchy known as peck order in a community of swordtails which reveals itself in the aquarium by one of the males tending to bully the rest. Indeed, these fishes seem to be unduly spiteful, especially in small aquaria. Dominance in a community of any species is decided and maintained by fighting, or at least, by aggressive displays, and is closely linked with the strength of the sex hormones. Experiments with swordtails have shown, however, that a female maintains her position in the social hierarchy for 1–3 months after being spayed and a castrated male retains his for $1-6\frac{1}{2}$ months. This is unusual because as a rule, when the gonads are removed, and with them the sex hormones, the individual usually drops more or less immediately to a subordinate rank in the social hierarchy.

△ *A male swordtail with a black-edged yellow 'sword' swims alongside a female.*
◁ *Red and green swordtails: two males with females and young.*

Mystery of sex-reversal

Swordtails first became aquarium fishes about 1910, and not long after this the idea began to be current that these fishes undergo a remarkable sex-reversal. In 1926 Essenberg reported that females, after having had several broods, may become fully functional males. From the many reports that followed this the impression is gained that this is commonplace. There have, for example, been several authoritative books on freshwater or aquarium fishes written during the years since Essenberg's report was published, and all have given prominence to this idea. Gunther Sterba in his book first published in 1959 speaks of the quite remarkable and always astonishing sex-reversal in swordtails. He claims that in some strains as many as 30% of females later change into males. Yet in 1957 Myron Gordon, who had made a special study of the species, had already claimed that such changes were extremely rare, quoting a substantial report on swordtails by Friess, in 1933, in support of his claim.

Subjects for heredity study
If the supposedly remarkable sex-reversal is still in doubt there are other aspects of the breeding for which we have more reliable information. Swordtails have been almost domesticated and by selective breeding a wide range of colour varieties exist, usually named according to their colours, such as the green, the red, the red-eyed red, the red-wag, the black, the golden, and the albino. According to Dr Myron Gordon, quoted by William T. Innes, there are wild specimens comparable to all the selected varieties produced up to 1935 except the golden. There have, however, been others since then, including the one seen below.

Swordtails have been much used for the study of genetics, by crossing the colour varieties. In addition many hybrids with the platy have been produced, which increases still further not only the range of colours but also the materials for further studies on heredity. These fishes are particularly suitable for laboratory work of this kind. The sexes can be readily recognized, which is always a help in such studies. The males not only differ from the females in having the 'sword', they also have a gonopodium for the insertion of milt, fertilisation being internal. They also breed rapidly. A brood may number up to 200, each $\frac{1}{4}$ in. long at birth. The newly-born must rise to the surface for air to fill the swim-bladder after which they can swim well and start to feed almost immediately. They also grow quickly. At first the sexes look alike but soon the males start to grow a sword. Swordtails live 2–3 years, so there is a rapid turn-over in populations. As a result swordtails, with their near relatives the platys, may be considered as a vertebrate equivalent of the fruit fly for genetical studies.

Hybridization
Probably the most remarkable feature of the sex life of the swordtail is the ease with which it hybridizes with platys in aquaria, yet although both species live virtually side by side in the fresh waters of Mexico and Guatemala no wild hybrids have been found. This is the more noteworthy since their breeding behaviour is so similar. There are, however, several small differences, hardly noticeable until close and critical study is made of them. To begin with, platys take about 5 minutes from the start of pre-mating behaviour to the actual mating, whereas swordtails take only one minute. The actual mating takes only half the time in platys that it does in swordtails and altogether the mating behaviour of platys is much the more vigorous. The differences are slight, and probably no one of them would be sufficient to form a barrier between the species, but taken as a whole they do. Under artificial conditions, as in an aquarium where the choice of mates is limited anyway, the barrier is readily overcome. In the wild, with a wide choice of mates, even small details count.

class	**Pisces**
order	Cypriniformes
family	Poeciliidae
genus & species	*Xiphophorus helleri*

▽ *Selective breeding results in a wide range of colour varieties: a recent breed is seen here.*

Zebra fish

There are several fishes with a common name that includes the word 'zebra'. The most noticeable of these is a small freshwater fish of Bengal and eastern India. Less than 2 in. long, it is called the zebra fish or zebra danio and is a member of the large carp family. It is an extremely popular fish with aquarists.

It is a slim fish with the body only slightly compressed. The single dorsal fin and the anal fins are fairly large, and it has a relatively large tailfin and small pelvic and pectoral fins. There are two pairs of barbels. The back is brownish-olive, the belly yellowish-white and the flanks are Prussian blue with four golden stripes from the gill cover to the base of the tail. The dorsal fin is also blue with yellow at its base and a white tip. The anal fin is again blue-gold barred, and so is the tailfin. The effect of the stripes is to make the fish look even more streamlined than it is, and to give an impression of movement even when the fish is stationary.

Beauty in repetition

As so often happens with a fish of outstanding colour, subsequently popular with aquarists, there is little that is zoologically striking in zebra fishes. They swim among water plants or in schools—it is when they are all aligned, swimming in formation, evenly spaced, and all travelling in the same direction that they most catch the eye. Almost certainly their attraction owes much to the repetition of their stripes—termed the 'beauty in repetition' by Dr Dilwyn John in 1947. In 1935, William T Innes came very near to saying this in his comprehensive book *Exotic Aquarium Fishes* when he described it as a fish 'to show to advantage moving in schools, it scarcely has an equal, for its beautiful horizontal stripes, repeated in each fish, give a streamline effect that might well be the envy of our best automobile designers'.

Special precautions

Zebra fishes are carnivorous, feeding on any small animals they can swallow, which usually means small insect larvae, crustaceans and worms. After their colour, their strongly carnivorous tendencies provide one of their more interesting features. They are egg-eaters, and those who breed zebra fish in aquaria need to take special precautions to achieve success.

There is little difference between the sexes except that the female, especially just before spawning, is more plump than the male, and her stripes are more silver and yellow than the golden stripes of the male. In the pre-spawning behaviour the male leads the female in among the water plants and the two take up position side by side, she to shed her ova, he to shed his milt over them to fertilise them. As the eggs slowly sink there is a tendency for the two to snap up the eggs. The first precaution for the aquarist is therefore to provide a breeding aquarium with water so shallow that the fish have no chance to catch the eggs before they sink to safety in the spaces between the gravel on the bottom. The correct size of gravel pebbles must be used or the adults may become trapped between them. Marbles have been used, or else some sort of trap. An early trap used was a series of slender glass rods held together at the ends with soft wire and raised just off the bottom of the aquarium. This was later superseded by fine metal mesh or nylon.

Each female lays about 200 eggs which hatch in two days. The larvae are at first fairly helpless and inactive, but two days later they can swim and start to feed on microscopic plankton animals. They begin to breed at a year old. At two years they are old-aged, and a zebra fish of three or more years old is an extreme rarity.

Question of stripes

The name 'zebra' is from an Amharic or Ethiopian word and first gained currency in Europe in 1600. By the early years of the 19th century its use had been extended not only to cover all manner of striped animals but also materials showing stripes, and especially to striped shawls and scarves. In the world of fishes there is the zebra shark of the Indian Ocean, with black or brown bars on the body, more like the stripes of a tiger. So we have the anomaly of the common name being zebra shark and the scientific name *Stegostoma tigrinum*. In the extreme south of South America is the zebra salmon *Haplochiton zebra*. In pisciculture there is a hybrid of the trout *Salmo trutta* and the American brook trout *Salvelinus fontinalis*, which is called the zebra hybrid. A foot-long marine fish of the Indo-Pacific *Therapon jarbua* is sometimes called the zebra or tiger fish. It is, however, among the aquarium fishes that the name is most used — the striped or zebra barb *Barbus fasciatus* of Malaya and the East Indies is an example. The common killifish *Fundulus heteroclitus*, of North America, is also called the zebra killie, while the zebra cichlid *Cichlasoma nigrofasciatum* is also — and more appropriately — called the convict fish. Some of these fish have horizontal stripes and others vertical, and there has been some disagreement over which are more correctly termed 'zebra'. However, since a glance at a photograph of a zebra shows that the stripes run in different directions on the different areas of the body, there seems no reason why the name should not be applied to all.

class	**Pisces**
order	**Atheriniformes**
family	**Cyprinodontidae**
genus & species	***Brachydanio rerio***

▽ *On the right lines: the popular zebra fish proves that parallel stripes never meet.*

Catfish

The European catfish, or wels, grows to 9 ft or more in the rivers of central and eastern Europe and western Asia, and is the most famous of a large group called the naked catfishes. Its head is large and broad, the mouth has a wide gape and around it are three pairs of barbels or 'whiskers', the feature of all catfishes. In the wels the three pairs of barbels can be moved about and one pair is very long. The eyes are small. The body is stout, almost cylindrical in front, and flattened from side to side in the rear portion. The skin is slimy and has no scales. The fins, except for the long anal fin, are small. The colour is dark olive-green to bluish-black on the back, the flanks being paler with a reddish sheen, the belly whitish, the whole body being marked with spots and blotches.

The wels has many common names: silurus, the name given it by the Romans, glanis, sheatfish, or sheathfish, said to be from a fanciful resemblance to a sword scabbard, and waller. It has been introduced to a number of lakes in different parts of England.

Night hunter

The European catfish lives in rivers or deep lakes with plenty of water plants. It spends the day under overhanging banks or on the mud in deep water, foraging in the mud with its barbels in search of small invertebrates. At night it hunts, feeding voraciously on fish, crustaceans, and frogs. The larger ones take small water birds and mammals.

In May to June, the breeding season, the catfish moves into shallow water, where the female lays her eggs in a depression in the mud formed by lashing movements of her tail. A large female may lay 100 000 eggs, which are said to be guarded by the male. The fry are black and tadpole-shaped.

Legendary criminal

It would be surprising if a large fish, with hearty appetite, that lurks in dark places did not gather an evil reputation. The wels has been accused of swallowing lambs, even children. Gesner, in the 16th century, reports that a human head and a hand bearing gold rings were taken from the stomach of one of these large catfish.

Many strange habits

Although related, the various naked catfishes show remarkable diversity in form and habits. The banjo catfishes of South America may live in rivers and brackish

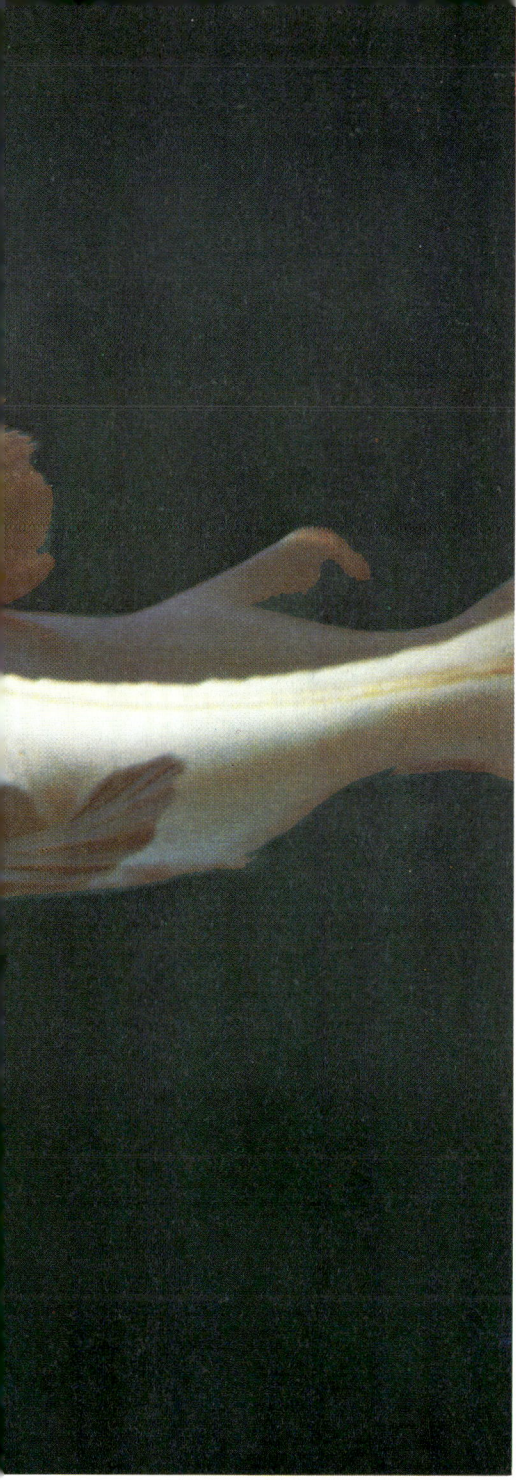

◁ *Most of the many different kinds of catfishes have three pairs of barbels round the mouth.*

△ *Glass catfish, like many catfishes, has no scales.*
▽ *The barbels are used to probe in mud for food.*

estuaries, some species in the sea. They are named for their flattened bodies with an unusually long tail. In one species *Aspredinichthys tibicen* the tail is three times the length of the body. In the breeding season, the females of this species grow a patch of spongy tentacles on the abdomen, and carry their eggs anchored to these.

Marine catfishes of the family Ariidae are mouth-breeders. That is, the male holds the eggs, which in some species are nearly 1 in. diameter, in his mouth, and when they hatch he continues to shelter the fry in the same way. For a month he must fast. Another name for these catfishes is crucifixion fish, because when the skull is cleaned, a fair representation of a crucifix is formed by the bones of the undersurface.

Another family of marine catfishes (Plotosidae) contains one of the most dangerous fishes of the coral reefs. The dorsal and the pectoral fins carry spines equipped with poison glands. Merely to brush the skin against these spines can produce painful wounds.

Equally dangerous are the parasitic catfishes. Some of this family (Trichomycteridae) are free-living but many attach themselves to other fishes using the spines on the gill-covers to hook themselves on, piercing the skin and gorging themselves on the blood. Others insinuate themselves into the gill-cavities, eating the gills. The candiru *Vandellia cirrhosa* is prone to make its way into the urethra of a naked person entering the water, especially, so it seems, if water is passed. A surgical operation may be necessary to remove the fish. Men and women in the unsophisticated areas of Brazil wear a special guard of palm fibres to protect themselves when wading into rivers.

North America has the flathead (family Ictaluridae), a useful catfish reaching 5½ ft long and 100 lb weight. The channel catfish is a most valuable foodfish. There are, however, the madtoms, 5 in. or less, but with pectoral spines and poison glands.

Mad in another sense are the upside-down catfishes of tropical African rivers. From swimming normally these catfishes may suddenly turn and swim upside-down, for no obvious reason. When courting, the male and female upside-down catfishes swim at each other and collide head-on, repeating this at half-minute intervals.

class	**Pisces**
order	**Siluriformes**
family	**Siluridae**
genus & species	*Silurus glanis* European catfish others

33

Seahorse

The seahorse is a strange animal which looks like the knight of a chess set, but that is not the end of its oddities. It can wrap its tail round a seaweed or similar object, as a South American monkey wraps its tail round a branch. Each of its eyes is on a turret and can move independently. Although many other fishes can also move their eyes independently, this ability is more pronounced in seahorses. A final oddity is that the male carries the babies in a pouch.

A seahorse has a large head with a tubular snout, a moveable neck, a rotund body and a long tapering, slender tail, with a total length of not more than 8 in. The neck, body and tail are marked with circular and longitudinal ridges, on which there are bony bumps, so the fish looks almost like a wood carving. There is a pair of small pectoral fins and a single small dorsal fin. The colours vary widely but are mostly light to medium brown, scattered with small white spots, and often there are ornamental fleshy strands.

There are 20 species, half of which live in the Indo-Australian region. The others live off the Atlantic coasts of Europe, Africa and North America, with two species on the Pacific coast of America.

Swimming upright

Seahorses live in shallow inshore waters among seaweeds or in beds of eelgrass in estuaries. They swim in a vertical position, propelling themselves by rapid waves of the dorsal fin. When swimming at full speed this fin may oscillate at a rate of 35 times a second—which makes it look like a revolving propeller. The pectoral fins oscillate at the same rate, and the head is used for steering, the fish turning its head in the direction it wants to go. When a seahorse clings to a support with its tail it still keeps its body upright. If the fins are damaged they can be regenerated relatively quickly.

Tiny mouth

The seahorse eats any kind of swimming animal small enough to enter its tiny mouth. Prey is located by sight and quickly snapped up, or is sucked in from as much as 1½ in. away. It is mainly tiny crustaceans such as copepods, but baby fishes are also eaten.

Male courts male

Breeding starts with males going through actions that look like a courtship, and a male seahorse of one species has even been seen to court a male of another species. This courtship probably brings him into condition to receive the eggs. He pairs up with a female, either swimming in front of her but without actually touching her or, in some species, the two may entwine tails. He seems to be bowing to her, but this is actually a pumping action to drive the water out of the pouch on his belly. The female inserts her long ovipositor into the opening of the pouch to lay her eggs, as many as 200 in some species. During this time the mouth of the pouch is large but when laying is finished it closes to a minute pore, and stays like this until the baby seahorses are ready to be born, in 4–5 weeks. They are about ½ in. long at birth, perfect miniatures of their parents and the first thing baby seahorses do is to swim to the surface to gulp air to fill their swimbladders. They feed ravenously on extremely small crustaceans, such as newly hatched brine shrimps, and grow rapidly. In the Steinhart Aquarium in the United States young seahorses *Hippocampus hudsonius* were found to grow from ⅜ in. at birth to 2½ in. in 2 months.

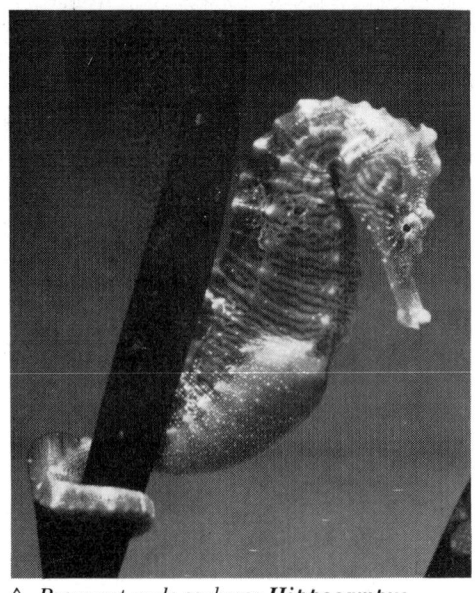

△ *Pregnant male seahorse* **Hippocampus erectus**, *his belly pouch extended with eggs.*
▽ *Proud parent with day-old young seahorses.*

▷ *The scene is set for the seahorse ballet; one wraps its prehensile tail round another.*
▽ *Young day-old seahorse (approx. × 7).*

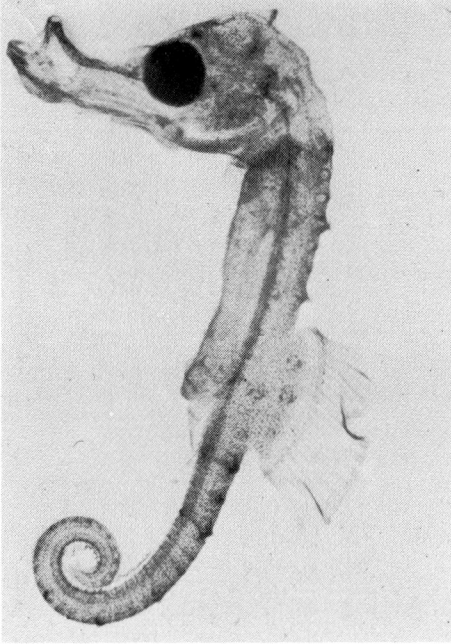

Placental fishes

The inside of the pouch changes just before and during courtship. The walls thicken and become spongy, and they are enriched with an abundant supply of blood vessels. As the female lays her eggs the male fertilises them and they become embedded in these spongy walls, which then act like a placenta. As the pouch is closed there must be some way by which oxygen reaches the eggs, and it is almost certain that the network of blood vessels in the wall of the pouch passes oxygen to the eggs and takes up carbon dioxide from them. Also food probably passes from the paternal blood into the eggs, just as it does from the mother's blood in the mammalian placenta.

Male labour

We are used to the idea that no matter what happens beforehand, in the actual bearing of offspring it is always the female that has the burden. In seahorses it is the reverse. As each batch of eggs is laid in his pouch the male seahorse goes through violent muscular spasms which work the eggs to the bottom of the pouch to make room for more. It seems also that there is a physiological reaction as the eggs sink into the spongy tissue, and he shows signs of exhaustion. When the young have hatched and are ready to leave the pouch, the mouth of the pouch opens wide. The male alternately bends and straightens his body in convulsive jerks and finally a baby seahorse is shot out through the mouth of the pouch. After each birth the male rests, and when all the babies are born he shows signs of extreme exhaustion. In aquaria the males often die after delivering their brood but this does not happen in a natural state, because the male soon looks around for another female to fill his pouch with eggs.

Seahorses have been described as having the head of a horse, the tail of a monkey, the pouch of a kangaroo, the hard outer skeleton of an insect and the independently moving eyes of a chameleon. It would, however, be difficult to find a suitable comparison for the labour pains of the father.

class	**Pisces**
order	**Gasterosteiformes**
family	**Syngnathidae**
genus & species	**Hippocampus brevirostris** **H. hippocampus**, others

*Marine angelfish, **Holacanthus**, living among the coral reefs of tropical seas, outstanding for its varied patterns and colours.*

Angelfish

*The name 'angelfish' has been used commonly for two types of fishes. Both of these types are bony fishes, one of which is marine, the other freshwater. The latter has long been a favourite with aquarists who, perhaps to avoid confusion of names, developed the habit of using its scientific name, which is **Scalare**. Since not everyone followed their example, however, at least part of the confusion remains. There is another perplexing usage. Some scientists 'lump' the marine angelfishes into the butterfly fish family (see page 16), but the butterfly fish is only distantly related to them and belongs to an entirely separate family.*

There is little to choose between these angelfishes and butterfly fishes. Most are brilliantly coloured, mainly coral-reef dwelling fishes; the angelfishes, however, have a sharp spine on the lower edge of the gill-cover which is lacking in the butterfly fishes.

It hardly needs explaining that these vernacular names are prompted by the enlarged flap-like or wing-like fins.

Most angelfish are small, up to 8 in. long, but the marine ones reach 2 ft in length. The outline of the body, because of the well-developed fins, has much the shape of a flint arrowhead.

Colourful and curious

The marine angelfishes, and the similar butterfly fishes, which together number more than 150 species, live mainly in shallow seas and a few enter estuaries. They live in pairs or small groups at most, around reefs, rocks or corals.

They are inoffensive as adults, they are peaceable, they do not dash away as most fishes do when, for example, a skin diver intrudes into their living space. They move away but slowly, every now and then tilting the body to take a closer look at the newcomer.

The outstanding feature of these fishes is the wide range and the beauty of their colours and patterns. In many of them the young fishes have the same colours as the adults, but in others the differences are so great that it looks as if there are two different species involved. Their behaviour tends to be different also. Quite small —that is, up to a few inches long—they tend to be solitary, and individuals are usually found in the same places day after day, in each case near a shelter into which the fish darts when disturbed. The shelter may be under a rock bed or among seaweed. A tin can lying on the sea-bed will readily be used for shelter. In an aquarium the sub-adults will be aggressive towards each other, but one kept on its own readily becomes tame and learns to feed from the hand.

Probably the most beautiful of the angels is the rock beauty, coloured jet black in front and yellow in its rear half, its fins bright yellow with red spots. It has a strong sense of curiosity that makes it draw near to the underwater swimmer. The queen angelfish, when small, is largely dark brown to black with three bluish vertical bands on the sides of the body and a bluish band along the dorsal fin. Adult, it is mainly a startlingly bright yellow with irregular and diffuse patches of violet or red on various parts of the body. The French angel is black with strongly contrasting bright yellow vertical bands and a yellow face (see illustration page 38).

Feeding

Angelfishes have small mouths armed with many small teeth and they use these when they browse on the algae and coral polyps or catch the small invertebrates on which they feed. In some species the snout is somewhat elongate, and may be inserted in cracks and crevices in rocks or coral to capture small animals for food.

In certain species of butterfly fishes, such as *Chelmon rostratus*, the snout is very long and tube-like with the small mouth at the end. This enables the fishes to probe even deeper into the crevices of coral rock for their food.

Parental care

Little is known of the breeding habits of marine angelfish, but they probably conform to the pattern of their better known relations in that they show quite close care of the eggs and fry.

Both fish clean a patch of flat rock, and the female lays her eggs on it, the male swimming close over them shedding sperm for fertilisation. The eggs are tended for 4–8 days by the parents, when the fry hatch, and sink to the bottom.

The parents guard them until they are sufficiently free-swimming to hide in crevices and weed. The fry are unlike the adults in that their bodies are long and slim. They do not not assume full adult shape before three or four months have passed.

Conspicuous colouring

All angelfishes and butterfly fishes are conspicuous. To the underwater swimmer

△ *Angelfish are strongly territorial and use their colours both to advertise possession of their territory and to warn off an intruder of their own species. One of these freshwater* **Scalare** *is displaying at the other with a sideways flick of its bright pectoral fins like flashing signals.*
▽ *These freshwater angelfish,* **Scalare***, are favourites with aquarists, being easy to care for and attractive to look at.*

their colours stand out and 'hit the eye'. Especially striking are the patterns of the imperial angelfish or blue angelfish, with their inscribed patterns of white and black curves and half circles on a rich blue and violet background, dazzling to the eye when seen at close quarters.

We are used to the idea of colours and colour-patterns serving as camouflage to hide an animal from its enemies or enable it, if a predatory animal, to steal close to its prey undetected. We are used also to conspicuous colours, especially combinations of yellow, black and red, serving as warning colours, the wearer of these colours being poisonous or bad-tasting or having a sting. The colours of angelfishes certainly fail to hide their wearer. Although one writer has described angelfishes as nestling among coral heads like hummingbirds among brilliant blossoms, most underwater swimmers agree you can see these fishes clearly at a distance. There is no indication that angelfishes are poisonous or unpalatable, or have a sting. They are eaten by the local peoples wherever they occur, although their skins are said to be tough.

Perhaps the comparison with hummingbirds is not so far-fetched as it appears at first sight. Conspicuous colours in birds are associated with displays, especially aggressive displays, as they are in lizards such as the anole and the same may be true of angelfishes. Experimentally, a mirror was placed in an aquarium with a French angelfish. The fish drew near, nibbled at its reflection in the mirror, then threw itself sideways and flicked its bright blue pectoral fins like flashing signals. This suggests that angelfishes are strongly territorial and use their colours both to advertise possession of a territory as well as to warn off an intruder of their own species.

There was at least one angelfish that escaped attention for a long time despite its colouring, a bright orange head with a glowing dark blue contrasting body. This, the pygmy angelfish, was wholly unknown until 1908, when one was brought up in the trawl off Bermuda from a depth of 540 ft. It was dead when it reached the surface and its carcase was committed to a jar of alcohol to preserve it. It became something of a mystery fish and it was not until 1951 that it was given a scientific name, when one scientist examining it realized it was a new species of angelfish. The next year a second specimen was taken from the stomach of a larger fish, a snapper, caught in 240 ft of water off Mexico. In 1959, this fish, believed to be so rare, was caught in fair numbers by a skin-diver off the Bahamas, in 40 ft of water.

class	**Pisces**
order	**Perciformes**
family	**Chaetodontidae**

◁ *Marine French angelfish,* **Pomacanthus paru***, showing one of the bizarre shapes and patterns typical of these fish, which look quite different when they are seen from the side than they do from the front view.*

Pompadour fish

This fish from the rivers of the Amazon basin has been described as the noblest among aquarium fishes. Its name of pompadour is then quite appropriate although it is also known as the discus from its shape. The pompadour fish and its relative, which is divided into subspecies known as the green discus, brown discus and blue discus, are almost disc-shaped when fully grown and up to 8 in. long. The long dorsal and anal fins make the otherwise oval body look more nearly circular. The body is covered with small scales but the cheeks and gill covers are more markedly scaly. The mouth is small, with thick lips. There is a single row of small conical teeth in the middle of each jaw and instead of the usual two pairs, there is a single pair of nostrils.

The colours are not easy to describe because they change with age. A young pompadour fish is brown with several vertical dark bars down each side. At 6 months old, flecks of blue appear on the head and gill covers, and these spread until the sides are coloured with alternating bands of blue and reddish brown and there are nine vertical dark bands, the first running through the eye. The fins become blue at their bases, pale blue and orange on the outer edges, and there are streaks of blue and orange between. The pelvic fins are red with orange tips. The green discus is mainly green with 9 dark vertical bars, the brown discus mainly brown with 9 dark bars and the blue discus brown with 9 blue bars.

△ Turning blue with age, pompadour fish **Symphysodon aequifasciata**. At 6 months the head and gill covers become flecked with blue and this gradually spreads across the sides.

Hanging by a thread

Pompadour fishes usually spend the day sheltering in the shadows of water plants when they are not feeding and they avoid strong sunlight. They eat water insects, especially the larvae of midges and small dragonflies, small worms and similar invertebrates. There is a brief courtship, during which the pair clean the surface of a broad leaf of a water plant. When this is ready, the female lays rows of eggs on it. Sometimes the surface of a stone is used but only after being meticulously cleaned. Once the eggs are laid the male swims over and fertilises them. The parents take it in turn to fan them with their fins and they hatch in about 50 hours. As each baby breaks out of the egg it is removed in the parents' mouth and placed on a leaf, where each hangs by a short thread for the next 60 hours. The parents continue to fan with their fins and when, at the end of this time, the babies are about to swim, they swarm on the side of one of the parents and appear to hang there. After a time the parent gives a wriggle and the fry are shaken off towards the side of the other parent, who is swimming nearby. When 3–4 weeks old the fry become independent and feed on small animal plankton such as very small water fleas or their larvae. At first they are the normal fish shape, if a little plump in the body. The discoid shape comes with age.

Feeding the fry

There can be little doubt that baby pompadours get protection by swarming on the side of the parent, although sometimes they are eaten by the parents, at least in aquaria. The question is whether they get something more. In 1959 Dr WH Hildeman reported observations that seemed to show that the babies fed on a slime secreted by the parents' skin. This seems to have been accepted by students of tropical fishes. In the 1969 edition of their book *All about tropical fish* Derek McInerny and Geoffry Gerard not only state that the parents secrete a whitish mucus over their bodies but that the fry will eat nothing else. They quote Mr R Skipper 'who has successfully raised several spawnings' and he claims they will not thrive on any alternative food. Indeed, he maintains the only hope of raising them is to leave them with their parents. Against this we have the words of Gunther Sterba, in his *Freshwater fishes of the world*, that not only do the young of some other cichlid fishes cling to the sides of their parents but that at least one aquarist has reared young pompadours away from the care and protection of parents.

One reason why pompadours are not more often kept in aquaria is that young ones taken in the wild are infected with microorganisms. The frequent changes of water necessary to keep them in captivity seem to favour the parasites, which get the upper hand and kill the pompadours.

class	**Pisces**
order	**Perciformes**
family	**Cichlidae**
genus & species	***Symphysodon aequifasciata*** brown, green and blue discus ***S. discus*** pompadour fish

▽ *Floating discs of colour,* **Symphysodon discus** *swim in the shadows.*

Moorish idol

This is one of the most striking of the small reef fishes. It has given inspiration to artists, designers and decorators and has been figured on wallpapers and fabrics. It is said to have been sold in the fish markets of Hawaii, and may still be sold there. It is mentioned and depicted in almost every book on fishes although practically nothing is known of its way of life or its life history.

There are three species of moorish idol, the largest being up to 8 in. long bu 4 in. is more usual. The body is strongly flattened from side to side, and when looked at from the side it is nearly circular. There is, however, a high dorsal fin in the mature fish and a triangular anal fin, making the outline almost diamond-shaped. In front the snout is drawn out and ends in a small mouth with small, very fine teeth in both upper and lower jaw. Two bony horns grow out over the eyes. The tail is short and it carries a tail fin that is almost triangular. The most striking feature is the colour pattern, the body being white and pale yellow with broad bands of brownish black running from top to bottom. The skin is shagreen-like, being covered with small sharp scales which have the effect of making it feel almost like fine sandpaper to the hand.

Moorish idols spread halfway round the world in tropical seas; they are found from East Africa around the coasts of the Indian Ocean, the East Indies, Melanesia, Micronesia and Polynesia to the coasts of Japan and the various islands off the Pacific coast of Mexico.

Hiding among coral
These fishes are often seen in shallow inshore waters but their real home is on the coral heads in deeper waters, in coral lagoons, especially in the surge channels through coral reefs, and along the outer edges of the reefs. Although the outward appearance and colours, the shapes of their fins and other physical features have been repeatedly described in great detail in one scientific paper after another, nothing has been recorded of how they swim or what is their food. At best we can only deduce something of this. They probably swim by waving their tails, dorsal and anal fins, with the tail fin used as a rudder. This is how the butterfly fishes and marine angelfishes, to which they are distantly related, also swim. It is the way fishes swim that spend their time among irregular reefs or coral where quick movements and sharp turns are needed rather than swift forward movement.

Tweezer jaws
The narrow jaws of a moorish idol, with small teeth in front, act almost like tweezers. The snout is very like that of the butterfly fishes. From looking at moorish idols in aquaria, as well as guessing from the shape of the jaws and teeth, they probably feed on small crustaceans and other small invertebrates picked out with the 'tweezers' from small crevices.

Knife-like spine
The spawning times and mating behaviour are unknown. Young moorish idols are seldom seen, probably because of the difficulty of collecting them from among the coral heads. The few that have been caught show that the young fishes, up to $\frac{1}{2}$ in. long, have much the same shape as the adults but with long, low dorsal and anal fins and only one black band running from the top of the head, through the large eye to the throat, where the pelvic fins are situated, the small pectoral fins being just behind the eye. In the front of the dorsal fin are three spines. Two of these are very short but the third is long and thin, about $1\frac{1}{2}$ times as long as the body, streaming out behind. As the fish grows this gets shorter and finally the whole dorsal fin assumes the well-known triangular shape. Another feature of the young fish is that it has a knife-like spine behind each corner of the mouth. These drop off when it has grown to about 3 in. long.

△ *At home among the colourful corals—the moorish idol has a very striking colour pattern and an exquisitely shaped dorsal fin.*

Why moorish idol?
Not the least puzzling aspect of these fishes is their common name. 'Moorish' is usually associated with the western Mediterranean region, where the Moors are best remembered for the way they spread across North Africa and into Spain centuries ago. But moorish idols do not live there. Moreover, the Moors would have nothing to do with idols. A possible key to the origin of the name may lie in the association of the word 'Moorish', meaning Mohammedan, with the language of southern India on the coasts of which the fish does live. This word is now obsolete but it was once used by Englishmen living in that part of India. Perhaps it would have been better to have adopted the name which the Hawaiians give to these fishes—*kihikihi*.

class	**Pisces**
order	**Perciformes**
family	**Acanthuridae**
genus & species	*Zanclus canescens* others

Mudskipper

Mudskippers are fish which, instead of retreating with the falling tide, usually remain on the exposed mud. They can breathe air and move quickly over the mud, using their pectoral fins. Among some of the largest members of the goby family, they live on mud flats and mangrove swamps from West Africa to southeast Asia and the southwestern Pacific.

Mudskippers are 5–12 in. long, almost tadpole-like with a heavy head and long body compressed from side to side. They could well be described as pop-eyed, with their conspicuous eyes, placed well up on the head. These eyes can move about in all directions. The front dorsal fin is high and spiny. The pectoral fins are fairly large and somewhat limb-like. The pelvic fins are joined to form a kind of sucker. The colour of the body varies from blue-grey to brownish, often with many small blue spots. The fins, especially the two dorsals, are decorated with coloured spots which vary according to the species.

In western Africa they live on the Saharan shores to the north and the Namibian shores to the south. In eastern Africa they range from East London to the Red Sea, and from there around the shores of the Indian Ocean and into the Indo-Australian region.

Three mud dwellers

Mudskippers show a zonation from the depths of the mangrove swamps, even up in the trees, through the mud of the forest floor down to the mid-tide level. There are three basic types of mudskippers. The eel-skippers *Scartelaos* so called because they have long slender bodies, live in the very soft mud at mid-tide level in the estuaries and are never far from water. Little is known of their habits. The second group, genus *Boleophthalmus*, live in large numbers on the mud at the seaward edge of mangrove forests. They may move into the margin of the forest, under the trees, but no more. They move their heads from side to side as they skitter over the mud skimming diatoms and algae from the surface. In a way not yet understood, they sort these out from the water in the mouth, swallow the diatoms and algae and spit out the water. The third group includes the genera *Periophthalmus* and *Periophthalmodon*, the commonest mudskippers, found along the banks of creeks and throughout the mangrove forests. These feed on insects that have fallen into the mud, on crabs, worms and the smaller mudskippers.

The species of *Periophthalmus* fall into two groups: those represented by *P. kalolo* in which the pelvic fins are still separate, and those represented by *P. chrysospilos* with the pelvic fins joined and forming a sucker. Mudskippers of the first group can climb only onto the exposed roots of mangroves whereas those of the second group are able to climb the vertical shoots and trunks by means of their suckers.

△ *Mudskipper profile: these are quite common in tropical parts of coastal Australia.*
◁ *Gill-chambers full of water, Malayan mudskippers* **Periophthalmus chrysopilos** *on mud.*

▽▷ *In these Malayan species the pelvic fins have moved anterior to the pectoral fins and joined to form a sucker which enables them to climb the vertical trunks of mangroves.*

Living in air
All mudskippers spend much of their time out of water, but they constantly return to the pools left by the tide. The gill chambers are much enlarged to carry a supply of water but this has to be continually renewed in the pools although they can breathe air through the membranes lining the back of the mouth and the throat which are richly supplied with blood vessels. Mudskippers are said to dip their tails in water because they breathe through them. This is not so at all. They need to keep their skin moist, so they often splash water over themselves with one of the pectoral fins. They also have to keep their eyes moist. We have a supply of fluid on the surface of the eye supplied by the tear gland, and every time we blink we draw the lids over the eyes and moisten them. Fishes have no tear glands and a mudskipper cleans and moistens its eyes by pulling them back into the head.

Double vision
The eyes themselves serve a dual purpose: the retina of the upper half is rich in rods, which means that it can detect small movements; the lower part has cones, which give colour vision. Presumably with the upper part of the eye they look down to detect insects and other small animals but watch other mudskippers for their colours, since these are used for signals. Eelskippers, when they meet, open their mouths at each other, showing the dark indigo blue inside. They also raise and lower the long spine of the dorsal fin. These movements are a challenge which may end in a pushing match, after which the two separate.

Most, if not all, mudskippers have some form of signal which is often used while they are moving about over the mud. Usually it is a matter of raising and lowering the brightly coloured first dorsal fin every few seconds. One species throws itself in the air at frequent intervals, seeming to stand for a split second on the tip of its very thin tail before flopping back on the mud. This appears to be a matter of making those around keep off its territory, so all have their own feeding ground.

The mudskipper's pectoral fins are broad and mounted on a stubby limb, a sort of arm. In moving over the mud it uses these as crutches. It anchors its body with the anal fin and presses downwards and backwards with the pectoral fins, so it moves with a similar action to a sealion. In the water it swims in the usual way, that is by wriggling its tail, usually keeping its head above water.

Gymnastic courtship
Except in the breeding season, when the male has brighter colours, it is impossible to distinguish the male from the female except by dissection. At the breeding season in *Periophthalmus chrysopilos*, the only species whose breeding behaviour is at all well known, the colours of the male intensify and he has a brilliantly golden chin and throat. He displays this by doing 'press-ups' at passing females until he attracts one. She then follows him to his burrow. Mating seems to take place in the burrow, and the eggs are also laid there.

Mud sappers

Mudskippers are truly amphibious, some species spending most of their time on land, others most of their time in water, being able to stay submerged for up to 2 hours. They have overcome problems of breathing and movement on land, and have also solved the problem of shelters, by burrowing in the mud. The burrows are made up of a saucer-shaped depression leading into a vertical tunnel, with a rampart of mud round the saucer. The saucer may be anything from 6 in. to 2 ft across. One species makes a Y-shaped burrow with twin turrets of mud at the surface. The burrow is dug with the mouth, the fish bringing out mouthfuls of mud and spitting them on to the rampart to build it.

Leaping as well as bounding

The actions of any mudskipper out of water are quite remarkable, as we have seen. There is, however, one species which does more than probably any other to justify the common name of these relatives of the gobies. This is *Periophthalmus koelreuteri*, which is the most widespread species, round the shores of the Indian Ocean. It spends a great deal of its time, when the tide is out, perched on the margins of small pools in the mangrove swamps with the tip of its tail just in the water. The usual size of this mudskipper is about 5 in. in length. When disturbed it jumps to the next pool, which may be anything up to 2 feet away. Moreover it seldom misses its target. Such jumps are made by curving the body and then straightening it suddenly.

class	**Pisces**
order	**Perciformes**
family	**Gobiidae**

▷ *A giant mudskipper* **Periophthalmus** *displays by raising and lowering its dorsal and tail fin. This species lives on the banks of Malayan rivers where they dig 'castles' for themselves. This is a small pool with a muddy wall and perhaps a tunnel in the pool for the fish to retreat into. This species is about twice the size of* **Scartelaos** *being about 9 in. and also much fatter. It will sit on its 'castle' wall and defend its territory, evicting all rivals.*

▷▷ *Tail standing. This mudskipper* **Scartelaos viridis** *was filmed at the mouth of a small river near a Chinese hamlet in Malaya. It lives on the mud flat and is exposed only at very low tide. Every so often, as the series of frames show, it throws itself upwards until it is almost standing on its tail before flopping back onto the mud. This appears to be a matter of showing itself to warn those around to keep off its territory so all have a reasonable amount of feeding ground.*

In the ring: two wary males circle each other during a lull in combat, seeking an opening to attack.

Fighting fish

Many fish fight, but the celebrated species is the fighting fish **Betta splendens** *of Thailand. This is one of 7 related species in southeast Asia, ranging from Thailand to Borneo. It has been selectively bred for fighting qualities and used for sport, with bets placed, in Thailand.*

The wild ancestor is 2 in. long, yellowish-brown with indistinct dark stripes along the flanks. In the breeding season the male becomes darker and rows of metallic green scales on its flanks become brighter. Its dorsal fin is medium-sized, metallic green tipped with red. The anal fin is large and red edged with blue and the small pelvic fins are red tipped with white. The tail fin is rounded. The female is smaller, less colourful, mainly yellowish brown.

Short-lived

Fighting fish live in clear but weedy rivers and lakes, in irrigation ditches and ponds, and two species are also found in mountain streams. They mature rapidly and grow quickly, and they do not live much longer than two years. Because of their rapid growth they feed heavily on all kinds of small aquatic animals such as water fleas, mosquito larvae, worms or small pieces of dead flesh.

Endurance tests

Male fighting fish are pugnacious towards each other—one species has been named *Betta pugnax*—but to nothing like the extent of the selectively bred descendants. Wild fighting fish rarely keep up their fights for 15 minutes and usually it is much less. The cultivated varieties are considered to be poor samples if they fight for less than an hour and some will continue to attack for up to 6 hours.

A raft of bubbles

Mating is preceded by the male swimming around the female, with heightened colours and fins spread. There follows what can only be called dancing and embracing. Before this takes place, however, the male has built a nest, a raft of bubbles. He takes in bubbles of air at the surface and these become enclosed in a sticky mucus in his mouth, so the bubbles last a long time.

The courtship ends with the male turning the female on her side and wrapping himself round her. Then he tightens his grip, turns her upside down, and in a short while lets go and, as she remains suspended in the upside-down position, he stations himself beneath her. She begins to lay 3–7 eggs at a time, to a total of several hundred. As these slowly sink the male catches each in turn in his mouth, coats it with mucus, then swims up to his raft and sticks it on the underside. This is repeated until all the eggs are laid, the male looping himself round the female each time to fertilise the eggs as she lays them. Finally, the male drives the female away. After that the male guards the nest. The young hatch 24–30 hours later, when the male's parental duties are at an end.

Head-on crash

The first *B. splendens* to be bred in Europe appeared in France in 1893 and in a very few years it was being kept by aquarists over a large part of the world. One of the earlier varieties was cream-coloured with flowing red fins. Then came the famous Cornflower Blue. After that there were various shades of blue, lavender, green and red ending in the best-known, the rich purplish-blue. All these varieties had flowing veil-like fins and, whatever their colour of body, all had red drooping pelvic fins.

There have been many stories, usually highly coloured, about the way the males fight. The facts are dramatic enough. When two males are put in an aquarium together their colours heighten and they take up position side by side, heads pointed in one direction, one fish slightly in advance of the other. Their fins are erected, their gill-covers expanded. Then, with lightning speed they attack. They try to bite each other's fins and in the end one may have some of its fins torn down to stumps. They may also bite patches of scales from each other's flanks. Sometimes they meet in a head-on clash with jaws interlocked.

Above: Male on the right surveys female. Below: Under the nest, a raft of bubbles, male mates with a female by wrapping himself round her.

The greatest damage is done when the cultivated fighting fish are unevenly matched. A small one matched against a large one is bound to suffer. So is a long-finned variety matched against a short-finned variety. Long flowing fins make it hard for their owner to turn quickly. Moreover, the fishes attack the rear half of their opponents, where the flowing fins are.

Exploding with rage

One of the more exaggerated stories to be published was collected by the distinguished American fish specialist, Hugh M Smith. It is quoted in *Exotic Aquarium Fishes* by WT Innes. It tells how you go out and catch your fighting fish—assuming you live in Thailand—and bring it home in a bottle. Your neighbour does the same. You stand the two bottles together. The two fishes see each other, flash their colours at each other and blow themselves up. They hurl themselves in vain at each other, until finally one of them becomes so angry it literally bursts. If this is your fish you lose your bet!

class	**Pisces**
order	**Perciformes**
family	**Anabantidae**
genus & species	***Betta splendens*** ***B. pugnax*** others

Kissing gourami

This is a popular aquarium fish that has achieved fame for a single trick of behaviour that looks uncommonly like a familiar human action. Other than this the species would have remained in relative obscurity. 'Kissing' is by no means confined to this gourami, which is chosen here to show an interesting facet of animal behaviour.

There are several species of gouramis, all from southeast Asia, where they grow to a foot or more and are used for food. The kissing gourami may grow to a foot long, but when kept in an aquarium it is usually well short of this. Its body is flattened from side to side, oval in outline, with a pointed head ending in a pair of thickened lips. The greenish to grey-yellow dorsal and anal fins are long and prominent and both slope upwards from front to rear. The normal colour of the body is silvery green with dark stripes on the flanks but there is another colour phase, pinkish-white and somewhat iridescent.

Thick lips for breathing and eating

The kissing and other gouramis belong to the labyrinth fishes, which means they have an accessory breathing organ in the gills for taking in air at the surface, as well as breathing by gills. The kissing gourami not only rises to the surface from time to time to gulp air, and therefore can live in water that is slightly fouled, but it also feeds at the surface. The thickened lips probably have an advantage in these two respects. The food consists of both animal and plant matter and in an aquarium kissing gouramis eat dried shrimps and powdered oatmeal, water fleas and dried spinach. To some extent they will feed on the small algae that grow on the sides of the aquarium.

Life history little known

There is still some doubt about their breeding habits. Many labyrinth fishes build bubble nests for their eggs but so far as we know kissing gouramis build no nest but lay 400–2 000 floating eggs. They seem to ignore these as well as the young which hatch in 24 hours. The baby fishes eat ciliated protistans for their first week, taking water fleas after this, graduating to the mixed diet as they grow older. They begin to breed when 3–5 in. long.

Mystery of the kiss

Nobody seems very clear whether this is an aggressive action or part of the courtship. Probably it enters into both. When several kissing gouramis are kept together in one aquarium the larger of them bother the smaller by 'sucking' at their flanks. They will do the same with fishes of other species. This is probably aggressive. When a pair are together, however, they can be seen to face each other, swaying backwards and forwards, as if hung on invisible threads, and then they come together, mouth to mouth, their thick lips firmly placed together in an exaggerated kissing action. Like other labyrinth fishes the male wraps himself around the body of the female when mating. This is preceded by the two swimming round and round each other in a circling movement, after which they again come together, lips to lips, in a seeming kiss.

A touching scene — like mirror images of each other two gouramis 'kiss'. It is not fully understood why this fish, a favourite among tropical fish fanciers, makes this familiar human action. It may be one of aggression but it also enters into the courtship ritual.

Mouth wrestling

The use of the mouth as a test of strength in fighting is common among the higher animals. It is frequently seen in aquarium fishes, especially among cichlids and labyrinth fishes. One fish butting another with its mouth is often used in courtship, especially by the smaller freshwater fishes, and it seems likely that the mouth-wrestling and the butting lead on to the kissing. At all events, A van der Nieuwenhuizen, in his book *Tropical Aquarium Fish*, takes the view that in the cichlid, known as the blue acara *Aequidens latifrons*, mouth-wrestling is used to defeat a rival as well as court a mate. He maintains that when a pair indulge in a bout of mouth-wrestling which ends in stalemate this means the two are physically and psychologically suited and the chances of their breeding are high. The mouth-tugging, as he calls it, may last for hours and be repeated day after day, to end in a genuine lovers' choice. The chances are that the kissing of the gourami has exactly the same importance, so it is a true lovers' kiss.

class	**Pisces**
order	**Perciformes**
family	**Anabantidae**
genus & species	***Helostoma temmincki***

The barracuda is one of the most feared and dangerous predatory fishes. Apparently they may be dangerous in one area and not in another.

Barracuda

Barracuda are pike-like fishes, not related to pike but having a similar long-bodied form, with a jutting lower jaw and a wicked-looking set of fangs. Fishermen, in handling even the dead fish, treat them with respect. There are more than 20 species, but most of them are harmless. The evil reputation of barracudas has perhaps been over-stated, and it is difficult to know what to believe. One eminent authority, speaking of the fear fishermen in the West Indies have for the barracuda, has referred to merciless struggles waged between man and barracuda in the shade of the mangroves. This is at variance with all that one hears from skindivers, as well as with what is said of the speedy attack by this fish. Nevertheless, there are a number of authentic records of attack, especially from the great barracuda, also called picuda, or becuna, the giant of the family, which ranges through tropical and subtropical waters the world over, and may reach a length of 8 ft or more. The northern barracuda, or sennet, of the western North Atlantic, reaches only 18 in., but the European barracuda, barracouta or spet, of the Mediterranean and eastern Atlantic, may reach 3 ft. Other species are the Indian barracuda and Commerson's barracuda, both of the Indian Ocean, and the California barracuda.

Most voracious fish

More fearful to some people than even the shark, the larger barracudas are among the most voracious of predatory fishes. Long and torpedo-shaped, the barracudas swim swiftly and feed voraciously, especially on plankton-feeding fishes, charging through their shoals, attacking with snapping bites. It is said that when a pack of barracuda has eaten enough, it herds the rest of the shoal it is attacking into shallow water and keeps guard over it until ready for another meal.

Small or half-grown barracudas swim in shoals, the larger individuals are solitary. A solitary barracuda attacks swiftly, bites cleanly and does not repeat its attack (shoaling barracuda seldom attack people). It hunts by sight rather than smell, as sharks do, and advice given to bathers and divers reflects this. For example, murky water should be avoided because the fish, aware of every movement you make through its keen sight, may over-estimate your size, thereby over-estimating the danger you represent to it, and attack. A metallic object flashing in clear water looks to a barracuda like a fish and stimulates attack. An underwater spear fisherman towing a fish may be in trouble also, and it is not unknown for a barracuda to snatch a captured fish from a skindiver's belt.

Virtually all the interest in this fish has been concentrated on its behaviour towards man, apart from its use for food. On two occasions American scientists have collected all reports of alleged attacks on human beings. It seems these amount to fewer than 40, making the barracuda less dangerous in aggregate than sharks. To a large extent the reputation of this fish is the result of what appears to be an insatiable curiosity. It will hang around a skin-diver, watching his movements and following him, generating in him a very uncomfortable feeling. There is evidence that a barracuda is most dangerous—some say only dangerous—when provoked. Even so, there are records of a person standing in no more than 1 ft of water having the flesh bitten from the lower leg, or the bone almost severed.

One feature of barracuda behaviour, for which there is as yet no explanation, is that the fish may be dangerous in one area and not in another. Barracuda in the Antilles, for example, should be avoided, but around Hawaii they seem to be harmless.

Barracuda spawn over deep water offshore in the Caribbean, ocean currents distributing the larvae and young.

Reputation prejudiced
All barracudas are regarded as good foodfishes, but there is some prejudice against the barracuda because its flesh is, on occasions, highly poisonous. This may be a seasonal danger, the flesh being poisonous at some times of the year and not at others, it may be due to the flesh being allowed to go slightly bad before being cooked, but it is also due to what is known as ciguatera, which is due to toxins, originating in toxic algae and diatoms, building up from plant-eating fish to predators, and concentrating. The toxin is the cause of sickness, and even death, in humans who eat the predator (for example the barracuda). In the Caribbean, some species of fish are safe to eat from only one side of an island.

Prejudice is not confined to the fish. Sir Hans Sloane, writing in 1707, maintained that barracudas were more fond of the flesh of dogs, horses and black men than that of white men. Père Labat, in 1742, carried this prejudiced statement further. He declared that, faced with a choice of a Frenchman and an Englishman, a barracuda would always choose the latter. He attributed this to the gross meat-eating habits of the Englishman, which produced a stronger 'exhalation' in the water, as compared with the more delicate exudations of a Frenchman, who is a daintier feeder.

class	**Pisces**
order	**Perciformes**
family	**Sphyraenidae**
genus & species	***Sphyraena barracuda*** great barracuda
	S. borealis northern barracuda
	S. sphyraena European barracuda
	others

△ The skull of the great barracuda showing its wicked-looking set of fangs and the jutting lower jaw.

▽ School of barracuda swimming past coral of the Great Barrier Reef, Australia. Shoaling barracuda seldom attack people.

Plaice

The plaice is one of the best known of the flatfishes and commercially the most important. It has a flattened body, with the dorsal fin extending from the head almost to the tailfin, and the anal fin from behind the gill cover to the same point. The brownish, upper, or right side is marked with red spots, each of which is surrounded by a white ring in the adult. These may be pale when the fish has been resting on whitish pebbles. The underside is pearly white but can be partially or wholly coloured, a condition known as ambicoloration. It may take the form of scattered brown or black spots or patches on the white undersurface. Alternatively, only the hindend may be completely coloured as on the upper surface, including the red spots. When the pigmentation extends along the whole underside the undersurface of the head is usually white, but in exceptional cases even this may be coloured. The mouth is twisted, with the lower, or blind, side more developed and armed with a greater number of teeth. The small scales are embedded in the skin and there are bony knobs between the eyes. Plaice can grow to almost 3 ft long, but the usual size is much less.

They range from Iceland and the White Sea, along the coasts of Scandinavia, south through the North Sea to the coasts of France and the western Mediterranean. Plaice are not identical throughout their range but split into a number of races. They vary in area of distribution, time and site of spawning, and in their degree of pigmentation.

Living magic carpet
Plaice live on sandy, gravelly or muddy bottoms, slightly buried, swimming just off the bottom at intervals through the day and night. They are said to be demersal or bottom-living fishes. They swim with vertical undulations of the flattened body, like a living magic carpet, then, holding the body rigid, they glide down. On touching bottom they undulate the fins to disturb sand or mud, which then settles on the fins, disguising the outline of the body. In this position a plaice breathes with a suction-pump action of the gill-covers.

Young plaice seem to go into a state resembling hibernation in winter. They remain quiescent in shallow water, slightly buried in the sand. At the appropriate time they move from shallow to deeper water.

Chisel and grinder
The teeth in the jaws of a plaice are chisel-like, but the throat teeth are blunt crushers. The food is mainly small molluscs but other small bottom-living invertebrates, such as worms, are eaten. Plaice swim over the shore at high tide to feed on the cockle and mussel beds. They hunt by sight not raising the head much off the bottom, but shooting forward horizontally with great accuracy to take the prey. Very small molluscs are taken whole into the stomach. Larger ones are crushed by the throat teeth. They also bite off the siphons of molluscs or the heads of worms sticking out of tubes.

Prolific spawnings
There is little in their outward appearance to tell male from female, but if at any time they are held up to the light the female roe shows as a small dark triangle. The male roe is a curved rounded line. The males reach the spawning grounds first and are still there after the females have gone. Spawning time differs from one part of the sea to another. Off the east coast of Scotland it is from early January to May, with a peak in March. In the Clyde estuary, on the west coast of Scotland, it is from February to June. In the southern North Sea it is from October to March.

To spawn, two plaice swim about $2\frac{1}{2}$ ft off the bottom, the female lying diagonally across the male, releasing a stream of eggs while he emits a stream of milt. Spawning lasts less than a minute, after which the two separate and return to the bottom. Each female lays 50–400 thousand eggs, the number depending, it seems, on the length of the fish. The transparent eggs, each in a tough capsule, are just under $\frac{1}{12}$ in. diameter.

△ *Face to face with the adult plaice. With distorted mouth and transposed eye it now lives permanently at the bottom of the sea, lying on its left side.*

In this plaice the upper surface is mottled light grey to suit its background of shell-gravel. The plaice in the bottom picture has a brown mottling because it is lying on differently coloured sandy gravel. A plaice can change its colour and patterns to blend in with its background. A hormone is secreted which alters the shape of the pigment cells thus changing the colour of the plaice's body.

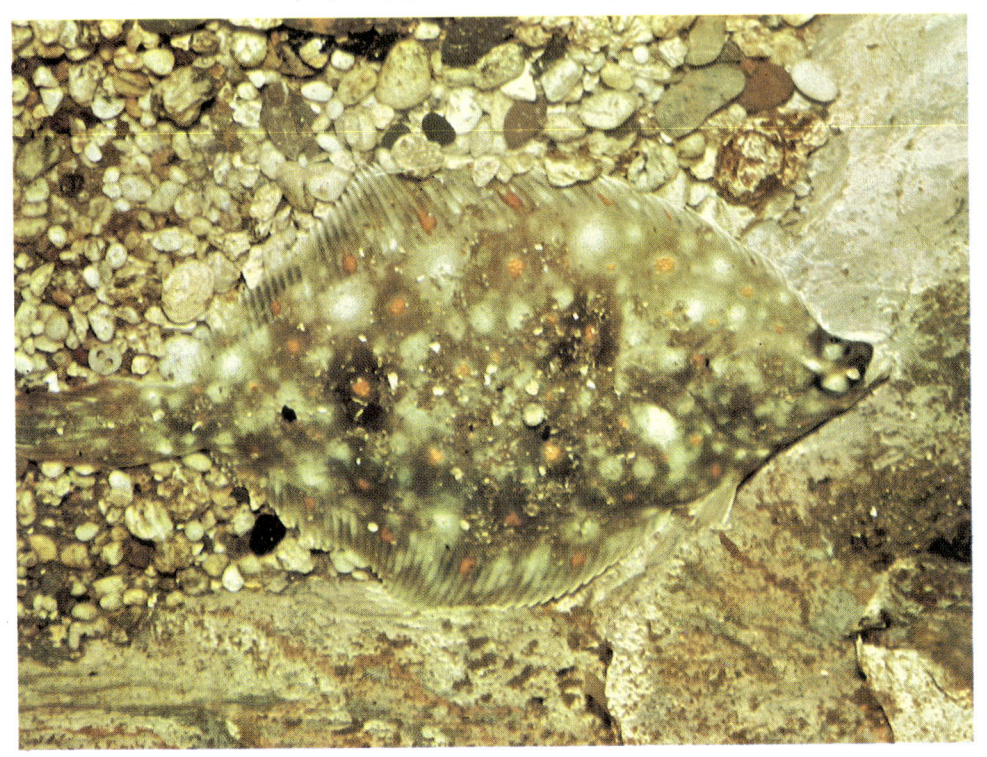

They float at or near the surface, and many are eaten before they can hatch, which they do in 8–21 days, according to the temperature of the water. The larvae are about ¼ in. long, without mouth or gills, and with the remains of a yolk sac attached which supplies them with food. This is the most vulnerable part of the life of a plaice. Apart from those eaten by other animals only 1 in every 100 thousand survive the first few weeks of larval life, or 2–5 for every pair of parent plaice. Although this seems disastrous the figures are put in perspective by the knowledge that in one area alone, halfway between the mouth of the Thames and the coast of Holland, 60 million plaice come together each year to spawn. The adults are probably protected by their colour and their habit of lying buried, but seals find them, and predatory fishes, such as cod, eat the small ones.

Plaice are of great economic value but of the tens of millions of plaice eaten each year in Europe, few are eaten at the right moment. Plaice has the best flavour when it is cooked immediately after being caught. The sole however, develops its characteristic taste 2–3 days after death due to the decomposition of the flesh with the formation of different chemical substances.

Baby food

As the contents of the yolk sac are being used up, the larval plaice starts to feed on diatoms. At this stage it has the normal fish larva shape, giving no indication of the adult shape to come. As it grows it graduates from small diatoms to larger diatoms then to larvae of small crustaceans, such as copepods, and molluscs. At this stage an important item is the planktonic food *Oikopleura*. After 2 months the larva gradually metamorphoses into a young flatfish, this takes about 2½ weeks. The body becomes flattened from side to side, the young plaice starts swimming on its side, the skull becomes twisted by growing more quickly on one side than the other, causing the left eye to be swung over to the right side. At the same time the young plaice leaves the upper waters for the seabed, settling on its left side, so its right side and both eyes are uppermost. As these changes have been taking place the young plaice (still only ½ in. long) has been carried by currents to its inshore nursery ground.

The account given above of the feeding of the larvae is only a generalization. The food taken varies in different places, the plaice taking whatever is available. In Scottish coastal waters they eat mainly worm larvae, crustacean eggs and larval molluscs. Off Plymouth, copepods and other small crustaceans are eaten, in the Irish Sea the larvae feed on small copepods, and spores of algae, and in southern North Sea it is mainly *Oikopleura*. The survival of the larvae can be seriously affected if supplies of these foods are low in the area where they form the staple diet of the larvae.

How they grow

After the ½in. young plaice has settled on the bottom it reaches 2¾ in. by the age of 1 year, 5 in. by 2 years, nearly 8 in. by 3 years, 10½ in. by 4 years and 13 in. by 5 years of age. These figures are for females, the males being smaller. On average, the males reach sexual maturity in 2–3 years, the females in 4–5 years. The figures must be read as approximations because average sizes of plaice have been found to vary: 17 in. in the North Sea, 15 in. in the English Channel, 13 in. in the Kattegat and 10 in. in the Baltic. These are, again, merely examples to show how size can vary, with environmental conditions. A 2ft plaice is 20 or more years old, and a 33in. plaice, which is one of the largest recorded, would be about 40 years old.

class	**Pisces**
order	**Pleuronectiformes**
family	**Pleuronectidae**
genus & species	***Pleuronectes platessa***

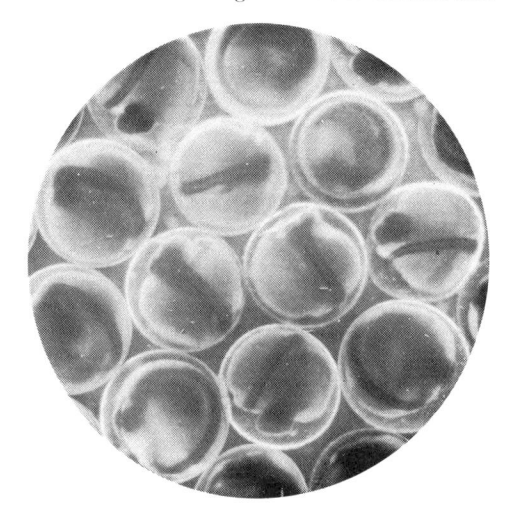

Plaice eggs with developing embryos.

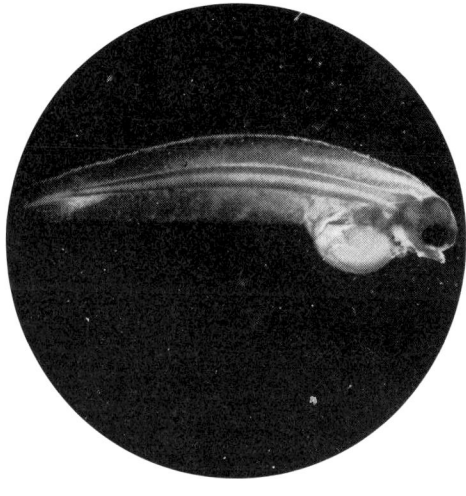

Larva lives in plankton, off its yolk sac.

As yolk sac is used up the mouth develops.

Like many marine fishes the plaice lays a large number of eggs to offset heavy predation. The dramatic part of the life cycle occurs after 2 months in preparation for life on the seabed. The body becomes flattened from side to side; the skull is twisted by growing more quickly on one side than the other, causing the left eye to migrate to the right side; then the young plaice settles with both eyes uppermost.

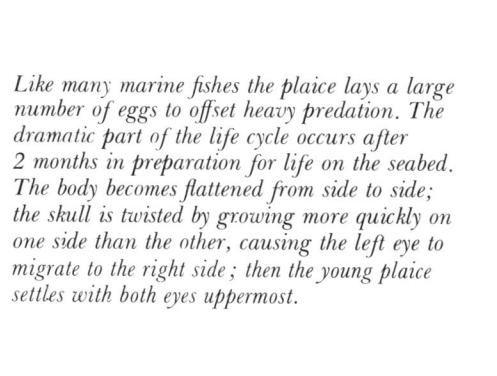

Left eye migrates as larva swims on its side.

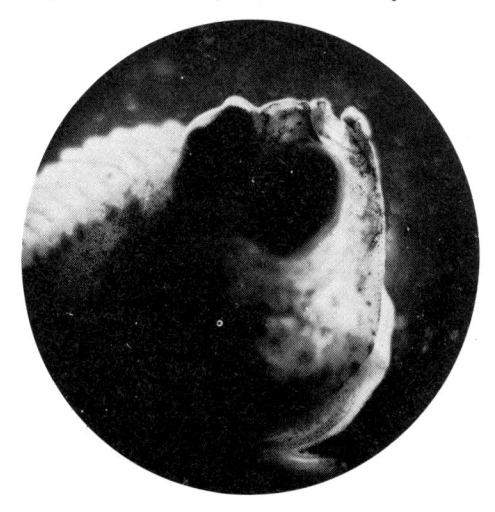

Eye migration complete, plaice settles on bottom.

Hippoglossus hippoglossus
The halibut is a rather mixed-up fish—being halfway between an ordinary fish and a proper flatfish.

Halibut

The halibut is little more than halfway between an ordinary fish and a thorough-going flatfish. It is longer in the body and more plump than most flatfishes, such as the plaice and the flounder. Its jaws have kept their original shape instead of being distorted, with one jaw weaker than the other, and they are armed with sharp teeth. The fringing fins (dorsal and anal) are somewhat triangular and the tail and tail fin are well-marked and powerful. The upper surface, which is in fact the right side, is uniformly olive brown, dark brown or black, the underside being pearly white.

There are two species, one in the North Atlantic, the other in the North Pacific. Exceptional heavy-weights have reached a length of 12 ft and a weight of 700 lb. Small halibut live inshore but, as they mature, move into deeper waters, onto sandy banks for preference, at depths of 1 200 ft or more.

Matching its background
A halibut lies on the seabed where it can pass unnoticed by its prey because of its colour. It leaves the bottom to chase after smaller fishes. Most flatfishes swim by undulations of their fringing fins, but halibut do so by vigorous movements of the body and the powerful tail. While on the bottom the halibut's upper side is coloured like the seabed. Lying on mud a halibut will be black. If it moves onto a patch of sand it begins to grow pale. One with its head on a patch of sand and its body on mud will have a pale head and a black body. These changes are governed through the eyes. A flatfish blinded by injury remains the same colour whatever it is lying on. If we watch a flatfish in an aquarium we see the eyes standing well out on the head, each moving independently of the other, and commanding a view of the bottom all around its head.

Bludgeoning its prey?
Halibut eat crabs, molluscs, worms and other bottom-living invertebrates, but their main food is fishes, especially herring, also flounder, cod, skate, and many others. The fish evidently has a reputation as a killer with fishermen. Dr GB Goode, former Commissioner of Fisheries in the United States, has stated that fishermen declare a halibut kills other fishes with blows of its tail. Whether this is true or not, it tells us something of what fishermen think of the halibut.

Floating eggs
Spawning takes place in the Atlantic during May to July at depths of about 1 200 ft. The Pacific halibut spawns in winter at depths of 900 ft. The female roe is large. In a 250lb fish it may be 2 ft long and weigh 40 lb. A mature female may lay $2\frac{3}{4}$ million eggs, each $\frac{1}{8}$ in. diameter and buoyant, so they float to the surface. The eggs hatch in a few days, the baby fish being the usual fish shape at first, with an eye on each side of the head. It remains at the surface and is carried by currents to inshore waters. After a while the left eye begins to migrate over the top of the head until it comes to lie close to the right eye. At the same time the young halibut turns more and more on to its left side while the dorsal and anal fins grow longer to become the fringing fins. As these changes are taking place the fish is sinking towards the bottom finally to rest on it, left side down. In about one in 5 000 it is the right eye that migrates and the fish then comes to rest on the right side. Until it comes to rest the young halibut is transparent, then it changes colour to become brown or black on the upper side. The halibut is fairly long-lived. One 4 ft long will be about 12 years old, and as much as 35 years of age has been recorded.

Evolution of flatfishes
In the Indian Ocean is one flatfish of the genus *Psettodes* that is more like sea perch to look at. The migrating eye stops short on top of the head, the dorsal fin begins farther back than in other flatfishes and both dorsal and anal fins have spiny instead of soft rays. They rest on their side on the bottom and, like the halibut, swim up to catch prey. Some sea perches also lie on their sides on the bottom to rest, although their shape is normal, and they and *Psettodes* suggest how the flatfish condition probably arose during the course of evolution.

Enemies of halibut?
There are few details known about the enemies of halibut but we can be reasonably sure, by comparison with what is known about other fishes laying huge numbers of eggs, that there is a heavy loss of eggs, fry and young. Later, the growing halibut will suffer from fish-eaters among other species of fish, doubtless also from porpoises, dolphins and seals. There is a steady drain on their numbers from commercial fisheries, halibut being taken by trawl and long line.

Name is mediaeval
Halibut must have been fished for a very long time since the name dates from mediaeval times. It is believed to mean holy turbot, from the Scandinavian word *butta* used for turbot. Captain John Smith, founder of Virginia, wrote of 'the large sized Halibut, or Turbot', and followed this with the strange remark that some are so big 'that the fisher men onley eat the heads & fins, and throw away the bodies'. Later, the halibut became known as the workhouse fish. This may have been a term of contempt or a reference to the fact that one halibut could be large enough to feed many hungry mouths. The fish finally came into its own, not only for the table but for medicinal purposes, in the present century. As we know, the cod was finally recognized in the 1920s as a supplier of cod liver oil for medicinal purposes. A decade or so later halibut oil became popular and almost displaced cod liver oil.

class	**Pisces**
order	**Pleuronectiformes**
family	**Pleuronectidae**
genus & species	***Hippoglossus hippoglossus*** *Atlantic halibut* ***H. stenolepis*** *Pacific halibut*

Anglerfishes

There are more than 350 species of anglerfish, the Pediculati, but because of the distinct differences between them it is convenient to consider them as two groups: anglerfishes (225 + species) and deep-sea anglers (125 species). All have developed the characteristic habits of anglers: they keep still most of the time, using a rod and line to catch small fishes. The rod of the anglerfish is a modified spiny ray of the dorsal fin. Habitual immobility means little expenditure of energy, and less need for breathing. This is reflected in the small gills of anglerfishes with only a small gill-opening.

'Pediculati', the old name for anglerfishes, means 'small foot', referring to the elbowed pectoral fins used like feet to move over the seabed in short jumps. The pelvic fins are also somewhat foot-like but they are small, usually hidden on the undersurface in advance of the pectoral fins. Because of their squat shape, bottom-living habits and method of locomotion the anglerfishes have been given a variety of descriptive vernacular names: goosefishes or monkfishes, frogfishes or fishing frogs (because of the wide mouth) and batfishes. One of the best-known is **Lophius piscatorius**, up to 4ft. long with a large head, about 2½ ft across, and a wide mouth. Although the fish is so ugly the flesh is highly palatable and is widely used as fried fish.

Camouflaged and immobile

Anglerfishes of one kind or another are found at all depths throughout tropical and temperate seas. Bottom-living for the most part, their bodies are ornamented with a variety of warts and irregularities, as well as small flaps of skin. These, with their usually drab colours arranged in a broken pattern, serve to camouflage the fish as it lies immobile among rocks and seaweed. The sargassum angler specializes more than most anglerfishes in camouflage. It lives exclusively among the weed of the Sargasso Sea, and uses its pectoral fins to grasp the weed, so that it is not easily shaken from its position.

Angling for food

The general method of feeding is to attract small fishes near the mouth with some form of lure. In the goosefishes or monkfishes this is a 'fishing rod' bearing a fleshy flap at its tip, which is waved slowly back and forth near the mouth. In others the rod lies hidden, folded back in a groove, or lying in a tube, and is periodically raised or pushed out and waved two or three times before being withdrawn. The lure at the end of the rod often is red and worm-like in shape. A small fish seeing it swims near and then suddenly disappears!

Breeding

Several deep-sea species of anglerfish show a peculiar relationship between male and female; the dwarf male, about ½in. long, attaches itself to the female (whose length is up to 45 in.) so securely that the two grow together, even sharing a blood system. The female is then, in effect, a self-fertilising hermaphrodite, the male being reduced to a mere sperm-producing organ.

Another outstanding feature of the breeding cycle of some anglerfishes is the size of the egg-masses. The female goosefish or monkfish lays eggs in a jelly-like mass, up to 40 ft long and 2 ft in width. This floats at the surface. The relatively large pear-shaped eggs are attached by the narrow end to a sheet of spawn, which floats at the surface, and may contain nearly 1½ million of them. The larva, even before it leaves the egg, begins to develop black pigment. Seen from above the spawn appears as a dark patch in the water, the enclosed larvae looking like currants in a cake. One of these masses, seen by rowers in a boat off Scapa Flow, was mistaken for a sea-monster and the rowers pulled away from it for dear life! The larva is in an advanced stage when hatched and already has the beginnings of its fishing rod. Later, other spines develop on the back and branched fins grow down from the throat, so the larva looks very unusual.

The compleat angler

It is an interesting pastime to list how many human inventions have been anticipated in the animal kingdom. Anglerfishes have used a rod and line (or a lure) long before man did. It is not surprising that both human and fish anglers should use similar methods because their aims are identical. But although attention is always drawn to this by writers on the subject, nobody seems to have commented on the other piece of apparatus the two have in common: the landing net. Both kinds of anglers play their fish but the anglerfish does not allow his quarry to take the bait. Instead, the lure is waved until a fish draws near, then it is lowered towards the mouth. As the victim closes in on it the rod and its lure is suddenly whipped away, the huge mouth is opened wide, water rushes into this capacious 'landing net' and the prey is sucked in, after which the mouth snaps shut. And it all takes place in a flash. Only when a fish is large, so that the tail protrudes from the mouth after the first bite, can we see what has happened. The anglerfish's ability to snap up its prey like lightning is quite remarkable. One moment the small fish is there near its mouth, the next moment it is no longer there, and the speed with which the anglerfish moves its jaws is too fast for the human eye to follow.

The batfishes take their angling to even greater lengths. The whiskery batfish, of the Caribbean, for example, is covered with outgrowths of skin that look exactly like small seaweeds and polyps known as seafire, that coat rocks like so much moss. Small fishes are deceived to the point where they will swim near and try to nibble the flaps of skin. The final touch to this masterpiece of deception lies in the batfish habit of gently rocking its body, making the flaps of skin sway from side to side, just as polyps and seaweed gently sway as the slow currents in the sea move back and forth. This is so much an ingrained habit that a batfish, removed from its surroundings and placed in an aquarium, will periodically rock itself even although it is surrounded only by clear water and glass.

When the small fish, deceived in this way, swims near, out comes the rod with its lure, looking like a wriggling worm. With this the batfish 'plays' its quarry. It will dangle the lure in front of the fish then withdraw it to entice the little fish nearer. It will vary the wriggling of the lure, now waggling it in an agitated manner, now moving it slowly. Watching this one gets the impression of a fish 'playing cat-and-mouse' with a smaller fish until—'snap'—and only the larger fish can be seen, motionless, and with a dead-pan expression.

Anglerfish's body is camouflaged by flaps of skin resembling surrounding seaweeds.

Small fishes attracted to the anglerfish's mouth by a lure are snapped up. (⅓ natural size.)

class	**Pisces**
order	**Lophiiformes**
families	**Lophiidae** *anglerfishes* **Antennariidae** *frogfishes* **Ogcocephalidae** *batfishes*

Amphibians and Reptiles

For reasons it would be difficult to define the custom has grown up of always speaking of amphibians and reptiles in one breath, as if the two must always be linked. Yet there is almost as much of a gulf between the living representatives of these two groups as between, say, birds and mammals. The features they have in common are that they are cold-blooded, air-breathing vertebrates typically living on land. The main differences between them are that amphibians, with rare exceptions, have a smooth scaleless skin whereas reptiles are scaly and that amphibians must go to water, or at least to a damp spot and this only exceptionally, to breed, whereas all reptiles have to come on land to lay their eggs.

The word 'amphibian' means more or less literally 'double life'. The typical amphibian spends the first part of its life in water and its adult life on land. There are plenty of exceptions to this, as there are to virtually every general statement made about living organisms. There are both salamanders and occasional toads that live their whole lives in water, examples being the salamander known as the olm and the Surinam toad. Conversely, there are frogs, the Stephens Island frog of New Zealand being one, that lay their eggs on land. The Stephens Island frog lives among boulders and its eggs are laid on damp earth. From them hatch fully formed froglets, the tadpole stage having been passed within the egg membrane.

The word 'reptile' is from the Latin *reptare* to creep and (very conveniently) *repere* to crawl. Therefore they should be, in fact, the 'creepy-crawlies' of modern vernacular, although this in practice embraces more commonly such creatures as centipedes, earthworms and slugs. Among reptiles the true creepers are the snakes and the few lizards, like the slow-worms, that are also legless. Tortoises and turtles may be said to crawl but most reptiles can employ a respectable walk, even a run, and it would tax the imagination to see in the Komodo dragon of today or the giant dinosaurs of past ages anything approaching a creepy-crawly.

Perhaps our habit of linking amphibians and reptiles dialectically is because of an intuitive feeling that both played an important part in the early colonization of the land masses by vertebrates. Among the diverse forms to emerge from among the multitudinous bony fishes were those that could breathe both by lungs and by gills. They were amphibious, and since they also had fins approximating to limbs, they could spend much time on land. There can be little doubt that it was from such pioneering fishes that the amphibians sprang.

The first fossil amphibians are found in the Lower Carboniferous rocks, 300 million years old. They are tailed amphibians of the type represented today by salamanders and newts. Tailless amphibians, the frogs and toads, did not appear for another 150 million years, in the Jurassic period. Meanwhile the first reptiles had put in an appearance in the Upper Carboniferous, and by the time frogs and toads had evolved reptiles were dominant on land and continued so into the Cretaceous period that followed, a period that was to become known as the Age of Reptiles.

The transition from an air-breathing fish to an undoubted amphibian is shown in one of the most complete series of fossils. A slightly less perfect series illustrates the development of reptiles from amphibian ancestors, but the indications that this was the true course of events are indisputable.

It is a common failing to think of the Age of Reptiles as including only the giant reptiles, the dinosaurs on land, the pterodactyls in the air and the plesiosaurs and ichthyosaurs in the water. In fact there were numerous other reptiles, small, medium and large, including the Rhynchocephalia, of which the tuatara is the only surviving representative, and the crocodiles and turtles, some of which also reached giant size. The lizards and snakes, by far the most numerous reptiles, came later, but meanwhile some groups of early reptiles had developed a temperature control and were partially warm-blooded (homoiothermic). One group gave rise to birds, the other to mammals, around 200 million years before the reptiles themselves achieved their domination in the Age of Reptiles.

The classification of Amphibians and Reptiles is as follows:

CLASS AMPHIBIA   3,000 species
Order Caudata or Urodela
  (salamanders, newts)
Order Anura or Salientia
  (frogs and toads)

CLASS REPTILIA   6,000 species
Order Rhynchocephalia (tuatara)
Order Crocodilia (crocodiles, alligators)
Order Testudines (tortoises, turtles)
Order Squamata
  suborder Sauria (lizards)
  suborder Serpentes (snakes)

Caecilian

The caecilian is a limbless amphibian with a long cylindrical body marked with rings, living wholly underground. The 158 species are worm-like or snake-like according to size, the smallest caecilian being only 4½ in. long, the largest, 4½ ft. Their colour is usually blackish but may be pale flesh-colour. The skin is smooth and slimy, but unlike that of other amphibians, it has small scales embedded in it, in most species. The eyes are small, sometimes covered with skin, and usually useless. There is a peculiar sensory organ; a tentacle on each side of the head lies in a groove running from eyes to tip of snout.

As in snakes, one lung is large and long, the other is reduced to a small lobe.

Caecilians live in warm regions, in America from Mexico to northern Argentina, in southern and south-east Asia and in the Seychelles and parts of Africa. They live from sea-level to about 6 000 ft.

Ancient burrower

Caecilians are the sole surviving relatives of the earliest land animals, large fossil amphibians which roamed the earth 400 million years ago. Burrows are made in soft earth, and caecilians seldom come above ground except when heavy rain floods the burrows. One species, at least, is aquatic, and a few species live in leaf litter which is found on the floor of rain forests.

Feeding

Little is known for certain but earthworms are probably the main diet for most species, and a few may eat termites. The sticky caecilian, of southeast Asia, the best-known species, also eats small burrowing snakes. They themselves are eaten by certain large burrowing snakes.

Life history

There is no difference between male and female externally. Fertilisation is internal and some species lays eggs, others bear live young.

More is known of the life history of the 15 in. sticky caecilian, the female of which lays some two dozen eggs, each about ¼ in. in diameter, connected in a jelly-like string. They are laid in a burrow near water, the female coiling her body around the egg-mass until they hatch. The larvae, which escape to water, have a breathing pore on either side of the head. This leads into internal gills, connected with the throat, as in fishes. External gills, present in the embryo, are lost before hatching. They have normal eyes, a flattened tail for swimming, and a head like a newt. At the end of its larval life the breathing pores close, lungs are developed and the young caecilian lives permanently on land, burrowing underground.

The aquatic species of caecilian has sometimes been observed swimming in an eel-like fashion.

Three-way links

The first mention of a caecilian was by Seba, in 1735, when he described it as a snake. Linnaeus, in 1754, also included it among the snakes. In 1811, Oppel put caecilians with frogs, toads and salamanders as amphibians, but these were generally regarded as reptiles as late as 1859. Then came a change, and the caecilians were thought to be degenerate salamanders. From 1908 on there followed studies of the anatomy, and it gradually became clear that caecilians provided an interesting link with the past.

Even now our knowledge of the caecilians is not extensive. They have always been regarded as rare animals, although it is now known that they are plentiful enough in suitable habitats. Yet, as with all animals living wholly underground, it is hard to find out anything about their way of life. What we can do, however, is study how they are made, and this is important, because it tells us that caecilians are a link with the large extinct amphibians that lived nearly 400 million years ago. Their large footprints are known from the Devonian rocks and their skeletons from the rocks of the next geological period, the Carboniferous (Coal Age). After that there is no trace of them, so they seem to have died out 300 million years ago. Some were crocodile-like, lived on land in the marshes where the coal measures were laid down, and they started life as aquatic larvae. They seemed to have been the first backboned animals to live permanently on land, and they almost certainly evolved from air-breathing fishes, the lobe-finned fishes which were the ancestors of the amphibians.

These ancient amphibians gave rise not only to the present-day amphibians but also to the reptiles. They link, therefore, the fishes, amphibians and reptiles, and the caecilians seem to be their direct surviving descendants. This relationship is seen not only in the degenerate scales found in the caecilian skin but also in the caecilian skull being so like that of these giant amphibians of 400 million years ago. It will be interesting to see if any fossil caecilians are found in the future and to compare them with the present day order. As yet no fossil caecilians have been found.

class	**Amphibia**
order	**Apoda or Gymnophiona**
family	**Caeciliidae**
genera	***Caecilia, Typhlonectes, Ichthyophis***, others

Feeding habits of many caecilians are still unknown, but earthworms are probably important in their diet, as in this species **Siphonops annulatus**.

Axolotl

The axolotl is the Peter Pan of the amphibian world, being able to reproduce its own kind while still in its aquatic larval stage. This is unlike the usual development of amphibians such as the common frog, toads and newts, which as larvae, or tadpoles, are confined to fresh water. In the adult form they can live in water and on land, reproducing in water in the breeding season. Certain amphibians, the Mexican axolotl being the most famous, are able to complete their life cycle without ever leaving the water, as sexual maturity is reached in the larval stage.

The axolotl is a newt-like creature, 4 – 7 in. long, usually black, or dark brown with black spots, but albinos are quite common. The legs and feet are small and weak, while the tail is long, with a fin running from the back of the head to the tail and along the underside of the tail. It breathes through the three pairs of feathery gills on the sides of the head.

Habits and habitat

Axolotls are quite often kept in aquaria, especially in schools. This is rather surprising as they are rather dull animals, spending most of their time at the bottom of the tank, occasionally swimming about lazily for a few seconds before sinking again. A probable reason is that the axolotl can reproduce its own kind without ever leaving the water. Newts and most salamanders, kept in captivity, need water, land and very careful keeping if they are to survive and breed successfully.

Axolotls cannot be kept together with complete safety as they are liable to bite off each other's gills and feet, and bite pieces out of the tail. If this does happen, however, and they are then separated, the missing pieces will regenerate.

In the wild, axolotls are confined to certain lakes around Mexico City, where they are regarded as delicacies when roasted. The name axolotl is Mexican for 'water sport'.

Zoologists were unable to decide where to place axolotls in the classification of amphibians, until 1865 when, at the Jardin des Plantes in Paris, the problem was solved. Several specimens had bred successfully, when one day it was noticed that the young of one brood had lost their gills and tails, and had quite a different coloration. They had, in fact, turned into salamanders. This was the secret of the axolotl. It is one of several species of salamander, an amphibian which normally has an aquatic tadpole resembling the axolotl, that normally changes straight into the adult. The axolotl, however, usually becomes sexually mature while still a larva. This is because the axolotl fails to metamorphose.

Sperm capsule

In most frogs and toads, fertilisation of the eggs takes place externally. In other words, the female sheds the eggs into the water and the male simply releases his sperm near them, to make their own way to the eggs. The axolotls, related salamanders, and newts have a system of internal fertilisation but it is different from the normal method in which the male introduces the sperm into the female's body to meet the eggs waiting there. Instead, the male axolotl sheds his sperm in a packet called a spermatophore. It sinks to the bottom and the female settles over it and picks it up with her cloaca.

Albino axolotl **Ambystoma mexicanum**. *Externally it seems to be juvenile, but internally it is a sexually mature adult. For years zoologists were unable to decide where axolotls fitted into the classification, until they were observed changing into adult salamanders.*

The male attracts the female by a courtship dance, secreting a chemical from glands in his abdomen and swishing his tail, presumably to spread the chemical until a female detects it and swims towards him.

About a week later, 200–600 eggs are laid, in April or May. They are sticky, and the female attaches them to plants with her back legs. The young axolotls hatch out a fortnight to three weeks later, depending on the temperature of the water. At this stage they are only about ½ in. long and remain on the plant where the eggs are laid. After a week they start swimming in search of food and, if the water is warm and food plentiful, they will be 5–7 in. long by winter. They will then hibernate, taking no food, if the water temperature drops below 10°C/50°F.

Carnivorous feeders
The youngest axolotls feed on plankton, minute organisms that float in water. Later they eat water fleas such as daphnia, and when fully grown they hunt for worms, tadpoles, insect larvae, crustaceans and wounded fish. Their prey has to move, however, and axolotls will ignore still, dead food given to them but will snap up a piece of food that is waved about in the water.

Precocious amphibians
The axolotl's habit of breeding while in the larval stage is known as neoteny, or the retention of juvenile characteristics in the adult form. By 'adult' is meant a sexually mature animal. This habit is not restricted to the axolotl. Other amphibians, including some salamanders, sometimes exhibit neoteny, failing to emerge onto land, but continuing to grow in the larval form.

The basic cause of neoteny seems to be a lack of thyroxine, the hormone secreted by the thyroid gland, which controls metabolism. If the secretion is upset in humans, several bodily disorders occur, including the formation of goitres, swellings in the neck caused by the thyroid gland enlarging. Administration of thyroid gland extracted from cattle, for instance, can often cure the goitre, and axolotls will change into adult salamanders if given thyroid gland.

It would seem, then, that there is something lacking in the diet of both axolotls and humans with goitres. In Wyoming and the Rocky Mountain area the tiger salamander regularly exhibits neoteny and humans are liable to get goitres. This has been traced to a lack of iodine in the water, for iodine is an essential component of thyroxine. In these cases the administration of iodine, rather than thyroxine, is all that is needed either to effect the metamorphosis of an amphibian or cure a goitre. However, iodine treatment is not the only way of making axolotls metamorphose. Sometimes a consignment sent to a dealer or a laboratory will change into adults shortly after being received. Apparently, the jolting during travel has been sufficient to start the change.

When faced with an odd occurrence like this, a zoologist asks whether it confers any advantage on the animal. The freshwater animal has an advantage over a land animal because it does not have to conserve its body water. This could well be the reason for the axolotl's neoteny. The lakes where it lives do not dry up and there is an abundance of water, so it is an advantage to live and breed there, rather than risk life on the dry, barren land around. If the lakes dry up, then it can still change into a salamander, having the best of both worlds.

△ It is now known that several species of salamanders are able to breed while still in the gilled stage. The eastern mud salamander **Pseudotriton montanus** is one such amphibian.

▽ Adult of **Ambystoma mexicanum**. The axolotl in juvenile form can be made to change into an adult salamander by giving it extract of thyroid, or sometimes when given a physical jolt.

class:	**Amphibia**
order:	**Caudata**
family	**Ambystomatidae**
genus & species	***Ambystoma mexicanum***

Newt

Newts are amphibians of the salamander family. They have a life history very similar to that of frogs and toads in that the adults spend most of their life on land but return to water to breed. They are different in form, however, having long, slender bodies like those of lizards with a tail that is flattened laterally. The name comes from the Anglo-Saxon *evete* which became *ewt* and finally a newt from the transcription of the 'n' in an *ewt*. In Britain, newt refers solely to the genus **Triturus** but in North America it has been applied to related animals which are sometimes, confusingly, called salamanders.

Newts of the genus **Triturus** are found in Europe, Asia, North Africa and North America. There are three species native to Britain. The most common is the smooth newt which is found all over Europe and is the only newt found in Ireland. The maximum length of smooth newts is 4 in. The colour of the body varies, but is mainly olive-brown with darker spots on the upper side and streaks on the head. The vermilion or orange underside has round black spots and the throat is yellow or white. The female is generally paler on the underside than the male and sometimes is unspotted. In the breeding season the male develops a wavy crest running along the back and tail. The palmate newt is very similar to the smooth newt, but about 1 in. shorter and with a square-sided body. In the breeding season the males of the two species can be told apart because black webs link the toes of the hindfeet of the palmate newts, and its crest is not wavy. In addition, the tail ends abruptly and a short thread, about $\frac{1}{8}-\frac{1}{4}$ in. long protrudes from the tip. The largest European newt is the crested or warty newt. It grows up to 6 in. long. The dark grey skin of the upperparts is covered with warts, while the underparts are yellow or orange and spotted with black. The distinguishing feature apart from its size is the crest of the male. From the head to the hips runs a tall, 'toothed' frill —its crest, which becomes the tail fin.

▽ A male smooth newt with its spotted front, as seen from below.

Hibernating on land

When they come out of hibernation in spring, newts make their way to ponds and other stretches of still water where water plants grow. They swim by lashing with their tails, but they spend much of their time resting on the mud or among the stems of plants. They can breathe through their skins but every now and then they rise to the surface to gulp air. Adult newts do not leave the water immediately breeding has finished but remain aquatic until July or August. When they come on land the crest is reabsorbed and the skin becomes rougher. The crested newt keeps its skin moist from the numerous mucus glands scattered over the surface of its body. A few individuals stay in the water all the year round, retaining their smooth skins and crests.

Hibernation begins in the autumn, when the newts crawl into crevices in the ground or under logs and stones. They cannot burrow but are very adept at squeezing themselves into cracks. Occasionally several will gather together in one place and hibernate in a tight mass.

Two rows of teeth

The jaws of newts are lined with tiny teeth and there are two rows of teeth on the roof of the mouth. These are not used for cutting food or for chewing but merely to hold slippery, often wriggling, prey. They feed on a variety of small animals such as worms, snails and insects when on land, and crustaceans, tadpoles and insect larvae while living in water. Unlike frogs and toads, newts do not use their hands to push the food into their mouths, but gulp it down with convulsive swallows. Snails are swallowed whole, caddis flies are eaten in their cases and crested newts eat smooth newts.

Internal fertilisation

The mating habits of newts are quite different from those of common frogs and common toads. Fertilisation is internal and is effected in a most unusual way. The male stimulates the female into breeding condition by nudging her with his snout and lashing the water with his tail. He positions himself in front of or beside her, bends his tail double and vibrates it rapidly, setting up vibrations in the water. The female is also stimulated by secretions from glands in the male's skin. At the end of the courtship the male emits a spermatophore which sinks to the bottom. The female newt positions herself over it, then picks it up with her cloaca by pressing her body onto it.

After fertilisation the 200–300 eggs are usually laid singly on the leaves of water plants, although some American newts lay their eggs in spherical clusters. The female newt tests the leaves by smell and touch. When she has chosen a suitable one she holds it with her hindfeet, then folds the leaf over to form a tube and lays an egg in it. The jelly surrounding the egg glues the leaf firmly in place to protect it.

The eggs hatch in about 3 weeks and a more streamlined tadpole than that of a frog or toad emerges. It is not very different from the adult newt except that it has a frill of gills and no legs. Development takes longer than in frog tadpoles but the young newts are ready to emerge by the end of summer. A few spend the winter as tadpoles, remaining in the pond until spring, even surviving being frozen into the ice.

Unpleasant secretion

Newts have many enemies: the young are eaten by aquatic insects and the adults by fishes, water birds, weasels, rats, hedgehogs and many other animals. The crested newt has an unpleasant secretion that is produced in the glands on the back and tail and is exuded when they are squeezed. Grass snakes are known to be dissuaded from eating crested newts because of this.

Newt's nerve poison

The poison of the crested newt is not only unpleasant, but men who have tasted it have found it to be burning. A far more potent poison is that of the California newt. The poison is found mainly in the skin, muscles and blood of the newt, as well as in its eggs. Analysis showed that the poison is a substance called tetrodotoxin, which is also found in puffer fish. Tetrodotoxin extracted from newts' eggs is so powerful that $\frac{1}{3000}$ oz. can kill 7 000 mice. It acts on the nerves, preventing impulses from being transmitted to the muscles. Somehow, in a manner that is not understood, California newts are not affected by their own posion. Their nerves still function when treated with a solution of tetrodotoxin 25 000 times stronger than that which will completely deaden a frog's nerves.

△ *Left: Segmenting embryo of a crested newt. Right: The legless tadpole of the crested newt.*
▽ *Alpine newt* **Triturus alpestris.**

class	**Amphibia**
order	**Caudata**
family	**Salamandridae**
genera & species	*Taricha torosa* California newt *Triturus cristatus* crested newt *T. helveticus* palmate newt *T. vulgaris* smooth newt others

Lungless salamander

The name 'lungless salamander' covers 200 species of salamanders living in Tropical and North America that have neither lungs nor gills but breathe through their skin and the lining of the mouth. A further peculiarity is that some of them cannot open their lower jaw to the normal gape. There is only one species outside America, **Hydromantes genei** represented by three subspecies.

Lungless salamanders range in size from 1½ to 8½ in. A few live permanently in water but most of them spend their lives on land. They are mainly sombrely coloured—black, grey or brown—but some have patches of red and the redbacked salamander occurs in 2 colour phases: red and grey with the belly of each spotted black and white. Varying proportions of red and grey individuals are found in any batch of larvae. Most lungless salamanders have the usual salamander shape, a long rounded body, tail about the same length, and short legs, the front legs with 4 toes, the back legs with 5. The four-toed lungless salamander has 4 toes on each foot. The longtailed salamander is so called because its 7 in. tail dwarfs a 4 in. body. The California slender salamander is snakelike, with vestigial legs, and lies under fallen logs, coiled up tightly like a watch-spring.

Some species are widespread. The dusky salamander ranges over the eastern United States from New Brunswick southwards to Georgia and Alabama and westwards to Oklahoma and Texas. Other species are very localised. The Ocoee salamander lives in damp crevices in rocks or on the waterfall-splashed faces of rocks in Ocoee Gorge, southeast Tennessee. One of the European subspecies lives in southeast France and north Italy, the second lives in Tuscany, the third in Sardinia.

From deep wells to tall trees

Lungless salamanders mostly live in damp places, under stones or logs, among moss, under leaf litter, near streams or seepages or even in surface burrows in damp soil. The shovel-nosed salamander lives in mountain streams all its life, hiding under stones by day. Others live on land but go into water to escape enemies. The pygmy salamander, 2 in. long, living in the mountains of Virginia and North Carolina, can climb the rough bark of trees to a height of several feet. The arboreal salamander does even better, climbing trees to a height of 60 ft, sometimes making its home in old birds' nests. The Californian flatheaded salamander uses webbed feet to walk over slippery rocks and swings its tail from side to side as it walks, to help itself up a slope. On descent its curled tail acts as a brake.

Several species live in caves or artesian and natural wells as much as 200 ft deep. All are blind, one retains its larval gills throughout life and one cave species spends its larval life in mountain streams but migrates to underground waters before metamorphosis. It then loses its sight.

Creeping, crawling food

All lungless salamanders eat small invertebrates. Those living in water feed mainly on aquatic insect larvae. Those on land hunt slugs, worms, woodlice and insect larvae. One group of lungless salamanders *Plethodon* are known as woodland salamanders. They live in rocky crevices or in holes underground and eat worms, beetles and ants. The slimy salamander also eats worms, hard-shelled beetles, ants and centipedes as well as shieldbugs, despite their obnoxious odour and unpalatable flavour. The European species catches food with a sticky tongue which it can push out 1 inch.

Different breeding habits

There is as much diversity in their breeding as in the way they live. Some lay their eggs in water and the larvae are fully aquatic;

△ Mountain salamander, **Desmognathus ochrophaeus** lives near springs and streams where the ground is saturated.
▷ Red-backed salamander, occupant of old garden plots where there are tree stumps, rotting logs and moisture-conserving debris.

others lay them on land, and among this second group are species in which the females curl themselves round their batches of 2–3 dozen eggs as if incubating. In a few species the female stays near her eggs until they hatch, but without incubating them or giving them any special care. The woodland salamanders lay their eggs in patches of moss or under logs and the larvae metamorphose before leaving the eggs. A typical species is the dusky salamander. The male deposits his sperm in a capsule or spermatophore. He then rubs noses with the female. A gland on his chin gives out a scent that stimulates the female to pick up the spermatophore with her cloaca. Her eggs are laid in clusters of two dozen in spring or

◁ *The long-tailed salamander has a tail nearly twice as long as its body. It spends most of the day hidden under logs and stones.*

early summer under logs or stones. Each egg is $\frac{3}{16}$ in. diameter and the larva on hatching is $\frac{5}{8}$ in. long. It has external gills and goes into water, where it lives until the following spring, when it metamorphoses. The adults, $5\frac{1}{4}$ in. long, are dark brown or grey. When it first metamorphoses the young salamander is brick-red and light cream in patches. Later it takes on the colours of the fully grown adult but has a light band down the back and a light line from the eye to the angle of the jaw.

Not so defenceless

Lungless salamanders, like other salamanders and newts, seldom have defensive weapons, a possible exception being the arboreal salamander with its fang-like teeth in the lower jaw. It is known to bite a finger when handled. The slimy salamander gives out a very sticky, glutinous secretion from its skin when handled and this possibly deters predators. The enemies are small snakes and frogs, which take their toll of the larvae and the young salamanders. It may be in an attempt to evade such enemies that the dusky salamander sometimes leaps about, several inches at a jump. The yellow blotched salamander, of California, has a curious behaviour that may be defensive. It raises itself on the tips of its toes, rocks its body backwards and forwards, arches its tail and swings it from side to side. It also gives out a milky astringent fluid from the tail. And it squeaks like a mouse.

Peculiar features

Peculiar features of these salamanders are that they lose their larval gills as they grow and they do not grow lungs. Instead, their skin has become the breathing organ with the skin lining the mouth acting the part of a lung by having a network of fine blood vessels in it, like the lining of a lung. The arboreal salamander has a similar network of fine blood vessels in the skin of its toes, which may play the part of lungs (or should they be called terrestrial gills?). Another extraordinary feature is that others, like the yellow-blotched salamander, squeak, although they have neither lungs nor voice box. They do this by contracting the throat to force air through the lips or nose.

The loss of lungs in the lungless salamanders must be seen as a secondary condition. That is, the ancestral salamander had lungs and these had been lost in the later evolution. The most reasonable explanation for this would be that the losses correlated with the brook-dwelling habits. In the normal salamander the lungs function not only as respiratory organs, but also as hydrostatic organs, decreasing the total specific gravity of the animal, so bringing the salamander very near to having neutral buoyancy. The salamander needs then only a flick of its tail or slight movement of the limbs to propel itself through water and, more especially, to make it rise towards the surface. When it then becomes immobile again it does not immediately sink, as it would do if its specific gravity was greater, but slowly sinks. With the loss of lungs the lungless salamanders have increased their specific gravity and are therefore able the more readily to keep near the bottom in fast moving water.

The loss of lungs is compensated by the greater oxygen content of moving water and so has made their respiratory function also less important. The loss of lungs could be a disadvantage in another respect and a special adaptation has been needed to counteract this. Lungless salamanders have a nasolabial groove running from each nostril to the lips. It is believed that these act as gutters carrying from the nostrils water that has collected there when the head has been submerged.

class	**Amphibia**
order	**Caudata**
family	**Plethodontidae**
genera & species	***Aneides lugubris*** *arboreal salamander* ***Batrachoseps attenuatus*** *California slender salamander* ***Desmognathus fuscus*** *dusky salamander* ***D. ocoee*** *Ocoee salamander* ***D. wrighti*** *pygmy salamander* ***Ensatina croceator*** *yellow-blotched salamander* ***Eurycea longicauda*** *long-tailed salamander* ***Hemidactylium scutatum*** *four-toed salamander* ***Leurognathus marmoratus*** *shovel-nosed salamander* ***Plethodon cinereus*** *red-backed salamander* ***P. glutinosus*** *slimy salamander*

Common toad

Despite a superficial resemblance to the common frog, few people have difficulty in recognising a common toad, even if they recoil in horror on seeing it. It has a flatter back and relatively shorter legs. Instead of the moist, bright skin of the frog, the toad has a dull, wrinkled, pimply skin. Its movements are slow and grovelling, and, although it can jump a short distance on all fours, it usually walks laboriously over the ground.

The rough skin blends well with the earth, so a toad can easily be overlooked as a clod of earth. This impression is heightened by the dark brown or grey colouring which can change, although only a little and slowly, to match the surroundings, becoming almost red in a sand pit, for instance. Its jewel-like eyes are golden or coppery-red, and behind them lie the bulges of the parotid glands that contain an acrid, poisonous fluid.

Male toads measure about 2½ in. and the females 1 in. longer.

The common toad ranges over Europe, north and temperate Asia and North Africa.

Common toads mating.

Hibernating toads

The common toad, like the common frog, hibernates from October to February, but in drier places. Dry banks and disused burrows of small mammals are chosen, and hibernating toads are sometimes found in cellars and outhouses. In the spring they migrate to breeding pools, preferring deeper water than frogs. Where the two are found in the same ponds, the frogs will be in the shallows and the toads in the middle.

The migrations of these toads are more spectacular. Toads give the impression of being slower movers and the migration route becomes littered with the remains of toads that have fallen foul of enemies. The route is especially well marked where it crosses a road and passing cars have run over the toads.

Although the migration may be long and arduous, perhaps covering 2 or 3 miles at a rate of $\frac{3}{4}$ mile in 24 hours, the toads are very persistent, and laboriously climb stone walls and banks.

Outside the breeding season toads live in hollows scooped out by the hindlegs. In soft earth they bury themselves completely, otherwise the hole is made under a log or stone. These homes are usually permanent, the toad returning to the same place day after day. One toad was recorded as living under a front-door step for 36 years until it was attacked by a raven. Occasionally the retreats may be in places that must cost the toad some effort to reach. One is known to have made its home in a privet hedge, 4 ft above the ground, and others have been found in birds' nests.

Every now and then there are stories of toads being found in even odder places. Quarrymen and miners tell of splitting open a rock or lump of coal revealing a cavity in which lies a toad that leaps out hale and hearty. Another story is told of two sawyers working in a saw pit, some 90 years ago. They were sawing the trunk of an oak into planks when they noticed blood dripping out of the wood. Examination revealed the now grisly remains of a toad in a cavity in the trunk. In every story there is speculation as to how the toads came to be imprisoned. It is hardly likely that they were trapped when the coal or rock was first formed millions of years ago, as was once believed. They could not have lived that long, as was shown by the following experiments performed over a century ago. Holes were drilled in blocks of sandstone and limestone, toads put in and the holes sealed with glass plates. The toads in the compact sandstone soon died but the ones in the porous limestone lived for a year or more. These rather macabre experiments suggest that the toads found in rocks and tree trunks could not have been there for long. It is most likely that either they had crawled into a crack or cavity which had later been filled in, or perhaps the miner or quarryman had hit a rock that happened to have a cavity in, thereby causing a toad hidden nearby to leap out suddenly, so creating the impression that it had come out of the hole.

Prey must be moving

At night and during wet weather, toads come out to feed on many kinds of small animals, but they must be moving because toads' eyes are adapted to react to moving objects. Any insect or other small invertebrate is taken, ants being especially favoured, and the stomach of one toad was found to contain 363 ants. Some distasteful animals such as burnet moth caterpillars or caterpillars covered with stiff hairs are left well alone, but toads are known to sit outside beehives in the evening and catch the workers as they come back home. Snails are crunched up and earthworms are pushed into the mouth by the forefeet which also scrape excess earth off them. Young newts, frogs, toads and even slowworms and grass snakes are eaten. One toad had five newly-hatched grass snakes in its stomach, while another had the head of an adder in its mouth. Toads will often return to a favourite retreat after hunting and will use the same home for years.

Spawn in strings

There is little to distinguish the breeding habits of common frogs and common toads. Both breed at roughly the same time of year and may be seen in the same pools. Male toads start arriving before the females but later the males may arrive already in amplexus on the females' backs. There is no external vocal sac and, unlike many of its relatives, a male common toad has a very weak croak.

The spawn is laid in strings rather than in a mass. The eggs are embedded three or four deep in threads of jelly that may be up to 15 ft long. Each female lays 3–4 thousand eggs, which are smaller than those of a frog, being less than $\frac{1}{16}$ in. in diameter. The jelly swells up but the spawn does not float, because it is wrapped round the stems of water plants.

The eggs hatch in 10–12 days and the tadpoles develop in the same manner as frog tadpoles, becoming shiny, black, $\frac{1}{2}$ in. toadlets in about 3 months. Sexual maturity is reached in 4 years, before the toads are fully grown.

Poisonous toads

Toads suffer from all the enemies to which frogs fall prey, despite the poisonous secretions of the parotid glands. The poison is certainly effective against dogs, that salivate copiously after mouthing a toad, and show all the signs of distress.

Toads react more strongly to danger signals than frogs do, possibly because, not being leapers, they are more vulnerable and need added protection from enemies. One

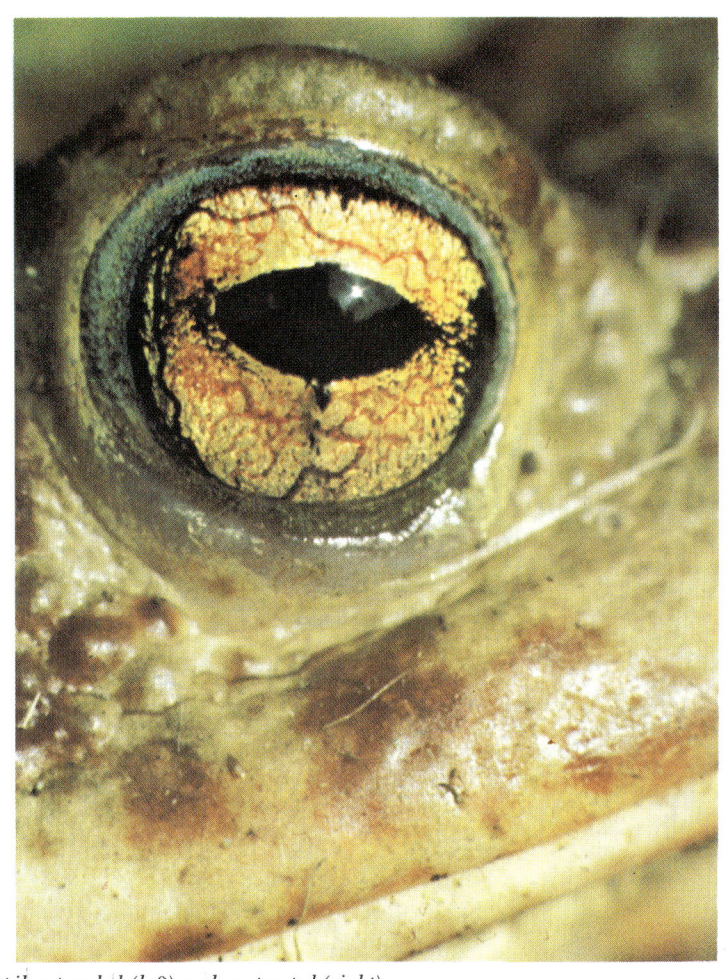

The coppery-golden eye of the toad, its most attractive feature, shown with pupil expanded (left) and contracted (right).

63

Strings of spawn rope through the water during mating, to be wrapped around the stems of water plants and convenient pebbles.

reaction is to inflate the lungs more than usual, so increasing the volume of the body by as much as 50%. Snakes, their chief enemies, know fairly accurately when an object is more than they can swallow, but how far the inflated body of the toad deceives them has never been tested.

Unless the snake is only small, the swelling of the toad will make little difference to the outcome if attacked by a constricting or a poisonous snake.

The defence mechanism of the toad of inflating itself against enemies is instinctive. This is seen by the following experiment. Any long cylindrical object, such as a length of thin rubber tubing, moved across its field of vision, will cause it to blow itself up. This reaction becomes progressively weaker when the experiment is repeated, and in a short time no reaction is produced.

In old age, toads fall victim to flesh-eating greenbottle flies, which lay their eggs on them. The larvae then crawl into the nostrils, hampering breathing, and eat their way into the toad's body, eventually killing it.

Many superstitions

Toads are often regarded with horror, and in folklore they generally play an unpleasant role. Their mere presence was said to pollute the soil, but one method of preventing this from happening was to plant rue, which toads could not abide. Without it, tragedies could occur of the kind that befell a mediaeval couple strolling in the garden. The young man plucked some leaves of sage, rubbed his teeth with them and promptly fell dead. His young woman was charged with murder and, to prove her innocence, took the judge and court to the garden to demonstrate what had happened, and fell dead too. The judge suspected the cause and had the sage dug up. There was a toad living in the ground beside it.

By contrast, 'the foule Toad has a faire stone in his heade', as the 16th-century writer John Lyly declared. To obtain this jewel the toad was placed on a scarlet cloth which pleased the toad so much that it cast the stone out. The toadstone was then set in a ring, for it had the valuable property of changing colour in the presence of any poison that an enemy might put in food and drink. It was also effective as a cure for snakebite and wasp-stings.

class	**Amphibia**
order	**Salientia**
family	**Bufonidae**
genus & species	***Bufo bufo***

Arrow-poison frog

Arrow-poison frogs are found only in Central and South America where the Indians have long extracted poison from their bodies for use on arrow-heads. Many amphibians have at least a trace of poison in their bodies or secrete poison from glands in the skin, and quite a few can cause a good deal of pain to any human that handles them. Only the arrow-poison frogs and one or two others secrete such a strong poison as to cause rapid death.

Most arrow-poison frogs can be distinguished by the nail-like plate on each toe. Many species are brilliantly coloured. The two-toned arrow-poison frog is brick red with patches of blue-black on its legs. More brilliant is the three-striped arrow-poison frog, which is yellow with stripes of black running lengthways down the head and body and around the limbs. Some species have 'flash colours' which are suddenly exposed as the frog jumps. It is thought that the bright colours, especially the 'flash colours' are warnings to other animals that they are not fit to eat.

A Cuban member of the family, **Sminthillus limbatus** *is the smallest frog in the world, measuring less than ½ in.*

Each female lays only one egg. The egg is large in comparison with the size of the mother's body and is laid in a moist spot on land, the larva completing its development and undergoing metamorphosis before hatching. This particular frog is by no means uncommon and its slow rate of breeding is in striking contrast to most frogs that ensure the perpetuation of the species by laying large numbers of eggs.

Habits

The various species of arrow-poison frogs are found in forests of different parts of Central and South America, some living in trees, others living on the forest floor.

Feeding

Arrow-poison frogs conform to the usual amphibian diet. As adults all amphibians are carnivorous. They take insects or other small invertebrates which are full of protein to restore worn-out tissue, and salts, fats, vitamins, and water needed for their metabolism. They also need carbohydrates which can be rebuilt from surplus protein.

Male carries the tadpoles

There are several peculiar features about the breeding habits of arrow-poison frogs. Courtship or courtship rituals are rare amongst frogs and toads, but the golden arrow-poison frogs, and probably other species, 'play' together for as much as two or three hours. They repeatedly jump at each other, sometimes landing on one another's backs, as if fighting. Following the 'play', the eggs are laid, but there is no 'amplexus', the process in which the male, as in the common frog, perches on the female's back and fertilises the eggs as they are laid. The female arrow-poison frog lays her eggs on the ground and the male, who has been waiting nearby, comes over and fertilises them.

The absence of amplexus may be linked with the occurrence of the courtship play, because in frogs using amplexus it is often the pressure of the male hugging the female that causes the eggs to be extruded. When there is no amplexus, it may be necessary for another stimulus, in this case leaping about with the male, to initiate egg-laying. Both methods ensure that there is a male present to fertilise the eggs which is the primary purpose of animal courtship.

When the eggs have been fertilised, the male carries them on his back where they become attached to his skin although how this is done remains to be discovered. After they hatch, the tadpoles remain on their father's back, getting no moisture except from rain. Up to twenty tadpoles can be found on one arrow-poison frog, and, as they grow, their father has to seek larger and larger holes in which to rest. Eventually he takes them down to the water and they swim away to lead an independent life.

Predator deterrent

Snakes, predatory birds and some carnivorous mammals will often prey on the majority of frogs. The arrow-poison frogs, however, possess the ultimate deterrent of the animal world—their flash colours give a warning to the predator, not to attempt to eat them because of their poisonous nature, giving the frogs a much safer life in their hazardous jungle existence.

It is very usual for an animal that carries a venom, or is in some other way unpleasant or unpalatable, to be brilliantly coloured in red, yellow or black or in some combination of these colours. Among arrow-poison frogs which are so highly poisonous these colours tend to predominate and are accentuated by the use of flash colours, as we have seen. This makes it even more puzzling that one species, *Dendrobates pumilio* should be dark blue and very difficult to see in the dark forests which are its home. The warning colours, red, yellow and black are very conspicuous, and it is their purpose to be conspicuous, because they are advertising a warning to predators. Yet *Dendrobates pumilio* seems to be doing its best to efface itself although it has eight times more poison in its skin than those arrow-poison frogs that are bright red and very conspicuous.

Self-effacing relative

Although it is usual to speak of the Dendrobatidae as the family of arrow-poison frogs, not all its members are poisonous. It is of interest to compare the case of a Brazilian species *Dendrophryniscus brevipollicatus* with other members of the family being discussed here. Apparently this particular species has no venom or very little of it. It is coloured brown, tan and buff, it lives among the leaf litter of the forest floor, and when molested its flattish body becomes stiff and the front part of the body bends upwards and backwards so that it looks like a dried leaf.

Poison arrows

The Indians of South America are renowned for their use of poisoned-tipped arrows, which are reputed to cause death if they do no more than scratch the skin of their target. The best known of the poisons is curare, which is extracted from certain plants, but even this is a mild poison compared with that of the arrow-poison frogs.

The Indians collect the poison by piercing the frog with a sharp stick, and holding it over a fire. The heat of the fire forces the poison through the skin where it collects in droplets. These are scraped off into a jar. The amount collected from each frog, and its potency, varies with the species. The kokoi frog of Colombia secretes the most powerful poison known. This is a substance called batrachotoxin which has recently been shown to be ten times more powerful than tetrodotoxin, the poison of the Japanese puffer fish which had previously held the record as the most powerful known animal venom. 1/100,000 oz. of batrachotoxin is sufficient to kill a man.

One kokoi frog, only 1 in. long, can supply enough venom to make 50 lethal arrows. But the arrow-poison frogs are now being sought for more peaceful purposes. In the same way as curare has become an important drug because of its muscle-relaxing properties, so the venom of arrow-poison frogs is now being used in the laboratory for studies on the nervous system. It has been found that it acts in the same way as the hormones secreted by the adrenal gland, blocking the transmission of messages between nerves and muscles. Large amounts rapidly cause death, but in tiny doses it could well have medicinal value.

△ *Golden arrow-poison frog (***Dendrobates auratus***).*
Overleaf: Arrow-poison frog **Dendrobates leucomelas.** *The poison secreted by these amphibians is so strong it kills very rapidly. Their bright colours give other animals warning of their poisonous nature so they are not eaten.*

class	**Amphibia**
order	**Salientia**
family	**Dendrobatidae**
genera	***Sminthillus***
	Dendrobates, Phyllobates

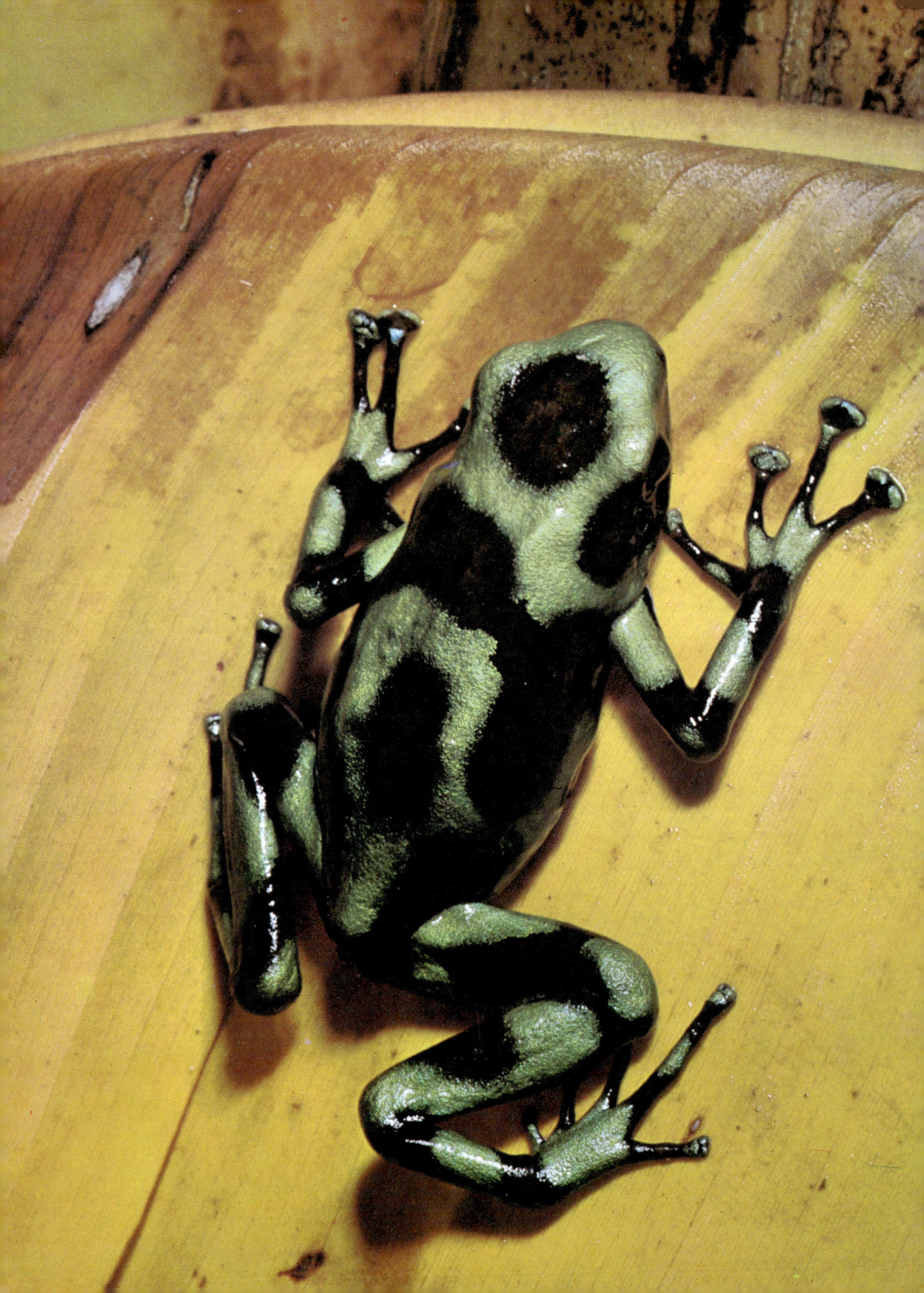

△ African bullfrog, **Pyxicephalus adspersus**, can puff out its vocal sacs to bellow like a calf.

△ With its powerful back legs, the bullfrog can leap over 3 ft. This ability helps in catching its prey; it lies in wait and leaps out on passing prey, catching it while it is in the air.

Bullfrog

The bullfrog is a large species of North American frog. The adult grows to be about 8 in. long. Its skin is usually smooth like that of a common frog but sometimes it is covered with small tubercles. The colour varies; on the upper parts it is usually greenish to black, sometimes with dark spots, the underparts are whitish with tinges of yellow. The females are browner and more spotted than the males. The best way of telling them apart is by comparing the size of the eye and the eardrum. In females they are equal, but in males the eardrum is larger than the eye.

The natural home of the bullfrog is in the United States, east of the Rockies, and on the northern borders of Mexico. They have also been introduced to the western states of America, as well as to Cuba, Hawaii, British Columbia, Canada.

The bullfrog's damp world

Bullfrogs are rarely found out of the water, except during very wet weather. They like to live near ponds and marshes or slow-flowing streams, lying idly along the water's edge under the shade of shrubs and reeds. In winter they hibernate, near the water, under logs and stones or in holes on the banks. How long they hibernate depends upon the climate. Usually they are the first amphibians in an area to retire and, in the spring, they are the last to emerge. In the northern parts of their range they usually emerge about the middle of May, but in Texas, for example, they may come out in February if the weather is mild enough. In the southern areas of their range they may not bother to hibernate at all.

A voracious appetite

The bullfrog gets most of its food from insects, earthworms, spiders, crayfish and snails. Many kinds of insects are caught including grasshoppers, beetles, flies, wasps and bees. The slow-moving larvae and immobile pupae, as well as the active adults, are taken. The unfortunate dragonfly is usually caught when it is in the middle of laying its eggs.

The bullfrog captures small, active prey like this by lying in wait and then leaping forward as the prey passes. Its tongue flies out by muscular contraction and wraps around the prey like a whiplash wrapping itself around a post. The frog then submerges to swallow its victim.

Its diet of insects, however, is usually supplemented by bigger prey. This can include other frogs and tadpoles and small terrapins and alligators. The bullfrog even eats snakes, including small garter and coral snakes. The fact that it eats these snakes is a measure of its voracity. Garter snakes themselves feed largely on amphibians and coral snakes are venomous. There is one case on record of a 17 in. coral snake being taken by a bullfrog. It can even capture small animals like mice and birds and especially ducklings. Even swallows, flying low over the water, are not safe from its voracious appetite and leaping ability.

Unusual mating call

When the water temperature reaches about 21°C/70°F mating takes place. This can be about February in the south of its range, to June or July in the northern parts. At night the males move out from the banks to call, while the females stay inshore. They join the male only when their eggs are ripe.

Find an empty barrel somewhere and shout into it, as deeply as possible, the word 'rum' and, according to Clifford Pope, the American herpetologist, the hollow, booming sound which will emerge is very like the mating call of the bullfrog. The call has also been described as sounding something like 'jug o' rum' or 'more rum' and the alcoholic allusion is carried a bit further in some parts by referring to the bullfrog as 'the jug o' rum'.

The bullfrog makes this extraordinary sound 3 or 4 times in a few seconds. Then, after an interval of about 5 minutes, it repeats it. The sound is made by air being passed back and forth along the bullfrog's windpipe, from lungs to mouth, with the nostrils closed. Some of the air enters the airsacs in the floor of the mouth and they swell out like balloons and act as resonators, amplifying the sound so that the noise can be heard half a mile away.

After the mating the female bullfrog lays 10–25 thousand eggs which float in a sheet on the surface of the water, in among the water plants. With its envelope of jelly, each egg is just over ½ in. It is black above and white below. The eggs usually hatch within a week of being laid. If the temperature is low, however, they may take 2 years, sometimes more, to change into an adult frog, by which time they are 2–3 in. long. They feed on algae and decaying vegetation with occasional meals of small pond animals. After about another 2 years the young bullfrogs are almost fully grown and are ready to breed.

Many enemies

Both the tadpole bullfrog and the adult have a lot of enemies. Fish, snakes, birds and mammals, such as skunks and raccoons, all take their toll. A particular enemy of the tadpoles is the backswimmer, which grapples with a tadpole, inserts its 'beak' and sucks out the body fluids. All the bullfrog can do to protect itself from any enemy, apart from hiding at the bottom of the pool or stream, is to use its tremendous jumping powers to leap several feet clear.

Man is another enemy of the bullfrog. Men hunt them for their legs which are considered as much of a delicacy as those of the edible frog. In California, where they multiplied rapidly after their introduction half a century ago, limits had to be set on the numbers that could be collected in an attempt to prevent them being wiped out altogether. The usual method of killing them is to search for them after dark, dazzle them with a flashlight and then shoot before they can leap clear.

The jumping-frog
There are many ancient legends about 'jumping-frogs' and how their owners have been double-crossed. Mark Twain tells one of the best versions in a short story about one Jim Smiley of Angel's Camp, Calveras County, California. In the story Jim Smiley catches a frog. He calls it Dan'l Webster. The frog is a terrific jumper and Jim makes a lot of money betting on it in contests with other frogs. Then a stranger arrives in the camp and says that he does not think that Dan'l, the frog, is that good a jumper. He's quite prepared to back his word with 40 dollars. The trouble is that, being a stranger, he does not have a frog. Unwilling to let 40 dollars slip by so easily Jim Smiley goes off to find a frog. He leaves his frog with the stranger.

Eventually the new frog is lined up alongside Dan'l Webster. The starting signal is given and both frogs are prodded. The new frog leaps away. Dan'l Webster doesn't move an inch. The stranger collects his 40 dollars and smugly takes his leave. Jim Smiley is baffled and furious.

He can't imagine what's happened to his champion frog. Maybe it's ill. So he picks it up to have a look.

'Why, bless my oats,' he exclaims, 'if he don't weigh a double handful of shot!' So he turns Dan'l Webster, the champion frog, upside down and out pours a couple of pounds of lead shot.

Mark Twain's story was a roaring success. In 1928 when a celebration was held in Angel's Camp, to mark the paving of the streets, the ceremonies included, naturally, a frog-jumping contest. The winner was an entrant called 'Jumping Frog of the San Joaquin' with a leap of 3 ft 4 in.

The contest became very popular and it is now held every year. Allowances are even made for the unpredictable natures of the frogs. Because the first jump might be short and the second record-breaking the contest is judged on the distance travelled by the frog in three consecutive leaps. The record now stands at over 16 ft. So many entries are attracted every year that a stringent set of rules is enforced. One can surely presume that all entries are weighed before jumping so that competitors are spared the embarrassing experience of Jim Smiley — whose tortured ghost is said still to haunt the arena.

class	**Amphibia**
order	**Salientia**
family	**Ranidae**
genus & species	***Rana catesbeiana*** *bullfrog*

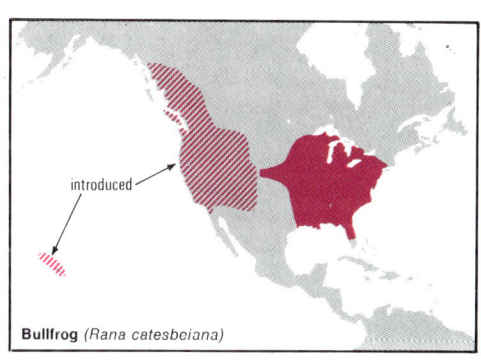

◁◁ Bullfrog, **Rana catesbeiana**. It will take quite large prey including other frogs, small terrapins and alligators, and even coral and garter snakes.
◁ Australian bullfrogs, **Limnodynastes dorsalis**. The female lays eggs in a mass of jelly which she beats up as the eggs are extruded so the eggs are coated and given protection.
▽ The bullfrog rarely leaves the water except during very wet weather. It lives in ponds, marshes or slow-flowing streams, and is often seen lying idly along the water's edge under the shade of reeds and shrubs.

Mouth-breeding frog

Also known as the vaquero, in Argentina, and as Darwin's frog and Darwin's toad, the mouth-breeding frog is probably the most remarkable of all the amphibians. First discovered by Darwin, it is only 1 in. long and its tadpoles mature to tiny froglets inside the father's vocal sacs.

This midget frog is an inconspicuous greenish brown with darker stripes and patches and a dark line running from behind each eye to the hind end of the body. There are many warts arranged in irregular rows on the body and legs. In front of the large eyes the snout rapidly narrows to a pointed, false nose, the nostrils lying halfway between the eyes and the tip of this 'proboscis'. The front legs are fairly short with long, slender toes, the hindlegs being long as in a normal frog.

The mouth-breeding frog was found by Darwin in the Argentine during his famous **Beagle** voyage, and has since been found to range through southern Chile as well as southern Argentina.

Weak voice

The home of this frog is in the beech woods where it hops around in a lively manner, rising well up on its hindlegs before making a short hop forward. The male has a small bell-like voice—weak for the size of the vocal sacs which, as we shall see, have a more important function. These form a large pouch under the throat which extends backwards under the belly to the groin and upwards on each side, almost to the backbone. Inside the mouth is a pair of slits, one on each side, that lead into the vocal sacs, which lie between the skin and the muscles of the body.

Strange nursery

In the breeding season the females lay 20–30 eggs over which the males stand guard for 10–20 days. As the eggs are about to hatch the males pick them up with their tongues, several at a time, and they slide through the slits into the vocal sacs which have now become much swollen. Each male may have anything up to 17 large eggs in his vocal sacs, and quite naturally he now becomes silent. The males do not have to fast while the tadpoles develop. The tadpoles can take no food, however, except for the yolk contained in the eggs which becomes enclosed in their intestines. When about ½ in. long, and with just a stump of a tail left, they leave the vocal sacs. Everything now goes back to normal in the male parent's body. The vocal sacs shrink and his shoulder girdle and internal organs, which had become distorted to make room for the growing tadpoles, go back to their former shape.

The males do not necessarily tend their own offspring; the females lay their eggs in masses and the males take whichever eggs are nearest at the time.

The mouth-breeding frog was first found by Darwin and so is named after him. It is just over 1 in. long and has a peculiar false nose.

The colouring and patterning of the skin of this tiny frog varies tremendously from one frog to another as pictures 1, 2 and 3 show.

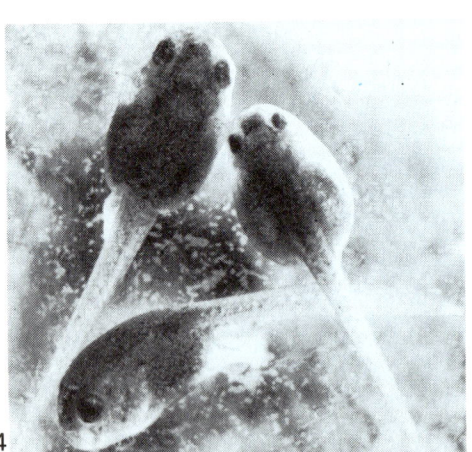

The earliest voice

The first voice in the history of the earth was probably that of a frog, and it may have sounded some 200 million years ago. Plenty of other animals made sounds, the crickets and grasshoppers, for example, as well as many fishes, but a voice-box in the throat came first in the tailless amphibians. Even the tailed amphibians, the salamanders and newts, who can hear, although they were once thought to be deaf, use only a very weak voice, though they have a larynx. By recording the calls of frogs and toads and playing these back to the animals during the breeding season and at other times the value of the voice was discovered. First and foremost, it seems, the voice is used as a mating call. The frogs and toads react most to calls when they are ready to breed. Males move towards any source of calls as a potential breeding site. Once the females have spawned, the voices of the males have no charms for them. So the mouth-breeding males suffer little from having to fall silent, as the females have already spawned. When the voice is used outside the breeding season it is to keep individuals spaced out.

class	**Amphibia**
order	**Salientia**
family	**Rhinodermatidae**
genus & species	***Rhinoderma darwinii***

The tadpoles, picture 4, develop in the swollen vocal sac of the male. This sac is opened, picture 5, showing the tadpoles inside.

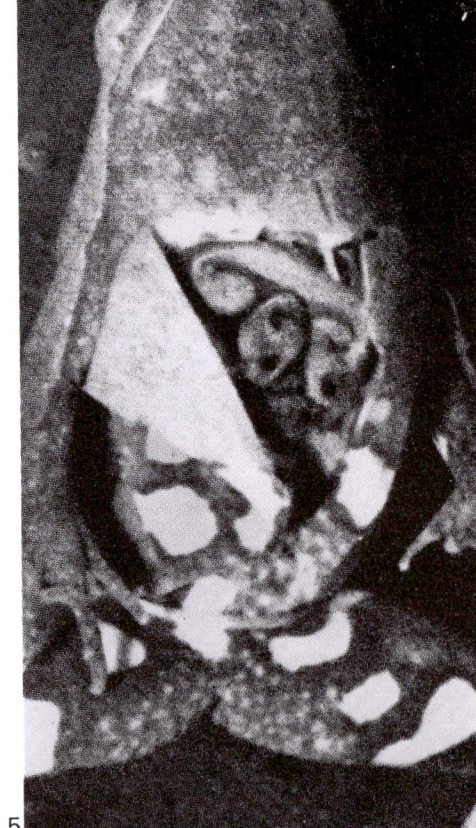

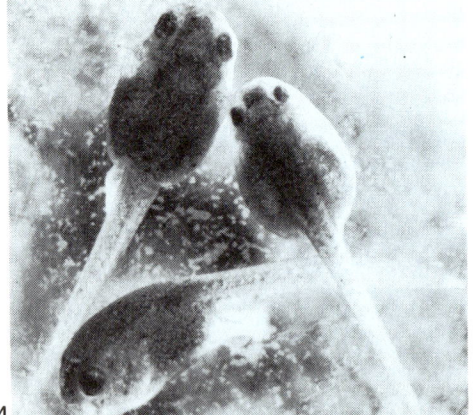

Reed frog

There are over 200 species of reed or sedge frogs, all living in Africa. Many are beautifully patterned and coloured, and can change colour in response to temperature or background. They are small, about 1 in. long. The five-lined reed frog, from Angola to Tanzania, is pale, almost golden brown with five mauve-brown stripes running down its back. These stripes are more distinct in the male than in the female. The painted or marbled reed frog has intricate patterns on its back. The patterns and their colours vary from frog to frog and with the background. Painted reed frogs may be black and white, black and green, black and yellow, brown and yellow as well as several other variations. The painted reed frog ranges from the Cape to Rhodesia and Angola. At the

△ A tiny painted reed frog clings onto a twig by the sucker-like discs on its fingers and toes. The beautiful pinky-red belly and markings on the head and arms are typical of this frog, which often proves difficult to identify because its colour and patterning varies so widely in different parts of its range.

◁ *Nocturnal serenade—a male reed frog sings to attract a female. Actually, both sexes sing but only the male has the well-developed vocal pouch. The noise is produced by the vibration of the elastic edges of a pair of skin folds in the vocal cords. Air is passed backwards and forwards between the lungs and the large pouch which inflates and deflates like a balloon.*
▽ *The long reed frog,* **Hyperolius nasutus**, *is widespread in the coastal belt of eastern southern Africa. Often seen sunbathing on reeds at the edges of swamps, it is said to feed mainly on mosquitoes.*

their new background. The arum frog basks with its legs drawn under it but it may suddenly stretch its legs and leap away. If only slightly disturbed, however, it swings around and disappears behind the lily.

class	**Amphibia**
order	**Salientia**
family	**Rhacophoridae**
genera & species	***Afrixalus*** *small golden spiny reed frog* **A. fornasinii** *brown and white spiny reed frog* **Hyperolius horstocki** *arum frog* **H. marmoratus** *painted reed frog* **H. tuberilinguis** *green reed frog* **H. quinquevittatus** *five-lined reed frog*

southern end of its range it is green or brown with light green spots, each spot ringed with a narrow black line. By contrast, the rare green reed frog is a plain brilliant green with no markings but is white on the belly and pink on the hindlegs.

The two spiny reed frogs live up to their name, for with the aid of a magnifying lens minute spines can be seen on their heads and backs. They differ from the other reed frogs in that the pupil of the eye is vertical instead of horizontal.

Sun-loving frogs

Apart from the spiny reed frogs, which hide during the day, reed frogs like to sunbathe, and can be found clinging to reeds or other plants even in hot sun. They are, however, always ready to leap to safety. Usually this means that they leap back into the pond but the painted reed frog that often lives miles from water escapes by long bounding leaps. During the dry season reed frogs disappear into cracks and crevices in the ground or bury themselves in the earth. Reed frogs feed on flying insects such as mosquitoes.

Varied breeding habits

The life histories of reed frogs have been largely made known through the studies of Vincent Wager, the South African expert on frogs. While the majority probably have life histories similar to other frogs such as the common, edible or bullfrogs, some reed frogs have unusual habits. The life history of the arum frog appears straightforward. Clusters of about 30 eggs are laid among water plants and the surrounding jelly is sticky so the eggs become camouflaged with mud. The tadpoles feed on minute floating organisms rather than scraping at the slime of algae on stones.

The giant reed frog lays its eggs above water. About 300–400 are laid in a sticky mass on floating plants or on the leaves of plants overhanging water. At first the jelly is stiff, then it softens and hangs down. The tadpoles develop within this mass and wriggle about until the jelly liquefies, when they break out and fall into the water. The painted reed frog lays its eggs in clusters on stones or plants underwater, but the southern spotted form, called the pondo reed frog, sometimes loses its eggs through an unusual habit. The mated pair jump onto an erect stalk and bend it over with their weight until its tip hangs into the water. Some eggs are laid on the submerged part which sometimes springs up again after the frogs have let go. The eggs dry out in the sun and die. The egg-laying habits of the spiny reed frogs recall those of newts (page 58). The eggs are stuck to a leaf which is folded over to make a protective tube. The golden spiny reed frog lays its eggs under water, the brown and white spiny reed frog on plants up to 3 ft above the water.

Flower frog

The arum frog lives in flowers of the arum lily, where its ivory colour makes it inconspicuous as it basks in the sun. It is also overlooked by insects that are attracted by the scent of the arum lily and so fall prey to the frog. When arum lilies are not in flower the frogs move to other plants and change their colour to dark brown to fit

Terrapin

The name terrapin is derived from an American Indian word for 'little turtle' and is one of those common words about which there is confusion as to the precise meaning, in the same way as there is confusion about 'turtle' and 'tortoise' (see tortoise, page 75). In Britain 'terrapin' is often used as the name for any small freshwater member of the order Testudines, particularly those kept as pets in aquaria. West of the Atlantic, however, the word has a more restricted meaning and some writers insist that terrapin should refer only to the diamondback terrapin **Malaclemys terrapin**. This is a very sensible idea and will certainly save the confusion that occurs when American natural history books are published in British editions with no explanation of the terms 'turtle', 'tortoise' and 'terrapin', and vice versa. The diamondback terrapin is well known gastronomically as the basic ingredient of 'Terrapin à la Maryland', and because of its economic importance as food, its biology has been studied in detail. It is so named because of the bold, rhomboidal or whorled markings etched in each plate of the carapace. The small plates that border the carapace like the scalloping on a pie crust, are hollowed and lighter in colour. The plastron is yellow and is speckled and lined with small black dots, as is the skin of the head and limbs. Female diamondback terrapins grow up to 8 in., the males to 6 in. and they weigh up to 2 lb. They range from Cape Cod, Massachusetts to Florida, Texas and Mexico.

Other freshwater turtles or tortoises sometimes known as terrapins, are the red-eared terrapin or pond terrapin **Pseudemys scripta**, the Spanish terrapin **Clemmys leprosa** of Spain, Portugal and North Africa and the geographic or map terrapin **Graptemys geographica** of the St Lawrence, the Great Lakes and the Missouri. Confusingly, the box turtles of North America are in the genus **Terrapene**.

Salt essential for health

The diamondback terrapin is never found far from the coast and is restricted to brackish waters, such as tidal estuaries and salt marshes, or the sea, where it may be found in bays. It is found up rivers only as far as the tide penetrates. It seems strange that diamondbacks should be restricted to brackish water but if captive terrapins are kept in fresh water they develop a fungus on the skin, which is cured by adding some salt to the water.

Terrapins come onto rocks to bask in the sun but they spend most of their time swimming with their webbed feet. They have the habit of floating with their shells hanging vertically with only the snout showing above water and with the hindfeet slowly moving to keep them steady. During the winter months terrapins hibernate under the mud of their habitat.

The diamondback terrapin, so called from the bold sculpturing of the plates of the carapace, is famous as a delicacy in the southern USA.

Crushed food
Apart from a few water plants, terrapins feed mainly on small animals such as fiddler crabs, periwinkles, insects and worms, which are crushed in the powerful jaws.

Males not always needed
Most of our knowledge of the breeding habits of diamondbacks comes from observations at terrapin farms where they are bred commercially for their flesh. In the wild, however, they lay their eggs in nests not far above the high water mark. The females, and probably the males as well, mature when about 7 years old. They may lay 1–5 clutches a year, younger terrapins laying fewer, and each clutch consists of 7–24 elliptical white eggs, 1½ by ¾ in. The laying season depends on the climate, being from early May to late July in North Carolina. The young hatch in about 90 days.

Observations at terrapin farms showed that female terrapins can lay fertile eggs although they have been separated from males for several years. In one test 10 females laid 124 eggs one year after being separated from males. Only one failed to hatch. After 3 years they laid 130 eggs and 91 failed to hatch but in the fourth year only 4 out of 108 hatched. It seems that the live sperms are stored in the ovaries and it is now known that this also occurs in other turtles and in snakes.

Gourmet's turtle
The diamondback terrapin has had a varied career as human food. During the 18th century it formed a cheap source of food for slaves, then over the course of the 19th century its fortunes changed as some whim of fashion decided its taste was superior to any other turtle. 'Terrapin à la Maryland' is a rich dish of terrapin meat cooked with vegetables, wine and eggs, with sherry added before serving. By 1920 diamondbacks were fetching $90 a dozen. As a result their numbers decreased so protection laws were passed and they were reared artificially. In recent years, however, there has been a decrease both in demand and price for terrapins.

class	**Reptilia**
order	**Testudines**
family	**Emydidae**
genus & species	***Malaclemys terrapin*** *diamondback terrapin*

▽ *Horny lips, goggle eyes and spotted wrinkled chin and throat – close-up of the diamondback terrapin.*

Tortoise

Tortoises are well known for their slowness of movement and for their long life span. They live longer than any other animal today; and they are about the most heavily armoured. There is a difference between American and British usage. In the United States the name 'tortoise' is used only for land-living chelonians belonging to the family Testudinidae. In British usage some water-living chelonians, such as the European pond tortoise, are also given the common name of tortoise.

There are about 40 land tortoises, the best known of which are the so-called garden tortoises and the giant tortoises. Since the way of life of all of them is much the same, most attention will be given here to the Iberian or Algerian tortoise and the Greek or Hermann's tortoise, both garden tortoises. They have high domed shells, up to 1 ft long. The legs are covered with hard scales which often have bony cores and the five toes on the forefoot and the four on the hindfoot all have stout claws. When disturbed a tortoise pulls its head and limbs into the shelter of the bony box covered with horn which is usually spoken of as its shell. The head is completely withdrawn. The front legs are pulled back to make the elbows meet in the middle, protecting the entrance with their scaly skin. The hindlegs and tail are similarly withdrawn, the soles of the hindfeet sealing the entrance.

Tortoises live in tropical and subtropical regions. The Iberian or Algerian tortoise is found in northwest Africa and Spain, the Balkans, Iraq and Iran. The Greek tortoise ranges from southern France through parts of Italy to the Balkans. The star tortoise of southern Asia has pale star-shaped markings on its shell. The gopher tortoises of the southern United States get their name from the French *gaufre*, a honeycomb, an allusion to their burrowing. There are other land tortoises in southern Asia, Africa, Madagascar and other islands of the Indian Ocean, South America and the Galapagos Islands.

The warmer, the faster

Tortoises live in sandy places or among rocks or in woodlands. They are active by day and generally slow in their movements, yet they can at times reach a speed of 2 mph over short distances. This may be slow compared with the speed of most quadrupeds but it is nearly the walking speed of a man and is faster than we normally consider tortoises' speed. The behaviour of a tortoise is geared to the temperature of the surrounding air. Its movements are faster in warmer temperatures but like other reptiles it is intolerant of the higher air temperatures. Tortoises spend some time every day basking. In temperate latitudes garden tortoises hibernate from October to March, fasting for a while prior to digging themselves into soft earth or under dead vegetation.

△ *A leopard tortoise* **Testudo pardalis** *about to enjoy a refreshing mouthful of cactus.*

Seedlings a favourite meal

It was once widely believed that the smaller tortoises fed on insects and slugs and for this reason people, in England at least, bought tortoises to keep in their gardens. The idea is not yet wholly dead. It may be that a garden tortoise will sometimes eat the smaller garden vermin, but anyone who has seen a tortoise travel along a row of seedlings just showing through the ground will need little convincing that tortoises are wholly or almost exclusively vegetarian, eating low growing vegetation such as seedlings, succulent leaves, flowers and fallen fruits, and only occasionally insects.

Battering ram courtship

Males and females look alike but in most species there is some small difference in shape. In Hermann's tortoise, for example, the plastron, or underside of the shell, is flat in the female, concave in the male. In the Iberian tortoise the tail shield is flat in the female, curved in the male. Another sign is that a male in breeding condition butts the female in the flank, at the same time hissing slightly. Male garden tortoises, when there is no female around, will butt the shoes of people sitting in the garden or the legs of garden chairs. The female lays 4–12 whitish spherical eggs, each 1½ in. diameter, in a hole which she digs in soft ground. The eggs hatch 3–4 months later.

Man the enemy today...

The solid box of bone with its horny covering and the tortoise's habit of withdrawing into this fortress at the slightest disturbance, seem the best possible protection against enemies. The Bearded Vulture is a traditional enemy, flying to some height with a tortoise and then letting it drop to the ground to crack its shell. Rats attack and eat tortoises. Apart from these the natural enemies must be limited. On the other hand, tortoises are probably very vulnerable to the elements, especially to such catastrophes as grass and woodland fires. After a grass fire the number of dead tortoises of all sizes, and especially the small ones, gives an indication of how numerous these animals can be in places where normally little is seen of them. The greatest danger today is the trade in tortoises for pets. Once a tortoise has been bought and installed in a garden it will be treated with the greatest care. The method of packing them for transport has meant, however, that in recent years there has been a hideously high mortality between their being collected, mainly in North Africa, and their reaching the dealers.

. . . and in the past
The four species of gopher tortoises, which may be up to 13 in. long, have also suffered from the pet trade. Two, the Texas tortoise and the desert tortoise, are now protected by law but the Mexican is very rare and may be extinct. The giant tortoises which live on the islands of the Galapagos and on islands in the Indian Ocean have also suffered in numbers, but in a different way. The largest of them have reached nearly 5 ft long, stood 2½ ft high and weighed 200–300 lb. Those of the Galapagos especially were taken by the crews of whalers, sealers and buccaneers for fresh meat. Between 1811 and 1844, a mere 105 whalers took 15 000. The giant tortoises of the Indian Ocean suffered even more, and in recent years a population on Aldabra Island was threatened through a proposal by the British Ministry of Defence to make the island an air staging post.

A ripe old age
Keeping tortoises as pets has been the only reliable way of estimating how long they can live.

The longest authentic record we have is for one of the giant tortoises, Marion's tortoise. It was taken to Mauritius, when full grown, by Marion de Fresne in 1766. In 1810 the British captured the island and the tortoise continued to live in the artillery barracks until 1918. It was, therefore, at least 152 years old, and probably 180 years or even more. Another famous giant was the Tonga tortoise, presented by Captain James Cook in 1774, when it was already 'a considerable age'. There is some doubt about this tortoise, largely because in Tonga the records are oral, not written, but there seems no reason why the present tortoise should not be the same as the one Captain Cook handed over.

class	**Reptilia**
order	**Testudines**
family	**Testudinidae**
genera & species	***Gopherus agassizi*** desert gopher tortoise ***G. berlandieri*** Texas ***G. flavomarginatus*** Mexican ***Geochelone elephantopus*** Galapagos giant ***G. gigantea*** Indian Ocean giant ***Testudo graeca*** Iberian or Algerian ***T. hermanni*** Greek, others

▷ *Galapagos giant tortoises: some of the few remaining members of a species once numerous enough to give its name to the islands but numbers are now greatly diminished. In the 19th century they were easy prey for the crews of passing ships, and their hardiness enabled them to be kept on board as a live source of meat.*

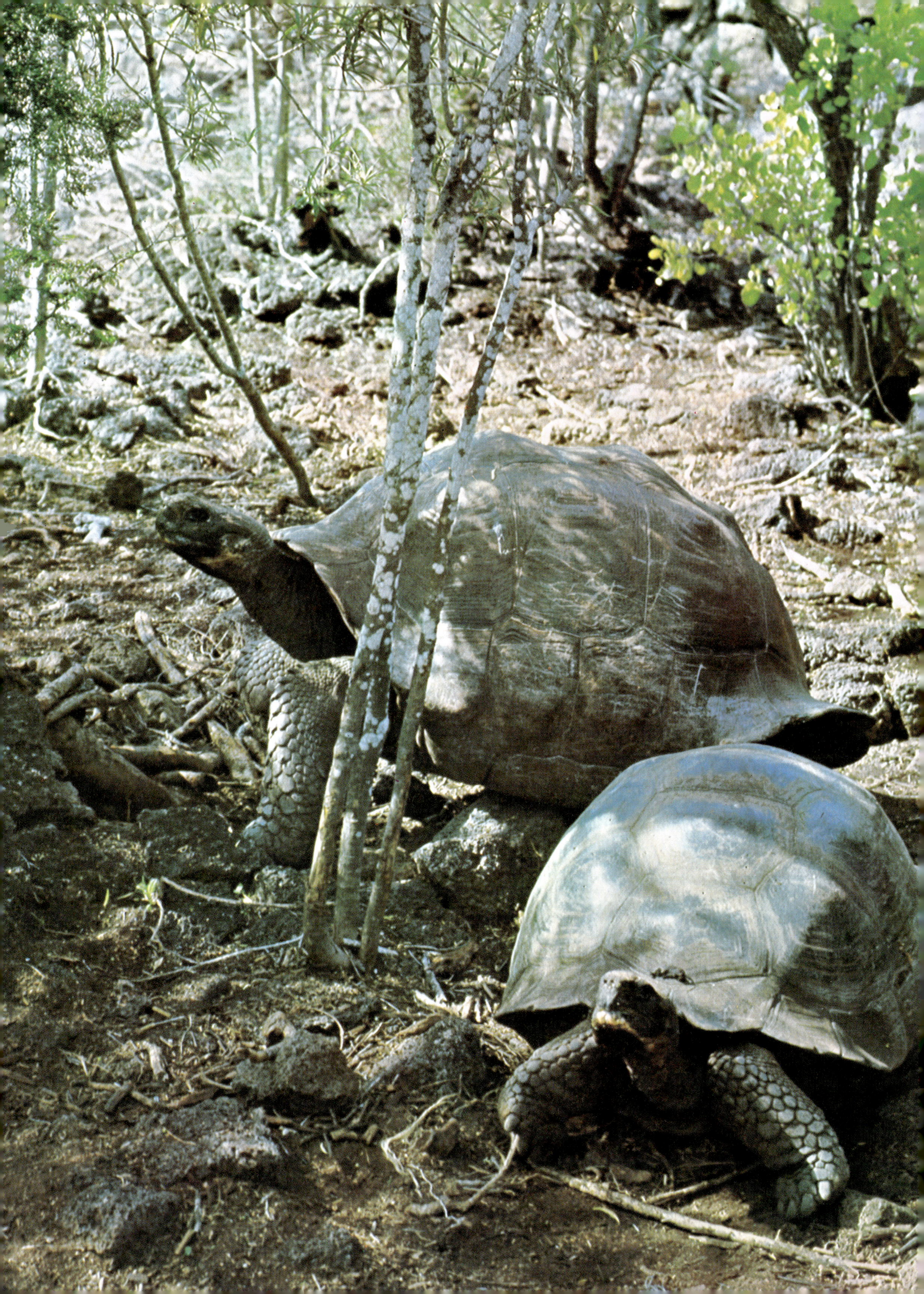

Early morning and the leathery turtle completes her task of egg-laying by filling in the nest hole. This rare sea turtle spends more time in deep water than any other turtle. The females come onto land only to lay eggs. Each comes ashore, usually late at night, about four times a season.

Leathery turtle

The leathery or leatherback turtle or luth is the largest sea turtle, and also differs from the others in the structure of its shell. The upper shell or carapace is made up of hundreds of irregular bony plates covered with a leathery skin instead of the characteristic plates of other turtles. There are seven ridges, which may be notched, running down the back, and five on the lower shell, or plastron.
Leathery turtles are dark brown or black with spots of yellow or white on the throat and flippers of young specimens. They grow to a maximum of 9 ft, the shell being up to 6 ft, and may weigh up to 1 800 lb. The foreflippers are very large; leathery turtles 7 ft long may have flippers spanning 9 ft.

Rare wanderer
The leathery turtle is the rarest sea turtle and lives in tropical waters, probably spending more time in deeper water than other turtles. Little is known about its habits and even its breeding haunts are not well known. Leathery turtles are known to breed in the West Indies, Florida, the northeastern coasts of South America, Senegal, Natal, Madagascar, Sri Lanka and Malaya. The breeding populations are quite small and predation of eggs by men and dogs endangers the populations of some beaches. Although generally restricted to warm waters, leathery turtles are occasionally found swimming in cooler waters or washed up on beaches, especially when carried by adverse winds or currents. They have been seen off Newfoundland and Norway in the north, occasionally straggling as far south as New Zealand.

Unlike some other turtles leathery turtles do not carry encrustations of barnacles and seaweeds. This may be due to the very oily skin. The oil has been found to have antibiotic properties but it is not known whether this prevents other organisms settling on the skin. Also, like the other turtles without barnacles, they are fast swimmers. Leathery turtles are regularly escorted by pilot fish, which are more commonly associated with other fishes, such as sharks.

Although the leathery turtle is described here as the rarest of the turtles, it is of interest to note that it has been increasingly reported in recent years, especially in the North Atlantic. One reason for this, possibly the main reason, is that fishermen have switched to faster, motorized vessels.

A soft diet
The stomach contents of leathery turtles show that they feed on jellyfish, salps, pteropods (planktonic sea snails) and other

soft bodied, slow-moving animals, including the amphipods and other animals that live in the bodies of jellyfish and salps. Leathery turtles have been seen congregating in shoals of jellyfish and the 2–3in. horny spines in the mouth and throat are probably a great help in holding slippery food.

Breeding in bands

Female leathery turtles come ashore in small bands to lay their eggs, usually late at night. They come straight up the shore to dry sand, stop, then start to dig the nest. They do not select the nest site, by digging exploratory pits and testing the sand, as in green turtles. A hollow is excavated with all four flippers working rhythmically until the turtle is hidden. She then digs the egg pit, scooping out sand with her hindflippers until she has dug as deep as she can reach. About 60–100 eggs, 2–2¼ in. diameter, are laid, then she fills the nest with sand and packs it down. Finally she masks the position of the nest by ploughing about and scattering sand, then makes her way back to the sea. Each female comes ashore to lay about four times in one season. The eggs hatch in 7 weeks and the babies emerge together and rush down the shore to the water.

The Soay beast

In September 1959 a large animal was seen in the sea off Soay, a small island off the Isle of Skye, western Scotland. There was much speculation at the time about what it could be. The two men who saw it gave a description and each made a rough sketch of it. The interest was increased by the fact that on at least one occasion many years previously a similar animal had been reported from these same waters. So the Soay Beast, as it came to be called, passed into history as an unsolved mystery, possibly a sea monster, probably one of the several different kinds of sea-serpent reported at various times. All these things seemed possible when one looked at an artist's impression published at the time. In due course Professor LD Brongersma had little difficulty in showing that, beyond reasonable doubt, the animal was nothing more than a large leathery turtle. In this he confirmed the opinion of Dr JH Fraser of Aberdeen, expressed in May 1960, a few months after the sighting was reported.

If the artist's impression was misleading we cannot blame him. He had only the verbal statements to go upon, together with two crude sketches. The real moral is that one should pay more attention to Occam's Razor. William of Occam (now Ockham) was a 14th century English scholar and philosopher who expounded the principle that if there are two or more theories to account for something, choose the simplest.

class	**Reptilia**
order	**Testudines**
family	**Dermochelidae**
genus & species	***Dermochelys coriacea***

△ *Why do leathery turtles cry? The answer might be to remove sand from its eyes on the rare occasions when the turtle comes ashore to nest and lay eggs. The accepted theory is that the tears a turtle sheds get rid of the excess salt that has been swallowed with gulps of sea water.*
▽ *The leathery turtle belongs to tropical waters, but sometimes ranges into temperate seas in summer.*

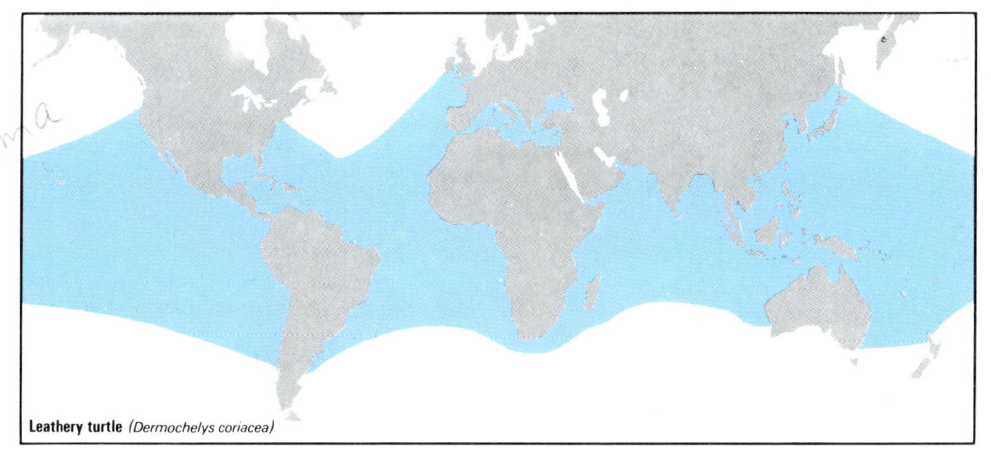

Leathery turtle (*Dermochelys coriacea*)

With a shell length of little more than 4 in. this tiny turtle, the common mud turtle, is one of the smallest freshwater turtles of North America.

The common musk turtle has a much reduced plastron without hinges. The shields of the plastron are separated along the mid-line by soft skin.

Mud turtle

The mud turtles and musk turtles of the family Trionychidae are some of the smallest North American turtles: the adult eastern mud turtle has a brown or olive shell which is little more than 4 in. long. The young of this species has three ridges on the carapace, the upper part of the shell, but these disappear as it grows up. The plastron, or underpart of the shell, is light brown or yellow and the turtles have yellowish green spots on the head. The central part of the plastron is joined to the carapace while its front and rear portions are hinged to this central portion by strong connective tissues forming movable lobes. When the turtle withdraws its head, limbs and tail it draws these lobes over the openings, completely sealing itself in. Musk turtles are similar to mud turtles except that the plastron is very much smaller in proportion to the carapace and is without hinges, but the two kinds of turtles are alike in having musk glands along the sides of the body. The musk is much stronger in the musk turtles which are often called stinkpots as a result. Male mud turtles differ from females in having larger heads and longer tails and, when adult, their plastrons are concave. They also have patches of horny scales on the hindlegs, which are used to hold the female in mating.

There are about 17 species of mud turtle, 4 or 5 in the United States, and the rest in Central and South America. One large South American mud turtle has enlarged lobes on the plastron that make a perfect fit with the edges of the carapace, so the turtle inside is fully protected. The musk turtles live in the United States.

Quiet life

Mud and musk turtles live in pools and sluggish streams where there are plenty of water plants. They crawl over the bottom and occasionally wander out over the land or bask on banks and tree stumps. The

Stinkpot—a three day old common musk turtle.

common musk turtle is rarely seen out of water but the keel-backed musk turtle of the southeastern United States often comes out to bask in the sun. The mud turtles are more likely to be found on land and they often live in very small pools and roadside ditches.

An unpleasant catch

Mud turtles and musk turtles feed on tadpoles, snails, worms, water insects and fish. They also eat a large amount of carrion and are unpopular with anglers because they often take their bait. After giving an angler the impression that he has hooked a large fish the turtle adds insult to injury by discharging its foul-smelling musk when lifted from the water.

Leisurely courtship

The courtship of mud turtles usually takes place in the water but the female comes on land to lay her eggs. To mate the male approaches the female from behind and noses her tail to confirm her sex. He then swims beside her, nudging her just behind her eye. She swims with him for some distance then stops suddenly. This is a signal for the male to climb onto her back, grasp the edges of her carapace with his toes and hold her tail to one side with the scaly patches on one of his hindlegs. Several fertile clutches may result from one mating and females isolated for 3–4 years have laid fertile eggs.

The eggs are laid under rotten logs and stumps or in nests dug in the earth. The musk turtles sometimes lay their eggs in muskrat nests. Up to 7 eggs with hard, brittle shells are laid in each clutch. They hatch in 60–90 days, depending on the heat provided by the sun and the decaying vegetation around them. The newly-hatched turtles have shells about 1 in. long. Males mature in 4–7 years and the females in 5–8 years. In captivity mud turtles have lived for 40 years but in the wild they fall prey to several predators; crows attack the adults, while king snakes, raccoons and skunks eat the eggs.

The turtle frame

It is natural to assume that the plastron is no more than a breast plate to protect the underside of a turtle or tortoise, but in some species it is so small that it can offer very little protection. Even so, it still has an important part to play. In all turtles and tortoises the ribs are incorporated into the carapace and the plastron takes over to some extent the work of the ribs in bracing the body and in providing an anchoring surface for the muscles of the shoulders and hips. In the snapping turtle, for instance, in which the plastron is very much reduced, scientists have calculated that this small plastron is just sufficient to give the necessary strength and support to the body. It is much the same in the mud and musk turtles when they are young; they have a soft carapace and a rigid plastron which braces the carapace. As the turtles grow older and the carapace hardens the plastron is freed from this duty. Then, in mud turtles, it develops the hinges which, acting like lids, close over the turtle when it withdraws into its shell so giving it maximum protection from its enemies.

class	**Reptilia**
order	**Testudines**
family	**Trionychidae**
genera & species	***Kinosternon subrubrum*** common mud turtle ***Sternotherus carinatus*** keel-backed musk turtle ***S. odoratus*** common musk turtle others

Crocodile

The crocodiles and their close relatives alligators, caimans and gharials are the sole survivors of the great group of reptiles, the Archosauria, that included the well-known and awe-inspiring dinosaurs. The crocodile family itself includes the dwarf crocodiles and the false gharial as well as the dozen or so species of true crocodiles.

Crocodiles are often distinguished by the shape of the snout. This is long and broad in the Nile crocodile, the best-known species, short in the Indian marsh crocodile or mugger, and long and narrow in the false gharial. The differences between crocodiles and alligators are set out under alligator, page 86.

As with many large, fearsome animals, the size of crocodiles has been exaggerated. There is reliable evidence for the Nile crocodile reaching 20 ft and American and Orinoco crocodiles have measured 23 ft. At the other extreme the Congo dwarf crocodile has never been found to exceed 3 ft 9 in. Now that crocodiles have been hunted too intensively, large ones have become extremely rare.

Cold-blooded lover of warmth

Crocodiles are found in the warmer parts of the world, in Africa, Asia, Australia and America. Unlike alligators, they are often found in brackish water and sometimes they even swim out to sea. Estuarine crocodiles swim between the islands of the Malay Archipelago and stray ones have been found in the Fijis and other remote islands.

▽ *Smaller relative, different jaw structure: the broad-fronted crocodile of West Africa only grows to 5–6 ft and does not attack man.*

△ *Saltwater or estuarine crocodile: one of the world's most dangerous crocodiles, it can reach lengths of over 20 ft.*

Reptiles are said to be cold-blooded because they cannot maintain their body temperatures within fine limits, as can mammals and birds. A reptile's body temperature is usually within a few degrees of that of its surroundings. It cannot shiver to keep warm or sweat to keep cool. Many reptiles, however, can keep their body temperatures from varying too much by following a daily routine to avoid extremes of temperature. Crocodiles do this. They come out of the water at sunrise and lie on the banks basking in the sun. When their bodies have warmed up, they either move into the shade or back into the water, escaping the full strength of the midday sun. Then in the late afternoon they bask again, and return to the water by nightfall. By staying underwater at night they conserve heat, because water holds its heat better than air.

Stones in their stomachs

When crocodiles come out of the water they generally stay near the bank, although occasionally they wander some distance in search of water, and can cause great consternation by appearing in towns. They are generally sluggish, but, considering their bulky bodies and relatively short legs, they are capable of unexpected bursts of speed. They have three distinct gaits. There is a normal walk, with the body

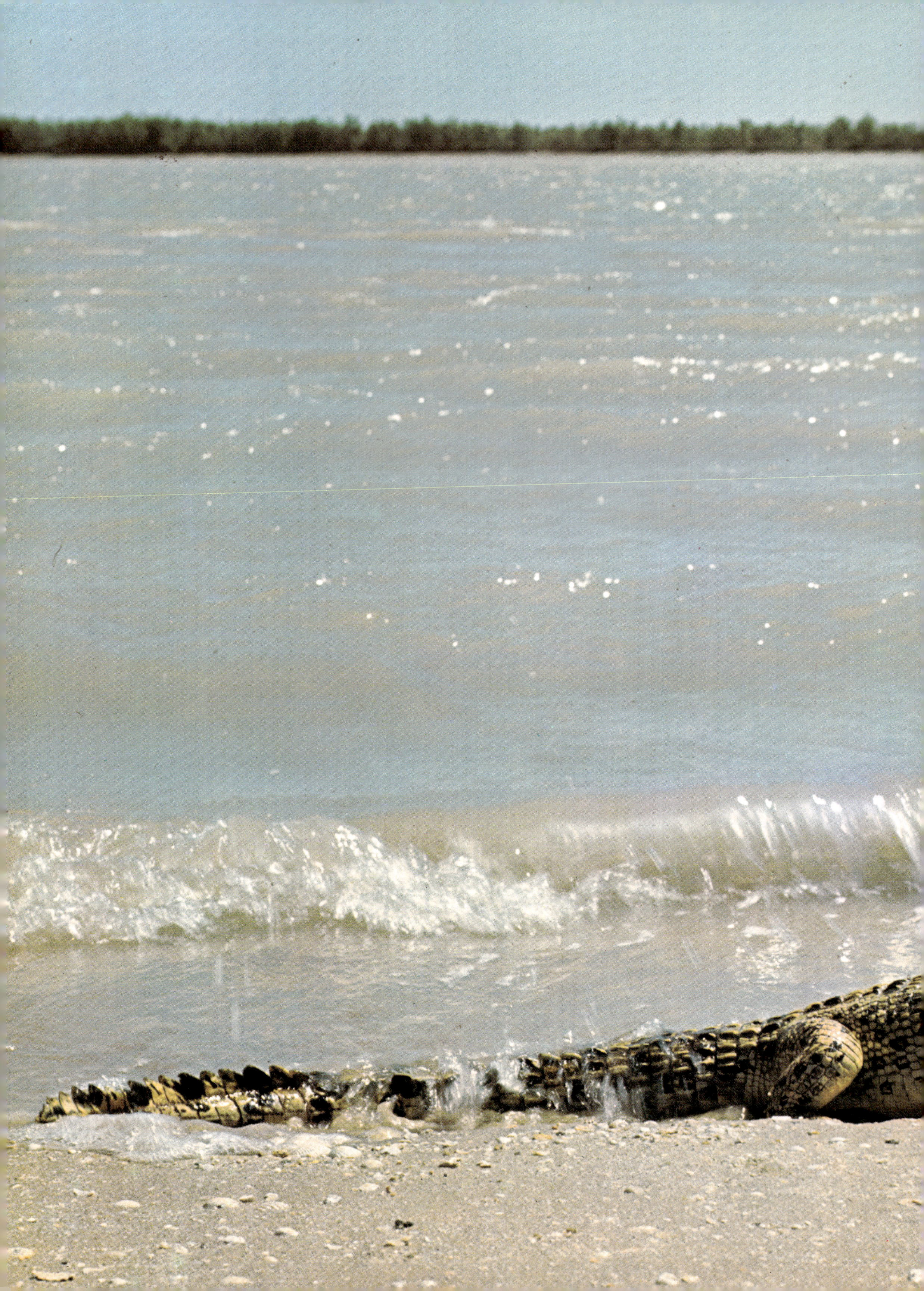

lifted well off the ground with the legs under the body – a gait most unlike the popular conception of a crocodile walking. More familiar is the tobogganing used when dashing into the water. The crocodile slides on its belly, using its legs as paddles. The third method is used by a young crocodile which will occasionally gallop along with the front and back legs working together, like a bounding squirrel.

In the water, crocodiles float very low, with little more than eyes and nostrils showing. They habitually carry several pounds of stones in their stomachs, which help to stabilise their bodies. The stones lie in the stomach, below the centre of gravity and work as a counterpoise to the buoyant lungs. This is particularly useful when the crocodiles are fairly young. At that age they are top heavy and cannot float easily at the surface.

Maneaters: myth and fact
For the first year of their lives, young crocodiles feed on small animals, frogs, dragonflies, crabs and even mosquito larvae. Young crocodiles have been seen cornering the larvae by curving their bodies and tails around them. Larger animals are stalked. The baby crocodile swims stealthily towards its prey then pounces, snapping at it with a sideways movement of the jaws, necessary because the crocodile's eyes are at the side of its head.

As a crocodile grows the amount of insects in its diet falls, and it turns to eating snails and fish. The adult crocodiles continue to catch fish but turn increasingly to trapping mammals and birds. They capture their prey by lying in wait near game trails or waterholes. When a victim approaches the crocodile will seize it and drag it underwater or knock it over with a blow from its tail or head. Once the victim is pulled into the water the crocodile has a definite advantage. Drowning soon stills the victim's struggles, and, grasping a limb in its jaws, the crocodile may roll over and over so that the victim is dismembered.

Crocodiles are well-known as maneaters – but how true is this reputation? The maneating habit varies and it may be that only certain individuals will attack man. In parts of Africa, crocodiles are not regarded as a menace at all, while elsewhere palisades have to be erected at the water's edge to allow the women to fetch water in safety. It seems that crocodiles are likely to be more aggressive when their streams and pools dry up so they cannot escape, or when they are guarding their young.

In the crocodile's nest
The Nile crocodile breeds when 5–10 years old. By this time it is 7–10 ft long. The full-grown males stake out their territories along the banks and share them with younger males and females. They defend the territories by fighting, which may sometimes end in one contestant being killed.

A male crocodile approaches a female

Like an extra for a film on the first amphibious reptiles, a small saltwater crocodile comes ashore in Queensland, Australia. Unlike alligators, crocodiles can be found in brackish waters, estuaries, and swimming out at sea.

crocodile and displays to her by thrashing the water with his snout and tail. They swim in circles with the male on the outside trying to get near her so he can put a forelimb over her body and mate.

Up to 90 eggs are laid during the dry season. They hatch 4 months later, during the rainy season when there are plenty of insects about for the babies to feed on.

The Nile crocodile and the marsh crocodile dig pits 2 ft deep for their nests, but the estuarine crocodile of northern Australia and southeast Asia makes a mound of leaves. The nests are built near water and shade, where the female can guard her brood and keep herself cool. During the incubation period she stays by the nest defending it against enemies, including other crocodiles, although in colonies they sometimes nest only a few yards apart.

The baby crocodiles begin to grunt before hatching. This is the signal for the mother to uncover the nest. The babies climb out and stay near her, yapping if they get lost. They follow her about like ducklings and forage for insects, even climbing trees, and grunting and snapping at one another. They disperse after a few days.

The young Nile crocodiles are about 1 ft long at hatching and for their first 7 years they grow at a rate of about 10 in. a year.

Cannibals

The mother crocodile has to be on her guard all the time as many animals will wait for their chance to eat the eggs or the baby crocodiles. Their main enemy is the monitor lizard. They are bold enough to dig underneath the crocodile as she lies over her nest, and once a male monitor was seen to decoy a crocodile away from the nest while the female stole the eggs. Other crocodiles, herons, mongooses, turtles, eagles and predatory fish all eat baby crocodiles. Adult crocodiles have been killed by lions, elephants, and leopards, and hippopotamuses will attack crocodiles in defence of their young.

Crocodiles are cannibals, so basking groups are always sorted out into parties of equal size and the smaller crocodiles keep well away from the bigger ones.

Crocodile tears

If we say that someone is shedding crocodile tears it means that they are showing grief or sympathy that they do not really mean. The idea that crocodiles are hypocrites is an ancient one, and is described in TH White's translation of a 12th century bestiary: 'Crocodiles lie by night in the water, by day on land, because hypocrites, however luxuriously they live by night, delight to be said to live holily and justly by day.' The hypocrisy seems to be manifested in the form of tears, and malicious or misunderstanding comparisons are made with women's tears. Thus when Desdemona weeps, Othello complains:

'O devil, devil!
If that the earth could teem with woman's tears,
Each drop she falls would prove a crocodile.'

John Hawkins explains crocodile's tears as meaning 'that as the Crocodile when he

△ *Hatching out: while still in the egg, baby Nile crocodiles grunt a signal to the mother to uncover the nest.*

▽ *Prelude to feeding: prey trapped in its vice-like jaws, a crocodile returns to the water where it will take its meal at leisure.*

crieth, goeth then about most to deceive, so doth a woman commonly when she weepeth'. The deception practised by the 'cruell craftie crocodile' is that it lures unwary travellers into drawing near to find out what is the matter.

The story, like many myths and legends, may have a basis of truth. It could have sprung from the plaintive howling that crocodiles make. Crocodiles, however, do have tear glands to keep their eyes moist and tears, or water trapped in their lids, may run from the corners of their eyes. This, with the permanent grin of their jaws, could have led to their legendary reputation as hypocrites.

class	**Reptilia**
order	**Crocodilia**
family	**Crocodylidae**
genera & species	***Crocodylus niloticus*** Nile crocodile ***C. porosus*** estuarine crocodile ***C. palustris*** marsh crocodile ***Osteolaemus*** dwarf crocodiles ***Tomistoma schlegeli*** false gharial

▷ *'African crocodiles at home': a romanticized print shows waterfowl scattering in panic from the threat of an evil-looking flock of crocodiles.*

▽ *Although in parts of Africa crocodiles are not regarded as maneaters, the Nile crocodile has a very bad reputation. One crocodile (15ft 3ins long) shot in the Kihange River, Central Africa, was reported to have killed 400 people over the years.*

When annoyed, alligators open their vast jaws and roar. Male alligators also roar during their quarrels in the breeding season and to attract females.

Alligator

Two species of reptiles which, with the caimans, belong to a family closely related to the crocodiles. Alligators and crocodiles look extremely alike: the main distinguishing feature is the teeth.
In a crocodile the teeth in the upper and lower jaws are in line, but in the alligator, when its mouth is shut, the upper teeth lie outside the lower. In both animals the fourth lower tooth on each side is perceptibly larger than the rest: in the crocodile this tooth fits into a notch in the upper jaw and is visible when the mouth is closed, whereas in the alligator, with the lower teeth inside the upper, it fits into a pit in the upper jaw and is lost to sight when the mouth is shut. In addition, the alligator's head is broader and shorter and the snout consequently blunter. Otherwise, especially in their adaptations to an aquatic life, alligators are very similar to crocodiles.

One of the two species is found in North America, the other in China. The Chinese alligator averages a little over 4 ft in length and has no webs between the toes. The American alligator is much larger, with a maximum recorded length of 19 ft 2 in.
This length, however, is seldom attained nowadays because the American alligator has been killed off for the sake of its skin; whenever there is intense persecution of an animal the larger ones are quickly eliminated and the average size of the remainder drops slowly as persecution proceeds.

It is sheer accident that two such similar reptiles as the alligator and the crocodile should so early have been given different common names. The reason is that when the Spanish seamen, who had presumably no knowledge of crocodiles, first saw large reptiles in the Central American rivers, they spoke of them as lizards – **el largato** in Spanish. The English sailors who followed later adopted the Spanish name but ran the two into one to make 'allagarter' – which was later further corrupted to 'alligator'.

Long lazy life
Alligators are more sluggish than crocodiles; this may possibly have an effect on their longevity. There is a record of an American alligator living for 56 years. They spend most of their time basking on river banks.

The American alligator is restricted to the south-eastern United States and does not penetrate further north than latitude 35. The Chinese alligator is found only in the Yangtse River basin.

Meat eaters
Alligators' food changes with age. The young feed on insects and on those crustaceans generally known as freshwater shrimps. As they grow older they eat frogs, snakes and fish; mature adults live mainly on fish but will catch muskrats and small mammals that go down to the water's edge to drink. They also take a certain amount of waterfowl. Very large alligators may occasionally pull large mammals such as deer or cows down into the water and drown them.

Alligator builds a nest
It seems that the female alligator plays the more active role in courtship and territorial defence. The males apparently spend much of the breeding season quarrelling among themselves, roaring and fighting and injuring each other. The roaring attracts the females to the males, as does a musky secretion from glands in the male's throat and cloaca. Courtship takes place usually at night, the pair swimming round faster and faster and finally mating in the water with jaws interlocked and the male's body arched over the female's.

A large nest-mound is made for the reception of the eggs. The female scoops up mud in her jaws and mixes it with decaying vegetation; the mixture is then deposited on the nest site until a mound 3 ft high is made. The eggs are hard-shelled and number 15–80; they are laid in a depression in the top of the mound and covered with more vegetation. The female remains by the eggs until they hatch 2–3 months later, incubated by the heat of the nest's rotting vegetation.

The hatchling alligators peep loudly and the female removes the layer of vegetation over the nest to help them escape. Baby alligators are 8 in. long when first hatched and grow 1 ft a year, reaching maturity at 6 years.

The biter bitten
Young alligators fall an easy prey to carnivorous fish, birds and mammals, and at all stages of growth they are attacked and eaten

by larger alligators. This natural predation was, in the past, just sufficient to keep the numbers of alligator populations steady. Then came the fashion for making women's shoes, handbags and other ornamental goods of alligator skin. So long as these articles remain in fashion and command a high price, men will be prepared to risk both the imprisonment consequent on the laws passed to protect alligators and the attacks of the alligators themselves.

There is also another commercial interest, detrimental both to the alligator and to the fashion industry. For, while the fashion for skins from larger individuals shows no sign of abating, a fashion for alligator pets also persists—though it may have dropped in intensity since its inception. Baby alligators are still being netted in large numbers for the pet shops, but—as so commonly happens with pets taken from the wild—not all those caught are eventually sold. Of a consignment of 1,000 hatchlings that reached New York City in 1967, 200 were already dead and putrefying, and many others were in a sorry condition and unlikely to survive.

In addition to persecution, land drainage has seriously affected the numbers of the American alligator. The Chinese alligator is an even worse case. Its flesh is eaten and the various parts of its body are used as charms, aphrodisiacs and for their supposed medicinal properties. The New York Zoological Park has recently announced plans to try and breed the Chinese alligator and so protect it from complete extermination.

Unwanted pets

The fashion for alligator pets has its disadvantages for owners as well as the alligator populations. Even setting aside the largest recorded lengths for the American species of 19 ft upwards, it still achieves too large a size to be convenient in the modern flat, and people who invest in an alligator often find it necessary to dispose of it. Zoos have proved unable to deal with the quantity offered them—Brookfield Zoo near Chicago has built up an enormous herd from unwanted pets—and it is widely said that unfortunate alligators are disposed of in such a way that they end up in the sewers. One result of this is that every now and then, despite official denials, reports have appeared in the press to the effect that the sewers of New York are teeming with alligators that prey on the rats and terrorise the sewermen.

△ *A female alligator builds a nest of rotting vegetation for her clutch of 15—80 eggs. She stays for 2—3 months by the nest until they hatch.*

▽ *Alligators spend much of their time basking on the banks of jungle rivers. Here they have made a lagoon by their thrashing about.*

class	**Reptilia**
order	**Crocodilia**
family	**Alligatoridae**
genus & species	***Alligator mississipiensis*** American alligator
	A. sinensis Chinese alligator

Gecko

Geckos form a family of lizards noted for the large number of species, the structure of their feet, their voices, the differences in the shape of their tails, and for the ease with which some of them will live in houses. The smallest is $1\frac{1}{3}$ in. long; the largest—the tokay—may be 14 in. long.

Geckos are found in all warm countries: 41 species in Africa, 50 in Madagascar, about 50 in Australia, the same in the West Indies, with others in southern and southeast Asia, Indonesia, the Pacific islands and New Zealand, and South America. There are geckos in the desert regions of Mexico and southern California. Several have been introduced into Florida from the Caribbean islands. Spain and Dalmatia, in southern Europe, have the same wall gecko as North Africa.

A liking for houses

The majority of geckos live in trees, some live among rocks, others live on the sandy ground of deserts. Tree geckos find in human habitations conditions similar to, or better than, those of their natural habitat: natural crevices in which to rest or take refuge and plenty of insects, especially at night when insects are attracted to lights. Because geckos can cling to walls or hang upside-down from ceilings they can take full advantage of these common insect resting places, and so many of them are now known as house geckos.

Hooked to the ceiling

Most geckos can cling to smooth surfaces. Their toes may be broad or expanded at the tips with flaps of skin (lamellae) arranged transversely or fanwise. The undersides of the toes bear pads furnished with numerous microscopic hook-like bristles that catch in slight irregularities, even in the surface of glass, or have bristles ending in minute suckers. So a gecko can cling to all but the most highly polished surfaces. The hooks are directed backwards and downwards and to disengage them the toe must be lifted upwards from the tip. As a result, a gecko running up a tree or a wall or along a ceiling must curl and uncurl its toes at each step with a speed faster than the eye can follow. Some of the hooks are so small the high power of a microscope is needed to see them, yet a single toe armed with numbers of these incredibly small hooks can support several times the weight of a gecko's body. In addition to the bristles, most species have the usual claw at the tip of the toe which also can be used in clinging. In one species there are microscopic hooks on the tip of the tail which enable the animal to cling.

△ *Close pursuit. As firm as the flies it is hunting, a diurnal gecko* **Phelsuma vinsoni** *pauses on a vertical tree-trunk, unaware of the apparent impossibility of its position.*
▷ *Living crampons. Geckos get a grip from tiny hooks in the flaps of skin on their feet.*
▷▷ *After partial loss, regrowth and healing, the result is a three-tailed gecko.*

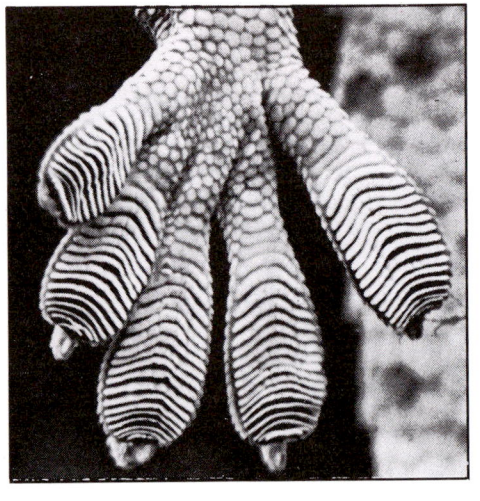

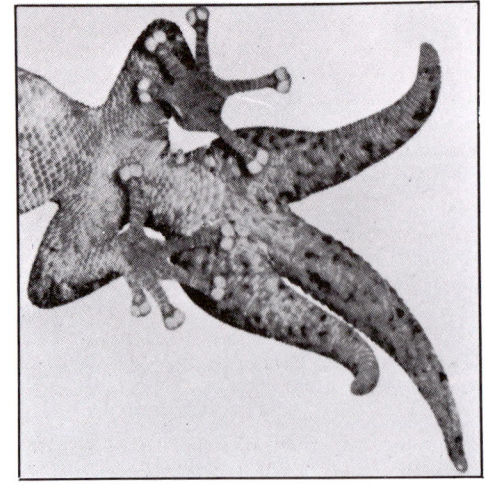

Leaf-like tail
The tail is long and tapering, rounded or slightly flattened and fringed with scales, according to the species, or it may be flattened and leaf-like. A South American gecko has a swollen turnip-shaped tail. It has been named *Thecadactylus rapicaudus* (*rapi* for turnip, *caudus* for tail). The flying gecko of southeast Asia has a leaf-like tail, a wide flap of skin along each flank, a narrow flap along each side of the head and flaps along the hind margins of the limbs. Should the gecko fall it spreads its limbs, the flaps spread and the reptile parachutes safely down.

Geckos can throw off their tails, like the more familiar lizards, and grow new ones. In some species 40% have re-grown tails. Sometimes the tail is incompletely thrown and hangs by a strip of skin. As a new tail grows the old one heals and a 2-tailed gecko results. Even 3-tailed geckos have been seen. Temperature is important in growing a new tail. It has been found that when the wall gecko of southern Europe and North Africa grows a new tail with the air temperature at 28°C/82°F it is short and covered with large overlapping scales. With the temperature around 35°C/95°F the new tail is long and is covered with small scales.

Cat-like eyes
One difference between snakes and lizards is that the former have no eyelids. In most geckos the eyelids are permanently joined and there is a transparent window in the lower lid. The few geckos that are active by day have rounded pupils to the eyes. The rest are active by night and have vertical slit-pupils like cats. In some species the sides of the pupils are lobed or notched in four places, and when the pupils contract they leave four apertures, the size of pinholes each one of which will focus the image onto the retina.

△ *Pinhole sight: pupils shrunk to four tiny holes, to keep out excessive glare of the sun.*

Surprisingly small clutches
All geckos except for a few species in New Zealand, which bear live young, lay eggs with a tough white shell. Usually there

are two in a clutch, sometimes only one. The eggs are laid under bark or under stones and take several months to hatch.

Harmless creatures
Geckos eat only insects. They are harmless and wholly beneficial to man, yet among the people of Africa, South America, Malaysia and the aboriginals of Australia there are widespread beliefs that their bite makes them dangerous to handle. Possibly such beliefs spring from some of the more remarkable species, like the gecko that stalks insects as a cat does a mouse, even lashing its tail from side to side just before the final pounce. Then there are the web-footed geckos living on the sand dunes of Southwest Africa. They not only use the webbed feet to run over loose sand but also to burrow. They scrape the sand away with the forefoot of one side and shovel it back with the hindfoot of the same side while balancing on the feet of the other side. Then they change over. They walk with the body raised high and the tail held up and arched.

One web-footed gecko has a delicate beauty. It is pinkish-brown with a lemon yellow stripe along its flank. Its eye has brilliant yellow lids, the iris is black, patterned with gold and coppery tints, while the edges of the vertical pupil are chalky white. Its skin is so transparent the spine and some internal organs can be seen clearly. In *African Wild Life*, GK Brain claims its two ear openings are almost in direct connection; by looking into one earhole light coming in

△ *A regrown tail shows that, despite excellent camouflage, only desperate measures saved this gecko's life.*

through the other can be seen.

class	**Reptilia**
order	**Squamata**
suborder	**Sauria**
family	**Gekkonidae**
genus & species	***Gekko gecko*** *others*

△ *Defiance: a cornered lizard unfurls its frill.*

Frilled lizard

One of the so-called dragons of Australia, the frilled lizard grows to about 3 ft long, with a slender body and long tail. It is pale brown, either uniformly coloured or with patches of yellow and darker brown. Its most conspicuous feature is the frill around the throat, like the ruff fashionable in Europe in the Middle Ages.

Apart from its size the only remarkable thing about this lizard is its frill. Normally this lies folded over the shoulders like a cape. It is a large area of skin supported by cartilaginous rods from the tongue bone which act like the ribs of an umbrella. In moments of excitement, muscles pulling on these raise the frill to 8 in. or more across, about as wide as the length of the head and body together.

It lives mainly in sandy semi-dry areas of northern and northeastern Australia.

Hindleg sprinter

The frilled lizard lives in rough-barked trees, coming to the ground after rainstorms, to feed. When disturbed on the ground it runs on its hindlegs with the frill laid back over the shoulders, tail raised, and the forelegs held close into the body. It may sprint for a considerable distance, or it may seek safety by climbing a tree. When brought to bay it turns, opens its mouth wide and extends its frill. The best description of what happens next is given by Harry Frauca in *The Book of Australian Wild Life*. It does not raise its tail, as it has often been reported to do, and as some other similar lizards are known to do, but keeps it flat on the ground. It sways from side to side and with its open mouth, coloured dark blue inside edged by pinkish yellow, surrounded by the greenish-yellow frill splashed with red, brown, white and black, it looks like a large flower among broad leaves. The colours of the lizard vary from one region to another. In Queensland the general colour is a sombre grey, in the Northern Territory it is pinkish, often with a black chest and throat. The colours of the mouth and frill also vary.

The open mouth and spread frill are a warning display. If the warning is ignored it passes to an aggressive display. The lizard steps boldly towards the intruder, keeping its mouth open and frill fully extended, and from the mouth comes a low hiss. The remarkable thing is that people who know very well the lizard can do nothing to harm them, tend nevertheless to be intimidated by all this show. Even a dog used to attacking larger lizards will retreat before it.

Meals of ants and eggs

The frilled lizard eats insects, including large quantities of ants, as well as spiders and small mammals. It is also said to be an egg thief. One of the many difficulties found in keeping this animal in captivity is that of getting enough of the right kind of food. In 1893, when the time it took to travel from Australia to Great Britain was much longer than it is today, the naturalist W Saville Kent brought a frilled lizard to London, the first to reach Europe alive. When it was exhibited before an audience of learned gentlemen one eminent zoologist is said to have followed it, in his excitement, on hands and knees, to watch it careering round on its hind legs and displaying its frill. Unfortunately, there is no record of how Saville Kent managed to feed his pet, but, like many reptiles, the frilled lizard can probably go without food for months.

Umbrella trick

Neither does history record whether any of the learned gentlemen noticed a comparison between the lizard and a lady. At that time ladies carried parasols and it was not uncommon for a lady, confronted by a cow as she crossed a field, to frighten the cow away by suddenly opening her parasol in its face. Konrad Lorenz, in *King Solomon's Ring*, tells how his wife kept geese from devastating her newly-planted flower beds. She carried a large scarlet umbrella and this she would suddenly unfold at the geese, with a jerk, causing the geese to take to the air with a thundering of wings. It is almost instinctive for a woman carrying an umbrella to use it in this way against a powerful and persistent opponent. It is a matter of no small interest to find that this same effective defence should have been evolved by a lizard.

class	**Reptilia**
order	**Squamata**
suborder	**Sauria**
family	**Agamidae**
genus & species	***Chlamydosaurus kingii***

Frilled lizard (*Chlamydosaurus kingii*)

Chameleon

The chameleons are a family of lizards renowned for several unusual features. The body is high in proportion to the length and is flattened from side to side. The tail in most species is prehensile, is often held in a tight coil, and can be wrapped round a twig for extra grip. The toes of each foot are joined, three on the inside of the front feet and on the outside of the hindfeet, resulting in feet like pairs of tongs that can give a tenacious grip on a perch. Above all, a chameleon is remembered for three things: its ability to change colour, its eyes set in turrets that can move independently of each other, and its highly extensible tongue which can be shot out at speed to a length greater than the chameleon's head and body. To add to their bizarre form, some species have rows of tubercles down the back or a 'helmet' or casque like the flap-necked chameleon or horns like Jackson's chameleon.

A few species grow to 2 ft long, while dwarf species measure less than 2 in.

There are about 80 species of chameleon most of which live in Africa south of the Sahara and including Madagascar. One species, the common chameleon, ranges from the Middle East along the coast of North Africa to southern Spain. Two others live in the southern end of the Arabian peninsula and a third in India and Sri Lanka.

Chameleons live in slow motion

Chameleons live mainly in forests, and seem to spend most of their time virtually rooted to the spot, the only movement being of the eyes, each independently sweeping from side to side searching for food or danger. When they move they creep slowly along a twig. Sloth-like, a fore foot is released on one side and the hind foot on the other, and both are slowly moved forward to renew their grip on the twig while, equally stealthily, the other two advance. Although most chameleons keep to the trees as much as possible, the stump-tailed chameleons can often be found on the ground.

Periodically chameleons shed their skins. Before it comes off the old skin comes away from the new skin under it, leaving an air-filled gap that gives the chameleon a pale, translucent appearance as if it were neatly wrapped in polythene. Then the old skin splits, first just behind the head, and chunks of it flake off exposing the brilliant new skin.

Extensible tongue

Chameleons eat the usual food of small reptiles, that is, insects and other small invertebrates, but the larger species will also catch small birds, lizards and mammals. The similarity with other reptiles ends here, for the method of capture is unique except in frogs and toads. Chameleons capture their prey by shooting out their long tongue, trapping the victim on the tip and carrying it back to the mouth. The whole

△ Portrait of **Chamaeleo bitaeniatus** taken on Mt Elgon, Kenya. It lives above 9 000 ft.

◁ A chameleon in the later stages of shedding its skin. A new skin has first grown under the old. Notice that it even sheds the skin on its eyelids.

△ Stage one: lining up on the target with tongue protruding. Note the spider in the top right corner.
▽ Stage two: muscles shoot the tongue to its full extent.

▽ Stage three: muscles contract, withdrawing the tongue. Despite its speed, the spider was quicker!

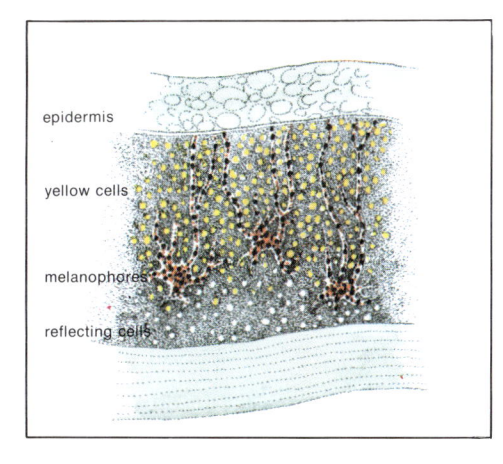

◁ Simplified diagram of section through skin: colour change is mainly due to melanophores moving dark pigment into or out of upper layers.
▷ Catapult mechanism of the chameleon's tongue: special bone with its own muscles pushes tongue forward and circular muscles squeeze it out. Longitudinal muscles withdraw the tongue.

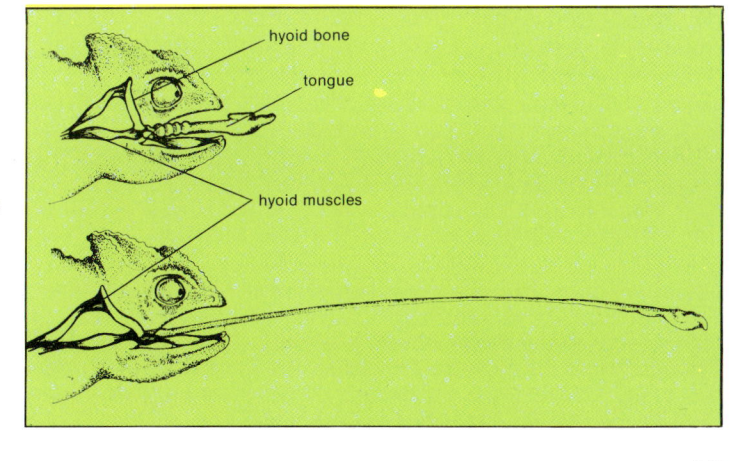

action is so rapid that high-speed photography is needed to show the mechanism at work. By using a ciné camera it has been found that a 5½ in. tongue can be extended in $\frac{1}{16}$ second and retracted in $\frac{1}{4}$ second. Without such aids all one sees is the chameleon watching its prey from its perch, or slowly edging towards it, for chameleons only take sitting prey. When in range it directs both eyes at its victim and rocks from side to side, improving its stereoscopic vision and range-finding capacity by looking at the target from different angles. While doing this the tip of the tongue protrudes from the mouth like a wad of chewing gum, then suddenly the insect disappears from its perch and is seen to be crushed in the chameleon's jaws. Young ones begin eating insects when a day old, and with a little practice become expert.

How the chameleon shoots out its tongue has been deduced by a careful study of its anatomy. Two mechanisms throw the tongue forward, both of them activated by powerful muscles. At the back of the jaw lies a V-shaped bone with the point of the V pointing backwards. Attached to this bone by a flexible joint is the tongue bone, over which the tongue fits like a glove on a finger. When the chameleon is about to shoot the V-bone is moved forward slightly to push the tip of the tongue out of the mouth. Then, the circular muscles in the thick tip of the tongue contract violently so that the tongue is forced out in the same way as an orange pip squeezed between the fingers, and simultaneously the V-bone is thrust further forward, giving added impetus.

The end of the tongue is sticky with saliva but an insect can settle on a chameleon's head and walk across its protruding tongue with no difficulty. On the other hand some people who have kept chameleons as pets report that the end of the tongue does feel adhesive, but this may be due to the minute hooks or hairs or other roughenings of its surface. Finally, there are photographs that show the tongue apparently grasping an insect. It may be that a combination of all three may be operating as in toads.

Breeding poses problems

Male chameleons hold territories which they guard against other males, keeping them out by bluff. The lungs of chameleons have branches spreading through the body and by inflating its lungs a chameleon can blow itself to a most impressive size. Females, of course, are allowed to enter the territories and the males chase after them and mate with them, unless dissuaded by a female already pregnant.

Some chameleons lay eggs, others bear their young alive. The former course has some disadvantages for chameleons lay up to 50 eggs in a clutch, each has a diameter of perhaps ½ in. Places to hide such a large clutch must be rare in a tree and the chameleon, who is bulky and ungainly when carrying her eggs, has to climb down the tree and dig a hole in the ground. A common South African chameleon has been described as digging the hole with her head and front feet, pushing the loose soil away with her hind feet. It takes a long time but eventually she has a hole nearly the length of the body. She then backs into it and lays

Independently-swivelling eyes and palsied gait.

her eggs, pressing each one into place with her hind legs. When she has finished she fills in the hole, tamps it down, camouflages it with sticks and pieces of grass and leaves it. In due course the young hatch out and fight their way to the surface.

Other chameleons bear their young alive. Before the birth the female's body becomes greatly distended. The young are born in a translucent membrane. As each one is due the mother presses her cloaca against the twig on which she is perching and the membrane sticks to it. After a short interval the baby chameleon struggles out and walks off down the twig. The mother takes no more interest in her offspring, except that, if she is very hungry, she may eat them. The young start to feed when a day old, and with a little practice become expert at catching insects.

Quick colour change

Although other reptiles, as well as many fish and squid, can change colour, it is the chameleon that is renowned as a quick change artist. This is epitomised by the story of the chameleon put on a red cloth that changed to red, then when put on a green cloth turned to green, but had an apoplectic stroke when placed on a Scottish tartan. This greatly exaggerates the chameleon's power of colour change. The truth is that most species of chameleon have a basic colour and pattern that suits their particular habitat and do not really change colour to resemble the background but in response to light intensity, temperature, or emotional state. Thus, colour change serves two purposes: to camouflage the chameleon and to act as a signal telling other chameleons its mood. An angry chameleon, for instance, goes black with rage. How the colour change is controlled is still not properly known. There is evidence for control by nerves and also by the secretion from the brain of chemicals which act on the colour cells; probably both act in different circumstances.

What is better known is the mechanics of colour change. The specialised colour cells lie under the transparent skin in four layers. The outermost is made up of xanthophores or yellow-bearers, together with erythrophores, the red-bearers. Under this layer are two reflecting layers, one reflecting blue light, the other white light. Beneath is the most important, and most complicated, layer of melanophores. These contain a dark brown pigment called melanin, the same substance that colours human skin brown or black. The main body of each melanophore lies under the reflecting layers but it sends tentacle-like arms up through the other layers.

To alter the colour of the skin, the colour cells alter in size, so that by variation of the amounts of yellow, red and dark brown, different colours are produced by mixing. The reflecting layers modify these effects. When the blue layer is under yellow cells, green is produced and where the blue layer is missing, light reflected from the white layer enhances the yellow or red coloration. The melanophores control the shading of the colours. When the colours are bright all the melanin is concentrated in the bodies of the melanophores. If the melanin spreads along the 'tentacles' to obscure the white layer, greens and reds become darker and if the melanin is dispersed completely, the chameleon becomes dark brown.

class	**Reptilia**
order	**Squamata**
suborder	**Sauria**
family	**Chamaeleontidae**
genera & species	***Chamaeleo chamaeleon*** common chameleon *C. dilepis* flap necked chameleon *C. oweni* three horned chameleon *C. jacksoni* Jackson's chameleon ***Brookesia*** spp. stump tailed chameleons others

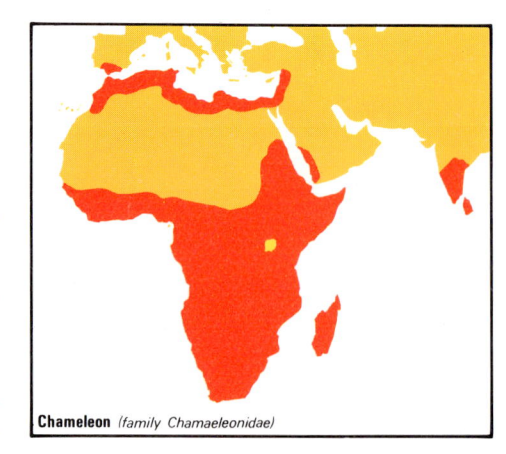

Chameleon (family Chamaeleonidae)

Iguana

The iguana family contains lizards such as the anole, the basilisk, the horned toad and many others, some of which are called iguanas in everyday English. The marine iguana is discussed under a separate heading; here we are dealing with the green iguana, the ground iguana, the land iguanas and the desert iguana or crested lizard.

The ground iguana is one of the most primitive members of the family. It has a crest like the teeth in a comb running down its back starting behind the head and petering out in the middle of the heavy tail.

One kind, the rhinoceros iguana, has two or three hornlike scales on its head and a large swelling on either side of the chin. Ground iguanas reach a length of 4 ft, 2 ft shorter than the green iguana which has been introduced to the Virgin Isles and the Lesser Antilles where it has driven out the ground iguana. The native home of the green iguana is Central and northern South America. It is pale green in colour, has a crest similar to that of the ground iguana and an erectable sac under the throat. The males are larger than the females, their crests are longer and their bodies are more orange or yellow compared with the females' light green. The males

△ Flowers on the menu: although it eats mainly insects when young, this green iguana seems to be interested in the more adult diet of tender young buds. They often clamber in trees.

also have a row of pores on the underside of each thigh, whose function is unknown.

The desert iguana lives in the deserts of North America. It measures 1 ft and is cream coloured with brown or black lines and spots. The land iguana of the Galapagos islands grows up to 5 ft. It is yellow with brown spots on the sides and legs.

High diver
The green iguana is an agile climber and adults are rarely found far from the trees of the tropical forests in which they live. It can scramble from one tree to another providing the twigs are interlaced to give reasonable support for iguanas cannot leap far. Green iguanas will, however, throw themselves from a branch 40–50 ft up and land on the ground unhurt, sprinting away to the undergrowth with barely a pause for breath. For an animal that appears so clumsy, with a heavy tail and legs splayed sideways, an iguana is remarkably fast and is extremely difficult to catch. Its reflexes are very rapid and unless one has nets the only way to catch an iguana is to throw oneself at it and even then a fullgrown iguana will be very hard to hold, as it can inflict nasty bites and scratches. Iguanas often take refuge in water and their favourite haunts are in trees overhanging pools and rivers. If disturbed they leap from the branch where they were lying and dive into the water. They swim underwater, propelling themselves with their tails, and surface under cover of vegetation along the bank.

The green iguana comes down to the ground in cold weather and hides under logs or in holes, but the other iguanas are usually ground-living and only occasionally climb trees. The desert iguana is a very fast runner and races about on its hindlegs.

Vegetarian lizards
As adults green iguanas eat a variety of plant foods, including young shoots, fruits, flowers and leaves, but the young ones also eat insects. Other iguanas are also vegetarian. The desert iguana prefers the yellow-flowered creosote bush but also eats other flowers, and after the flowering season is over it eats insects and carrion. Land iguanas feed on cactus and the larger species eat small rodents.

Eggs need constant temperature
Male land iguanas of the Galapagos form territories which they defend against other males. Each keeps watch from a rock and if another male intrudes he climbs down from his vantage point, walks slowly over to his rival and displays at him, pointing his snout at the sky and jerking his head up and down. If this does not scare the intruder into running away a fight breaks out, each trying to grab the loose skin on the other's flanks.

The female land iguanas live in the same burrows as their mates or in separate burrows alongside. Iguanas generally lay their eggs in nests well separated from each other but on a small island in Panama green iguanas were found nesting in great numbers close together on a sandy beach. Each female spent up to 2 weeks on the shore. For the first few days she probed the sand and dug small holes seeking a suitable site. Then she dug a large burrow 1–2 yd long and 2–3 ft deep. Because the beach was so crowded some were seen digging up other nests and scattering the eggs. Eggs were laid at the bottom of the burrow which was

▷ *The Barrington Island iguana of the Galapagos* **Conolophus pallidus**. *Local people prize its flesh, goats destroy its home.*

◁◁ *The aptly named rhinoceros iguana, with two horn-like scales on the top of its nose.*
◁ *A green iguana pauses, throat sac down and crest erect, to fight or flee an intruder, its partly missing tail witness of a past escape.*

filled in afterwards. The females spent some time filling the hole and at the same time filling in adjacent holes. Sometimes this meant filling in the burrows of other females who might be trapped and buried.

The green iguana lays 20–70 eggs in a clutch. The eggs are spherical, white and about 1½ in. diameter. They hatch in 3 months and it has been found that an almost constant temperature is needed for their development. A few degrees too high or too low and they fail to hatch. Although the female abandons her eggs after they are laid she ensures their survival by burying them in a suitable part of the beach. She chooses a spot where the temperature fluctuates only 1°–2° either side of 30°C/86°F. The young iguanas measure about 10 in. when they hatch and grow to 3 ft in one year.

Fooling the iguanas
Man and his domestic animals are the iguanas' worst enemies. Their flesh is relished in many parts of the world. Hawks are also serious enemies, for they catch iguanas as they lie basking in trees. In parts of South America iguanas are hunted by men imitating the screams of hawks. The iguanas' reaction to the cries is to 'freeze' and they are then easily caught. Snakes also hunt iguanas; a 6 ft boa constrictor has been found with an adult green iguana in its stomach.

Vanishing iguanas
When Charles Darwin visited the Galapagos islands in 1835 land iguanas were extremely abundant. Darwin wrote 'I cannot give a more forcible proof of their numbers than by stating that when we were left at James Island, we could not for some time find a spot free from their burrows to pitch our single tent.' Since then man has settled on the island, bringing with him dogs, cats, pigs, rats, goats and other animals and the iguana population is now a fraction of its former size. On some islands, however, where there are no goats, there are still large numbers of iguanas. The link between goats and iguanas is that goats strip the vegetation, depriving iguanas of cover. Some islands seem to be populated by adult iguanas only. They can survive in the open but young iguanas need cover to protect them from the Galapagos hawk. Without this cover they are killed off, and when the old lizards die there will be none left.

class	**Reptilia**
order	**Squamata**
suborder	**Sauria**
family	**Iguanidae**
genera & species	**Conolophus subcristatus** land iguana **Cyclura cornuta** rhinoceros iguana **Dipsosaurus dorsalis** desert iguana **Iguana iguana** green iguana

Marine iguana

The marine iguana is unique in its way of life, being the only truly marine lizard. It is found only in the Galapagos Islands, some 600 miles west of Ecuador. Because of its exceptional home, it is of great interest, but physically it is not so exciting. The accounts of early visitors to the Galapagos testify to the marine iguana's ugly appearance. One account describes them as having the most hideous appearance imaginable, and the same author, a captain of the Royal Navy, says that 'so disgusting is their appearance that no one on board could be prevailed on, to take them as food'. Marine iguanas grow up to 4 ft long. They have blunt snouts, heavy bodies, clumsy-looking legs with long toes and a crest that runs from the neck to the tail. The tail is flattened sideways and is used for swimming. Most marine iguanas are black or very dark grey, but on Hood Island at the south of the Galapagos Archipelago their bodies are mottled with black, orange and red and their front legs and crests are green.

Lizard heaps

Outside the breeding season, when they are not feeding at sea, marine iguanas gather in tight bunches, sometimes even piling on top of each other. They lie on the lava fields that are prominent but unpleasant features of the Galapagos. In the heat of the day they seek shelter under boulders, in crevices or in the shade of mangroves. At the beginning of the breeding season, the males establish small territories, so small that one iguana may be on top of a boulder while another lies at the foot. Fights occasionally break out but disputes are generally settled by displays. A male marine iguana threatens an intruder by raising itself on stiff legs and bobbing its head with mouth agape, showing a red lining. If this does not deter an intruder, the owner of the territory advances and a butting match takes place. The two push with their bony heads until one gives way and retreats.

While marine iguanas are basking, large red crabs will walk over them, pausing every now and then to pull at the iguanas' skin. The lizards do not resent this pulling and pinching and with good reason, because the crabs are removing ticks from their skin. Darwin's finches (named after Charles Darwin) perform the same service.

▽ 'It's a hideous looking creature of a dirty black colour, stupid and sluggish in its movements. The usual length of a fullgrown one is about a yard, some even 4 ft long.' Voyage of HMS Beagle, Charles Darwin 1890.

Diving for a living

As the tide goes down the marine iguanas take to the water and eat the algae exposed on the reefs and shores. They cling to the rocks with their sharp claws, so as not to be dislodged by the surf, and slowly work their way over the rocks tearing strands of algae by gripping them in the sides of their mouths and twisting to wrench them off. At intervals they pause to swallow and rest. Some marine iguanas swim out beyond the surf and dive to feed on the seabed. They have been recorded as feeding at depths of 35 ft but usually they stay at about 15 ft. The length of each dive is about 15–20 minutes but they can stay under for much longer. When Darwin visited the Galapagos in HMS *Beagle* he noted that a sailor tried to drown one by sinking it with a heavy weight. An hour later it was drawn back to the surface and found to be quite active.

Marine iguanas normally eat nothing but marine algae. Unusual exceptions are the marine iguanas that haunt the home of Carl Angermeyer. He has trained them to come at his whistle to be fed on raw goat meat, rice and oatmeal.

Easy courtship

When the males have formed their territories, the females join them. They are free to move from one territory to another but the males soon gather harems of females around them and mating takes place without interference from other males. Courtship is simple: a male walks up behind a female, bobbing his head, then grabs her by the neck and clasps her with his legs.

When the males leave their territories, the females gather at the nesting beaches. There is competition for nest sites and fighting breaks out. Each female digs a 2ft tunnel in the sand, scraping with all four feet. Sometimes they are trapped and killed when the roof falls in or when a neighbour scrapes sand into the hole.

Only 2 or 3 white eggs, $3\frac{1}{4}$ by $1\frac{3}{4}$ in., are

△ *Like a lichen encrusted monument — the marine iguana presents his best side to the camera and shows off his metallic colours. In profile his snout is seen to be blunt and the clumsiness of his legs and heavy body is apparent. But against the blue sky the red and green mottling of this otherwise rather grotesque reptile is given full due.*
▽ *The marine iguana is the only modern lizard that uses the sea as a source of food. It is herbivorous, and feeds exclusively on seaweeds.*

laid. Then the female iguana fills up and camouflages the tunnel. When the eggs hatch in about 110 days, 9in. iguanas emerge.

Apart from man the main enemies of full grown marine iguanas are sharks, but the iguanas usually stay inshore where sharks are not likely to venture. Young iguanas are caught by herons, gulls and Galapagos hawks, as well as introduced cats.

Warmer on land

While he was on the Galapagos, Darwin found that it was impossible to drive marine iguanas into the sea. They would rather let themselves be caught than pushed in and if thrown into the sea they would hurriedly make for the edge and clamber out. This is a surprising habit for an aquatic animal as most animals that habitually swim, such as turtles and seals, make for the safety of the sea when frightened. Darwin assumed that the marine iguana behaved in this strange way because it had no natural enemies on land but that the sharks were waiting for it in the sea. If this were so, it would mean that marine iguanas would have to be pretty hungry before setting out to feed. Recently another explanation has been put forward. While basking, marine iguanas regulate their body temperatures to within a range of 35–37°C/95–99°F. The sea temperature around the Galapagos is 10°C/50°F less, so the marine iguanas are reluctant to escape into the sea, as this makes them too cool.

class	Reptilia
order	Squamata
suborder	Sauria
family	Iguanidae
genus & species	*Amblyrhynchus cristatus*

Skink

Skinks have none of the frills or decorations found in other lizard families; they all have an ordinary 'lizard shape' with a rather heavy tail and very often limbs that are reduced or missing. These are adaptations to the burrowing way of life which is characteristic of skinks and many spend most of their lives underground. Skinks are usually only a few inches long, the largest being the giant skink of the Solomon Islands, which is 2 ft long. The skink family contains over 600 species, and they are found all over the warmer parts of the world. In some areas, such as the forests of Africa, they are the most abundant lizards.

Within the skink family there are all gradations from a running to a burrowing way of life. The little brown skink of the southeastern United States has well-developed legs and toes and is a surface dweller; the burrowing Florida sand skink is almost limbless. In the **Scelotes** *genus of Africa there is a whole range of limb reduction. Bojer's skink of Mauritius has well-developed legs; the black-sided skink of Madagascar has very short legs; others have lost their forelegs altogether and have a reduced number of toes on the hindlegs; and the plain skink of South Africa has completely lost all its legs.*

Other adaptations for burrowing include the streamlining of the scales, the provision of a transparent 'spectacle' over the eye and the sinking of the eardrum into a narrow tube.

Diverse habits

Skinks are found in a variety of habitats, both on the ground and beneath the surface, from the damp soil of forests to the sands of deserts. A few live in trees, but only one has any adaptation for aboreal life. This is the giant skink which has a prehensile tail. Some skinks, such as the keel-bearing skinks, named after the projections on their scales, live on the banks of streams and dive into the water if alarmed. Some of the snake-eyed skinks live among rocks on the shore and feed on sea creatures such as small crabs and marine worms.

▷ *A young* **Eumeces skiltonianus**. *Like many other lizards skinks can shed their tails when they are attacked by a predator. The young of some skinks, including the type shown, have bright blue tails as an added safety device. When attacked the tail is broken off and it bounds continually; as it is the most conspicuous thing in sight, the predator is confused and the skink can scuttle safely away while the predator pursues the bounding tail. The tail is bright blue only when the skink is young, when the hazards of life are greatest. The blue-tailed Polynesian skink is exceptional in retaining its blue tail throughout its life.*

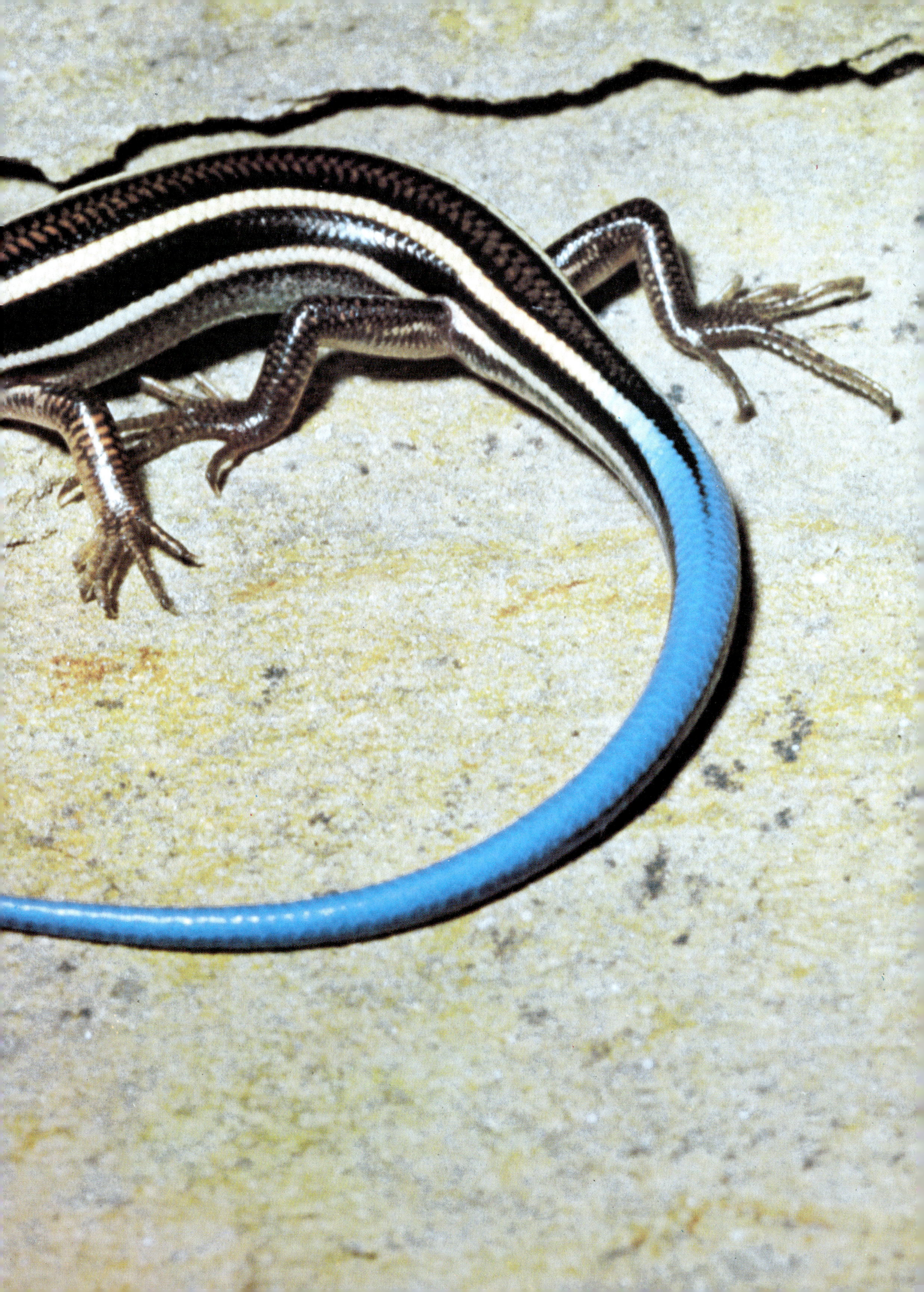

◁ *Foot-long mother* **Tiliqua rugosa** *and enormous newly-born.*

◁ ▽ *The largest of the skinks – the prehensile-tailed giant skink of the Solomon Islands.*

Teeth to fit the diet

The main food of skinks is insects and other small animals, including young mice and birds' eggs. The insect-eating skinks have pointed teeth with which they crush their hard-bodied prey and some types of skink which feed on earthworms have backwardly curving teeth which prevent the worms from escaping as they are being swallowed. The larger skinks are vegetarians and have broad, flat-topped teeth used for chewing.

Some lay eggs

Skinks lack the wattles and fans which other lizards use to display their superiority to rivals, but some male skinks develop bright colours during the breeding season. When they meet the males fight vigorously and may wound each other. Courtship is simple: the male follows a female, who allows him to catch her if she is ready to breed.

About half the skinks lay eggs; the others bear their young alive, the eggs being hatched just before they leave the mother's body. The eggs are usually laid under a log or rock and some skinks such as the five-lined skink of North America guard their eggs. The female curls around the eggs and stays with them until they hatch 4–6 weeks later, only leaving them to feed. As with other reptiles which stay with their eggs, it is difficult to decide what function they are performing. There is no evidence that skinks incubate the eggs and they desert them if disturbed, but it is known that skinks regularly turn their eggs which may be to prevent them from rotting.

Swimming in the sand

Some of the desert skinks are called sandfish from the way they appear to swim through the sand. Their legs are well-developed but they are held close into the body when moving. Propulsion comes from the flattened tail which is reminiscent of the tails of amphibians or aquatic reptiles such as the marine iguana (page 98). Another adaptation is a sharp chisel-like snout that can cleave a way through the sand. Like other lizards, skinks have flexible skulls but their heads are strengthened for sand-swimming and burrowing by the fusing of the scales on the head.

class	**Reptilia**
order	**Squamata**
suborder	**Sauria**
family	**Scincidae**
genera & species	***Corucia zebrata*** *giant skink* ***Eumeces fasciatus*** *five-lined skink* ***Lygosoma laterale*** *little brown skink* ***Neoseps reynoldsi*** *Florida sand skink* ***Scelotes bojeri*** *Bojer's skink* ***S. inornatus*** *plain skink* ***S. melanopleura*** *black-sided skink* *others*

Green lizard

This is the second largest lizard in Europe; the male is 15 in. long, of which 10 in. is tail. Europe's largest lizard is the eyed lizard, 24 in. long of which 16 in. is tail, and there are records of 36 in. total length. The eyed lizard is often dark green spotted with yellow and black. There are blue spots forming rosettes on the flanks.

The head of the green lizard is large, its legs stout and the toes, especially on the hindfeet, long. The length of the toes is most marked in the males although the females are usually slightly larger than the males in total body size. The colour varies and while usually bright green in the male it may be yellowish-green or brown and yellow on the flanks of the female. Males are noticeably thick at the root of the tail.

Green lizards range across southern Europe from northern Spain and the south of France to southwest Russia and northwards to parts of Germany. They are also found in the Channel Islands, but attempts to acclimatize them a few degrees farther north, in southwest England, have failed.

△ *Green lizards fighting.*
▽ *The second largest lizard in Europe.*

Lovers of dampness

Green lizards live among rocks and on rough ground especially along the margins of woods, where the ground is not too dry. They are particularly found on river banks, but they may also occur in meadows, especially where there are damp ditches. They climb well and are reputed to be good swimmers and to take readily to water when disturbed and seek refuge on the bottom. They are active by day, hunting or basking, but seek the shade when the sun is hot. Hibernation is from October to March, in holes in the ground, under buttress roots of trees or under vegetation litter, the period of hibernation being shorter in the southern than in the northern parts of the range.

Shell-cracker jaws

Green lizards feed on insects, spiders, woodlice, earthworms and other small invertebrates but also eat smaller lizards and small rodents. They sometimes take birds' eggs, cracking the shells with their powerful jaws which can give a strong but non-venomous bite on the hand. They occasionally eat fruit.

Submissive females

The breeding season starts in late April and continues into May. The male's throat goes cobalt blue, and is used as a threat in the many contests that take place between males. He also uses the same intimidating displays towards females and it is the fact that she responds submissively, that is, she does not return his menacing attitude, which tells him she is a female. A short time after mating the female lays 5–21 dull white oval eggs, about ¾ in. long, in soft earth. She stays near her eggs and will come back to them even after being driven off. They hatch 2–3 months later, the newly-hatched young being 2–3½ in. long, brown with one or two rows of yellowish-white spots. They gradually turn

△ A meal of a brimstone butterfly.
▽ A male in the mating season.

green as they reach maturity. Green lizards may live for 10 years in captivity although their life in the wild is doubtless generally less than this.

Victims of pet-keepers
This lizard is attacked by the usual enemies of lizards, particularly the larger birds of prey, and it has the usual lizard defence of casting its tail and growing a new one. The chief danger to the green lizard, as with several other southern European reptiles, notably the Greek tortoise and the wall lizard, is their export for pet-keeping. Thousands each year find their way northwards to central and northern Europe to be kept in vivaria, to be used in laboratories, or to re-stock the many zoos.

Unsuccessful habitat
Some idea of the traffic in these attractive reptiles can be gained from the attempts to naturalize them in England. In 1899 an unspecified number of green lizards were liberated in the Isle of Wight and for a while they bred there. The last were seen in 1936. In 1931 some were introduced into Caernarvonshire, in North Wales. These did not breed and survived for only 4 years or so. In 1937, 100 green lizards were set free at Paignton, in south Devon. A few were still alive in 1952.

The wall lizard, a medium-sized European lizard, 8 in. long, was also introduced at Paignton in 1937, 200 being set free. They lasted only a few years, yet the wall lizard is a more northerly species than the green lizard, ranging from Jersey, in the Channel Isles, across Holland, Germany and Poland to the southern European mountain ranges.

South Devon is only a few degrees farther north than the Channel Islands, but it seems this is enough to make the difference between survival and extinction for the green lizard. Subtropical plants grow well in south Devon so, while temperature may be important, there must be other factors working against the lizards. An animal set down in a foreign environment must find suitable hiding places, suitable food and other necessities for successful living. Everything around is strange and, far more than for a plant, it is a gamble whether an animal will settle down. Nevertheless, we have the instances in which one group of green lizards survived in the Isle of Wight for at least 37 years and another group in South Devon continued for at least 15 years. The climate of the British Isles is said to be slowly getting warmer. It may well be that future attempts at acclimatization might prove more successful, provided there is then more sunshine than is usual now. Experience with captive green lizards shows that without sufficient sunlight they are prone to skin complaints that shorten their lives.

class	**Reptilia**
order	**Squamata**
suborder	**Sauria**
family	**Lacertidae**
genus & species	***Lacerta viridis*** green lizard *L. lepida* eyed lizard

Anaconda

The largest snakes are to be found in the boa family, and the largest of these is **Eunectes murinus**, *the anaconda or water boa. Probably no animal has been the subject of such exaggeration in respect of size. The name itself is said to come from the Tamil words* **anai** *for elephant and* **kolra** *for killer. Properly this name must have originally referred to the anaconda's relative, the Indian python. Claims for 140-ft anacondas have been made and 40 ft often occurs in travel literature. The famous explorer, Colonel Fawcett, claimed to have killed a 62-ft anaconda and was pronounced 'an utter liar' by London opinion. In fact, a 20-ft anaconda is a large specimen, although it must be presumed that larger individuals do occur. It is difficult to find an authentic record for the largest anacondas. The measurement of $37\frac{1}{2}$ ft for one specimen has been widely accepted by scientists but not by all. Long ago, the New York Zoological Society offered a prize of 5,000 dollars for a 30-ft anaconda. This has never been won.*

The anaconda is olive green with large, round black spots along the length of its body and two light longitudinal stripes on the head. It lives throughout tropical South America, east of the Andes, mainly in the Amazon and Orinoco basins, and in the Guianas. It extends north to Trinidad. The species is variable in colour and size giving rise to numerous sub-specific names. However, these can be regarded as merely geographical variations. The closely related **Eunectes notaeus** *of Paraguay is known as the Paraguayan or southern anaconda.*

Life by jungle streams and swamps

Water boa is a good alternative name for the anaconda, the most aquatic of the boas. It is apparently never found far from water; sluggish or still waters being preferred to rapid streams. It is this preference that limits the species to the basins east of the Andes. Swamps are a favourite haunt.

Anacondas have, as a rule, fixed hunting grounds and generally live alone, but they are occasionally seen in groups.

Largely nocturnal in habit, anacondas lie up during the day in the shallows or sunbathe on low branches, usually over water. On land they are relatively sluggish, but they are able to swim rapidly and often float motionless, allowing the current to carry them downstream.

Killing by constriction

Anacondas usually lie in wait for their prey to come down to the water's edge to drink, whereupon they strike quickly with the head, grabbing the luckless prey and dragging it underwater so that it drowns. At other times anacondas may actively hunt prey on land.

The usual prey caught by lying in wait are birds and small mammals—deer, peccaries

Anaconda is the largest of snakes, reaching up to 37 ft, although exaggerated claims give lengths of 140 ft. They kill their prey by constricting. Each time the victim breathes out, the anaconda tightens its coils until the animal dies of suffocation.

and large rodents such as agoutis. Fish also form a large part of the diet, a fact not surprising in so aquatic an animal. More surprisingly, turtles and caimans are sometimes attacked. There is a record of a 25-ft anaconda killing a 6-ft caiman. The special jaw attachment that snakes have allows an anaconda to swallow such a large victim. After a meal of this size, which will suffice an anaconda for several weeks, the snake rests for a week or more until digestion has taken place. Normally the diet will consist of more frequent smaller meals.

Most snakes are adapted for swallowing prey wider than themselves: the upper and lower jaws are only loosely attached, and the brain protected from pressure by massive bones. Also a valve on the breathing tube allows the snake to breathe while swallowing.

The method of killing the prey is the same as in other constricting snakes such as the pythons. The prey is not crushed, but merely contained; each time the victim exhales, the coils of the anaconda tighten around its chest so that the ribs cannot expand, thus preventing inhalation until it suffocates. Stories in travelogues refer to anacondas' prey having every bone in the body broken and being squashed to pulp. In reality, bones are rarely broken during the process just described, which is one of strangulation. The fallacy is due to confusion between freshly-killed and regurgitated prey. This is covered with mucus, which gave rise to the story that anacondas smear their prey with saliva to facilitate swallowing.

Breeding

Few observations have been made on the breeding cycle of the anaconda. Males of southern anacondas studied in captivity were apparently aroused by the scent of the females. The male moves up alongside the female, flicking his tongue over her, until his head is resting over her neck. When in this position, he erects his spurs, two claw-like projections which are the last visible remnants of the hind limbs. The spurs are moved backwards and forwards against the female's skin and when the cloacal regions are in opposition, a hemipenis is inserted and copulation takes place.

Anacondas, like other boas, are viviparous. From 20–40, sometimes up to 100 young are born in the early part of the year. Each baby is 2–3 ft long.

Anacondas in folklore

It is not surprising that such a large, and malevolent-looking creature should be the subject of folklore and fallacy. The South American Indians have numerous stories about the anaconda, from the belief that it turns itself into a boat with white sails at night, to the mythology of the Taruma Indians who claimed to be descended from an anaconda. Several factors have led to tales of giant snakes. For one thing size is notoriously difficult to estimate unless a comparison can be made with something of known dimensions. Exaggeration is more likely if the animal is moving and writhing around, or if the observer has had a shock, as he might well have on suddenly seeing an anaconda Secondly, snake skins stretch very easily when being prepared so that the length of a skin gives no concrete evidence. It is not therefore difficult to see how stories of giant snakes could have arisen, and, once started, how this has led to unwitting or deliberate embroidery. Along with stories of venomous qualities and body size, there is exaggeration about the danger involved in meeting an anaconda. This is not unique; all large carnivorous animals become surrounded by stories of their man-eating habits. Many accounts are pure fiction. Only a few years ago a book was published describing a 140-ft anaconda, and how the author narrowly escaped from a 45-ft specimen by shooting its head off.

Other stories are reported truthfully but are not evidence of man-eating habits, but of self-defence, for when man blunders into an animal it is not surprising that it tries to defend itself. There are, however, remarkably few authentic stories of people killed and eaten. Rolf Blomberg, who has made many searches for record-sized specimens, has been able to find only two fairly definite instances of anacondas killing human beings. In only one case was it claimed that the victim, a 13-year-old boy, was eaten. Even this was somewhat doubtful because the story goes that he disappeared while bathing with friends. On discovering his absence, one of them dived down to search and saw an anaconda. The victim's father then hunted down the snake and shot it. Blomberg states that the boy's body had been vomited up but does not say whether,

△ *An alternative name for the anaconda is water boa as it is never found far from the sluggish forest streams or swamps. Anacondas move relatively slowly on land but can swim rapidly and often float motionless, allowing the current to carry them downstream.*

▽ *Anacondas often lie up during the day in branches over the water's edge and wait for their prey to come down at night to drink, when they strike quickly with the head, grab the prey in their coils, often dragging it down into the water, to drown.*

in fact, it was recovered or whether this was only surmise. In the other incident a grown man was captured by an anaconda while swimming and was drowned. His body, when later found, had distinct marks of having been subjected to a powerful squeeze, but there was no indication of his having been swallowed.

Here then are two reports of the death of human beings, caused by anacondas. As we have seen, there is some doubt about one of them and in the second the man may have been killed but there is nothing to show he was eaten. In fact, few anacondas would be large enough to swallow a man. Nevertheless, such stories, perhaps in a garbled form, would travel through the country, so giving the impression that anacondas are man-eaters. After this, anyone who disappeared and was last seen at the water's edge would be presumed to have been eaten by the anaconda, especially if one of these large snakes was seen in the vicinity. Such stories are so sensational that nobody asks for details or unequivocal evidence and the travellers would then take home a supposedly authentic story to relate to eager and uncritical audiences.

class	**Reptilia**
order	**Squamata**
suborder	**Serpentes**
family	**Boidae**
genus & species	***Eunectes murinus*** *E. notaeus*

Python

Pythons are the Old World equivalent of the New World boas. Like the boas they have small spurs that represent the vestiges of hind limbs. The largest and best-known pythons belong to the genus **Python.** Not only are these large pythons at home in jungles, climbing trees, but they are often found near water. The African rock python which reaches about 32 ft long is not quite as long as the accepted record figure for the anaconda ($37\frac{1}{2}$ ft.), the largest of the boas. It lives in most parts of Africa in open country except the deserts. The other African pythons are the ball python and Angolan python of West Africa. There are no pythons in southwest Asia but several species are found from India to China and the East Indies. The Indian python reaches about 20 ft and ranges through southeast Asia from India to China and on some of the islands of the East Indies. The reticulated python, reaching a length of 33 ft, has a more easterly distribution, from Burma to the Philippine Islands and Timor. The short-tailed python lives in the Malayan Peninsula, Borneo and Sumatra and the Timor python lives on the islands of Timor and Flores in Indonesia.

As well as the true pythons there are several other genera of pythons, including the carpet snake, that are found in the East Indies and Australia. Of the rock pythons the largest is the 20ft amethystine rock python or scrub python. A smaller group is the Australian womas which eat other snakes. The green tree python of New Guinea hunts in trees. The burrowing python, which lives in West Africa, in Liberia and throughout the rain forest of Zaire, spends its time underground chasing rodents and shrews.

Good travellers

The large pythons are often found near water and the Indian python is almost semi-aquatic. They also live in jungles and climb trees, except for the African python which prefers open country. The reticulated python shows a preference for living near human settlements. At one time it was a regular inhabitant of Bangkok, hiding up by day and coming out at night to feed on rats, cats, dogs and poultry. One individual was caught in the King's palace. This habit of associating with buildings must account for its turning up in ships' cargoes. One reached London in good condition; but it is a good traveller under its own steam. It swims out to sea and was one of the first reptiles to reach the island of Krakatoa in the Malay archipelago, after it erupted in 1888, destroying all life.

Any live prey accepted

Pythons kill their prey by constriction, wrapping themselves around the body of the

△ *A green tree python wraps its coils around itself as it waits for some unsuspecting prey which it grasps with its enlarged front teeth. Its leaf-green colour with white spots along its back and its extremely prehensile tail, make it admirably adapted for life in the trees.*

prey so that it cannot breathe. The coils then hold the body steady while the python works it into its mouth. Prey is caught by ambush; the python lies in wait then springs out knocking the animal with its head and seizing it with its jaws until it can wrap its body round it. The list of animals eaten by pythons is too long to enumerate. Mammals are preferred, followed by birds, but young rock pythons have been caught in fish traps. African pythons eat many small antelopes such as duikers, gazelle, impala and bushbuck. A large python can swallow prey weighing up to 120 lb but this is exceptional and usually smaller animals are taken such as dassies, hares, rats, pigeons and ducks. Jackals and monkeys are sometimes eaten and one 18 ft African python is known to have eaten a leopard, with very little damage being sustained in the process of catching it. Pythons sometimes suffer from their meals. They have been found with porcupine quills and antelope horns sticking through their stomach wall. Usually such dangerous projections are digested before causing any serious damage.

A large animal will last a python for a long time but they sometimes kill several small animals in quick succession. An African python has been credited with capturing and eating three jackals and a small python was seen to kill two sparrows in quick succession, then pin down a third with its tail.

There are a few authentic accounts of men being attacked by pythons, and there is good reason to believe the case of the 14 year old Malay boy attacked and eaten on the island of Salebabu.

Devoted mother pythons

The courtship of pythons is less lively than that of smaller snakes. The male crawls after the female, trying to climb over her and sometimes they rear up and sway to and fro. The spurs or vestigial limbs that lie either side of the cloaca are used by the male to scratch the female and stimulate her to raise her body so that he can wrap his body around hers and bring the two cloacas together. The eggs, 100 in a single clutch, are laid 3–4 months after mating. The female gathers the eggs into a pile and wraps herself around them, brooding them throughout the 2–3 month incubation period, only leaving them for occasional visits to water and more rarely to eat. Most pythons merely guard their eggs but the Indian python incubates them by keeping her body a few degrees above that of the surrounding air. Reticulated pythons are 2–2½ ft long when they hatch and for the first few years they grow rapidly at a rate of about 2 ft or more a year. An Indian python nearly trebled its length in its first year of life. Pythons may live for over 20 years.

Courageous otters

Even the great snakes are not free from enemies. Young pythons have many enemies but as they grow larger fewer animals can overcome them. Crocodiles, hyaenas and tigers have been found with the remains of pythons in their stomachs and Jim Corbett writes of finding a 17ft Indian python killed by a pair of otters which had apparently attacked from either side, avoiding harm by their agility. When the ball python of Africa is molested it rolls itself into a tight, almost uniformly round ball, its head tucked well inside.

Beating elephants

Both African and Indian pythons were well known to the Greeks and Romans and have taken their place in folklore and religion. They are, for instance, responsible for one of the many dragon legends. Dragon is derived from the Greek word for snake, and the ancient writers were obviously talking about big snakes. It was mediaeval naturalists who turned them into fabulous creatures. Edward Topsell has left us a delightful description of how dragons capture elephants. In his *Historie of Serpentes* 1608 he writes how they 'hide themselves in trees covering their head and letting the other part hang down like a rope. In those trees they watch until the Elephant comes to eat and croppe off the branches, then suddainly, before he be aware, they leape into his face and digge out his eyes, and with their tayles or hinder partes, beate and vexe the Elephant, untill they have made him breathlesse, for they strangle him with theyr foreparts, as they beat him with the hinder.' Apart from the impracticability of an elephant being attacked, this is a reasonable account of a python killing its prey.

◁ *Strangled! A flying fox, caught in the jaws of a scrub python, is being strangled to death by the python's tightening coils.*

△ *A carpet python* **Morelia spilotes** *curls over and around her eggs, rarely leaving them. The temperature within her coils is up to 12F° warmer than the surrounding atmosphere.*

▷△ *A ball python emerges from its egg, after an incubation period of up to 80 days. It may be one of a hundred snakes in the clutch.*

▷ *Superfluous legs. The two claws (arrowed) on either side of the anal vent of this African python are vestigial hind limbs, reminding us that snakes evolved from legged reptiles.*

▽ *The African python's skull shows the typical arrangement of teeth of a non-poisonous snake. The even sized teeth all point backwards, which ensures a firm and fatal grip on their prey.*

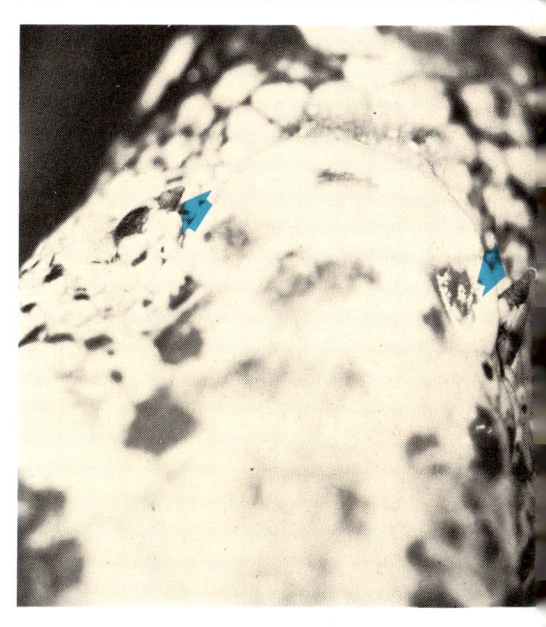

class	**Reptilia**
order	**Squamata**
suborder	**Serpentes**
family	**Pythonidae**
genera & species	***Calabaria reinhardti*** *burrowing python* ***Chondropython viridis*** *green tree python* ***Liasis amethystinus*** *amethystine rock python* ***Morelia argus*** *carpet snake* ***Python anchietae*** *Angolan python* ***P. curtus*** *short-tailed python* ***P. molurus*** *Indian python* ***P. regius*** *ball python* ***P. reticulatus*** *reticulated python* ***P. sebae*** *African python* ***P. timorensis*** *Timor python*

Cobra

*Immortalised in Kipling's story of the hardy mongoose Rikki-Tikki-Tavi, the true cobras of the genus **Naja**, from the Sanskrit word 'naga' for snake, are medium-sized snakes. Several species average 6 or 7 ft. The Indian cobra has a dark body encircled by a series of light rings, and like all cobras, it has the characteristic hood behind the neck. The neck is flattened horizontally by long, moveable ribs being swung out to stretch the loose skin of the neck, rather like the ribs of an umbrella stretching out the fabric. The cobra rears up and expands the hood when frightened or excited, and, in the Indian cobra, this displays the distinctive spectacled pattern the hood has the typical 'spectacle' markings, but towards the eastern side of India a single ring-like marking becomes more common, while in the Kashmir and Caspian region the hood is marked with black transverse bars.*

There are four species in Africa, the black-and-white cobra, the Cape cobra, the spitting cobra and the Egyptian cobra, which is also found in Asia.

Some cobras, such as the Egyptian cobra, are diurnal, others nocturnal like the Indian cobra, retiring by day to a favoured shelter in a burrow or under rocks. Some are found only near water.

Inoculating nerve-poisons

The cobra's venom is secreted from glands which lie just behind the eyes. It runs down

One of the four African species, the Cape cobra eats snakes as well as rodents, and is not averse to cannibalism.

Indian cobra, with its distinctive pattern. A cobra's hood works like an umbrella, with long, flexible ribs spreading the thin skin.

The Indian cobra is regarded by many experts as being one of the most dangerous snakes and death has been recorded as little as 15 minutes after the bite. Figures of 10 000 deaths a year have been given for India, which represents 1 in 30 000 of the population. Snakebite is so common in Asia and Africa because so many of the country people go about barefooted. Some cobras, notably the spitting cobra, of Africa, defend themselves by spitting venom over a distance of up to 12 ft. They aim for the face and the venom causes great pain and temporary blindness if it gets in the eyes.

Cobra venom has a different effect on the body than that of vipers which acts principally on the blood system, destroying tissues. Some tissue damage is done by cobra venom causing swelling and haemorr-

as the scales slide apart. The pattern is on the back of the neck but it can be seen from the front as the stretched skin is translucent.

Another well-known species is the Egyptian cobra, depicted on Ancient Egyptian headdresses rearing up with its hood inflated. Average length of adults is 5½–6 ft and there are reports of their reaching 10 ft, although the longest reliable measurement is over 8 ft. The body is yellowish to almost black, the lighter forms often having darker spots.

Cobras are found in Africa and Asia, although fossils have been found in Europe, presumably dating from a time when the climate was warmer. There are two or four species in Asia, the number depending on different authorities' methods of classification. One of these is the Indian cobra that is found from the Caspian across Asia, south of the Himalayas to southern China and the Philippines, and south to Bali in Indonesia. Throughout its range, the markings vary. In the west

ducts to the fangs that grow from the front of the upper jaw. Each fang has a canal along the front edge, and in some species the sides of the canal fold over to form a hollow tube like a hypodermic needle, so resembling the hollow fangs of vipers. The cobra strikes upwards, with the snout curled back so that the fangs protrude. As soon as they pierce the victim's flesh, venom is squirted down the fangs by muscles that squeeze the venom gland. When a very aggressive cobra tightens these muscles too early venom dribbles from its mouth.

Cobras' fangs are fairly short, but after it has struck the snake hangs on, chewing at the wound and injecting large quantities of venom. The seriousness of the bite depends very much on how long the cobra is allowed to chew. If it is struck off immediately, the bite will probably not be too serious. It is always difficult to assess the dangers of snake bite. Even where good medical records are kept, some of the less severe cases will probably not be reported, and the severity depends so much on the condition of the victim. Young and old people and those who are sick, especially with weak hearts, are most likely to succumb.

hage, but the principal ingredients are neurotoxins acting on the nervous system causing paralysis, nausea, difficulty in breathing and, perhaps, eventually death through heart and breathing failure.

Rat-catching snakes

Cobras eat mainly rodents, coming into homes after rats, which is a cause of many accidents. Frogs, toads and birds are also eaten, the cobras climbing trees to plunder nests. The Egyptian cobra often raids poultry runs. The Cape cobra often eats snakes, including its fellows, and the black-and-white cobra is reported to hunt fish. When food is short they will eat grasshoppers and other large insects.

Cobras' mating dance

Before mating, the pair 'dance', raising their heads a foot or more off the ground and weaving to and fro. This may continue for an hour before mating takes place, when the male presses his cloaca to the female's and ripples run through his body.

The Cape cobra mates between September and October and the eggs are laid a month later. These dates vary through the cobras' range as they mate and lay eggs at the season most likely to provide abundant food for the young. Eggs number 8–20, and are laid in a hole in the ground or in a tree. The female may stand guard and during the breeding period is irritable and aggressive. She is liable to attack without provocation with dire results for passers-by if her nest is near a footpath. Newly-hatched cobras measure about 10 in.

Enemies

The traditional enemies of cobras are the mongooses, but genets also attack them. The mongoose's tactics are to leap backwards and forwards, around the cobra, keeping it continually on the alert until it tires and cannot hold its body raised in striking position. The mongoose is protected by the speed of its movements and by being very resistant to the cobra's venom. Mongooses do not always win, however. It has been suggested that the inflated hood serves as a protection, making it difficult for any enemy to bite the cobra's neck. Cobras also sham dead, going limp until danger passes.

Snake-charmer's bluff

Cobras, especially the Indian and Egyptian species, are the favourite performers in the snake-charmer's act. It is perhaps fairly common knowledge now that the snakes are not reacting to the music but to the rhythmic movements of the charmer. The pipe is merely a stage prop, and is not used by all performers, because snakes are deaf, or, in other words, they cannot perceive airborne vibrations. They have no eardrum that in most other terrestrial animals vibrates in time to the airborne waves, and they do not have the systems of bones and ducts that convey the vibrations from the eardrum to the sense cells of the inner ear. They can, however, detect vibrations through the earth.

The explanation of the cobras' dance is that the basket is suddenly opened, exposing the snakes to the glare of daylight. Half-blinded and somewhat shocked, they rear up in the defensive position with hoods inflated. Their attention is caught by the first moving object they see, which is the swaying snake-charmer, whose actions they follow.

Part of the act consists of the cobras being handled and even kissed on the head. This is not such a dare-devil act of bravado as it may seem for it is said that cobras cannot strike accurately in the full light of day, and, anyway, their fangs will have been drawn or their lips sewn up. If this has not been done, the chances are that the charmer is immune to their venom.

class	**Reptilia**
order	**Squamata**
suborder	**Serpentes**
family	**Elapidae**
genus & species	*Naja naja* Indian cobra *N. haje* Egyptian cobra *N. nivea* Cape cobra *N. nigricollis* spitting cobra *N. melanoleuca* black-and-white cobra others

The legendary 'asp' or Egyptian cobra may grow to a length of 8 ft; and length for length it is much heavier than the Indian cobra.

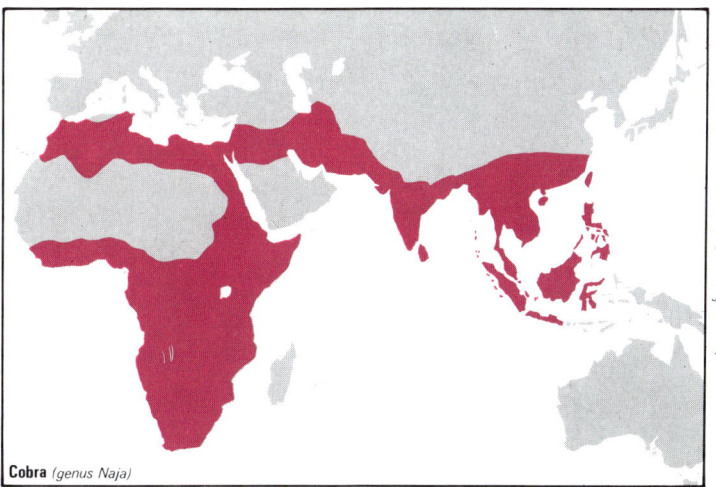

△ *When cobras 'dance' for snake-charmers it is because, shocked and half-blinded by sudden exposure to daylight, they rear into their typical defensive position with their attention fixed on the first moving object they see—the hand or pipe of the snake-charmer.*

Cobra (genus *Naja*)

Adder

A snake, member of the viper family, the adder has a relatively stout body and a short tail. The average male is 21 in. long, the female 2 ft – the record length is 2 ft 8 in. The head is flat, broadening behind the eyes to form an arrow-head shape.

The colour and body-markings vary considerably; adders are among the few snakes in which male and female are coloured differently. Generally the ground colour is a shade of brown, olive, grey or cream; but black varieties in which all patterning is obliterated are fairly common. The most characteristic marking is the dark zig-zag line down the back with a series of spots on either side; the head carries a pair of dark bands, often forming an X or a V.

It is often possible to distinguish the sex of an adder by its colour. Those which are cream, dirty yellow, silvery or pale grey, or light olive, with black markings, are usually males; females are red, reddish brown or gold, with darker red or brown markings. The throat of the male is black, or whitish with the scales spotted or edged with black; females have a yellowish-white chin sometimes tinged with red.

Distribution and habits

The adder ranges throughout Europe and across Asia to Sakhalin Island, north of Japan. In the British Isles it is absent from Ireland and the northern isles. It is usually to be seen in dry places such as sandy heaths, moors and the sunny slopes of hills where it often basks in the sun on hedge-banks, logs and piles of stones. It is, however, also found in damp situations.

Its tolerance of cold allows the adder to live as far north as Finland, beyond the Arctic Circle. It escapes cold weather by hibernation, which starts when the shade temperature falls below 9°C/49°F. It emerges again when the air temperature rises above 8°C/46°F – even coming out onto snow –

▽ *The hedgehog is one of the adder's arch-enemies. It is protected by its spines while it alternately bites and rolls up, until the adder is dead.*

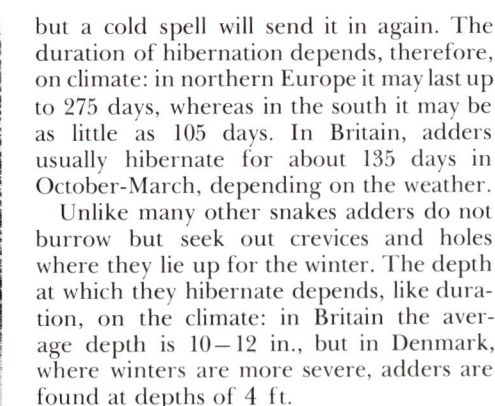

△ *The adder's tongue looks menacing but is harmless. It is a smell-taste organ, picking up particles from the air and withdrawing them for analysis in the mouth.*

but a cold spell will send it in again. The duration of hibernation depends, therefore, on climate: in northern Europe it may last up to 275 days, whereas in the south it may be as little as 105 days. In Britain, adders usually hibernate for about 135 days in October-March, depending on the weather.

Unlike many other snakes adders do not burrow but seek out crevices and holes where they lie up for the winter. The depth at which they hibernate depends, like duration, on the climate: in Britain the average depth is 10–12 in., but in Denmark, where winters are more severe, adders are found at depths of 4 ft.

Very often many adders will be found in one den, or hibernaculum. As many as 40 have been found coiled up together, along with a number of toads and lizards. This massing together is a method of preventing heat loss, but it is not known how the adders come to congregate in the hibernacula, which are used year after year. It may be that they can detect the scent left from previous years.

It is uncertain whether adders are nocturnal or diurnal. Their eyes are typical of nocturnal animals in that they are rich in the very sensitive rod cells: such eyes will see well at night, but during the day they need protection, and the adder's slit pupils cut down the intensity of light. On the other hand, despite these adaptations, adders are often active during the day. Courtship and some feeding are definitely diurnal; feeding depends on how hungry the adder is.

Rodent killer
The adder's main prey is lizards, mice, voles and shrews. Young adders subsist at first

A black adder. Adders range in colour from cream, through dirty yellow to silvery grey or olive (male); and from red to gold (female).

on insects and worms. Larger victims are killed by a poisonous bite, the effects of which vary with the size of the prey. A lizard will be dead within a few minutes, or even within 30 seconds; but an adder's bite is rarely fatal to humans. There were only seven authenticated records of fatalities through snakebite in England and Wales in the first half of this century, and four of these were children.

The adder's method of hunting is to follow its prey by scent, then poison it with a quick strike of the head. While the venom acts, the victim may have time to escape to cover, in which case the snake will wait for a while then follow to eat its dead prey.

Dance of the adders
The mating period is from the end of March to early May, though it has been known to last until autumn. In the north of Europe the summer is too short for the eggs to mature in one year, so breeding takes place in alternate years.

At the beginning of the breeding season, there is a good deal of territorial rivalry between males, culminating in the 'dance of the adders'. Two males face each other with head erect and the forepart of the body held off the ground. They sway from side to side, then with bodies entwined each attempts to force the other to the ground by pushing and thrusting. They do not attempt to bite each other.

Finally one gives up and departs. The female, who is frequently waiting close at hand, will accept any victorious male, if she is ready, and a male will mate with any female. He crawls up behind her and loops his coils over her body, rubbing his chin (which has especially sensitive skin) on her back until he reaches the back of her neck, and mating takes place.

Adders are ovoviviparous: that is, the eggs remain inside the mother's body until they are fully developed, and the young are born coiled up in a membrane which is ruptured by their convulsive movements. They have an egg tooth, which in other animals is used to rupture the egg membranes, but in adders it is degenerate as they have no need of it, and the tooth is so situated that it is of no use for this purpose. It is shed a few days after birth.

The young are born in August or September and the number ranges from five to 20: 10-14 are most common, each measuring 6-8 inches in length. They are immediately capable of independent existence, but often they appear to stay with the mother. Young adders disappear so quickly when disturbed that there is an ancient legend, an account of which appears in Holinshed's Chronicle of 1577, that in times of danger the mother adder swallows her offspring. This legend could be due to early observers cutting up an ovoviviparous mother and finding unborn adders inside. Not knowing that adders hatch from the egg inside the parent they would think she had swallowed them.

△ *Male (left) and female adders are always differently coloured.*
▽ *Adder with day-old young.*

The adder has no external ear or ear drum, but picks up vibrations from the ground through its lower jaw. The vertical slit pupil gives quick perception of horizontal movement.

Enemies although poisonous
Like most animals—even those well capable of defending themselves—adders are most likely to flee if confronted with danger, and they usually bite only if suddenly frightened. But, despite not having the excuse of self-defence, man is their chief enemy. However, the killing of adders on sight has not led to their decline, although nowadays increased urbanisation is destroying their habitat.

Undoubtedly many carnivores will take adders. Foxes and badgers kill them, and they have been found in the stomachs of pike and eels. Surprisingly, perhaps, the hedgehog is a great adversary of adders: one reason is that it can tolerate large doses of venom without harm. Its method of killing is to bite the adder, then curl up leaving nothing but a palisade of spines for the snake to strike at. It repeats the process of biting and curling until the snake is dead, after which the hedgehog eats it.

A confusion of names
The Anglo-Saxon name for the adder was *naedre,* which became 'a nadder' or 'a nedder' in Middle English. Later the *n* was transposed, so that we now have 'an adder'. The alternative name viper comes from the Anglo-Saxon *vipere* or *vipre*, itself derived from the Latin *vipera*. This was a contraction of *vivipara*, from *vivus* (alive) and *parere* (to bring forth)—alluding to the animal's method of reproduction. In general 'viper' was used to mean any venomous snake. There being only one such snake in England, viper and adder became synonymous for the one species (viper also being used to describe a venomous or spiteful person).

The two words have spread with the English language all over the world, being used not only for snakes of the genus *Vipera*. There are the near relatives such as the gaboon viper, more distant, like the pit vipers and mole vipers, and the death adder, which is not even in the viper family.

class	**Reptilia**
order	**Squamata**
suborder	**Serpentes**
family	**Viperidae**
genus & species	***Vipera berus***

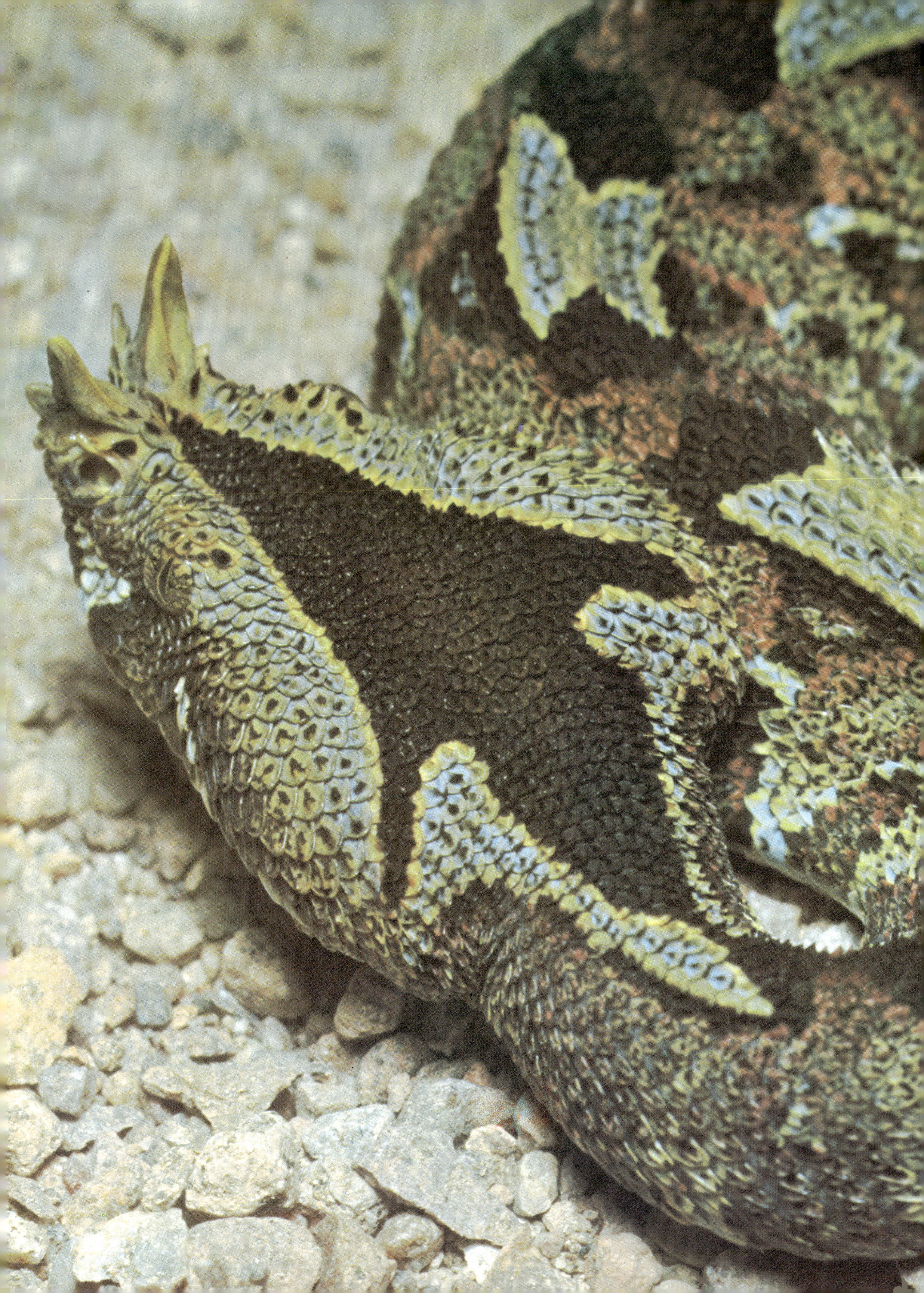

Puff adder

There are 8 species of puff adder in Africa and they range in size from the Peringuey's desert adder, 1 ft long, to the Gaboon viper, 6 ft or more long. They are stout bodied snakes with short tails. The head is very broad compared with the neck, and is covered with small overlapping scales. There is a deep pit of unknown function above the nostrils, and in many species one or more erectile scales on the snout form 'horns', as in the rhinoceros viper. Not all puff adders are given this name, although they all belong to the same genus, and they fall into two groups. These are the highly coloured Gaboon viper and rhinoceros viper, of the tropical African forests, and the sombrely coloured brown and grey puff adders of the savannah and deserts. One of this second group, the common puff adder, is yellow to brown with darker bars or chevrons on the back. It ranges from Morocco southwards across the Sahara to the Cape and is also found in Arabia. The others have less extensive ranges, the Cape puff adder, for example, being found only in the mountains of Cape Province, South Africa.

Melting into the background

Savannah and desert puff adders, with their duller colourings, tend to harmonize with the differently coloured soils on which they are living. So also do the Gaboon and rhinoceros vipers in spite of their bright colours, for their colour patterns are disruptive. The Gaboon viper has a gaudy pattern of yellow, purple and brown arranged in geometric forms. The rhinoceros viper, even more brilliantly coloured with more purple, and blue as well, has green triangles margined with black and blue on its sides. But both snakes are virtually invisible on the carpet of dead and green leaves on the forest floor. The smaller species of puff adder live on sandy soils. Several of these smaller adders are able to climb into bushes, but generally puff adders keep to the ground, hunting mainly during the night.

Inoffensive yet deadly

The broad head of the puff adder houses the large venom glands and although the effect of this snake's bite is less rapid than that of a mamba or a cobra it is just as deadly. Fortunately, these snakes strike only to disable prey or in self-defence, and need a fair amount of provocation to make them hit back. Africans are said to be more afraid of harmless geckos than of the Gaboon viper, and Herbert Lang tells of a small boy dragging a 5 ft live specimen into his camp to sell it to him. If their venom is slow-acting it is nonetheless potent. R Marlin Perkins, curator of reptiles in the St Louis Zoological Gardens, nearly died from the bite of a Gaboon viper. Some years later, in 1964, the Director of the Salt Lake City Zoo died from a puff adder bite received while handling the snake. Puff adders can give out as much as 15 drops of venom at a time—4 drops are enough to kill a man. But usually snakes give a first warning by hissing. The hissing sound is produced by forcing air from the lungs and windpipe through the glottis. Puff adders have an especially loud hiss. Their puff makes a sound more like the noise of a horse when it forces air through its lips.

◁ *The attractive 'horned' head of the rhinoceros viper is deceptive; it houses the venom glands.*

Beckoning their food

The food of puff adders varies widely between the species. Small prey, such as a frog, is grabbed and swallowed without being poisoned. Larger prey is struck with the fangs and allowed to run away to die. The snake later follows its trail to eat it. The carcase is dragged into the snake's mouth by the teeth in the lower jaw. Once part of the victim has reached the throat, muscular swallowing movements carry it down, the snake holding its head up to assist this. Some scientists claim that the long fangs, which may be 2 in. long in a 5ft Gaboon viper, are used to drag the victim into the snake's mouth. South African herpetologists do not support this, but suggest the long fangs make it possible to inject the venom deeply.

The common puff adder and the Gaboon viper eat rats and mice, ground-living birds, frogs, toads and lizards. The Cape Mountain adder feeds on the same but is known to eat other snakes. The many-horned adder and the horned puff adder bury themselves in the sand, except for the eyes and snout, to catch lizards. The horned puff adder leaves the tip of its tail sticking out of the sand and waggles it to attract its victims within striking distance.

An enemy to many small animals, the puff adder has few adversaries itself, mainly birds of prey, mongooses and warthogs, and man. Puff adders can store large quantities of fat and this is sold by African herbalists as a cure for rheumatism.

Large families

Puff adders are ovoviviparous. That is, the eggs are hatched inside the mother so the young are born alive or else they wriggle out of the egg capsule soon after it is laid. Mating is usually from October to December, the young being born in March and April. The young from a mother 3 ft long, are about 8 in. at birth. There are 8–15 in the litter of the smallest species, 70–80 or more in the large puff adders.

Fasting to grow

The paradoxical frog is named because of the paradox that the tadpole is much greater than the froglet into which it changes. The puzzle is, where does all the spare flesh go? The situation is reversed in the baby puff adder. As soon as it is born it can kill and eat small mice although it moults first before looking for food. It can, however, happily go without food for as much as 3 months. The ability to fast is not unusual. What is extraordinary is that the baby puff adder still grows 25% in length and increases its girth by a quarter while doing so.

△ Sedate mating, two love-locked common puff adders, the male is on the right. Mating usually takes place from October to December. Fertilisation is internal and sperm may survive inside the female for long periods. Most reptiles lay their eggs but puff adders are ovoviviparous, the female retains the eggs until the young are ready or nearly ready to hatch 5–6 months later.

◁ Submerged for the day, a small Peringuey's puff adder spends the day well hidden. Alerted by the photographer the snake raises its head so giving its position away. But its sandy colouring blends well with the soil making the snake very inconspicuous.

class	**Reptilia**
order	**Squamata**
suborder	**Serpentes**
family	**Viperidae**
genus & species	**Bitis arietans** *common puff adder* **B. atropos** *Cape Mountain adder* **B. caudalis** *horned puff adder* **B. cornuta** *manyhorned adder* **B. gabonica** *Gaboon viper* **B. inornata** *Cape puff adder* **B. nasicornis** *rhinoceros viper* **B. peringueyi** *Peringuey's puff adder*

Pit viper

Some of the most-feared snakes are to be found among the 60 species of pit vipers (family Crotalidae) including well known forms like the fer de lance, (named so because of its lance-shaped head and body), and the sidewinder and the rattlesnakes, which we shall come to later. Here we shall consider others, such as the American water moccasin, copperhead and bushmaster, as well as the Asiatic pit vipers. Pit vipers are a diverse group with several interesting specializations, which is why we have given them three entries. Here, while dealing with the family in general terms, we pay special attention to what has been called their sixth sense, the two pits on the head that give them their name.

Pit vipers are solenoglyph. That is, they have fangs which fold back and are erected when about to be used. Most pit vipers are land-living, some are tree-dwellers, a few have taken to water and others lead a partially burrowing life. Water moccasins are heavy-bodied, up to 5 ft long, and while living on land they readily take to water when disturbed and they hunt in water. They are slate black to olive or tan with indistinct brown bands. The copperhead, a brown snake with hourglass markings along the back, is up to 3 ft long. It lives in rocky outcrops and quarries and among piles of rotting logs. The bushmaster is the longest of the American pit vipers, up to 12 ft, mainly grey and brown with large diamond blotches along the back. It has large venom glands and unusually long fangs. Its generic name **Lachesis** is from one of the Fates that influenced the length of life of people – a grim pun by the scientist who named it, for the bushmaster is one of the most dangerous of snakes. The Asiatic pit vipers are of two kinds, tree-dwelling and ground-living, the first having prehensile tails that assist their climbing. The Himalayan pit viper lives at altitudes of 7 000–16 000 ft, sometimes being found even at the foot of glaciers.

The Asiatic pit vipers are found mainly in eastern and southeast Asia with one species extending as far west as the mouth of the River Volga. Wagler's pit viper is kept in large numbers in the Snake Temple in Penang. The water moccasin and the copperhead are widespread over the eastern and middle United States, the bushmaster ranges from Costa Rica and Panama to northern South America.

Warm-blooded food

The warning posture of the water moccasin, mouth open showing its white lining, gives it the alternative name of cottonmouth. It also vibrates its tail at the same time, like its relatives the rattlesnakes, although it has no rattle to make a warning sound. Pit vipers, apart from their pits, are very ordinary snakes. Some take a wide range of foods, like the water moccasin which eats rabbits, muskrats, ducks, fish, frogs, other snakes, birds' eggs, and nestlings. The copperhead eats small rodents, especially the woodmouse, other snakes, frogs, toads, and insects, including caterpillars and cicadas. The bushmaster, by contrast, takes mainly mammals, and pit vipers generally tend to hunt warm-blooded animals more than cold-blooded, as one would expect from snakes with heat-detector pits. They have one on each side of the head between the eye and the nostril. Using these a pit viper can pick up the trail of a warm-blooded animal.

'Seeing' heat

Each pit is $\frac{1}{8}$ in. across and $\frac{1}{4}$ in. deep. A thin membrane is stretched near the bottom and temperature receptors, 500–1 500 per sq mm, are packed within this membrane. These receptors are so sensitive they can respond to changes as small as 0·002 of a C°, and they allow a snake to locate objects 0·1 of a C° warmer or cooler than the surroundings. In more understandable terms a pit viper could detect the warmth of the human hand held a foot from its head. The membrane with its receptors can be compared to an eye with its retina. The overhanging lip of the pit casts 'heat shadows' onto it, so the snake is aware of direction, and since the 'fields of view' of the two pits overlap there is the equivalent of stereoscopic vision, giving a rangefinder. A pit viper hunting by day has the advantage of being able to follow an animal's heat trail through low vegetation after the animal has passed out of sight. It could, of course, do this equally well by scent. The facial pits come into their own in night hunting, when prey can be tracked by scent with the facial pits guiding the final strike. At first it was thought they had something to do with an accessory aid to smell or as an organ of hearing – snakes have no ears. Another suggestion was that they might be organs for picking up low-frequency air vibrations. Then, as late as 1892, it was noticed that a rattlesnake, one of the pit vipers, was attracted to a lighted match. Then came the discovery that pythons have pits on their lips that are sensitive to heat. The first experiments on pit vipers were made in 1937, and left no doubt that the pits are heat detectors and further studies since have shown just how delicate they are.

△ *Trimeresurus gramineus.*

Snakes in cold climates

Pit vipers usually bear living young. There are a few exceptions, the bushmaster being one, and that lives in the tropics. Pit vipers extend from the Volga across Asia and across America. There may be a direct connection between these two facts. One of the advantages of bearing living young, as against laying eggs, is that the offspring are protected not only against enemies but also against low temperatures until they are at an advanced stage of development. At some time pit vipers must have crossed the land bridge that used to exist where the Bering Straits are now. This is well north, and it would have been far easier for snakes able to bear live young to survive in these latitudes and so make the crossing. It probably explains also why the Himalayan pit viper can live so near glaciers, and why the most southerly of all snakes is a pit viper named *Bothrops ammodytoides*, living in the Santa Cruz province of Argentina.

class	**Reptilia**
order	**Squamata**
suborder	**Serpentes**
family	**Crotalidae**
genera & species	***Ancistrodon contortrix*** copperhead *A. himalayanus* Himalayan pit viper *A. piscivorus* water moccasin ***Trimeresurus wagleri*** Wagler's pit viper

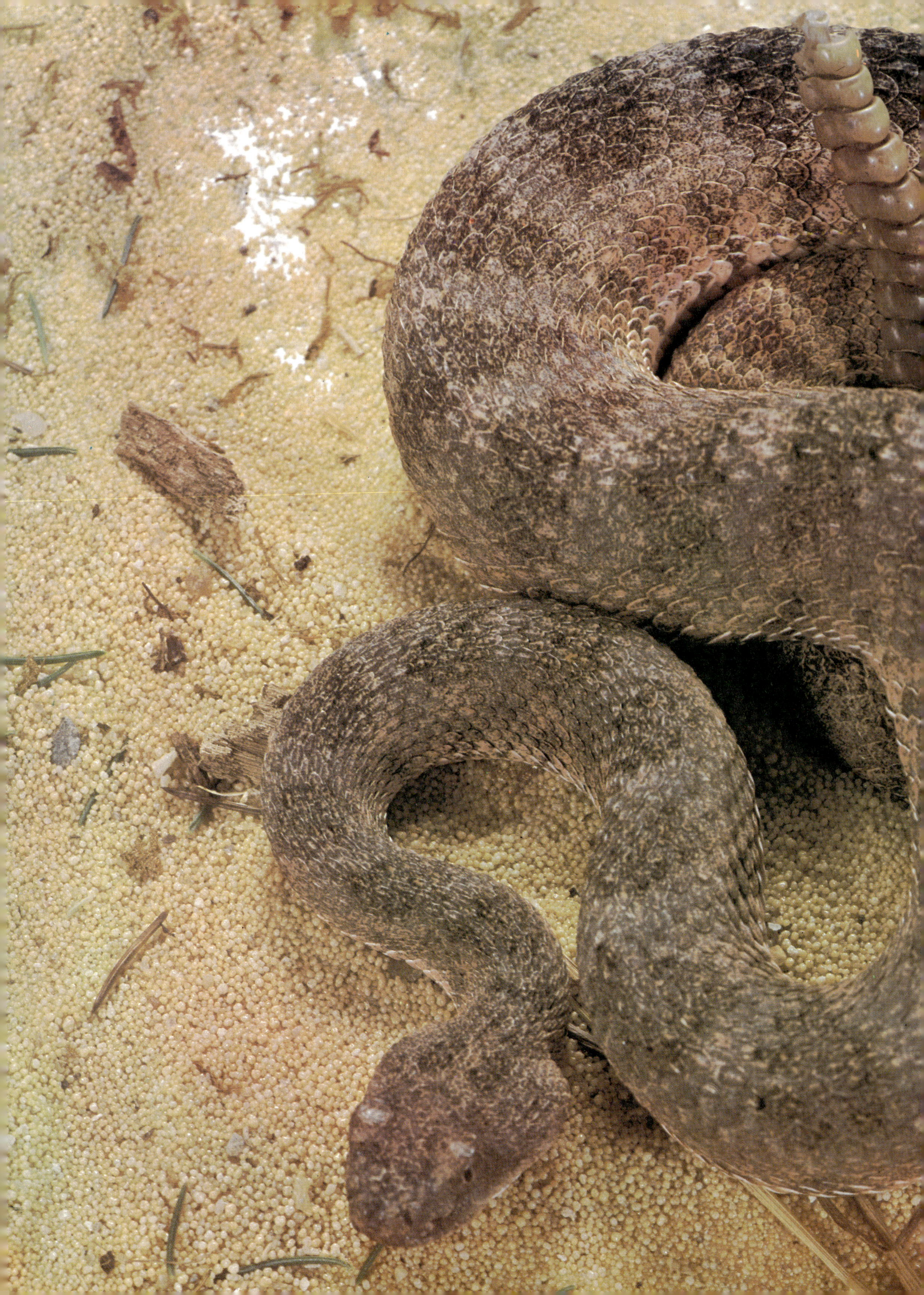

Rattlesnake

These are heavy-bodied and usually highly venomous snakes, best known for the rattle, sometimes called a bell, cloche, buzzer or whirrer, on the tail. When disturbed the rattlesnake vibrates its tail, or rattle, as if giving warning that it is about to strike. Rattlesnakes are found almost entirely in North America, from southern Canada to Mexico, where there are 30 species and over 60 subspecies, with one species in South America.

There are two groups of rattlesnakes, each represented by one genus: the pygmy rattlesnakes **Sistrurus** *have short slender tails and very tiny rattles, and they never exceed 2 ft in length; and the rattlesnakes proper* **Crotalus**, *which are usually around $3\frac{1}{2}$–5 ft but exceptionally grow to 8 ft or more. The timber or banded rattlesnake of the eastern States is marked with dark chevrons on the back. In the prairie rattlesnake the markings are irregularly oblong. Most others have diamond markings. Rattlesnakes share with other pit vipers (page 117) a tolerance of low temperatures. The Mexican dusky rattlesnake lives at altitudes of up to 14 500 ft.*

Sound varies with size

The rattle is made up of a number of loosely interlocked shells each of which was the scale originally covering the tip of the tail. Usually in snakes this scale is a simple hollow cone which is shed with the rest of the skin at each moult. In rattlesnakes it is larger than usual, much thicker and has one or two constrictions. Except at the first moult, the scale is not shed but remains loosely attached to the new scale, and at each moult a new one is added. The rattle does not grow in length indefinitely. The end scales tend to wear out, so there can be a different number of segments to the rattle in different individuals of the same age, depending on how much the end of the rattle is abraded. It seldom exceeds 14 segments in wild rattlesnakes no matter how old they may be, but snakes in zoos, leading a more untroubled life, and not rubbing the rattle on hard objects, may have as many as 29 pieces in a rattle. The longer the rattle the more the sound is deadened, 8 being the most effective number to give the loudest noise. The volume of sound not only varies with the size of the snake and the length of the rattle, but it also varies from species to species. At best it can be heard only a few feet away.

◁ *Threatening tiger rattlesnake. Between its coils is a large rattle, a unique organ composed of horny segments of unshed skin. The fact that rattlesnakes shed their skin three or four times a year during the first years of their lives disposes of the popular idea that the number of rattles corresponds to the years of the snake's age. The best reason to be found for the evolution of the rattle in an animal that is deaf is that it acts as a warning device to large animals that may molest or tread on the snake.*

Rattlers not all black

It is hard to generalize on the size and effectiveness of the rattle as it is on any other feature of rattlesnakes. For example, these snakes have a reputation for attacking people, and of being bad tempered. It applies only to some of them. Unless provoked or roughly treated the red diamond rattlesnake may make no attempt to strike when handled. It may not even sound its rattle. The eastern and western diamond backs, by contrast, not only rattle a warning but they will also pursue an intruder, lunging at it again and again. How poisonous a snake is also depends on several things, such as its age – the younger it is the less the amount of poison it can inject – and whether it has recently struck at another victim, when the amount of venom it can use will be reduced. Cases are known in which a snake has taken nearly two months to replenish its venom to full capacity. Rattlesnakes of the same species from one part of the range may be more venomous than those from another part. Prairie rattlesnakes of the plains are about three times as venomous as those of California, and half as poisonous again as those of the Grand Canyon.

Waterproof skin

Rattlesnakes feed on much the same prey as other pit vipers (page *117*), mainly small warm-blooded animals and especially rodents, cottontail rabbits and young jack rabbits. Young rattlesnakes, including the pygmy rattlesnakes, take a larger proportion of coldblooded animals, such as frogs, salamanders and lizards. Studies have also been made on how much rattlesnakes drink, and the remarks that follow probably apply to all snakes. Their needs are not as great as those of active and warm-blooded animals because the water loss from the body is not high. They need about one-tenth as much water as a mammal of similar size. In one test it was found that twice as much water is lost from a rattlesnake's head, and this mainly in its breath, as from the whole of the rest of its body, which suggests that its skin is almost waterproof. When it does drink it sucks up water from a pond or stream. There is no evidence that it laps it with the tongue, as is sometimes stated, or that it drinks dew.

Two years to be born

All rattlesnakes give birth to live young. Whether they have one litter a year or less depends on the climate. The prairie rattlesnake has one litter a year in the southern part of its range, but in the northern part it may be two years before the young are ready to be born. Mating is in spring and the number in a litter may vary from 1 to 60 according to the size of the mother, the usual number being between 10 and 20.

Slaughter of infants

Their venom does not spare rattlesnakes from being killed and eaten. Hawks of all kinds kill them, so do skunks and snake-eating snakes. Pigs, deer and other hoofed animals trample them, especially the young ones, and many die of cold or excessive heat, or from starvation. Indeed few from a litter survive their first year.

Sensitive eyes

Snakes are known to be deaf yet they often seem to be reacting to sounds. In fact, they seem at first glance to be able to hear but there is more to it than this, as Laurence Klauber found in his celebrated tests on rattlesnakes. First, having placed a rattlesnake under a table, he clapped two sticks together making sure his hands and the sticks could not be seen by the snake. It reacted, apparently to the sound. Puzzled at first, Klauber finally found the reason. He was sitting on a stool, his feet dangling, and every time he clapped the sticks together his feet moved and the snake reacted to sight of them. So he put a screen between the snake and his feet, and still the snake reacted when he clapped the sticks – it was seeing a reflection of Klauber's feet in a nearby window.

He found his red diamond rattler highly sensitive to footsteps on a concrete floor 15 ft away, and it still reacted to footsteps that distance away after he had placed it on a blanket. He decided to test this further. He put the snake in a fibreboard box, suspended this by a rubber band from a stick held each end on a pillow, to insulate it from vibrations through the ground. It still reacted to clapped sticks and to the radio. It was, in fact, as Klauber finally found, picking up the heat from the valves of the radio as these warmed up, and it was reacting to vibrations in the floor and sides of the fibreboard box, against which its body rested. So the box was changed for a Chinese woven bamboo basket hung from the same stick. Still the snake appeared to react to sound, but further tests showed it was reacting to Klauber's hand movements seen through the very tiny cracks between the bamboo withies. Apart from anything else, these experiments show how hard it can sometimes be to test a particular animal sense. They also show, among other things, how sensitive a snake's eyes are to small movements.

class	**Reptilia**
order	**Squamata**
suborder	**Serpentes**
family	**Crotalidae**
genus & species	***Crotalus adamanteus*** eastern diamond back ***C. atrox*** western diamond back ***C. horridus*** timber or banded rattlesnake ***C. pusillus*** Mexican dusky rattlesnake ***C. ruber*** red diamond back ***C. tigris*** tiger rattlesnake ***C. viridis*** prairie rattlesnake

◁ *Sparring partners – two western diamond back rattlesnakes engage in combat. Although it is difficult to observe both snakes simultaneously during the fight it seems that the twining of the necks is a manoeuvre for an advantageous position from which one snake may forcefully throw his opponent.*

Sidewinder

Also known as the horned rattlesnake, the sidewinder is named after its peculiar form of locomotion which allows it to move over soft sand. Sidewinders are small rattlesnakes, the adults being only 1½–2 ft long. The females are usually larger than the males, whereas in other rattlesnakes it is the reverse. The body is stout, tapering to a narrow neck with a broad head like an arrowhead. Above each eye there is a scale that projects as a small horn. There is a dark stripe running backwards from each eye. The body is pale grey or light brown with a row of large dark brown spots running down the back and smaller ones on each side. The tail is marked with alternate light and dark bands and the underparts of the body and tail are white.

The single species of sidewinder lives in the deserts of the southwest United States, including Nevada, Utah, California, Arizona and in the northern part of the state of Baja California in Mexico.

Sand snake

Sidewinders are most common in areas of loose, windblown sand and although they can be found among rocks or on compacted sand there is usually loose sand nearby. Although other rattlesnakes live in deserts and can be found on loose sand, the sidewinder is the most characteristic of this type of habitat. It is likely that in this habitat the sidewinder has an advantage over the other snakes. By adapting to life in moving sand the sidewinder does not compete with other snakes. These can move over sand by the usual eel-like wriggling. The sidewinder's unusual looping movement enables it to get a good grip on loose sand and so move faster.

Sidewinders are most active in the early part of the night when air temperatures are not dangerously high and when their prey is also active. They spend the day in mouse-holes or buried in sand, usually under the shelter of a creosote bush or a yucca. They bury themselves by shovelling sand over themselves with looping movements of the body until they are coiled like springs, flush with the surface of the sand. Their mottled brown colour makes them very difficult to see as they lie there half buried.

Desert prey

The shallow saucers in the sand where sidewinders have been resting are often found near mouse and rat burrows as the sidewinders are probably attracted to these areas where they will find prey plentiful. Their main food is small rodents, such as deer mice, kangaroo rats and spiny pocket mice, and lizards such as the tree-climbing utas and other sand-dwelling iguanids. Sidewinders also eat a few snakes, such as the glossy snake and even other sidewinders, and a few small birds.

The breeding habits of sidewinders are the same as those of other rattlesnakes (page *119*). Mating takes place when they emerge from hibernation in spring and the young are born alive.

The sidewinder is a small squat rattlesnake that is perfectly adapted for living in deserts.

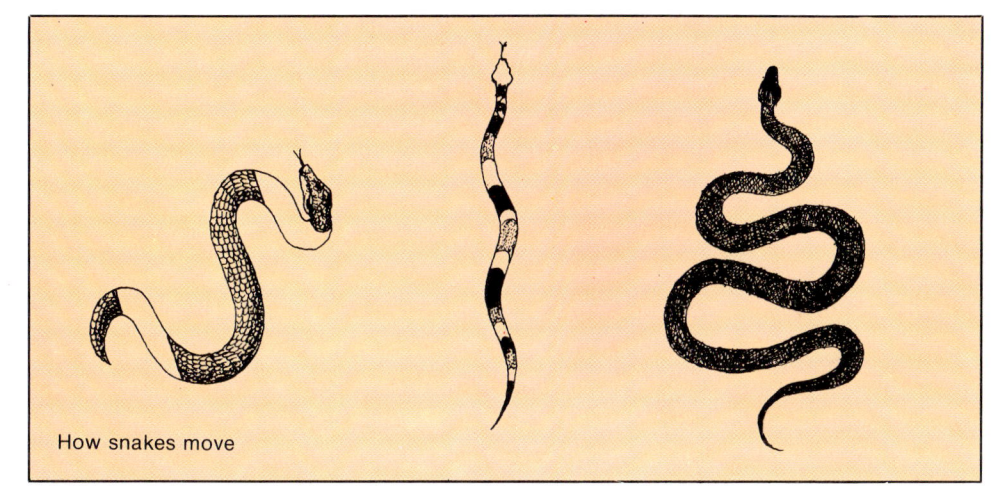

How snakes move

Sidewinding is like a coiled wire rolled along the sand making a series of oblique parallel tracks. Only the white areas touch the ground.

In serpentine movement the body literally skates along in a series of shallow curves which get a grip on any projecting object.

Concertina movement: with the tail anchored the head and neck dart forward, the neck grips the ground and the rest of the body is then pulled up.

Sidewinding

Many snakes will perform 'sidewinding' movements if placed on a sheet of glass, throwing their bodies into loops to get a grip on the smooth surface. The sidewinder, and the horned viper and puff adder of African deserts, make a habit of sidewinding, leaving characteristic tracks in the sand. These are a series of parallel, wavering lines each with a hook at one end made by the sidewinder's tail.

It is very difficult to see how the track is made without seeing a sidewinder in action. In normal, or rectilinear, movement, a series of waves passes down a snake's body, pushing against the ground and driving the snake in the opposite direction to the waves. Sidewinding is very different; it is more like a coil spring being rolled or the movement of the tracks of a caterpillar tractor. The snake throws its body into curves and, when moving, only two points of the body touch the ground. These two points remain stationary while the raised parts move at an angle to the direction of the waves that pass along its body. As the snake progresses the part of the body immediately behind is raised, so that the body is laid down and taken up like a caterpillar track. When the point of contact reaches the tip of the tail, a new point is started at the head end and the snake moves along a series of parallel tracks.

class	**Reptilia**
order	**Sauria**
suborder	**Serpentes**
family	**Crotalidae**
genus & species	*Crotalus cerastes*

Birds

There is no doubt that among non-scientists birds are the most favoured of all animals, largely because they are the most obvious, because of their colours and their songs. They have also received more than their fair share of attention from scientists and one result of this is that it is unlikely that new species will be discovered in the future.

Another consequence of this attention is that the classification of birds has reached a stable form. In this classification 27 orders of living birds are enumerated, with two more for the recently extinct moas of New Zealand and elephant-birds of Madagascar. This is a higher proportion of orders to a single class of animals than in any other area of the animal kingdom.

Side by side with this, it has to be recognized that there are few, if any, other major groups of animals so poorly represented by fossils, as are birds. Fortunately, there are the remarkably complete fossils of the earliest known bird, the Archaeopteryx, the so-called lizard-bird, that indicate very clearly the evolution of birds from reptilian ancestors. This paucity of fossils is probably to be correlated with the flying habits, so that, as has often been said by palaeontologists, "birds do not make good fossils". The situation is similar for bats – but not for the pterodactyls or flying reptiles. This absence of all but a few scattered fossils is the more remarkable when it is recalled that birds have certainly been in existence for about 180 million years.

The class Aves used to be divided into two main divisions: the Ratitae and the Carinatae, the first including the large, flightless, running birds, such as ostrich, emu, cassowary, rhea and kiwi, the second including all the rest. Today, both names are used, if at all, merely as convenient group names, the surviving ratites being assigned to four separate orders, the Struthioniformes (ostriches), Rheiformes (rheas), Casuariiformes (emus, cassowaries) and Apterygiformes (kiwis), on the assumption that these birds are not necessarily related but look alike as a result of convergent evolution.

Of the remaining 23 orders, one is by far the largest and contains the most familiar of all birds. It is named the Passeriformes, after *Passer domesticus*, the house sparrow, the most familiar of all birds in the western world, where the main work on the early classification of birds was carried out. This order, sometimes referred to merely as Passeres, contains more than half the known species of living birds and includes 56 of the 149 families of the 'Carinatae'.

In its turn, the Passeriformes, also known as the perching birds, is divided into four suborders, the Eurylaimi (broadbills), Tyranni (woodcreepers, antbirds, antpipits, ovenbirds, tapaculos and others), Menurae (lyrebirds, scrub-birds) and Oscines (songbirds). The first three of these account for only 15 of the 56 families and about 1040 species out of the 5000 or more species of Passeriformes.

The Passeriformes therefore bear comparison with bony fishes in having been evolved, geologically speaking, in a very short space of time. They have proliferated into numerous species, are worldwide, have successfully adapted to environments most of which are man-made, nesting or roosting on buildings and making use very often of 'unnatural' foods. Like the bony fishes, they have exploited a wide variety of habitats. Since they use agricultural land and buildings so much they are brought into close contact with people, whether in rural or urban districts, so that the Passeriformes can reasonably be said to have played a major role in the social phenomenon of the 20th century known as bird-watching.

It has been said, doubtless with a fair degree of truth, that we hold as favourites those animals having characteristics similar to our own. The passerines have these in generous degree. Most birds are deficient in the sense of smell, and this is especially true of passerines. With rare exceptions, birds are 'eyesight animals', like humans, meaning that sight is the most important sense. Above all, the Passeriformes are especially vocal, if not vociferous, a feature of human behaviour almost without parallel in the animal kingdom.

Ostrich

The ostrich is the largest living bird and one of the most familiar because of its bizarre appearance. A large male may stand 8 ft high of which nearly half is neck. The plumage of the male is black except for the white plumes on the wings and tail. It is these plumes that first led to the numbers of ostriches being greatly reduced in many places and later to ostriches being raised on farms. The plumage of the females is brown with pale edging to the feathers. The head, most of the neck and the legs are almost naked, but the eyelids have long, black eyelashes. There are two strong toes on each foot, the longest being armed with a large claw.

A few million years ago, in the Pliocene era, there were nine species of ostriches, but only one survives today. About 200 years ago five subspecies of this species ranged over much of Africa, Syria and Arabia, in desert and bush regions. They are now extinct or very rare over most of this area. The Asian subspecies was last recorded in 1941. Ostriches are still plentiful in East Africa, and they live wild in a few places in south Australia where they were introduced.

Strange social life
Ostriches are extremely wary, their long necks enabling them to detect disturbances from quite a distance. As a result it is very difficult to study ostriches in the wild and until recently our knowledge has been based mainly on observations on domesticated ostriches. Incomplete observations in the wild have led to many mistaken ideas about the habits of these birds which have now become legendary. A husband and wife team of zoologists, the Sauers, studied ostriches in South West Africa by the ingenious method of disguising their hide as a termite mound. Ostriches and several other animals treated this hide with complete indifference with the result that the Sauers were afforded a grandstand view of ostrich social life, and they found that in some respects this is almost as strange as the legends.

Ostriches often live in very dry areas and they move about in search of food, often in quite large groups. During wet spells the herds break up into family groups, consisting of a pair with chicks and immatures. The herd is led by a cock or hen that chooses grazing grounds and makes decisions as to when to move. If the herd leaves familiar territory or comes to a water hole where no other animals are drinking, the dominant ostriches push the immature birds forward to spring any ambushes.

Eats nearly anything
Ostriches feed mainly on plants including fruits, seeds and leaves. In deserts they get their water from succulent plants. They also eat small animals and are even said to eat lizards and tortoises. Their reputation for eating almost anything including lumps of metal and tins of paint is widespread and perhaps exaggerated but ostriches swallow considerable amounts of sand to aid digestion and it is said that it is possible to trace the movements of an ostrich by examining the kinds of sand and gravel in its stomach.

Unstable society
Until recently there was considerable doubt as to whether ostriches were polygamous or monogamous. Proponents of monogamy pointed out that there was never more than one male or one female seen at a nest or leading a group of chicks. It is now known that ostriches may be monogamous but more usually they are polygamous. The Sauers found that the social organisation of ostriches is very flexible and that a male accompanying a female with chicks need not be the father of the chicks.

Breeding takes place at any time of the year, depending on the time of the rainy season. At first the males develop a red pigment on their heads and feet and they display to each other, chasing around in groups with wings held out to show off the white plumes. Later they establish territories away from the communal feeding grounds, and here they are joined by the females. A male ostrich usually has three hens in his harem but it is not unknown for him to have up to five.

The courtship ceremony is elaborate. The male separates one female from the group and the pair feed together, synchronising the movements of head and neck. The male then sits down and opens his wings to show the white plumes. At the same time he rocks from side to side and twists his neck in a corkscrew. The female walks around him and eventually drops into the mating position.

Each female lays 6—8 eggs which are about 6 in. long and weigh up to $2\frac{1}{2}$ lb. The members of a harem all lay in one nest, which consists of a depression in the ground that may be about 3 yd across. It may take nearly 3 weeks for all the eggs to be laid, after which the dominant hen drives the others away and the nest is guarded by the single hen and the cock. Incubation consists of keeping the eggs cool by shading them rather than keeping them warm. Towards the end of the 6-week incubation period some eggs are rolled into pits on the edge of the nest. These eggs are those that are most advanced and this is probably a mechanism to synchronise the hatching of the eggs as much as possible.

The chicks can run almost as soon as they hatch and after a month can attain a speed of 35 mph. When they leave their parents they form large bands, breeding when 4—5 years old.

Running to safety
Adult ostriches have little to fear from predators. They are very wary and can run at 40 mph, but the eggs and young ostriches may fall prey to jackals and other predators. The adults lead their chicks away from enemies and perform distraction displays while the chicks scatter and crouch.

▷ *A bizarre creature with a long naked neck: the ostrich is the largest living bird.*

Beating their wings and calling loudly the ostriches run to and fro presenting a broadside to the enemy and occasionally dropping to the ground and setting up a cloud of dust with the wings. Sometimes the male continues the display while the female leads the chicks away.

Burying their heads
One of the popular notions about ostriches is that they bury their heads in the sand when danger threatens. The action is used to describe the behaviour of a person who thinks that a problem can be solved by ignoring it, and has been the subject of many jokes and cartoons. This idea is very old, for the Roman writer Pliny says '... the veriest fools they be of all others, for as high as the rest of their body is, yet if they thrust their head and neck once into any shrub or bush, and get it hidden, they think then

◁ *Too many eggs? At the end of the incubation period the most advanced eggs are rolled into a pit beside the nest to synchronize hatching.*
▽ *Arrival date. Ostrich chicks hatching.*

they are safe enough, and that no man seeth them.'

Like so many legends there is a basis of truth in the ostrich burying its head and the story is probably due to the difficulty in observing ostriches. When an ostrich is sitting on the nest, its reaction to disturbance is to lower its head until the neck is held horizontally a few inches above the ground. The ostrich is then very inconspicuous and the small head may well be hidden behind a small plant or hummock.

class	**Aves**
order	**Struthioniformes**
family	**Struthionidae**
genus & species	*Struthio camelus*

▷ *A handsome male ostrich gives chase to two females busy displaying.*
▽ *Ostriches on the march. Flocks of them move about in the dry season, looking for food.*

125

Emu

One of Australia's flightless birds, the emu is the second biggest bird in existence. It stands 5–6 ft high, 2–3 ft less than the ostrich and dwarfed by the giant moas of New Zealand that became extinct a few centuries ago. Emus are related to cassowaries and share with them the coarse, drooping plumage and small wings hidden by the feathers. The feathers are double, as in cassowaries, with the aftershaft—the small tuft at the base of the vane in many birds—the same length as the main vane. The feathers are also downy, like the feathers of chicks, for the barbs do not have hooks linking them to make the stiff vane. The downy feathers, together with other anatomical features, suggest that emus and the other flightless birds known as ratites, such as ostriches, rheas and kiwis, are neotenous—that is, that juvenile characters have been retained in the adult (see axolotl, page 56).

Before Europeans settled in Australia there were several species of emu, but all except one have been wiped out. At one time Tasmania, Kangaroo, Flinders and other islands, had their own emus, but they were killed off so rapidly that hardly any specimens reached museums.

Apart from the female being slightly the larger, it is difficult to tell male and female emus apart. Their voices, however, are very different. The male makes guttural cries, whereas the female has a resonant booming call made by a large air sac connected to the windpipe.

△ *The second largest of living birds—the emu. The external ear opening is visible as only downy feathers cover the head and neck.*

▽ *In the nonbreeding season these huge Australian birds congregate in small flocks, moving through the outback in search of food and water.*

Pests in the dry season

Emus live in most parts of Australia, except where building and agriculture have driven them out. They are found in the deserts, on plains and in forests—but not in the dense rain forests of northeast Australia, where their place is taken by the cassowary. Outside the breeding season emus live in small parties, sometimes banding together into large herds. They are nomadic, moving about the country in search of food and water. In the dry season they become a pest. They move from the arid areas into agricultural land, raiding crops and using water holes that in bad years are barely enough to support domestic stock and farmers shoot on sight of them.

Like their flightless relatives, emus are strong runners. When pressed they reach 40 mph in short bursts, covering over 9 ft in one stride. Normally they run at a slower and steadier cruising speed that enables them to cover long distances. They are extremely inquisitive, investigating any new object. This may explain the habit, shared with ostriches, of swallowing all sorts of strange objects: keys, nails, bottle tops, coins and so on. One emu is reported to have drunk the contents of a tin of paint, then eaten the tin. Another chased a man for 4 miles, having been attracted to his shiny bicycle; but they will follow men apparently just to look at them.

Keeping down harmful insects

Fruit of many plants, leaves, grass and insects are the food of emus. During the winter months insects, especially caterpillars probably make up the bulk of the diet. Wheat crops are attacked when they ripen and for this reason emus are often persecuted. Nevertheless, eating insects must repay the debt to a large extent. One emu killed in an official campaign had nearly 3 000 harmful caterpillars in its stomach.

Father guards the eggs

Emus breed when 2 years old, laying their eggs in February or March, the Australian autumn. The male builds the nest, about 3 ft across, making a shallow bowl of grass and weeds, usually under a tree or bush. After the female has laid her clutch of 8–10 dark green eggs, she leaves the nest and the male incubates them for 8 weeks. During this time he rarely leaves the nest, and when he does, he may cover it with leaves to make the already inconspicuous eggs almost impossible to find.

At the end of the 8 weeks the eggs, which were rough, have become smoother and darker. They are often collected and turned into curios or souvenirs by etching the thick shell, revealing the paler layers under the surface in a cameo-like effect.

The chicks leave the nest shortly after hatching. They are miniature versions of the adults but very pale grey with conspicuous black stripes running along the body. The father guards the chicks for up to 18 months, until they are nearly mature. The young chicks feed themselves, mainly on insects, but there is a legend that emus lay a sterile egg either for the chicks to eat or to support a colony of fly maggots for the chicks to eat after hatching.

Oil and outsize omelettes

The natural enemies are wedge-tailed eagles that take young emus; and nest robbers such as various lizards, mammals and birds raid unguarded nests. Black-breasted buzzards, however, drive male emus off their nests then drop stones on the eggs to break them.

The early destruction of emus living on islands was brought about by seal hunters and early settlers killing the emus not only for their flesh but for the oil that can be extracted from their bodies. About 4 gallons of oil can be got from one emu, and it was used for lighting and as an embrocation. Eggs were also taken, if they could be found. To make an omelette, the egg was broken into a basin and left overnight so that the oil could be skimmed off before cooking it in the morning. One emu egg, weighing 1½lb, made an omelette sufficient for the hungriest of families to go to work on and feel well-filled.

The great emu war

It is ironical that both the emu and the kangaroo, which appear on the Australian coat-of-arms, should be considered vermin. Both have had bounties on their heads, and in Queensland 121 768 emus and 109 345 eggs were destroyed in one two-year period alone. This slaughter had its lighter side, however. In 1932 some farmers persuaded the government to declare war on the emus on a large scale. On November 2 a battery of the Royal Australian Artillery engaged the emus with machine-gun fire, but the emus resorted to guerilla tactics and split into small parties, so spoiling the hopes of pouring a hail of fire into the serried ranks of birds. Next, ambushes were tried, with the emus being driven towards the guns. When the emus were at point-blank range the gunners opened fire. A dozen birds fell and the gun jammed. From then on the war got bogged down and after a month the offensive was discontinued.

The government, feeling perhaps that public money had been wasted, asked the farmers for £24 each to offset the cost of ammunition. In reply they received the following claim from one of them:

To victualling H.M.'s troops.................£ 9
To transporting of troops...................£10
To damage of transport vehicles..........£ 5

£24

A 4 days old emu chick surveys a 1½lb emu egg. The father guards the 8–10 chicks for 18 months. The chicks feed mainly on insects, but there is a legend that emus lay a sterile egg either for the chicks to eat or to support a colony of fly maggots for the chicks to eat after hatching.

class	**Aves**
order	**Casuariiformes**
family	**Dromaiidae**
genus & species	***Dromaius novaehollandiae***

Kiwi

The kiwi is the smallest flightless running bird in the southern hemisphere, the other runners being the emu, cassowary, ostrich and rhea. There are three species in New Zealand, each about the size of a domestic fowl, with a rounded body, no tail, stout but short legs, strong claws on their three toes and a long slender bill with slit-like nostrils at its tip. They range in size from a bantam to an Orpington and in weight from 3–9 lb, the females being larger than the males. The wings are very small, 2 in. long, and completely hidden by the hair-like body feathers that make up the plumage. The eyes are small but there are many long bristles at the base of the bill which are probably used as organs of touch. The ears are large and are the chief sensory organs used in detecting danger.

Kiwis are so different anatomically from the other running birds that they are probably only distantly related to them. They are more closely related to the extinct moas of New Zealand.

Waddling nightbird

The home of the kiwi is in the kauri pine forests with their tree ferns and swampy ground. Here they spend the day in burrows or under buttress roots of large trees. They are shy, retiring and hard to see in the forest because of the gloom and the birds' dark brown colouring. They come out at night and waddle along, their legs being set well apart. Their run is a long-striding waddle, with the bill held well out in front.

Food for all seasons

When feeding a kiwi moves quietly, probably feeling its way to a large extent with the bill bristles. At the slightest alarm it dashes rapidly to cover. Its main food, when the ground is moist, is earthworms and insects and their larvae. The tip of the long bill overlaps the lower half, so the bill can be thrust deep in the ground, driven by the short, thick neck. The bird tracks its prey mainly by smell. When the ground is dry in summer, the kiwi picks up fallen forest fruits and eats a large number of leaves.

Testing its sense of smell

It has always been assumed that the kiwi finds its food by smell, although most birds have a weak sense of smell. In December 1968, Bernice M Wenzel, of the University of California, published an account in *Nature* (Vol 220, p 1133) of a series of experiments carried out in New Zealand. Sets of tapering aluminium tubes were sunk into the ground in two kiwi aviaries. The tests, repeated over a period of 3 months, consisted of placing food in one tube, earth in another and a strong odorant in a third. By ringing the changes, such as using different odorants and different ways of masking the contents of the various tubes, it was proved beyond doubt that a kiwi can smell food several inches down in a way that no other bird is able to do.

Unusually large eggs

Although kiwis' nests have often been found, not much is known about the breeding or nesting habits. The nest is made in a hollow log or among the roots of a large tree. Sometimes it is in a hole or burrow in a soft bank, enlarged by the bird itself. Kiwis lay 1 or 2 very large chalky-white eggs, each about 5 in. long, weighing about a pound. This is $\frac{1}{8}$ of the hen kiwi's body weight, not $\frac{1}{4}$ as is sometimes stated. The male, as is usual with running birds, does the incubating, which lasts for 75–80 days. The chicks are small balls of soft hair-like feathers with a spindly beak. They remain in the nest for 6 days after hatching, receiving no food during this time. Then they follow their parents on their nightly forays, finding their own food, after the male has helped by clearing the ground for them. The normal call of the male is thin and reedy; that of the female is more hoarse. It is a two-note call, made only at night, and sounds like 'k-wee', with the accent on the second part.

At Hawke's Bay a colony of kiwis is kept under protection. Nesting boxes are provided and there it was noticed that during the incubation period the hen tapped at intervals on the box and the male inside tapped back. This may be a means of communication between the two partners.

Increased popularity

The kiwi population has decreased over the past century. They were prized by the Maoris as a delicacy, and their feathers were woven into cloaks for the chieftains. Then the early settlers hunted them for food. The birds also suffered from dogs, cats, stoats, weasels and other introduced animals. Their habitat has been reduced through the country being opened up for agriculture. In contrast with their falling numbers, their popularity has increased. Their image is seen on postage stamps and coins and on the trademarks of many products from shoe polish to textiles. The name became most familiar to people in Britain and in other parts of the world during the First World War because the New Zealand troops were called Kiwis. The Royal Air Force also perpetuated the name to some extent when its non-flying members were nicknamed Kiwis.

class	**Aves**
order	**Apterygiformes**
family	**Apterygidae**
genus & species	***Apteryx australis*** common or brown kiwi ***A. haasti*** great spotted or large grey kiwi ***A. oweni*** little spotted or little grey kiwi

The flightless kiwi of New Zealand, with beak outstretched, walks through undergrowth in long-striding waddles, in search of earthworms.

Tinamou

The tinamous are partridge-like birds that present a fine puzzle; in spite of looking like small game birds they are probably more nearly related to the large South American running birds, the rheas. They range in size from a quail, 7 in. long, to a grouse, 14 in. long. They have rounded, bulky bodies in which the well-developed feathers on the rump often hide the very short tail feathers. The wings are short and rounded, the legs short, with the hind toe, or hallux, minute or missing. The head is small and the neck slender. The plumage is dull, brown or grey with spots and bands, so tinamous are extremely inconspicuous. They have some powder-down plumage, like herons and parrots.

The martineta or crested tinamou is large, about 14½ in. long. It is a dull mottled brown with a long crest that is spread when the bird is excited. The ornate tinamou also has a crest which can be erected when excited. One of the smallest tinamous is the 9 in. little tinamou. Its upperparts are rich brown with the sides of the head grey and the chin and throat white, gradually turning grey on the underparts of the tinamou.

The 50 or so species of tinamous live in the New World from southern Mexico to southern Chile and Argentina, including the island of Trinidad.

△ Grey outlook of a martineta tinamou.

Accident prone birds

Tinamous live in a variety of habitats from wet rain forests to open scrubland and the ornate tinamou can be found at over 13 000 ft in the Andes. They spend most of their time on the ground, keeping in touch with each other by attractive, fluting calls. They take flight only when startled, suddenly exploding into the air with a rush of wings, but they never fly far. Although their flight muscles are well-developed, sustained flight seems to be impossible because the heart and lungs are small. The tinamous' powers of co-ordination also seem to be limited as, when flushed, they sometimes hurtle headlong into branches and may kill themselves. Similarly, although fast runners, they soon tire and if pressed they may stumble. As tinamous are widely hunted for their extremely palatable flesh, it is surprising that these clumsy birds have survived; but they escape detection by remaining motionless or slipping quietly away through the undergrowth, camouflaged by their drab plumage.

A wide diet

Tinamous feed mainly on plants, particularly seeds and fruit, but they also eat insects and other small invertebrates. The ornate tinamou eats more animal food than most tinamous, including beetles, caterpillars and grasshoppers. Occasionally tinamous have been seen eating larger animals, such as mice. The plant food includes small leaves, flowers, fruits, seeds and, very occasionally, roots.

Father plays mother

Outside the breeding season tinamous are solitary. During the breeding season they are seen in twos and threes, and towards the end small coveys, consisting of parents with half-grown young, are formed. The breeding habits of tinamous are unusual in that the birds are usually polygamous and the females, which are slightly larger, with brighter colours than the males, play the dominant role in courtship. Some species live in pairs, as in the ornate tinamou where the sex ratio is 1:1, but in the variegated tinamou there are four times as many males as females. Each female may lay eggs in more than one nest, and several females may lay in a single nest. This is possible because the males build the nest and also incubate the eggs.

In the ornate tinamou courtship is fairly simple. The female is the most aggressive in defending the 6-acre territory and she courts the male by following him, both feeding as they go. The male displays by raising his rump and spreading the feathers to show a conspicuous dark patch. The variegated tinamou has a more elaborate courtship. The female runs to and fro, calling to attract the male and on approaching him, she lowers her wings and raises the tail and rump feathers to display a beautiful and elaborate pattern.

The male tinamou builds a nest in the undergrowth, which is little more than a poorly lined depression in the ground. The number of eggs that he incubates varies from 1 to 12 and they hatch in a little less than 3 weeks. The male may sit so tight during incubation that he can be lifted off the nest. After the chicks have left the nest he stays with them and defends them.

Doubtful honours

Tinamous are probably preyed upon, as partridge and grouse are, by both birds of prey and ground predators, such as foxes and the small and medium-sized members of the cat family. Sportsmen rate them as one of the finest gamebirds—always an unhappy situation for a bird. Frozen tinamou have also been exported to the United States as 'South American quail'.

Resembles the rhea

The tinamous are classed in their own order the Tinamiformes, low down in the scale of bird classification. They are not closely related to any other birds. Their resemblance to guineafowl, partridges and their relatives is only external, a consequence of their similar, ground-living habits. From a study of their anatomy it seems that tinamous are most closely related to the rheas, although the latter are flightless ratites, a group which includes ostriches and emus, that lack a keel on the breastbone. Yet the tinamous are 'carinates'. That is, they have a well-developed carina or keel on the breastbone, like the great majority of living birds. The breeding habits of tinamous are like those of rheas, with aggressive females and motherly males. There are physical similarities in the structure of the palate and in the shape of the rhamphotheca—the horny covering of the bill, and also there are chemical similarities in the composition of the eggs.

class	**Aves**
order	**Tinamiformes**
family	**Tinamidae**
genera & species	***Crypturellus soui*** little tinamou *C. variegatus* variegated tinamou ***Eudromia elegans*** martineta tinamou ***Nothoprocta ornata*** ornate tinamou, others

King penguin

King penguins look very much like emperor penguins, to which they are very closely related. They have the same stately walk as the emperors, with their long knife-shaped bills held up. King penguins are the smaller of the two, 3 ft long instead of 4 ft, but are otherwise similar in appearance. They both have blue-black backs and white fronts with yellow and orange patches around the neck, but in the king penguin the patches are separated into two comma-shapes on the side of the neck with a 'bib' of yellow on the breast.

King penguins live farther north than emperor penguins, in the ice-free sub-Antarctic seas between the Falkland Islands southwards to the South Sandwich Islands and Heard Island. There are very small colonies on Staten Island, near Cape Horn, and on the Falkland Islands. The largest colonies are found on islands such as South Georgia, Kerguelen, Macquarie and Marion.

Feeding at sea

Like other penguins, king penguins live at sea when they are not breeding and sometimes swim long distances, turning up on the fringes of the Antarctic pack ice. The latitudes in which the king penguins live are those of the roaring westerly gales, but these are unlikely to affect the penguins much except to drive them off course. Penguins are perfectly adapted to life at sea. Their bodies are streamlined and a layer of blubber under the skin insulates them from the cold water. The large king and emperor penguins can dive to considerable depths to hunt squid and fish which they catch in their sharp bills. The eyes of aquatic animals are designed to see underwater. Light is not bent so much as it passes from water into the eye as when it passes from air. To compensate, the lens is very strong. As a result aquatic animals are short-sighted out of water.

Prolonged childhood

The king penguin has the same problem of child care as the emperor penguin. Both are very large birds and their chicks take a long time to grow, yet the Antarctic summer is very short. The emperor penguin has solved the problem in an unexpected way by starting the 7-month nursery period in midwinter so the chicks become independent before the following winter. The king penguin has a different method. It lives farther north where the sea does not freeze and the adults are able to feed near the colony. So instead of laying their eggs in midwinter, the king penguins lay in spring or summer and when the chick hatches after 7½ weeks it is fed throughout the following winter, becoming independent the next summer.

Just before they start breeding king penguins come ashore to moult. They spend a fortnight ashore shedding their old feathers to reveal the brilliant new coat, then retire to sea to feed and build up reserves of food before breeding. Returning to land, they make their way to the colony among the tussack grass and mud where each male takes up position and advertises for a mate. He stretches his neck, ruffs out his feathers and tilts his head back and calls, braying like a donkey. If an unmated female hears him, she wanders over and the two penguins introduce themselves by flagging their bills up and down. They then set off on an 'advertisement walk', strutting along on their toes, waving their heads from side to side, showing off their brilliant patches of colour. The colours are important—if they are covered with black paint a penguin stands no chance of getting a mate.

At first these partnerships do not last very long. The male displays at any female and keeps company with a succession of prospective mates. Gradually, however, he pays attention to one particular female and the bond between them strengthens and they perform another display; standing side by side they raise their beaks and stand on their toes as if stretching themselves.

The king penguin, like the emperor penguin, makes no nest but balances the single large egg on his feet, protected by a fold of skin. He does, however, defend a small territory rather than wander about with his egg. The first eggs are laid in November,

*Yetis of the Antarctic! The little sheath bill **Chionis** is dwarfed by the big brown penguin chicks.*

and more are laid until April. After laying the female goes off to feed and make up the food reserves she lost forming the egg. The male is left guarding the egg until the female's return 2 weeks later. Thereafter, there is a shuttle service, each parent taking a turn in guarding the egg or chick.

As the chicks get older they spend more time on their own and eventually form crèches where they huddle together while parents go fishing. On its return a parent king penguin finds its chick by sound. It walks up to the crèche and calls, and one chick out of hundreds replies. They both walk towards each other, calling, and may even walk past, until another call brings them back to each other. Several pounds of food are transferred at each feed and the chicks put on weight rapidly, but as winter sets in feeding becomes very infrequent and the chicks huddle in their crèches, protected by their thick, woolly down but gradually losing weight. Then, in spring, when food becomes abundant again, the chicks put on weight, lose their down and the adult plumage emerges.

The chicks take to the sea 2 months later and learn to fish for themselves. This is well-timed because food is abundant at this season. The young king penguins stay at sea for most of their early life, spending more time ashore as they get older and begin to practise their courtship displays. At 6 years old, they come ashore and start courting in earnest.

Boiled for blubber

The enemies of king penguins are leopard seals. They lie in wait off the colonies, but the seals will find them difficult to catch as the penguins have an alarm system. When a king penguin sees a leopard seal, it panics and rushes towards the shore. Its flippers beat on the surface of the water and the clattering sound they make alerts other king penguins, and they all rush clattering to the shore. Not only are all the penguins alerted but the leopard seals are probably confused and will be able to catch only weak or unwary penguins.

At one time, man was a far greater enemy. As elephant and fur seals became scarce sealers killed king penguins for their blubber, which was used for tanning leather. Their eggs were taken and their skins sometimes used for fancy clothing.

Slow breeding

It took only a few years for the sealers to reduce the numbers in a king penguin colony to such an extent that it was not worth their while to exploit them further. The reason for this is the extremely slow rate of breeding. After the egg has been laid, a pair of king penguins spends a year incubating, guarding or collecting food. By the time they are free of their offspring it is too late in the year to begin again and they leave the colony to feed during the winter and start breeding the following spring.

Therefore, king penguins, like the larger albatrosses (page *134*) which also spend their first winter on the nest, cannot raise more than one young every two years. Furthermore, not all their offspring survive the first winter. If the egg is laid too late in the summer the chick will not have had time to accumulate enough fat with which to survive the winter. Without the attentions of the sealers, king penguins flourish; they are long-lived and generally survive to rear enough offspring to keep numbers constant.

class	**Aves**
order	**Sphenisciformes**
family	**Spheniscidae**
genus & species	***Aptenodytes patagonica***

131

Grebe

Grebes are waterbirds with long necks and short tails that give them a distinct, blunt-ended appearance. Many species have plumes on the head. The feet are set well back on the body, as in the divers. They are not webbed but each toe has a horny fringe that acts as a paddle. The feet are used for steering both in the air and in the water, the vestigial tail being useless for this purpose.

The largest grebe is the 19in. long great crested grebe, whose behaviour has been studied in great detail. It is found in most of Europe except northern Scandinavia, in many parts of Asia, Africa and in Australia and New Zealand. Its upperparts are light brown and the underparts white. The black ear tufts and, in the breeding season, chestnut and black frills on the sides of the head are particularly distinctive. The Slavonian grebe is darker on the upperparts than the great crested grebe. In the breeding season it has a glossy black head with a golden stripe running through the eye, and chestnut neck and flanks. Its range is circumpolar, from Iceland, Faeroes and Scotland through parts of Scandinavia and a broad belt across Asia to North America. Another widespread species is the little grebe or dabchick, the smallest of grebes, which has dark plumage. It breeds in Europe as far north as southern Sweden, in Asia as far as the East Indies and Japan and in most of Africa.

Of the 18 species of grebe, 10 are confined to the New World. In comparison with the wide-ranging species described above, others are extremely restricted. One is restricted to Madagascar, another to New Zealand and a third to the Falkland Islands. In the highlands of South America there are three species tied to single lakes. The flightless Titicaca grebe lives on Lake Titicaca, 2 miles high in the Andes, another lives on Lake Junin in Peru, while the giant pied-billed grebe, also flightless, lives on Lake Atitlan in Guatemala.

Shy stay-at-homes

Grebes live on lakes, reservoirs and flooded gravel pits, only rarely on slow-moving rivers. Some stay in one place all the year round but others, such as the great crested grebe, migrate to the coast in winter. Generally, however, grebes do not fly much and have to run across the water to take off. When disturbed they scutter to safety or dive and, like cormorants and darters, can swim half submerged by flattening their plumage, so squeezing the air out. Grebes are not gregarious, only occasionally are they seen in small parties. More often they live in pairs not straying from their territories, which in great crested grebes are about 2 acres. The great crested grebe can often be seen swimming slowly about in open water and can be watched diving re-

Penguin dance: a rare and complicated ceremony in which both male and female come high up out of the water and shake their heads with nesting materials in their bills.

Rearing display: the male, or the female, climbs onto the nest, rears up, and with bent neck moves the head from side to side as an invitation to coupling.

Invitation to coupling: as courtship proceeds the female takes more turns at mounting the nest (often only a copulation platform) and makes this final display.

Mating begins as the male jumps onto the female. This remarkable series of photographs by George Rüppell illustrates the now famous observations of JS Huxley in 1914 and KEL Simmons in 1955

peatedly for food, but the little grebe lives a very secluded life among reeds and other vegetation surrounding its lake or pond. It can be seen only by accident or by patiently waiting for its occasional trip from one reed bed to another.

Eating fish and feathers

Grebes eat fish, aquatic insects and crustaceans together with a few newts, tadpoles and some plant matter which they find by swimming underwater. A grebe usually stays underwater for $\frac{1}{2}$ minute or less, depending no doubt on the depth of the water, abundance of food and so on. They have been known to stay submerged for as long as 3 minutes. In calm, clear water a grebe can easily spot its prey while swimming with its neck raised, but in ruffled water or if searching for small animals it may swim with its head just underwater, waiting to submerge suddenly and plunge after its prey. Insects are sometimes picked off the surface or snatched out of the air.

Fish are swallowed alive, head-first. They may have to be juggled before being in the right position for swallowing. Grebes usually eat 4–6 in. fish, but larger ones are sometimes caught and the grebe can only gulp them down slowly. It is not unusual for dabchicks, and other waterbirds, to be choked by the spines of bullheads they are attempting to swallow.

A strange habit of grebes is feather eating. They regularly eat their body feathers, or soak them, and give them to their young. In the stomach the feathers break down to a felt-like mush which is thought to make sharp fish bones easier to regurgitate.

Floating nests

Grebes are famed for their spectacular courtship dances. Both sexes have plumes and ear tufts and both take the initiative in courtship. The great crested grebe has several displays with various functions. They vary from simple head-shaking to the penguin dance. Both birds dive, surfacing with weed in their bills, then rise up breast to breast and sway from side to side before relaxing. In the 'cat display' the grebe lowers its head with ear tufts spread and holds its wings out with the forward edges turned downwards. The western grebe of North America performs incredible dashes over the water. The two grebes rear up out of the water and dash across the surface side by side with their necks arched forwards. The dash is ended by both birds diving.

Some of the courtship is carried out on the nest, which is a large pile of waterweed built by both birds among the weeds, or occasionally floating freely. The adults take turns in incubating 3–10 faint white or blue-green eggs. If they are frightened off the nest they will often cover the eggs with nest material before creeping away.

The eggs of large grebes hatch in a month and those of small grebes in 3 weeks. The nest is abandoned as soon as the chicks dry out and the young chicks are carried on the parents' backs for a week or more. They occasionally get carried under when the parent dives or carried aloft when it flies. As they grow older they spend less time on the parent. This behaviour protects them from enemies, the worst of which, in Europe, is the pike. In a survey carried out in Britain, pike were the main cause of chick mortality, followed by foxes, otters, herons, trout and eels.

The young begin to dive when 6 weeks old and are independent by 10 weeks. Some species raise two broods in a season, the male guarding the first clutch while the female incubates the second.

Save the grebes
In 1860 the British population of great crested grebes fell to below 50 pairs because grebe feathers were once in great demand as decorations for women's hats. Since then, however, their numbers have increased, and now the bird is by no means rare. It is now the turn of another species, the giant pied-billed grebe, to be endangered. It is one of the rarest birds in America, only 100 surviving in 1965 on the 10 by 12 mile Lake Atitlan. The reason for their decrease seems to have been the introduction of largemouth bass as a gamefish. This on the face of it was an admirable scheme designed to enrich the area, but as all too often happens the project backfired. Largemouth bass, which weigh 10–12 lb, are predatory and live on the same small fish and crustaceans that the grebes hunt, and it seems that they also take young grebes. More seriously the bass have upset the delicate balance of the lake animals and the 50 000 people living round the lake are feeling the effects of this on their important fishing industry.

Steps have been taken to save the grebes. A small bay has been isolated from the lake by wire mesh, the bass killed off and grebes introduced. Rigorous patrolling against poaching has allowed the grebe population to increase. This is very encouraging, but expensive and one wonders whether it will be possible to eliminate the bass to allow both grebes and men to continue their fishing in peace.

class	**Aves**
order	**Podicipediformes**
family	**Podicipedidae**
genera & species	***Podiceps auratus*** Slavonian grebe *P. cristatus* great crested grebe *P. ruficollis* little grebe ***Podilymbus gigas*** giant pied-billed grebe others

Changeover: great crested grebe male takes on the job of incubating the last egg of the clutch while his mate prepares to leave with the chick.

Albatross

A family of birds in the petrel order. They are the largest members of the order and among the largest of flying birds. They have goose-sized bodies with very long, slender wings: of the 13 species, the largest is the wandering albatross, which has a wingspan sometimes exceeding 12 ft. The plumage is black and white or, in a few species, brown. In only some of the species is it possible to tell the sexes apart.

Ocean wanderers
Nine species of albatross are confined to the Southern Hemisphere, breeding mainly on the sub-Antarctic and oceanic islands. The other four are found in the North Pacific. None breed in the North Atlantic, although fossil remains have been found in England and a few have been recorded as vagrants in modern times. These vagrants include wandering, black-browed, yellow-nosed, grey-headed, and light-mantled sooty albatrosses. One black-browed albatross appeared in a Faroese gannet colony in 1860 and for 30 years—until it was shot—it accompanied the gannets on their annual migrations. Another visited the Bass Rock gannet colony off the Scottish coast in 1967 and returned in 1968.

The doldrums, the windless belt around the Equator, are possibly one of the reasons why so few albatrosses have been recorded in the North Atlantic, as albatrosses need a sustained wind for flight. They are heavy birds with comparatively small wing muscles, but they can remain airborne for long periods and cover vast distances because of the difference in the speed of the wind at the water's surface and some 50 ft above, due to friction slowing down the air at the surface. The albatross glides swiftly downwind and surfacewards, gathering speed. When just above the water it swings sharply round into the wind and soars up. As it rises it loses momentum and its ground speed (*i.e.* in relation to the water surface) decreases. Its air speed, however, does not decrease so fast, as the bird is rising and so continually meeting faster wind currents. By the time the air speed has dropped completely the albatross will have gained sufficient height to start the downward glide again. Thus it progresses in a series of zig-zags.

*1. Yellow-nosed albatross (**Diomedea chlororhyncha**) landing, showing its large wingspan. This enables it to soar for hours in the oceanic air currents.*
2. The albatross nests on cliff tops where it can easily take off. The chick is guarded by its parents for several weeks.
3. Later both parents can be away feeding for ten days at a time.
*4. Black-browed albatross (**Diomedea melanophrys**) ranges over the oceans between 30° and 60° latitude south, breeding on such islands as Tristan da Cunha, South Georgia, and the Kerguelen and Auckland Islands. It has been recorded as a vagrant to the British Isles and even to the Arctic.*

The main haunt of albatrosses is the sub-Antarctic zone where the Roaring Forties and Howling Fifties sweep around the world and there is nearly always enough wind to keep the albatrosses aloft—although they can glide in quite gentle breezes. To increase speed the albatross 'close-hauls', partly closing its wings to reduce air resistance without seriously affecting lift.

With their great wingspan and weak wing muscles albatrosses have difficulty in taking off. When there is enough wind—especially if there are thermal currents or eddies around the cliffs on which they nest—takeoff is not so difficult; but on still days they have to taxi, running along and flapping their wings until they have gained sufficient air speed to take off.

Some species are fairly confined in their range, like Buller's albatross in New Zealand; others, like the wandering, black-browed and sooty albatrosses circle the world from Tropics to Antarctic.

Marine feeders

All species of albatross feed on marine organisms living at the surface of the sea, such as fish, squid and crustaceans. They also take small sea birds on occasions, and they like refuse from ships, flopping down into the water as soon as a bucketful is tipped overboard. Sailors who have fallen overboard have reputedly been viciously attacked by albatrosses.

Cliff top breeding sites

Breeding grounds, where albatrosses gather in tens of thousands, are usually on the top of cliffs where the birds can take off easily. They are extremely faithful to their nest sites, and populations have survived such calamities as volcanic eruptions or pillage by man because the immature birds that were absent at the time later returned to breed.

Albatrosses are very long-lived birds: one recaptured 19 years after being ringed as an adult must have been at least 26 years old. They do not start breeding until at least seven years old, but young birds return to the breeding ground before then and court halfheartedly. Courtship displays, which are to be seen throughout the breeding season, are most spectacular. The two birds of a pair dance grotesquely and awkwardly with outstretched wings to the accompaniment of nasal groans and bill snapping. At the beginning of the breeding season several males may dance around one female.

A single egg is laid in a cup-shaped nest of mud and is incubated by both parents for periods ranging from 65 days in the smaller species to 81 days in the larger ones. The chick is also brooded for a short time and is guarded by the adults for several weeks. It is then left by itself and both parents can be away feeding at once. They return every 10 days to give the chick a huge meal of regurgitated squid and fish. The young of the smaller albatrosses fledge in two to three months, but larger ones may spend eight or nine months in the colony, sitting out the severe southern winter until the following summer. The parents feed them the whole time, so breeding is only possible in alternate years.

The young albatrosses leave the breeding grounds to glide away around the world, driven by the winds of the Westerly Drift. Before they return to start courting several years later they may circle the globe many times.

No natural enemies

Albatrosses have no natural enemies, living as they do on remote islands. Any introduced carnivores would, however, wreak havoc among the densely packed nests, for the sitting albatross's reaction to disturbance is just to sit tight on the nest and clack its bill. It also spits oil from digested crustaceans and fish—as does the chick—but this is hardly likely to discourage a determined predator.

The sailors' curse

Albatrosses have been known to sailors since the days of Magellan. Their inexpressive, fixed facial expression as they glide alongside a ship for miles on end without a flicker of the eye has brought them various nicknames: Mollymawk (from the Dutch Mallemok, 'stupid gull'), Gooney (English/American for a stupid person), Bakadori (Japanese for 'fowl-birds').

But they not only had a reputation for idiocy; they were considered to be harbingers of wind and storms—not, perhaps, surprising in view of their difficulty in remaining aloft in calm weather. They were also regarded as the reincarnations of seamen washed overboard, and it was thought extremely unlucky to kill them.

But, despite the chance of having an albatross hung round one's neck and suffering the far worse experience that later befell the Ancient Mariner, sailors have not always treated albatrosses kindly. Their capture on baited hooks trailed from the stern of a ship often relieved the monotony of life and diet.

More seriously, albatrosses were once favourite material for the 19th-century millinery trade, the wings sometimes being cut off the still-living birds. The North Pacific colonies bore the brunt of this fashion for plumage which, luckily, ceased before all the birds were dead.

Since the Second World War there has been another crisis for the albatross. Long-range aircraft flights have made oceanic islands necessary as staging posts, and one such is Midway Island, the home of the Laysan albatross. Not only are albatrosses using the United States Navy's runways for taking off, they also soar in the thermals above them, providing a serious danger to aircraft. Of the many methods that have been tried to reduce this danger, the most effective has been the bulldozing of dunes by the runways which cause the updraughts that the albatrosses need for flying.

class	**Aves**
order	**Procellariiformes**
family	**Diomedeidae**
genus & species	***Diomedea spp.*** ***Phoebetria spp.***

Pelicans often found their colonies in tall trees. The nests, unlined structures of dry twigs, are large and ungainly.

Pelican

The pelican is known to many people only from seeing it in zoos or on ornamental lakes where its ungainly appearance often makes it the subject of ridicule. In the wild, however, it is a superb flier and swimmer.

There are eight species, two of which occur in the New World and six in the Old, distributed over the tropical and warm temperate parts of the globe. The species differ only in the smaller details of size, colour and geographical range. Both sexes are alike and all have massive bodies, supported on short legs with strong webbed feet. They have long necks, small heads and a thick, harsh plumage. They are among the largest living birds, from 50–72 in. long. The most conspicuous feature is the enormous beak; the upper part is flattened and the lower part carries a pouch that can be distended to grotesque proportions. It can hold about 17 pints of water and is used, not for storing food, but as a dip net for catching fish.

Apart from the brown pelican, in the majority of the species the adult plumage is mainly white, tinged with pink in the breeding season in some species such as the pink-backed pelican of Africa. The primaries are black or dark. Some species have crests and in some there is yellow, orange or red on the bill, pouch and bare part of the face. The brown pelican, the smallest member of the family, with a wing-span of up to $6\frac{1}{2}$ ft and weighing about 8 lb, has a white head with a yellow tinge. In the breeding season the neck turns a rich brown with a white stripe running down each side. The wings and underparts are dark brown. The larger white species may have a wing-span of 10 ft and weigh 24 lb.

The brown pelican, which is a sea bird that does not venture far from the shore and breeds on small islands, is found along the south Atlantic and Gulf coasts of North America through the West Indies to Venezuela. Along the Pacific it ranges from central California to Chile with one population on the Galapagos Islands. The other New World species is the American white pelican that breeds on inland lakes from western Canada to southern Texas. In the Old World there are pelicans in Africa, southern Asia, including the Philippines, and Australia and in southeast Europe there are isolated colonies of the large silvery white Dalmatian pelican which ranges eastward from there into central Asia, visiting Egypt and northern India in winter. It nested at least as far north as Hungary until the middle of the last century and according to Pliny it nested in the estuaries of the Elbe, Rhine and Scheldt.

Fishing cooperation

Pelicans feed mainly on fish but crustaceans are also taken. The white pelicans fish while floating on the surface or wading about in the shallows. They thrust their heads under the water, using their pouches as dip nets to catch the fish. Occasionally a large flock of birds will cooperate by forming a line across the water and swimming abreast, beating the surface violently with their wings to drive schools of small fish into shallow water where they can easily scoop them up.

Community breeding

Pelicans are very sociable and all the species nest in large colonies sometimes of tens of thousands. Most of the white species breed on isolated islands in large inland lakes usually making their nests on the ground but occasionally they nest in low trees. On the ground the nest is sometimes just a depression scooped out of the earth. The brown pelican which breeds on small islands on the coast, makes a loose nest of sticks in mangrove trees and low shrubs or sometimes on the ground.

In all species the breeding season varies from place to place and from year to year. In some tropical areas they may even breed throughout the year. Chalky white eggs numbering 1–4 are laid which both parents help to incubate for 29–30 days. The babies are born naked and blind but quickly grow a soft white down. Both parents feed the young, at first dribbling regurgitated food out of the ends of their beaks into the chicks' open mouths, but after a few days the chicks are strong enough to stick their heads into their parents' pouches to get the food. Before the chicks are 2 weeks old they leave the nest and form noisy juvenile groups but the parents continue to feed them for some time. The young mature slowly, only acquiring adult plumage after several years. They seldom breed until they are 4 years old. Pelicans are long lived birds. Although the accepted record is 52 years, there are less well authenticated accounts of birds living to a much greater age. The Emperor Maximilian is said to have had a pelican which lived for more than 80 years.

Many hazards for the young

Mature pelicans have few natural enemies. Sometimes they may be killed by sea lions in the Pacific or occasionally eaten by sharks but among the young mortality is very high. When the young birds congregate after leaving the nest many fall from trees or get caught in the branches or even trampled on by clumsy adults. When a baby pelican is hurt a larger fledgling is likely to eat it. The adult birds do little to protect their young and sometimes entire nesting colonies are wiped out by predatory animals. It is doubtful if even half the young birds survive. Fishermen have been known to destroy colonies of pelicans to prevent them taking so much fish. At Pelican Island, Florida, in 1911 a plague of mosquitoes caused an entire colony of breeding birds to abandon the rookery, leaving 600 nests containing nestlings. In Peru the guano diggers often damage the nests, knocking young birds out of the way and frightening away the parents, so leaving the chicks an easy prey for predators. Nowadays the pelican colonies are often in danger when marshes are drained or lakes dry up due to large water schemes.

Superb in flight

The pelican has often been described as a clumsy bird, a statement no more justified than it would be to speak of a duck or a swan as clumsy merely because they walk on

△ *Fish scoop. A yawning common white pelican shows its enormous pouch for catching fish.*

land with a waddle and because the body is heavily built. When a pelican has managed after much effort and flapping to become airborne it is a strong and graceful flier, and it is no less graceful in the water. With legs up, head well back on the shoulders and its large bill resting on the front of the neck it can sail through the air with little effort.

Pelicans seem to possess quite unnecessary powers of flight considering that all their food is taken from the water and everything about them suggests adaptation to an aquatic mode of living. They fly at about 26 mph and there is an authentic record of their having maintained this speed for 8 miles, so it seems they also have the quality of endurance in flight. There is one record of the common pelican having achieved 51 mph. They regularly fly in formation either in line astern or in V-formation, all members of the flight beating their wings in perfect unison. The sight of a flock gliding down like a squadron of flying-boats is spectacular. They also have the vulture's trick of using thermal currents, soaring in spirals to a great height, even as much as 8 000 ft, where by alternately flapping and gliding they may circle for hours.

Symbol of piety
The principal myth concerning the pelican is that the parent bird, if unable to find food for her brood, pierced her breast with the tip of her bill and fed the youngsters on her own blood, and that is how the bird is figured in the earliest pictures of it. It was because of this belief that the pelican was chosen as an emblem of charity and piety and became a favourite heraldic emblazonment. There is a different version of the story according to Bartholomew. Writing in 1535 he says that the young pelicans smite the parents in the face, whereupon the mother retaliates, hitting them back and killing them. Then, on the third day, the mother smites herself in the side until the blood runs out onto the bodies of her youngsters, bringing them to life again.

These two stories may have arisen because in feeding its young the parent presses its bill against its neck and breast in order to make the contents of the pouch more readily available to the young, who thrust their bills into the pouch to take the food. The red tip on the common pelican's mandible may also have made the story more plausible.

class	**Aves**
order	**Pelecaniformes**
family	**Pelecanidae**
genus & species	***Pelecanus crispus*** *Dalmatian pelican* ***P. erythrorhynchos*** *American white pelican* ***P. occidentalis*** *brown pelican* ***P. onocrotalus*** *common white pelican* ***P. rufescens*** *pink-backed pelican* *others*

Flamingo

Beautiful but bizarre, flamingos, like giraffes, have an appearance of unreality bordering on disbelief. Their necks and legs are proportionately longer than in any other bird; they feed with their heads upside down in foul, alkaline or saline water yet keep their delicately pink plumage immaculate.

There are four species of flamingo in both Old and New Worlds. Their plumage is tinged with pink, except for the black flight feathers. The greater flamingo, standing about 4 ft high, is found in America from the Bahamas to Tierra del Fuego, including the Galapagos Islands, and in the Old World from southern Europe to South Africa across to India. The lesser flamingo lives in eastern Africa and India. The two remaining species live in the Andes, 14 000 ft above sea level, in Bolivia, Chile, and Argentina. The Andean flamingo is common locally, but the James'-flamingo is very rare and at one time was feared to be extinct.

Vast flocks of beautiful waders

Flamingos are gregarious, living in vast flocks of many thousands. One colony of the lesser flamingo in East Africa, the commonest species, numbers at least 1 million pairs. Flamingos breed, feed and travel in flocks and a flock of flamingos wading or swimming in a lake or flying in skeins, like geese, with necks and legs outstretched and wings slowly beating must be amongst the most beautiful sights in the world.

Flamingos are always found on lakes or lagoons of brackish water, where they breed and feed in shallow water. Many of them are migratory, and in recent years greater flamingos from the Camargue have been found to be flying south across the Mediterranean to spend the winter in Africa on the same lakes as the lesser flamingos.

Upside-down filter feeding

Shallow lakes and lagoons are the invariable homes of flamingos because it is here that minute plants and animals exist in the vast concentrations needed to feed the flamingo flocks. Flamingos extract their food from the water by a filtering mechanism which is very similar to that used by the blue whale. They wade through the water with necks lowered and heads upside down, sweeping from side to side. They adopt this unlikely position to sieve their food from the water. The upper and lower mandibles of the bill are fringed with bristles which trap particles as the flamingo sucks in water. The outer layer of coarse bristles keep out large particles while minute algae such as diatoms are collected on an array of bristles inside the bill. The collected algae are then worked off onto the tongue and swallowed after the water has been expelled.

The greater flamingo has a more varied diet than other species. The other flamingos sweep their heads through the surface water but the greater flamingo feeds nearer the bottom. Its bill has fewer filtering bristles and has a flatter upper mandible. With it the greater flamingo sweeps up small snails and shrimps, as well as quantities of mud from which it extracts the organic matter, rejecting the inedible silt. The greater and lesser flamingos feed together in mixed flocks in the lakes of eastern Africa as the slight difference in feeding ground and feeding habits is sufficient to prevent them from competing for food.

They nest on hummocks

Flamingos breed in colonies. In East Africa where they are most abundant the colonies may be enormous. Several with over 900 000 pairs are known and at one time it was estimated that one had over 1 million pairs. Sometimes a particular colony may be deserted for several years in succession. Then the flamingos may perhaps rear two broods in very quick succession.

The erratic nature of the breeding is most likely due to changes in the water level of the breeding lake. The nests are towers of mud some 6–14 in. high with a depression in the top for the eggs. The water level has only to rise a foot or so for the colony to be

▷ *Rarity in captivity: the James' flamingo, which lives in the Andes, 14 000 ft above sea level. Very scarce, it was once believed extinct.*

▽ *A stilt-legged trio of greater flamingos, showing off their balance on dry land.*

A scintillating moment of breathtaking beauty as greater flamingos take to the air.

Aftermath of disaster: smashed and deserted eggs in the potash-ridden waters of Lake Magadi, Kenya.

inundated. On the other hand, if the water level of an alkaline lake drops, thick deposits may form and become caked on the legs of flamingo chicks when they leave their nests. In 1962 Lake Natron in Kenya was flooded and the flamingos moved to Lake Magadi to breed. Thousands of chicks perished, caked with soda that formed heavy anklets round their legs. A rescue operation was launched and many chicks were saved. A flamingo is long lived, however, and produces many chicks in its lifetime, so it is very unlikely that such a catastrophe would have a serious long term effect on the population.

At the beginning of the breeding season the flamingos indulge in spectacular courtship displays. Banding together in tightly-bunched flocks the male flamingos run to and fro with the necks held straight up and bills pointed skyward. At the same time there is a continual guttural uproar while the flock appears to be shimmering because the flamingos are jerking their heads sideways, fitfully and never in unison. At other times they bend their necks, sweeping their bills across their backs. Within the colony of thousands of flamingos these tightly-knit flocks of males flow and eddy.

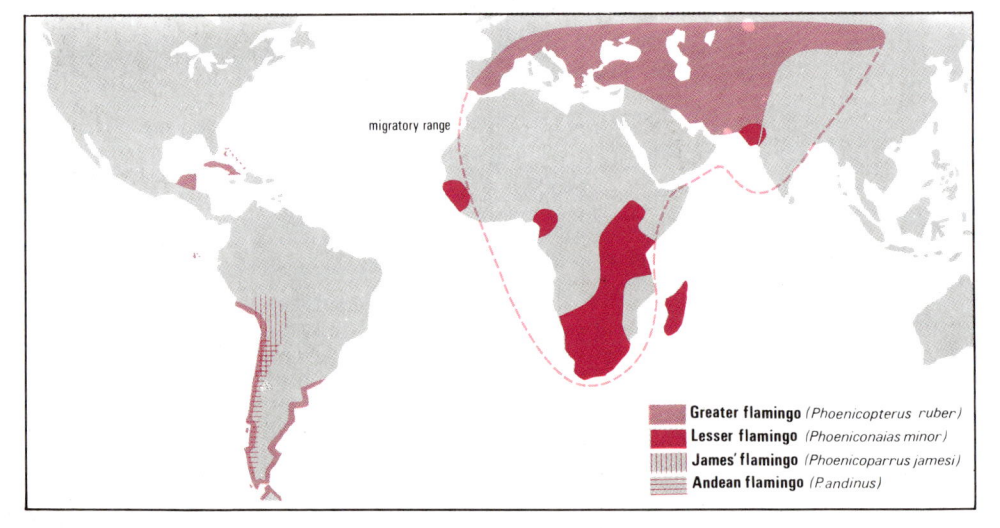

A single egg is laid in the saucer-shaped depression in the nest and is incubated for a month by both parents in turn. After the chicks hatch they stay on the nest for 2–3 days then they join the other chicks in bands which can run readily, and swim when 10 days old. The chicks look very much like goslings. They are covered in grey down and their bills are straight, not sickle-shaped like their parents'. Because of the resemblance of young flamingos to goslings and the goose-like flight of the adults, flamingos have been thought to be related to geese, but most ornithologists now think that the flamingos are related to storks and ibises.

Until its bill has developed the characteristic shape, a young flamingo is unable to feed itself and has to rely on its parents. To feed a chick a parent stands behind it and lowers its neck so the chick may take the tip of its bill in its own. The adult regurgitates liquefied food which runs down into the chick's mouth. The parents seem to be able to recognise their own chicks even when they are among a dense crowd of other chicks which may be running or swimming together. The crowds of chicks are always accompanied by adults that lead them away from danger.

Many enemies
The main enemies of flamingos are the fish eagles that can pick the young flamingos out of the rafts and carry them off. Hyaenas, cheetahs and jackals also kill any stragglers they find. In Roman times flamingo tongues were a delicacy and flamingos are still eaten by local hunters. At one time they were prized for their plumage but now the main human menace to them is disturbance of the breeding colonies, especially by low flying aircraft.

How do they sit down?
While idly looking at the more grotesque animals at the zoo, one is often led to wonder how they carry out simple everyday functions. How, for instance, does a heron or a flamingo sit down on its nest? Strangely, this was long in dispute, perhaps because the ornithologists writing about flamingos had never seen them at their nests and could only theorise. In 1697 William Dampier thought that the flamingo leaned back on its nest as if sitting on a shooting-stick. Even a century ago there were still some strange ideas on this point. One was that it sat astride its nest, another that it sat with the legs sticking straight out behind. The correct answer is that it sits like any other bird. The legs are doubled up beneath it, the 'knees' (actually the ankles) hinge backwards, so the folded legs stick out behind the sitting bird.

class	**Aves**
order	**Ciconiiformes**
family	**Phoenicopteridae**
genera & species	***Phoenicopterus ruber*** *greater flamingo* ***Phoeniconaias minor*** *lesser flamingo* ***Phoenicoparrus jamesi*** *James' flamingo* ***P. andinus*** *Andean flamingo*

Greater flamingo (*Phoenicopterus ruber*)
Lesser flamingo (*Phoeniconaias minor*)
James' flamingo (*Phoenicoparrus jamesi*)
Andean flamingo (*P andinus*)

140

Mallard

Although there are many species of wild duck the mallard is the one that most people think of as the 'wild duck'. It is the ancestor of most of the domesticated ducks. It is about 2 ft long and weighs 2½ lb. The male, or drake, is brightly coloured from September to June. His belly and most of his back are grey. His head and neck are a dark glossy green and a white ring at the base of the neck separates the green from the brown of the breast. He has small curled feathers on the tail and his voice is a low hoarse call. The female, or duck, is a mottled brown, her voice is a loud quack and she has no curly tail feathers. From July to August the drake is in eclipse plumage, and is unable to fly. That is, he moults his colourful feathers at the end of June, is clothed in a mottling similar to that of the duck, and resumes his coloured plumage at the end of August. Both sexes have wing patches (specula), which are dark or purplish-blue with white edges.

Mallard breed in Europe and Asia from the Arctic Circle southwards to the Mediterranean, Iran, Tibet and Central China, and in northern and central North America. Throughout the range there is a movement south in autumn to Africa, southern Asia and, in America, to Mexico and Florida.

Make your own duck pond

Wild duck are attracted to any water: from a small pond in woodland to large lakes, to rivers, streams and marshes, although they often live on dry land well away from water. This habit is taken advantage of by wildfowlers and bird-lovers alike as they can be encouraged to breed quite easily by digging a pond with small islands or floating basket nests. Mallard spend much time on land even when water is available, but whether on water or on land, and apart from feeding, they do little more than stand or sit about, preening from time to time. Indeed, ducks spend a large part of their time simply doing nothing. On land they waddle apparently awkwardly; on water they swim easily and dive only when alarmed. In the air they fly with rapid wingbeats and with neck outstretched, taking off in a steep ascent.

Wide choice of food

Mallard feed by day or by night, mainly on leaves and seeds, grain, berries, acorns, as well as much small animal life such as insects and their larvae, worms, tadpoles, frogs' spawn, small frogs and small fishes. They dabble in mud on land and at the edge of water and upend in deeper water to feed from the mud at the bottom.

Ritual courtship

Mallard form pairs in autumn and begin breeding in spring. Pairing is preceded by a ritualized courtship. This is initiated by a duck swimming rapidly among a group of drakes with an action that has been called nod-swimming or coquette-swimming. She swims with the neck outstretched and just above water and head nodding. This makes the drakes come together in a tighter group and they begin their communal displays. These are made up of stereotyped actions known as mock drinking, false preening, shaking, grunt-whistling, head-up-tail-up and up-and-down movements. These same movements are seen more easily when the drake and duck are courting.

The duck chooses a drake, who follows her away from the group. She symbolically looks back by turning her head, inciting him to drive away other drakes that may be following. The 'inciting' has become ritualized and is carried out even if no other drakes are there. Mock drinking is a formalized gesture of peace and two drakes meeting head on will 'pretend' to drink. It is a sign they have no intention of attacking each other. In false preening a drake lifts one wing slightly, reaches behind it with his bill as if to preen. Instead, he rubs the bill over the heel of the wing making a rattling sound. In shaking the drake draws his head back between his shoulders so the white ring disappears. The feathers on the underside of the body are fluffed out, so the drake appears to ride high on the water. The head feathers are raised so the green sheen disappears and the head rises high so he is almost sitting on his tail on the water, and then he shakes his head up and down.

When a drake grunt-whistles he thrusts his bill almost vertically into the water then throws his head back, scattering a shower of water drops, and as he does this he grunts. Head-up-tail-up is fully descriptive of the

▽ *Tired of just dabbling in things, a pair of mallard take to deeper water. The male will lose his lovely plumage once the breeding season is over.*

next movement, and in the up-and-down movement the bill is quickly thrust into the water and jerked up again with the breast held low in the water. Another movement is known as gasping; one drake utters a low whistle and the rest give a kind of grunt.

These actions may be made in sequence by a group of drakes facing into the centre or by one or two drakes, or between drake and duck. Also, one or other may be seen as isolated actions. Together they form a ritual pattern of courtship carried out in the autumn but actual mating does not take place until spring. More remarkable, in spite of the complicated courtship, there is a high degree of promiscuity in mallard; a drake will mate with a duck while the drake with whom she is paired looks on.

High-diving ducklings

The nest, built by the duck, is a shallow saucer of grass, dry leaves and feathers lined with down. It may be on the ground, usually under cover of bushes or in a pollarded willow, in the disused nest of a large bird such as a crow, or in a hollow in a tree up to 40 ft from the ground. Up to 16, usually 10–12, greyish, green or greenish-buff eggs are laid, from March to October, incubated by the duck alone, for 22–28 days. When the ducklings have dried, soon after hatching, the duck calls them off the nest and leads them to water, or if far from water to a feeding ground. Sometimes the drake is in attendance but takes no part in the care of the ducklings. Even when the nest is 40 ft up in a hollow tree the ducklings leave the nest when the duck calls, each in turn tumbling to the ground without injury. The ducklings are covered with yellowish down broken with large patches of brown. They take nearly 2 months to fledge.

Mother is one enemy

The natural enemies of mallard are birds of prey and ground predators such as foxes. These probably have little effect on mallard populations. The main losses are at the duckling stage. A duck may hatch a brood of 12 and in a fortnight be left with only one duckling. Crows, rooks, magpies, rats and other ducks attack the ducklings. The duck herself may tread on one or more or sit on them in the water, drowning one or two. By contrast, the same duck may then lay a second clutch of 12 and rear all the ducklings to fledging.

Tongue acts as a piston

When a duck dabbles its bill in mud it is doing much the same as when a large whalebone whale opens its huge mouth and swims through a mass of krill. Both are using a highly efficient filter in which transverse plates on the inner edges of the duck's bill play the part of the baleen plates of the whale. As the duck dabbles its tongue acts as a piston sucking water or mud into the mouth and driving it out again. Only the edible particles are left behind on the transverse plates, but how the sorting out is done nobody knows. It used to be thought birds had no taste buds, the groups of cells on the tongue that give a sense of taste. Mallard have, however, 200 arranged in rows along the sides of the tongue. It may be these that tell the duck how to sort out edible from inedible particles.

class	**Aves**
order	**Anseriformes**
family	**Anatidae**
genus & species	***Anas platyrhynchos***

▽ *These obedient children always follow when their mother calls them to water very soon after they have dried out from hatching.*

Swan

The six species of swan are very closely related to the geese. Together they make up a tribe of the order Anseriformes separate from the various tribes of ducks. One possible exception is the Coscoroba swan of South America, which is the smallest swan and has a comparatively short neck; it is thought to be in some way related to the whistling or tree ducks.

The most familiar swan is the mute swan that originally bred in parts of Europe and Asia, but has been domesticated and introduced to many parts of the world such as North America and Australia where it has gone wild. It is thought that it was introduced to Britain by the Romans. The mute swan is 5 ft long and weighs about 35 lb. The plumage is all white and the bill is orange with a prominent black knob at the base. The Bewick's swan and the whooper swan are two other species that breed in Eurasia. Bewick's swan breeds in the tundra of northern Russia and Siberia and visits Europe in the winter. The whooper swan breeds farther south, including northern Scandinavia and Iceland, with a few pairs nesting sporadically in Scotland. Both have black bills with a yellow base, the pattern differing slightly between the two, and Bewick's swan is rather smaller than the whooper with a shorter neck. There are two swans in North America; the whistling swan has a black bill, sometimes with a yellow spot at the base, and is smaller than the trumpeter with a completely black bill. The whistling swan breeds mainly north of the Arctic Circle and migrates to the southern coast of the United States. The trumpeter used to breed over much of North America but is now confined to the northwest United States and southwest Canada where there are now about 1 500 individuals under protection. The only swans in the southern hemisphere, apart from the Coscoroba swan, are the black swan of Australia, and the black-necked swan of South America, from Brazil to Tierra del Fuego and the Falkland Islands. The black swan is all black but with white primary wing feathers, and a red bill. It has been introduced to New Zealand. The black-necked swan has a black head and neck, a white eyestripe and a red bill.

▽ *Mute swan takeoff. Their heavy bodies clear the water of the pond with difficulty.*

Not so mute

Compared with other swans the mute swan is quiet, but its name is a misnomer for it has a variety of calls. A flock of mute swans can be heard quietly grunting to each other as they swim along a river. When disturbed or in defence of the nest mute swans hiss violently. The sighing noise during flight is caused by the wings. The whooper swan has a bugle-like call when flying and a variety of quiet calls when grounded. Bewick's swan has a pleasant variety of honks and other sounds and the trumpeter is named after the trombone-like calls produced in the long, coiled windpipe. It is said that the swan-song, the legendary song of a dying swan, is based on a final slow expiration producing a wailing noise as it passes through the long windpipe.

A danger to cables

Despite their great weight swans are strong fliers. They have four times the wing loading (the body weight divided by the surface area of the wings) of a herring gull or crow and they have to beat their wings rapidly to remain airborne. A high wing loading makes take-off and landing difficult and swans require a long stretch of water over which they can run to gain flying speed or surge to a halt when landing. Swans are also unable to manoeuvre in flight and the chief cause of mortality in built-up parts of the world is collision with overhead cables.

Shallow water feeders

Swans feed mainly on plants but they also feed on water animals such as small fish, tadpoles, insects and molluscs. They often feed on land, grazing on grass like geese, but more often they feed on water plants, which they may collect from the bottom by lowering their long necks underwater, sometimes upending like ducks. This limits the swans' distribution to shallow water because they very rarely dive and are only occasionally seen on deep water.

Centuries-old colonies

Swans nest near water. Male mute swans set up territories, each defending a stretch of river from which they drive other males and young swans. Intruders are threatened

1 *Profile: head of a whooper swan.*
2 *Swan song? A black swan stretches up its neck and wails through its long windpipe.*
3 *Reflecting swan: the Coscoroba swan has features of both ducks and swans.*
4 *Black-necked swans guard their young.*
5 *A pair of Bewick's swans sit upright on the water while their young paddle around.*

△ *A pair of nesting mute swans, seen through the reeds, renovate their nest.*

by an aggressive display in which the neck is drawn back, the wings arched over the back and the swan propels itself in jerks with the webbed feet thrusting powerfully in unison, instead of alternately as in normal walking. There are a variety of displays between the male, the cob, and the female, the pen, involving tossing and swinging the head and dipping it into the water.

Mute swans mate for life and nest in the same territory each year, some violent fights taking place if a new pair tries to usurp the territory. The nest is a mass of water plants and twigs, roughly circular and cone-shaped with a depression in the centre. Wild mute swans nest among reeds on small islands in pools but semi-domesticated ones may nest in the banks of ponds in parks or in other inhabited places. Occasionally, mute swans nest in colonies rather than spaced out territories.

There are usually 5–7 eggs, sometimes twice as many, and they are incubated mainly by the female, the male taking over only when she leaves to feed. In the smaller swans incubation lasts 4 weeks, but it is 5 weeks in the larger species and $5\frac{1}{2}$ weeks in the black swan. While the last eggs are being brooded by the female the male takes the cygnets to the water. The family stays together until the cygnets fledge at 4–5 months. When young they swim together in a tight bunch with the female leading and rooting up plants for them to eat.

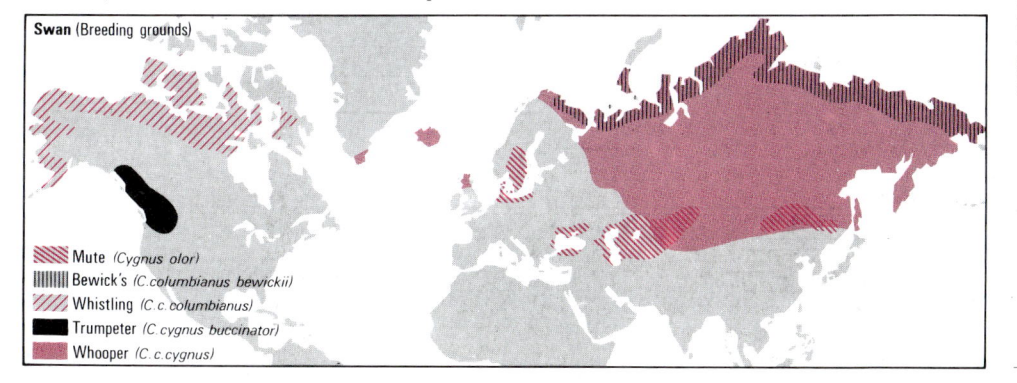

Swan (Breeding grounds)
- Mute (*Cygnus olor*)
- Bewick's (*C. columbianus bewickii*)
- Whistling (*C. columbianus*)
- Trumpeter (*C. cygnus buccinator*)
- Whooper (*C. c. cygnus*)

class	**Aves**
order	**Anseriformes**
family	**Anatidae**
genera & species	***Coscoroba coscoroba*** *Coscoroba swan* ***Cygnus atratus*** *black swan* ***C. columbianus bewickii*** *Bewick's swan* ***C. c. columbianus*** *whistling swan* ***C. cygnus buccinator*** *trumpeter swan* ***C. c. cygnus*** *whooper swan* ***C. melanocoryphus*** *black-necked swan* ***C. olor*** *mute swan*

Martial eagle

The martial eagle is the largest of the African eagles. Like many other eagles it bears a crest. It has long wings and a relatively short tail and in flight can be confused with only one other eagle, the serpent eagle. The upperparts are dark grey with light grey bars on wings and tail. The underparts, including the feather 'leggings', are white, barred and spotted with black. The bill is black and the legs and toes, which are armed with long curved talons, are blue-grey. The total wingspan may be as much as 8 ft. The females have larger spans than the males and are more powerfully built. They are easily distinguished, being more spotted on the underparts than the males.

The martial eagle lives in Africa from the southern borders of the Sahara to the Cape, but not in the thickly forested regions such as Zaire.

Shy eagle

A pair of martial eagles inhabits a range of as much as 50 sq miles, soaring over the countryside for hours at a time, often at great heights where they are almost invisible to the naked eye. Martial eagles are shy birds as compared with other eagles, and shun human settlements, which is to their advantage as they are often persecuted for taking farm stock. Because of persecution and their dislike of inhabited areas, martial eagles are much rarer than they once were. They are found in savannah, semi-desert and other

▷ *A martial eagle discourages intruders on its reptile repast – monitor lizard.*
▽ *A golden glower from Africa's largest eagle.*
▽▷ *Grounded: sub-adult martial eagle showing its white chest and abdomen.*

open country, and breed only in forested regions when there is open country nearby.

Swoops down on prey

Martial eagles spot their prey from a great height, swooping down on it in a well-controlled glide. The speed of the descent is regulated by the angle at which the wings are held over the back. When they are held almost horizontal the glide is shallow and the descent slow, but if the wings are raised in a 'V' they get less lift and the eagle drops at a steep angle.

They usually prey on small mammals and birds that live in the open, but the species vary from place to place. Their favourite foods seem to be game birds such as francolin, bustard and guinea fowl and mammals, like hyraxes. They will even eat impala calves. Jackals, snakes and lizards are sometimes taken but martial eagles rarely eat carrion. Domestic poultry, lambs and young goats are often eaten, but Leslie Brown, the authority on African eagles, has suggested that on the whole martial eagles are beneficial to man and that their destruction of livestock has been exaggerated.

Choice of nests

Martial eagles build large nests of sticks in tall trees, often on hillsides so there is a clear run-in to the nest. The female builds the nest, which may be 4 ft across and 4 ft deep, while the male collects sticks, or even small branches. The nests are used year after year and usually the female has to do no more than repair the nest and add a lining of fresh green leaves. Some pairs of martial eagles have two nests, each being used in alternate years.

Nest repair may take several weeks and when complete a single white or pale greenish-blue egg with brown markings is laid. The laying date varies between November in Sudan to July in South Africa. The female alone incubates and broods the chick when it hatches out after about 45 days. For about 2 months the male brings food to the female who then gives it to the chick. Later, the female also hunts for food for the chick. The chick makes its first flight when it is about 100 days old. For some days it returns to the nest to roost and thereafter it stays fairly near the nest. Young martial eagles have been seen near their parents' nest when 3 years old. Unlike the crowned eagle that breeds in alternate years, the martial eagle may breed several years in succession, then fail to do so for several years.

Separate interests

In the course of his remarkable studies on African eagles, Leslie Brown found a hill on which five, and in one year six, species of eagles nested. The hill was appropriately named 'Eagle Hill'. There seemed to be no reason for this gathering except a natural gregariousness; there was no special abundance of food and there were plenty of other suitable nesting places nearby.

While on 'Eagle Hill' the different species did not interfere or compete with each other. The martial eagles fed on game birds caught in open country whereas African hawk-eagles hunted those in bush country. Brown snake-eagles caught snakes. Verreaux's eagles ate hyraxes that they hunted among rocks; the crowned eagles preyed on duikers and monkeys in the forests and Ayres' hawk-eagles took small birds from the trees. So, although crowded, the eagles did not have to compete for food.

class	**Aves**
order	**Falconiformes**
family	**Accipitridae**
genus & species	***Polemaetus bellicosus***

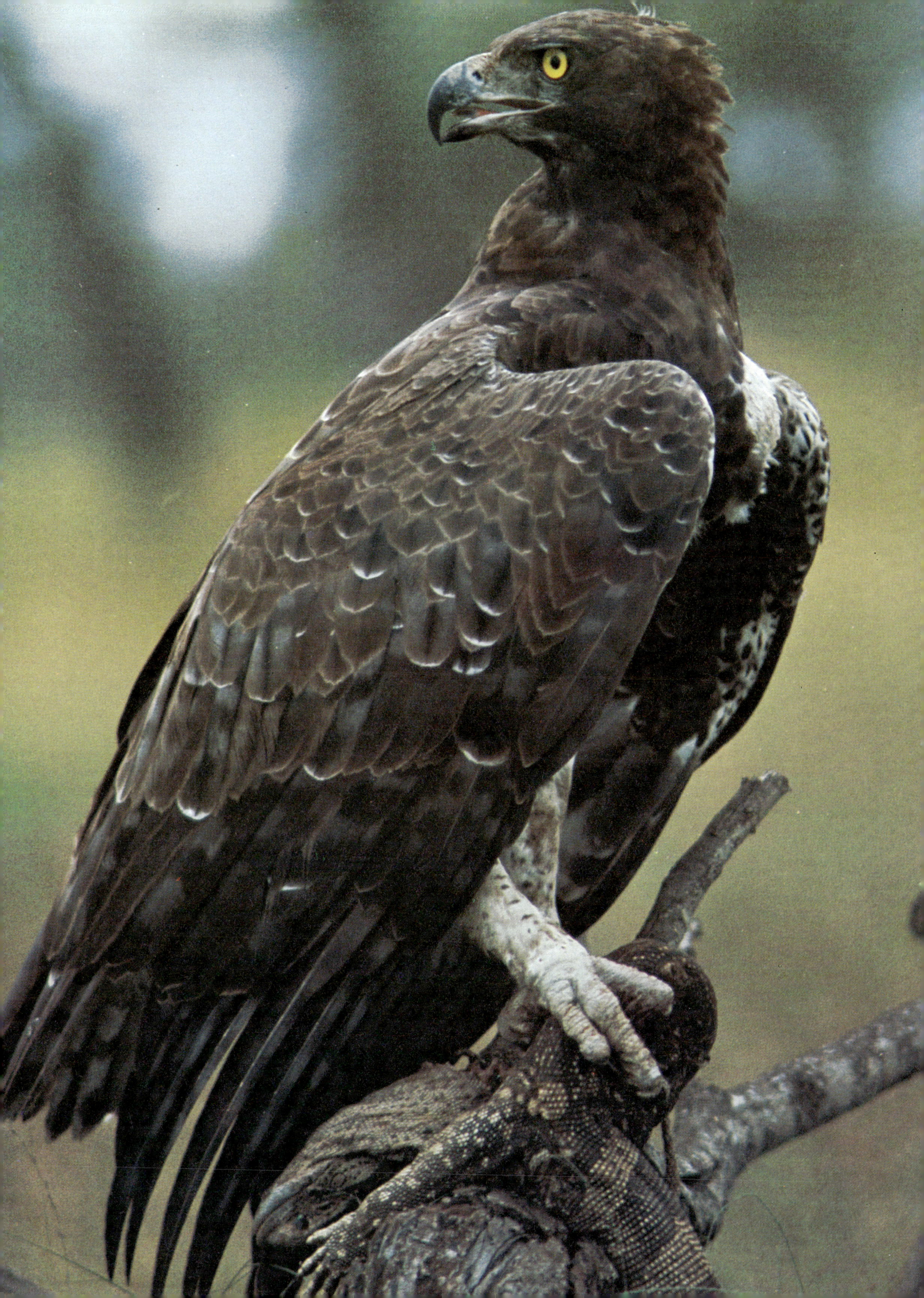

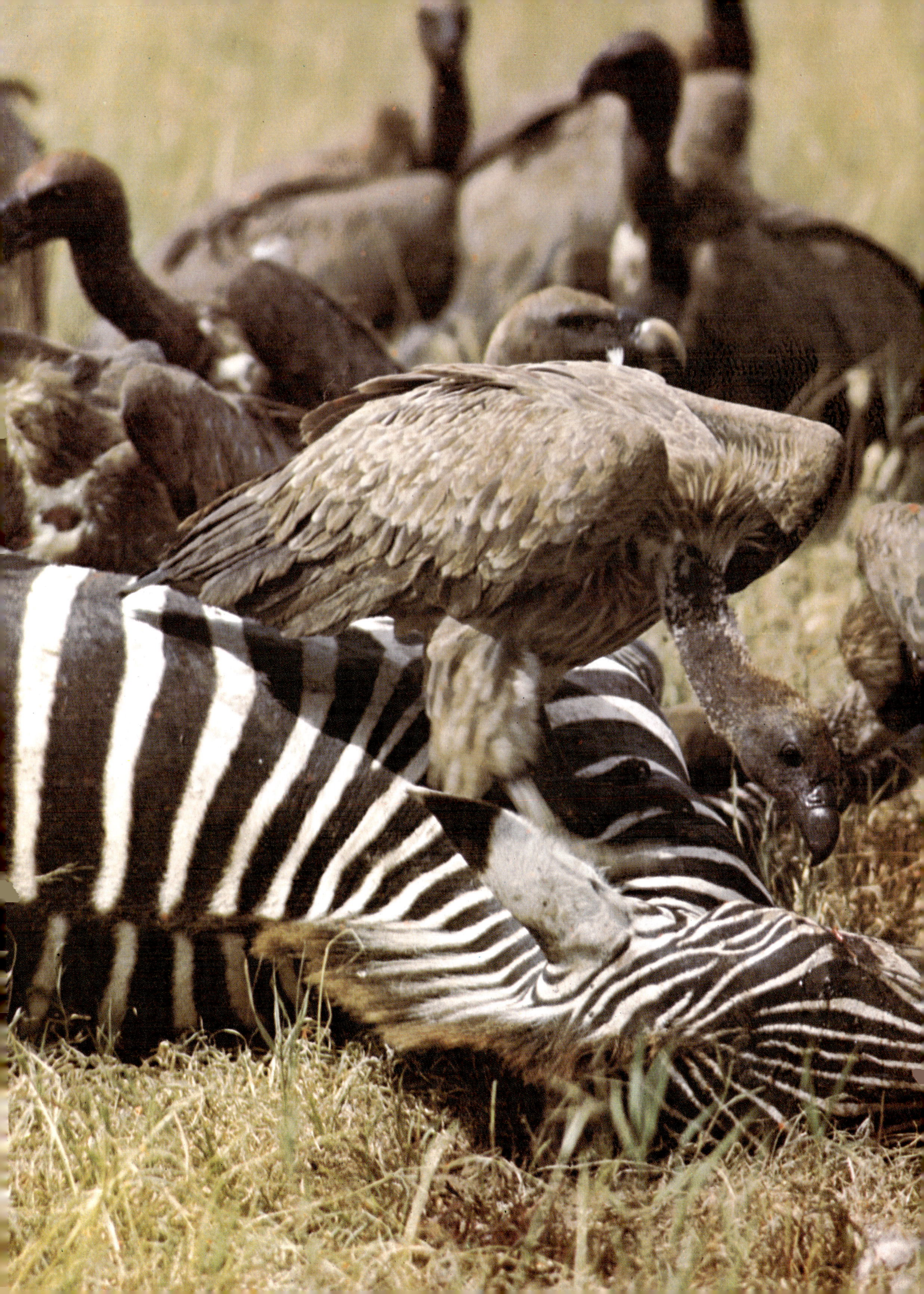

Vulture

The name 'vulture' was originally applied to only the large, scavenging birds of prey of the Old World, but after the discovery of America the term was extended to the condors, turkey vultures and other members of the New World family of birds of prey. They resemble the Old World vultures in appearance, presumably through convergent evolution, both groups having similar habits.

Vultures have naked or nearly naked heads, and sometimes naked necks, which is an asset to birds that regularly thrust their heads into carcases. Unlike other birds of prey, which kill their food, they have relatively weak feet which are adapted for running rather than holding prey. Both groups of vultures have heavy bodies but they soar effortlessly for hours on their long, broad wings.

There are 15 species of Old World vultures, with dark brown or black plumage, except in a few cases. The bare skin of the head and neck may, however, be orange, pink or white. The European black vulture is the largest bird in the Old World. It has a wingspan of over 8 ft and weighs over 15 lb. The plumage is almost wholly dark brown or black, with pale skin on the head and neck. It ranges from Spain to Korea and Japan. At the other end of the scale there is the lammergeier, or bearded vulture, and the Egyptian vulture. The latter has a wingspan of over 5 ft and is almost pure white except for black on the wings. The Egyptian vulture ranges through Africa, southern Europe, the Middle East and India. Only a little larger is the hooded vulture which is dark brown with a pinkish head and neck. It is very common in Africa south of the Sahara. The seven species of griffon and white-backed vultures are, perhaps, the 'typical' vultures. They are found throughout southern Europe, Africa and Asia, often in large groups, and they nest in colonies. They are medium-sized and have a ruff of long feathers around the naked neck. The remaining vultures are the palm-nut vulture, which has a feathered neck and black and white plumage, the white-headed vulture with blue at the base of the bill and the lappet-faced vulture. All of these live in Africa and have wattle-like folds of skin on the head and neck. There is also the Asian black vulture, which has a bright red head and neck.

◁ *Gregarious griffons. Cape vultures gorge on a common zebra carcase. Most vultures are not strong enough to rip the hide so have to wait for it to decompose.*

△ White-backed vultures: **Gyps africanus**.

Ripe food only
Vultures hunt by sight, detecting carrion from vast distances by watching the behaviour of other vultures and other carrion-eating animals. Large carcases may attract large flocks of vultures but despite their heavy bills most vultures have difficulty in breaking through the skins of large animals. Therefore they have to wait for the carcase to decompose or for another animal to attack it. The large vultures, such as the lappet-faced vulture, are powerful enough to rip through hide and, although solitary in habits, they take precedence over the gregarious griffon and white-backed vultures at a carcase. These, in turn, keep away the small vultures which have to be content with scraps.

The rasp-like tongues of vultures enable them to pull flesh into the mouth and their long necks allow them to probe deep into a large carcase, while the lack of feathers means that they have no problems about preening blood-stained feathers. Vultures do not feed on carrion exclusively, however. The largest vultures sometimes prey on the chicks of flamingos or on small rodents and the palm-nut vulture feeds on oil-palm nuts as well as shellfish from the seashore and sometimes hunts in shallow water for small fish.

Huge nests
Unlike the condors and many other birds of prey, the Old World vultures build their own nests instead of laying their eggs on the ground or in the abandoned nests of other birds. The lammergeier and the Egyptian vulture nest in caves or rock crevices, as do the griffon vultures which nest in colonies of over 100 on cliffs. The Indian griffon and the white-backed vultures often nest in trees, with up to a dozen nests in one large tree. The large vultures, the hooded vulture and the palm-nut vulture, nest singly in trees. The nests are huge cups of sticks and twigs lined with leaves, pieces of hide and refuse.

There is usually a single egg, two in smaller species, which is incubated by the female. Incubation ranges from 46 to 53 days, depending on the size of the vulture, and the chicks stay in the nest for up to 4½ months. The male feeds the female while she is incubating, then both parents feed the chicks by regurgitation.

Decreasing scavengers
Vulture numbers are decreasing wherever modern agricultural methods and methods of hygiene are being introduced; there are fewer carcases left lying about, and those that remain have often been poisoned. Although the vultures are not so useful nowadays as scavengers around human settlements they still help to clear up the carcases of stock, which are a potential source of infection. Unfortunately they are not always seen in this light and are persecuted for allegedly killing livestock, although only the largest vultures could possibly attempt to do so.

Riding the thermals
Vultures are most common in dry, open country where they can soar effortlessly in ascending air currents. They are also found in mountain country, up to 20 000 feet. Apart from supplying the air currents necessary for flight, these areas are also those where there is likely to be an abundance of carcases of large animals easily visible from the air. Vultures are rarely found in forests, except for the hooded vulture. This is the most widespread, although not the commonest vulture in Africa. It regularly scavenges around towns and villages, providing a valuable garbage disposal service, and even follows people as they till the soil, to feed on insects that are turned up. Because of its exploitation of man it is able to penetrate forests where there are human settlements.

To be able to soar at great heights, the heavy-bodied vultures make use of thermals, the 'bubbles' of hot air that rise from the ground as it heats up. A thermal is like a smoke-ring with a stream of air rising through the centre of the ring, which is spinning rapidly. The vultures glide around inside the ring, using the rising air to hold them aloft. This is the same principle as is used by glider pilots. The dependence of vultures on thermals is shown by their daily habits. They do not take off in the morning until the ground has warmed up and thermals begin to form. The lighter species of vulture take off before the heavier vultures, which need more lift.

Tool-users
There are very few animals that use tools – the Galapagos woodpecker finch, the chimpanzee and the sea otter are probably the best known examples – but in 1966 another was added to the list. This is the Egyptian vulture, which throws stones at eggs. The habit is so well developed in a population in Tanzania studied by Jane Goodall that it is surprising that there are no previous records. These vultures smash the tough shells of ostrich eggs either by throwing them against a rock or another egg, or by throwing a stone at them. If there is no stone nearby a vulture may search for one up to 50 yards away, fly back with it in its bill then sling it with a violent downward movement of the head. The action is repeated until the shell cracks. One vulture managed to throw a 2lb rock, and continued to do so for some time, no mean feat for a raven-sized bird.

class	**Aves**
order	**Falconiformes**
family	**Accipitridae**
genera & species	**Aegypius monachus** European black vulture **Gypohierax angolensis** palm-nut vulture **Gyps africanus** white-backed vulture **G. coprotheres** Cape vulture **G. indicus** Indian griffon **Necrosyrtes monachus** hooded vulture **Neophron percnopterus** Egyptian vulture **Sarcogyps calvus** Indian black vulture **Torgos tracheliotus** lappet-faced vulture **Trigonoceps occipitalis** white-headed vulture, others

Chicken

When we say somebody 'keeps chickens' in his backyard, we mean that the person owns domesticated fowls of the kind known scientifically as **Gallus gallus.** This is also the name of the red jungle fowl of southern and south west Asia, from the foothills of the Himalayas to Java. It is from this the domestic fowl is believed to have been bred, although some scientists believe that other wild fowl of the same region may have been involved, and they prefer to call the domestic fowl **Gallus domesticus.** The red jungle fowl lives in forests from sea level to 5 000 ft.

The cock of the wild fowl is mainly red and black, the black feathers having a greenish iridescence. The hen is russet and brown. The cock has a high arched tail, twin wattles on the throat and a saw-edge comb. The beak is short and strong, the legs powerful, the toes on each foot are armed with strong claws used in scratching the earth. Of the four toes one is directed backwards, set at a higher level than the rest and, in the cock, armed with a long spur. The wings are small and rounded, capable of strong but not sustained flight, consisting of bursts of wing beats alternating with glides. Their food is leaves, roots, bulbs, seeds and berries, earthworms and insects. The nest is on the ground. The chicks, able to run about soon after hatching, feed mainly on insects.

The cock's voice is a loud crowing, used to advertise his possession of a territory. He is polygamous and defends his territory if necessary by fighting with beak and spurs.

Early domestication

The date of domestication of the jungle fowl is uncertain. It may have been as early as 3 200 BC but had certainly taken place by 2 000 BC in India. There were domestic chickens in China by 1 400 BC as well as in Egypt and Crete, and they reached southeastern Europe by 700 BC.

The evidence from archaeological relics, such as pottery, figurines, coins and mosaics, suggests that the birds were kept primarily for religious and sacrificial purposes, as well as for the sport of cockfighting. They were later valued for their egg-laying. According to Aristophanes (about 400 BC) every Athenian, even the poorest, kept his hen for laying eggs. The Greeks also invented the capon, or castrated cock, for fattening, but the eating of chicken flesh was the least of the economic uses until the 19th century. Another use for the bird was as an 'alarm clock' for the farmer.

From Ancient Greece to Ancient Rome was but a short step, and with the Roman conquest of much of Europe the domestic chicken was taken farther afield, although it seems also to have been taken along the trade routes in advance of the Roman legions. The Celts of northern Europe, for example, had it before Caesar invaded Britain.

▽ *Barnyard family. Cockerels are polygamous and defend their territories, if necessary, by fighting with beak and spurs. There are more than 100 breeds or varieties of chickens, but the number kept for egg or meat production is limited. Modern farming is so specialised that hens are now rarely found scratching around for a living. They tend to be kept in large flocks under standard conditions by poultry farmers only, either in deep litter houses or in batteries of cages. Separate units are maintained with some breeds kept as table birds and others as layers.*

Ornamental and commercial breeds

The modern breeds are divided into Mediterranean and Asiatic types. Of the former there are now 37 breeds used commercially, as well as 24 ornamental breeds. In addition to show birds and fighting cockerels, the breeds tend to be grouped into prolific layers and table birds. The names of some are almost household words: the white leghorn, the best egg-layer, closely followed by the Rhode Island red and the Plymouth. Among the ornamental breeds the most spectacular is the long-tailed Yokohama, bred for the long tail, which in the cock may reach 20 ft.

The peck order

In the scientific field chickens have been responsible for one of the biggest advances in our knowledge of animal behaviour. In 1922 the idea of a peck order was first published. It was discovered by observation of the common or farmyard domestic hen. Briefly, it amounts to this: if a dozen hens new to each other are put into an enclosure, they will separate into couples and start to fight. One of each couple will triumph over the other, either because she is stronger than her opponent or because her opponent refuses to fight. She will be dominant, the other will be subordinate.

Then the dominants will face each other in couples, from which half will emerge once more as dominants, the other half as subordinates. In the end a hierarchy will have been established which can be expressed as follows. If we identify the hens by the letters A to L there will be the boss hen (A) which can peck all the others and they will not peck back. The next in succession (B) will be able to peck all except A, C can peck D–L, but not A and B, and so it will go down the line, until the lowest in the hierarchy (L) will be subordinate to all the rest, the one which gets pecked by all the others.

Any hen can change her position in the hierarchy by winning a fight with a superior hen, but without such a challenge the positions in the hierarchy are accepted by all.

This is a simplified version but the principle is there, and subsequent research in a large number of animal species has confirmed it. In most animal communities (including our own) there is a social order of dominance and subordinance, among males as well as females. It is generally referred to as a peck order, because the first discovery was with domestic hens. And the discovery has revolutionized our study of the social behaviour of animals as well as human beings.

Chicken fortune tellers

The behaviour of chickens in their peck order has become almost a symbol in the philosophy of the modern scientist. Chickens have served as symbols in other ways in earlier civilizations. Hens were symbols of fertility, because of their egg-laying, and this was later transferred to the cock, largely from the elaborate display he uses in wooing the hen. He became an erotic symbol as well as a symbol of health.

The Romans went further and used chickens for prophecy, the *oraculum ex tripudio*. Hens were put in a cage with food. If they ate greedily, the omens were good. Should they show little taste for food, the omens were unfavourable. The method was open to abuse. One had only to starve the hens beforehand to obtain a good omen.

In the first Punic War a consul, angry with his hens because they refused to eat when he needed a good omen, cast them into the sea saying: 'Let them drink if they won't eat.' He was subsequently defeated in a battle at sea, a fate which the people of Rome attributed to his lack of respect for the hens.

△△ *Wild relative – the jungle fowl, which lives in forests from sea level to 5 000 feet. It is characterised by the iridescence of its feathers.*

△ *One of the more exotic breeds: the long-tailed Yokohama. Many varieties have been specially bred for their attractive plumage patterns.*

class	**Aves**
order	**Galliformes**
family	**Phasianidae**
genus & species	***Gallus gallus***

Sunbittern

The sunbittern is a large and little-known inhabitant of tropical American forests. It is related to the coots, cranes and bustards rather than the true bitterns of the heron family. It is, however, heron-like in appearance, about 18 in. long, with a long slender neck, small head and long bill. The bright orange legs are also long and slender and the toes are unwebbed. The wings and tail are broad. The plumage is soft like that of an owl and is mainly brown and grey with black bars and spots. The crown of the head is black and two white streaks run across the face. There are two broad black bands across the tail. The bill is black on the upper mandible, yellow on the lower. When a sunbittern opens its wings a pattern of chestnut and orange becomes visible on the back with white and black patches on the wings.

Sunbitterns are found from southern Mexico to Bolivia and central Brazil.

Sunset display

Sunbitterns, like herons, live singly or in pairs along the banks of rivers or in swampy woodland and wade slowly through the shallows in search of food. Captive sunbitterns have been described as standing with their bodies swaying from side to side in the same manner as bitterns, reputedly to make them less conspicuous among the waving reeds. They also spend a considerable time motionless with the neck withdrawn as herons do. Sunbitterns are reluctant to fly preferring to walk and to swim across streams. When disturbed, however, they fly into trees. Their flight is very quiet, presumably because of the soft plumage, and their broad wings give them the appearance of gigantic fluttering moths. Sunbitterns are usually silent but sometimes they utter quiet whistles or rattles.

The display of the sunbittern is most spectacular. The forepart of the body is lowered while the head is raised and the wings are spread with the rear edges raised and the tail fanned and brought up, so that the whole of the beautifully patterned plumage is displayed in a semi-circle. The bright chestnut and orange of the back and wings have been described by Alexander Skutch as looking like 'a sun darkly glowing in a sunset-tinted sky'. During the display a harsh rattle is given. This display is used during courtship and also as a threat.

Sunbitterns feed on insects, crustaceans, small fish and other small animals found in shallow water along the banks. Their feeding behaviour is very much like that of herons; they stalk slowly or stand motionless then suddenly shoot out their necks and grab their prey in the dagger-like bill.

Nests rarely seen

Very few sunbittern nests have been found in the wild. Alexander Skutch describes one which consisted of a 12in. mass of decaying leaves, twigs, moss and mud, lined with green

△ *Out on a limb: an unusual photograph of a brooding sunbittern on its nest of moss and mud.*

leaves and perched on a 2in. branch. A tree is the usual place for a sunbittern to build its nest but they may build on the ground.

The first record of the nesting behaviour of the sunbittern was the description given of a pair that nested in London Zoo in 1865, and a century later it is still the most detailed account, although sunbitterns have since nested in other zoos. The pair built their nest of straw, grass, mud and clay on a specially provided platform, 10 ft up. The first egg was found broken under the nest but a second was laid shortly afterwards and was incubated by both parents for 27 days. The chick was like that of a snipe and was fed by both parents on food carried in their bills until its wing feathers had grown enough for it to fly to the ground, at the age of 21 days. The parents continued to feed it and 2 months after it had hatched another egg was laid and incubated mainly by the male while the female continued to feed the original chick. In the wild the normal clutch seems to be 2 eggs.

Mixed crowd

The order Gruiformes, to which the sunbittern belongs, contains some unusual birds. There is the large family of rails, some of which are flightless, the buttonquails in which the female plays the leading role in courtship, the mesites of Madagascar which are probably flightless, the cranes, finfoots and the bustards. Some of the Gruiformes resemble birds outside the order, such as the stork-like kagu, the ibis-like limpkin and the heron-like sunbittern. Despite a variety of external form and habit the gruiform birds have many similarities in the form of their skeletons and muscles. One habit which is, however, very common in the group is that of nesting on the ground and producing chicks that can walk soon after hatching. The sunbittern is an exception because it nests in trees and although its chicks are hatched with a coat of down and appear well-developed, they are fed in the nest for some time.

class	**Aves**
order	**Gruiformes**
family	**Eurypygidae**
genus & species	***Eurypyga helias***

Oystercatcher

The oystercatchers are large waders that are found in many parts of the world. Some species have black and white plumage, hence the old name of 'sea-pie' but others are all black. The most widespread oystercatcher **Haematopus ostralagus** *is found in Europe, the Canaries, South Africa, Asia, Australia, New Zealand and North and South America. It is largely black above with white underparts and has a long red bill and pink legs. Another pied oystercatcher is the American oystercatcher* **H. palliatus** *that ranges from New Jersey and California to Argentina and Chile, while a third* **H. leucopodus** *lives in southern South America. The sooty oystercatcher* **H. fuliginosus** *lives on the coast of Australia and other black oystercatchers* **H. bachmani** *and* **H. ater** *live in western North America, southern South America and Australia. In some places the common oystercatcher is all black, as in the Canaries, Africa and America.*

Moving inland

Oystercatchers are usually seen on rocky shores or sandy beaches, on mudflats, or in sand dune areas just behind the shore but they sometimes breed inland. They have nested inland in Scotland for centuries and they are now breeding inland in northern England. In New Zealand, oystercatchers are found by the snow rivers of South Island. Outside the breeding season oystercatchers gather in large flocks, and those that breed in high latitudes migrate to warmer regions in the winter. The Burry Inlet in South Wales, for instance, is the winter home of oystercatchers from Scotland, Iceland, the Faeroes and Norway.

The pied plumage and red bill of the oystercatcher are unmistakable, yet, surprisingly, they are sometimes difficult to see if they are motionless. They often give away their presence by their loud shrill calls of 'kleep-kleep' or a shorter, rapid 'kic-kic'. Oystercatchers are wary and run rapidly or take flight when approached.

Musselcatchers

It is difficult to see how the oystercatcher got its name. The authoritative *Handbook of British Birds* does not include oysters in the diet of the oystercatcher, and it would be surprising if it did because oysters live below the lowtide mark and oystercatchers feed between the tides or on land. A better name would be the old local name of musselpecker. Mussels, together with limpets, cockles, winkles, crabs and worms, make up a large part of the oystercatchers' diet. Cockles and worms are found by probing the sand with their bills. They also eat insects, especially their larvae, some plant food and occasionally eggs of other birds. The composition of the diet depends on the animal life living in the oystercatchers' habitat; whether sandy or rocky shores, farmland and so on.

The methods by which oystercatchers eat molluscs that are protected by strong shells, have been studied in detail. Limpets are dealt a sharp blow with the tip of the bill. Small ones are dislodged and large ones are shifted so they can be levered off or holed. The oystercatcher can then insert its bill and tear the strong muscles that hold the limpet down. Two different ways are used for opening bivalve molluscs such as mussels and cockles. If the shellfish is covered with water and its valves, or shells, are agape, the oystercatcher stabs downward then levers and twists to sever the adductor muscle that closes the valves. These fall open and the flesh is rapidly pecked out. If the shellfish are exposed to the air and firmly closed the oystercatcher has to smash its way in. Examination of mussel shells that were the remains of oystercatcher meals, shows that they are regularly smashed on the bottom edge and tests have shown that this side of the shell is much weaker than the top edge even in large mussels. The oystercatcher carries a mussel or cockle to a patch of firm sand, places it with its ventral margin upwards, and starts to hammer it. If the shell falls over it is righted or if it sinks it is carried to a firmer patch. On average, five blows of the bill are needed to penetrate a mussel shell and the bill is then inserted to cut the adductor muscle and prise the two halves apart. Cockle shells are not attacked in any particular position as their shells are weaker than those of mussels. Small crabs are flipped onto their backs and killed with a stab through the brain. The shell is then prised off and the flesh cut out with the same scissoring movements that are used for eating other shellfish.

In some places, such as the Burry Inlet

Posed on a cliff top beside a clump of thrift before flying down to feed at the mussel beds between the tide lines below. The strong red bill for prising open mussels and the thick red legs add flashes of colour to the oystercatcher's stark black and white plumage.

S. African black oystercatcher **Haematopus moquini**.

in Britain, oystercatchers are considered a pest because of the damage they do to the cockle beds. Each oystercatcher eats about one cockle every minute and consumes on average 336 cockles per tide. As flocks number several thousands, they eat many millions of cockles each winter; but oystercatchers are only one of several enemies of cockles and it is debatable whether they seriously affect the cockle industry. In the Faeroes, they are considered beneficial as most of their food is insects and other invertebrates in grassland.

Piping display

Oystercatchers arrive at their breeding grounds in flocks but then split up into pairs. Each pair forms a territory which it defends against the other oystercatchers. Among their several displays there is the quite spectacular piping display in which a group of birds, or sometimes just a pair, run rapidly to and fro with necks outstretched and open bills pointing at the ground. At the same time they utter a piping call that varies from a clear 'kleep-kleep' to a quavering trill.

The nest is a shallow depression in shingle, sand or turf, sometimes with no lining but at other times lined with stones, shells, or dead plants. There are usually three eggs, yellowish or light brown with spots or streaks of dark brown. Both parents incubate the eggs which hatch in 24–27 days. The chicks leave the nest after a day or two and are fed by both parents. They fly in about 5 weeks and are fed by their parents for another 5 weeks.

Family traits

The careful study of the way oystercatchers open mussels was made by M Norton-Griffiths of Oxford University. He found that some oystercatchers regularly stabbed open mussels while others hammered the shells. Furthermore, young oystercatchers developed the same feeding habits as their parents. This is, perhaps, not so surprising as the chicks were learning to feed on only those animals which their parents brought to them. First the chicks practise pecking empty shells and picking up pieces of flesh left in them, learning the scissoring movements of the adults. Later they take opened shellfish from their parents and remove the flesh by themselves. Eventually they open the shells themselves, starting on small ones and graduating to large ones as they become more proficient. Norton-Griffiths never saw a 'crab-eating' chick attack a mussel and when a 'mussel-eating' chick found a crab it was frightened of it. The differences in feeding habits are so marked that a population of oystercatchers is distinctly divided by them and 'mussel-eaters' mate only with 'mussel-eaters' and 'cockle-eaters' with 'cockle-eaters'.

class	**Aves**
order	**Charadriiformes**
family	**Haematopodidae**
genus & species	***Haematopus ostralagus*** *oystercatcher, others*

Puffin

The puffin, a small auk about 12 in. long, with a massive, brilliantly coloured and decidedly bizarre bill, is perhaps the most popular and well known of sea birds. The comical effect of the bill is enhanced by coloured horny patches above and below the eyes. The plumage is basically the same as that of other auks; black above and white underneath, with the black extending around the neck as a collar. The legs are bright orange and the sides of the face ashy grey. The triangular bill has red, yellow and blue stripes with a thick yellow skin in the corners of the mouth. Outside the breeding season the basal part of the horny covering of the bill, including the blue parts and the yellow skin, are shed, leaving the base of the bill narrower and horn-coloured. At the same time the red tip becomes yellow. The bill of young puffins is more conventional, narrower and plainly coloured, the inner half greyish brown, the outer half reddish brown.

   The puffin breeds along the coasts of the North Atlantic from Greenland to the Gulf of the St Lawrence in the west and from Spitzbergen and Novaya Zemlya to the British Isles and northern France in the east. Some spread as far south as the Canaries and into the Mediterranean as far as the Adriatic. British puffins have been found wintering in American waters but not all puffins migrate away from their breeding places. Puffins regularly spend the winter in Baffin Bay and in mild winters they stay near Amsterdam Island, north of Spitzbergen, despite the low temperatures and continual darkness of the Arctic winter. The horned puffin, which lives in the North Pacific and is a close relative of the Atlantic puffin, has fleshy growths over the eyes and differs in the colouring of the bill. It breeds on either side of the Bering Sea. Another Pacific puffin is the tufted puffin, all black but for a white face and long tufted feathers sprouting from above the eyes. The bill is red and green.

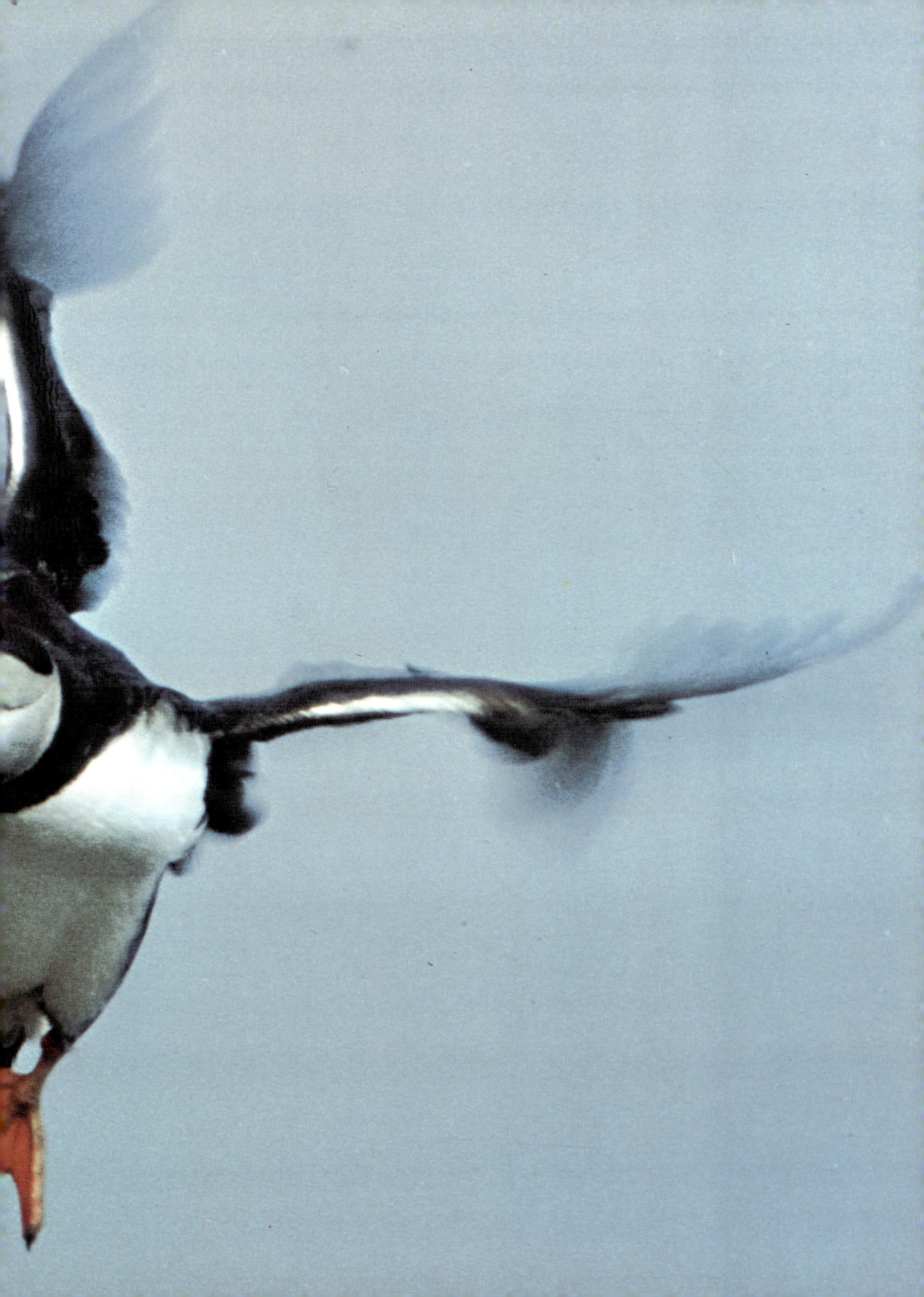

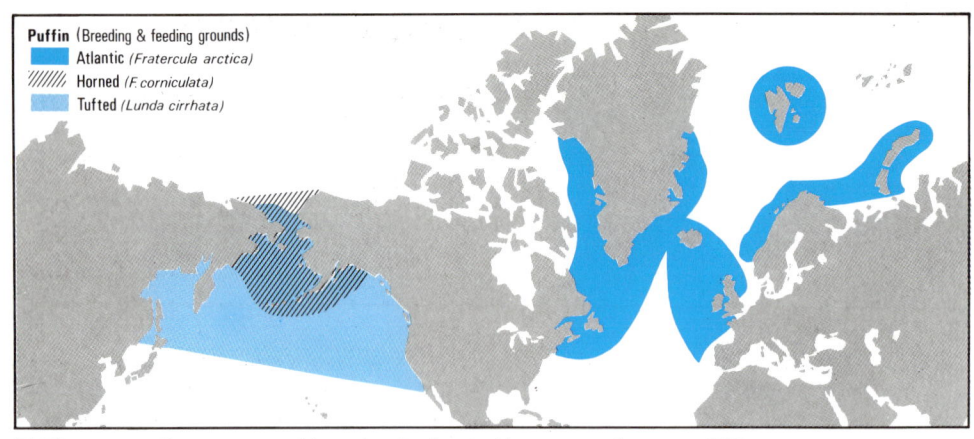

▽ *These two puffins are engaged in a ritualised courtship ceremony known as billing.*

Cliff nester
From spring until the end of the breeding season puffins contribute to the masses of auks that fly continually to and from the nesting cliffs. Instead of shuffling on their haunches like other auks such as the guillemots, puffins walk quite easily with a waddling gait. When they take off from the cliffs their wings appear to be too small to support them and they plunge steeply until their rapidly whirring wings become effective. When cornering in flight or coming in to land the orange feet are spread out to help in steering or braking.

Mysterious fish stackers
Puffins feed on small fish, such as sand eels and cod fry, together with crustaceans, floating molluscs and other planktonic animals. Outside the breeding season they go far out to sea, usually out of sight of land. Food is caught by diving, the puffins swimming underwater with their wings. If puffins have chicks to feed they carry their catch back in the bill. Puffins are quite tame on their breeding cliffs and can be watched from close quarters landing with fish draped crossways in the bill. They can carry up to 30 fish in this way, but this is exceptional. How they arrange the fish in the bill is still a mystery. Presumably each fish is killed by a nip with the bill but how it is then placed alongside ones caught previously without dropping them is difficult to visualize. The tongue and the serrated floor of the upper mandible may be used to manoeuvre and hold them. Pictures of puffins with fish arranged in the bill head-to-head or alternating head-to-tail are based on either imagination or coincidence. Working the fish into a pattern would be very difficult and would serve no useful purpose.

Slow development
When puffins arrive at the breeding ground they start digging burrows or clearing out old ones. They dig with their heavy bills and scrape the loosened soil out with their feet. In large colonies burrowing can be so extensive as to cause a landslide. Sometimes they take over shearwater or rabbit burrows.

Puffins arrive at the breeding grounds already paired but there is a considerable amount of displaying around the burrows. The large colourful bill is used as a signal, being thrust forward in threat or shaken in appeasement. Mating takes place on the water after the male has chased the female.

A single egg, white with faint markings, is incubated for 40–43 days. The parents share the task, but at intervals they leave the egg and parade together outside the burrow. The chick is fed on fish by both parents, but when 6 weeks old it is deserted by the parents who go out to sea to moult, during which time they become flightless. The chick stays in the burrow for another week then flutters down from the cliffs and paddles out to sea. The young puffins leave the burrows at night when there is less danger from gulls and skuas. Until they can fly they avoid danger by diving. Seven weeks is a very long fledging period for an auk, but puffins are reared in the safety of a burrow, whereas guillemots, razorbills and other auks breed on cliff ledges where their chicks are vulnerable to predation by gulls. These auks also leave the nest before they can fly, but unlike puffins are not independent and remain in the care of the adults.

Rat and oil problems
A certain number of puffins fall prey to gulls and skuas; on the island of Foula in the Shetlands, for instance, the cliffs are sometimes littered with the remains of puffins eaten by skuas, but their numbers are more severely reduced when rats are introduced to their breeding grounds. At one time the puffin population of Ailsa Craig was described as phenomenal, but in 1889, rats got ashore from a wreck and the population has since declined almost to extinction. A similar decrease has also occurred on Lundy, the name of this island being Norse for Puffin Island.

Recently there has been another threat to puffins, and other auks. Oil pollution is particularly serious to auks, because of their gregariousness and their habit of diving out of trouble and resurfacing in the oil patch. They are also particularly vulnerable when flightless during the moult.

Cliff crop
Man is another predator of puffins. The islanders of Faeroe, Shetland, St Kilda and other places have for a long time relied on sea birds for food, although the practice has declined in recent years. On St Kilda where sea birds formed the mainstay of the islanders, more puffins were killed than any other bird, including gannets and fulmars. They were the main food during the summer, eaten roasted, and their feathers were collected and sold. Catching puffins was usually the women's work, assisted by dogs who helped locate nests. They were hauled out of their burrows, snared or caught in nets as they flew in. On Foula, the sheer cliffs where many of the puffins nested were divided so that each man had a section where he could hazardously collect his crop.

class	**Aves**
order	**Charadriiformes**
family	**Alcidae**
genera & species	***Fratercula arctica*** *Atlantic puffin* **F. corniculata** *horned puffin* **Lunda cirrhata** *tufted puffin*

Wood pigeon

From being a harmless rarity up to the end of the 18th century, the wood pigeon, or ring dove, has become one of the most common and most destructive pests of agricultural land, especially in certain parts of Europe. It is a handsome, rather heavily built bird, about 16 in. long with a wing span of about 18 in. The upper parts are bluish-grey with darker grey on the upper wings and black on the upper tail and wing quills. The breast is vinous shading to pale grey or lavender on the belly, flanks and under the tail. The rump and head are a bluer grey than the rest and the sides of the neck are a metallic purple and green. The base of the bill is pink, the rest yellow shading to pale brown on the tip. The base of the bill expands into a soft fleshy lump over the nostrils. The legs and feet are pink with a mauve tinge. The straw colour of the eye and its unusual pear-shaped iris give the bird a very alert expression. The wood pigeon can always be distinguished from other doves by the white patch on the sides of the neck, which is absent in young birds, and the broad white band across the wing. The male and female are alike except that the males tend to be slightly larger and their plumage brighter.

The typical race of the wood pigeon is found throughout Europe, except in the extreme north. It ranges eastwards to Russia and in the south extends to the north coast of the Mediterranean and to the various Mediterranean islands from the Balearics to Cyprus, and around the Black Sea. It is replaced by allied races in northwest Africa, the Azores, Madeira, Turkestan and Transcaspia to Iran, Baluchistan, Kashmir and Sikkim.

Wary in the country

The wood pigeon is primarily a bird of the woods but since the spread of agriculture it has taken to feeding on cultivated land. It is also a familiar bird in town parks and suburban gardens and is often found on downs and on coasts, some way from woods.

From autumn to spring and sometimes also in summer it congregates in large flocks to feed, although single birds and small groups may also be seen. In the towns and parks it may become quite tame but in the open country it is wary of humans and will

△ *Just beginning to lose their sparse yellow down, a pair of large young wood pigeons wait for the arrival of one or other of their parents with some food. After their first three days, when they are fed with pigeon's milk, their main diet is ripe cereal grain.*
◁ *One of the greatest enemies of farmers in Europe, the gentle-looking wood pigeon is easily distinguishable from other doves by the white patch on the sides of its neck. In order to reduce their numbers, the most effective method has proved to be nest destruction.*

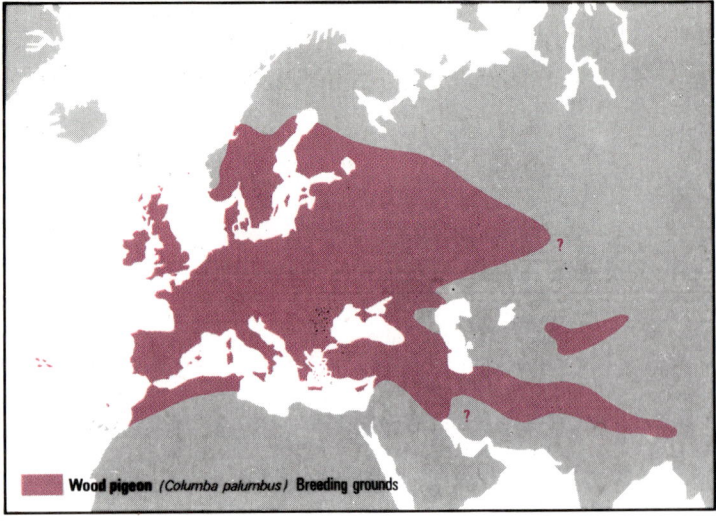

△ *Two greedy young wood pigeons eagerly reach out of the nest trying to get more food from their ever-patient parent.*

take off with a loud clatter of wings at the slightest disturbance. Its normal flight is fast and strong with quick regular wingbeats and occasional glides. On the ground it struts about, restlessly moving its head to and fro. It roosts in trees, sometimes in large numbers.

The wood pigeon's voice, which is heard at all times of the year but more frequently in March and April, is often said to be a series of coos but the phrase 'two coos, Taffy take' repeated several times gives a better idea. The alarm note is a short, sharp 'roo' sound.

Agricultural menace
Originally the wood pigeon fed on acorns and beech mast as well as seeds, nuts, berries and the young leaves of many trees. Since the spread of agriculture and the disappearance of many woods it has turned, to a large extent, in many areas to cultivated crops and found them just as palatable and in greater abundance. Cereal grains are the most important food for both adults and young in late summer and autumn and in some areas peas and beans are taken in large quantities. In winter the birds depend mainly on clover, turnip tops and young greens. The pronounced hook at the end of the bill makes it easy for the pigeon to tear off the leaves of these plants. Some animal food is taken including caterpillars, earthworms, slugs, snails and insects.

The wood pigeon needs quite a large quantity of water and drinks greedily, not in sips like most other birds.

Billing and cooing
The courtship of a pair of wood pigeons begins while they are still in flocks. A pair separate from the main body and on the ground or a perch in a tree they bow to each other, their breasts touching the ground or perch, with their tails raised and spread, all the time cooing to each other. This bowing and cooing is often interrupted by a nuptial display flight in which the bird rises steeply with strong wingbeats then glides down and rises again with stiff set wings in an undulating course. At the top of its rising flight it usually makes several claps with its wings, caused by a strong downbeat of the wings and not, as so often supposed, by the wings clapping together. Also at this time pairs of birds start to establish territories in the trees, the males driving away any intruders with aggressive posturing or actual attacks.

Young fed on milk
The breeding season is long, usually from April to September, but there are records of nests in every month of the year for the southern parts of the wood pigeon's range. The peak of breeding activity seems to be July, August and September in the British Isles when there is plenty of ripe corn for feeding the young. There are usually three broods a year. The nest is built in almost any kind of tree or in tall hedgerows, sometimes on top of the old nest of crows or sparrowhawks or on a squirrel's drey. Very occasionally it is built close to the ground or on ledges of rocks. In towns, buildings are used. The nest is a flimsy structure of intertwined sticks, often used for several years in succession. The male brings the material but only the female builds. Usually two, occasionally one or three, white, fairly glossy eggs are laid and are incubated for about 18 days, by both parents.

When the young birds hatch they are covered in sparse yellow down and for the first three days are fed at frequent intervals on a fluid from the parents' crops known as 'pigeon's milk'. After this, ripe cereal grain is the main food with some green food and weed seeds supplemented with animal foods. They stay in the nest for about 22 days, and afterwards are still fed by one or both parents for at least another week.

The average age attained by a wood pigeon in the wild in the British Isles is only 38 months but the oldest one recorded was in its 14th year.

Large numbers shot
Apart from man the adult wood pigeon has few enemies, but many of their eggs are taken by jays and magpies. The losses among young birds are due mainly to starvation, especially when they leave the nests and compete for food with the adult birds. In really severe winters the mortality among wood pigeons is very high but their numbers soon seem to increase again.

Owing to the widespread destruction of crops by wood pigeons a great deal of research has been done into methods of keeping down their numbers. Shooting the birds is still the most widely used method although some sportsmen contend that wood pigeons are difficult to shoot as the shot glances off their feathers. There is no evidence to show that widescale shooting makes any impression on their numbers.

Migrant or not?
The subject of migration of wood pigeons to and from the British Isles has provided a constant source of argument amongst countrymen, sportsmen and bird-watchers for many years. Apparently the wood pigeons in the British Isles are mainly sedentary but with a tendency to move south in the winter. Only a small proportion of the population undertakes long flights and these are usually young birds. There is probably a latent urge, inherited from migratory ancestors, which shows itself in only a few individuals. The only birds recovered abroad reached no farther than France. In continental Europe the migratory behaviour is rather different. Wood pigeons in Scandinavia and the Baltic are forced to migrate south in winter to escape the snow and some of these do arrive on the east coast of Britain, but the numbers vary considerably from year to year. Observers have told of hordes of wood pigeons arriving from the Continent and although large numbers may arrive in some years, confusion very often arises because of the flocks of wood pigeons that seem to fly out to sea from the British Isles and then fly back again!

class	**Aves**
order	**Columbiformes**
family	**Columbidae**
genus & species	***Columba palumbus***

Macaw

The 18 species of macaw include the largest and most colourful members of the parrot family. They live in tropical America, from southern Mexico through Central America to Paraguay. They have large beaks, the upper mandible being long and strongly hooked. The skin on the cheeks and around the eyes is naked except for a scattering of very small feathers.

The largest is the scarlet or red and blue macaw, of Mexico to Bolivia, 3 ft long, of which 2 ft is tail. It is mainly scarlet except for the yellow wing coverts and the blue of the flight feathers, the lower back feathers and outer tail feathers. The blue and yellow macaw, ranging from Panama to Paraguay, is only slightly smaller. It is a rich blue on the crown, nape, back, wings and upperside of tail, golden yellow on the underside, including the underside of the tail. There is a large black patch on the throat, the bill is black and the white sides of the face are marked with black wavy lines. The military or great green macaw, 30 in. long and ranging from Mexico to Brazil, is green, shading to blue on flight feathers, rump and tail coverts, with a crimson band on the forehead and red on the upperside of the tail. Less gaudy but probably more beautiful, certainly more prized by fanciers, is the hyacinthine macaw, 34 in. long, a cobalt blue throughout its plumage. Its range is limited to the interior jungles of the Amazon basin. The smaller species are usually green.

Commuting parrots

Macaws move about in screeching flocks except when breeding. Their day starts with a screeching chorus as individual birds leave their roosts to gather in a tree. There they bask in the early morning sun before setting off to feed. As the midday heat builds up they seek the shade, but when the sun's rays begin to weaken they come out again to feed. At dusk they return to their assembly point, usually a bare tree, before dispersing to roost.

Steamhammer beaks

Most macaws feed on seeds, nuts and fruits, the larger of them cracking even hard-shelled nuts such as Brazil nuts with their beaks and extracting the kernels with the

▽ *Rendezvous at Felipe Benavides Fountain — red and blue and blue and yellow macaws.*

◁ *Rhapsody in blue: hyacinthines preening.*

beak helped by the fleshy tongue. Precise details of their feeding in the wild are hard to come by, but in captivity, although these form their basic foods, they seem to show a liking for such things as bread and butter and cake, and tame macaws have been known to take meat readily. It may be, therefore, that they take some insect food in the wild. This possibly explains, at least in part, their readiness to pull wooden structures to pieces, such as the edges of nesting boxes or woodwork frames in the aviary. In the wild the same activities would expose insect grubs.

Bashful male
Except for the hyacinthine macaw, which is said to nest in holes in earth banks, macaws nest in hollows in trees, sometimes high up from the ground. Once the eggs are laid macaws are aggressive towards anyone approaching their nest. Even tame macaws will defy their owners trying to see what is happening. A fairly clear account can, however, be given of the breeding behaviour of the blue and yellow macaw, based mainly on observations published by Mr Donald Risdon, in the *Avicultural Magazine* for 1965. He found little distinction between male and female except that the male blushes when excited, the bare skin of his face going a deep pink. The female seldom blushes and when she does the colour hardly shows. At the same time as he blushes the male nods his head up and down and contracts the pupils of his eyes. When Risdon's pair showed signs of breeding he gave them rotten wood, which they chewed up in typical macaw fashion. The eggs are slightly larger than pigeon's eggs. The nestling is still naked and blind at a week old. The wing quills begin to erupt at 4 weeks, the bill darkens and the eyes open. The back then begins to grow feathers followed by the tail and later the rest of the body and head, the young macaw becoming fully feathered by 10 weeks of age. It does not leave the nest for another 3 weeks, except to sit at the entrance. The parents feed it during this time by regurgitation. At 6 months the young macaw is as large as its parents and looks like them.

Vulnerability
With so formidable a beak a macaw could be a match for most small predators. Its main enemy is the harpy eagle. Their habit of feeding in flocks combined with their garish colours have made macaws vulnerable to the South American Indians with their blowpipes and arrows.

class	**Aves**
order	**Psittaciformes**
family	**Psittacidae**
genera & species	***Anodorhynchus hyacinthinus*** hyacinthine macaw **Ara ararauna** blue and yellow macaw ***A. macao*** scarlet macaw ***A. militaris*** military macaw, others

Cuckoo

The cuckoo is regarded in sharply contrasting ways; it is to some the harbinger of spring, to others, a base parasite. Of the many species, only the common cuckoo of Europe and Asia gives the loud insistent call that has given rise to the name. It is called **coucou** *in French,* **Kuckuck** *in German,* **Kukushka** *in Russian and* **Kak-ko** *in Japanese.*

The common cuckoo has distinctive black and white barring on the underparts and a grey head and neck. The tail is long and the wings narrow, so in flight the cuckoo looks very much like a hawk. It can be distinguished, however, by its longer neck, the shape of the head and a pale streak under the wing.

Other cuckoos are gaudy by comparison with the common cuckoo. The red-winged Indian cuckoo has a magpie-like tail and a black head, back and tail. Related to it is the great spotted cuckoo, similar in shape but with white spots on the wings and back. The emerald cuckoo of South Africa is a brilliant golden green, except for a yellow belly.

Cuckoos belong to two subfamilies, with their relatives the anis, roadrunners, couas and coucals in other subfamilies. One subfamily, to which the common cuckoo belongs, ranges across the Old World from western Europe to Polynesia, while the other belongs to both Old and New Worlds. The former are all parasitic; the female lays her eggs in other birds' nests. It is for this habit that the cuckoos are best known, but it is by no means widespread in the family as a whole.

Long migrations

Many cuckoos migrate over thousands of miles, from the tropics to the temperate regions. The common cuckoos begin to arrive in the British Isles in the last few days of March and leave during July to early September, each bird flying on its own bound for tropical Africa although exactly where is not known. The shining cuckoo of New Zealand makes an even more impressive migration, across 2 000 miles of ocean to the Solomon Islands. How they find their way over vast distances is especially puzzling as the young birds migrate from the breeding grounds several weeks after the adults have gone. This is sure proof that the urge to migrate, the ability to navigate, and the knowledge of the route are inherited, for there is absolutely no chance of the young cuckoos learning from their elders.

Feeds on many pests

Cuckoos eat insects, especially the larvae, but they will also eat worms, spiders, and centipedes. The beetles, flies, dragonflies, butterflies and moths eaten often include those harmful to agriculture; for instance, cockchafers, cabbage white butterflies and wireworms. In particular they eat hairy or toxic caterpillars including those of the cinnabar moth which are usually left alone by other birds. The yellow-billed and black-billed cuckoos of North America are useful because they eat the tent caterpillars that weave large communal shelters, from which they sally forth to strip trees of their leaves. Fruit is sometimes eaten, especially by the koel, a cuckoo of Asia and Australia.

The lodger awaits acceptance in hedge sparrow's nest. When the foster parent is away the cuckoo flies down, lifts an egg out, swallows it or drops it and lays one of her own in its place.

Boarding out the children

It has been well-known since ancient times that the common cuckoo does not build a nest of its own, but lays its eggs in those of other birds. Other members of the cuckoo family do the same, as do other kinds of birds; for example, the cowbird and the honeyguide. It is far from easy to watch the cuckoo lay an egg in the host nest as so much depends on being in the right place at the right time. Nevertheless, the amazing ways in which she ensures that her offspring have a good chance of surviving until independent are now well-known.

The female cuckoo keeps a watch for small birds building their nests. When the nest is complete and the unwitting foster parent has laid an egg, the cuckoo flies down. Choosing a time when the foster parent is away, she lifts an egg out of the nest, swallows or drops it, and very quickly lays one of her own in its place and departs before the foster parent returns.

Cuckoo eggs are sometimes found in domed nests of willow warblers and it was once thought that the cuckoo laid her egg on the ground then carried it to the nest in her bill, but it is now known that she presses her body against the nest and ejects the egg through the entrance. In Australia and New Zealand the shining cuckoo lays in domed nests of wrens by forcing its head in through the entrance then out through the far wall. The egg is laid while it straddles the nest, then it scrambles out through the hole it has made. The foster parent, when it returns, merely repairs the gap in the nest.

Observations have shown that clutches with a cuckoo egg are more likely to be deserted than normal clutches, but usually the cuckoo egg is accepted. It hatches in $12\frac{1}{2}$ days and often the chick emerges before its nestmates. This advantage is used by the baby cuckoo to evict the other eggs and any newly hatched young. It is perhaps this part of the parasitic habit, more than any other, that has earned the cuckoo its bad name. The baby cuckoo manoeuvres itself in the bottom of the nest so that an egg or chick becomes balanced on its back, between the wings. It then hoists the unfortunate creature out of the nest, to be followed by the others. Occasionally two cuckoo eggs may be laid in one nest, when two female cuckoos are keeping watch in one area. After a few days jostling, the urge to empty the nest of competitors dies away and both young cuckoos grow together.

If the cuckoo did not evict its nestmates they would surely die in any case, for the young cuckoo grows rapidly, and its foster parents are hard put to feed it. After 3 weeks it leaves the nest which it has outgrown, and the foster parents keep feeding it, often having to perch on its back to drop insects in the gaping beak.

The African emerald cuckoo is a brilliant golden green.

Almost ready to moult at the end of the season, hedge sparrow feeds its giant foster child.

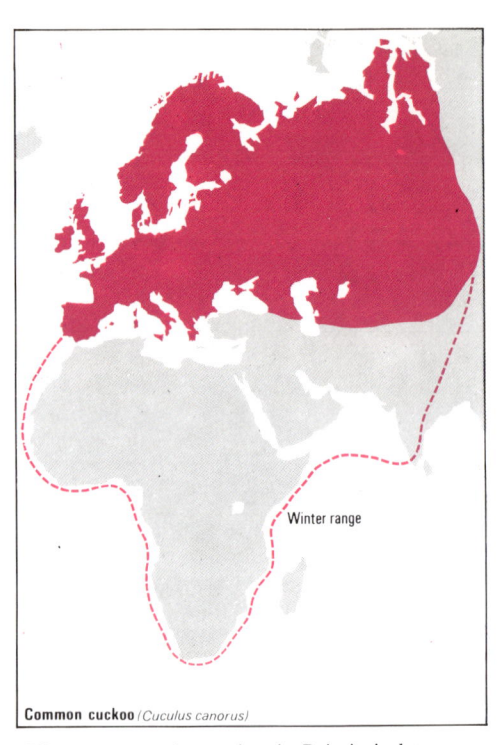

The common cuckoo arrives in Britain in late March leaving between July and September.

The baby cuckoo usually hatches first and begins to evict the other eggs.

The second egg does not survive long, being ejected from the nest in the same manner.

A newly-hatched tree pipit receives the same treatment being unable to defend itself.

Matching egg colours

Surveys of clutches containing cuckoo eggs show that the cuckoo egg is often very similar to the foster parents' eggs, and it has also been found that in any area cuckoos use certain host nests more than others. In Hungary, the chief dupe of the common cuckoo is the great reed warbler; and the cuckoo lays greenish eggs blotched with brown and black, like those of the warbler. In Finland, cuckoos' eggs are blue like those of its hosts the whinchat and redstart. Nearly all over its range, there are these preferences for certain hosts with a mimicking of their eggs. It seems that this reduces the chance of the foster parent abandoning the nest.

In the British Isles, however, cuckoo eggs differ surprisingly from their hosts'—yet they all tend to be of one pattern. The explanation for this seems to be that a cuckoo may lay in nests of another host if it cannot find the right one, and in Britain, where the countryside is divided into many small habitats with a large variety of possible host species, the cuckoo has not been able to form any set preferences for any particular host.

The final deception

Before the mysteries of bird migration were revealed it was thought the cuckoos turned into sparrowhawks in the winter and, even now, it is not unusual for a cuckoo to be mistaken for a sparrowhawk because of the similarity of shape and plumage. Bird watchers are not the only ones to be deceived as, when the cuckoo returns in spring, small birds will gather to mob it as if it were a hawk. There is some evidence that the cuckoos make use of this mistake. Cuckoos have been seen flying in an even more hawk-like fashion than usual, flapping and gliding in a soaring flight very much like a bird of prey. When they settle they are sometimes mobbed by meadow pipits and other small birds. On a few occasions this behaviour has been followed by the cuckoo alighting near a meadow pipit's nest, and one was seen flying away with a pipit's egg which it swallowed. It seems then that the cuckoo indulges in this hawk-like flight just before egg-laying, to lure the owners of the nest away by false pretences so that it can sneak in and lay its own egg.

Evidence for this is not conclusive but similar behaviour has been seen in other cuckoos. An Indian hawk-cuckoo that imitates sparrowhawks has been seen to lure birds from their nests in a more positive fashion, and the koel mimics a crow which is its main host in India. The male koel is black and it flies up to the host nest, calling, and is promptly chased away by the crows. Apparently they do this not so much to ward off a parasitic bird but for the same reason of ownership for which they would drive away another crow. Meanwhile the brown female koel slips in to lay her egg. The baby koel, moreover, does not eject its nestmates but it looks so like a young crow that it is hardly distinguishable from its fellow nestlings.

Of all the parasitic birds, however, the cuckoos, by reducing egg size and incubation time, and by mimicry of host birds' eggs, have applied the greatest resource to their underhand art.

class	**Aves**
order	**Cuculiformes**
family	**Culculidae**
genera & species	***Cuculus canorus*** common cuckoo ***C. varius*** hawk-cuckoo ***Clamator coromandus*** red-winged Indian cuckoo ***C. glandarius*** greater spotted cuckoo ***Chrysococcyx cupreus*** emerald cuckoo ***Chalcites lucidus*** shining cuckoo ***Coccyzus erythrophthalmus*** black-billed cuckoo ***C. americanus*** yellow-billed cuckoo ***Eudynamys scolopacea*** koel others

Barn owl

The barn owl's body is not as white as it appears when it is seen flying about at dusk. The upper parts are orange-buff, often speckled with grey and white. The underparts and face are pure white.

Although widespread, barn owls are not common throughout the British Isles, and are absent from the North of Scotland. In North America they do not breed north of Massachusetts, southern Ontario and Michigan, Iowa, Nebraska and northern California but they are regularly recorded as visitors farther north.

There are ten species of barn owl in various parts of the world. They differ from other owls in small details of the skeleton and proportionately smaller eyes set in a heart-shaped facial disc.

The typical barn owl is widespread, found in most parts of Europe, America, Africa, India, South-east Asia and Australia. There are about 32 races.

Ghost-like habits

The barn owl has probably given rise to many ghost stories. It often lives in churches or empty houses and is likely to give anyone not expecting it a bad shock, when it flies silently past them, a ghostly white in the gloom of night, or when they hear its eerie, long drawn out shrieks.

In Britain barn owls were formerly subject to unnecessary persecution, especially by gamekeepers. In the early 20th century, however, they made some recovery, but in the late 1940's a general decrease became apparent and by 1955 they had disappeared from many areas, especially in eastern Britain. The decrease is largely the the result of the owls' dependence on man. Old buildings and hollow trees provided roosts and nest sites and the barn owls' main prey were the rats, voles and mice that fed on man's crops. Since the Second World War, agriculture in Britain has been changing. Derelict stables and rotten trees are no longer tolerated and intensive agriculture has changed those parts of the countryside that barn owls used to frequent. The most rapid decrease in numbers over the last decade or so has, without much doubt, been due to the increased use of pesticides sprayed onto crops. These poisons accumulate in the bodies of the small animals that eat the crops and are then accumulated even further when they are eaten by owls, with the result that the barn owls often become sterile and their eggs fail to hatch.

Sometimes barn owls may be seen in broad daylight, but more usually they come out at twilight. With their white plumage, they are easy to see, flying about 15–20 ft above the ground, with fairly rapid but long wing-beats. They have regular routes which they patrol night after night, circling about and occasionally dropping to the ground to catch their prey.

Prey is taken to the nest or to a regular roost, which is identifiable by the pellets of indigestible bones, insect bodies and fur

△ *Barn owl having just swallowed its prey, indicated by the blood on the ground.*
▽ *Parent barn owls with 3-month-old chicks. At 4 months the young fly off to find their own territories.*

that are regurgitated and dropped, littering the ground about the roost. The barn owl's pellets are blackish with a varnished appearance, easily distinguishable from the greyish, soft pellets of tawny owls.

Owl pellets identify prey

It is from their pellets that the food of barn owls, and other predatory birds, can be identified. As the owls regurgitate their pellets in set places and the pellets accumulate, it is possible to get a very good idea of the diet by collecting them at intervals and pulling them apart to find the bones and other remains of the owls' prey.

A few years ago a large number of pellets were analysed in Poland. The remains of nearly 16 000 vertebrates (back-boned animals) were found and identified. Of these, 95.5% were of small mammals, 4.2% birds and the small remainder, amphibians. In Britain, similar proportions have been found. Mammal remains appear in the following order of frequency: common shrew, long-tailed field mouse, field vole and bank vole. Others, such as brown rats, house mice, even moles, bats and rabbits are taken, while several species of bird, night-flying beetles and moths, and occasional frogs and fish are found in the pellets. It is this kind of analysis which exposes the folly of persecution. Barn owls, as we now see, rarely take birds and are not a significant menace to poultry or pheasants.

Rodent control

The large number of small mammals included in the barn owls' diet shows the useful role they play, for these mammals feed on man's crops. The numbers that a barn owl can catch are shown by the observation made on an American barn owl. In only 20 minutes it had caught 16 mice, three gophers, one rat and one squirrel. It must be added that this impressive number of animals was captured for the owl's babies.

A nest of pellets

In April or May, and again in July, piles of prey can be found at a barn owl's nest site. This is a sign that they are about to breed, for the male collects extra food to feed to the female. There is no nest made, the eggs are merely laid on an accumulation of pellets. Usually four to seven white eggs are laid, but there may be as few as three or as many as eleven. They are incubated for nearly 5 weeks by the female alone, who remains on the nest, being fed by the male.

The young hatch out at different times because the female begins incubating the first egg as soon as it is laid, so each egg begins its development before the next is laid. It has been suggested that the staggered hatching of barn owls' eggs helps to reduce the strain of providing enough food for them, because they will not all be requiring large quantities of food at once. The chicks leave the nest after 9–12 weeks to find territories of their own, where they stay for the rest of their lives.

At one time it was thought that barn owls hunted by sight. But experiments have shown that they can catch their prey in total darkness, where it is absolutely impossible to see anything. A tame barn owl was put in a pitch black room and a mouse was allowed to scuffle through leaf litter on the floor. After a short pause the owl would swoop at the ground and when the lights were put on it was back on its perch with the mouse. The experiment was repeated 17 times, and the only four misses were near misses.

A detailed examination of a barn owl's ears shows them to be very well developed, and there are flaps of skin forming 'outer ears', hidden under the feathers. These flaps are not placed symmetrically about the head, so sound coming to one ear follows a slightly different path from that going to the other ear. Thus a sound is picked up by one ear slightly before or after the other. It is this slight difference that enables an owl to judge the prey's position.

To make life even more hazardous for a small animal, the long, flight feathers of an owl's wings are tipped with down on the leading, trailing and upper surfaces. This deadens the noise of the owl's wingbeats so the intended prey has no warning of attack, unless they, too, have specially sensitive ears.

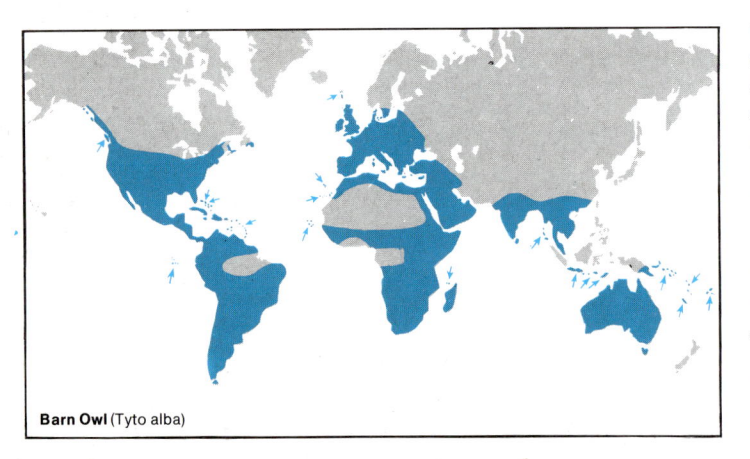

The barn owl has the distinction of being the most widely spread land bird in the world; varieties are found in every continent except Antarctica.
△ *Barn owl returning to its nest after a successful foray.*
▷ *Barn owl with captured prey.*

Barn Owl (Tyto alba)

class	**Aves**
order	**Strigiformes**
family	**Tytonidae**
genus & species	***Tyto alba***

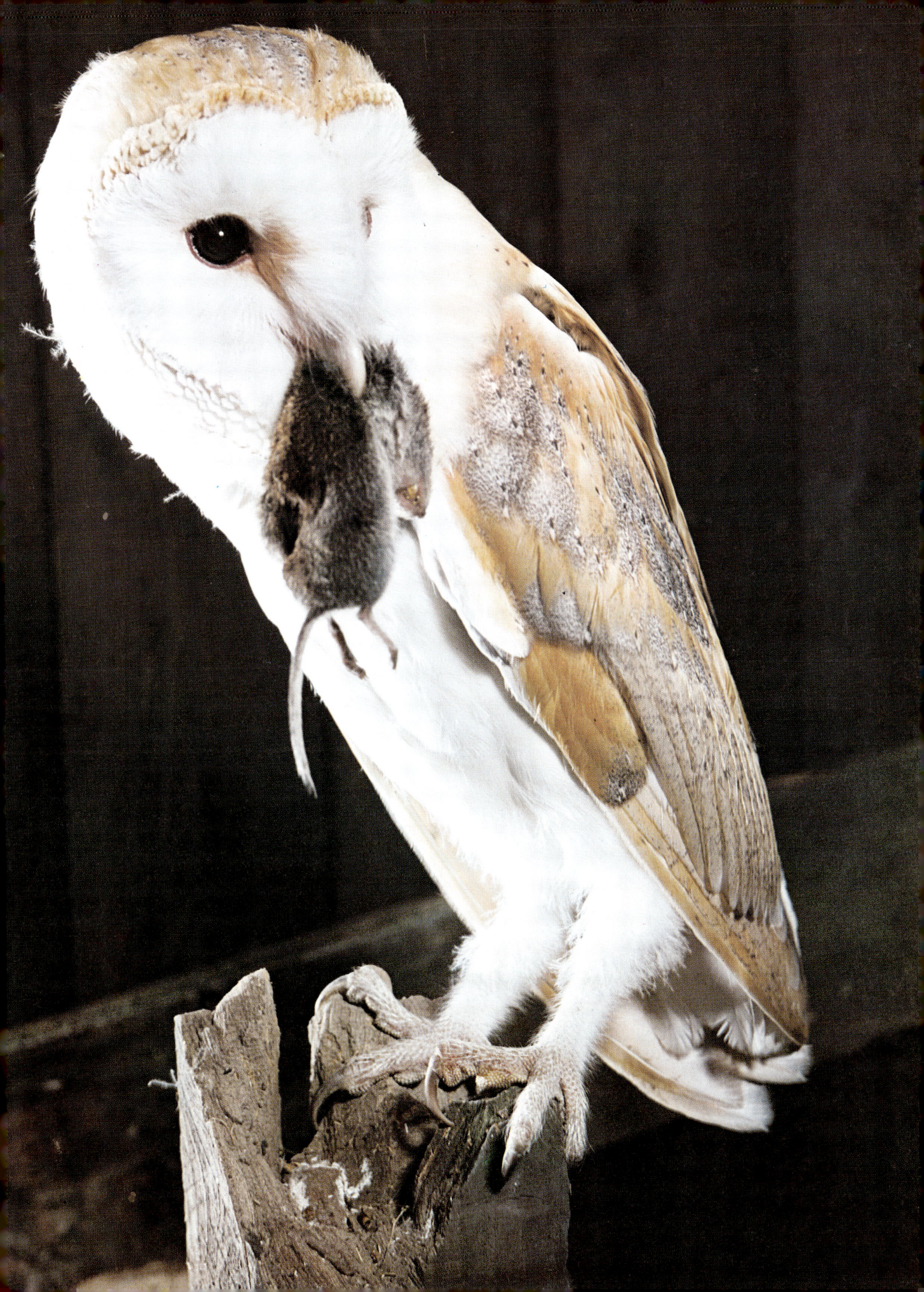

Hummingbird

There are over 300 species of these minute, beautiful birds living in the New World. The largest is the giant hummingbird, an 8½ in. monster compared with the bee hummingbird of Cuba which is little more than 2 in. long; half this length is bill and tail, the body being the same size as a bumblebee. Hummingbirds are very diverse in form, although all of them are small and have the characteristic rapid wingbeats producing the hum that gives them their name. They have brilliant, often iridescent, plumage which has led to their being given names like 'ruby' and 'topaz' – and also to their being killed in thousands and their skins exported to Europe for use in ornaments. A feature of many hummingbirds is the long narrow bill, often straight but sometimes curved, as in the sicklebill. The sword-billed hummingbird has a straight bill as long as the head, body and tail put together.

Hummingbirds are most common in the forests of South America, but they range from southern Alaska to Tierra del Fuego. Some species are so rare that they are known only from collections of hummingbirds' skin exported to Europe. Loddige's racket-tail was known from a single skin found in 1840 and was not found alive for another 40 years, when it was discovered in a small valley high in the Andes.

Hummingbird stamina . . .

Considering the diversity of habitats and food in the South American forests it is not surprising that there should be so many kinds of hummingbirds living there. It is rather surprising, however, to learn that hummingbirds breed as far north as southeast Alaska, or in the heights of the Andes. The rufous hummingbird breeds in Alaska, migrating to South America for the winter, an incredible journey for so small a bird. The ruby-throated hummingbird also migrates to and from North America, crossing the Gulf of Mexico on each trip. Unlike non-migratory hummingbirds, it stores a layer of fat equal to half its body weight before setting off. At a normal rate of use, however, this would not last through a non-stop crossing of the Gulf. Yet the hummingbirds complete this marathon, so we must presume that they have some method of economising on food reserves.

. . . and speed

Even ignoring the mystery of their migration, the flight of hummingbirds is truly remarkable. Their wings beat so fast they appear as a blur. Small species have wingbeats of 50–80 per second and in courtship displays even higher rates have been recorded. The fast wingbeats enable the hummingbirds to dart to and fro, jerking to a halt to hover steadily. They are also extremely fast in straight flight – speeds of 71 mph have been recorded. Specialised filming has shown that hummingbirds do not take off by leaping into the air like other birds but lift off with rapid wingbeats. The photographs showed that a hummingbird on a thin twig actually pulls the twig up as it rises before letting go.

Flying with such rapid wingbeats requires a large amount of energy, so hummingbirds must either feed constantly or have plentiful reserves. Even at rest their metabolism – the rate at which they produce energy – is 25 times faster than a chicken's. At night when they cannot feed they conserve their food reserves by becoming torpid – going into a form of nightly hibernation. In the Andes a hummingbird's temperature drops from 38°C/100°F to 14°C/57°F, about the temperature of the surrounding air – and their metabolism is reduced six times.

Nectar seekers

Hummingbirds feed on nectar and small soft-bodied animals. To sip nectar they hover in front of flowers and insert their pointed bills down the corolla or, if that is too long, pierce it near the base. The nectar is sucked through a tubular tongue that is very similar to those of flowerpeckers. Pollen is often brushed onto the hummingbirds' heads and transferred to other flowers, so pollinating them. To the flowers of the South American jungle, hummingbirds are as important as pollinators as bees are in a clover field. Hummingbirds can readily be attracted to tubes containing sugar-water and they become so tame they will feed at a tube held in the hand.

Small insects are caught on the wing and spiders are taken from their webs. Most hummingbirds are unable to manipulate insects in their bills and have to rush at them so they are forced into the mouth. Some pick insects and spiders from flowers.

Tiny babies

Courtship antics of hummingbirds are difficult to watch as they flit about among dense vegetation too fast for accurate observation. The males fly about in arcs, singing songs that are almost too high-pitched for humans to hear. They are usually promiscuous, mating in the air with several females, but in a few species such as the violet-eared hummingbirds (which have similar plumage for males and females) the male helps rear the family. The nest is a delicate cup of moss, lichen and spiders' webs placed on a twig or amongst foliage. The two eggs are incubated for 2–3 weeks and minute naked chicks hatch out. They are fed by the parent hovering alongside, putting its bill into theirs and pumping out nectar. The chicks grow very rapidly and leave the nest when 3 weeks old.

Hovering skill

When feeding, hummingbirds can be seen hovering steadily and even flying backwards. They can do this because their wings can swivel in all directions from the shoulder. When hovering the body hangs at an angle of about 45 degrees so the wings are beating backwards and forwards instead of up and down. In each complete beat the wing describes a figure of eight. As it moves forwards (the downstroke) the wings are tilted so they force air downwards and the bird upwards. At the end of the stroke they flip over so that the back of the wing is facing downwards and on the upstroke air is again forced downwards. To fly backwards the wings are tilted slightly so air is forced forwards as well, and the hummingbird is driven back.

The flight of a hummingbird can be compared with that of a helicopter with its blades moving in a circle to achieve the same effect of driving air downwards as the hummingbird's wings do by moving back and forth. In the flight of most birds the power is in the downstroke, the upstroke being merely a recovery phase, but in hummingbirds both strokes are powerful. The breast muscles of a hummingbird weigh a third of its total weight and the muscles drawing the wings upward are half as powerful as those driving the wings down. Non-hovering species have comparatively much smaller muscles for the upstroke.

class	Aves
order	Apodiformes
family	Trochilidae
genera & species	**Archilochus colubris** ruby-throated hummingbird **Ensifera ensifera** sword-billed hummingbird **Eutoxeres aquila** sickle-billed hummingbird **Loddigesia mirabilis** Loddige's racket-tail **Mellisuga helenae** bee hummingbird **Patagona gigas** giant hummingbird **Selasphorus rufus** rufous hummingbird, others

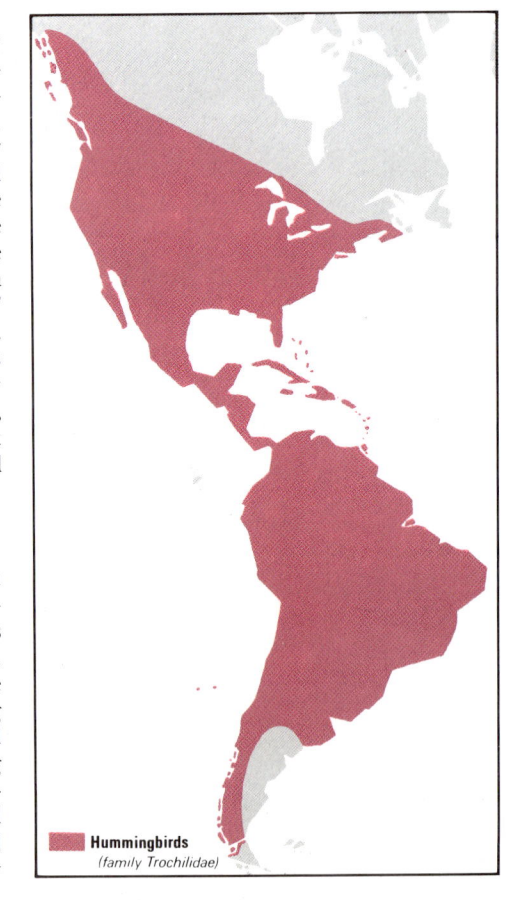

Hummingbirds (family Trochilidae)

The form of individual species of hummingbird is very varied. This male black-throated train-bearer **Lesbia victoriae**, from Ecuador, has long ornamental feathers that do not appear to hinder its aerial acrobatics. Its body is only 2 in. long but the tail is 6 in. with widely forked feathers which help make a marvellous picture when it turns sharply doing its fast manoeuvres in the air. The iridescent throat is absent in the female.

Top: Banana-boat feeder. A male velvet-purple coronet **Boissonneaua jardini** greedily sips nectar from **Heliconia jaquinii**, a relative of the bananas. Centre: The white-lipped sicklebill is perfectly adapted for sucking nectar from flowers. Bottom: The tiny ruby-topaz hummingbird **Chrysolampis mosquitus**, a beautiful Brazilian species, vibrates its wings at about 100 beats per second, fast even for the hummingbirds.

Kingfisher

There are over 80 species of kingfisher living mainly in the tropics. They are stockily built with long bills, quite short tails and often brilliant plumage, of which the common kingfisher of Europe and Asia is a good example. The common kingfisher is found throughout much of Europe and Asia, south into North Africa and east to the Solomon Islands and Japan. It is one of the most beautiful of birds, 6½ in. long with a 1½ in. dagger-like bill, its upperparts a shining iridescent blue or green.

▷ *Psychedelic forest kingfisher of Malaya.*
▽ *A giant kingfisher **Megaceryle maxima** glares from a vantage point over a stream.*

▷ *King of the world: perched aloft, a grey-headed kingfisher **Halcyon leucocephala** watches carefully for passing insects. It also feeds on beetles, grasshoppers and small reptiles.*

The underparts are chestnut, the legs red and there are patches of white on the neck. The pied kingfisher of Africa south of the Sahara and southwest Asia is dull-coloured for a kingfisher but is nevertheless striking with its black and white plumage. Like many kingfishers it has a crest. The Amazon kingfisher, also crested, has brilliant green upperparts and white underparts, with a chestnut breast in the male. The Texas kingfisher, ranging into the southern USA, is very similar.
In some species where the sexes differ in plumage, the female is the more brilliant. On the other side of the Pacific the yellow sacred kingfisher is found in many parts of Australia and is the only kingfisher in New Zealand.

A blur of colour

Kingfishers are usually seen as little more than a blur of colour as they fly low over the water on whirring wings to disappear into waterside undergrowth. If lucky one sees it perched on a branch, rock or post on the bank and its true colours can then be appreciated. Kingfishers are very much alike in habit as well as form; their feeding and breeding behaviour follow a pattern although some kingfishers rarely, if ever, go near water. Even the common kingfisher, associated so much with streams and rivers, sometimes nests some distance from water.

When thousands of exotic birds were being slaughtered and their carcases and feathers sent to Europe and North America as decorations and ornaments, it is not surprising that the dazzling kingfisher did not escape persecution. It was used for decorating hats and stuffed kingfishers in glass cases were a common household ornament. Later kingfishers were shot because they were alleged to eat enough trout fry to damage breeding stocks. The pollution of rivers and streams now threatens their wellbeing. Hard winters have a very severe effect on kingfisher populations.

Fishing over land and water

The method of catching prey is similar in nearly all species. The kingfisher waits on a perch, then darts out, catches its prey and carries it back to its perch. The common kingfisher flies out, hovers momentarily just over the water then dives in. Having caught a small fish or water insect it uses its wings to 'fly' through the water then up into the air without pausing. Larger prey are beaten against the perch to subdue them and may be tossed and caught again to get them into a suitable position for swallowing. Common kingfishers take mainly fish such as minnows, sticklebacks and gudgeon, also small perch and small trout. These last two are the reason for the persecution of kingfishers, but they also feed on water beetles, dragonfly larvae and waterboatmen which also kill small fish. Small frogs, tadpoles and pond snails are also taken.

The majority of kingfishers, however, take mainly land animals, although they hunt from a perch like the common kingfisher. They dart down from their perches like shrikes or they hawk passing insects like flycatchers. The racquet-tailed kingfisher, living in the area from the Moluccas to northeast Australia, hunts for lizards, centipedes and insects in the leaf litter of humid forests, swooping on them and sometimes driving its bill into the soft earth. The stork-billed kingfisher of India, 14 in. long with a large scarlet bill, catches fish as well as frogs, lizards, crabs and insects. It also robs other birds' nests, taking nestlings even from nests in holes in trees, but, true to its kind, it returns to its perch to swallow its prey. An exception to this is the shoe-billed kingfisher of the forests of New Guinea. It digs for earthworms with its flattened bill.

◁ *Malachite kingfisher **Corythornis cristata**, a very common African species. It feeds on fish, water invertebrates and flies.*

Common kingfisher with a prospective meal.

Hole nesting

Kingfishers nest in holes, those that hunt fish usually nesting in holes in banks near water while the more land-living kingfishers nest in holes in trees or abandoned termite nests. The striped kingfisher of Africa uses ready-made holes and may even dispossess swallows from their nests under eaves.

The nest hole is dug by the kingfishers repeatedly flying at one spot on the bank, loosening a bit of soil with their bills each time. When they have formed a ledge they can perch and dig more rapidly until the tunnel is 1½–3 ft long. The 6 or 7 spherical white eggs are laid on the floor of the tunnel and incubated for 3 weeks. During this time a revolting pile of fish bones and droppings piles up around the eggs, a squalid contrast with the magnificent plumage of the adult birds. Until Ron and Rose Eastman made their prizewinning film 'The Private Life of a Kingfisher' in 1966 it was thought that pieces of fish were fed to the young. Their remarkable patience and technique, however, showed the young inside the nest burrow swallowing whole fish almost as big as themselves, the bones being later regurgitated. The chicks, which live in the tunnel for 3–4 weeks, are hatched naked but soon acquire a covering of bristle-like wax sheaths which are shed to reveal a plumage like that of the parents just before they leave the nest.

class	**Aves**
order	**Coraciiformes**
family	**Alcedinidae**
genera & species	***Alcedo atthis*** common kingfisher ***Ceryle rudis*** pied kingfisher ***Chloroceryle amazona*** Amazon kingfisher ***C. americana*** Texas kingfisher ***Clytoceyx rex*** shoe-billed kingfisher ***Halcyon chelicuti*** striped kingfisher ***H. sancta*** sacred kingfisher ***Pelargopsis capensis*** stork-billed kingfisher ***Tanysiptera galatea*** racquet-tailed kingfisher

Woodpecker

No birds are better adapted for a life on the branches and trunks of trees than the woodpecker.

There are about 200 species of woodpecker which are spread over the wooded parts of the world, except Madagascar, Australia and oceanic islands. They are up to nearly 2 ft long and are usually brightly-coloured with patterns of black, white, green or red. A few woodpeckers have crests. The bill is straight and pointed, the legs short with two toes facing backwards and the tail is made up of pointed feathers with stiff shafts.

The 15 species of green woodpeckers inhabit the woods and forests of Europe and Asia from the British Isles to Borneo and Java. The familiar green woodpecker of Europe is 12 in. long, and has a green plumage, which is brighter below, a bright yellowish rump and a red crown. The male has a red and black stripe under the eye, while the female has a plain black stripe. The pied or spotted woodpeckers form a widespread group, the 30-odd species being distributed across North America, Europe and Asia. They are black or grey with white patches, bars or mottling. The males often have red crowns. The three-toed woodpeckers are unusual in having one toe missing from each foot. They too have a circumpolar distribution. The ivorybills of America are the largest woodpeckers and inhabit forests of large trees. As a result of these forests being cut down these species are in danger of extinction. The ivory-billed woodpecker of North America and Cuba was thought to be extinct but in 1966 a few pairs were found in Texas.

Expert tree climbers

Woodpeckers are usually seen as just a flash of colour disappearing through the trees. They live solitarily in woods and can be identified by their characteristic undulating flight: 3–4 rapid wingbeats carrying them up, followed by a downward glide. They are more likely to be given away by their harsh or ringing calls, such as the loud laugh of the green woodpecker, or by their drumming, a rapid tattoo which they make with their bills on dead branches, or even on metal roofs.

Woodpeckers spend most of their time hopping up tree trunks in spirals, searching for insects. When a woodpecker has searched one tree it flies to the base of the next and repeats the operation. In climbing vertical trunks, woodpeckers are assisted by having two backward-facing toes, sharp claws, and stiff tail feathers, which are used as a prop while climbing, rather like a shooting stick.

Above: Female African **Campethera abingoni**. *Below: Great spotted woodpecker* **Dendrocopos major**.

Boring for insects

The woodpecker's food is largely insects and their larvae. The green woodpeckers often hunt on the ground for ants and sometimes attack bee hives. The red-headed woodpecker of North America catches insects on the wing. Otherwise woodpeckers feed on insects which are prised out of crevices in the bark or drilled out of the wood. The pointed bill is an excellent chisel and the skull is toughened to withstand the shock of hammering. When drilling, a woodpecker aims its blows alternately from one side then the other, like a woodman felling a tree. Insects are removed from the hole by using the woodpecker's second useful tool — an extremely long tongue; it can protrude up to 6 in. from the tip of the bill in the green woodpecker. The tongue is protruded by muscles running round the back and top of the skulls. It is often tipped with barbs or bristles or coated with mucus for brushing up the insects.

Some woodpeckers eat fruit and seeds or drink sap. Red-headed woodpeckers and acorn woodpeckers store acorns, drilling separate holes in trees for each acorn or else using a natural cavity. There is a story of an acorn woodpecker that spent an autumn feeding acorns into a knothole in the wall of a cabin. As the hole never filled, the woodpecker 'posted' several hundred acorns in it.

Nesting in holes

With the exception of the African ground woodpecker, which burrows in the ground, woodpeckers nest in holes that they excavate in trees. They drill into a trunk then tunnel downwards to make a cavity up to 1 ft deep. There is no nest lining and the 2–8 white eggs rest on the bottom of the cavity. The eggs hatch in 11–17 days and the chicks fledge in 2–3 weeks, depending on the size of the woodpecker. Both sexes bore the nest hole, and takes turns at incubating and feeding the chicks.

Evacuating the home

Boring a nest hole several inches across does considerable damage to a tree and may weaken it sufficiently for it to fall. This happened at a nest of a pileated woodpecker observed by FK Truslow in the Everglades National Park. The tree split off at the level of the entrance to the nest, revealing that the trunk had been hollowed to leave a shell only $\frac{1}{4}-\frac{1}{2}$ in. thick. Truslow stayed in his hide hoping to watch the reactions of the woodpeckers — the female was incubating at the time. About 10 minutes later the female woodpecker did a most remarkable thing. She returned to the tree, disappeared into the nest cavity and reappeared with an egg in her bill. She then flew off with it and did not drop it for the 75 yd she was in sight. All three eggs were removed in this manner. Unfortunately this extraordinary story has no satisfactory ending as he never found out what became of the eggs. It is, however, one of the few positive records we have of birds rescuing their eggs by carrying them away.

▷ *The lesser spotted woodpecker is widespread in the woods of Europe; but, although numerous, it is seldom seen.*

class	**Aves**
order	**Piciformes**
family	**Picidae**
genera & species	***Campephilus principalis*** ivory-billed woodpecker *** Dendrocopos major*** great spotted woodpecker ***D. minor*** lesser spotted woodpecker ***Dryocopus pileatus*** pileated woodpecker ***Geocolaptes olivaceus*** ground woodpecker ***Melanerpes erythrocephalus*** red-headed woodpecker ***M. formicivorus*** acorn woodpecker ***Picoides tridactylus*** three-toed woodpecker ***Picus viridis*** green woodpecker

Goldfinch

The goldfinch is a very handsome bird, $5\frac{1}{4}$ in. long, named for the golden-yellow bar on each wing. Its back is a tawny brown, its underparts paler. The head is boldly marked with red, white and black. The wings are black with a gold bar and white tips to the flight feathers. The forked tail is black with white tips. The beak is short and conical: a seed-eater's beak.

The young goldfinch lacks the red, white and black of the adult's head. Instead it has lines of spots or streaks on head, back and breast and, except for the golden bar on the wing, looks very like several other closely related finches. One of these is the siskin **Carduelis spinus**, *which is about the same size and belongs to the same genus but has more yellow in its plumage. It spends the summer in pine-woods and the winter among the alders along the riverside. Another is the twite* **Carduelis flavirostris**, *a finch of Scandinavia and northern Britain. The serin* **Serinus dermus** *is very like the siskin in appearance and habits. It is a European bird that occasionally visits Britain, which also has the lines of dark streaks. In an evolutionary sense all three are less 'grown up' than the goldfinch and show their immaturity in the streaked plumage of the adult.*

The goldfinch ranges across Europe into western and southwestern Asia, also North Africa.

A charm of goldfinches
The goldfinch is a showy bird that appears to come from nowhere at certain seasons, especially late summer, when it feeds on the seed heads of herbaceous plants. Except in the breeding season, it goes about in small flocks and attracts attention by its musical twittering and its bold and conspicuous colours seen at close range. When not feeding it perches high up in trees, on the outer twigs, and seen then in silhouette so that its coloured head is obscured, it passes for any one of a half-a-dozen small finches. At night the flocks roost in trees and in winter use oak and beech, especially those in hedges, that are late in shedding their dead leaves. As with other small finches the flight is bounding or undulating.

A flock is usually spoken of as a charm of goldfinches. Originally this was spelled 'chirm', and meant a chorus of sounds and was applied to the chatter of any birds. In recent years it has become restricted to goldfinches. It was this musical twittering that made goldfinches, as well as the related linnets, popular as cage birds.

Diet of seeds
Goldfinches seldom feed on the ground although they may take insects, especially in summer. Their feeding is traditionally associated with the seeding thistle heads but they will visit the seeding heads of other members of the daisy family Compositae. They also take seeds of pine and birch and may visit alders to feed from their catkins, in company with siskins, serins and redpolls. One goldfinch was seen to climb a dandelion stem until it bent over, then nip it, the stem folding at the weakened point. Then she held the top of the stem, as well as the part she was standing on, in her feet and ate the seeds. She did this repeatedly.

An agility at performing tricks with string made the goldfinch a popular cage bird in the past.

Away from the comparative safety of the nest, a young goldfinch faces the world.

Resourceful goldfinch hen
The breeding season begins early in May. The male flashes his golden wing bars at the female, as part of his courtship display, while swaying from side to side. The nest of interwoven roots, bents, wool, moss and lichens, lined with thistledown and wool, is built by the hen, usually well out on a branch but sometimes in a hedge. There have been a number of instances of goldfinches untying the strings of labels used on fruit bushes and weaving the strings into the nests. The 5–6 eggs are bluish white with red spots and streaks, each nearly $\frac{3}{4}$ in. by $\frac{1}{2}$ in. The hen alone incubates for 12–13 days, fed by the cock, but both parents feed the chicks by regurgitation for another 12–13 days. There are sometimes 3 broods a year.

Hauling in the lines
The note included above under breeding behaviour, about goldfinches untying the strings of labels, may appear remarkable, but this is not beyond their known abilities. We are used to stories of tits pulling up strings of nuts to a perch in order to eat but for centuries, according to Dr WH Thorpe, the eminent authority on animal behaviour, goldfinches have been kept in special cages so people could watch what they do. In the 16th century the goldfinch was called the draw-water or its equivalent in several European languages. These captive goldfinches were in cages so designed that to survive they had to do precisely this. On one side was a little cart containing seed and this was held by a string. The goldfinch had to pull the string with its beak, hold the loop with one foot, then pull in another loop with the beak, hold that, and so on until it could take the seeds. Another string held a thimble of water. To drink, the bird had to draw this up in the same way.

Canaries and other captive birds have been seen to do similar things, and the performances are not confined to cage birds. In 1957, it was reported from Norway and Sweden that hooded crows were stealing fish and bait from fishermen's lines set through holes in the ice. A crow would take the line in its beak and walk backwards away from the hole. Then it would walk forward again, carefully treading on the line to stop it slipping back. It would repeat this until the fish or the bait was drawn to the edge of the ice, when it would seize it.

class	**Aves**
order	**Passeriformes**
family	**Fringillidae**
genus & species	***Carduelis carduelis***

Waxbill

The waxbills are a group of small, colourful, seed-eating birds, that are popular cage birds. Waxbills are related to the sparrows and weavers and the waxbill subfamily includes the mannikins, munias, cordon-bleus, silvereyes and many others well known to bird fanciers. Unfortunately, several have different common names which makes the term waxbill open to confusion. The cordon-bleus, for instance, are also called blue waxbills. The waxbills proper belong to the genus **Estrilda** *which also includes the striking avadavat.*

Waxbills are small, usually about 4 in. long and many have finely barred upperparts. The species, known as the Waxbill, the common waxbill or sometimes the St Helena waxbill, is brown with fine barring. There is a scarlet patch around the eye, the cheeks and throat are white and in the male there is a pink tinge to the underparts. It is found in many parts of Africa and has been introduced to St Helena and Brazil. Other waxbills have a similar confusion of names. The grey or red-eared waxbill is also called the common waxbill. The upperparts are grey-brown with a pink tinge and the underparts light grey with a pink tinge turning to crimson on the belly. There is a crimson stripe through the eye and the rump is black. The grey waxbill has recently become established in Portugal from aviary escapes. One of the smallest is the $3\frac{1}{2}$in. locust finch that flies in dense swarms. Its plumage is almost black with red on the face and throat. The smallest waxbill of all is the zebra or orange-breasted waxbill with a crimson streak through the eye and a crimson rump. The throat is yellow becoming scarlet underneath and the sides are barred with yellow. Waxbills live in Africa south of the Sahara apart from the avadavat in Asia and the Sydney waxbill that lives in eastern Australia.

Grain eaters

Outside the breeding season waxbills are gregarious, living in parties, sometimes of only a few birds, but others, such as the locust bird, in large flocks. The members of a party continually call to each other with shrill or soft monosyllables designed to inform each waxbill of its fellow's position and to keep the party together. Waxbills are mainly found near rivers or in swampy country where they feed on seeds, particularly those of grasses, and are particularly abundant in grassland and in crops of cereals, in association with other seedeaters such as mannikins and whydahs. In Sierra Leone the flocks are followed by rats which feed on the seeds they spill. In general, waxbills occur in too few numbers to be pests. They also eat some insects and catch flying termites.

△ *The distinctive southern grey waxbill of western Africa.*

Husband's annexe or decoy?

The typical waxbills differ from their near relatives by building nests with tubular entrances projecting from a ball of grass that are very much like the nests of sparrows and weavers. The nest is built of grass stems or flowering heads woven into an untidy mass and fastened to vertical stems or placed on the ground among grass or herbage. Some waxbills decorate the nest with paper, damp earth, feathers and other materials and a peculiar feature of the nests of true waxbills is that there is a so-called 'cock nest' incorporated into the top or side of the nest or built a short distance away. It has been said that the cock nest is used as a roost by the member of the pair that is not incubating the eggs. There is, however, no proof of this and Derek Goodwin has suggested that the cock nests may mislead predatory birds into overlooking the real nest.

The nest is built by the female waxbill but the male helps with the decoration and with lining the nest with feathers. Both sexes incubate the 4–6 white eggs, which hatch in 2 weeks. They feed the chicks by regurgitating seeds when chicks solicit by gripping their parents' bills with their own. The young waxbills are able to fly in 16–17 days.

Getting their own back?

Many waxbills are parasitised by some of the related whydahs, also known as widow birds. The whydahs lay their eggs in the waxbills' nests and their young are brought up with the young waxbills. Not all the whydahs are, however, parasites and one waxbill, the zebra waxbill, has to a certain extent reversed the situation: it lays its eggs in the nests of whydahs and bishops, but only when they have been abandoned. Bishops and whydahs finish nesting in March and the waxbills then start their nesting season taking over the nests of the bishops and whydahs and relining them.

class	**Aves**
order	**Passeriformes**
family	**Ploceidae**
genus & species	***Estrilda astrild*** common waxbill ***E. locustella*** locust finch ***E. melpoda*** orange cheeked waxbill ***E. perreini*** southern grey waxbill ***E. subflava*** zebra waxbill ***E. temporalis*** Sydney waxbill ***E. troglodytes*** northern grey waxbill others

Mammals

Although mammals, like birds, are descended from reptiles, the two groups are sharply contrasted in form and behaviour. They share a warm-blooded (homoiothermic) physiology and are air-breathing. But whereas all birds lay eggs, the characteristic feature of mammals is that the females bear their young alive. The bodies of birds, moreover, are clothed in feathers, those of mammals bear hair. Birds use sight as the main sense, mammals use smell except for the Primates (lemurs, monkeys, apes and man) which are mainly 'eyesight animals'. Except for man, mammals are relatively silent animals although all have voices, which mainly come into use at the breeding season.

One of the features of birds which lends credibility to the notion that they are descended from reptiles is the presence on their bodies of scales. It is true these are restricted to the legs and feet, but there they so strongly recall the corresponding structures on reptiles as to still any remaining doubts of the close relationship of birds to reptiles. When scales do occur in mammals these are of a different character and structure. Thus, the scales of the scaly-anteater or pangolin are made up of what can conveniently be called compressed hair.

When Captain James Cook visited Australia and opened the way to the settlement of that continent by Europeans, he could not have foreseen that one result would be to rescue the zoologists of those times from a dilemma. It would have been hard to convince anyone that mammals are descendants of reptilian stock without knowledge of the duckbill or platypus, of Australia, and the echidna or spiny anteater, of Australia (and also New Guinea) which the early settlers found when they first arrived there.

Both these are undoubted mammals. They both have hair on the body and the females nourish their young in the early stages of life with milk. But both lay eggs, a feature unique among mammals. Moreover, in the shape of some of their bones, in certain other features of their skeleton, as well as in the anatomy of their reproductive, excretory and digestive systems, they bear the hallmarks of true reptiles.

Also in Australia, though not exclusively so because they occur as well in adjacent islands and in America, are the marsupials or pouch-bearers, epitomized for most people by the kangaroo. These are also undoubted mammals but they are only a degree or so removed from the egg-laying mammals in possessing some undoubted reptilian characters.

We have travelled far in this book from the point where reference was made to the phrase 'from amoeba to man'. Although in principle it is still valid and useful as a convenient catchphrase, it has been rendered outmoded, and the history of this sheds an important light on the classification of mammals.

Man has always placed his own species at the apex of the pyramid formed by the animal kingdom. Consequently, when constructing a classification of mammals, he began with the most primitive, the egg-laying mammals, and ended with the Primates, those with the most highly-organized brains, of which man is a member. This classification was accepted and used for decades.

In 1945, the eminent zoologist, Dr George Gaylord Simpson published a monograph in which he suggested a new classification of mammals. The revolutionary idea it embodied was to give first consideration to the physical or bodily specializations, ignoring the matter of brain-development. The result can be seen in the table of classification appended here.

The classification of mammals is as follows:

Class Mammalia   3,700 species
SUBCLASS PROTOTHERIA
Order Monotremata
   (egg-laying mammals)
INFRACLASS METATHERIA
Order Marsupialia
   (marsupials or pouch-bearers)
SUBCLASS THERIA
Order Insectivora
   (shrews, moles, tenrecs)
Order Dermoptera (flying lemur)
Order Tupaioidea (tree shrews)
Order Chiroptera (bats)
Order Primates
   (lemurs, monkeys, apes, man)
Order Edentata
   (anteaters, sloths, armadillos)
Order Pholidota (pangolins)
Order Lagomorpha (pikas, rabbits, hares)
Order Rodentia (rodents)
Order Carnivora (dogs, bears, cats, etc.)
Order Pinnipedia (seals, sealions, walrus)
Order Tubulidentata (aardvark)
Order Sirenia (dugong, manatee)
Order Perissodactyla
   (horse, ass, rhinoceros, tapir)
Order Artiodactyla
   (pig, hippopotamus and other cloven-hoofed animals)
Order Cetacea
   (whales, dolphins, porpoises)

Platypus

Today the platypus is accepted as an unusual animal of quaint appearance, but it is not difficult to imagine its impact on the scientific world when it was first discovered. So strange did the creature appear that one scientist named it **paradoxus,** and a paradox it was with duck-like bill, furry mammalian coat and webbed feet.

Known as the duckbill, watermole or duckmole, the platypus is one of Australia's two egg-laying mammals, the other being the spiny anteater. The platypus is about 2 ft long including a 6in. beaver-like tail and weighs about $4\frac{1}{2}$ lb, the males being slightly larger than the females. The 'bill' is a sensitive elongated snout and is soft, like doeskin, not horny as is popularly supposed.

Although bizarre in appearance, the platypus is well adapted to its semi-aquatic life. The legs are short with strong claws on the toes and the feet are webbed. The webbing on the forefeet extends well beyond the toes, but can be turned back when on land, leaving the claws free for walking and digging. The eye and the opening to the inner ear lie on each side of the head in a furrow which can be closed when the platypus submerges. There are no external ears, thus the platypus is blind and deaf when under water. Young have teeth, but these are replaced in the adult by horny ridges.

Thick loose skin makes the barrel-shaped body of the platypus appear larger than it is. The pelt consists of a dense woolly undercoat and long shiny guard hairs. The colour varies from sepia brown to almost black above and is silver, tinged with pink or yellow underneath; females can be identified by the more pronounced reddish tint of their fur. Adult males have hollow spurs, connected to venom glands, on the ankle of each hind limb. The poison from them can be quite harmful to a man, although not fatal.

The platypus was not discovered until 1796, nearly 200 years after the first wallaby, for instance, had been seen by a European. This is not as strange as might appear at first sight, for aquatic animals tend to be elusive particularly if, like the platypus, they are nocturnal.

Its range can be seen on the map. The western limits are the Leichhardt River in North Queensland, and the Murray, Onkaparinga and Glenelg rivers, just within the border of South Australia. It is found in all fresh water, from clear icy streams at 5 000 ft to lakes and warm coastal rivers.

▷ *Out of its front door and into the river. When underwater the platypus is blind and deaf so it relies mainly on its sense of touch, highly developed in the soft rubbery bill.*

Hearty appetite
Like many small energetic animals the platypus has a voracious appetite, and probably needs more food, relative to its weight, than any other mammal. It feeds mainly in the early morning and late evening, on crayfish, worms and other small water animals. It probes for these with its bill and at the same time takes in mud and sand, which are apparently necessary for breaking up the food. During the day the platypus rests in burrows dug out of the banks, coming out at night to forage for food in the mud of the river-bottom.

Egg-laying mammal
The breeding season is from August to November and mating takes place in the water, after an elaborate and unusual courtship. Among other manoeuvres, the male will grasp the female's tail and the two will then swim slowly in circles. The female digs a winding, intricate burrow in a bank 25–35 ft, sometimes as much as 60 ft, long, 12–15 in. below the surface of the ground. At the end, a nesting chamber is excavated and lined with wet grass and leaves. The female carries these by wrapping her tail around a bundle. Usually two soft-shelled white eggs are laid, each $\frac{1}{2}$ in. diameter. They often stick together, which prevents them rolling, and the wet leaves and grass keep them from drying out. Before retiring to lay her eggs, 2 weeks after mating, the female blocks the tunnel at intervals with earth, up to 8 in. thick, which she tamps into position with her tail. During the incubation period of 7–10 days she rarely leaves the nest but each time she does so these earth blocks are rebuilt. Presumably this is a defensive measure, but in fact today the platypus has virtually no natural enemies, although a carpet-snake or goanna may occasionally catch one. The inference is that in past ages natural enemies did exist in some numbers and the earth-block defences were very necessary. This is an example of what is known as 'fossil behaviour' and the platypus itself is a living fossil.

Blind for 11 weeks
The young platypus is naked and blind, and its eyes do not open for 11 weeks. It is weaned when nearly 4 months old, at which age it takes to the water. The mother has no teats; milk merely oozes through slits on her abdomen where it is licked up by the babies. A platypus matures at about $2\frac{1}{2}$ years and has a life span of 10 years or more.

Competing with rabbits
Formerly hunted ruthlessly for its beaver-like pelt, the platypus is now rigidly protected. Too often, however, it falls foul of wire cages set under water for fish. Should the platypus enter one it cannot escape and will drown, as it is not able to stay under water for much more than 5 minutes. The introduced rabbit of Australia threatens the platypus in a different way. Where rabbits have driven too many tunnels the platypus cannot breed: it needs undisturbed soil for its breeding burrows. Fortunately, although reduced in numbers, it is now well protected by the Australian authorities and it is in no danger of extinction.

Creature of contrast
Fortunately for the sanity of naturalists, the paradoxical facts that the platypus, a mammal, laid eggs and suckled its young were not known when it was first discovered. In 1884, WH Caldwell, who had gone to Australia specially to study the platypus, dissected a female which had already laid one egg and was ready to lay another. Thrilled by this discovery he electrified members of the British Association for the Advancement of Science, then meeting in Montreal, with his laconic telegram – 'Monotremes oviparus, ovum meroblastic' (monotremes egg-laying, egg only partially divides). Delegates stood and cheered, for controversy over this point had raged in the scientific world for some years.

Long before this, in 1799, the first dried skin reached London and came into the hands of Dr Shaw, then assistant-keeper in the Natural History section of the British Museum. When Dr Shaw saw the skin he literally could not believe what he saw. At that time visitors to the Far East were bringing back fakes such as the 'eastern-mermaid', made from the skin of a monkey skilfully sewn to the tail of a fish. It is not surprising, therefore, that Dr Shaw should suspect someone had grafted the bill of a duck on to the body of a quadruped. He tried to prise off the bill, and today the marks of his scissors can still be seen on the original skin which is preserved in the British Museum (Natural History).

class	**Mammalia**
order	**Monotremata**
family	**Ornithorhynchidae**
genus & species	***Ornithorhynchus anatinus platypus***

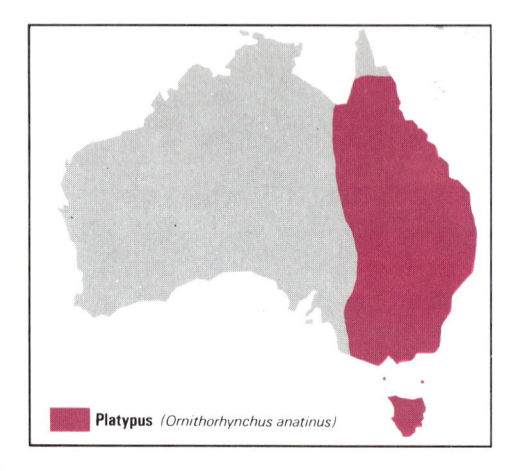

▽ *In the water the platypus uses its strong webbed forefeet for swimming and its hind legs as rudders. On land its forefeet are used for digging and to press the water out of its fur before it enters its burrow.*

Kangaroo

The best-known of the five kangaroos are the great grey and the red. The great grey or forester is up to 6 ft high, exceptionally 7 ft, with a weight of up to 200 lb. Its head is small with large ears, its forelimbs are very small by comparison with the powerful hindlimbs and the strong tail is 4 ft long. The colour is variable but is mainly grey with whitish underparts and white on the legs and underside of the tail. The muzzle is hairy between the nostrils. The male is known as a boomer, the female as a flyer and the young as a Joey. The great grey lives in open forest browsing the vegetation. The red kangaroo is similar to the great grey in size and build but the male has a reddish coat, the adult female is smoky blue, and the muzzle is less hairy. Unlike the great grey kangaroo it lives on open plains, is more a grazer than a browser, and lives more in herds or mobs, usually of a dozen animals.

The 55 species of kangaroo, wallaby and wallaroo make up the family Macropodidae (**macropus** = big foot). Only two are called kangaroos but there are 10 rat kangaroos and two tree kangaroos. A third species is known as the rock kangaroo or wallaroo. There is no brief way of describing the difference between a kangaroo and a wallaby except to say that the first is larger than the second. An arbitrary rule is that a kangaroo has hindfeet more than 10 in. long.

The red is found all over Australia. The great grey lives mainly in eastern Australia but there are three races of it, formerly regarded as species: the grey kangaroo or western forester of the southwest; that on Kangaroo Island off Yorke Peninsula, South Australia; and the Tasmanian kangaroo or forester. The wallaroo or euro lives among rocks especially in coastal areas. It has shorter and more stockily built hindlegs than the red or the great grey.

Leaps and bounds

When feeding, and so moving slowly, kangaroos balance themselves on their small forelegs and strong tail and swing the large hindlegs forward. They then bring their arms and tail up to complete the second stage of the movement. When travelling fast, only the two hindfeet are used with the tail held almost horizontally as a balancer. They clear obstacles in the same way, with leaps of up to 26 ft long. Usually the leap does not carry them more than 5 ft off the ground but there are reports of these large kangaroos clearing fences up to 9 ft. Their top speed is always a matter for dispute. They seem to be capable of 25 mph over a 300yd stretch but some people claim a higher speed for them.

Eating down the grass

Kangaroos feed mainly by night resting during the heat of the day. The red kangaroo, because it eats grass, has become a serious competitor with sheep, important in Australia's economy. By creating grasslands man has helped the kangaroo increase in numbers. In turn the kangaroo tends to outgraze the sheep, for which the pastures were grown, not only through its increased numbers but by its manner of feeding. Sheep have teeth (incisors) in only the lower-front jaw, with a dental pad in the upper jaw. Kangaroos have front teeth in both lower and upper jaw which means they crop grass more closely than sheep. At times, it is reported, they also dig out the grass roots. They can go without water for long periods, which suggests they were originally animals of desert or semi-desert, but where water is supplied for sheep kangaroos will, if not kept out, take the greater share.

Kangaroos set a problem

Enemies of the larger kangaroos are few now that the Tasmanian wolf has been banished. The introduced dingo still claims its victims but that is shot at sight. The loss of natural enemies, the creation of wide areas of grassland and the kangaroo being

A place in the sun: a red kangaroo group whiles away a lazy sociable afternoon. The powerful hindlegs and long tails can be clearly seen.

Full steam ahead: a shallow water sprint shows the versatility of bounding movement.

able to breed throughout most of the year, has created a problem, especially for sheep graziers, in Australia. Fencing in the pastures, often thousands of acres in extent, is costly – over £200 a mile – and kangaroos have a trick of squeezing under the fence at any weak spot. So kangaroos are shot. In one year, on nine sheep properties totalling 1 540 000 acres, 140 000 kangaroos were shot and it would have needed double this number of kills to keep the properties clear of them. Another problem is that kangaroos often bound across roads at night and collide with cars causing costly damage and endangering those in the cars.

Bean-sized baby

The manner in which baby kangaroos are born and reach the pouch had been in dispute for well over a century. In 1959-60 all doubts were set at rest when the birth process of the red kangaroo was filmed at Adelaide University. About 33 days after mating the female red kangaroo begins to clean her pouch, holding it open with the forepaws and licking the inside. She then takes up the 'birth position' sitting on the base of her tail with the hindlegs extended forwards and her tail passed forward between them. She then licks the opening of her birth canal or cloaca. The newborn kangaroo, ¾in. long, appears headfirst and grasps its mother's fur with the claws on its forefeet. Its hindlegs are at this time very small. In 3 minutes it has dragged itself to the pouch, entered it and seized one of the four teats in its mouth. The birth is the same for the great grey except that the female stands, with her tail straight out behind her. The baby kangaroo, born at an early stage of development, weighs $\frac{1}{35}$ oz at birth. It remains in the pouch for 8 months, by which time it weighs nearly 10 lb. It continues to be suckled for nearly 6 months after it has left the pouch and can run about, putting its head in to grasp a teat. Meanwhile, another baby has probably been born and is in the pouch. The red kangaroo has lived for 16 years in captivity.

Overlooking the obvious

The truth about kangaroo birth took a long time to be established. In 1629 Francois Pelsaert, a Dutch sea captain, wrecked on the Abrolhos Islands off southwest Australia, was the first to discover the baby in the pouch of a female wallaby. He thought it was born in the pouch. This is what the Aborigines also believed. In 1830 Alexander Collie, a ship's surgeon on a sloop lying in Cockburn Sound, Western Australia, investigated the birth and showed that the baby was born in the usual manner and made its way unaided into the pouch. From then on various suggestions were put forward: that the mother lifted the newborn baby with her forepaws or her lips and placed it in the pouch, or that the baby was budded off from the teat. In 1883 Sir Richard Owen, distinguished anatomist, came down heavily on the side of those who said the mother placed the baby in her pouch holding it in her lips, yet in 1882 the Hon L Hope had shown Collie to be correct. In 1913 Mr A Goerling wrote a letter to the Perth *Western Mail* describing how he had watched the baby make its way to the pouch with no help from the mother. It was not until 1923, however, that this view was generally accepted, when Dr WT Hornaday, Director of the New York Zoological Gardens, watched and described the birth. Finally, in 1959-60, the whole process of birth was filmed by GB Sharman, JC Merchant, Phyllis Pilton and Meredith Clark, at Adelaide University, setting the matter at rest for all time. It seems so obvious to us now!

class	**Mammalia**
order	**Marsupialia**
family	**Macropodidae**
genus & species	***Macropus giganteus*** *great grey kangaroo* ***M. robustus*** *rock kangaroo or wallaroo* ***Megaleia rufa*** *red kangaroo*

Koala

The koala is probably Australia's favourite animal. It is known affectionately as the Australian teddy bear although there are a dozen names to choose from. At various times it has been called bangaroo, koolewong, narnagoon, buidelbeer, native bear, karbor, cullawine, colo, koala wombat and New Holland sloth! The last two have an especial interest. For a long time it was believed the koala was most nearly related to the wombat and was placed in a family on its own, the Phascolarctidae, near that of the wombat. Now it is placed in the Phalangeridae with the opossums. In habits the koala recalls the slow loris and the sloth, two very different animals which also move in a lethargic way.

The koala is like a small bear, 2 ft high, up to 33 lb weight, with tufted ears, small eyes with a vertical slit pupil and a prominent beak-like snout. Tailless except for a very short rounded stump, it has a thick ash-grey fur with a tinge of brown on the upper parts, yellowish white on the hindquarters and white on the under parts. It has cheek pouches for storing food and the brood pouch of the female opens backwards. All four feet are grasping. On the front feet the first two of the five toes are opposed to the rest and the first toe on the hindfoot is opposed. Also on the hindfoot the second and third toes are joined in a common skin.

Ace tree-climbers

The koala is essentially tree-living, only occasionally descending to lick earth—apparently to aid digestion—or to shuffle slowly to another tree. If forced to the ground its main concern is to reach another tree and climb it, scrambling up even smooth trunks to the swaying topmost branches where it clings with the powerful grip of all four feet. Although its legs are short they are strong and there are sharp claws on the toes. When climbing a trunk its forelegs reach out at an angle of 45° while the hindlegs are directly under the body. It climbs in a series of jumps of 4–5 in. at a time. During the day it sleeps curled up in a tree-fork. It never enters hollows in trees. Koalas are inoffensive although they have harsh grating voices, said to be like a handsaw cutting through a thin board; it has been claimed that they have the loudest Australian voice, other than the flying phalanger.

▽ *A koala squatting up a telegraph pole on Phillip Island, off eastern Australia.*

▷ *Year-old koala who will soon leave mother.*

Fussy feeders
At night the koala climbs to the topmost branches to find its only food: the tender shoots of eucalyptus, 12 species of which are eaten. A koala is said to smell strongly of eucalyptus. Bernhard Grzimek, well-known German zoologist and ethologist, has spoken of koalas as smelling like cough lozenges. Their feeding is, however, more restricted than this. Different races of koala eat only certain species of gum tree. Koalas on the east coast of Australia feed only on the spotted gum and the tallow wood, in Victoria only the red gum. Even then they cannot use all the leaves on a chosen gum. At certain times the older leaves, sometimes the young leaves at the tips of the branches, release prussic acid—a deadly poison—when chewed. So, as more and more gum trees have been felled, koalas have become increasingly hemmed in, prisoners of their specialised diet. One of the difficulties of saving the koala by having special reserves is to supply enough trees for them of the right kind. Koalas are said to eat mistletoe and box leaves as well, and a koala in captivity was persuaded to eat bread and milk, but without gum leaves they cannot survive.

Get off my back!
Another drawback to preserving the koala is that it is a slow breeder. Usually the animal is solitary or lives in small groups. At breeding time a boss male forms a small harem which he guards. The gestation period is 25–35 days and there is normally only one young at a birth, $\frac{3}{4}$ in. long and $\frac{1}{5}$ oz weight. It is fully furred at 6 months but continues to stay with the mother for another 6 months after leaving the pouch, riding pick-a-back on her, which has led to many endearing photographs. On weaning it obtains nourishment by eating partially digested food that has passed through the mother's digestive tract. The young koala is sexually mature at 4 years, and the longest lived koala was 20 years old when it died.

Pitiless persecution
Until less than a century ago there were millions of koalas, especially in eastern Australia. Now they are numbered in thousands. In 1887–89 and again in 1900–1903 epidemics swept through them, killing large numbers. This was at a time when it was a favourite 'sport' to shoot these sitting targets, often taking several shots to finish one animal which meanwhile cried piteously, like a human baby, a fact that caused Australian naturalists to condemn the sport as the most callous. At all times koalas are a prey to forest fires as well as to land clearance for human settlement. Moreover a market was developed for their pelts, their fur being thick and able to withstand hard usage. In 1908 nearly 58 000 koala pelts were marketed in Sydney alone. In 1920–21 a total of 205 679 were marketed and in 1924 over two million were exported. By this time public opinion was being aroused and before long efforts were being made to protect the surviving populations and to establish sanctuaries for them and ensure their future.

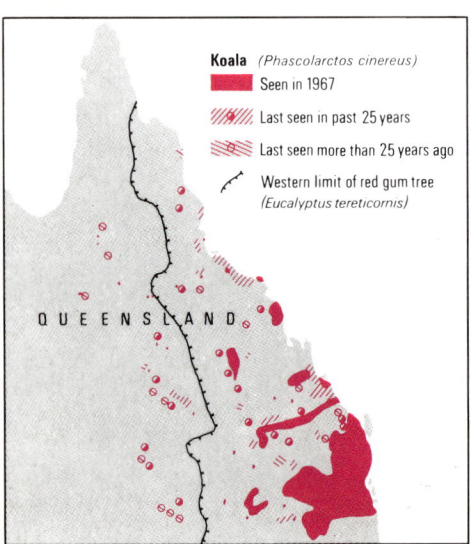

Curious cuddly: favourite of millions, the koala is the Australian teddy bear. It spends most of its time shuffling about its eucalyptus tree-top home. The baby above has climbed onto its mother's back from a downward opening pouch. At a year it will be ready to leave its mother and find its own gum tree. Numbers have seriously decreased in the last 100 years mainly due to fires destroying their gum trees and from persecution by man. From a 1967 survey in Queensland the present-day distribution was established in that state (left).

class	**Mammalia**
order	**Marsupialia**
family	**Phalangeridae**
genus & species	*Phascolarctos cinereus koala*

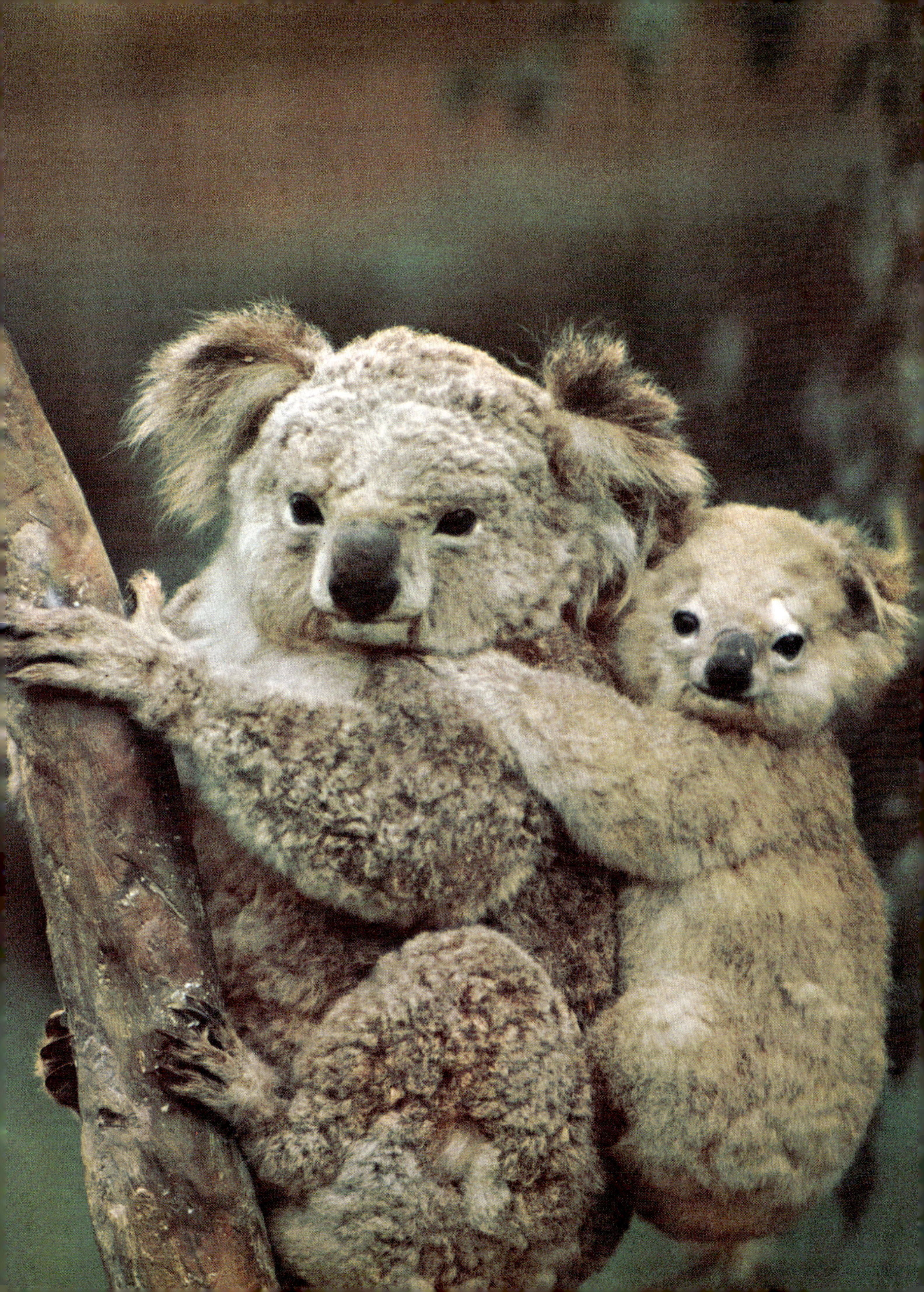

Chimpanzee

One of the great apes and the nearest in intelligence to man, the chimpanzee is one of the most studied and popular of animals. Scientists have examined its mental capacities and sent it into space in anticipation of man. To the general public, the chimpanzee is the familiar clown of circus acts and tea parties at the zoo. Yet despite all our knowledge of the chimpanzee's capabilities in the laboratory, it is only recently that its habits in the wild have been studied, and these are proving to be more remarkable than its antics in captivity.

Chimpanzees need little description. Being apes and not monkeys, they have no tail. Their arms are longer than their legs and they normally run on all fours, but they can walk upright, with toes turned outwards. When erect they stand 3–5 ft high. The hair is long and coarse, black except for a white patch near the rump. The face, ears, hands and feet are naked and, except for the black face, flesh coloured.

Forest families

The single species of chimpanzee lives in the tropical rain forests of Africa, roughly from the Niger basin to Angola. They are at home in the trees, making nests of branches and vines each night to sleep in, but they often come down to the ground to search for food. Whereas their normal gait on the ground is all fours, they will run on three legs, leaving one free to hold food, or on their hind legs, in an amusing waddling gait, when carrying an armful of food.

Chimpanzees live in small parties, occasionally numbering up to 40, but the bonds between the members of a party are weak. There is no fixed social structure like that found in baboon troops. A chimpanzee party is constantly varying in size as members leave to wander off in the forests by themselves or return from such a wandering. The only constant unit of social life is a mother with her young. She may have two or three of different ages with her at any time because they stay with her for several years. The usual size of a group is from 3–6, but numbers increase as chimpanzees gather at a source of plentiful and tasty food, or if a female comes on heat when the males will gather round her for several days.

Within a party, the males are arranged in a social order, the inferior ones respecting the superior ones. Dominance is related to age; a chimpanzee gradually rises in social position from the time he is physically mature and leaves the protection of his mother. The status of a male seems to be partly determined by noisy displays, charging about waving branches or rocks or drumming the feet on the plank-like buttresses of the forest trees. This behaviour is sometimes sparked off by frustration brought on by seeing more dominant males enjoying food without sharing it. Yet the chimpanzees recognize the right of owner-ship sufficiently to prevent a dominant male from wresting food from one of his inferiors.

The gamut of emotions

△ *'I'm content'* — relaxed and normal.

△ *'Hello'* — the greeting pout.

△ *'I'm happy'* smile, showing bottom teeth only.
▽ Tantrum, showing top and bottom teeth.

First aid and affection

When chimpanzees meet after having been apart they greet each other in a very human way, by touching each other or even clasping hands and kissing. The arrival of a dominant male is the signal for the rest to hurry over and pay their respects to him. The members of a party also spend a considerable amount of time grooming each other, and themselves. Mothers carefully go through the fur of their babies for any foreign particles, spending more and more time on the task as the babies grow older. Dirt, burrs, dried skin and ticks are plucked off and splinters may be removed by pinching them out with forefingers or lips. Such mutual help may lead to further first aid. A captive female was once seen to approach her male companion, whimpering. She sat down while the other chimpanzee sat opposite her and, holding her head steady with one hand, pulled the lower lid of one eye down with the other. After a short inspection he removed a speck of grit from her eye with his finger, to her evident relief.

Hunting for meat

About 7 hours a day may be spent feeding either up trees or on the ground. The chimpanzees investigate any source likely to produce food. Crevices in logs are searched for insects and nests are robbed of eggs and chicks, but their usual food consists of fruits, leaves and roots. Ripening fruit crops, of bananas, pawpaws or wild figs, are a special attraction to them and they are sometimes a nuisance when they attack plantations. A big male chimpanzee can eat over 50 bananas at one sitting.

Until recently it was thought that the only flesh eaten by chimpanzees was that of insects and occasionally birds and small rodents. They have now been found to hunt larger animals, some individuals apparently being particularly fond of meat. Young bushbucks and bushpigs have been seen caught by chimpanzees, as well as colobus monkeys and young baboons. Jane Goodall, the British naturalist who spent several years in Africa studying chimpanzees in the wild, has given a very graphic description of a chimpanzee catching a young baboon and killing it by holding its back legs and smashing its head against the ground.

Obedient children

Chimpanzees are promiscuous. When a female comes on heat the males gather round her, bounding and leaping through the branches. All of them mate with her, no matter what their social standing. She remains on heat for several days, then the males lose interest.

A single baby—twins are rare—is born after about 230 days. If it is the female's first baby, she does not at first seem to know what to do with it, but by a combination of instinct, knowledge gained from having seen other babies, and learning, she soon starts to care for it. For 2 years the baby will be completely dependent on her. At first she carries it to her breast, but as it grows larger it rides pick-a-back.

The standard of baby care shown by

*Top: Young chimps, Primrose (left) and Peter.
Right: Chimpanzees are the best tool-users apart from man, using natural objects to gather food, crack nuts, and drive off enemies.*

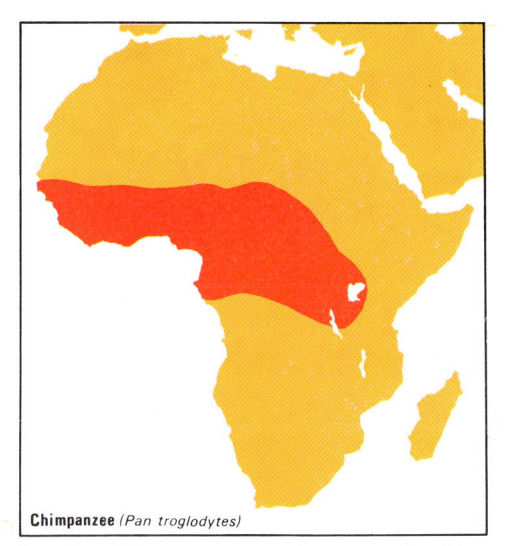

Chimpanzee (Pan troglodytes)

female chimpanzees varies considerably. Some are ideal mothers, caring for their babies zealously and caressing and kissing them. Others are over-attentive, and the babies are 'spoilt'; and yet others neglect their children. The standard of care and education, however, is on the whole exemplary. The babies are not usually bullied or spoiled, yet they obey the parents' orders instantly. When they leave their mother's back they have considerable freedom, and can climb over dominant males without fear.

The babies are carried for varying periods. Sometimes they are still riding on their mothers when 4 years old. By this time the mother will have another baby and the elder one has to fend more for itself, but chimpanzees have been seen hand feeding young that are 6 or 7 years old.

Tools for chimpanzees

Man is sometimes called the toolmaker to distinguish him from other animals. It is difficult to decide when our ancestors became human-like rather than ape-like, and toolmaking is one factor used as a line of contrast. Upright gait and speech are others, but it is difficult to make rigid pronouncements about features that must have evolved gradually.

Tools can be regarded as extensions of the body used to help with certain tasks. Few animals are known to use tools, but the real difference that separates man and the rest of the animal world is that he not only uses a variety of tools, he makes them, fashioning natural objects to suit his purpose. In this way, opening a nut with a stone is tool using, but shaping the stone into an axe is toolmaking.

Chimpanzees are the best tool-users apart from man. In captivity, they have been seen to throw stones and brandish clubs when put in a cage near a leopard and they are mentally well equipped to work out how to use tools, which are used by some other animals more or less instinctively. Chimpanzees have solved such problems as fitting two sticks together or balancing boxes on top of each other to get at otherwise inaccessible bananas.

The observations by Jane Goodall and others on wild chimpanzees have shown that they also use a variety of tools. The most common use is to extract honey, ants or termites from nests. Sticks 2–3 ft long are picked off the ground or broken from branches and pushed into nests, then withdrawn, and the honey or insects licked off. Stones are used to crack nuts, or as missiles to drive humans or baboons away from the chimpanzees' food. The stones, which sometimes weigh several pounds, are thrown, overarm, not very accurately but definitely aimed. Another material used for tools is leaves. Chimpanzees have been seen plucking leaves, chewing them up, and using the resultant mass as a sponge. Water, in a natural bowl in a tree, was soaked up into the sponge and squeezed out into the chimpanzee's mouth. Whole leaves have also been used for wiping sticky lips and hands after eating bananas.

The variety of tools used by the chimpanzees is made more interesting because they actually make some of their implements. To make a suitable rod to extract insects, the chimpanzees will strip the leaves off a twig or tear shreds off a grass stem to make it narrower. These are clear signs of modifying natural material for a specific use, as is the chewing of leaves to make a sponge. So man is not the only toolmaker, merely better at it than his relatives.

A final point arises from these observations on wild chimpanzees. Babies were seen to play with tools discarded by their elders after having watched them being used. At first their efforts at imitation were clumsy but by 3 years of age they were using them competently. Here is the beginning of a culture in which individuals learn skills passed on from generation to generation.

class	**Mammalia**
order	**Primates**
family	**Pongidae**
genus & species	**Pan troglodytes**

△ △ *Chimpanzee first-aid: incredible instance of male removing grit from his mate's eye.*
△ *A mother suckles her baby. Chimpanzees show great affection to their young, and discipline is good without the need for bullying.*

Growing old. Youngsters (above) stay with their mother for 5 years but they are 10 or 12 before they are mature and they may live to 40.

Orang utan

The orang utan is one of our more interesting relatives. It occupies an intermediate place within the Hominoidea, the superfamily that comprises the apes and man, as it is less closely related to man than the gorilla or chimpanzee, but more man-like than the gibbon.

The big male orang stands $4\frac{1}{2}$ ft high when upright, and may weigh as much as a man. Females stand only 3 ft 10 in. at the most, and weigh half as much as the male. The arms are $1\frac{1}{2}$ times as long as the legs, both hands and feet are long and narrow and suited for grasping, and the thumb and great toe are very short since they would only 'get in the way' of the hook-like function of the hand. The skin is coarse and dark grey, and the hair, which is reddish, is sparse, so the skin can be seen through it in many places. The male develops large cheek-flanges of unknown function, and grows a beard or moustache, the rest of the face being virtually hairless. There is a great deal of variation in facial appearance; orangs are as individual and instantly recognisable as human beings. Both sexes have a laryngeal pouch, which in the male can be quite large, giving it a flabby appearance on the neck and chest. The forehead is high and rounded, and the jaws are prominent. Youngsters have a blue tinge to the face.

Orang utans are found on Borneo and Sumatra. There are slight differences between the two races, and these are more marked in the male. The Borneo race is maroon-tinted, and the male looks really grotesque, with enormous cheek-flanges and great dewlaps formed by the laryngeal sac. The Sumatran race is slimmer and lighter-coloured, and males can look quite startlingly human, with only small flanges and sac, a long narrow face, and a long gingery moustache.

Old man of the woods

The orang utan is strictly a tropical forest animal. It generally lives in low-lying, even swampy forests, but is also found at 6 000 ft on mountains in Borneo. Here, at any rate, most individuals are entirely arboreal. They swing from branch to branch by their arms, though they may use their feet as well, or walk upright along a branch, steadying themselves with their hands round the branch above. It is reported by the Dyaks of Borneo that big old males become too heavy to live in the trees, so they spend most of their time on the ground.

When they are on the ground, orangs move quadrupedally, with the feet bent inwards and clenched, and the hands either clenched or flat on the ground. This contrasts with the gorilla and chimpanzee, which live mainly on the ground and 'knuckle-walk', with their feet flat on the ground and their hands supported on their knuckles. In captivity, orangs easily learn — or discover for themselves — how to walk erect, but because the leg muscles are insufficiently developed to do this easily, the knee is kept locked and the leg straight.

Anti-social 'burping'

At night the orang utan makes a nest, between 30 and 70 ft above the ground. There is often a kind of sheltering roof over this nest, to protect the orang from the rain—a structure which is not found in nests made by chimps or gorillas. The nest is otherwise much more sketchily made than that of chimps or gorillas. It takes only 5 minutes to make and the orang usually moves on and makes a new nest at its next night's stopping place. Sometimes the same one is used again and the previous night's nest may be used for a daytime nap.

Unlike gorillas and chimpanzees, orang utans seem to have no large social groupings. A female with her infant often travels with other such females for a while, forming something like a smaller version of the chimpanzee's 'nursery group'. A male may join this group, but adult males live alone most of the time. Adolescents of both sexes tend to travel around in groups of twos or threes. It is possible that male orangs, like gibbon families, may be territorial, spacing themselves vocally. The laryngeal sac is filled with air, making the animal swell up terrifyingly, and the air is then released to produce what has been described as a 'loud, two-tone booming burp'. They communicate within a group by making a smacking sound with their lips every few seconds. The most terrifying sound which an orang makes is a roar. This begins on a high note and the tone gets deeper and deeper as the laryngeal sac fills with air. Roaring is heard at night and before dawn, and orangs are said

▽ *An aggressive orang utan burps defiantly.*

to make the same noise when wounded. The Dyaks report that male orangs fight and scars are quite common.

There is no special birth season, food being available all the year round in the Indonesian rain forest. Gestation lasts 9 months. The young orang weighs only 3½–4 lb at birth, and is sparsely covered with hairs on the back and head. At first it clings to its mother's fur, usually slung on her hip, but when it is a little older, it wanders about on its own, sometimes walking along the branch behind its mother, clinging to her rump hairs. At about 5 years or so, orangs seem to leave their mothers and form adolescent bands.

Source of contention
Man is the principal enemy of the orang utan. Orangs love the juicy, evil-smelling durian fruit, and so do human beings, so this is often a source of contention. An orang will react to a human intruder by making a great deal of the smacking sound, and breaking off branches, keeping up a continuous shower of them which is often annoying enough to drive the humans away. A Dyak recently reported that he was attacked for no reason by a huge male orang that he came upon unexpectedly on the ground. It has few other enemies. There are no tigers in Borneo—Dyaks claim to have exterminated them about 1000 years ago—and in Sumatra there are only a few. Leopards are unknown on both islands.

Zoos are a danger
The orang's distribution has been steadily declining. Its ancestors' remains have been found in 14 million-year-old deposits in the Siwalik Hills, Punjab, India. In the Pleistocene, 500 000 years ago, the orang was found as far north as China, and as far south as Java. Today it occurs all over Borneo—the largest and least populated of the East Indian islands—and in the north of Sumatra. It seems that deforestation and heavy human populations have affected its distribution very adversely and there are now fears that it may become extinct altogether in the wild. One reason for its decline is its slow breeding rate. A female breeds every fourth year or so, and usually not until the previous young has left her. It is possible that the average female may bear only three or four young in her life.

The biggest threat, however, to the orang's survival is, sad to say, the zoo trade. Every zoo wants a young ape to display to its visitors, and orangs are the easiest to obtain. Many unscrupulous private zoos, especially in the United States, have paid high prices for baby orangs, and there has been quite a lucrative trade in them in Southeast Asia. Baby orangs are obtained by shooting their mothers. The dealer does not make much effort to ensure the captive's welfare as he probably bought it from the hunter at a low fee, so many youngsters die. For every one orang that reaches a zoo alive, ten orangs have probably died. It is now illegal in Singapore to possess orangs, and smugglers are penalised, but other ports in Southeast Asia are still open for this trade. There is now a list of animals in danger of extinction which, under an international convention, cannot normally be imported into the countries, including the United States, which signed the convention. They can only be imported under special licence, usually for research purposes. This may have some effect on the situation. The deforestation problem, however, remains.

In 1963 Barbara Harrisson, working with her husband, Tom, then Government Ethnologist and Curator of Sarawak Museum, estimated that only 2 000 wild

◁ *A mature orang utan.* ▽ *Brotherly love.* △ *The old man of the woods. A male orang with his large cheek flanges.*

orangs remained in Sabah, 1000 in Kalimantan (Indonesian Borneo), 700 in Sarawak and 1000 in Sumatra. Of these, only the Sabah population seems to be anything like adequately protected. In 1964 another estimate put the Sumatra population at only 100. Tom and Barbara Harrisson undertook a programme in Sarawak of reintroducing into the wild, young orangs which had been illegally bought by people. This has met with a certain amount of success. There are about 300 in zoos all over the world and breeding has been achieved several times. Most zoos that breed them now keep the Bornean and Sumatran races separate, which will help to save the Sumatran race.

class	**Mammalia**
order	**Primates**
family	**Pongidae**
genus & species	***Pongo pygmaeus pygmaeus*** Bornean orang utan ***P. p. abeli*** Sumatran orang utan

Jack rabbit

The jack rabbits of the western United States are hares belonging to the genus **Lepus**—they are close relatives of the brown hare, the varying hare and the snowshoe rabbit. The white-tailed jack rabbit, also known as the plains or prairie hare, has a brownish coat in the summer which changes to white in the winter. Only the 6in. black-tipped ears and 4in. white tail remain unchanged all the year round. This jack rabbit, which weighs up to 10 lb, lives in the prairies of the northwest, but to the south lives the smaller black-tailed or jackass hare. The latter name is derived from the 8in. black-tipped ears. The coat is sandy except for the black upper surface of the tail. It does not turn white in winter. This species lives in the arid country from Oregon to Mexico and eastwards to Texas. There is also a small population in Florida which has come from imported jack rabbits, used in training greyhounds, that have gone wild.

The remaining jack rabbits, the two species of antelope or white-sided jack rabbits, live in restricted areas of Arizona and New Mexico.

Safety in bounding leaps

Like all hares, jack rabbits live on the surface of the ground and do not burrow. The exception is the white-tailed jack rabbit which in winter burrows under the snow for warmth and also gains protection against predators such as owls. Otherwise jack rabbits escape detection by crouching among the sparse vegetation of the prairies and semi-desert countryside. They lie up in shade during the day and come out in the evening. Each jack rabbit has several forms, hollows in the ground shaded and con-

Hare of the plain and prairie: the jack rabbit of the western United States has two obvious adaptations for grassland life—very long ears, useful for detecting predators at a distance, and long hind legs with which it runs up to 45 mph in a series of bounding leaps.

cealed by plants, within its home range. If flushed, jack rabbits will run extremely fast, sometimes reaching 45 mph in a series of 20ft springing bounds like animated rubber balls. Every so often they leap up 4 or 5 ft to clear the surrounding vegetation and look out for enemies.

Water from cacti

Jack rabbits feed mainly on grass and plants such as sagebrush or snakeweed, and often become serious pests where their numbers build up. To protect crops and to save the grazing for domestic stock, hunts are organised or poisoned bait put down. In the arid parts of their range, when the grass has dried up, jack rabbits survive on mesquite and cacti. They can get all the water they need from cacti providing they do not lose too much moisture in keeping cool. To eat a prickly cactus a jack rabbit carefully chews around a spiny area and pulls out the loosened section. Then it puts its head into the hole and eats the moist, fleshy pulp which it finds inside.

Born in the open

The length of the breeding season varies according to the range of the jack rabbit, being shorter in the north. At the onset of breeding jack rabbits indulge in the typical mad antics of hares. The males chase to and fro and fight each other. They rear up, sometimes growling, and batter each other with their forepaws. They also bite each other, tearing out tufts of fur or even flesh and occasionally violent kicks are delivered with the hindlegs. A carefully-aimed kick can wound the recipient severely; otherwise the fight continues until one of the combatants turns tail and flees.

The baby jack rabbits are born in open nests concealed by brush or grass and lined with fur which the female pulls from her body. The litters are usually of three or four young but there may be as few as one or as many as eight. The babies weigh 2–6 oz and can stand and walk a few steps immediately after birth, but they do not leave the nest for about 4 weeks.

Precarious heat balance

Large ears are a characteristic of desert animals, such as bat-eared and fennec foxes, and it is usually supposed that as well as improving the animal's hearing they act as radiators for keeping the body cool. There is, however, a drawback to this idea. If heat can be lost from the ears it can also be absorbed. The problem has now been resolved because it has been realised that a clear sky has a low radiant temperature and acts as a heat sink. In the semi-arid home of the black-tailed jack rabbit a clear, blue sky may have a temperature of 10–15°C/50–59°F to which heat can be radiated from the jack rabbit's ears that have a temperature of 38°C/100°F. Only a slight difference in temperature is needed for radiation to take place and the large difference between ears and sky allows efficient heat transfer.

Jack rabbits rely on radiation to keep them cool, for, as we have seen, they do not get enough water to be able to use evaporation as a means of cooling. In hot weather jack rabbits make use of every bit of shade and in their forms the ground temperature is lower than the air or body temperature and so acts as another heat sink.

The heat balance of a jack rabbit is, however, very precarious. On a hot day it is possible for two men easily to run down a jack rabbit. By continually flushing it and keeping it in the open the jack rabbit soon collapses from heat exhaustion and is soon ready for the pot!

class	**Mammalia**
order	**Lagomorpha**
family	**Leporidae**
genus & species	***Lepus californicus*** black-tailed jack rabbit ***L. townsendi*** white-tailed jack rabbit others

◁▽ *On the look-out. White-tailed jack rabbit crouches by sparse vegetation of the prairies.*
▽ *Black-tailed portrait. Named jackass hare, after its 8in. black-tipped ears, this jack rabbit does not change to white in winter as does the white-tailed jack rabbit.*

191

Beaver

The beaver is the second largest rodent, exceeded in size only by the capybara. Stout-bodied, with a dark brown fur, it is up to 3½ ft long including 1 ft of broad scaly tail, and it may weigh between 30 and 75 lb. Its muzzle is blunt, ears small, and it has five toes on each foot. Those on the front feet are strongly clawed, used for digging, manipulating food and carrying. The hind feet are webbed, with two split claws for grooming the fur and spreading waterproofing oil. The body oil, as well as the dense underfur and the heavy outer coat of guard hairs, not only act as waterproofing but also as insulation against the cold. When a beaver submerges, its nostrils and ears are closed by valves, and it can remain underwater for 15 minutes. The tail is used for steering and sometimes for propulsion through the water. It also forms a tripod with the hind legs when the beaver stands up to gnaw trees or when carrying, with the fore feet, mud or stones for building.

There are two species of beaver, both so alike in appearance and habits that we are fully justified in speaking merely of the beaver. The first, the European beaver, must at one time have been very abundant throughout Europe, even in England, where its bones may still be found. On the Continent of Europe it is still present in small numbers in Scandinavia, along rivers in European Russia, in the Elbe and Rhône valleys, and, where given protection, it shows signs of increasing numbers.

The Canadian beaver formerly enjoyed a wide range across the North American continent, from northern Canada south to beyond the US–Mexico border. Today, in severely depleted numbers, its range extends from Canada into some parts of the northern US.

Habits

Beavers live in loose colonies, each made up of a family unit of up to 12, including the parents, which mate for life. Their home may be in a burrow in a bank, with an underwater entrance or in a lodge in a 'beaver pond', a pool made by damming a river until it overflows. The lodge is built of sticks and mud, often against a clump of young trees, with underwater entrances, a central chamber which is above water level and a ventilating chimney connecting the chamber with the top of the lodge. Secondary dams are built upstream of the lodge, with usually one secondary dam downstream of the main dam. Young trees are felled, cut up and carried to the site, and, if necessary, canals are dug to float logs to the pond.

Intelligence of beavers

Many people are convinced that beavers are unusually intelligent, largely because their dams are such fine examples of engineering works. The structure of the

△ *Beaver in the Canadian autumn. Its tail makes a tripod with the back legs so it can sit up and gnaw tree tunks.*

▽ *A beaver lodge. It is made of sticks and mud, in a pond, which is made by the beavers damming a stream so it overflows.*

Beaver swimming. It can dive instantly if danger threatens, simply by depressing its rudder-like tail, here stretched out behind. When submerged its nostrils and ears are closed by valves and it can stay underwater for 15 minutes.

beaver brain, however, gives no indication of any greater mental capacity than is found in other rodents. Moreover, some of a beaver's actions which appear to be the result of a high order of reasoning can be shown to be due to instinct, the result of an inborn pattern of behaviour.

The lodge is a conical pile of branches and sticks 2–6 ft long, compacted with mud and stones, the upper half of which projects above the surface of the water. From an engineering standpoint it could hardly be improved. It has a central chamber just above water level, one or more escape tunnels leading from the chamber to below-water exits, well-insulated walls and a vertical chimney or ventilating shaft for regulating the temperature inside and to give air-conditioning. The evidence gained from dissecting a lodge suggests that it is built by laying sticks more or less horizontally to construct a pile, with an admixture of mud which stops short a foot or so from the top of the pile. Then the beavers chew their way in, to make the entrance tunnels and the central chamber. The absence of mud packing from the top of the pile means that spaces between the sticks serve for ventilation. In other words, there is no more intelligence required than any other rodent uses to dig in the ground.

The dams are text-book examples of engineering, and beaver dams give way no more frequently than do man-made dams.

One reason for this is that a beaver dam is resilient, subject to immediate repair, is under constant surveillance and is supported by subsidiary dams. All the actions used in its construction can, however, be shown to be the result of a succession of instinctive actions, just as are those that result in the building of a bird's nest.

It is often said that beavers not only show skill in felling trees but use intelligence, by dropping the trees so that they fall towards the nearest water. This is not the case. Moreover, beavers are not uncommonly killed by the trees they fell falling on them.

Beavers often do other stupid things. The classic example is of a small lake in New York that was created by an artificial barrier of stones and cement litter. This was occupied by a family of beavers who were seen to 'repair' the dam with branches and mud although it was fully effective without these. Moreover, although the level of the pond was, so far as could be seen, satisfactory for their needs, the beavers built a subsidiary dam upstream of the pond, the only result of which was to flood the adjacent land to no purpose.

Everything considered, the achievements of beavers are more a tribute to the effectiveness of evolution in developing inherited behaviour patterns than a sign of unusual intelligence. There is, however, one qualification to be made. Young beavers stay with the parents for 2 years. During that time they must learn a great deal by following the example of the adults. It may be justifiable, therefore, to speak in terms of a cultural inheritance, and this alone would give an appearance of a greater intelligence.

Further evidence for the theory of innate behaviour can be added. Until a few years ago, beavers in the Rhone valley were hunted and they had long taken to burrowing in the river banks. Then they were protected by law, and shortly afterwards they began once more to build lodges and dams. A beaver may live for 20 years, but here they were reverting to a former pattern of behaviour after centuries of suppression due to persecution, using techniques they could not have learned. Only great intelligence, or a very strong instinct, could have brought about this behaviour.

Aspen and willow as food
Beavers eat bark, mainly of aspen and willow, from the smaller branches cut when building. Twigs and branches are stored around the base of the lodge. These have always been regarded as for the winter use of all members of the colony. Recent research has shown that the bulk of these are eaten by youngsters; older beavers live on their fat and eat little during winter.

Life history
Beavers, which are monogamous, mate in January to February. Gestation is 65–128

193

days and in April, May or early June two to eight kits, sometimes more, are born, with a coat of soft fur and eyes open. At birth each weighs about 1 lb and is 15 in. long including 3½ in. of tail. At one month, each will find and eat solid food, but weaning is not complete until 6 weeks old. Young remain with parents for 2 years, becoming sexually mature at 2–3 years.

Enemies

As with all rodents, beavers are preyed upon by any carnivores of approximately their own weight or more. In this instance the enemies include wolverine, lynx, coyote, wolf, bobcat, puma and bear. A beaver's alarm signal when a predator is in sight is to bring the tail over the back then smack it down with such force on the water that the sound can be heard up to ½ mile away.

Decline of the European beaver

Beavers were once common in Switzerland, as shown by the place names Biberach, Bibersee, Biberstein and Bibermukle (biber is German for beaver). Their extermination was due partly to their valuable fur, but more particularly to slaughter for their glandular secretion used to mark their territories. This, known as castoreum, enjoyed a vogue as a cure-all in the 16th and 17th centuries, with a resulting insensate slaughter of the luckless animals. Analysis has shown castoreum to contain salicylic acid, one of the ingredients of aspirin.

The former presence of beavers in the British Isles, too, is commemorated in many place-names, such as Beverley, Beverege, Bevercotes, Beverstone and Beversbrook in England, and Losleathan in Scotland and Llostlydan in Wales, both meaning broadtail. The animal seems to have still been plentiful in Britain up to the mid-16th century. The value of its fur can be gauged from prices fixed by the Welsh prince, Howel Dha, in the 10th century, at 120 pence a skin as compared with 24 pence for a marten pelt and 18 pence for otter, wolf and fox. This undoubtedly led to the animal's extermination, and in France to its almost complete elimination except in the Rhône Valley. In the 16th century, Henry IV of France, impressed by the demand for beaver pelts for hats, trimmings, fur linings and leather for shoes, sought to increase the economic strength of his country by sending men to Nova Scotia and Newfoundland. In due course the British gained this resource, largely through the Hudson Bay Company, and it was the search for more and more furs, particularly beaver, that led to Canada being opened up.

Profit versus protection

In America, with the arrival of the early settlers, the beaver was recognised as a valuable source of both meat and fur. Trade was soon established with the Indians, who wisely killed only mature animals, so that their hunting could have done little to impair the number of beavers. The brisk fur trade with England that sprang up roused the old spirit of avarice, and before long white trappers joined their efforts with those of the Indians—and killed indiscriminately.

In about 150 years the beaver had been exterminated in the coastal regions of the Eastern States, and seriously reduced elsewhere. The story is, however, patchy, for in some spots their numbers remained relatively unimpaired. Also, beavers in deep rivers were less easy to catch than those in, say, mountain streams. As the North American continent was more and more opened up, so the trade continued unabated, with similar results to those seen in the Eastern States, but on a wider scale.

The Hudson Bay Trading Company was formed in 1670 and such was the growth of its beaver trade that between 1853 and 1877 it marketed nearly 3 million beaver pelts. This steady drain brought about a serious depletion which has been rectified to some extent by official conservation measures.

Beavers were not always killed for profit. At times the animal became a nuisance, either through its inroads on timber, in settled areas, or when it took a liking to the stalks of corn. In places, too, it became a menace to river banks. Nevertheless, it was early recognised that only harm could result from its total elimination. As early as 1866, it became protected by law in the State of Maine, with the result that by the early years of the present century it had increased so much in numbers that some control had to be imposed to protect plantations.

Since that time, both in the USA and in Canada, with increasing speed to the present day, there have been many efforts made at conservation, either by individual landowners, by public bodies, or by Government action, State or Federal. In some cases the reason behind it has been no more than a desire to preserve an interesting animal. In others it is due to a realisation that the work of beavers contributes to the conservation of water in the land and to the preservation of trout streams. It has been found that it is possible, by the intelligent use of closed seasons, limiting the numbers of pelts taken and having them taken only under licence, not only to bring about increased beaver populations locally, but to derive revenue from the surplus. Consequently, there has been considerable reintroductions to re-stock areas where they had been exterminated.

The conservation of water may be summed up in the following quotation from an American water company's report: 'On almost all the mountain streams they (the beaver) should be protected and encouraged. A series of beaver ponds and dams along the headwaters of a mountain stream would hold back large quantities of mountain water during the dangerous flood season and equalise the flow of the streams so that during the driest seasons the water supply would be greatly increased in the valleys. Beaver-ponds not only hold water but distribute it through the surrounding soil for long distances, acting as enormous sponges as well as reservoirs. A series of ponds also increases the fishing capacity and furnishes a safe retreat for the smaller trout and protection from their enemies.'

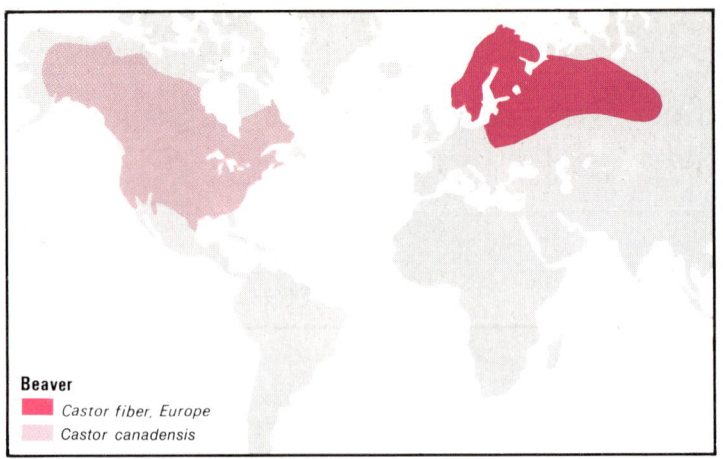

The beaver was on the way to extinction in Europe and America in the 19th century, but has since been rigorously protected and the populations are increasing. They have been so successful in some places that control is necessary.

Beaver
Castor fiber, Europe
Castor canadensis

Fear and flight having failed to rescue this beaver, caught away from the relative safety of its pool, it must now turn and fight for its life against the hungry hunting coyote.

class	**Mammalia**
order	**Rodentia**
family	**Castoridae**
genus & species	***Castor fiber*** European beaver ***C. canadensis*** Canadian beaver

Deer mouse

Meal among the toadstools: a deer mouse strikes a Disneylike pose while taking a snack.

Deer mice are American, very similar to the European long-tailed fieldmouse, both in appearance and in habits, but the two belong to different families. There are about 20 species, varying in colour from sandy or grey to dark brown. Some are almost white and others nearly black, but in general those living in woods are darkish, and those living in open or arid country are pale. The underparts and feet are white, hence the alternative name of white-footed mouse. A deer mouse measures 5–15 in. from nose to tip of tail, the tail varying from 1½–8 in. in different species.

They are found over most of North America, from Alaska and Labrador southwards, and one species extends into South America, reaching the extreme north of Colombia. They inhabit many kinds of country from swamps and forests to arid, almost desert, country, but each species usually has only a limited habitat and consequently is found only in a relatively small part of the total deer mouse range.

195

Overlapping territories

Deer mice are nocturnal, coming out during the day only if they are very hungry, or if there is a cover of snow that allows them to forage under its shelter. During the evening they can be heard trilling or buzzing, a noise quite unlike the squeaks of other mice, and in some parts of the United States this has led to their being called vesper mice. They also drum with the front feet when excited.

Each deer mouse has a home range which it covers regularly in search of food. The extent of the range varies considerably and depends on the amount of food available. In the grasslands of south Michigan the average size of the ranges of male deer mice is ⅗ of an acre, while those of the females are slightly smaller. The home range of a mammal is not strictly comparable with the territory of a bird. Only a few birds keep a territory all through the year, but more important, a mammal does not defend its range so vigorously. The borders of neighbouring ranges overlap, sometimes considerably, and the ranges of two females may be almost identical, but it is only the inner parts of the territory around the nest that will be defended vigorously.

Within its range, a deer mouse may have several refuges in abandoned burrows or birds' nests, under logs or in crevices. Sometimes a deer mouse will come indoors and make its nest in an attic or storage room. Each nest is used for a short time, being abandoned when it becomes soiled, for deer mice limit hygiene to cleaning their fur.

Burrows with a bolt hole

The nest is an untidy mass of grass and leaves, lined with moss, fine grass or feathers. Sometimes the deer mice make their own burrows. The Oldfield mouse, a species of deer mouse living in Alabama and Florida, makes a burrow leading down to a nest which is 1 ft underground. Then from the other side another burrow leads up again but stops just short of the surface. This presumably serves as a bolt hole in case a snake or other narrow-bodied enemy finds its way in. A traditional way of catching these mice is to push a pliable switch or wand down the hole, twiddle it about until it can be pushed up the escape burrow, and catch the mouse as it breaks out.

Are they a pest?

Seeds and berries are the main food of deer mice but they also eat many insects such as beetles, moths and grasshoppers, which are chased and bitten or beaten to death. Insect larvae, snails and slugs are devoured, and deer mice also eat carrion such as dead birds and mammals, and they will gnaw cast antlers.

Deer mice are something of a problem in plantations or on farms, where they eat seeds of new-sown crops which they smell out and dig up. But even when abundant, they are not as much of a pest as meadow voles and other small rodents. To even the score, deer mice are helpful because they eat chafer grubs that damage the roots of young trees.

Hanging on to mother

In spring the males search for mates, perhaps finding females whose ranges overlap theirs. At first their advances are repulsed but the males eventually move into the females' nests, staying there for a few days only but sometimes, it is thought, forming permanent pairs.

The female gives birth to a litter of 1–9 young after 3 or 4 weeks. At birth the young mice are blind, deaf, and apart from their whiskers, naked. They hang firmly to their mother's teats and she can walk around with them trailing behind. If the nest is disturbed she will drag them in this manner to a new site. Any baby that does fall off is picked up and carried in its mother's mouth.

Litters of deer mice can be found from spring to autumn but more are born in spring and autumn than during the summer, and if the winter is mild, breeding will continue through it. Females begin breeding at 7 weeks, only a few weeks after leaving their mothers, and have up to 4 litters a year.

Many nocturnal enemies

Most deer mice live less than two years, and many never reach maturity but provide food for the many predators that hunt at night. Foxes, weasels, coyotes, bobcats, owls and snakes, all feed on deer mice, and even shrews will occasionally eat them.

Racial 'segregation'

Although similar, the 20 different deer mice can easily be told apart by the specialist in classification, and, one must presume, by the mice themselves. Otherwise they would mix and interbreed and their differences would disappear, especially when different kinds live in the same habitat. Experiments by an American scientist using a Rocky Mountain deer mouse and a Florida deer mouse, which are closely related, showed how the deer mice are segregated.

Special cages were made, each with two side compartments. In preparation for the experiment a Rocky Mountain mouse was put in one compartment and a Florida mouse in the other, and this was repeated for all the cages. After these had remained long enough to impart their smell to the compartments they were taken out. Now, into each cage were put either a Rocky Mountain mouse or a Florida mouse, and these naturally made full use of the available space, including wandering into each compartment. By timing the period each mouse spent in each of the two side compartments of its cage the scientist found that in all cases the test mouse was very obviously drawn to that compartment which carried the smell of its own species. This almost certainly is how mice of the same species, even when sharing a habitat with another species, would be drawn together to breed, for it was noticed that males reacted particularly strongly to the smell of females of their own species on heat. So although it may sometimes appear that there are mixed populations of deer mice, the different species are really living separately.

There was, however, one difference between the Rocky Mountain mice and the Florida mice: the latter were much more likely to spend time in compartments smelling of Rocky Mountain mice. The reason for this seems to be that in Florida there is only one species of deer mouse, and discrimination is no longer necessary; but in the west there are many species and if their strains are to be kept pure, they must be able to distinguish between their own fellows and those of closely related species.

class	**Mammalia**
order	**Rodentia**
family	**Cricetidae**
genus & species	*Peromyscus maniculatus* others

Deer mouse cleaning and drying its fur—its only hygienic habit.

Porcupine

The tree porcupines of North and South America are very different from the porcupines of the Old World. To begin with, they live mainly in trees and their hindfeet are adapted for climbing. Some species also have a prehensile tail. The best known, the Canadian or North American porcupine, is up to $3\frac{1}{2}$ ft long, of which 1 ft is tail, and has an average weight of 15 lb although large males may weigh up to 40 lb. It is heavy and clumsily built with a small head, short legs and a short, stout, spiny tail. The hindfoot has a well-developed great toe and very long, powerful claws to help the animal climb. The long fur on the upper parts is brownish-black, sprinkled with long white hairs that conceal the short, barbed spines, which are yellowish-white tipped with black.

The South American tree porcupines, of which the Brazilian tree porcupine is typical, differ from the North American species in having a long, prehensile tail, the tip of which is hairless and by having only four toes on the hindfeet with a broad fleshy pad, opposable to the toes, used rather like a thumb in gripping branches when the animal is climbing. It is of lighter build with short, closely set spines, sometimes concealed by long hairs.

The Canadian porcupine inhabits most of the timbered areas of Alaska, Canada and the United States (except the southeastern quarter), south to the extreme north of Mexico. South American porcupines extend from Mexico through Central America to Colombia, Venezuela, Brazil, Bolivia, Peru and Ecuador in South America.

△ Long fur conceals the porcupine's spines.
▽ North American porcupine revealing its arsenal of over 20 000 sharp-tipped quills.

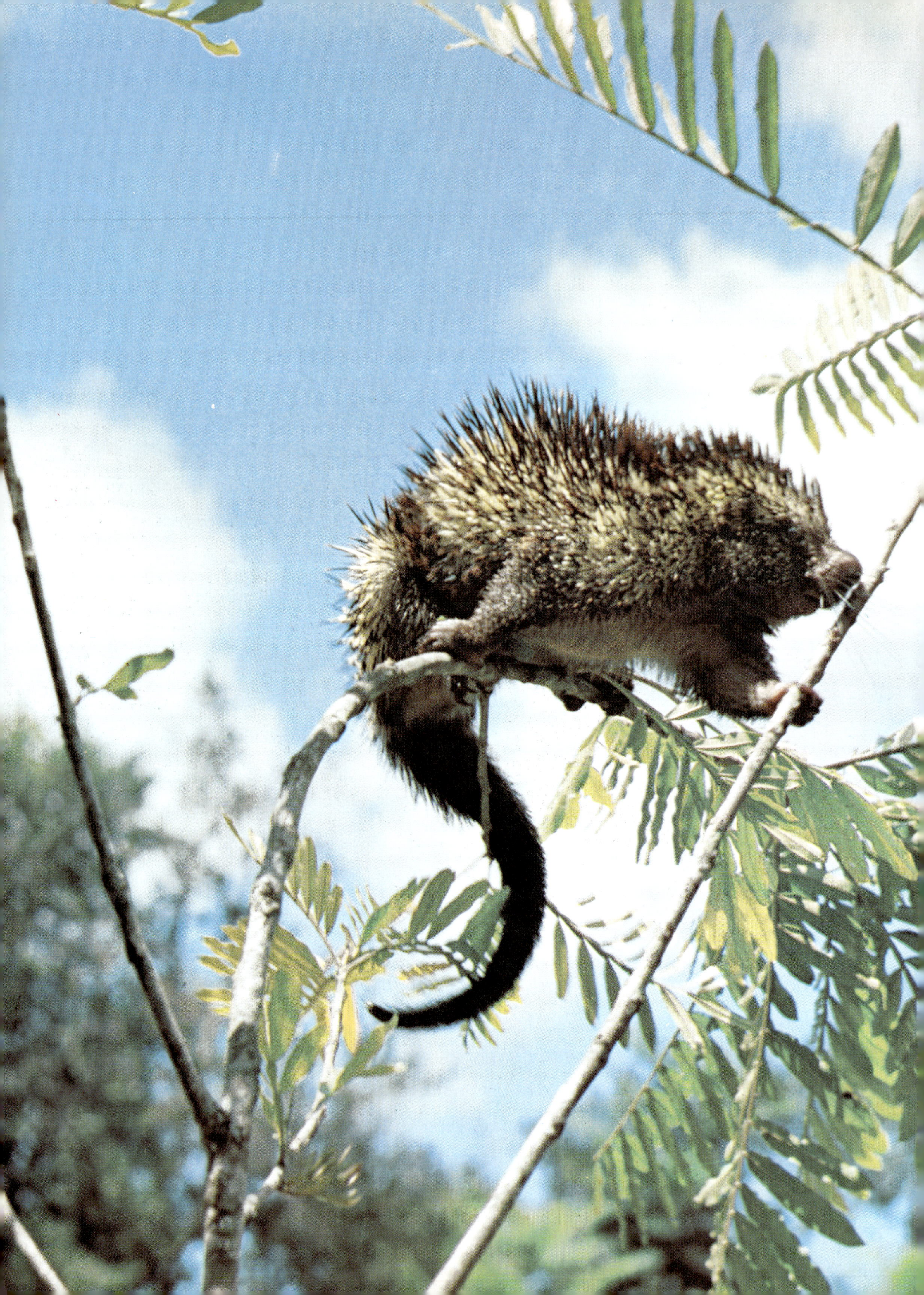

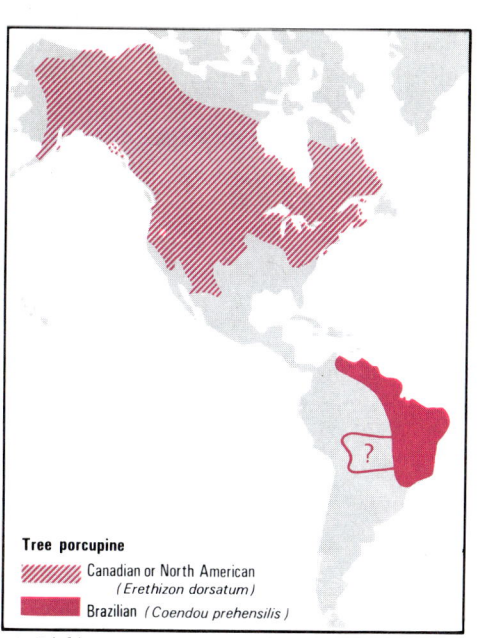

◁ *Picking a precarious path, a South American porcupine* Coendou *sp. seeks its typically rodent diet of bark, stems and leaves.*

Tree porcupine
- Canadian or North American (*Erethizon dorsatum*)
- Brazilian (*Coendou prehensilis*)

No hibernation
All the tree porcupines live in wooded areas, the North American species preferring woods of conifers, junipers and poplars. Although clumsily built they can climb well and they will also swim. They lie up during the day among rocks or in hollow trees and feed mainly at dusk and at dawn. They are usually solitary but occasionally several Canadian tree porcupines may shelter together in the same den, especially in winter. They do not hibernate but they take to dens during bad weather.

Salt addicts
The Canadian tree porcupine varies its food with the seasons. In spring it eats the flowers and catkins of the willow, maple and poplar. Later it turns to the new leaves of aspen and larch. In summer it feeds more on herbaceous plants and in winter on evergreens like the hemlock and pine. Its principal food in winter, however, is bark and the porcupines do much damage by ring-barking trees. The young red firs of the Sierra Nevada in California are occasionally destroyed by tree porcupines. When the weather is bad and the snow deep an animal may live in one tree and not leave it until all the bark above the snow-line has been stripped. Tree porcupines also have a strong liking for sweet corn and a few of these animals can completely ravage a field of it.

A more peculiar taste is the porcupine's craving for salt. Handles of farm implements which have been touched by hands moistened with sweat, leaving a trace of salt, will be gnawed. So will gloves, boots, and saddles; even the steering wheel of a car has been gnawed away. The porcupine will also gnaw bones and antlers dropped by deer. But its crowning achievement is to gnaw glass bottles thrown away by campers, presumably for the salt in the glass.

The South American tree porcupines also eat the bark and leaves of trees and tender stems but in addition they eat fruit such as bananas, and occasionally corn.

Well-developed babies
The Canadian tree porcupines mate in the fall or early winter. During courtship the male rubs noses with the female and often urinates over her. Generally a single young is born after a gestation period of 210–217 days. The young are very well-developed at birth; their eyes are open and they are born with long black hair and short soft quills. They weigh about 20 oz and can climb trees when 2 days old. They are weaned in 10 days, and become sexually mature in their second year.

Little is known of the breeding habits of the South American tree porcupines. There is usually a single young at a birth, born from February to May. The young of the Brazilian tree porcupine are comparatively large at birth and are covered with long, reddish hair. Their backs are covered with short spines, which are flexible at birth.

Few natural enemies
Few animals prey on the porcupine because of its spines, but the wolverine, puma and fisher marten will attack the North American species. A tree porcupine is said never to attack an enemy. If cornered, however, it will erect its quills and turn its back on its adversary, striking out repeatedly with its tail. A porcupine does not shoot its quills but they are so lightly attached that when they enter the skin of the enemy they become detached from the porcupine.

Skulls identify species
The crested porcupine is the best known species in the Old World family Hystricidae. Not all the porcupines in that family have such prominent quills as the crested porcupine. One *Trichys lipura* living in Borneo, for example, lacks true quills. It has only short, flat, weak spines and its long tail has a brush of bristles on the end. At first sight it appears not to be a porcupine at all. The same thing can be said of some of the family Erethizontidae. Since the crested and the Canadian porcupines look so alike, the question arises: What is the essential difference between the Old World porcupines and the New World porcupines? The fact that they are widely separated geographically is not important. Both families agree in having species that show a varying tendency to grow quills among the bristly coat, and both families contain a diversity of species. Therefore, those who classify these rodents have to look for something more stable upon which to separate them. They find this in the skull. Any Old World porcupine, whatever it may have in the way of quills, has a very rounded skull which has quite obviously a different shape from that of the New World porcupines.

class	**Mammalia**
order	**Rodentia**
family	**Erethizontidae**
genera & species	***Erethizon dorsatum*** Canadian or North American porcupine ***Coendou prehensilis*** Brazilian tree porcupine, others

Black bear

There are five species of black bear, each placed in a separate genus. All are smaller than the brown bears, and all are sufficiently similar for one of them, the one most studied, to serve as a type for the other four. This is the American black bear which originally inhabited practically all the wooded areas of North America from Central Mexico northwards. Its numbers are much reduced now and it has been eliminated from much of its former range, but in national parks its numbers are increasing and elsewhere it survives close to human settlement. Up to 5 ft long with a 4½ in. tail, and weighing 200–500 lb, it has shorter fur, shorter claws and shorter hind feet than the brown bears. The species also shows a number of colour phases: black, chocolate brown, cinnamon brown, blue-black and white with buff on the head and in the middle of the back. This last is most common in British Columbia, where it has been known as Kermode's bear. These different colour phases may occur in the same litter.

△ *Twin cubs being escorted by their mother. They stay with her until at least 6 months old.*

Friendly habits
Black bears are good tree climbers, powerful, quick to react, harmless to people except when provoked, cornered or injured – or through sheer friendliness. In national parks, where they are familiar with human beings and come begging food, visitors to the parks must keep to the protection of cars to avoid inadvertent injury from the bears' claws. Black bears are solitary except during the breeding season, the two partners separating after mating, to wander far in search of food. The American black bear sleeps through the winter – not hibernation in the usual sense – after laying in fat by heavy autumn feeding. It does not feed during the winter although it may leave its den, a hollow tree or similar shelter, for brief excursions during mild spells. When startled, the adult gives a 'woof', otherwise it is silent. The cubs, when distressed, utter shrill howls.

Mixed diet
Insects, berries and fruits, eggs and young of ground-nesting birds, rodents and carrion form its main foods, but young of deer and pronghorn are killed and eaten. Porcupines are killed, the bear flipping them over with its paw and attacking the soft under-belly, often to its own detriment from the quills. Black bears have been found dead with quills embedded in the mouth. Sometimes a black bear may turn cattle-killer.

Enemies
Old or sickly adults are occasionally killed by pumas and wintering bears may be attacked by wolves.

Life history
The breeding month is June and the gestation period is 100 to 210 days. Usually there are two or three cubs in a litter, exceptionally four, rarely five, born in January and February. At birth the 8 in., 9–12 oz cubs are blind, toothless and naked except for scanty dark hair. The mother continues to sleep for two months after the birth, having roused herself sufficiently to bite through the umbilical cords. The cubs alternately suck and sleep during these two months. They stay with the mother for at least six months, and she mates only every other year.

The original Teddy Bear
In 1902, Theodore (Teddy) Roosevelt, who was a keen naturalist as well as President of the United States, captured a black bear cub on a hunting trip, which he adopted as a pet. Morris Michton, a Brooklyn doll manufacturer, used this bear as model for the first Teddy Bear, so named with the President's permission. The popularity of the Teddy Bear as a toy was immediate and world-wide. The black bear, as already stated, is such a favourite in American national parks that they take liberties with visitors. In European zoos a prime favourite with visitors is the Himalayan black bear. Such general favouritism owes much to the human-like qualities of the bears.

We tend to favour in animals, qualities which reflect our own, as with birds that talk or animals that stand erect such as penguins, owls and bears. In man the bipedal stance is habitual; in bears it is but occasional, the usual way of walking being on all-fours. That does not invalidate the comparison, and the effect of the bears' ability to stand erect at times is reinforced by the way they will sit upright, as if on a chair, and also by the characteristic way a bear will wave a fore-paw (or hand) when soliciting food. Another trait which enables us to see ourselves in bears is their way of lying prone, on their backs.

Bears also appear to be intelligent. Whether they are more intelligent than their near relatives, the cats and dogs, has never been adequately tested. At least we know that the cubs stay with the mother for six months, often longer, and some may stay with her until her next cubs are born. A long period of parental care allows for learning by example and a longer period for experience with security. And if bears are by nature solitary they can, if circumstances compel them, as in bear-pits in zoos, live together with little discord, showing they are, like us, fundamentally friendly.

Yet in spite of the comparisons that can be drawn between bears and ourselves, and in spite of our fondness for Teddy Bears, the fact remains that the American black bear, like all other bears, has long been a target for the hunter's gun – and not only the hunter's. In 1953, 700 black bears were killed in British Columbia to provide bearskins, the ceremonial headwear, for the Brigade of Guards, for the coronation of Queen Elizabeth II. An American writer drily remarked: 'Fortunately for the black bear Great Britain's coronations are infrequent . . .'

class	**Mammalia**
order	**Carnivora**
family	**Ursidae**
genus & species	***Euarctos americanus*** American black bear

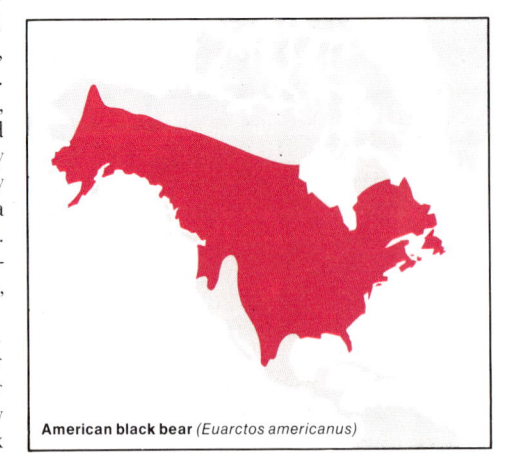

American black bear (*Euarctos americanus*)

Returning to their earth after a hunt: North American red fox and two cubs. Night hunting is a way of teaching the cubs how to fend for themselves.

Red fox

It is usually assumed that, but for its careful preservation by the various 'hunts', the red fox would have become extinct long ago in the British Isles except in the wildest and most remote corners. For centuries it has been persecuted outside the hunt areas because of its alleged poultry-killing habits and even today the killing of a fox is still looked on with approval. Yet, in spite of all this, the fox has survived and at times is unusually numerous.

The head and body of the red fox measure just over 2 ft with a 16in. tail, but there are records which greatly exceed these measurements, especially in Scotland. A well grown fox stands only about 14 in. at the shoulder. The dog-fox and vixen are alike except that the vixen is slightly smaller and has a narrower face as she lacks the cheek ruffs of the male. The fur is sandy russet or red-brown above and white on the underparts. The backs of the ears are black, as are the fronts of the legs, but these may be brown, and can change from one colour to the other with the moult. The colours may vary, however, not only between one individual and another, but in the same individual from season to season. The foxes (Tods) of Scotland, although of the same species, usually have greyer fur than the English fox. When fully haired the tail is known as a brush. The tip (or tag) is white but may be black. Weights vary considerably but on average a dog-fox weighs 15 lb, a vixen 12 lb.

The sharp-pointed muzzle, the erect ears and quick movements of the eye with its elliptical pupil combine to give the fox an alert, cunning appearance, so many stories of its astuteness have been invented in the past. At the moult, in July and August, foxes lose their characteristic appearance and look thin-bodied, long-legged and slender of tail.

The red fox ranges over Europe and over Asia as far south as central India, as well as northwest Africa. It is found throughout the British Isles, except for Orkney, Shetland and all Scottish islands, but not Skye. In central Asia it lives up to 14 000 ft above sea-level. The North American red fox ***Vulpes fulva*** is very like the Old World red fox in build and habits. There are several mutants, the cross fox is red with a black band across the shoulders, and the silver fox has a lustrous black coat with white tips to the guard hairs.

Tree-climbing foxes

The red fox's traditional cunning is a reflection of its adaptability. It prefers wooded or bushy areas but is found in a variety of habitats. Many foxes today are even found living in urban areas or even near large towns, where they probably live off rats and mice and scavenge in dustbins. Although the fox lives mainly on the ground there are many instances of it climbing trees. Usually this occurs when a tree is leaning or when there is a trailing bough that has broken and is hanging down to the ground, up which the fox can clamber. There is one recorded instance, however, of a fox having its sleeping nest at the top of a bole of an elm, 14 ft from the ground, with no branches between it and the ground. Foxes are largely nocturnal, but they can often be seen during the day. Except at the breeding season the dog-fox and vixen lead solitary lives. Most of the day is spent in an 'earth' which is more of a cavity in the ground than a burrow. They may make this themselves or use a badger's set or rabbit burrow.

Foxes use a great variety of calls, the most familiar being the barking of both the dog-fox and the vixen in winter and the screaming of the vixen, generally during the breeding season. It has now been established that, contrary to common opinion, the dog-fox may also scream sometimes.

Poultry killer?

A great deal has been written about the fox prowling round farms looking for an opportunity to kill an unguarded fowl. Certainly foxes will take poultry and they will take lambs, but these habits tend to be local. A vixen that has taken to killing poultry will teach her cubs to do the same. But not all foxes are habitual poultry stealers and there have been instances of foxes repeatedly visiting poultry farms or private gardens containing a few poultry and never molesting them.

More solid information about their food comes from a Ministry of Agriculture investigation of the stomach contents of dead foxes. This showed that, now that rabbits are scarce, the chief items of food are rats, mice and bank voles. Hedgehogs, squirrels, voles, frogs, even snails and beetles are, however, also eaten, as well as a great deal of vegetable matter. Birds such as partridges and pheasants will also be taken. A fox will soon discover offal or carrion, even if buried 2 ft in the earth. Foxes also visit dustbins and a feature of the many foxes now living in towns is that they have turned scavenger. Railway marshalling yards also have their foxes, probably feeding on food thrown out from restaurant cars or on rats living on this food.

Teaching the cubs

Mating takes place from late December to February. The gestation period is 51–52 days. About April the vixen produces her single litter for the year, usually of four cubs. They are blind until 10 days old, and remain in the earth until nearly a month old, the vixen staying close beside them, while the dog plays a large part in supplying the food. When about a month old the cubs come out in the evening and can be seen playing as a group with the parents outside the earth. This continues for several weeks.

After the cubs are weaned it has been noted, in semi-captivity, that the dog-fox continues to bring food for them and the cubs will take the food from his mouth themselves, or the vixen may take it and the cubs take it from her mouth. The cubs have to jump up to reach the parent's mouth and all the time the parent is moving its head, from side to side or up and down. In this way the cubs are being exercised so developing their limbs, and also learning to co-ordinate movements and senses. During this time the dog plays a great deal with them, more so than the vixen.

Later the vixen takes them hunting at night, so they learn from her example how to fend for themselves. The cubs leave their parents when about 2 months old, reach adult size 6 months after birth, and become sexually mature in their first winter.

'Charming'

Foxes are credited with resorting to a particular stratagem, called 'charming', to attain their end. A story is usually told of a fox which, seeing a party of rabbits feeding and knowing that they will bolt to their holes on its approach, starts rolling about at a safe distance to attract their attention. Then like a kitten it begins chasing its tail, while the rabbits gaze, apparently spellbound, at the performance. The fox continues without a pause, as though oblivious to the presence of spectators, but all the time it is contriving to get nearer, until a sudden straightening of the body enables it to grab the nearest rabbit in its jaws.

There are too many authentic accounts of foxes charming to leave much doubt about the matter. From these, a more likely explanation evolves: foxes are naturally playful. Like some other mammals they will, without obvious cause, suddenly behave as if they have taken leave of their senses, bounding about, bucking, somersaulting, and so on. Rabbits and birds on seeing these antics are drawn to watch out of curiosity. If the fox is hungry then the spectators suffer. It is possible that a fox playing in this way and finding birds and rabbits attracted to it, might use this tactic again, deliberately. Such learning by experience would not be beyond a fox's intelligence, but there is much to be said for the view that charming, as such, is not primarily a deliberate stratagem.

class	**Mammalia**
order	**Carnivora**
family	**Canidae**
genus & species	***Vulpes vulpes*** *European red fox*

▷ *With ears pricked, wary eyes glinting from its mask, the red fox with its magnificent brush is a very wily, sometimes vicious, and yet most handsome animal.*

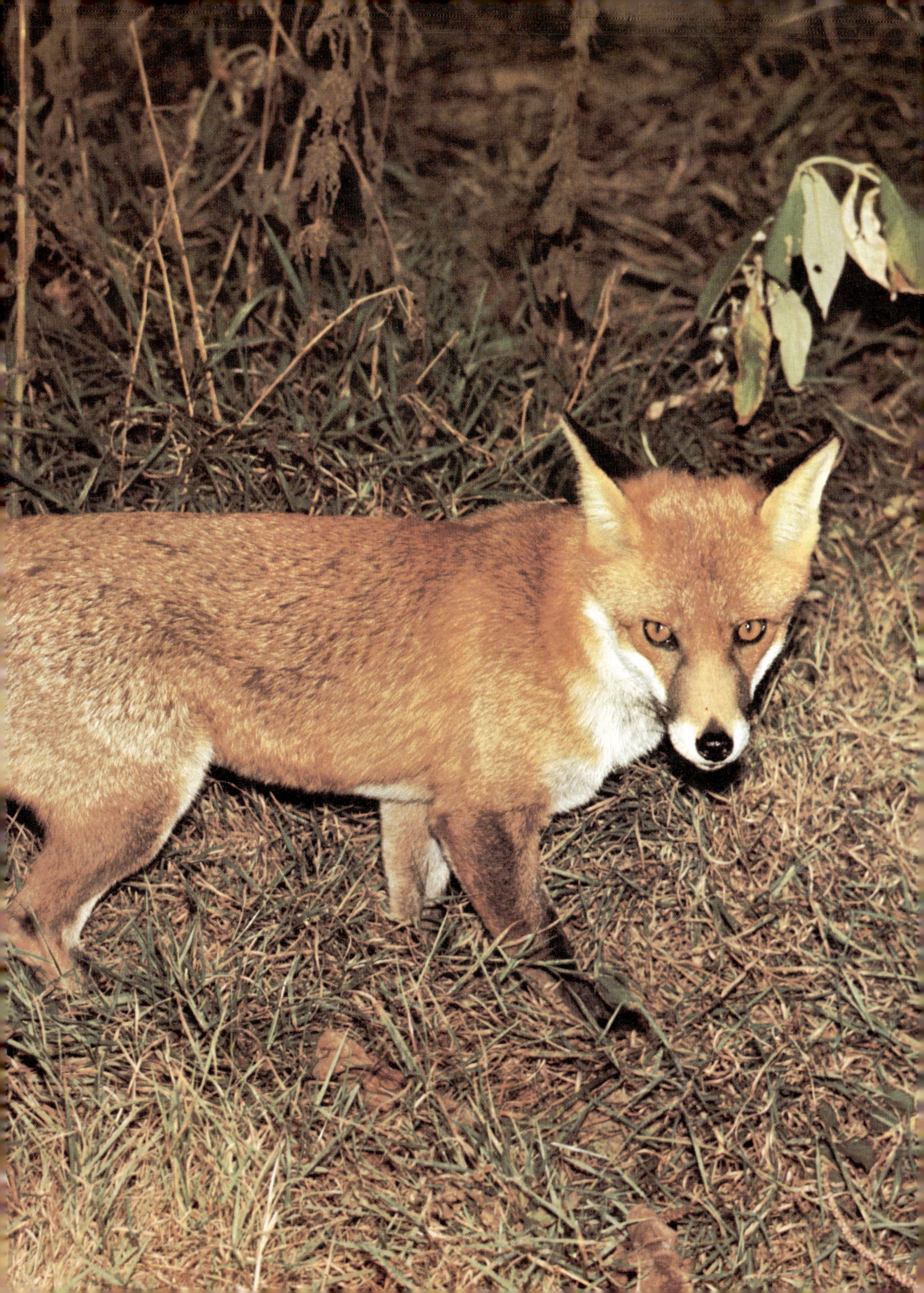

Giant Panda

This black and white bear-like carnivore has leapt from obscurity to worldwide fame in less than a century. Also called the panda and, by the Chinese, **beishung**, *the white bear, it was first made known to the western world in 1869, by the French missionary, Père David.*

The giant panda is stockily built, with a 6 ft long body and a mere stump of a tail and weighs 300 lb. Its thick, dense fur is white except for the black legs and ears, black round the eyes and on the shoulders. There are 5 clawed toes on each foot and each forefoot has a small pad which acts as a thumb for grasping. The cheek teeth are broad and the skull is deep with prominent ridges for the attachment of strong muscles needed in chewing fibrous shoots. It lives in the cold damp bamboo forests on the hillsides of eastern Tibet and Szechwan in southwest China.

Habits unknown . . .

Giant pandas are solitary animals except in the breeding season. They live mainly on the ground but will climb trees when pursued by dogs. They are active all the year. Little more is known of the habits in the wild of this secretive animal which lives in inaccessible country. When live giant pandas were first taken to zoos it was thought they lived solely on bamboo shoots. Later it was learned that during the 10—12 hours a day they spend feeding they eat other plants, such as grasses, gentians, irises and crocuses, and also some animal food. This last includes small rodents, small birds and fishes flipped out of water with their paws.

Breeding unknown . . .

Little is known about the giant panda's breeding habits in spite of attempts to induce a mating between An-an, the male giant panda belonging to the Moscow zoo, and Chi-chi, the female in the London zoo. In 1966 Chi-chi was taken to Moscow but no mating took place, and An-an was brought to London in 1968 with no more success. It is believed that giant pandas mate in spring, and that probably one or two cubs are born in the following January, each cub weighing 3 lb at birth. Several cubs have been born in Chinese zoos. On September 9, 1963, a male cub Ming-ming was born to Li-li and Pi-pi in Peking zoo, and a female cub, Ling-ling, was born on September 4, 1964, to the same parents. A third cub Hua-hua, a male, was born to Chiao-chiao on October 10, 1965.

Bad treatment

In 1869 Père Armand David of the Lazarist Missionary Society, and an experienced naturalist, came upon the skin of an animal

Chinese mother love. Although breeding has not been achieved in the western world, despite the efforts of the Moscow zoo and London zoo to breed An-An and Chi-Chi, there are more than a dozen giant pandas in Chinese zoos, and they have been bred successfully.

in a Chinese farmhouse in Szechwan which he did not recognise. He sent it to Paris and later sent more skins. Not until 1937, however, was the first live giant panda seen outside China. Theodore and Kermit Roosevelt had shot one in the 1920's and in 1936 two other Americans, Ruth and William Harkness, with the animal collector Tangier Smith, captured several. They quarrelled, presumably over the spoils, and all the giant pandas died except one, which Ruth Harkness delivered to the Chicago zoo where it was named Su-lin. Another, given the name Mei-mei, reached the same zoo in 1938. In December the same year a young female, Ming, aged 7 months and two young males, Tang and Sung, reached the London zoo. The two males died before the female reached maturity, and she died in December 1944. In May 1946, the government of the Szechwan Province presented a male, Lien-ho, to the London zoo and he lived until 1950. By 1967 there were a score of giant pandas in various zoos, 16 or more in Chinese zoos, An-an in Moscow and Chi-chi in London.

Although the species is now protected it was formerly hunted by the local Chinese, and the history of western animal collectors does nothing to offset this. The story of Chi-chi gives point to this. In 1957, Heini Demmer, then living in Nairobi, was commissioned by an American zoo to negotiate the exchange of a collection of East African animals for a giant panda. He reached Peking zoo with his cargo, was given the choice of one of three giant pandas, chose Chi-chi, the youngest, and took charge of her on May 5 1958. Chi-chi had been captured by a Chinese team of collectors on July 5 1957, and was reckoned then to be 6 months old. She had been taken to Peking zoo and cared for night and day by a Chinese girl. By the time Demmer had taken charge of Chi-chi the United States had broken off diplomatic relations with the Chinese People's Republic, so she became automatically a banned import.

Bamboo shoots are not the sole food of giant pandas

Demmer took her on a tour of European zoos during the summer of 1958, reaching the London zoo on September 26.

After such treatment perhaps it is not surprising she refused to be mated! She died on July 21 1972.

London Zoo now has two 3 year-old pandas, Ching-Ching and Chia-Chia, which were presented to Mr Heath during his visit to Peking. Mr Nixon was similarly honoured on his visit there in 1973. In 1974 Tokyo had two pandas, and Korea and Paris owned one each.

class	**Mammalia**
order	**Carnivora**
family	**Procyonidae**
genus & species	***Ailuropoda melanoleuca***

Raccoon

Commonly known as 'coons', raccoons are one of the most familiar North American animals, if only in folklore and stories. Their adaptability has allowed them to withstand drastic changes in the countryside while their intelligence, cleanliness and appealing looks have combined to make them popular. Their head and body length is 16–24 in. with a tail of 8–16 in. and they weigh up to 45 lb. Their fur is grey to black with black rings on the tail and a distinctive black 'burglar mask' over their eyes. Their feet have long toes and the front paws are almost hand-like and very dexterous.

Raccoons are relatives of pandas, kinkajous and coatis. There are seven species, the best known ranges from Canada to Central America. The crab-eating raccoon lives in southern Costa Rica, Panama and the northern regions of South America. The other species are found on islands.

Adaptable coons

Raccoons originally lived in woods and brushy country, usually near water, but as the woods have been cut down they have adapted to life in open country. They are solitary, each one living in a home range of about 4 acres, with a den in a hollow tree or in a rock crevice. They come out more at night, and are good climbers and swimmers. In the northern part of their range raccoons grow a thick coat and sleep through cold spells. The raccoons of southern USA and southwards, are active throughout the year. Where trees have been cut down raccoons move into fox burrows or barns and they have been known to spread into towns, even to the middle of cities where they live in attics and sheds and raid garbage bins for food.

Raiding garbage bins is one of the raccoon's less popular traits. Apart from the mess, the bins are sometimes carried away bodily. There are stories of ropes securing the bins being untied, rather than bitten through. This is evidence of the raccoon's extreme dexterity. They use their hands almost as skilfully as monkeys; experiments have shown that their sense of touch is very well developed.

Varied diet

Raccoons eat a very wide variety of both plant and animal food. It is the ability to take so many kinds of food that is probably the secret of the raccoon's success and of its ability to survive changes in the countryside. Raccoons are primarily carnivores; earthworms, insects, frogs and other small creatures are included in their diet, and raccoons also search in swamps and streams for crayfish and along the shore for shellfish. The eggs and chicks of birds, both ground and tree nesters, are eaten and raccoons are sometimes pests on poultry

Appealing look from large bundle of fur – a raccoon up a tree.

farms and in waterfowl breeding grounds. They are also pests on agricultural land because they invade fields of corn, ripping off the ears and scattering them half-eaten. Fruits, berries and nuts are also eaten.

Irresponsible fathers
Raccoons mate in January or February, each male mating with several females then leaving them to raise the family. The young, usually 3 or 4 in a litter, are born from April to June, after 60-70 days gestation. They weigh 2½ oz at birth and are clad in a coat of fuzzy fur, already bearing the characteristic black mask. Their eyes open in 18 days and at about 10 weeks they emerge from the nest for short trips with their mother. The trips get longer as the young learn to forage for themselves but they stay with their mother until about one year old. Raccoons live as long as 13 years.

Coon currency
Raccoons are a match for most predators and when hunted with dogs the raccoon may come off best, especially if it can lure the hound into water and drown it. Raccoons have always been trapped and hunted in large numbers by Indians and Europeans, both for their hard-wearing fur and because of their attacks on crops. Their fur was the main cause for killing them and even in the 17th century efforts were made by imposing taxes and bans to prevent too many raccoon pelts from being exported. At one time the skins were used as currency and when the frontiersmen of Tennessee set up the State of Franklin, the secretary to the governor received 500 coonskins a year while each member of the assembly drew three a day. Nowadays coonskin is not valuable unless there is a sudden fashion as there was for coonskin hats following the film on Davy Crockett, King of the Wild Frontier.

Why so fastidious?
In the *Systema Naturae* Linnaeus called the raccoon *Ursus* (later *Procyon*) *lotor*, or the 'washing bear'. In other languages the raccoon is similarly named *ratons laveur*, *ositos lavadores* and *Waschbaren*. Their names testify to the strange habit raccoons have of appearing to wash their food before eating it. This apparently hygienic behaviour has become part of the raccoon folklore and only recently have proper attempts been made to explain it.

Some books state that raccoons always wash their food, others say that the habit may be more common in captive animals, yet there are no authentic reports of food washing in the wild. Naturalists who have studied raccoons deny ever seeing this take place. Food washing must, therefore, be an unnatural habit of captive raccoons.

The first scientific study of food washing was made by Malcolm Lyall-Watson at London Zoo. First, he showed that raccoons do not really wash their food but immerse it, manipulate it, then retrieve it. He suggested that the habit should, therefore, be called dousing.

Lyall-Watson gave a large variety of foods to a number of raccoons. Animal food was doused more often than plant, yet earthworms, the only food that needed cleaning, were doused least of all. In another series of experiments it was shown that the shape, smell and size of food objects governed dousing to some extent, but most important was the distance of the food from water. The nearer the water, the more likely is food to be doused.

The conclusion drawn by Lyall-Watson explains why dousing only occurs in captivity. In the wild, raccoons feed on food found on land and food found in water. In captivity all their food is on land, so they 'go through the motions' of foraging in water by taking their food to water, dropping it then searching for it in an action that has for so long been described as washing. Similar behaviour is seen in captive cats. When presented with dead animals, they often throw them about and pounce on them, 'pretending' to hunt them.

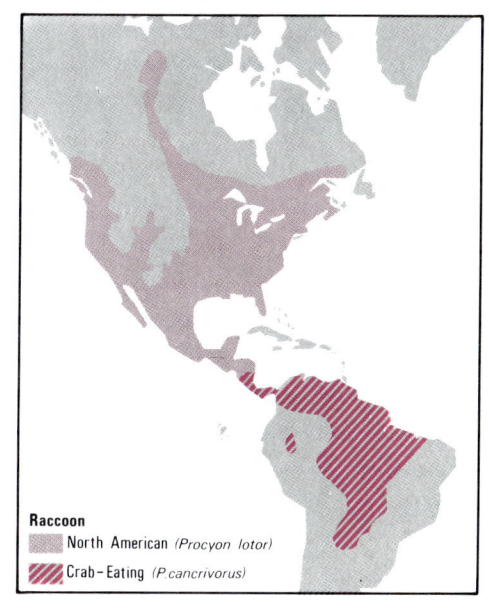

Raccoon	
▓ North American (*Procyon lotor*)	
▨ Crab-Eating (*P. cancrivorus*)	

class	**Mammalia**
order	**Carnivora**
family	**Procyonidae**
genus & species	***Procyon lotor*** North American raccoon ***P. cancrivorus*** crab-eating raccoon others

▽ *An unsuspecting raccoon enjoys the shallow waters, unaware of the threatened danger of a puma waiting for the moment to pounce.*

Otter

The various species of otter are all much alike in appearance and habits. They are long-bodied, short-legged mammals, with a stout tail thickened at the root and tapering towards the tip. There is a pair of scent-glands under the tail. The head is flattened with a broad muzzle and numerous bristling whiskers. The ears are small and almost hidden in the fur. The sleek, dark brown fur consists of a close fawn underfur which is waterproof and an outer layer of long stiff guard hairs, which are grey at their bases and brown at their tips. The throat is whitish and the underparts pale brown. Each foot has five toes, bearing claws in most species, the forefeet are small, the hindfeet large and webbed.

The common or European otter ranges across Europe and parts of Asia, to Japan and the Kurile Islands. It is 4 ft long, including the tail, but may reach $5\frac{1}{2}$ ft, and weighs up to 25 lb. The bitch is smaller than the dog otter. The Canadian otter, of Canada and the United States, is very similar to the European but has an average larger size. It is sometimes spoken of as the river otter, to distinguish it from the sea otter, a markedly different animal. The small-clawed otter, of India and southeast Asia, is much smaller than the European species but the clawless otter of western and southern Africa is larger and is a marsh dweller, feeding on frogs and molluscs. The giant Brazilian otter is the largest of all the otters. It reaches $6\frac{1}{2}$ ft in length, and has a tail that is flattened from side to side.

Solitary and elusive

Except during the mating season otters are solitary, extremely elusive and secretive, and always alert for any sign of disturbance. They will submerge in a flash, leaving few ripples or, when on land, they will disappear among vegetation. Their ability to merge into their background on land is helped by the 'boneless' contortions of the body and the changing shades of colour in the coat which is aided by the movements and changes in the guard hairs. For example, the coat can readily pass from looking sleek and smooth to looking, when damp, spiny and almost porcupine-like.

Otters do not hibernate. They will fish under ice with periodic visits to a breathing hole. It has been said that otters will use a trick known in aquatic insects; that is, to come up under ice and breathe out, allowing the 'bubble' to take in oxygen from the air trapped in the ice and lose carbon dioxide to the ice and water, then inhale the re-vitalised 'bubble'. This has not yet been proved, however.

▽ *Prenuptial affectionate play. Usually solitary, otters are sociable in the mating season.*

Master-swimmers

At the surface an otter swims characteristically showing three humps each separated by 5–8 in. of water. The humps are the head, the humped back and the end of the tail curved above the water line. When drifting with the current only the head may be in view. Occasionally an otter may swim with the forelegs held against the flanks, the hindlegs moving so rapidly as to be a blur. When this is done at the surface there is a small area of foam around the hindquarters, with a wake rising in a series of hump-like waves. It will also use this method when submerged, although more commonly it swims with all four legs drawn into the body which, with the tail, is wriggled sinuously, as in an eel. Leaping from the water and plunging in again, in the manner of a dolphin, is another way in which an otter can gain speed in pursuit of a large fish. Underwater it will often progress in a similar, but smoother undulating manner.

An otter shows its skill better in its ability to manoeuvre. It will roll at the surface, or when submerged, pivoting on its long axis, using flicks of the tail to give momentum. It can turn at speed in half its own length, using tail and hindquarters as a rudder, or it may swim round and round in tight circles, creating a vortex that brings mud up from the bottom. This last tactic is used to drag small fishes up that have taken refuge under an overhanging bank.

When an otter surfaces it stretches its neck and turns its flattened, almost reptilian head from side-to-side reconnoitring before swimming at the surface or coming out on land.

Otters are nomads, fishing a river or lake then moving on to take their next meal elsewhere. They are said at times to cover up to 16 miles overland in a night. Certainly the European and Canadian otters are met at times far from the nearest water. Overland they move by humping the back. A favourite trick is to take a couple of bounds then slide on the belly for 4–5 ft. On a steep slope the glide may take them 40–50 ft. On a muddy or snow-covered slope the slide becomes tobogganing, otters often retracing their steps to slide repeatedly down the slope in a form of play.

Otters live in rivers and lakes, especially small rivers running to the sea or to large lakes. They particularly like those free of weed and undisturbed by human beings. In times of scarcity otters will move to the coast and are then spoken of as 'sea-otters', not to be confused with the real sea otters.

Eels and crayfish favoured

The European otter has a varied diet of fish, small invertebrates, particularly crayfish and freshwater mussels, birds, small mammals, frogs and some vegetable matter. The main fish food seems to be eels and slow-moving fishes but salmon and trout are also eaten.

Otter families play sea-serpents

Mating takes place in water, at any time of the year, with a peak in spring and early summer. After a gestation of about 61 days 2 or 3 cubs, exceptionally 4 or 5, are born, blind and toothless, with a silky coat of dark hair. There is uncertainty about when the eyes open, the only reliable record being 35 days after birth. The cubs stay in the nest for the first 8 weeks and do not leave their mother until just before she mates again.

Young otters swim naturally, as is shown by cubs hand-reared in isolation. The indications are, however, that the mother must coax them, or push them, into the water for their first swim. In the early days of taking to water a cub will sometimes climb onto the mother's back, but normally the cubs swim behind their mother. On rare occasions two or more family parties will swim one behind the other. When this does happen a line of humps is seen, and as the leading otter periodically raises her head to take a look around the procession resembles the traditional picture of the sea-serpent.

Otters as lake monsters

It has been said that any schoolboy knows an otter when he sees one. This is so only as long as the otter runs true to form, but otters are quick-change artists and highly deceptive. Sir Herbert Maxwell has recorded how, at the turn of the century, four gentlemen crossing Loch Arkaig in a steam pinnace saw a 'monster' rise from the depths almost under the bows of their boat, create a tremendous flurry of water at the surface, then dive again out of sight. All were puzzled as to its identity, but when the stalker, a Highlander, present with them in the boat, was questioned later, he was in no doubt that the 'monster' was an otter.

The monster of Loch Morar, near Loch Arkaig, is traditionally 'like an overturned boat towing three overturned dinghies', which could serve as a reasonable description of a bitch otter followed by her three cubs. The ogo-pogo of Canada is believed to be founded on otters swimming in line, and at least one lake monster in Kenya was proved to be a line of otters.

When President Theodore Roosevelt was big game hunting in 1911 he was out in a boat on Lake Naivasha, in Kenya, when the three humps of the local monster appeared. Roosevelt fired once, two humps disappeared, the third stayed on the surface. The skin of the otter was sent to the American Museum of Natural History in New York.

△ *A backflip from a European otter. This photo caught an otter leaping playfully into the water for the pure joy of living.*

△ *The African clawless otter has only a small connecting web at the base of the toes.*

class	**Mammalia**
order	**Carnivora**
family	**Mustelidae**
genera & species	***Amblonyx cinerea*** Indian small-clawed otter ***Aonyx capensis*** clawless otter ***Lutra canadensis*** Canadian otter ***L. lutra*** European otter ***Pteronura brasiliensis*** giant Brazilian otter others

Tiger

One of the largest of the 'big cats', the tiger's sinuous grace, splendid carriage and distinctive colouring make it one of the most magnificent of all animals. A large male averages 9 ft – 9 ft 3 in. in length including a 3ft tail. It stands 3 ft or more at the shoulder and weighs 400 – 500 lb. Females are a foot or so less in length and weigh about 100 lb less. The various races of tigers vary considerably in size from the small Bali Island tiger to the outsized tiger found in Manchuria which may reach 12 ft in total length. The ground colour of the coat is fawn to rufous red, becoming progressively darker southwards through the animal's range, the Balinese tiger being the darkest. The underparts are white. There have been rare cases of white tigers in India. The coat is overlaid with black to blackish-brown transverse stripes, and these contrasting colours provide an excellent camouflage in forest regions.

In cold climates such as Siberia and Manchuria, tigers have thick, shaggy coats which become shorter and denser in the warmer climates. The hair round the face is longer than on the rest of the body, forming a distinct ruff in adult males.

From its original home in Siberia, the tiger spread across almost the whole of Eurasia during the Ice Ages. Today it is found only in Asia where a number of geographical races are recognised, including those of Siberia, Manchuria, Iran, India, China, Sumatra, Java and Bali. The races differ only in size, colour and markings.

▷ *Solitary splendour: tiger caught by flash.*
▷▷ *Transport solution: a helpless tiger cub is carried in the same way as a domestic kitten.*

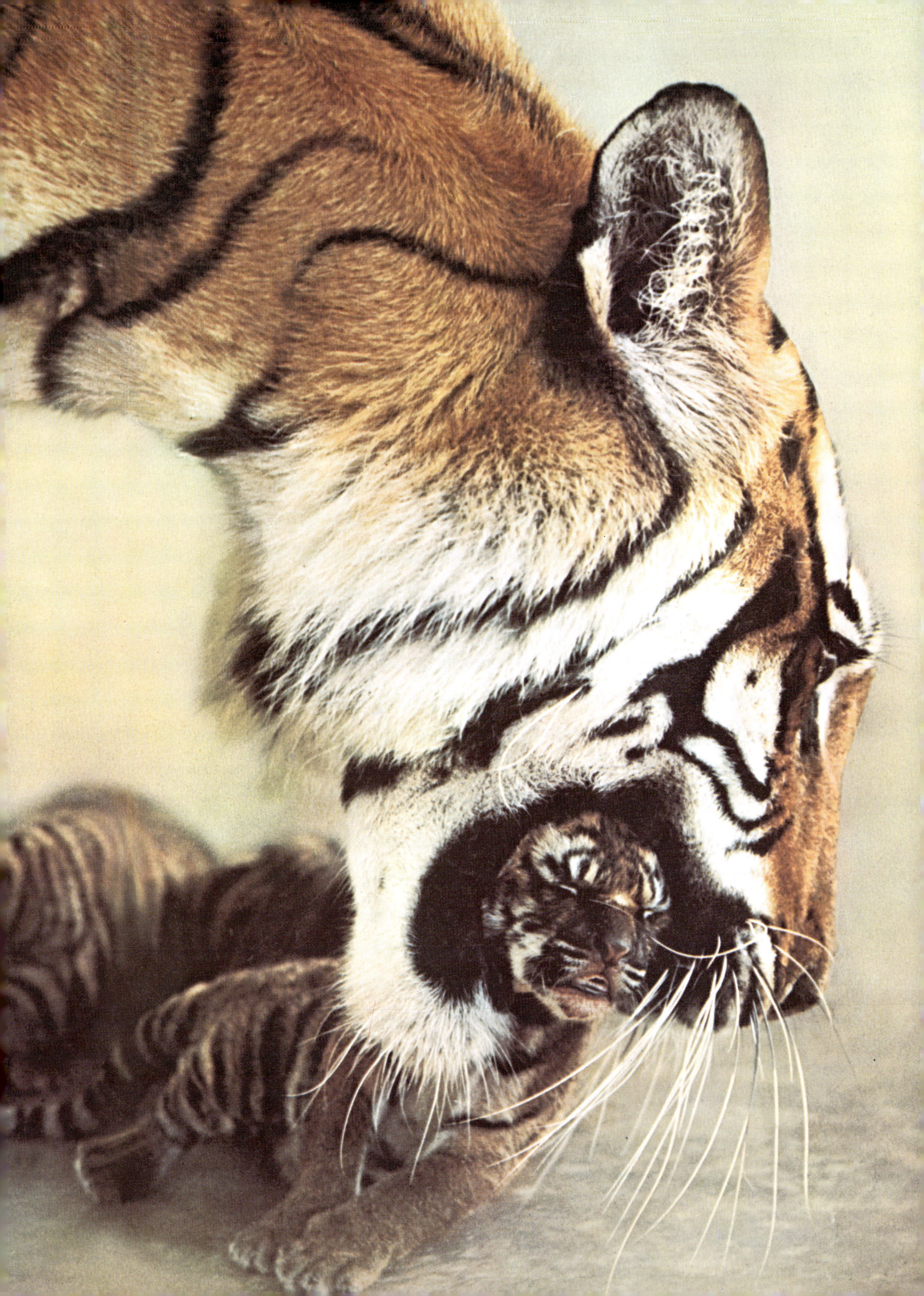

Solitary prowler

Although its original home was in the snowy wastes of Siberia the tiger's natural preference is for thick cover. It has, however, become adapted to life in rocky mountainous regions, the reed beds of the Caspian, and the dense steaming jungles of Malaya and islands such as Java and Bali. It cannot, however, tolerate excessive heat and during the heat of the day it will lie up in long grass, caves, ruined buildings, or even in swamps or shallow water.

The tiger is an excellent swimmer and in times of flood has been known to swim from one island to another in search of food. Unlike most members of the cat family it is not a good climber and seldom takes to the trees, but there is a record of a tiger taking a single leap of 18 ft from the ground to pull a man off a tree. Its hearing is very good and is the sense most used in stalking prey. It does not appear able to see unmoving animals, even at a short distance.

The tiger has a variety of calls ranging from a loud 'whoof' of surprise or resentment to a full-throated roar when disturbed or about to launch an attack.

Strength widens choice of prey

A tiger preys on deer, antelope, wild pig and smaller animals such as monkeys and porcupines. It will take fish and turtles in times of flood and locusts in a swarm. It occasionally attacks larger animals such as wild bull buffaloes, springing on their backs and breaking their necks. When food is short it may steal cattle, and an old or injured tiger too weak to hunt may attack humans. Game is, however, its natural food and it is interesting that tigers have completely deserted some forested areas of India where game animals have disappeared even though there were still plenty of wandering cattle about.

A tiger stalks using stealth for the first part of its hunt, finally attacking with a rush at its victim, grasping a shoulder with one paw and then seizing the throat. It then presses upwards, often breaking the neck in the process. After a kill it withdraws to a secluded spot, preferably under cover, taking its prey with it. If it cannot do this, or hide its kill near its lying-up place, it is forced to have a hurried meal and leave the rest of the carcase to the hyaenas and vultures and other carrion eaters.

Small striped cubs

Only while the tigress is in season do male and female tigers come together; according to some authorities, this could be for less than two weeks. During this time a tiger will not allow another male near him and will fight, sometimes to the death, over possession of the female. In India the mating season is variable, but in Malaya it is from November to March and in Manchuria it is during December. A female starts to breed at about 3 years of age and then has a litter every third year, or sometimes sooner. After a gestation of 105–113 days, 3–4 cubs are born, occasionally as many as 6. The mortality among cubs is high and usually no more than two survive to adulthood. They are born blind and helpless, weighing only 2–3 lb, but they have their parents' distinctive striped pattern from the beginning. The cubs grow rapidly; their eyes open after 14 days and they are weaned at 6 weeks. At 7 months they can kill for themselves, but stay with their mother until 2 years old, during which time she trains them in hunting. They are fully grown at 3 years.

Man the hunter

Although the tiger has few natural enemies it has been hunted by man from very early times, at first by the local people and later for sport. In India especially, the coming of the British and the introduction of firearms was disastrous to the tiger and it is estimated that in 1877 alone 1 579 tigers were shot in British India. Today the reduction of game animals and the reduction of its natural habitat is further diminishing its numbers, and as a result six of the eight races of tiger are listed as being in danger of extinction.

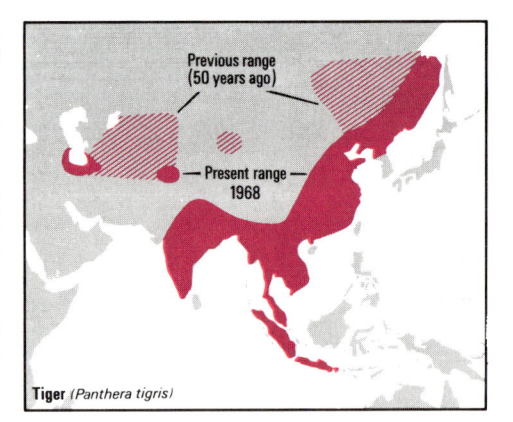

△ *Reflected glory: unlike many of the cat family, tigers often take to the water and are strong swimmers. In times of flood they have been known to feed on fish and turtles and to swim in search of stranded prey. They cannot bear excessive heat and will sometimes sit in shallow water in an attempt to keep cool.*

Not normally dangerous

Tigers have a respect and fear for man which is difficult to explain. Even if harassed by curious humans or sportsmen a tiger will not normally react until its patience is well-nigh exhausted. Normally a man can walk in a tiger's habitat without fear or hindrance and there have been several instances of a tiger approaching a man while sitting quietly near his camp and passing by, doing no harm even though it was obvious that it had seen him. Men have been followed for many miles by tigers and have come to no harm; they were probably being escorted off the territory. It is only when its normal hunting routine is disturbed that it becomes really dangerous. It may then become a man-eater, especially when shot at indiscriminately, incapacitating it rather than killing it. A wounded tiger left to its fate, without the strength to hunt, will resort to man-eating or cattle killing, out of necessity, as it will when injured by natural mishap. One of the commonest causes of injury is damage by porcupine quills. If the quills enter the paws or lower limbs the tiger cannot pull down and kill natural prey or cattle. Occasionally the quills may even penetrate the tiger's jaw and the animal starves to death. Old age may also cause a tiger to attack cattle or humans. Once a tiger has turned man-eater or cattle-killer, for whatever reason, every man's hand is against it. Whole villages will turn out and not rest until it is killed, even in areas where the tiger is protected by law.

Tiger (Panthera tigris)

class	**Mammalia**
order	**Carnivora**
family	**Felidae**
genus & species	***Panthera tigris*** *tiger*

Lion

Lions were once common throughout southern Europe and southern Asia eastwards to northern and central India and over the whole of Africa. The last lion died in Europe between 80–100 AD. By 1884 the only lions left in India were in the Gir forest where only a dozen were left, and they were probably extinct elsewhere in southern Asia, for example, in Iran and Iraq, soon after that date. Since the beginning of this century the Gir lions have been protected and a few years ago they were estimated to number 300. A census taken in 1968, however, puts the figure at about 170. Lions have been wiped out in northern Africa, and in southern Africa, outside the Kruger Park.

The total length of a lion may be up to 9 ft of which 3 ft is tail, the height at the shoulder is $3\frac{1}{2}$ ft and the weight up to 550 lb. The lioness is smaller. The coat is tawny; the mane of the male is tawny to black, dense or thin, and maneless lions occur in some districts. The mane grows on the head, neck and shoulders and may extend to the belly.

▷Shady business: lioness evades the heat.
▷▷An aspiring lion claims a higher position.
▽Pride of the bush: lionesses with their cubs.

Prides and the hunting urge

Lions live in open country with scrub, spreading trees or reedbeds. The only sociable member of the cat family, they live in groups known as prides of up to 20, exceptionally 30, made up of one or more mature lions and a number of lionesses with juveniles or cubs. Members of a pride will co-operate in hunting, to stalk or ambush prey, and they combine for defence. The roar is usually not used when hunting although lions have been heard to roar and to give a grunting roar to keep in touch when stalking. A lion is capable of speeds of up to 40 mph but only in short bursts. It can make standing jumps of up to 12 ft high and leaps of 40 ft. Lions will not normally climb trees but lionesses may jump onto low branches to sun themselves and they as well as lions will sometimes climb trees to reach a kill cached in a fork by a leopard. There is one record of a lioness chasing a leopard, apparently with the intent to kill it, into a tree, but she was foiled by the leopard going into the slender top branches which failed to bear the lioness's weight.

Not wholly carnivorous

Although strongly carnivorous lions take fallen fruit at times. Normally, in addition to the protein, fat, carbohydrate and mineral salts, lions get their vitamins from the entrails of the herbivores they kill. Typically, lions first eat the entrails and hindquarters working forward to the head. In captivity, lions flourish best and breed successfully when vitamins are added to a raw meat diet. Although lionesses often make the kill the lions eat first (hence, 'the lion's share') the lionesses coming next and the cubs last. In general, antelopes and zebra form the bulk of lions' kills but almost anything animal will be taken, from cane rats to elephant, hippopotamus, giraffe, buffalo and even ostrich.

A survey in the Kruger Park showed that in order of numbers killed the prey-species were: wildebeest, impala, zebra, waterbuck, kudu, giraffe, buffalo. A later survey showed a preference descending through waterbuck, wildebeest, kudu, giraffe, sable, tsessebe, zebra, buffalo, reed-buck, impala. When age or injury prevents a lion catching agile prey it may turn to porcupines and smaller rodents, to sheep

▽ *Violence afoot: hampered by the water around them, a pair of paddling lions make the opening moves of a soggy trial of strength.*

and goats, or turn man-killer, taking children and women more particularly. Man-eating can become a habit, however; once a small group of lions at Tsavo held up the building of the Uganda railway through their attacks on the labourers. Dogs may be killed but not eaten.

Exaggerated story of strength
A favourite story is of a lion entering a compound, killing a cow and jumping with it over the stockade. R Hewitt Ivy argues in *African Wild Life* for June 1960 that this is impossible. His explanation is that lions visiting a cattle compound do not all go inside. Possibly one leaps the fence, makes a kill and drags it under the fence to those waiting outside. Should the cattle panic and one leap the fence it will be pulled down by the rest of the pride outside and there eaten.

The lion hunts in silence and it is the lioness that most often kills the prey. The usual method of killing is to leap at the prey and break the neck with the front paws. Alternatively a lion may seize it by the throat with its teeth or throttle it with the forepaws, on the throat or nostrils. Another method is to leap at the hindquarters and pull the prey down. A lion will kill a hippopotamus by scoring its flesh with the claws in a running battle. Lions will kill and eat a crocodile and will also eat carrion, especially if it is fresh, and lion will eat dead lion. An old story tells of the lion's habit of lashing itself into a fury with a spur on the end of its tail, in order to drive itself to attack. Some lions do have what appears to be a claw at the tip of the tail. But this is only the last one or two vertebrae in the tail out of place, due to injury.

Natural control of populations
Lions begin to breed at 2 years but reach their prime at 5 years. The males are polygamous. There is a good deal of roaring before and during mating, and fights with intruding males may take place. Gestation is 105–112 days, the number of cubs in a litter is 2–5, born blind and with a spotted coat. The eyes open at 6 days, weaning is at 3 months after which the lioness teaches the cubs to hunt, which they can do for themselves at a year old. There is a high death rate among cubs because they feed last, so suffering from a diet deficiency, especially of vitamins. This serves as a natural check

▽ *On firmer ground. The skirmish begins as one lion lumbers up onto his rear legs and lunges at his equally cumbersome opponent.*

on numbers. Should numbers fall unduly in a district—as when lions are hunted by man or culled in national parks—prey is more easily killed and there is more food to spare. Lionesses will then kill for their cubs and then the cubs eat first. This richer diet makes for a high survival rate among the cubs, so restoring the balance in the population number.

Dangers for the King of Beasts
There are no natural enemies as such, apart from man, but lions are prone to casualties, especially the young and inexperienced. A zebra stallion may lash out and kick a lion in the teeth, after which the lion may have to hunt small game. The sable antelope is more than a match for a single lion and other antelopes have sometimes impaled lions on their horns. A herd of buffalo may trample a lion or toss it from one set of horns to another until it is dead, although two lions will overcome one large buffalo. One female giraffe attacked a lioness trying to kill her calf. Using hoofs of fore and hindlegs, as well as beating the lioness with her neck, she severely mauled her—and chased the lioness away over a distance of 100 yards. This is a better performance than a rhinoceros can manage. A lion will kill rhino up to three-quarters grown.

class	**Mammalia**
order	**Carnivora**
family	**Felidae**
genus & species	**Panthera leo** *lion*

△▷ *Plan of campaign: lion's strategy observed in Kruger Park. Detecting wildebeest, 16 lions deliberated and split into three parties.*
▷ *Drink up! One lioness remains on watch.*
▽▷ *Lioness casually accepts a mother's duty.*
▽ *An affectionate nudge from mother.*

Walrus

Although hunted since the time of the Vikings, almost to the point of extinction, the walrus has survived and today, with strict conservation measures, some herds are very slowly recovering their numbers. The two subspecies, the Pacific walrus and the Atlantic walrus, differ in only minor details. The Pacific bulls average $11-11\frac{1}{2}$ ft long and weigh a little over 2 000 lb but they can reach $13\frac{3}{4}$ ft and weigh up to 3 700 lb when carrying maximum blubber. The Atlantic bulls average 10 ft long and up to 1 650 lb in weight but may reach 12 ft and weigh 2 800 lb. The cows of both subspecies are smaller, $8\frac{1}{2}-9\frac{1}{2}$ ft and 1 250 lb, but large Pacific cows may reach almost $12\frac{1}{2}$ ft and a weight of 1 750 lb.

The walrus is heavily built, adult bulls carrying sometimes 900 lb of blubber in winter. The head and muzzle are broad and the neck short, the muzzle being deeper in the Pacific walrus. The cheek teeth are few and of simple structure but the upper canines are elongated to form large ivory tusks, which may reach 3 ft in length and are even longer in the Pacific subspecies. The nostrils in the Pacific subspecies are placed higher on the head. The moustachial bristles are very conspicuous, especially at the corners of the mouth where they may reach a length of 4 or 5 in. The foreflippers are strong and oar-like, being about a quarter the length of the body. The hindflippers are about 6 in. shorter, very broad, but with little real power in them.

The walrus's skin is tough, wrinkled and covered with short hair, reddish-brown or pink in bulls and brown in the cows. The hair becomes scanty after middle age and old males may be almost hairless, with their hide thrown into deep folds.

The Pacific walrus lives mainly in the waters adjacent to Alaska and the Chukchi Sea in the USSR. The Alaskan herds migrate south in the autumn into the Bering Sea and Bristol Bay to escape the encroaching Arctic ice, moving northwards again in spring when it breaks up.

The Atlantic walrus is sparsely distributed from northern Arctic Canada eastward to western Greenland, with small isolated groups on the east Greenland coast, Spitzbergen, Franz Josef Land and the Barents and Kara Seas. They migrate southward for the winter.

Walruses also inhabit the Laptev Sea near Russia and do not migrate in the winter. It is thought that this herd may be a race midway between the Atlantic and Pacific subspecies.

◁ *A long-in-the-tooth bull walrus of the Pacific subspecies. The elongated upper canine teeth are put to a variety of uses, among them defence and digging for clams.*

◁ *Playful pups: young walruses nuzzle each other with their sensitive moustaches.*

Tooth-walking bulls
Walruses associate in family herds of cows, calves and young bulls of up to 100 individuals. Except in the breeding season the adult bulls usually form separate herds. They live mainly in shallow coastal waters, sheltering on isolated rocky coasts and islands or congregating on ice floes. Since their persecution by man, however, walruses have learnt to avoid land as much as possible and to keep to the ice floes, sometimes far out to sea. They are normally timid but are readily aroused to belligerence in the face of danger. There seems to be intense devotion to the young, and the killing of a young one will rouse the mother to a fighting fury, quickly joined by the rest.

Walruses can move overland as fast as a man can run and because of their formidable tusks hunters, having roused a herd, have often been hard put to it to keep them at bay. Walruses have even been known to spear the sides of a boat with their tusks or to hook them over the gunwales.

As well as using them as weapons of offence and defence the walrus makes good use of its large tusks for digging food out of the mud and for keeping breathing holes open in the ice. It also uses them as grapnels for hauling itself out onto the ice, heaving up to bring the foreflippers onto the ice. The horny casing of bare hard skin on the palms of the flippers prevents the walrus from slipping. The walrus also uses its tusks for hauling itself along on the ice – indeed the family name Odobenidae means 'those that walk with their teeth'.

Walruses sunbathe and sleep packed close together on the ice floes with their tusks resting on each other's bodies. If the water is not too rough, adult walruses can also sleep vertically in the water by inflating the airsacs under their throats.

Monstrous swine
The walrus was associated in the Middle Ages with a variety of sea monsters. Named the whale-elephant in the 13th century it also became the model for the original seahorse and sea-cow. In addition it was described as 'a monstrous swine . . . which by means of its teeth climbs to the top of cliffs as up a ladder and then rolls from the summit down into the sea again.'

Clam grubbers
The walrus's diet consists principally of clams, which it grubs out of the mud with its tusks, and sea snails. It will also take mussels and cockles. The snout bristles help in detecting the shellfish. Clams are swallowed whole and no shells have ever been found in the stomach of a walrus, although it is not known how they are disposed of. A walrus also swallows a quantity of pebbles and stones, possibly for helping to crush the food in its stomach. Walruses usually dive for their food in shallow water of about 180 ft or less but occasionally they go down to 300 ft. Probably they deal with pressure problems at such depths by reducing the rate of blood flow as seals do.

Occasionally a walrus, usually an adult bull, will turn carnivorous and feed on whale carcases or it may kill small ringed or bearded seals. Having sampled flesh it may continue to eat it in preference to shellfish.

Hitch-hiking pup
Most matings take place from late April to early June and after a gestation of just over a year one pup is born, every alternate year. Birth takes place on an ice floe. The new-born pup is 4 ft long with a coat of short silver grey hair and weighs 100–150 lb. It is able to swim immediately, although not very expertly, and follows its mother in the water. After a week or two it can swim and dive well. Even so, it usually rides on its mother's back for some time after birth, gripping with its flippers. After a month or two the silver grey hair is replaced by a sparser dark brown coat of stiff hairs. The cow nurses the pup for 18 months to two years but they remain together for several months after weaning. The pups grow quickly, males becoming sexually mature at about 5–6 years, the females at about 4–5 years.

Killed in the rush
Killer whales and polar bears attack walruses but not often, the polar bear particularly being wary of attacking an adult bull even when he is ashore and therefore more vulnerable. Panic when killer whales are near may, however, cause high mortality. In 1936 a large herd was attacked by killer whales and driven ashore on St Lawrence Island. They hauled out onto the beach in such panic that they piled up on each other and 200 of them are said to have been smothered or crushed to death.

Slaughter by man
Walruses have been hunted by man from early times. The Eskimo and Chukchee have always depended on the annual kill to supply all their major needs, including meat, blubber, oil, clothing, boat coverings and sled harnesses. Even today they are largely dependent on it. The annual killings by the local people, however, had no very marked effect on the numbers of the herds. It was the coming of commercially-minded Europeans to the Arctic that started the real extermination. From the 15th century onwards they used the walrus's habit of hauling out on the beaches in massed herds to massacre large numbers in the space of a few hours. After 1861, when whales had become scarce, whalers from New England started harpooning walruses. Then they started using rifles and the Eskimos followed suit. More walruses could be killed but large numbers of carcases fell into the water and could not be recovered. An even greater wastage has been that caused by ivory hunters, who kill for the tusks and discard the rest of the carcase.

By the 1930's the world population of walruses had been reduced to less than 100 000 and strict conservation measures have now been enforced. The Pacific walrus now seems safe from extinction but the Atlantic walrus is still in danger.

class	**Mammalia**
order	**Pinnipedia**
family	**Odobenidae**
genus	***Odobenus rosmarus divergens*** *Pacific walrus* ***O. r. rosmarus*** *Atlantic walrus*

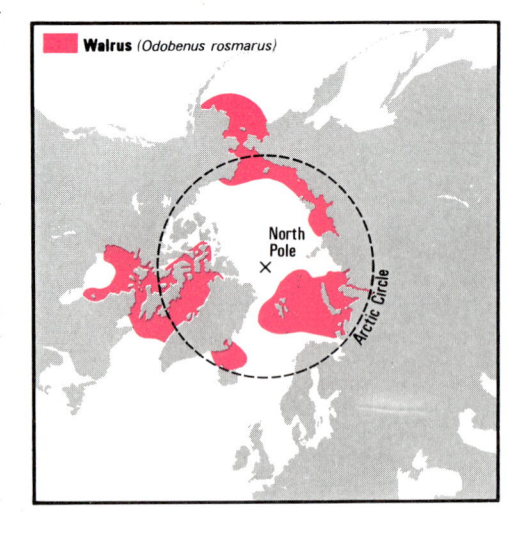

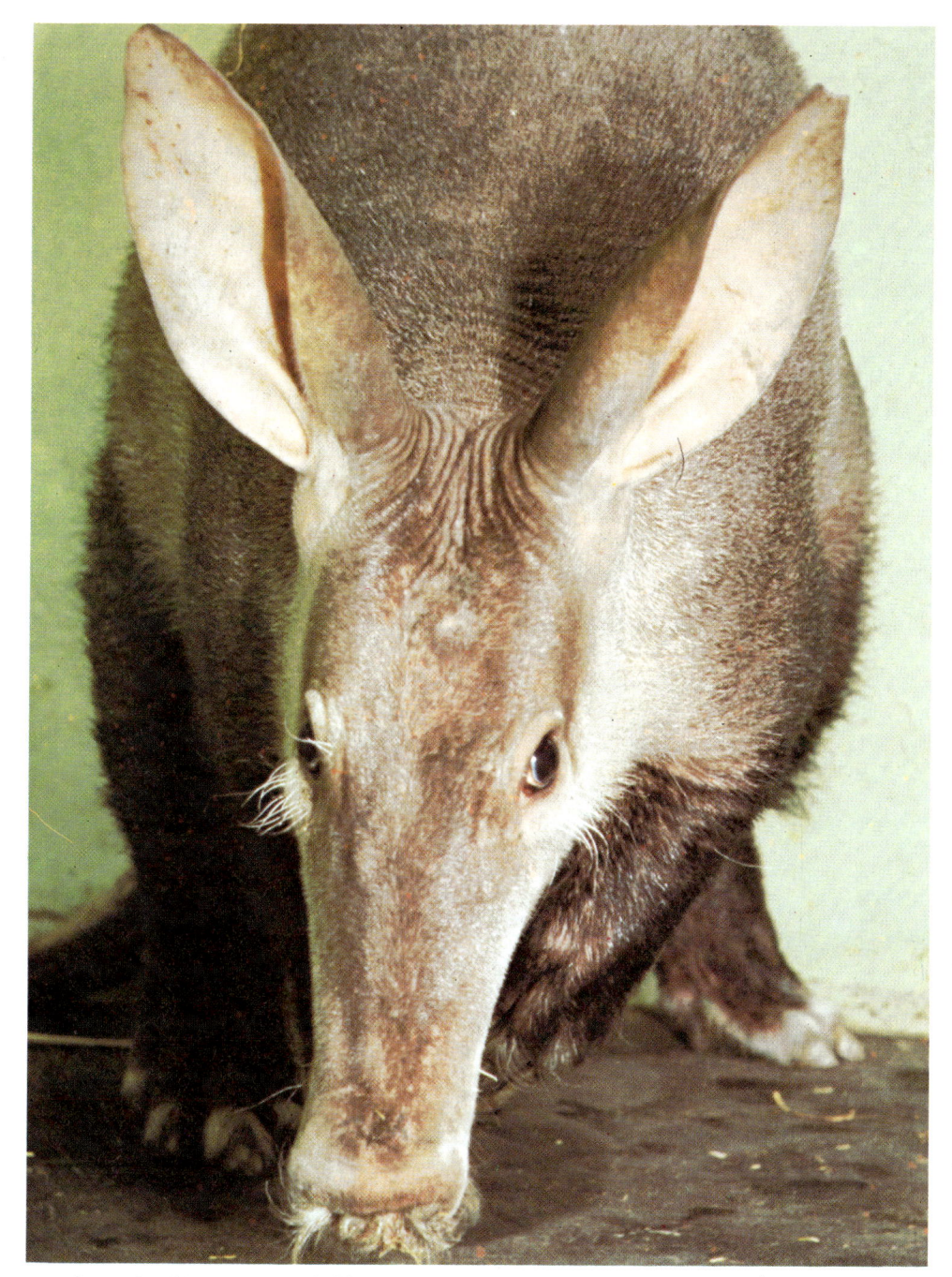

Aardvark

African mammal with a bulky body, 6 ft long including a 2 ft tail, and standing 2 ft high at the shoulder. Its tough grey skin is so sparsely covered with hair that it often appears naked except for areas on the legs and hind quarters. The head is long and narrow, the ears donkey-like; the snout bears a round pig-like muzzle and a small mouth. The tail tapers from a broad root. The feet have very strong claws—four on the front feet and five on the hind feet. The name is the Afrikaans for 'earth-pig'.

Distribution and habits

The aardvark has powerful limbs and sharp claws so it can burrow into earth at high speed. This it does if disturbed away from its accustomed burrow. There are records of it digging faster than a team of men with spades. When digging, an aardvark rests on its hind legs and tail and pushes the soil back under its body with its powerful fore feet, dispersing it with the hind legs.

The normal burrow, usually occupied by a lone aardvark, is 3–4 yd long, with a sleeping chamber at the end, big enough to allow the animal to turn round. Each animal has several burrows, some of them miles apart. Abandoned ones may be taken over by warthogs and other creatures.

Years can be spent in Africa without seeing an aardvark, although it is found throughout Africa south of the Sahara, except in dense forest. Little is known of its habits as it is nocturnal and secretive, though it may go long distances for food, unlike other burrowing animals.

Termite feeder

The aardvark's principal food is termites. With its powerful claws it can rip through the wall of termite nests that are difficult for a man to break down even with a pick.

Its method is to tear a small hole in the wall with its claws; at this disturbance the termites swarm, and the aardvark then inserts its slender 18 in. tongue into the hole and picks the insects out. It is protected from their attacks by very tough skin and the ability to close its nostrils—further guarded by a palisade of stiff bristles.

As well as tearing open nests, the aardvark will seek out termites in rotten wood or while they are on the march. It also eats other soft-bodied insects and some fruit.

Breeding cycle

The single young (twins happen occasionally) is born in midsummer in its mother's burrow, emerging after two weeks to accompany her on feeding trips. For the next few months it moves with her from burrow to burrow, and at six months is able to dig its own.

△ *The aardvark's nose is guarded by a fringe of bristles and it can also close its nostrils, as a protection against termites.*

◁ *Aardvark at home in African scrub close to a termites' nest where it has been feeding on these soft-bodied insects.*

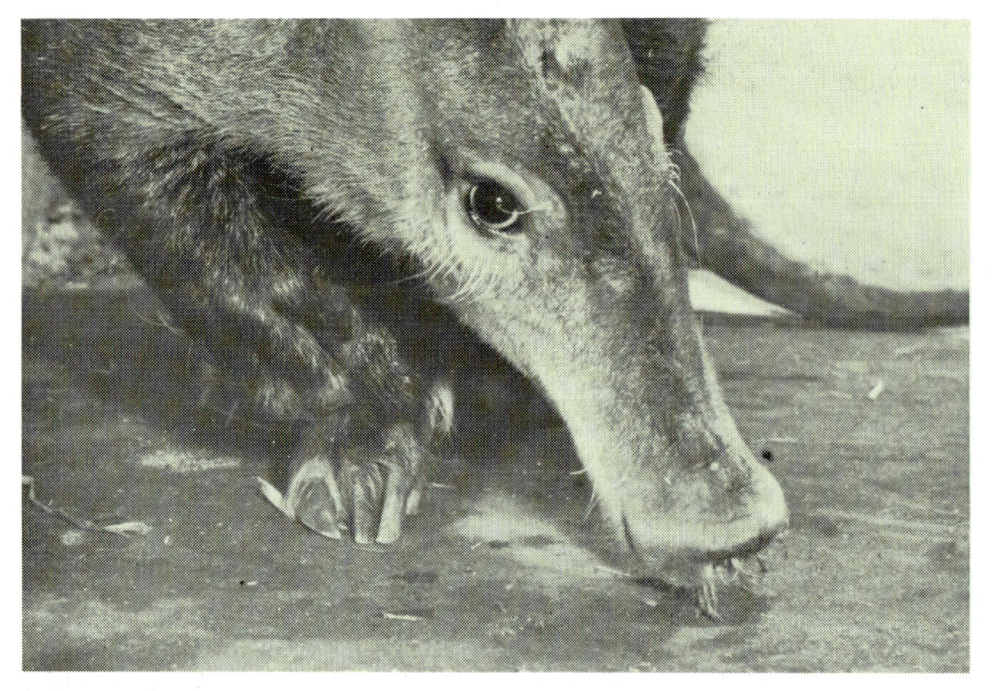

Digs to escape enemies

The aardvark's main enemies are man, hunting dogs, pythons, lions, cheetahs and leopards, and also the honey badger or ratel, while warthogs will eat the young. When suspicious it sits up kangaroo-like on its hind quarters, supported by its tail, the better to detect danger. If the danger is imminent it runs to its burrow or digs a new one; if cornered, it fights back by striking with the tail or feet, even rolling on its back to strike with all four feet together.

On one occasion, when an aardvark had been killed by a lion, the ground was torn up in all directions, suggesting that the termite-eater had given the carnivore a tough struggle for its meal. However, flight and — above all — superb digging ability are the aardvark's first lines of defence for, as with other animals with acute senses like moles and shrews, even a moderate blow on the head is fatal.

The last of its line

One of the most remarkable things about the aardvark is the difficulty zoologists have had in finding it a place in the scientific classification of animals. At first it was placed in the order Edentata (the toothless ones) along with the armadillos and sloths, simply because of its lack of front teeth (incisors and canines). Now it is placed by itself in the order Tubulidentata (the tube-toothed) so called because of the fine tubes radiating through each tooth. These teeth are in themselves very remarkable, for they have no roots or enamel.

So the aardvark is out on an evolutionary limb, a species all on its own with no close living relatives. Or perhaps we should say rather that it is on an evolutionary dead stump, the last of its line.

What is more, although fossil aardvarks have been found — but very few of them — in North America, Asia, Europe and Africa, they give us no real clue to the aardvark's ancestry or its connections with other animals.

class	**Mammalia**
order	**Tubulidentata** sole representative
family	**Orycteropidae**
genus & species	*Orycteropus afer*

◁ *The claws of the aardvark are so powerful that it can easily rip through the wall of a termite nest which is so hard it is difficult for a man to break down even with a pick-axe.*

The termites are so disturbed by having their nest opened that they swarm about and the aardvark then puts its pig-like muzzle into the nest to eat them.

It has an 18 in. long, slender, sticky tongue with which it captures and eats the swarming termites that make up the main food of aardvarks.

▷ *A day-old aardvark. It depends on its mother for six months until it can dig its own burrow. The aardvark's snout and round, pig-like muzzle earn it the Afrikaans name for 'earth-pig'.*

Disturbed away from its burrow, the aardvark can escape its enemies by digging at incredible speed. It forces the soil back with its fore feet and kicks it away with its strong hind legs, 'so fast that it can outstrip a team of six men with spades'.

Elephant

The elephant is the largest living land animal and there are two species, the African and the Indian. During fairly recent geological times elephants of many species making up six families ranged over the world except for Australia and Antarctica. The African elephant, the larger of the two surviving species, is up to $11\frac{1}{2}$ ft high and weighs up to 6 tons.

Elephants have a massive body, large head, short neck and stout pillar-like legs. The feet are short and broad with an elastic pad on the sole and hoof-like nails, five on each foot except for the hind foot of the African elephant, which has three. The bones of the skeleton are large, and instead of marrow cavities they are filled with spongy bone. The outstanding feature of elephants is that the snout is remarkably long, forming a flexible trunk with the nostrils at the tip. The trunk is used for carrying food and water to the mouth, for spraying water over the body in bathing or spraying dust in dust-bathing, and for lifting objects, as well as being used for smelling. The single incisor teeth on either side of the upper jaw are elongated and form tusks.

The main differences between the two living species are the larger ears and tusks of the African, its sloping forehead and hollow back, and two 'lips' at the end of the trunk compared with one lip in the Indian elephant.

The African elephant is found in most parts of Africa south of the Sahara, in savannah, bush, forest, river valley or semi-desert. It lives in herds of bulls and cows, each herd being led by an elderly cow, while the older bulls live solitary and join the herd only to mate. The Indian elephant is also native to Sri Lanka, Burma, Thailand, Malaya and Sumatra, living in dense forests. More correctly it should be called Asiatic, not Indian, but the use of 'Indian elephant' is now too deeply rooted for change. The social structure of its herds is much the same as in the African species.

Keeping its skin in condition

Elephants are sometimes grouped with rhinoceroses and hippopotamuses under the loose heading of pachyderms (thick-skins). In all the skin is thick and only sparsely haired, and all need to keep the skin in condition by wallowing. An elephant will bathe in water, almost completely submerging itself and will also spray water over itself with its trunk. It indulges in dust baths, too, and if water is scarce it will wallow in mud. The African elephant at least is adept at finding water in times of drought, boring holes in the ground using one of its tusks as a large awl. The requirements of the two species differ because the Indian elephant keeps mainly to dense shade. This also influences other aspects of their behaviour. The African elephant, for example, must seek what shade it can from the midday sun and cool its body by waving its large ears. The enormous surface these present allows for loss of body heat, which is helped by waving the ears back and forth. The Indian elephant, with much smaller ears, keeps itself to dense shade.

Asleep on their feet

A vexed question of long standing is how elephants sleep. Both species can sleep standing, or lying on one side. To lie down an elephant uses similar movements to a horse, but it does what no horse will do: it will sometimes use a pillow of vegetation pulled together on which to rest its head. When standing asleep an elephant breathes at the normal rate. Lying down it breathes at half this rate. When 17 elephants were kept under observation it was found they usually slept for 5 hours each night, in two equal periods. Of this 20 minutes were slept standing, the rest lying down.

Dangers of over-population

The diet is entirely vegetarian and includes grass, foliage and branches of trees and fruit. The trunk is used to gather these and convey them to the mouth. African elephants, living where bushes and trees are scattered, will use the forehead to push over small trees to get at the top foliage. When an area becomes over-populated the loss of trees can be serious. In national parks in Africa the populations of elephants, under protection, tend to increase so much that their ranks have to be thinned out by selective shooting, usually spoken of as culling, to prevent destruction of the habitat. Otherwise all the elephants in the area would be in danger from starvation.

Under free conditions elephant herds trek from one area to another, often seasonally in search of particular fruits. Long distances may then be covered, and this relieves the strain on the vegetation, which can regenerate in their absence.

△ Family group – the youngsters stay with the adults until their teens.

◁ Feeding time. At birth the baby is 3 ft high and weighs some 200 lb. It uses its mouth when suckling from the mother's nipples, situated between the cow's forelegs.

▷ Largest land animals alive today – African elephants feeding and drinking on the river bank. Their vegetarian diet includes grass, foliage and branches of trees and fruit. The mobile trunk is used to gather and carry food to the mouth.

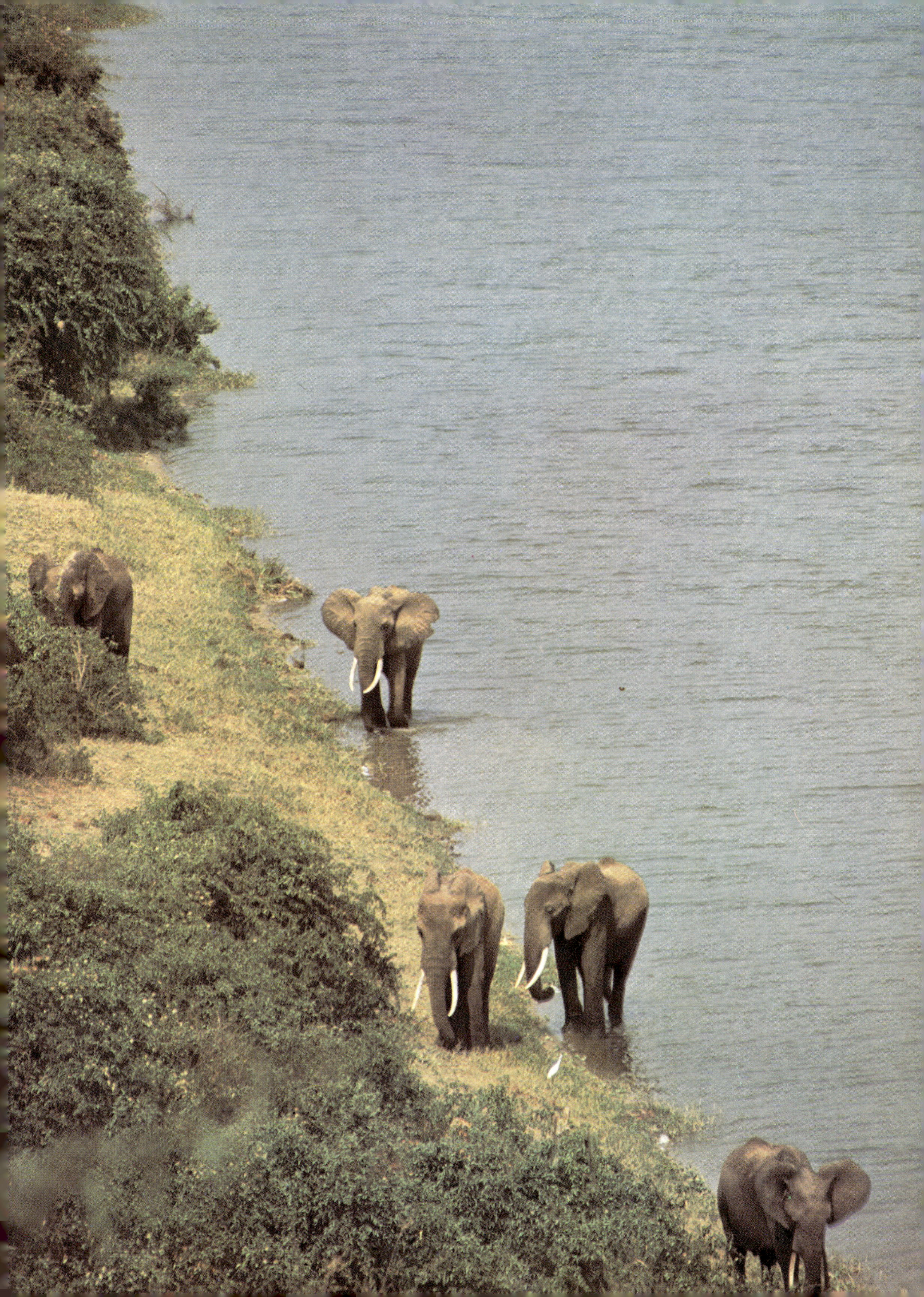

The molars of elephants have broad crushing surfaces for chewing fibrous vegetation. The wear on them is considerable. Every elephant in its lifetime, assuming it dies of old age (70 years in the Indian, 50 years in the African elephant) has 7 teeth in each half of both upper and lower jaws, exclusive of the tusks. The first are 4 milk teeth which are soon shed. After that a succession of 6 teeth moves down each half of both jaws on a conveyor-belt principle. The first is in use alone but as its surface is getting worn down the next tooth behind it is moving forward, to push out the worn stump and take its place. When the last teeth have come forward and been worn down the elephant must die from starvation, if nothing else.

Purring from the stomach

For a long time big-game hunters and naturalists were perplexed by one feature of elephant behaviour: their tummy-rumblings. Nobody was surprised that these abdominal noises should be so loud and persistent, in view of the enormous quantities of food the huge pachyderms must eat. What puzzled people was that the elephants could apparently control the noises, stopping suddenly when someone approached. Within the last few years it has been discovered that these noises have nothing to do with digestion. When elephants are out of sight of each other they keep up this sort of purring. When danger approaches one of them, it becomes silent. The sudden silence alerts the rest of the herd, which also grows silent. Only when danger has passed is the purring resumed, by which the elephants tell each other that all is well.

Trumpet Voluntary

Apart from these sounds elephants will 'trumpet'. The sound is as startling and as loud, if less pure in tone, as that from the brass wind instrument. In paintings of elephants made in the Middle Ages, or even later, the trunk was always given a trumpet-shaped end, the artists being influenced by travellers' stories of the elephants' trumpeting.

Elephant 'midwives'

Mating is preceded by affectionate play, especially with the bull and the cow entwining trunks or caressing each other's head or shoulders with the trunk. The gestation period is 515–760 days, mostly about 22 months. The single baby—twins are rare—is about 3 ft high and weighs about 200 lb. On several occasions hunters or naturalists have seen a cow elephant retire into a thicket accompanied by another cow. Some time later the two come out again accompanied by a baby. Nobody knows whether the second cow acts as midwife or merely

◁ *Woe betide those who ignore this warning notice.*
▷ *Dressed up for a reception at Bahawalpur, West Pakistan, an Indian elephant looks very decorative. It is distinguished from its larger African relative by its smaller ears, arched back, domed forehead and smoother trunk which has only one 'finger' or lobe at its end compared with the African's two (below). In general, the Indian elephant appears to be an animal of jungle or bush country, although it is found in grassland areas.*
▽ *Enjoying a dustbath, an elephant uses its hose-like trunk to snort dirt over its body.*

stands guard while the calf is being born. The baby is able to walk soon after birth and can keep up with the herd in two days.

Hefty train-stoppers

Such large and powerful animals have few enemies. In India a tiger may kill a baby and in Africa the large predators, such as the lion, may do the same. The power of an elephant in defence can be gauged by the several stories told of a bull elephant meeting a train on a railway and charging the engine head on. In all reports it is stated how the engine driver drew the train to a halt and the elephant charged the engine repeatedly, doing itself great injury yet persisting in the attack. Another feature of elephant defence is the close co-operation between members of a herd. Hunters have reported seeing a shot elephant being helped away by two others ranged either side of it, keeping it upright on its feet. On one occasion the herd combined to drag the carcase of one of their fellows throughout the night, in an abortive attempt at rescue. In 1951, in the Johannesburg *Star*, Major JF Cumming was reported as having seen some elephants dig a grave to bury a dead comrade!

Do they fear mice?

In contrast with the elephant's comparative freedom from large enemies is the long-standing belief that elephants are afraid of mice. Lupton, in his *A Thousand Notable Things,* published in 1595, wrote: 'Elephants of all other beasts do chiefly hate the mouse.' The idea still persists, helped no doubt by such stories as that of the elephant in a zoo found dead from a haemorrhage and with a mouse jammed in its trunk.

In 1938 Francis G Benedict and Robert C Lee, American zoologists, tested zoo elephants with rats and mice in their hay, and by putting rats and mice in the elephants' house. The pachyderms showed no concern even when the rodents ran over their feet or climbed on their trunks. White mice were also put in the elephants' enclosure, again without result. There was, however, one moment when a rat ran over a piece of paper lying on the ground. The unfamiliar noise of rustling paper set the nearest elephant trumpeting and before long all the others were joining in the chorus.

class	**Mammalia**
order	**Proboscidea**
family	**Elephantidae**
genera & species	***Elephas indicus*** *Indian elephant* ***Loxodonta africana*** *African elephant*

△ *Bulls contest for the cow who appears to be rather uninterested in the combat.*
▽ *African elephants were thought to be untameable but the Belgians succeeded at the turn of the century by training immature ones for work using kindness and patience rather than brutality.*

Zebra

Zebras are distinguished from horses and asses by the stripes on their bodies. Their mane is neat and upright. The tail is tufted as in asses, but the hard wart-like knobs known as 'chestnuts', are found on the forelegs only, and not on the hindlegs as in horses. There are differences from both the horse and the ass in the skull and teeth. Three species of zebra live in Africa today. The commonest and best-known is Burchell's zebra, which extends from Zululand in the southeast, and from Etosha Pan in southwest Africa, north as far as southern Somalia and southern Sudan. In this species the stripes reach under the belly, and on the flanks they broaden and bend backwards towards the rump, forming a Y-shaped 'saddle' pattern. Although the races in the southern and northern parts of the range look quite different, the differences are only clinal. That is, there are gradual changes from south to north, but they all belong to one species. In the southernmost race, the 'true' Burchell's zebra, now extinct but once living in the Orange Free State and neighbouring areas, the ground colour was yellowish rather than white; the legs were white and unstriped; the stripes often did not reach under the belly; and between the broad main stripes of the hindquarters and neck were lighter, smudge-grey alternating stripes commonly known as 'shadow-stripes'.

Further north a race known as Chapman's zebra is still found. It has a lighter ground colour than the true Burchell's, the stripes reach further down the legs—usually to below the knees—and the shadow-stripes are still present. All zebras still living from Zululand north to the Zambezi are referred to as members of this race; but at Etosha Pan there are some zebras that have almost no leg stripes and closely resemble 'true' Burchell's.

North of the Zambezi is the East African race, known as Grant's zebra. Its ground colour is white, the stripes continue all the way down to the hoofs and there are rarely any shadow-stripes. Grant's zebra is smaller than the southern races, about 50 in. high, weighs 500–600 lb, and has a smaller mane. In the northern districts the mane has disappeared altogether. Maneless zebras occur in southern Sudan, the Karamoja district of Uganda and the Juba valley of Somalia.

South and southwest of the Burchell's zebras' range lives the mountain zebra, about the same size as Burchell's but with a prominent dewlap halfway between the jaw angle and the forelegs. Its stripes always stop short of the white belly. Its ground colour is whitish and, although the stripes on the flanks bend back to the rump, as in Burchell's, the vertical bands continue as well, giving a 'grid iron' effect. The southern race, the stockily built, broad-banded Cape mountain zebra, is nearly extinct, preserved only on a few private properties. The race in southwest Africa, Hartmann's zebra, is still fairly common. It is larger and longer-limbed than the Cape mountain zebra, with narrower stripes and a buff ground colour.

The third species is Grévy's zebra, from Somalia, eastern Ethiopia and northern Kenya, a very striking, tall zebra. The belly is white and unstriped, and there are no stripes on the hindquarters, except the dorsal stripe which bisects it. On the haunches the stripes from the flanks, rump and hindlegs seem to bend towards each other and join up.

▽ *At the waterhole: a herd of southeast African Burchell's zebra. This race generally has striped legs and a paler ground colour than the now extinct true Burchell's zebra.*

Belligerent stallions

Burchell's zebras are strongly gregarious. Groups of 1–6 mares with their foals keep together under the leadership of a stallion, who protects them and also wards off other stallions. Sometimes, for no apparent reason, the male simply disappears and another one takes his place. The surplus stallions live singly, or in bachelor groups of up to 15 members. Burchell's zebras are rather tame, not showing as much fear of man as the gnu with which they associate. When alarmed they utter their barking alarm call, a hoarse 'kwa-ha, kwa-ha', ending with a whinny. Then the herd wheels off, following the gnu. When cornered, however, the herd stallion puts up a stiff resistance, kicking and biting.

Mountain zebras, said to be more savage than Burchell's, live in herds of up to six, although sometimes they assemble in large numbers where food is plentiful. They seem to have regular paths over the rugged hills and move along them in single file. The call of the mountain zebra has been described as a low, snuffling whinny, quite different from that of the Burchell's.

Although in Grévy's zebra there are family groups as well as bachelor herds, the biggest and strongest stallions, weighing up to 1 000 lb, are solitary, each occupying a territory of about a mile in diameter.

Slow breeding rate

A newborn foal has brown stripes and is short-bodied and high-legged like the foal of a domestic horse. It is born after a gestation of 370 days. It weighs 66–77 lb and stands about 33 in. high. The mares come into season again a few days after foaling, but only 15% are fertilised a second time; usually a mare has one foal every three years. They reach sexual maturity at a little over 1 year, but do not seem to be fertile before about 2 years. Young males leave the herd between 1 and 3 years and join the bachelor herd. At 5 or 6 years many of them attempt to kidnap young females and if successful a new one-male herd is formed. The unsuccessful ones remain in the bachelor herd, or become solitary. Zebras live about as long as horses.

Lions beware

Man still hunts the zebra for meat but in protected areas, at least, very little of this continues. The zebra, with the gnu, is the lion's favourite prey. Because zebras are potentially dangerous, the lion must make a swift kill and young lions have been routed by zebra stallions that turned on them. Astley Maberley, the wildlife artist and writer, tells the story of an African poacher who was killed and fearfully mangled by an irate troop of Burchell's zebras after he had killed a foal.

(1) Linear line-up: a row of Grévy's zebra, large, handsomely-marked animals recognised by the huge ears and narrowly-spaced stripes.
(2) Topi antelope and Grant's zebra—a species having stripes that reach below the knees. The odd-looking animal on the left of the picture is a rare melanistic form of Grant's zebra.
(3) Grant's zebra spar in the dust of Ngorongoro crater. Zebra stallions are aggressive not only to males of the same species but also to predators, including man.

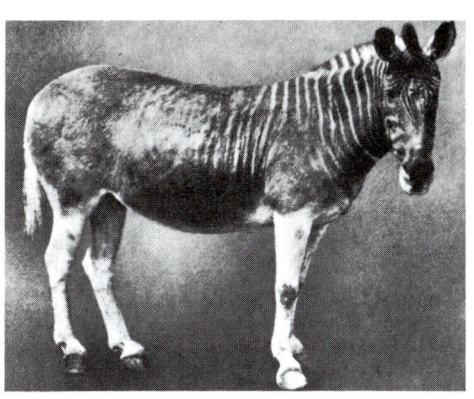

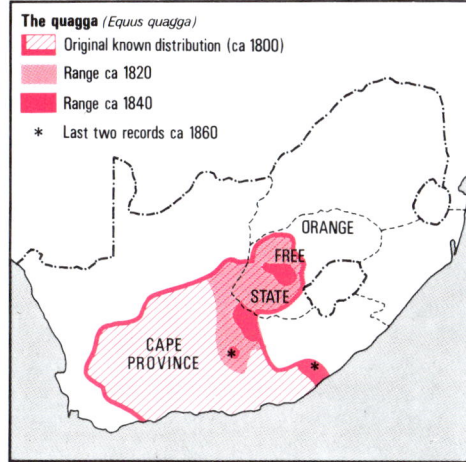

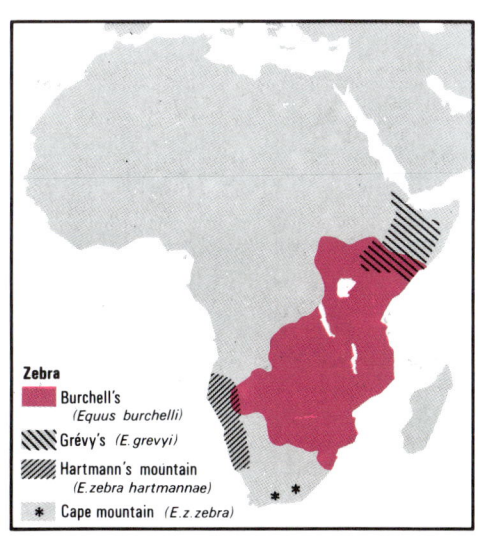

The lost quagga

A fourth species of zebra, the quagga, was extremely common in South Africa 150 years ago. It has since been completely exterminated. Most closely resembling Burchell's zebra, the quagga was distinctly striped brown and off-white on the head and neck only. Along the flanks the stripes gradually faded out to a plain brown, sometimes extending to just behind the shoulders, sometimes reaching the haunches. The legs and belly were white. Its barking, high-pitched cry, after which it was named, was rather like that of the Burchell's zebra.

The early explorers, around 1750–1800, met quaggas as far southwest as the Swellendam and Ceres districts, a short way inland from Cape Town. The Boer farmers did not appreciate quaggas except as food for their Hottentot servants. Their method of hunting was to take a train of wagons out onto the veldt and blaze away at everything within sight. Then large numbers of carcases would be loaded onto the wagons, and the rest of the dead and dying animals were simply left to rot. It is no wonder that today Cape Province is virtually denuded of wild game. When Cape Province was emptied, the trekkers to the Orange Free State repeated the process there. By 1820 the quaggas' range was already severely curtailed; they were almost gone even from the broad plains of the Great Fish River, which had been named 'Quagga's Flats' from the vast numbers of them roaming there. A few lingered for another 20 years or so in the far east of Cape Province and in the Orange Free State, the last wild ones being shot near Aberdeen, CP, in 1858, and near Kingwilliamstown in 1861. Strange to say, no one realised that they were even endangered. Zoos looking for replacements for their quaggas that had died were quite shocked to be told, 'But there aren't any more'.

class	**Mammalia**
order	**Perissodactyla**
family	**Equidae**
genus & species	*Equus burchelli burchelli* true Burchell's zebra or bontequagga *E. b. antiquorum* Chapman's or southeast African Burchell's *E. b. boehmi* Grant's or East African Burchell's *E. b. borensis* maneless zebra *E. grevyi* Grévy's zebra *E. quagga* quagga *E. zebra zebra* Cape mountain zebra *E. z. hartmannae* Hartmann's mountain zebra

(4) '... along a mountain track'—Hartmann's mountain zebra, a race of the Cape mountain zebra described in 1898, has a large dewlap between chin and forelegs and stripes that end short of the belly. The stripes form a 'gridiron' effect on the rump.
(5) Nearly extinct: less than 200 Cape mountain zebra live in specially protected areas of high tableland in western Cape province.
(6) Extinct: the quagga was hunted in large numbers by early white settlers to South Africa.

Hippopotamus

Distantly related to the pigs, the hippopotamus rivals the great Indian rhinoceros as the second largest living land animal. Up to 14 ft long and 4 ft 10 in. at the shoulder it weighs up to 4 tons. The enormous body is supported on short pillar-like legs, each with four toes ending in hoof-like nails, placed well apart. A hippo trail in swamps shows as two deep ruts made by the feet with a dip in the middle made by the belly. The eyes are raised on top of the large flattish head, the ears are small and the nostrils slit-like and high up on the muzzle. The body is hairless except for sparse bristles on the muzzle, inside the ears and on the tip of the short tail. There is a thick layer of fat under the skin and there are pores in the skin which give out an oily pink fluid, known as pink sweat. This lubricates the skin. The mouth is armed with large canine tusks; these average $2\frac{1}{2}$ ft long but may be over 5 ft long including the long root embedded in the gums.

Once numerous in rivers throughout Africa, the hippopotamus is now extinct north of Khartoum and south of the Zambezi river, except for some that are found in a few protected areas such as the Kruger National Park.

The pygmy hippopotamus, a separate species, lives in Liberia, Sierra Leone and parts of southern Nigeria in forest streams. It is 5 ft long, 2 ft 8 in. at the shoulder and weighs up to 600 lb. Its head is smaller in proportion to the body, and it lives singly or in pairs.

Rulebook of the river-horse

The name means literally river-horse and the hippopotamus spends most of its time in water, but comes on land to feed, mainly at night. It can remain submerged for up to $4\frac{1}{2}$ minutes and spends the day basking lethargically on a sandbar, or lazing in the water with little more than ears, eyes and nostrils showing above water, at most with its back and upper part of the head exposed. Where heavily persecuted, hippopotamuses keep to reed beds. Each group, sometimes spoken of as a school, numbers around 20–100 and its territory is made up of a central crèche occupied by females and juveniles with separate areas, known as refuges, around its perimeter each occupied by an adult male. The crèche is on a sandbar in midstream or on a raised bank of the river or lake. Special paths lead from the males' refuges to the feeding grounds, each male marking his own path with his dung. The females have their own paths but are less exclusive.

The organisation of the territories is preserved by rules of behaviour which, in some of their aspects, resemble rules of committees. Outside the breeding season a female may pay a social call on a male and he may return this, but on the female's terms. He must enter the crèche with no sign of aggression and should one of the females rise on her feet he must lie down. Only when she lies down again may he rise. A male failing to observe these rules will be driven out by the adult females attacking him *en masse*.

Matriarch hippos

It was long thought that a hippopotamus school was led by the oldest male. It is in fact a matriarchy. For example, young males, on leaving the crèche, are forced to take up a refuge beyond the ring of refuges lying on the perimeter of the crèche. From there each must win his way to an inner refuge, which entitles him to mate with one of the females, by fighting. Should a young male be over-persecuted by the senior males he can re-enter the crèche for sanctuary, protected by the combined weight of the females.

The characteristic yawning has nothing to do with sleep. It is an aggressive gesture, a preliminary challenge to fight. Combats are vigorous, the two contestants rearing up out of the water, enormous mouths wide open, seeking to deliver slashing cuts with the long tusks. Frightful gashes are inflicted and a wounded hippo falling back into water screams with pain, but the wounds quickly heal. The aim of the fighting is for one hippo to break a foreleg of his opponent. This is fatal because the animal can no longer walk on land to feed.

Nightly wanderings

Hippos feed mostly at night, coming on land to eat mainly grass. During one night an individual may wander anything up to 20 miles but usually does not venture far from water. Hippos have been known to wander through the outskirts of large towns at times, and two surprised just before dawn by a motorist entering Nairobi showed him they could run at 30 mph.

Babies in nursery school

When in season the female goes out to choose her mate and he must treat her with deference as she enters his refuge. The baby is born 210–255 days later. It is 3 ft long, $1\frac{1}{2}$ ft high and 60 lb weight. Birth may take place in water but normally it is on land, the mother preparing a bed of trampled reeds. The baby can walk, run or swim 5 minutes after birth. Outside the crèche

A trio of hippos in single file moves ponderously through a mixed throng of cormorants, pelicans and gulls, with a hippo youngster in the lead.

A mournful-looking pygmy hippo **Choeropsis liberiensis**, *from West Africa. Its well-oiled look is due to the secretion of a clear, viscous material through its skin pores. When frightened, the pygmy hippo prefers to head for the undergrowth, whereas the big hippos invariably seek safety in water.*

the organisation of the school is dependent on fighting and the females educate the young accordingly. This is one of the few instances of deliberate teaching in the animal kingdom. In a short while after its birth the baby hippo is taken on land for walks, not along the usual paths used when going to pasture but in a random promenade. The youngster must walk level with the mother's neck presumably so she can keep an eye on it. If the mother quickens her pace, the baby must do the same. If she stops, it must stop. In water the baby must swim level with her shoulder. On land the lighter female is more agile than the male, so she can defend her baby without difficulty. In the water the larger male, with his longer tusks, has the advantage, so the baby must be where the mother can quickly interpose her own body to protect her offspring from an aggressive male. Later, when she takes it to pasture, the baby must walk at heel, and if she has more than one youngster with her, which can happen because her offspring stay with her for several years, they walk behind her in order of precedence, the elder bringing up the rear.

Obedience, or else . . .

The youngsters must show strict obedience, and the penalty for failing to do so is punishment, the mother lashing the erring youngster with her head, often rolling it over and over. She may even slash it with her tusks. The punishment continues until the youngster cowers in submission, when the mother licks and caresses it.

Babysitting was not invented by the human race: hippos brought it to a fine art long ago. If a female leaves the crèche for feeding or mating she places her youngster in charge of another female, who may already have several others under her supervision. The way for this is made easy, for hippo mothers with young of similar age tend to keep together in the crèche.

The young hippos play with others of similar age, the young females together playing a form of hide-and-seek or rolling over in the water with stiff legs. The young males play together but they indulge in mock fights in addition to the other games.

Few enemies for the hippo

Hippos have few enemies apart from man, the most important being the lion which may occasionally spring on the back of a hippo on land, raking its hide with its claws. But even this is rare.

The wanderlust hippo

Many animals sometimes wander well inland for no obvious reason. Huberta was a famous hippopotamus that wandered a thousand miles. She left St Lucia Bay, in Zululand, in 1928 and wandered on and on until in 1931 she reached Cape Province. Each day she stopped to wallow in a river or lake, and her passage was noted in the local newspapers all along her route, so her journey is fully documented. Throughout that time she never came into contact with another hippo. Huberta became almost a pet of the people of South Africa and a law was passed to protect her. She was finally shot, however, by a trigger-happy person in April 1931, and was then found to be a male. So, it will never be known how much farther Hubert might have wandered.

class	**Mammalia**
order	**Artiodactyla**
family	**Hippopotamidae**
genera & species	*Hippopotamus amphibius* *Choeropsis liberiensis* pygmy hippo

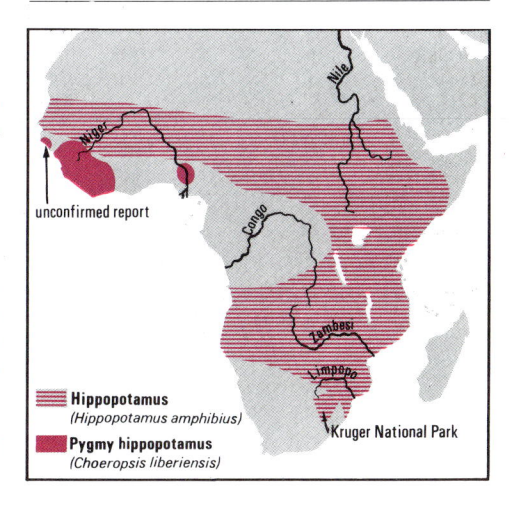

Camel

There are two species of camel: the Arabian or one-humped and the Bactrian or two-humped. The first is not known as a wild animal, though the second survives in the wild in the Gobi desert. A dromedary is a special breed of the one-humped camel, used for riding, although the name is commonly but wrongly used to denote the Arabian camel as a whole.

Camels have long legs and a long neck, coarse hair and tufted tails. Their feet have two toes united by a tough web, with nails and tough padded soles. The length of head, neck and body is up to 10 ft, the tail is 1½ ft long, height at the shoulder is up to 6 ft, and the weight is up to 1100 lb.

Habits

The wild camels of the Gobi desert are active by day, associating in groups of half-a-dozen, made up of one male and the rest females. They are extremely shy and make off at first sight of an intruder, moving with a characteristic swaying stride, due to the

One-humped camels drinking at a water-hole in the desert. Having taken their fill of water, camels can survive for several days in the desert without drinking, or for several weeks if they have access to succulent desert plants. Water is drawn from the body tissues to maintain the fluid in the blood.

fore and hind legs on each side moving together. Their shyness may be partly due to persecution in former times.

It is often said that a camel cannot swim. Reports suggest they do not readily take to water, but they have been seen swimming.

Adaptations to desert life

Everything about a camel, both its external features and its physiology, show it to be adapted to life in deserts. Its eyes have long lashes which protect them from wind-blown sand. The nostrils are muscular so they can be readily closed, or partly closed to keep out sand. The form of the body, with the long neck and long legs, provides a large surface area relative to the volume of the body, which allows for easy loss of heat.

The camel's physiology shows other adaptations which provide protection from overheating, and help it to withstand desiccation and to indulge in physical exertion with a minimum of feeding and drinking. These characteristics are often seen in stories of journeys made across waterless deserts. Many of these are exaggerated, but even those that are true are remarkable enough. There is one instance of a march through Somalia of 8 days without water and in Northern Australia a journey of 537 miles was made, using camels which were without a drink for 34 days. Most of the camels in this second journey died, but a few that were able to graze dew-wetted vegetation survived.

Most desert journeys are made in winter, however, and during that season even a man can go without drinking if he feeds largely on juicy fruits and vegetables. Knut Schmidt-Nielsen tested camels in the desert winter and found that even on a completely dry diet, camels could go several weeks without drinking, although they lost water steadily through their skin and their breath as well as in the urine and faeces. Normally, however, a camel feeds on desert plants with a high water content.

Do camels store water?

There are many stories of travellers in the desert killing a camel and drinking the water contained in its stomach. From these arose the myth, which has not yet been completely killed, that a camel stores water in its stomach. Pliny (AD 23-79), the Roman naturalist, first set it on record. Buffon (1707-1788) and Cuvier (1769-1832), celebrated French scientists, accepted it. Owen (1804-1892) and Lyddeker (1849-1915), British anatomists and zoologists, supported it.

In 1801 George Shaw, British zoologist, wrote of a camel having four stomachs with a fifth bag which serves as a reservoir for water. Everard Home, the Scottish surgeon, dissected a camel and in 1806 published his celebrated drawing of alleged water pockets in the first two compartments of the stomach, a drawing which has many times been reproduced in books, and which has served to bolster the story. It was not until the researches of Schmidt-Nielsen and his team, working in the Sahara in 1953-4, that the full story emerged. In the living camel, these pockets are filled with an evil-smelling soup, the liquefied masticated food, which might be drunk, so saving his life, by a man crazy for water—but not otherwise.

Another of the camel's achievements which served to support the story is its ability to drink 27 gallons of water, or more, in 10 minutes. It will do so only to replenish the body supply after intense desiccation. In those 10 minutes a camel will pass from an emaciated animal, showing its ribs, to a normal condition. This is something few other animals can do. But the water does not stay in the stomach; it passes into the tissues, and a camel after a long drink looks swollen.

A camel can lose water equal to 25% of its body weight and show no signs of distress. A man losing 12% of his body water is in dire distress because this water is drawn from his tissues and his blood. The blood becomes thick and sticky, so that the heart has greater difficulty in pumping. A camel loses water from its tissues but not from the blood, so there is no strain on the heart, and an emaciated camel is capable of the same physical exertion as normal. The mechanism for this is not known. The only obvious difference between the blood of a camel and any other mammal is that its red corpuscles are oval instead of being discoid.

The camel's hump

The hump contains a store of fat and it has often been argued that this can be converted to water, and therefore the hump is a water reserve. The hump of the Arabian camel may contain as much as 100 lb of fat, each pound of which can yield 1·1 lb of water, or over 13 gallons for a 100 lb hump. To convert this, however, extra oxygen is needed, and it has been calculated that the breathing needed to get this extra oxygen would itself lead to the loss of more than 13 gallons of water as vapour in the breath. The fat stored in the hump is broken down to supply energy, releasing water which is lost. The hump is thus really a reserve of energy.

Other physiological advantages possessed by a camel are that in summer it excretes less urine and, more important, it sweats little. The highest daytime temperature is 40°C/105°F but during the night it drops to 34°C/93°F. A man's temperature remains constant at just under 39°C/100°F and as soon as the day starts to warm up he begins to feel the heat. A camel starts with a temperature of 34°C/93°F at dawn and does not heat up to 40°C/105°F until nearly midday. A camel's coat provides insulation against the heat of the day and it keeps the animal warm during the cold desert nights.

With all these advantages, camels should be even-tempered, but everyone agrees that they are bad-tempered to a degree. One writer has described them as stupid, unwilling, recalcitrant, obnoxious, untrustworthy and openly vicious, with an ability to bite destructively. There is a traditional joke that there are no wild camels, nor any tame ones.

The power of the bite is linked with the camel's unusual dentition. At birth it has six incisors in both upper and lower jaws, a canine on each side, then a premolar followed by a gap before the cheek teeth are reached. As the young camel grows, it quickly loses all but the outside incisors of the six in the upper jaw and these take on a similar shape to the canines. So in making a slashing bite a camel has, in effect, double the fang capacity of a dog.

Breeding

A baby camel is a miniature of its parents, apart from its incisors, its soft fleece, lack of knee pads and hump. There is a single calf, exceptionally two, born 370–440 days after conception. Its only call is a soft *baa*. It can walk freely at the end of the first day but is not fully independent until 4 years old, and becomes sexually mature at 5 years. Maximum recorded life is 50 years.

Origins of the camel

Camels originated in North America, where many fossils have been found of camels, small and large, with short necks or long, as in the giraffe-like camels. The smallest was the size of a hare, the largest stood 15 ft at the shoulder. As the species multiplied there was one migration southwards into South America and another northwestwards, and then across the land-bridge where the Bering Straits now are, into Asia. As the numerous species died out, over the last 45 million years, the survivors remained as the S. American llamas and Asiatic camels.

A few species reached eastern Europe and died out. None reached Africa. Until 6 000 years or more ago there was only the one species in Asia, the two-humped Bactrian camel. The date is impossible to fix with

In a sandstorm the long lashes protect the camel's eyes, and its nostrils can readily be closed to keep the sand out.

Camels have been used as pack animals since early times, and can carry a load of about 400 lb for long distances.

certainty, as is the date when the one-humped camel came into existence, but the evidence suggests that it is a domesticated form derived from the Bactrian camel. Both readily interbreed, and the offspring usually have two humps, the hind hump smaller than that in front.

Surprisingly, the first record of a one-humped camel is on pottery from the sixth dynasty of Ancient Egypt (about 3500 BC) for the camel was not known in the Nile Valley until 3 000 years later. Its representation on the pottery may have been inspired by a wandering camel train from Asia Minor. Meanwhile, on Assyrian monuments dated 1115–1102 BC, and from then onwards, the camel appears quite often, and when the Queen of Sheba visited King Solomon in Jerusalem, in 955 BC, she brought with her draught camels. The name seems to be from the Semitic *gamal* or *hamal*, meaning 'carrying a burden'.

The one-humped camel was presumably selectively bred from domesticated two-humped camels, in Central Asia, by peoples who left no records. It is also suggested that the nickname 'ship of the desert' is derived from 'animal brought in a ship from the desert' by mis-translation—a reference to the Assyrian habit of naming an animal according to the place from which it came. Presumably this would mean camels were brought by ship across the Persian Gulf.

Feral camels

Today the Bactrian camel is confined to Asia but most of the 3 million Arabian camels are on African soil. Some have, however, been introduced into countries far from Africa or Asia. In 1622 some were taken to Tuscany where a herd still lives on the sandy plains near Pisa. On the plains of the Guadalquivir are feral camels taken to Spain by the Moors earlier still. Camels were taken to South America in the 16th century

◁ *Camel herd of an Arabian caravan. A miniature from a manuscript of about the 12th century illustrates the work of the poet Harari. (Cairo)*

▷ *Camels develop leathery callosities on their knees and other joints through kneeling down for loading.*

234

by the Spanish conquistadors but these have died out. Others were taken to Virginia in 1701, and there was a second importation into the United States in 1856. The survivors from these were still running wild in the deserts of Arizona and Nevada in 1915. Camels were taken to Northern Australia, and there also they have reverted to the wild.

For a long time text books reiterated that no camels are now known in the wild state, although they had been mentioned in Chinese literature since the 5th century, and Marco Polo wrote about them. Then, in 1879, Nikolai Przewalski reported wild two-humped camels still living around Lake Lob, southeast of the Gobi desert. The local people told him they had been numerous a few decades prior to his visit but that they hunted them for their hides and flesh. There were reports also of camels in the Gobi, but nobody was prepared to say whether these were truly wild or merely feral camels. In 1945, the Soviet zoologist AG Bannikov rediscovered them and in 1955 a Mongolian film unit secured several shots of them.

These Gobi camels are two-humped but the humps are small. They are swift, with long slender legs, small feet and no knee pads. Their coat is short, the ears smaller than in the domesticated camels, and the coat is a brownish-red.

The Mongolian film shows the Gobi camel to be different from the typical Bactrian and Arabian camels, and it would be not unreasonable to conclude that it represents the ancestral stock from which the other two were domesticated.

class	**Mammalia**
order	**Artiodactyla**
suborder	**Tylopoda**
family	**Camelidae**
genus & species	***Camelus dromedarius*** 1-humped camel *Camelus bactrianus* 2-humped camel

△ *The camel draws water from the well while his keeper sleeps peacefully.*

▽ *Dromedaries are the riding strain of the one-humped camel, and can travel 100 miles in a day*

Reindeer

Some scientists regard the reindeer of Northern Europe and the caribou of North America as varieties of one species. The reindeer, of arctic Europe and Asia, are now domesticated or at least semi-domesticated. They are up to 43 in. at the shoulder, and a good bull may weigh 224 lb. Reindeer are perhaps the tamest of all domesticated animals, and it is said that even a child can manage a herd of them. The domestication of the reindeer is thought to have begun in the 5th century when they were used as decoys for hunting wild reindeer. The hunter, with four or five tame beasts on ropes, and himself in the middle, would approach a wild herd without alarming them, and then loose his arrows at short range. One tribe in Siberia is known to have used tame hinds in the rutting season to attract wild stags, which were then shot. In time, the tame hinds produced enough fawns to build up herds, and the domestication of the reindeer gradually came about in this way.

Reindeer are all profit

Reindeer are to the Lapps and the northern tribes of the USSR what cattle were to early man farther south. They provide everything he needs. The hide makes a soft leather used for clothing and a variety of other purposes, such as cushions and curtains. Reindeer give milk, cheese and flesh. Their sinews can be used for sewing boots or for covering a canoe, and their bones for needles. The stretched bowel makes a window covering or bag for minced meat.

Reindeer are used as pack animals or for drawing sleighs, and are most economical animals to keep as they can withstand exposure and so need no stabling, and they can forage for themselves, digging down through the snow for the spongy lichen known as reindeer moss. Today, however, the use of reindeer products is declining in favour of manufactured goods or preserved foods especially where towns are accessible.

Man the parasite

The reindeer is a nomad like the people who domesticated it. One valuable quality of the reindeer is its ability to find its way in a snowstorm, and this and its nomadism, together with its many other uses, has made some scientists speak of man's social parasitism on the reindeer. In the association between the animal and the human, the animal gains little besides protection from enemies—an advantage largely offset by man killing some of them for food. Otherwise the advantages are all with the human.

The reindeer's achievements as a draught animal are greater than those of horse or dog over uneven or frozen ground. A reindeer will pull 300 lb at an average of 8 mph, and while a daily journey averages 25–35 miles, up to 75–100 miles a day have been recorded. In an annual race in Sweden

▷ *Reindeer, the cattle of the Scandinavian Arctic, provide all the Lapps' requirements.*

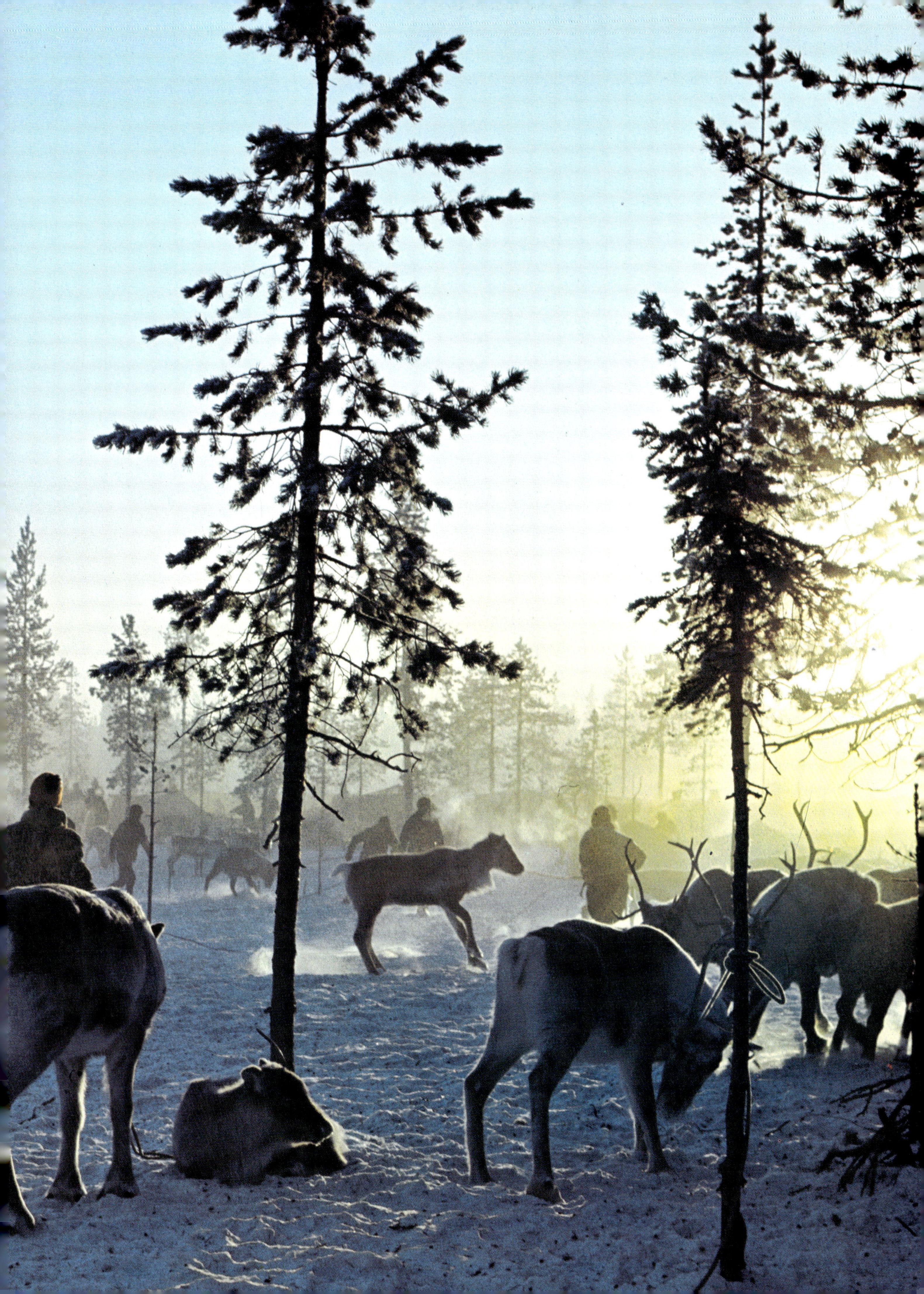

two reindeer pulled a sledge and driver 5 miles in 14½ minutes. At a reindeer festival held on Christmas day on the Kola peninsula a mile course has been covered in 2½ minutes. At Nome in Alaska in an annual race a 10-mile course was invariably covered in under half an hour.

Why reindeer cows have antlers
Because reindeer are domesticated it has been possible to experiment on some aspects of their behaviour. For example, why do female reindeer have antlers, the only deer apart from caribou to do so? A possible answer lies in an experiment carried out in 1962-3 by Yngve Espmark of the University of Stockholm. A group of 16 reindeer were marked and kept in an enclosure, and at the same time observations were made on free-ranging reindeer. The social hierarchy—usually called the peck-order—changes during the course of a season, but generally speaking the larger the antlers the higher the male is in the social order. During the rut the mature bulls, with their large antlers, are the bosses. After the rut the males shed their antlers before the females, and then the females become boss. Moreover, each calf shares its mother's rank. The importance of the antlers was tested by cutting off the antlers of some of the males, who then dropped in the social ranking. One male was castrated and from what is known in other species he should have fallen to a very subordinate rank. He did not and all the circumstances suggest that an old male, experienced in fighting and in holding his rank, has learned to 'know his own strength', which may explain how stags without antlers hold their own.

During the winter the calf stays with its mother and feeds from the 'crater' she makes in the snow. If she had no antlers there is a fair chance both might be driven from the crater by other members of the herd looking for an easy meal, and the calf would starve.

Epic arctic journey
Reindeer once took part in an historic drive across Arctic Canada. In the 1890's a herd of 171 was taken into Alaska from Siberia to save the Eskimos from starvation. These

flourished and increased in numbers, but many mistakes were made, such as poor herding, and by the mid 1940's the number had dropped to 120 000, from a peak of nearly a million 10 years previously. In 1929 the Canadian government introduced reindeer into its Northwestern Territory to build up an industry for the Eskimos there. A herd of 3 400 left Kotzebue Sound in Alaska under the supervision of a Lapp, Andrew Bahr, who delivered 2 370 animals at the Mackenzie River delta 5 years later. The journey was made across unknown territory and included crossing a mountain range, fording one river after another and by-passing lakes. Wolves harried the flanks of the herd, taking a continual toll. Plagues of mosquitoes in summer sometimes held the herd up as did the blizzards in winter, for the journey was made well within the Arctic Circle. On arrival less than 20% of the original herd remained, the rest having been born on the journey.

◁ *Man and his beasts; or beasts and their man? Many think the reindeer domesticated the Lapps.*
◁▽ *Reindeer keep their heads above water.*
▽ *Reindeer crocodile. A Lapp leads the way.*
▽▽ *Reindeer camp. They do not need stabling.*

class	**Mammalia**
order	**Artiodactyla**
family	**Cervidae**
genus & species	***Rangifer tarandus*** *reindeer*

Giraffe

Tallest animal in the world, the giraffe is remarkable for its long legs and long neck. An old bull may be 18 ft to the top of his head. Females are smaller. The head tapers to mobile hairy lips, the tongue is extensile and the eyes are large. There are 2—5 horns, bony knobs covered with skin, including one pair on the forehead, a boss in front, and, in some races, a small pair farther back. The shoulders are high and the back slopes down to a long tufted tail. The coat is boldly spotted and irregularly blotched chestnut, dark brown or liver-coloured on a pale buff ground, giving the effect of a network of light-coloured lines. A number of species and races have been recognised in the past, differing mainly in details of colour and number of horns, but the current view is that all belong to one species. The number of races recognised, however, varies between 8 and 13 species depending on the authority.

The present-day range of the giraffe is the dry savannah and semi-desert of Africa south of the Sahara although it was formerly more widespread. Its range today is from Sudan and Somalia south to South Africa and westwards to northern Nigeria. In many parts of its former range it has been wiped out for its hide.

A leisurely anarchy

Giraffes live in herds with a fairly casual social structure. It seems that males live in groups in forested zones, the old males often solitary, and the females and young live apart from them in more open country. Males visit these herds mainly for mating.

Giraffes do not move about much, and tend to walk at a leisurely pace unless disturbed. When walking slowly the legs move in much the same way as those of a horse. That is, the right hindleg touches the ground just after the right foreleg leaves it, and a little later the left legs make the same movement. The body is therefore supported on three legs most of the time while walking. As the pace quickens to a gallop the giraffe's leg movements change to the legs on each side moving forward together, the two right hoofs hitting the ground together followed by the two left legs moving together.

The long neck not only allows a giraffe to browse high foliage, the eyes set on top of the high head form a sort of watch-tower to look out for enemies. In addition, the long neck and heavy head assist movement by acting as a counterpoise. When resting crouched, with legs folded under the body the neck may be held erect or, if sleeping, the giraffe lays its neck along its back. To rise, the forelegs are half-unfolded, the neck being swung back to take the weight off the forequarters. Then it is swung forwards to take the weight off the hindlegs, for them to be unfolded. By repeated movements of this kind the animal finally gets to its feet.

Necking parties

The habit of 'necking' has been something of a puzzle. Two giraffes stand side-by-side and belabour each other with their heads, swinging their long necks slowly and forcibly. Only rarely does any injury result, and the necking seems to be a ritualised fighting, to establish dominance, and confined exclusively, or nearly so, to the male herds.

Not so dumb

One long-standing puzzle concerns the voice. For a long time everyone accepted the idea that giraffes are mute—yet they have an unusually large voice-box. During the last 25 years it has been found that a young giraffe will bleat like the calf of domestic cattle, that the adult female makes a sound like 'wa-ray' and that adult bulls, and sometimes cows, will make a husky grunt or cough. Nevertheless, there are many zoo-keepers who have never heard a giraffe utter a call and there is still the puzzle why there should be such a large voice-box when so little use is made of it. Some zoologists have suggested the giraffe may use ultra-sonics.

Controlled blood pressure

In feeding, leaves are grasped with the long tongue and mobile lips. Trees and bushes tend to become hourglass-shaped from giraffes browsing all round at a particular level. Acacia is the main source of food but many others are browsed, giraffes showing definite preferences for some species of trees or bushes over others.

Giraffes drink regularly when water is available but can go long periods without drinking. They straddle the front legs widely to bring the head down to water, or else straddle them slightly and then bend them at the knees. Another long-standing puzzle concerns the blood pressure in the head, some zoologists maintaining a giraffe must lower and raise its head slowly to prevent a rush of blood to the head. In fact, the blood vessels have valves, reservoirs of blood in the head and alternative routes for the blood, and so there is no upset from changes in the level of the head, no matter how quickly the giraffe moves.

Casual mothers

Mating and calving appear to take place all the year, with peak periods which may vary from one region to another. The gestation period is 420—468 days, the single calf being able to walk within an hour of birth, when it is 6 ft to the top of the head and weighs 117 lb. Reports vary about the suckling which is said to continue for 9 months, but in one study the calves were browsing at the age of one week and were not seen suckling after that. The bond between mother and infant is, in any case, a loose one. Giraffe milk has a high fat content and the young grow fast. Captive giraffes often live for over 20 years.

Defensive hoofs

Giraffes have few enemies. A lion may take a young calf or several lions may combine to kill an adult. Even these events are rare because the long legs and heavy hoofs can be used to deadly effect, striking down at an attacker.

Symbol of friendliness

Rock engravings of giraffes have been found over the whole of Africa and some of the most imposing are at Fezzan in the middle of what is now the Sahara desert. The animal must have lingered on in North Africa until 500 B.C. Some of the engravings are life size, or even larger, and many depict the trap used to capture giraffes, while others show typical features of its behaviour, including the necking. The engravings also show ostriches, dibatag, and gerenuk. Giraffes were also figured on the slate palettes, used for grinding malachite and haematite for eye-shadows, the cosmetics used by ladies of rank in Ancient Egypt. The last giraffe depicted in Egyptian antiquities is on the tomb of Rameses the Great, 1225 BC.

There are references to the animal in Greek and Roman writings and a few pictures survive from the Roman era, but from then until the 7th or 8th century AD the principal records are in Arabic literature. The description given by Zakariya al-Qaswini in his 13th-century *Marvels of Creation* reflects the accepted view, that 'the giraffe is produced by the camel mare, the male hyaena and the wild cow'. The giraffe was taken to India by the Arabs, and from there to China, the first arriving in 1414 in the Imperial Zoological Garden in Peking. To the Chinese it symbolised gentleness and peace and the Arabs adopted this symbolism, so a gift of a giraffe became a sign of peace and friendliness between rulers.

In medieval Europe, and until the end of the 18th century, knowledge of the giraffe was based on descriptions in Greek and Roman writings and on hearsay accounts. It was at best a legendary beast.

class	**Mammalia**
order	**Artiodactyla**
family	**Giraffidae**
genus & species	***Giraffa camelopardalis***

▷ *Dappled freaks of the African veld: a group of giraffes rear their extraordinary necks against the skyline of a pale sunset. Wiped out for its hide in many parts of its range, the present day distribution of the giraffe is much reduced. A number of races are recognised within the single species.*

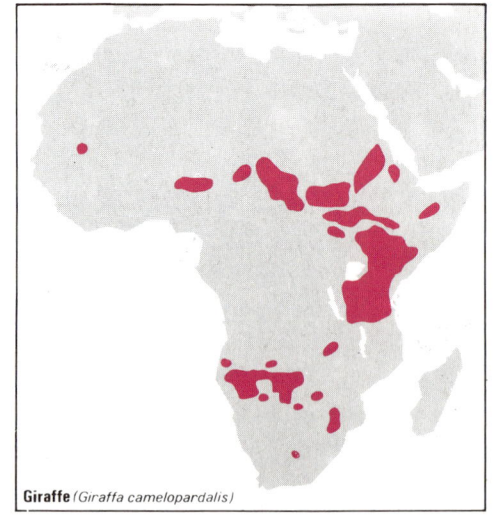

Giraffe (*Giraffa camelopardalis*)

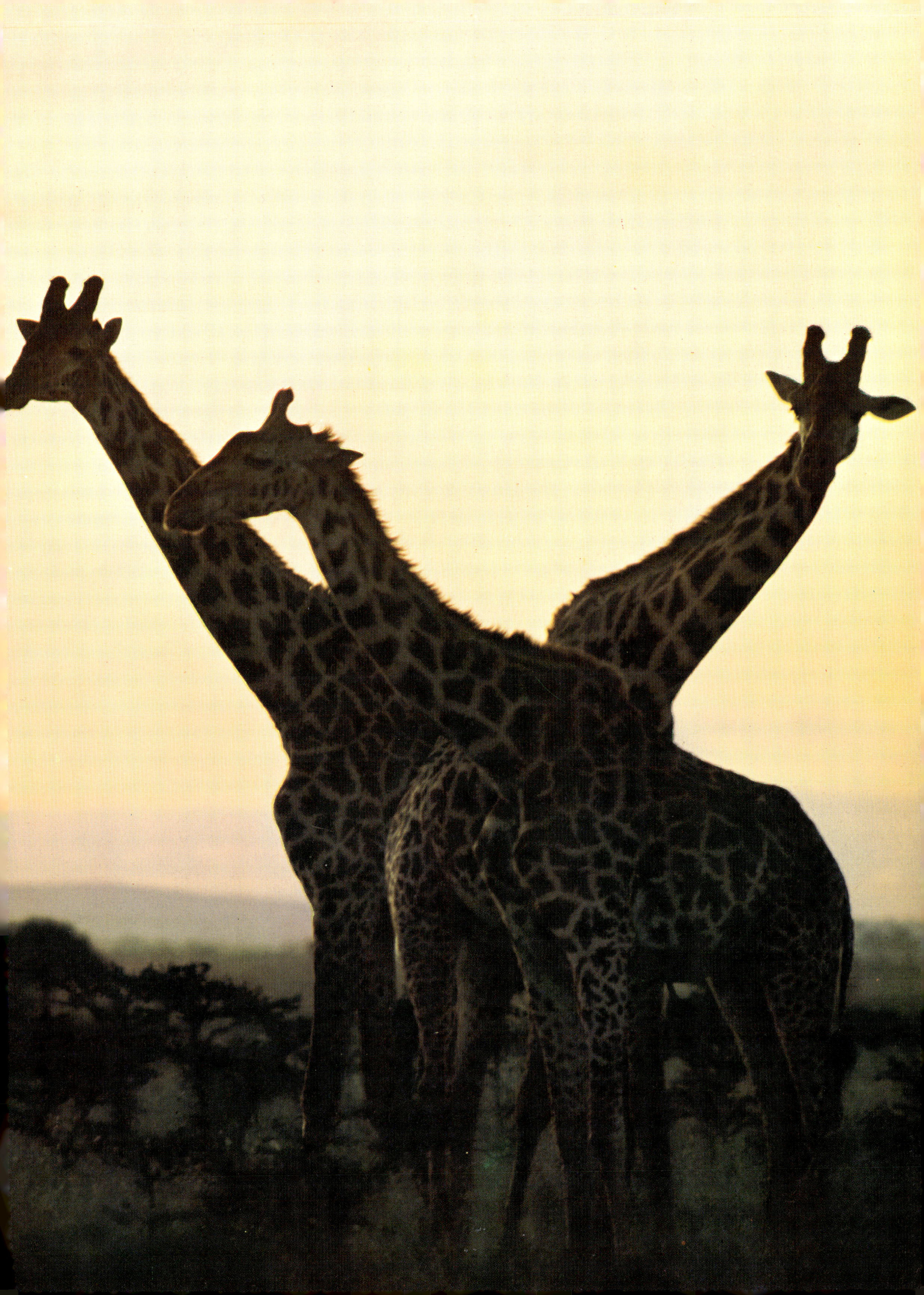

Impala

The impala is one of the most graceful of the antelopes. About 30–40 in. high, weighing 140–160 lb, it is chestnut brown with a lighter brown area on the flanks and a sharply defined white belly. The male has lyre-shaped, ribbed horns, 20–30 in. long, which make one spiral turn; the female is hornless. The neck and limbs are slender and delicate. The impala occupies a rather isolated position in the family Bovidae. In the past there have been divided opinions on whether it was more nearly related to the gazelles or to the reedbuck. Recently Alan Gentry has suggested, on a study of the skull, teeth and horn-cores, that the impala is more nearly related to the hartebeest and gnu.

Taking to cover

Impala inhabit a wide area of East and South Africa. They seem to like being near water and they avoid open country, being more usually found where there are low trees and tall shrubs, without much ground cover, in scrub and thornbush country especially. Their distribution is patchy because they do not venture much into either overgrown or open land. So, although abundant in most of the Kruger National Park, they are absent from much of its northern end.

△ Poise in triplicate: a female impala trio nose down in their local river. Impala seldom stray far from water, and will not venture into arid surroundings or bushy thickets.

According to its suitability for the impala, an area may have a density of anything from seven to over 200 per square mile; the usual figure is 50–70. Concentrations are highest in the dry season, as with most African ungulates; this also happens to be the time of the rut. In the wet season, impala are more scattered, and occupy small home ranges; but they may wander as much as 15 miles for water.

Impala both graze and browse, but in most areas they eat mainly grass.

Born when the grass sprouts

The rut takes place in the beginning of the dry season. The lambs are born, one to each ewe, after a gestation of 180–210 days, early in the wet season when there is most food for them.

In Rhodesia, the first lambs are dropped in early December and the peak of lambing is from December 15 to January 1. Two-year-old ewes, breeding for the first time, give birth later in the season than older ones. The young grow rapidly – in young males the horns begin to sprout in late February – and are usually weaned before the next rut, at which time they may form separate bands. In the rut nearly all ewes breed, at least 97% of the older ones, and 85% of the two-year-olds.

The rut begins when the males set up their territories in late May or early June. Surplus rams attach themselves to small groups of ewes, and the yearlings form small bands by themselves. The ewes live in herds the year round. At the end of the lambing season these may number (including lambs) as much as 100. At Fort Tuli, Rhodesia, herds of 200–300 have been counted. These large herds stay together from January to May, and only a few males associate with them; then in May they break into smaller groups, which pass through the rams' territories and are covered by them. After the rut, the ram groups re-form but groups of mixed sex and age predominate. By December, the groups are reduced in size to ten or less; the ewes become secretive, separating off for a while to give birth.

The main predator is probably the leopard. Existing populations of impala are often subject to poaching, but this does not severely affect their numbers.

△ *The roving eye: a handsome male runs a casual glance over the scrubland.*

▽ *Poetry in motion: female in full flight.*

Switchback fugitives

Impala rams become quite aggressive in the rutting season, especially when setting up territories. At this time, fighting and chasing are common. The rams, once the territories are set up, leave their bases to drink at the waterholes, which are a no-man's-land. But the most conspicuous piece of impala behaviour is their alarm reaction. When disturbed, the whole group indulge in a magnificent display of leaping. They jump forward, straight up or with side turns, as much as 10 ft into the air, up and down, round and in all directions. What is the function of this behaviour? It has been suggested that in reality its purpose is to confuse a predator, such as a big cat who is trying to single out one animal from the group it is attacking. The leaping impala, helped by their contrasting colours, seem to be wholly successful in preventing this, and completely confuse the attacker.

A number of animals show this sort of behaviour when alarmed by a predator. Instead of putting as much ground between themselves and their adversary they jink to and fro to cause confusion. The jinking of hares is an example that readily comes to mind and it has been suggested that continually changing direction prevents an enemy from cutting off its prey.

class	**Mammalia**
order	**Artiodactyla**
family	**Bovidae**
genus & species	*Aepyceros melampus*

Bottlenose dolphin

Also often known as the common porpoise, this is the animal that in the last 20 years has become a star performer in the seaquaria of the United States. It is up to 12 ft long, weighs as much as 440 lb and is black above and white underneath, with a bulbous head and a marked snout. The forehead of the male is more protruding than that of the female. The moderate-sized flippers taper to a point and the fin in the middle of the back has a sharply-pointed apex directed backwards, making the hinder margin concave. It has 20–22 conical teeth in each half of both upper and lower jaw. Although as well suited to life in the water as any fish it is in fact a mammal like whales or, for that matter, man, giving birth to fully-developed young which are suckled on milk. The bottlenose is the commonest cetacean (family name of the whales) off the Atlantic coast of North America, from Florida to Maine. It occurs in the Bay of Biscay and Mediterranean also. It occasionally ranges to Britain, and is also found off West Africa, south to Dakar.

Cooperative schools

Bottlenose dolphins live in schools containing individuals of both sexes and all ages. Apparently there is no leader, but males in the school observe a 'peck order' based on size. When food is plentiful the schools may be large, breaking into smaller schools when it is scarce. The dolphins pack together at times of danger. They also assist an injured member of the school by one ranging either side of it and, pushing their heads under its flippers, raising it to the surface to breathe. In schools they keep in touch by sounds.

They sleep by night and are active by day, although each feeding session is followed by an hour's doze. Females sleep at the surface with only the blowhole exposed and this periodically opens and closes, as it does in stranded dolphins, by reflex action. The males sleep a foot below the surface, periodically rising to breathe.

The main swimming action is in the tail, with its horizontal flukes. This, the flexible part of the animal, is used with an up-and-down movement in swimming, quite unlike that of fishes, with only an occasional sideways movement. The flippers help in steering and balance. The dorsal fin also aids stability, but it is the lungs placed high up in the body that are chiefly responsible for keeping a dolphin balanced.

The depths to which bottle-nosed dolphins can dive has to be deduced from the remains of fishes in their stomachs. These show they go down for food to at least 70 ft, and they can stay submerged for up to 15 minutes. Their lung capacity is half as much again as that of a land animal and in addition they fill their lungs to capacity. Land animals, including ourselves, use only about half the lung capacity and change only 10–15% of the air in the lungs with each breath. A dolphin changes up to 90%.

Tame dolphin leaping some 30 ft into the air to take fish accurately, which proves that its small eyes are still quite useful out of water.

Well equipped for marine life

Since a dolphin's lungs are compressed when diving, air would be squeezed into the bronchial tubes, where no gaseous exchange would take place, unless this were prevented by valves. There are 25–40 of these in the bronchial tubes of the bottlenose dolphin and they act as a series of taps controlling the pressure in the lungs according to whether the animal is diving, swimming on the level or rising to the surface.

At the surface the pulse of the bottlenose dolphin is 110 a minute. When submerged it drops to 50 a minute and starts to increase as the animal nears the surface. The drop is related to the way the blood circulation is shut off so that the oxygen supply goes mainly to essential organs, notably the heart and brain. This extends the time of submergence by reducing the frequency with which visits need be made to the surface to breathe.

Whales and dolphins have an insulating layer of blubber, but they have no sweat glands and they cannot pant, so other means are needed to lose excess body heat. The tail flukes and the flippers are always warmer to the touch than the rest of the body and their temperature is not only higher than that of other parts of the body but varies through a greater range. They also have a much thinner layer of blubber. It is assumed therefore that these parts lose heat to the surrounding water. In brief, whales and dolphins keep cool through their flukes and flippers.

A dolphin's eyesight is not particularly good. Yet the animal can move its eyelids, shut its eyes, even wink. At one time it was thought the eyes were of little value and were quite useless out of water. This last seems proved wrong by the way dolphins in seaquaria will leap out of water and accurately snatch fish from the attendant's hand. Moreover, the visual fields of left and right eyes overlap, so presumably they have partially stereoscopic vision. The sense of smell is, however, either non-existent or almost wholly so.

Hearing is the main sense, apart from taste and touch. This is acute and is especially sensitive to high tones. It is probably second only to the hearing of bats. A dolphin is sensitive to the pulses of an echosounder or asdic and will respond to frequencies as high as 120 kilocycles or beyond, whereas we can hear 30 kilocycles at the most. At sea it has been noticed that bottlenose dolphins will avoid a boat that has been used for hunting them but will not be disturbed by other boats. The assumption is that they can recognize individual boats by the sounds they make.

Feeding

Fish form one of the main items in the diet but a fair amount of cuttlefish is eaten, the dolphin spitting out the chalky cuttlebone and swallowing only the soft parts. Shrimps also are eaten. In captivity a bottlenose will eat 22 lb of fish a day, yielding 237 calories per pound of its body weight, compared with the 116 calories/lb taken by man.

Life history

Bottlenose dolphins become sexually mature

at 5–6 years. The breeding season extends from spring to summer. The gestation period is 11–12 months, births taking place mainly from March to May. The baby is born tail-first and as soon as free it rises to the surface to take a breath, often assisted by the mother usually using her snout to lift it gently up. Just prior to the birth the cow slows down and at the moment of birth she is accompanied by two other cows. These swim one either side of her, their role being protective, especially against sharks, who may be attracted to the spot by the smell of blood lost during the birth process. Weaning may take place between 6–18 months; reports vary considerably.

For the first 2 weeks the calf stays close beside the mother, being able to swim rapidly soon after birth. Then it begins to move away, even to chase fish, although quite ineffectively. However, it readily dashes back to its mother's side or to its 'aunt', the latter being another female that attaches herself to the mother and shares in the care of the calf. The aunt is the only one the mother allows near her offspring.

The calf is born with the teeth still embedded in the gums. These begin to erupt in the first weeks of life but the calf makes little attempt to chew until 5 months old and some take much longer before they attempt to swallow solid food. Even then there may be difficulties and in captivity a calf at about this time has been seen to bring up its first meal, the mother then massaging its belly with her snout.

Suckling is under water. The mother's nipples are small and each lies in a groove on the abdomen. The mother slows down to feed her calf which comes in behind her and lies slightly to one side, taking a nipple between its tongue and the palate. The mother then, by muscular pressure on the mammary glands, squirts the milk into its mouth. Should the calf let go the nipple the milk continues to squirt out. The baby bottlenose must come to the surface to breathe every half minute, so suckling must be rapid. In this species it consists of one to nine sucks, each lasting a few seconds. For the first 2 weeks the calf is suckled about twice an hour, night and day, but by 6 months it is down to six feeds a day.

Can dolphins talk?

It is not all that time ago that it was generally believed that whales, porpoises and dolphins were more or less mute, although the whalers themselves held very definite views to the contrary. It was not until after World War II, when bottlenose dolphins were being first kept in captivity in the large seaquaria, first in Florida and later in California and elsewhere, that it began to be realized fully that they have a wide vocabulary of sounds. Then, a few years ago, came the startling suggestion that these cetaceans might be capable of imitating human speech, even perhaps of being able to talk to people, in a sort of Donald Duck language in which words are 'gabbled' in a very high pitch. These high hopes do not seem to have been realised, but apart from this much has been learned about the noises they make.

One thing that has long been known is that air can be released from the blowhole

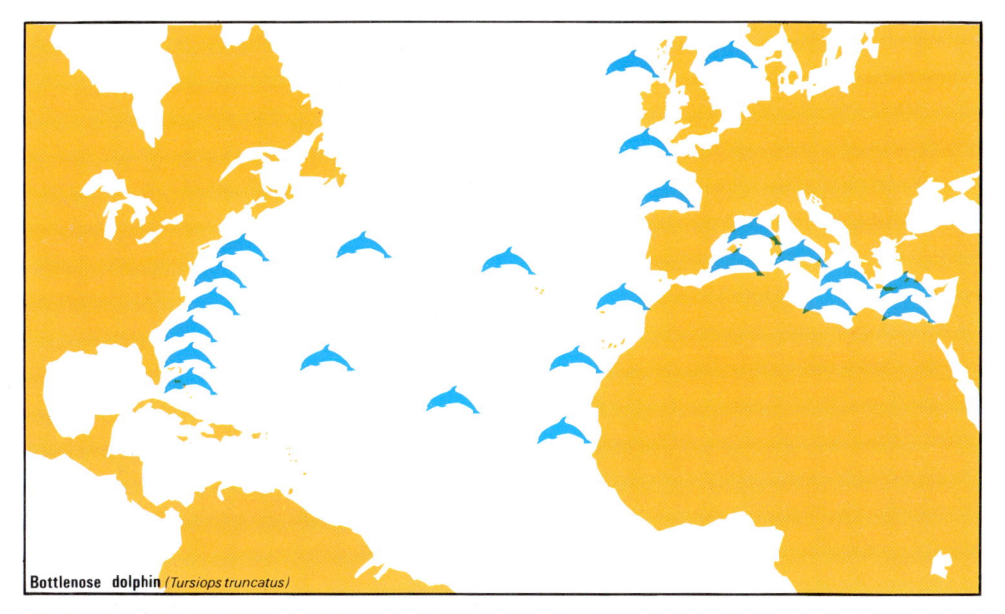

△△ *Bottlenose dolphin jaws are well armed with teeth that help it catch its mainly cuttlefish food.*
△ *Baby dolphin with its mother. As with most mammals it stays with its mother for some time and is suckled on milk, being weaned after 5 months or more. Note the blowhole or nostril on top of the head.*

245

while the animal is still submerged. This can be seen, by direct observation, emerging as a stream of bubbles. It can be used to produce sounds, and part of the mechanism for it is the many small pouches around the exit from the blowhole which act as safety valves, preventing any inrush of water.

It has been known for some time that some cetaceans are attracted over long distances by the cries of their fellows in distress. Conversely, people have been calling the animals to them by using whistles emitting sounds similar to their calls. Pliny, the Roman naturalist of the first century AD, knew of this, and in modern times the people on the Black Sea coasts have continued to do this. Sir Arthur Grimble also left us an account of what he called porpoise calling in South Pacific Islands. He described how local peoples in this area would call the porpoises from a distance to the shore. These items indicate an acute sense of hearing in dolphins and porpoises and a potentiality for communication by sounds on their part.

Underwater microphones as well as more direct observations in the various seaquaria have established that these cetaceans use a wide range of sounds. These have been variously described as whistles, squawks, clicks, creaks, quacks and blats, singing notes and wailings. It has been found that two dolphins which have been companions will, if separated, call to each other, and that a calf separated from its mother will call to her. Dolphins trained to leap out of water for food have been heard to make sounds at their attendants.

These are, however, only the sounds audible to our ears, which can deal only with the lower frequencies. Much of dolphin language is in the ultrasonic range, and if they are able to understand what we are saying, as one investigator has somewhat unconvincingly suggested, they could be using their own vocalizations to call us by rude names without our knowing it!

It has often been said that if whales cried out in pain we might be less ready to slaughter them. Scattered reports suggest that in fact they do precisely this. Freshly captured bottlenose dolphins placed in the tanks in Florida's Marineland have been heard through the thick plate glass windows to cry with shrill notes of discomfort and alarm. At sea similar distress calls have been heard from injured or wounded whales, porpoises and dolphins.

class	**Mammalia**
order	**Cetacea**
family	**Delphinidae**
genus & species	***Tursiops truncatus***

Bottlenose dolphins leaping out of the water in formation. This demonstrates the powerful swimming action of the tail with its horizontal fluke unlike a fish's tailfin which is vertical. It also shows their sociability.

Dolphins try to find each other by echo-locating 'clicks'. Then they talk in 'whistles' with a few 'grunts' and 'cracks'. Their sounds were analysed in 1965 when TG Lang and HAP Smith of the US Naval Ordnance Test Station put two newly captured bottlenose dolphins, Doris and Dash, in separate tanks linked by a two-way hydrophone system so the experimenters could tap their conversations. The first 4 of a total of 16 two-minute periods shown here indicate how the animals conversed when they were linked by phone and how sporadic noises were made when the line was 'dead'.

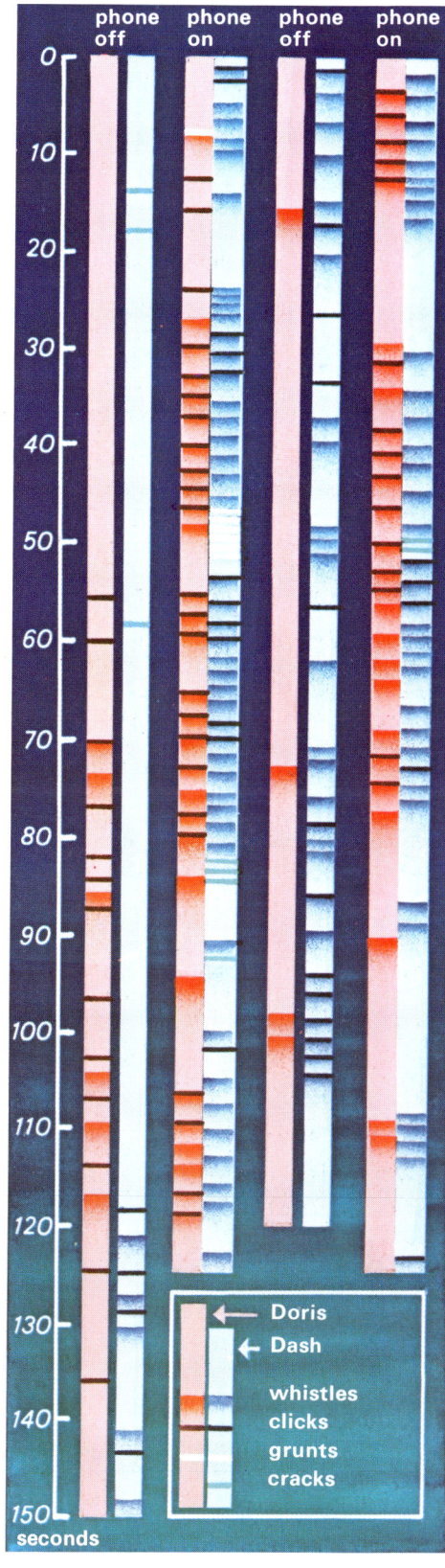

Killer whale

The killer whale is closely related to the false killer whale and also the pilot whale. It has a very bad reputation for ferocity which is probably unjustified. Killer whales are small for whales, the females growing up to a maximum of about 15 ft, but an old male may be as long as 30 ft. They are one of the few whales in which there is a marked difference in size between the sexes, the sperm whale being another example. The colour is very striking and distinctive, both sexes having similar markings, which are black on the back and white on the underside. Occasionally the white is somewhat yellowish. The chin is white and there is a characteristic white oval patch just above and behind the eye. There is a small whitish patch just behind the dorsal fin which varies quite considerably in shape and hue in different animals. The white on the underside sweeps up towards the tail and the flanks are white between the dorsal fin and the tail. The flippers, which are broad and rounded, are black all over, but the underside of the tail flukes are white. The dorsal fin is very conspicuous, usually about 2 ft high, but in the old males it may be 6 ft. The oldest males also have very long flippers, up to $\frac{1}{5}$ the animal's total length, the average length of the flipper in juvenile males and adult females being $\frac{1}{9}$ only.

Killer whales are found in all seas but are particularly numerous in the Arctic and Antarctic where there is abundant food to satisfy their voracious appetite. They are not uncommon around the British Isles, where a number have been stranded, mainly on the north and east coasts. These strandings take place in most months of the year. A larger number than usual were stranded on British coasts during the last war, mostly on the North Sea coast, probably due in part at least to anti-submarine activities.

Killer whale showing off its strength and beauty. Despite their reputation for ferocity, killer whales kept in oceanaria have been unaggressive and many are hand-tame.

△ *Running at the surface with blowhole open, a killer whale in relaxed mood.*

▽ *Affectionate play between a pair of killers. Sensory pits can be seen on the head.*

Living in packs

Killer whales hunt together in packs made up of both sexes. They are inquisitive and appear to take a close interest in anything likely to be edible. Nothing is known about their movements in the oceans or how much, if at all, the populations in different oceans mix. In the Antarctic they are often seen around whaling factory ships and probably they tend to follow the ships around as they offer an easy source of food. Otherwise very little is known about their habits.

Ruthless hunters

The killer whale is a voracious feeder and will take anything that swims in the sea. Included in its diet are whales, dolphins, seals, penguins, fish and squid. It will attack even the larger blue whales and quite often killers will hunt in packs numbering from two or three up to as many as 40 or more. When attacking a large whale they are said to work as a team. First one or two will seize the tail flukes to stop the whale thrashing about and slow it down, then others will attack the head and try to bite the lips. Gradually the whale becomes exhausted and its tongue lolls from its mouth—to be immediately seized by the killers. At this point all is over for the whale: the tongue is rapidly removed and the killers take their fill, seeming to favour a meal from around the head of their monster victim.

Apart from attacking fully-grown and healthy whales, killers have earned the hate of whalers because they often take the tongues from whales that have been harpooned and are lying alongside the factory ship waiting to be processed. They will even take the tongue from whales being towed by the catcher boat, and in an effort to stop this looting a man may be posted with a rifle to deter the killers. If he should injure a killer all the others in the pack turn on it and it very soon becomes their next meal.

Killer whales also eat seals and porpoises, and there are a number of records of complete seals found in a killer's stomach. The greatest number recorded is the remains of 13 porpoises and 14 seals that were taken from the stomach of one killer whale, while another contained remains of 32 seals. Off the Pribilof Islands in the Bering Sea, killer whales are often seen lying in wait for the young fur seal pups swimming out into the open sea for the first time. The number of seals actually taken by killers is not certain but it is likely that large numbers of pups must meet their end in this way before they reach the age of one year.

In the Antarctic, penguins form an important part of the killer whale diet. On many occasions killer whales have been seen swimming underneath ice floes, either singly or sometimes several at a time, and then coming up quickly under the floe either to tip it or break it up, thereby causing the penguins to fall into the water and into the waiting jaws of the killers.

Once killer whales were seen cruising close to an island where there was a colony of grey seals. As the killers came close in the seals hurried ashore in spite of a couple of people standing nearby. The certain danger from killer whales was more important to the seals than possible danger from man. It is said that when killer whales attack grey whales, these become so terrified that they just float on their backs unable to make any effort to escape.

Seven-footer calves

Very little is known about the breeding habits of the whale. They are thought to produce their young towards the end of the year, in November and December after a 16-month gestation. This is supported by examination of some of the stranded whales washed up on the beach and found to be pregnant. The calf at birth is about 7 ft long. The females suckle the young in the same way as other whales, but how long this lasts is not known.

No enemies

The killer whale probably has no real enemies. A few are killed by man, usually irate whalers. They are not a very valuable catch to a whaler although some Russian whaling fleets do catch a few, usually if there is nothing else worth shooting.

Chased by killers

The most famous story of killer whales is that told by Herbert Ponting who was the official photographer to the British *Terra Nova* Antarctic expedition led by Captain Scott in 1911. While the ship's cargo was being unloaded onto the ice some killer whales appeared nearby. Ponting went to take some photographs carrying the bulky photographic apparatus of those days over the floes. As he went across the ice the killers thrust up alongside and then followed him as he crossed the floes, tipping them from beneath. Ponting just managed to get to the safety of the fast ice in front of the killers—a lucky escape.

Ponting's experience must have been terrifying, yet it is often found that a reputation for ferocity is unfounded. Divers who have met killer whales have not been molested and several killer whales have been kept in oceanaria. All have been unaggressive or even hand-tame. One story tells of a fisherman of Long Island, New York, who threw a harpoon at a killer whale. The whale pulled free and followed the boat and its terrified occupants to shallow water, but it made no attempt to harm them despite such severe provocation.

class	**Mammalia**
order	**Cetacea**
family	**Delphinidae**
genus & species	*Orcinus orca* killer whale

◁ *Flukes aloft, a killer sounds with a minimum of splash—a tribute to its streamlining.*
△ *A killer pack surges round the edges of encroaching ice.* ▽ *Killer curiosity.*

Grey whale Eschrichtius glaucus.

Grey whale

At one time the Californian grey whale lived in the Atlantic Ocean, for its remains have been found in reclaimed land in the Zuider Zee. Now it is confined to the North Pacific where there are populations on both sides of that ocean.

It is a rather unusual whale, having points in common with both the rorqual (family Balaenopteridae) and right whales (family Balaenidae). It is about the size of the right whales, reaching 45 ft long and 20 tons in weight. The flukes of the tail are proportionally longer and more delicate than those of right whales, but more stubby than those of rorquals. The dorsal fin is replaced by 8–10 small humps along the tail just in front of the flukes. On the throat the grey whale has 2–3, rarely 4, grooves extending a short distance as compared with the 40–100 grooves extending to the belly in rorquals and the complete absence of grooves in right whales.

As the name implies, the grey whale is usually dark slate-grey but it may sometimes be blackish. It is lighter on the belly than on the back, as is usual in marine animals. Many grey whales have crescent-shaped marks or patches on the skin, especially on the back. These are caused either by lampreys or by barnacles.

Sluggish swimmers

Grey whales are very slow, usually swimming at 2–3 knots with bursts of 6–7 knots when alarmed, compared with 20 knots of a fin whale. As they also come very close inshore this makes them very vulnerable to hunters. In early spring the grey whales migrate down the west coast of North America. In 1840 there were estimated to be around 25 000 grey whales but soon after this there was very intense hunting all along the coast. By 1875 it was unusual to see more than 50 migrating whales at a time, although they used to be seen by the thousand. While the whales were in the Arctic Ocean they were hunted by Eskimos; in the Bay of Vancouver and around the Queen Charlotte Islands they were attacked by Indians from canoes, and farther south the Yankee whalers chased them in sailing boats.

Dog food or tourist bait?

By 1936 the world population was thought to be as low as 100–200. Then the governments of America, Japan and Russia came to an agreement on the future of the grey whale and declared it a protected species. This protection, together with the animal's fairly high rate of reproduction, has resulted in a gradual build-up of the population and it is now thought that they number between 5 and 10 thousand. But the grey whale's future is still dubious: it has recently been reported that the Mexican government is planning to kill grey whales when they migrate south to Mexican water, the idea being to use the carcases as dog food. This is a short-sighted plan: far more could be made out of tourism, for each year thousands of tourists gather on the west coast to watch the grey whales come down from the Bering Sea to give birth to their calves in the shallow and sheltered coastal waters of California and Mexico.

Straining out their food

Like the rarer blue whale the grey whales collect their food by means of rows of baleen plates in their mouths. Various crustaceans and molluscs floating in the sea are eaten in this manner.

Swimming south to breed

The migration of the grey whale is one of the better known aspects of its behaviour. They spend the summer months in the far north, principally in the Bering Sea, where they live in mixed herds. As summer draws to a close they swim slowly southwards and come in close to the coast, particularly so when they approach California where they can be seen swimming only a mile or so offshore. Here the herds segregate; the females stay together and led by an older cow come really close into the bays and lagoons where they get shelter from the weather to give birth to the calves. These are usually born at about the end of January, measuring about 15 ft in length and weighing around 1 500 lb. Normally only a single calf is produced but twin births have been recorded, the calves suckling for about 9–10 months. As spring approaches the migration is reversed. The males, who have been waiting in deeper water, join the females with their newborn calves and the herds make their way back to the northern oceans to feed again in the colder waters where food is more abundant.

Chivalrous males

It has sometimes been noticed that grey whales show a one-sided faithfulness. If a female is injured or gets into difficulties one or more males may go to her aid, either to keep her at the surface where she can breathe, or to defend her from the attacks of killer whales. But if a male gets into similar difficulties, the females have been seen swimming away from the scene of trouble!

After man, killer whales are the greatest danger to grey whales. It is said that when a small school of grey whales are attacked by a large group of killers they may become so terrified by the attacks that they just float at the surface, belly uppermost, paralysed by fear and making themselves extremely vulnerable to further attack. The grey whales' habit of coming close inshore during the breeding season probably keeps them fairly clear of the attacks of killer whales who prefer deeper water. Sometimes grey whales have come so close inshore that they have practically run aground, and on one occasion a grey whale was seen playing about in the surf like a seal. They have also been found stranded at low tide, apparently without ill effect as they just floated off again at the next high water. This is most unusual since, for almost every other species of whale, stranding means death.

class	**Mammalia**
order	**Cetacea**
family	**Eschrichtidae**
genus & species	*Eschrichtius glaucus* *grey whale*

Index

Note: page numbers in italics denote illustrations

aardvark 219-21
Acipenser :
   ruthenus 11
   sturio 11
   transmontanum 11
adder 112-13
   puff 115-16
Aegypius monachus 150
Aepyceros melampos 243
Aequidens latifrons 47
Afrixalus 72
   fornasinii 72
Age of Fishes 6
Age of Reptiles 54
Ailuropoda melanoleuca 205
alarm call 131
albatross 131, 134-5
Alcedo atthis 171
alligator 81, 86-7
   difference between crocodile and 83, 86
Alligator :
   mississipiensis 87
   sinensis 87
Amblonyx cinerea 209
Amblyrhynchus cristatus 99
Ambystoma mexicanum 56, 57
ammocoete 8
amphibians 54
Amphioxides 7
Amphioxus 7
anaconda 105-6
Anas playrhynchos 142
Ancistrodon :
   contortrix 117
   himalayanus 117
   piscivorus 117
Aneides lugmbris 61
ani 163
angelfish 36-8
anglerfish 53
Anodorhynchus hyacinthinus 162
anole 38
antbaths 38
anteater:
   scaly 176
   spiny 176, 177
antelope:
   impala 242-3
   sable 216
antlers: importance of 238
Aonyx capensis 209
Aptenodytes patagonica 131
Apteryx :
   australis 128
   haasti 128
   oweni 128
Ara :
   ararauna 162
   macao 162
   militaris 162

Archaeopteryx 122
Archilochus colubris 168
Aristophanes 151
asp 111
Aspredinichthys tibicen 33
ass: difference between zebra and 226
auk 158
axolotl 56-7

baboon 184
babysitting 231
bakadori 135
barb: zebra 31
Barbus fasciatus 31
barracuda 48-9
batfish 53
Batracloseps attenuatus 61
batrachotoxin 65
bear: black 200
beaver 192-4
becuna 48
behaviour:
   defensive 61
   fossil 178
   innate 193
beluga 10, 11
Betta :
   pugnax 45-6
   splendens 45-6
birds 122, 176
   flightless 122, 123-8, 130-1, 132
Bitis :
   arietans 116
   atropos 116
   caudalis 116
   cornuta 116
   gabonica 116
   inornata 116
   nasicornis 116
   peringueyi 116
bittern 153
blood:
   differences between camel's and other mammals' 233
   effect of loss of body water on 233
blue acara 47
boa: water 105
Boissonneaua jardini 169
Boleophthalmus 42
boxfish 23
Brachydanio rerio 31
branchial basket 7
Branchiostoma :
   californiense 7
   lanceolatum 7
   lubricum 7
breathing without lungs or gills 61
Brookesia 94
buffalo 216

Bufo bufo 64
bullfrog 67-9
burial: of animals by others in herd 225
bushmaster 117
butterfly fish 16-18
button-quail 153

Caecilia 55
caecilian 55
caiman 81
Calabaria reinhardti 109
camel 232-5
Camelus :
   bactrianus 235
   dromedarius 235
camouflage:
   colour 50
   governed by eyes 52
   colour and form 53, 65
Campephilus principalis 173
Campethera abingoni 172
candiru 33
capybara 192
Carcharodon carcharias 9
Carduelis :
   carduelis 174
   flavirostris 174
   spinus 174
carinates 129
carp 26-7
carpet snake 107
cassowary 126
Castor :
   canadensis 194
   fiber 194
castoreum 194
catfish 32-33
   electric 22
caviare 10
Ceryle rudis 171
Chaetodon 17
Chalcites lucidus 164
Chamaeleo :
   bitaeniatus 92
   chamaeleon 94
   dilepis 94
   jacksoni 94
   oweni 94
chameleon 92-4
charming 202
Chelmon rostratus 36
chicken 151-2
chimpanzee 150, 184-6, 187
Chionis 131
Chlamydosaurus kingii 91
Chloroceryle :
   amazona 171
   americana 171
Choeropsis liberiensis 231
Chondropython viridis 109

Chrysococcyx cupreus 164
Chrysolampis mosquitus 169
Cichlasoma nigrofasciatum 191
cichlid: zebra 31
ciguatera 49
Clamator :
   coromandus 164
   glandarius 164
Clemmys leprosa 73
Clytoceyx rex 171
cobra 110-11
Coccyzus :
   americanus 164
   erythrophthalmus 164
Coendou 198-9
   prehensilis 199
cofferfish 23
cold-blooded reptiles:
   temperature control 81
Columba palumbus 160
colour:
   as camouflage 50, 53
   governed by eyes 52
   changing 93
   mechanics 94
   purposes 94
   in courtship 43
   flash coloration 65
   uses 38
   as warning 65
condor 149
Conolophus :
   pallidus 96
   subcristatus 97
constriction 105, 107-8
convict fish 31
copperhead 117
cordon-bleu 175
Corucia zebrata 102
Corythornis cristata 170
Coscoroba coscoroba 145
cottonmouth 117
coua 163
coucal 163
courtship:
   aimed at inanimate objects 75
   dances 57, 110, 132, *132*, 135
   display 129, 140, 153
   female active in 86
   gymnastic 43
   purpose of 65
   ritual 34, 59, 65, 123, 131, 141-2, *158*, 160, 178
cowbird 163
cowfish 24
crocodile 81-5
   difference between alligator and 83, 86
crocodile tears 84
Crocodylus :
   niloticus 85

palustris 85
porosus 85
Crotalus 119
    adamanteus 120
    atrox 120
    cerastes 121
    horridus 120
    pusillus 120
    ruber 120
    tigris 120
    viridis 120
crucifixion fish 33
Crypturellus soui 129
cuckoo 163-4
Cuculus:
    canorus 164
    varlus 164
curare 65
Cyclura cornuta 97
Cygnus:
    atratus 145
    columblanus bewickii 145
    c. columbianus 145
    cygnus buccinator 145
    c. cygnus 145
    melanocoryphus 145
    olor 145
Cyprinus carpio 27

dances:
    courtship 57, 110, 132, *132*, 135
    territorial 113
danio: zebra 31
Darwin, Charles 97, 99
defence mechanisms:
    hiss 91
    inflating body 63-4
    tail-shedding 100
defensive behaviour 61
dehydration 233
Dendrobates:
    auratus 65
    leucomelas 65, *66*
    pumilio 65
Dendrobocopos:
    major 172
    minor 173
Dendrophryniscus brevipollicatus 65
Dermochelys coriacea 79
Desmognathus:
    fuscus 61
    ochrophaeus 60
    ocoee 61
    wrightii 61
deterrents, *see* defence mechanisms
dingleberry 25
Dipsosaurus dorsalls 177
discus 39
display:
    aggressive 91
    alarm reaction 243
    courtship 129, 140, 153
    distraction 123-4
    territorial 43, *44*, 98, 113
    threatening 98, 153
distraction displays 123-4
Dolly Varden 14
dolphin: bottlenose 244-7
dove 159

dragon 109
Dromalus novaehollandiae 127
dromedary 232
Drycopus pileatus 173
duck: mallard 141-2
duckbill 176, 177
duckmole 177

eagle:
    hawk- 146
    martial 146-7
    snake- 146
    Verreaux's 146
echidna 176
eclipse plumage 141
education: of young by female 231
eel, electric 22
eelskipper 42, 43
electric eel 22
electricity: study of 22
Electrophorus electricus 22
elephant 140-3
Elephas indicus 225
emu 126-7
Ensatina croceator 61
Ensifera ensifera 168
Equus:
    burchelli antiquorum 229
    b. boehmi 229
    b. borensis 229
    b. burchelli 229
    grevyi 229
    quagga 229
    zebra hartmannae 229
    z. zebra 229
Erethizon dorsatum 199
Eschrichtius glaucus 251
Essenberg 29
Estrilda:
    astrild 175
    locustella 175
    melpoda 175
    perreini 175
    subflava 175
    temporalis 175
    troglodytes 175
Euarctos americanus 200
Eudromia elegans 129
Eudynamys scolopacea 164
Eumeces:
    fasciatus 102
    skiltonlanus 100
Eunectes:
    murinus 105
    notaeus 105
euro, 179
Eurycea longicauda 61
Eurypyga helias 153
Eutoxeres aquila 168
extinction, animals in danger of 189
eyes:
    effect of light on 89
    sensitivity of 120

fighting:
    between males 45-6, 191, 230
    ritualised 240
    with mouth 47
fighting fish 45-6

fishes 6
    groups 6
fishing: by fish 53
fishing frogs 53
flamingo 138-40
flathead 33
flying fish 17, 18
folklore, myths and legends 64, 109, 137
fossil behaviour 178
fossils:
    of amphibians 54
    of birds 122
    of fishes 6
    living 178
fowl:
    domestic 151-2
    jungle *152*
fox: red 201-2
Fraterculla:
    arctica 158
    corniculata 158
Friess 30
frog:
    arrow-poison 65-6
    arum 72
    bull 67-9
    common 63
    jumping 68
    kokoi 65
    mouth-breeding 70
    paradoxical 115
    reed 71-2
    sedge 71
    Stephens Island 54
frogfish 53
Fundulus heteroclitus 31

Gallus:
    domesticus 151
    gallus 151-2
grebe 132-3
gecko 88-90
Gekko gekko 90
Geocolaptes olivaceus 173
Geotria 8
gharial 81
    false 81
gibbon 187
Giraffa camelopardalis 240
giraffe 216, 240-1
glanis 32
gnu 228
goby 6
goldfinch 174
gooney 135
goosefish 53
Gopherus:
    agassizi 76
    berlandieri 76
    flavomarginatus 76
    gigantea 76
gorilla 187
gourami, kissing 47
Graptemys geographica 73
griffon *148-9*, 149
guillemot 158
Gypohlerax angolensis 150
Gyps:

africanus 150
coprotheres 150
indicus 150

Haematopus:
    ater 154
    bachmani 154
    fuliginosus 154
    leucopodus 154
    moquini 155
    ostralagus 154-5
    palliatus 154
hagfish 8
Halcyon:
    chelicuti 171
    leucocephala 170
    sancta 171
halibut 52
Haplochiton zebra 31
hare:
    jackass (black-tailed) 190
    jack rabbit 190-1
    prairie 190
hatchet fish 18
heat: detecting 117
hedgehog *112*, 113
Helostoma temmincki 47
Hemidacylium scutatum 61
Heniochus acuminatus 17
heron 153
Hi-goi 26
Hippocampus:
    brevirostris 34
    erectus 34
    hippocampus 34
    hudsonius 34
Hippoglossus:
    hippoglossus 52, *52*
    stenolepis 52
hippopotamus 230-1
Hippopotamus amphibius 231
Holacanthus 36
honeyguide 163
horse: difference between zebra and 226
hummingbird 168-9
Huso huso 11
hybridization 30
Hydromantes genei 60
Hyperolius:
    horstocki 72
    marmoratus 72
    nasutus 72
    quinquevittatus 72
    tuberilingius 72

Ichthyophis 55
iguana 95-7
    marine 98-9
Iguana iguana 97
impala 242-3
injured: helped by others in herd or pack 225, 244, 251

jack rabbit 190-1
jug o' rum 67
jungle fowl *152*

kagu 153

kangaroo 179-80
kihikihi 209
killifish 41
kingfisher 170-1
Kinosternon subrubrum 80
kissing gourami 47
kiwi 28
knifefish 22
koala 181-3
koel 163
kokoi frog 65

labyrinth fish 47
Lacerta :
    lepida 104
    viridis 104
Lachesis 117
Lactophrys :
    bicaudalis 25
    quadricornis 25
lammergeier 149
lampern 8
Lampetra:
    fluviatilis 8
    planeri 8
lamprey 8
lancelet 6, 7
legends, *see* folklore, myths and legends
Lepus :
    californicus 191
    townsendi 191
Lesbia victoriae 169
Leurognathus marmoratus 61
Liasis amethystinus 109
Limax. lanceolatus 7
Lymnodynastes dorsalis 69
limpkin 153
lion 213-6
lizard:
    crested 95
    eyed 103
    frilled 91
    green 103-4
    wall 104
lizard-bird 122
llama 233
Loddigesia mirabilis 168
Lophius piscatorius 53
Loxodonta africana 225
Lunda cirrhata 158
lungs:
    capacity and air change 244
    as hydrostatic organs 61
    inflating 94
    mouth lining acting as 61
luth 78
Lutra :
    canadensis 209
    lutra 209
Lygosoma laterale 102

macaw 161-2
Macropus :
    giganteus 180
    robustus 180
madtoms 33
mako 9
Malaclemys terrapin 73, 74

mallard 141-2
mammals 176
    egg-laying 177
mannikin 175
marsupials 176
mating:
    see courtship, reproduction
matriarchy 230
medicine:
    folk 115, 194
    use of poison in 65
Megaceryle maxima 170
Megaleia rufa 180
Melanerpes :
    erythrocephalus 173
    formicivorus 173
Mellisuga helenae 168
mesites 153
moa 126
mollymawk 135
mongoose 111
monkfish 53
monsters:
    lake 209
    sea 218
moorish idol 41
Mordacia 8
Morelia :
    argus 109
    spilotes 109
mouse:
    deer- (white-footed) 195-6
    elephant and 225
    Oldfield 196
    vesper 196
mouth:
    lining acting as lungs 61
    wrestling with 47
mouthbreeding (mouthbrooding) 33
mudskipper 42-44
mugger 81
muscular motion 22
musselpecker 154
myths, *see* folklore, myths and legends

Naja 110-11
    haje 111
    melanoleuca 111
    nigricollis 111
    naja 111
    nivea 111
Necrosyrtes monachus 150
Neophron percnopterus 150
Neoseps reynoldsi 102
neoteny 7, 57
Nests of fish 8, 45
    made of bubbles 45, *46*
neurotoxin 110
newt 58-9
Nothoprocta ornata 129

Occam's Razor 79
Odobenus :
    rosmarus divergens 218
    r. rosmarus 218
ogo-pogo 209
olm 54
Oncorhynchus :

    gorbuscha 13
    keta 13
    kisutch 13
    masou 13
    nerka 13
    tshawytscha 13
orang utan 187-9
Orcinus orca 250
Ornithorhynchus anatinus 178
Orycteropus afer 220
Osteolaemus 85
Ostracion :
    cornutus 25
    lentiginosus 25
    meleagris 23
ostrich 123-4
otter 208-9
    sea 150
owl: barn 165-7
oystercatcher 154-5

pachyderms 222
Pan troglodytes 186
panda, giant 204-5
pangolin 176, 219
Panthera :
    leo 216
    tigris 212
Pantodon buchholzi 18
parachute 89
parasitism:
    laying eggs in host nest 163-4, 175
    social: man's 236
Patagona gigas 168
peck order 29, 152, 238
Pelargopsis capensis 171
Pelecanus :
    crispus 137
    erythrorhynchos 137
    occidentalis 137
    onocrotalus 137
    rufescens 137
pelican 136-7
pellets of predatory birds 165
penguin:
    emperor 130-1
    king 130-1
perch: sea 52
Periophthalmus 44
    chrysospilos 42, *42*, 43
    kalolo 42
    koelreuteri 44
Peromyscus maniculatus 196
Petromyzon marinus 8
pets, unsuitable 87
Phascolarctos cinereus 182
Phelsuma vinsoni 88
Phoebetria 135
Phoeniconatas minor 140
Phoeniconparrus :
    andinus 140
    jamesi 140
Phoenicopterus ruber 140
Phyllobates 65
Picoides tridactylus 173
picuda 48
Picus viridis 173
pigeon, wood 159-60

pigeon's milk 160
pilot fish 78
pink sweat 230
piranha (piraya) 19-21
plaice 51-2
plastron 80
platy 30
platypus 176, 177-8
play 209
Plethodon 60
    cinereus 61
    glutinosus 61
Pleuronectes platessa 51
Plotosidae 33
plumage, eclipse 141
Podiceps :
    auratus 133
    cristatus 133
    ruficollis 133
Podilymbus gigas 133
poison:
    acting on blood system 110
    affecting nervous system 59, 110
    collecting 65
    for arrow heads 65
    injected through fangs 110
    most powerful 65
    snake's: replenishing 120
    use in medicine 65
Polemaetus bellicosus 146
Pomacanthus paru 38
pompadour fish 39-40
Pongo :
    pongo abeli 189
    pygmaeus pygmaeus 189
porcupine 197-19
porpoise 244, 245
pride 8
Procyon :
    cancrivorus 207
    lotor 207
prophecy: hens used in 152
Psettodes 52
Pseudemys scripta 73
Pseudotriton montanus 57
Pteronura brasiliensis 209
puff adder 114-6
puffin 156-8
python 107-9, 117
Python :
    anchietae 109
    curtus 109
    molurus 109
    regius 109
    reticulatus 109
    sebae 109
    timorensis 109
Pyxicephalus adspersus 67

quagga 229

rabbit, jack 190-1
raccoon 206-7
rails 153
Rana :
    catesbeiana 68, *68*, 69
Rangifer tarandus 239
ratites 126, 129
rattlesnake 45-6

horned 121
razorbill 158
redd 15
redpoll 174
regeneration 56, *88*, 90
    effect of temperature on 89
reindeer 236-9
reproduction:
    by attached male 53
    juvenile (neoteny) 7, 57
    male emitting spermatophore 59
    mouthbreeding 33, 70, *70*
    neoteny 7, 57
    ovoviviparous 311, 113
    viviparous 106
reptiles 54
Rhinoderma darwinii 70
roadrunner 163
rock beauty 36
rorqual 251

salamander 56-7
    lungless 60-1
    olm 54
Salmo :
    aguabonita 15
    clarki 15
    gairdneri 15
    trutta 15
salmon:
    Pacific 12-13
    zebra 31
Salvelinus :
    fontinalis 15
    malina 15
    namaycush 15
sandfish 102
Sarcogyps calvus 150
Scalare 37
scales: size in relation to speed of fish 19
Scaphirhynchus platorhynchus 11
Scartelaos 42
    viridis 44
Scelotes 100
    bojeri 102
    inornatus 102
    melanopleura 102
seahorse 34-5
sea-pie 154
Selasphorus rufus 168
sennet 448
serin 174
Serinus dermus 174
Serrasalmus :
    nattereri *19*, 20
    piraya 19
    rhombeus 19
    spilopleura 20
sex: reversal 29-30
shark
    great white 9
    maneater 9
    zebra 31
sheatfish (sheathfish) 32
sidewinder 121
silurus 32
Silurus glanis 33
Siphonops annulatus 55

siskin 174
Sistrurus 119
skink 100-2
Sminthillus limbatus 65
snake-charmer 111, *111*
snakes:
    drinking 120
    replenishing poison 120
Soay Beast 79
social order 184
    peck order 29, 152, 238
sole 51
sound:
    carrying power 67
    dolphins': analysis 247
    hissing 115
    production 72
    vocabulary of 245-6
spet 448
Sphyraena :
    barracuda 49
    borealis 49
    sphyraena 49
Stegostoma tigrinum 31
sterlet 10
Sternotherus :
    carinatus 80
    odoratus 80
stinkpot *80*
Struthio camelus 125
sturgeon 10-11
    shovelnose 11
sunbittern 153
swan 143-5
swordtail 28-30
Symphysodon :
    aequifasclata 38
    discus 40
tail: shedding as decoy 100
Tanysiptera galatea 171
Taricha torosa 59
teddy bear 200
teeth:
    egg 113
    for holding prey 59, 102, *109*
    moving round jaw 224
    tubes in 220
temperature:
    control in cold-blooded animals 81
    effect on regeneration 89
    receptors detecting 117
Terrapene 73
terrapin 73-4
Testudo :
    graeca 76
    hermanni 76
    pardalis 75
tetrodotoxin 59
Thecadactylus rapicaudus 89
Therapon jarbua 31
thyroxine 57
tiger 210-2
tiger fish 31
Tilaqua rugosa 102
tinamou 129
toad:
    common 62-4
    Surinam 54

toadstone 64
tokay 88
Tomistoma schlegeli 85
tools:
    made by animals 186
    used by animals 150, 185-6
Torgos tracheliotus 150
tortoise 75-7
    Greek 104
Trichomycteridae 33
Trichys lipura 199
Trigonoceps occipitalis 150
Trimeresurus :
    gramineus 117
    wagleri 117
Triturus 58-9
    alpestris 59
    cristatus 59
    helveticus 59
    vulgaris 59
trout 14-15
trunkfish 23-5
Tursiops truncatus 246
turtle:
    box 73
    leathery (leatherback) 78-9
    mud 80
    musk 80
    snapping 80
twite 174
Typhlonectes 55
Tyto alba 166

Ursus lotor 207

Vandellia cirrhosa 33
vaquero 70
vertebrates: first 6
viper 110, 113
    Gaboon 115
    pit 117-18
    rhinoceros 115
Vipera berus 113
vocal sac: breeding in 70, *70*
voice: purpose 70
    See also sound
voice-box: unused 240
Vulpes vulpes 202
vulture 149-50

wallaby 177, 179, 180
wallaroo 179
waller 32
walrus 217-18
warthog 219
water: loss from body 233
water moccasin 117
watermole 177
waxbill 175
wels 32-3
whale 245
    blue 251
    fin 251
    grey 251
    killer 248-50
    right 251
whale-elephant 218
whydah 175
womas 107

woodpecker finch 150
wood pigeon 159-60

Xiphophorus helleri 30

Zanclus canescens 41
zebra 226-9
    comparison with horse and ass 226
    name 31
zebra fish 31

Acknowledgments

This book is adapted from *Purnell's Encyclopedia of Animal Life*, published in the United States under the title of *International Wild Life*.

AFA: F.G.H. Allen; E.H. Herbert, Geoffrey Kinns, A.C. Wheeler; J. Allan Cash; Heather Angel; Toni Angermayer; R. Apfelbach; Atlas: Drogesco; Australian News and Inflormation Bureau; M.E. Bacchus; Barnabys; Bavaria: Sune Berkeman, W. Harstrick, Helmut Heinpel, B. Leidmann, W. Rohdich, H.W. Silvester, A. Sycholt; S. Beaufoy; S. Bisserot; R. Boardman; K. Boldt; Michael Boorer; British Antarctic Survey; British Museum, Natural History; Alice Brown; Fred Bruemmer; Ralph Buchsbaum; Kent Burgess; Jane Burton; Robert Burton; H.R. Bustard; Colin Butler; N.A. Callow; Camera Press; Carolina Biological Supply Co; James Carr; Centre de Documentation du CNRS; A. Christiansen; John Clegg; F. Collet; Dolly Connelly; J.A.L. Cooke; Gene Cox; Micro-colour Int.; Ben Cropp; Gerald Cubitt; Cyr Colour Agency; Peter David; W.T. Davidson; R.B. Davies; T. Dennett; Colin Doeg; G.T. Dunger; Herman Eisenbeiss; Andre Fatras; Douglas Faulkner; Forestry, Fish & Game Commission, USA; Harry & Claudy Frauca; J.B. Free; Carl Gans; G.S. Giacomelli; John Goddard; E. Grave; Hans Gundel; W.D. Haacke; H. Hansen; R.A. Harris & K. R. Duff; Bruce Hayward; Robert C. Hermes; Peter Hill; M.J. Hirons; E.S. Hobson; W. Hoflinger; E.O. Hoppe; Eric Hosking; Chris Howell-Jones; David Hughes; G.E. Hyde; Jacana: Brosset, A.R. Devez, J. & M. Fievel, Gerard, P. Summ, B. Tollu, J.P. Varin, P. & C. Vasselet, J. Vasserot, Bel G. Vienne, A. Visage; Roy Jarris; Michael Johns; Palle Johnsen; Peter Johnson; Keystone; G.E. Kirkpatrick; E.F. Kilian; H. Klingel; A.B. Klots; A. Kress; H.V. Lacey; Yves Lanceau; Leonard Lee Rue III; Henning Lender; D.B. Lewis; E. Lindsey; H.A.E Lucas; Wolfgang Lummer; Michael Lyster; Kendall McDonald; Malcolm McGregor; Steve McGutcheon; Mansell; Aldo Margiocco; Marineland, Florida, USA; John Markham; Meston; Walter Miles; Carl Mills; Lorus & Margery Milne; G. Mundey; N. Myers; Natural History Museum; K.B. Newman; NHPA: Andrew Anderson, F. Baillie, Anthony Bannister, F. Blackburn, Joe Blossom, N.A. Callow, J.M. Clayton, Stephen Dalton, E. Elkan, C. McDermot, W.J.C. Murray, Hugh Newman, Brian O'Donnell, Graham Pizzey, Gordon F. Woods; Okapia; Oxford Scientific Films; Ram Panjabi; Klaus Paysan; B. Pengilley; Photographic Library of Australia; Photo Library Inc; Photo Res: Des Bartlett, Jane Burton, Bob Campbell, C. Ciapanna, Jack Dermid, Peter Jackson, Russ Kinne, N. Myers, R.T. Peterson, D.C. Pike, Masood Quarishy, Dick Robinson, H.W. Silvester, Vincent Serventy, James Simon, Tomanek, Simon Trevor, Howard E. Uible, Joe Van Wormer; Graham Pizzey; Joyce Pope; Popperfoto; Roebild; Root/Okapia; G. Puppell; Walter Scheilhauer; Friedel Schox; Philippa Scott; Gunter Senfft; M. Severn; Shell Photograph; H. Shrempp; E. Slater; M.F. Soper; South African Tourist Corporation: A.J. Southward; Helmut Stellrucht; W.M. Stephens; John Tashjian at Arizona Sonard Desert Museum, Fort Worth Zoo, San Diego Zoo, Steinhart Aquarium, Tacoma Aquarium, Vancouver Aquarium; Ron Taylor; Ronald Thompson; Sally Anne Thompson; Time Life Inc; William Vandivert; John Visser; J.J. Ward; P. Ward; John Warham; Constance P. Warner; A.N. Warren; Birgit Webb; We-Ha; Alison Wilson; D.P. Wilson; M.A. Wilson; Gene Wolfsheimer; John Norris Wood; Zoological Society, London.

¡Viva!

**AQA GCSE Spanish
Higher**

Rachel Hawkes, Christopher Lillington

ALWAYS LEARNING　　　　PEARSON

Published by Pearson Education Limited, 80 Strand, London, WC2R 0RL.

www.pearsonschoolsandfecolleges.co.uk

Copies of official specifications for all Edexcel qualifications may be found on the website: www.edexcel.com

Text © Pearson Education Limited, 2016

Written by Rachel Hawkes and Christopher Lillington
Additional material written by Leanda Reeves

Designed and typeset by Tek-Art Ltd.

Illustrated by: Tek-Art Ltd., Oxford Designers and Illustrators Ltd., KJA Artists (Mark, Andy), Beehive Illustration (Alan Rowe, Peter Lubach, Esther Pérez-Cuadrado) and John Hallett.

First published 2016

19 18 17
10 9 8 7 6 5

British Library Cataloguing in Publication Data
A catalogue record for this book is available from the British Library

ISBN 9781292118963

All rights reserved. No part of this publication may be reproduced in any form or by any means (including photocopying or storing it in any medium by electronic means and whether or not transiently or incidentally to some other use of this publication) without the written permission of the copyright owner, except in accordance with the provisions of the Copyright, Designs and Patents Act 1988 or under the terms of a licence issued by the Copyright Licensing Agency, Saffron House, 6–10 Kirby Street, London EC1N 8TS (www.cla.co.uk). Applications for the copyright owner's written permission should be addressed to the publisher.

Printed in Slovakia by Neografia

Acknowledgements

We would like to thank Christopher Lillington, Rachel Hawkes, Leanda Reeves, Teresa Martínez-Arteaga, Samantha Alzuria, Marina Barrull, Clive Bell, Gillian Eades, Nicola Lester, Ruth Manteca, Clare Dobson for their invaluable help in the development and trialling of this course. We would also like to thank María José Sierras Jimeno at the Colegio M. Mª Rosa Molas, Zaragoza, Spain. We would also like to thank María José Sierras Jimeno at the Colegio M. Mª Rosa Molas, Zaragoza, Spain.

The authors and publisher would like to thank the following individuals and organisations for permission to reproduce photographs:

(Key: b-bottom; c-centre; l-left; r-right; t-top)

123RF.com: 6, 7 (i), 14 (c), 53 (a), 53 (b), 167 (b), Andrey Tsidvintsev 142 (a), Anna Lurye 108, Anton Gvozdikov 77 (a), Antonio Diaz 43 (b), Burmakin Andrey 196, Cathy Yeulet 36 (c), 47, 117, Daniel Ernst 34 (a), Deborah Kolb 33 (a), Dmitrijs Gerciks 7 (p), Fabio Lamanna 148 (a), fiphoto 100 (f), 104 (c), HONGQI ZHANG 43 (a), joserpizarro 232, mitarart 213 (b), nito500 203 (a), Tami Freed 182; **© 2016 Maraworld :** 128 (b); **Alamy Images:** age fotostock 103, 122 (b), Agencja Fotograficzna Caro 40 (a), Alex Segre 189, 192, Alibi Productions 7 (e), Angela Hampton Picture Library 36 (d), Azk Waters 98 (c), Bill Cheyrou 62 (c), Cal Vornberger 22, Chris Mattison 14 (e), Christian Bertrand 129 (b), Christopher Scott 154, Citrus Stock 97 (h), Classic Image Stock 59, colau 160, dbimages 32 (c), Denkou Images 132, Doug Houghton 96 (d), dpa picture alliance 185, epa european pressphoto agency b.v 122 (a), epa european pressphoto agency b.v. 84 (a), Faiz Balabil 176, Finnbar Webster 13 (c), Francisco Javier Fernandez Bordonarda 7 (k), Greg Balfour Evans 96 (f), Hero Images Inc. 25, Iain Sharp 110, Ian Dagnall 39 (b), Image Source 88, Image Source Plus 130, imageBROKER 99 (e), Images & Stories 200, Izel Photography 113, Jack Sullivan 96 (c), Jean Schweitzer 31, Jeffrey Blackler 100 (g), JLImages 57 (b), Julie Woodhouse 98 (d), Ken Welsh 82 (c), 96 (g), 104 (g), Marc Hill 36 (i), Maria Galan 174, Matt Fowler Photography 100 (e), Michael Dwyer 30 (a), 30 (b), Nick Lylak 40 (b), Paula Solloway 63 (b), philipus 38 (f), Prisma Bildagentur AG 135, Radius Images 145 (c), Robert Harding World Imagery 122 (c), Rolf Richardson 16, RosalreneBetancourt 1 145 (b), Sergio Azenha 13 (1), Simon Reddy 14 (d), Speedpix 96 (a), 170 (a), Steve Davey 119, ton koene 146 (a), Travel Pictures 106 (c), Warren Faidley / Corbis 172 (e), WENN Ltd 171, xixia 34 (b), YAY Media AS 97 (a), Zuma Press Inc 146 (b); **Art Directors and TRIP Photo Library:** Helene Rogers 97 (d), 97 (i), 97 (m); **Colegio M.M.Rosa Molas:** 38 (b), 38 (c), 38 (d), 38 (e), 38 (h), 38 (i); **Corbis:** Bernd Vogel 82 (b), FRANCK ROBICHON / epa 91, Imageshop 213 (a), Liu Dawei / Xinhua Press 140, Michele Falzone 106 (d), Pascal Saez / Demotix 164 (b), Ricardo Romero / epa 172 (f), Xinhua 172 (b); **Fotolia.com:** 104 (b), alain wacquier 116 (h), Aleksandar Todorovic 101 (b), amophoto.net 38 (g), Andres Rodriguesz 138 (c), Andriy Petrenko 69, Andy Dean 32 (b), 198 (b), AntonioDiaz 199, asife 61, asikkk 7 (a), atomfotolia 7 (n), Axel Bueckert 151 (b), BlueSkyImages 141 (b), bzyxx 129 (a), canovass 116 (g), Christian Schwier 72 (b), 187, corepics 29 (e), Darren Baker 65, DragonImages 87, efired 7 (m), Eugenio Marongiu 56, fotos 593 104 (e), GalinaSt 198 (a), Gelia 7 (l), gemenacom 96 (e), Gina Sanders 99 (a), goodluz 104 (d), Halfpoint 131, Hugo Felix 63 (a), Igor Mojzes 138 (f), Iurii Sokolov 8 (a), JackF 13 (b), Javier Castro 57 (a), JJAVA 164 (e), Joanna wnuk 39 (c), Kablonk Micro 62 (d), kitzcorner 116 (e), Konstantin Kulikov 197, Leonid Andronov 96 (b), lldi 121 (b), lom742

15 (b), M.Studio 116 (a), Maksym Gorpenyuk 107 (a), Maria 20, Martinan 169, mathess 107 (b), Max Topchii 8 (b), Maygutyak 7 (h), Mila Supynska 195 (c), Monart Design 32 (a), Monkey Business 78 (c), Monkey Business Images 7 (f), 35 (a), 62 (c), Morenovel 170 (c), Morten Elm 105, mr.markin 78 (a), Nina Nagovitsina 100 (d), Noam 8 (c), Nobilior 39 (a), Olaf Speier 116 (l), papa 81 (a), pedrosala 202 (b), phanuwatnandee 36 (e), Brad Pict 99 (b), Sergey Chayko 172 (d), SOMATUSCANI 104 (f), steheap 166, Theirry Ryo 7 (o), uzkiland 18 (a), Valeriy Velikov 121 (a), ViewApart 55, Viktor 116 (d), Vladislav Gajic 7 (j), Volker Z 34 (c), WavebreakmediaMicro 75 (b), xalanx 142 (b), Yuri Timofeyev 10 (a), Yury Gubin 166 (d); **Fran Fernandez Photography/Photographers Direct:** 97 (c), 97 (k); **Getty Images:** AFP 138 (d), AFP / Stringer 167 (a), Alfredo Maiquez 18 (b), altrendo images 44, Anadolu Agency / Contributor 179, Ariel Skelley 204, / Bloomberg 126 (b), Brent Winebrenner 35 (c), C Flanigan 77 (b), Catherine Lane 164 (d), CBS Photo Archive 81 (b), ChinaFotoPress 84 (b), Christopher Futcher 35 (b), Credit: Trevor Williams 10 (b), Dave M. Benett 75 (a), Dennis Doyle 201, Fuse 83 (a), Gaelle Beri 128, Ingolf Pompe / Look Foto 13 (d), JOHN GURZINSKI / Stringer 79 (b), JTB Photo 99 (d), Jupiter Images 161, Katarnina Wittkamp 36 (a), Michael Tran 52, MIGUEL ROJO / Staff 84 (c), Nigel Waldren 85, Pacific Press / Contributor 164 (a), Rubberball / Mike Kemp 36 (j), Sergei Supkinsky 145 (a), Shane Hansen 78 (d), Stockbyte 170 (b); **IOC Museums Collection © IOC :** 73 (a); ; **Ira de Reuver/Photographers Direct:** Ira de Reuver 121 (c); **© Juma, 2011:** 125; **Kin Camp SA de CV:** 9; **Sergio Santana** 38(j); **Pearson Education Ltd:** Chris Parker 144, Gareth Boden 7 (g), 141 (a), 173 (b), 186 (a), 186 (b), 188, Handan Erek 40 (c), John Pallister 15 (a), Jules Selmes 104 (a), 217, National Geophysical Data Center 172 (a), Rafal Trubisz 36 (g), Sozaijiten 116 (f), Studio 8 100 (a), 100 (b), 101 (a), 102 (a), 102 (b), 102 (c), 102 (d), 102 (e), 102 (f); **Peter Menzel/menzelphoto.com:** 120 (a), 120 (b); **PhotoDisc:** Kevin Sanchez, Cole Publishing Group 116 (k); **Reuters:** David Mercado 165; **ShelterBox:** 173 (a); **Shutterstock.com:** Alex Yeung 99 (f), Alexander Raths 33 (a), Andresr 195 (b), Anna-Mari West 209, Bananastock 36 (b), bikeriderlondon 34 (h), 66, blvdone 104 (h), Chris Pole 7 (c), Dainis Derics 166 (a), 172 (c), Darren Baker 82 (a), David Pereiras 62 (b), Dieter H. 106 (b), dotshock 151 (a), Elzbieta Sekowska 14 (b), everydaysunshine 116 (j), Fotokostic 79 (a), g-Stockstudio 100 (c), Galina Barskaya 190, Gordon Swanson 124, Greg Blok 221, holbox 138 (a), iko 195 (a), Ivan Cuzmin 99 (c), Ivan Smuk 166 (e), J Fox Photography 148 (b), Jason Stitt. 59 (b), JeniFoto 7 (d), Konstantin Chagin. 152, Ksenia Ragozina 98 (a), Kzenon 203 (b), / macro meyer 116 (b), mangostock 146 (c), marekuliasz 97 (b), Martin Good 73 (b), Matthew Gough 166 (b), Mikadun 164 (c), Minerva Studio 36 (f), Monkey Buiness Images 29 (b), Monkey Business Images 51, 54, 138 (b), 225, Nathalie Speliers Ufermann 123, Niv Koren 202 (a), paol_ok 126 (c), Parinya 97 (f), Poznyakov 29 (a), Pressmaster 29 (c), 184, Quality Master 97 (e), 97 (j), Rob Bayer 62 (a), Robert Wolkaniec 97 (g), 97 (l), Rose Hayes 72 (a), savageultralight 62 (f), Serg Zastavkin 19, sianc. 86 (a), Signature Message 166 (f), slava296 14 (a), Subbotina Anna 116 (i), svry 116 (c), Tatiana Popova 98 (b), Timothy Epp 106 (a), Tissiana Kelley 86 (a), Tom Wang 175, Tracey Whiteside 53 (c), Tyler Olson 33 (a), u20 138 (e), vichie81 126 (a), Victor Torres 73 (a), Wavebreakmedia 29 (a), WDG Photo 7 (a), YanLev. 157; **www.imagesource.com:** Corbis / Bridge 78 (b), Moosboard 83 (b)

Cover images: Front: **Shutterstock.com:** David Pereiras

All other images © Pearson Education

Every effort has been made to contact copyright holders of material reproduced in this book. Any omissions will be rectified in subsequent printings if notice is given to the publishers. We are grateful to the following organisations for permission to reproduce copyright material:

©Kin Camp SA de CV p9; ©Grupo 20minutos S.L. p11; ©María Pineda & Logitravel S.L. p20; ©Alfaguara (Frisa, M 2013) p21; ©Just Landed p30; ©Mano a Mano Bolivia p35; ©Información Eroski Consumer p42; ©Quino, Caminito S.A.S. p60; ©Antonia Kerrigan Agencia Literaria p64; ©Dolors Reig p65; ©Agencia EFE p72; ©Academia de las Artes y las Ciencias Cinematográficas de España p75; ©INJUVE - Instituto de la Juventud p76; ©Laura Gallego p86; ©Repsol S.A. p99; ©Huffington Post p108; ©AG Balcells (Allende, I 1982) p108; ©El Tiempo p109; ©Editorial Iparraguirre SA p109; ©Sandra Bruna Agencia Literaria S.L. (Palomas, A 2014) p125; ©Línea Directa Aseguradora S.A. p130; ©Organice su evento (Digital Marketing) p130; ©Blogestudio S.L. p141; ©Jordi Galceran p153. For play inquiries, please contact the Gurman Agency LLC (www.gurmanagency.com); ©Antonia Kerrigan Agencia Literaria (Ruiz Zafón, C 1993) p174; ©Ocio por Madrid p174; ©Agencia EFE p175; ©AG Balcells (Allende, I 2003) p185; ©BodaMás Gestión S.L. p202; ©Grupo 20minutos S.L. p203; ©Grupo Anaya SA (Alcolea, A 2007) p204; ©Sabática Consultores S.L. p206; ©VeoVerde Betazeta Networks S.A. p207

Websites

Pearson Education Limited is not responsible for the content of any external internet sites. It is essential for tutors to preview each website before using it in class so as to ensure that the URL is still accurate, relevant and appropriate. We suggest that tutors bookmark useful websites and consider enabling students to access them through the school/college intranet.

Contenidos

Módulo 1 ¡Desconéctate! *Theme 2: Local, national, international and global areas of interest*

Punto de partida 6
- Discussing holidays and weather
- Revising the present and preterite tenses

Unidad 1 ¿Qué haces en verano? 8
- Saying what you do in summer
- Using the present tense
- Listening to identify the person of the verb

Unidad 2 ¿Cómo prefieres pasar las vacaciones? 10
- Talking about holiday preferences
- Using verbs of opinion to refer to different people
- Understanding percentages

Unidad 3 ¡Destino Barcelona! 12
- Saying what you did on holiday
- Using the preterite tense
- Using different structures to give opinions

Unidad 4 ¿Cómo era? 14
- Describing where you stayed
- Using the imperfect tense
- Working out the meaning of new words

Unidad 5 Quisiera reservar… 16
- Booking accommodation and dealing with problems
- Using verbs with *usted*
- Using questions to form answers

Unidad 6 Mis vacaciones desastrosas 18
- Giving an account of a holiday in the past
- Using three tenses together
- Identifying positive and negative opinions

Leer y escuchar 20
Prueba oral 22
Prueba escrita 24
Palabras 26

Módulo 2 Mi vida en el insti *Theme 3: Current and future study and employment*

Punto de partida 1 28
- Giving opinions about school subjects
- Describing school facilities

Punto de partida 2 30
- Describing school uniform and the school day
- Using adjectives

Unidad 1 ¿Qué tal los estudios? 32
- Talking about subjects and teachers
- Using comparatives and superlatives
- Justifying opinions using a range of language

Unidad 2 ¡Mi nuevo insti! 34
- Describing your school
- Using negatives
- Comparing then and now

Unidad 3 ¡Está prohibido! 36
- Talking about school rules and problems
- Using phrases followed by the infinitive
- Tackling harder listening exercises

Unidad 4 ¡Destino Zaragoza! 38
- Talking about plans for a school exchange
- Using the near future tense
- Asking and answering questions

Unidad 5 Mis clubs y mis éxitos 40
- Talking about activities and achievements
- Using object pronouns
- Saying how long you have been doing something

Leer y escuchar 42
Prueba oral 44
Prueba escrita 46
Palabras 48

Módulo 3 Mi gente *Theme 1: Identity and culture*

Punto de partida 1 50
- Talking about socialising and family
- Using verbs in the present tense

Punto de partida 2 52
- Describing people
- Using adjectival agreement

Unidad 1 Mis aplicaciones favoritas 54
- Talking about social networks
- Using *para* with infinitives
- Extending responses by referring to others

Unidad 2 ¿Qué estás haciendo? 56
- Making arrangements
- Using the present continuous tense
- Improvising dialogues

Unidad 3 Leer es un placer 58
- Talking about reading preferences
- Using a range of connectives
- Recognising similar ideas expressed differently

Unidad 4 Retratos 60
- Describing people
- Using *ser* and *estar*
- Understanding more detailed descriptions

Unidad 5 Relaciones 62
- Talking about friends and family
- Using a range of relationship verbs
- Referring to the present and past

Leer y escuchar 64
Prueba oral 66
Prueba escrita 68
Palabras 70

tres 3

Contenidos

Módulo 4   Intereses e influencias   *Theme 1: Identity and culture*

Punto de partida 1 72
- Talking about free-time activities
- Using stem-changing verbs

Punto de partida 2 74
- Talking about TV programmes and films
- Using adjectives of nationality

Unidad 1 *¿Qué sueles hacer?* 76
- Talking about what you usually do
- Using *soler* + infinitive
- Identifying correct statements about a text

Unidad 2 *¡Fanático del deporte!* 78
- Talking about sports
- Using the imperfect tense to say what you used to do
- Listening for different tenses

Unidad 3 *#Temas del momento* 80
- Talking about what's trending
- Using the perfect tense
- Using words which have more than one meaning

Unidad 4 *En directo* 82
- Discussing different types of entertainment
- Using *algunos / ciertos / otros / muchos / demasiados / todos*
- Adapting a model dialogue to fit different situations

Unidad 5 *Modelos a seguir* 84
- Talking about who inspires you
- Using a range of past tenses
- Talking about dates

Leer y escuchar 86
Prueba oral 88
Prueba escrita 90
Palabras 92

Módulo 5   Ciudades   *Theme 2: Local, national, international and global areas of interest*

Punto de partida 1 94
- Talking about places in a town
- Asking for and understanding directions

Punto de partida 2 96
- Talking about shops
- Shopping for souvenirs

Unidad 1 *¿Cómo es tu zona?* 98
- Describing the features of a region
- Using *se puede* and *se pueden*
- Asking and responding to questions

Unidad 2 *¿Qué haremos mañana?* 100
- Planning what to do
- Using the future tense
- Understanding the geography of Spain

Unidad 3 *De compras* 102
- Shopping for clothes and presents
- Using demonstrative adjectives
- Explaining preferences

Unidad 4 *Los pros y los contras de la ciudad* 104
- Talking about problems in a town
- Using the conditional
- Using synonyms and antonyms

Unidad 5 *¡Destino Arequipa!* 106
- Describing a visit in the past
- Using different tenses together
- Recognising and using idioms

Leer y escuchar 108
Prueba oral 110
Prueba escrita 112
Palabras 114

Módulo 6   De costumbre   *Theme 1: Identity and culture*

Punto de partida 1 116
- Describing mealtimes
- Talking about daily routine

Punto de partida 2 118
- Talking about illnesses and injuries
- Asking for help at the pharmacy

Unidad 1 *Sabores del mundo* 120
- Talking about typical foods
- Using the passive
- Spotting words which indicate an increase/decrease

Unidad 2 *¡De fiesta!* 122
- Comparing different festivals
- Avoiding the passive
- Paying attention to question words

Unidad 3 *Un día especial* 124
- Describing a special day
- Using reflexive verbs in the preterite
- Inferring meaning in literary texts

Unidad 4 *¡A comer!* 126
- Ordering in a restaurant
- Using absolute superlatives
- Spotting irregular verb patterns in the preterite

Unidad 5 *El festival de música* 128
- Talking about a music festival
- Using expressions followed by the infinitive
- Adding interest when narrating a story

Leer y escuchar 130
Prueba oral 132
Prueba escrita 134
Palabras 136

cuatro

Contenidos

Módulo 7 ¡A currar!   *Theme 3: Current and future study and employment*

Punto de partida 138
- Talking about different jobs
- Discussing job preferences

Unidad 1 ¿Qué haces para ganar dinero? 140
- Talking about how you earn money
- Using *soler* in the imperfect tense
- Using verbs in different forms

Unidad 2 Mis prácticas laborales 142
- Talking about work experience
- Using the preterite and imperfect together
- Using alternatives to 'and'

Unidad 3 ¿Por qué aprender idiomas? 144
- Talking about the importance of learning languages
- Using the present and the present continuous
- Using *saber* and *conocer*

Unidad 4 Solicitando un trabajo 146
- Applying for a summer job
- Using indirect object pronouns
- Writing a formal letter

Unidad 5 Un año sabático 148
- Discussing gap years
- Revising the conditional
- Using the 24-hour clock

Unidad 6 El futuro 150
- Discussing plans for the future
- Using the subjunctive with *cuando*
- Using different ways to express future plans

Leer y escuchar 152
Prueba oral 154
Prueba escrita 156
Palabras 158

Módulo 8 Hacia un mundo mejor   *Theme 2: Local, national, international and global areas of interest*

Punto de partida 1 160
- Describing types of houses
- Talking about the environment

Punto de partida 2 162
- Talking about healthy eating
- Discussing diet-related problems

Unidad 1 ¡Piensa globalmente…! 164
- Considering global issues
- Using the present subjunctive
- Listening for high numbers

Unidad 2 ¡Actúa localmente! 166
- Talking about local actions
- Using the subjunctive in commands
- Presenting a written argument

Unidad 3 ¡Vivir a tope! 168
- Discussing healthy lifestyles
- Understanding different tenses
- Giving extended reasons

Unidad 4 ¡El deporte nos une! 170
- Talking about international sporting events
- Using the pluperfect tense
- Explaining your point of view

Unidad 5 ¡Apúntate! 172
- Talking about natural disasters
- Using the imperfect continuous
- Using grammar knowledge in translation

Leer y escuchar 174
Prueba oral 176
Prueba escrita 178
Palabras 180

¡A repasar!

Módulo 1 *¡Desconéctate!* 182
Módulo 2 *Mi vida en el insti* 184
Módulo 3 *Mi gente* 186
Módulo 4 *Intereses e influencias* 188
Módulo 5 *Ciudades* 190
Módulo 6 *De costumbre* 192
Módulo 7 *¡A currar!* 194
Módulo 8 *Hacia un mundo mejor* 196
General Conversation Questions 198

Te toca a ti 200
Gramática 208
Verb Tables 237

cinco 5

1 ¡Desconéctate!
Punto de partida

- Discussing holidays and weather
- Revising the present and preterite tenses

1 Completa las frases con los verbos del recuadro. Sobran <u>dos</u> verbos. Traduce las palabras en **negrita** al inglés.

1 **A menudo** ——— a caballo con mi hermano.
2 **Nunca** ——— para mi familia.
3 ——— la guitarra **todos los días**.
4 **Casi nunca** ——— canciones o vídeos.
5 **De vez en cuando** ——— al polideportivo.
6 ——— al baloncesto **dos o tres veces al año**.

llevo	monto	juego
toco	cocino	voy
veo	descargo

2 Escucha. Escribe las <u>dos</u> letras correctas y apunta las actividades. (1–4)

Ejemplo: **1** *a – goes to park, …*

| ¿Qué haces en verano? |
| Cuando | hace | buen tiempo / mal tiempo… calor / frío / sol / viento… |
| | llueve / nieva… |

3 Traduce las palabras en violeta al inglés. ¿Qué significan las preguntas?

a **¿Dónde** te gusta ir de compras?
b **¿Cuándo** te gusta hacer deporte?
c **¿Con qué frecuencia** te gusta leer?
d **¿Por qué** te gusta escuchar música?
e **¿Con quién** te gusta ir al cine?
f **¿Qué** no te gusta hacer?

Pedro

4 Escucha a Pedro y apunta los datos (1–6):
- la expresión que usa
- la pregunta del ejercicio 3 que contesta.

Ejemplo: **1** *me mola, b*

⭐ Use different opinion phrases to add variety to your answers:
Prefiero
Me chifla
Me encanta
Me mola   } + infinitive
Me flipa   (e.g. *leer, escuchar,* etc.)
No me gusta (nada)
Odio

5 Con tu compañero/a, haz diálogos con las preguntas del ejercicio 3.

● ¿Dónde te gusta ir de compras?
■ Me chifla ir de compras a un centro comercial.

seis

Módulo 1

6 Escucha y escribe las <u>cuatro</u> o <u>cinco</u> letras correctas. (1–5)
Ejemplo: **1** d, g, …

¿Adónde fuiste de vacaciones?
Fui de vacaciones a…

- a Francia.
- b Turquía.
- c Gales.
- d Italia.

¿Con quién fuiste?
Fui…

- e con mi insti.
- f con mi familia.
- g con mi mejor amig**o/a**.
- h sol**o/a**.

¿Cómo viajaste?
Viajé…

- i en avión.
- j en coche y en barco.
- k en tren.
- l en autocar.

¿Qué hiciste?

- m Hice turismo y saqué fotos.
- n Compré recuerdos.
- o Tomé el sol y descansé.
- p Comí muchos helados.

7 Escucha. Copia y completa la tabla en inglés. (1–7)

	day	what he/she did	what weather was like
1	Tues	visited castle	stormy

¿Qué tiempo hizo?	
Hizo	buen tiempo / mal tiempo calor / frío / sol / viento
Hubo	tormenta / niebla
Llovió / Nevó	

8 Con tu compañero/a, haz diálogos. Inventa actividades para cada día.
- ¿Qué hiciste durante tus vacaciones?
- El <u>lunes</u> <u>fui</u> <u>a la playa</u> porque <u>hizo sol</u>.
- ¿Y qué hiciste el <u>martes</u>?
- …

G Hacer *in the preterite tense* ▶ Page 212

The verb **hacer** is irregular in the **preterite tense**.

	hacer (to do/make)
(yo)	hice
(tú)	hiciste
(él/ella/usted)	hi**z**o
(nosotros/as)	hicimos
(vosotros/as)	hicisteis
(ellos/ellas/ustedes)	hicieron

Many activities which use 'to go' in English are translated by **hacer** in Spanish:
Hice alpinismo.   **I went** mountain climbing.

siete 7

1 ¿Qué haces en verano?

- *Saying what you do in summer*
- *Using the present tense*
- *Listening to identify the person of the verb*

1 Escucha y lee. ¿Qué significan las frases en **negrita**? Luego copia y completa la tabla en inglés.

	lives	weather	how often / activities
Maisie	Edinburgh, east…	changeable, …	sometimes – goes…,

¿Qué haces en verano?

Vivo en Edimburgo, en el este de Escocia. En verano **el tiempo es variable**. A veces voy de paseo con mis amigos, pero casi nunca hacemos una barbacoa porque **hay chubascos** a menudo (siempre llevo un paraguas cuando salgo, ¡por si acaso!).
Maisie

el paraguas — umbrella

Vivo en Valle Nevado, en el centro de Chile. En invierno siempre hago esquí, pero en verano, no. Normalmente hace sol, pero a veces **está nublado** o **hay niebla** (¡no se puede ver nada!). Una vez a la semana trabajo como voluntario en un refugio de animales.
Jaime

Vivo en Mazatlán, en el noroeste de México. El clima **es muy soleado y caluroso** en verano, con temperaturas de más de 30 grados. ¡Qué calor! Todos los días nado en el mar. ¡Soy una fanática de la playa! De vez en cuando **hay tormenta** y por eso no salgo – chateo en la red.
Florencia

⭐ Can you work out the pronunciation of these words?

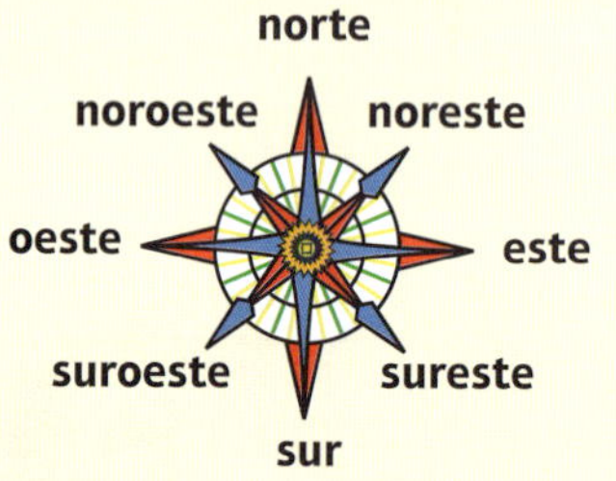

norte
noroeste   noreste
oeste   este
suroeste   sureste
sur

2 Lee los textos del ejercicio 1 otra vez. Busca <u>ocho</u> verbos diferentes. Traduce los verbos al inglés y escribe el infinitivo.

Ejemplo: salgo (I go out) – salir

G The present tense
> Pages **208, 210**

Remember how the present tense works:

	regular			**irregular**
	nad**ar** (to swim)	le**er** (to read)	viv**ir** (to live)	**ser** (to be)
(yo)	nad**o**	le**o**	viv**o**	soy
(tú)	nad**as**	le**es**	viv**es**	eres
(él/ella/usted)	nad**a**	le**e**	viv**e**	es
(nosotros/as)	nad**amos**	le**emos**	viv**imos**	somos
(vosotros/as)	nad**áis**	le**éis**	viv**ís**	sois
(ellos/ellas/ustedes)	nad**an**	le**en**	viv**en**	son

Some verbs change their stem: *jue*go (jugar – to play)

Some verbs are irregular in the 'I' form only: ha**go** (hacer – to do/make), sal**go** (salir – to go out), v**eo** (ver – to see/watch)

3 Imagina que vives en otro país. Con tu compañero/a, haz diálogos.

- ¿Dónde vives?
- ¿Qué tiempo hace en verano?
- ¿Qué actividades haces en verano?

■ Vivo en…, en…
■ Normalmente…
■ A menudo…, pero…

⭐ Make use of the new weather expressions from exercise 1 to add variety.

In addition, mention lots of different activities using a range of verbs. Look back at your list of verbs from exercise 2 for ideas.

8   *ocho*

Módulo 1

4 Escucha y escribe los verbos en español. Luego traduce los verbos al inglés. (1–8)

Ejemplo: **1** *nadan – they swim*

> ⭐ Listen for verb endings as clues:
> | Verbs ending in… | usually refer to… |
> |---|---|
> | –o | I |
> | –s | you |
> | –mos | we |
> | –n | they |

5 Escucha a David y lee las frases. Identifica las <u>tres</u> frases correctas.

a David vive en el suroeste de su país.
b Hay muchos chubascos en su región.
c David es adicto a la tele.
d David y sus amigos practican mucho deporte.
e David y sus amigos nunca hacen natación.
f David toca un instrumento.

6 Escribe un texto sobre tus vacaciones.

- Say where you live.
- Say what the weather is like in summer.
- Say what activities you do.
- Say what activities your friends do.

Vivo en…, en el… de…
En verano normalmente…
Todos los días… También… porque…
Mis amigos…

7 Lee el texto y completa las frases en inglés.

Campamentos de verano con Kin Camp en México

¡El mejor verano de tu vida!

Verano Senior es la experiencia perfecta para adolescentes (de 13 a 17 años), con una combinación de diversión, juegos, deportes, aventura y amistad.

El campamento tiene actividades especiales como escalada, pista comando, tiro con arco y canoas. Además, aprendes a:
- ser un líder
- trabajar en equipo
- y lo más importante, ¡echar relajo!

Tienes la oportunidad de ir de excursión a lugares de interés increíbles. Y también ofrecemos diferentes talleres creativos de teatro, música, pintura, escultura y baile, porque ¡TODOS tenemos un artista dentro!

| ¡echar relajo! | to go wild! (Mexican slang) |

1 The summer camp is aimed at…
2 It offers a combination of fun, …
3 Special activities include climbing, …
4 You also learn to…
5 Creative workshops include theatre, …

Zona Cultura
Cada año muchos jóvenes en España y Latinoamérica pasan quince días, o más, en un **campamento de verano**, donde disfrutan de actividades educativas, deportivas y recreativas.

nueve

2 ¿Cómo prefieres pasar las vacaciones?

- Talking about holiday preferences
- Using verbs of opinion to refer to different people
- Understanding percentages

1 leer
Lee y completa los textos con la opinión correcta. Sobra una opinión.

a me mola leer
b le encanta hacer deportes acuáticos
c nos apasiona hacer ciclismo
d nos flipa ver películas
e odio ir de compras
f prefiero estar al aire libre

En España tenemos por lo menos once semanas de vacaciones en junio, julio y agosto. ¡Qué suerte! En verano no veo la tele en casa porque **1** _____ cuando hace sol. Todos los días mi mejor amigo y yo montamos en bici, dado que **2** _____.
Íñigo

En Argentina tenemos las vacaciones de verano en enero y febrero. **3** _____ y por eso compro un montón de revistas en verano porque tengo más tiempo libre. A menudo voy a la pista de hielo con mi hermana y también vamos al cine, puesto que **4** _____. Mi padre bucea en el mar, ya que **5** _____.
Ana

2 escuchar
Escucha y comprueba tus respuestas.

⭐ The following all mean 'since' or 'given that':
dado que
puesto que
ya que

G Verbs of opinion ▶ Page 228

Many verbs for giving opinions need a pronoun like **me**. These verbs all take pronouns: gustar, encantar, chiflar, molar, apasionar, flipar.

Change the pronoun to talk about other people:

me gusta	I like	**nos** gusta	we like
te gusta	you (sing) like	**os** gusta	you (pl) like
le gusta	he/she likes	**les** gusta	they like

To give your opinion of an activity, use the **infinitive** after these verbs.
If you mention another person directly (for example by using their name), you need to add the word **a**.

A <u>mi padre</u> **le** chifla cocinar.   My dad loves cooking.
También **le** gusta bailar.   He also likes dancing.

3 leer
Lee los textos del ejercicio 1 otra vez. Busca las expresiones en español en el texto.

1 loads of magazines
2 What luck!
3 at least
4 (he) goes diving
5 I go to the ice rink
6 I have more free time

4 escuchar
Escucha a Alejandra. Apunta las personas y las actividades en inglés.

Ejemplo: Brother – loves shopping, hates…

5 hablar
Imagina que hablas con tu compañero/a español(a). Haz diálogos.

● ¿Cuándo tienes vacaciones?
■ En <u>Inglaterra</u> tenemos…
● ¿Qué haces durante las vacaciones?
■ A veces hago… porque me chifla… Cuando hace calor mi hermano y yo, …

⭐ Give reasons for <u>activities</u> you do by referring to **your wider interests**. For example:
<u>Compro muchas revistas</u> porque **me chifla leer**.
Which activities could you connect with these interests?

hacer deportes acuáticos
hacer artes marciales
estar al aire libre
estar en contacto con los amigos
usar el ordenador

Módulo 1

6 Lee el artículo. Apunta ocho detalles en inglés.

Ejemplo: 17% prefer to go abroad

Los españoles prefieren las vacaciones... en España.

- Según una encuesta, el 83% de los españoles prefiere veranear en España y solo un 17% en el extranjero.

- La costa es el destino preferido de los españoles para las vacaciones (60%), comparado con el campo (17%), la montaña (14%) y la ciudad (9%).

- Alicante, Cádiz y Málaga son los tres destinos preferidos.

En términos de alojamiento, aunque la opción preferida es ir a un hotel (33%), la segunda opción es alquilar un apartamento o una casa rural (27%). El 15% tiene una segunda residencia, y solo el 6% prefiere los campings.

| según | according to |
| veranear | to spend the summer holidays |

G Preferir, tener and ir

> Page 210

Preferir is a stem-changing verb. **Tener** and **ir** are irregular in the present tense.

	prefer**ir** (to prefer)	**tener** (to have)	**ir** (to go)
(yo)	pref**ie**ro	ten**go**	**voy**
(tú)	pref**ie**res	t**ie**nes	**vas**
(él/ella/usted)	pref**ie**re	t**ie**ne	**va**
(nosotros/as)	preferimos	tenemos	**vamos**
(vosotros/as)	preferís	tenéis	**vais**
(ellos/ellas/ustedes)	pref**ie**ren	t**ie**nen	**van**

7 Escucha la información sobre los argentinos. Copia y completa la tabla.

a	b	c	d	e
%	%	%	%	%

⭐ Percentages are usually preceded by the word **un** or **el**. Listen out for the word **y** to help you work out numbers above 30.

cuarenta **y** nueve — 49
ochenta **y** cinco — 85

When listening, take extra care with the numbers se<u>s</u>enta (60) and se<u>t</u>enta (70).

8 Traduce las frases al español.
1. My best friend prefers to spend the summer holidays abroad.
2. You have at least ten weeks of holidays and you live on the coast. What luck!
3. They like to go to the ice rink in summer since they have more free time.
4. My brother and I go diving when it's hot given that we love doing watersports.

once

3 ¡Destino Barcelona!

- *Saying what you did on holiday*
- *Using the preterite tense*
- *Using different structures to give opinions*

1 Escucha. Copia y completa la tabla en inglés. (1–4)

	when visited	best thing	worst thing
1	two years ago	b	

Hace una semana / un mes / un año…
Hace dos semanas / meses / años…

Zona Cultura

Destino:	BARCELONA
Ubicación:	Noreste de España, en la costa
Población:	1,6 millones de habitantes (2ª ciudad de España)
Famosa por:	Los Juegos Olímpicos de 1992
	La arquitectura de Antoni Gaudí
	El club de fútbol FC Barcelona ('el Barça')

Lo mejor fue cuando…

a vi un partido en el Camp Nou.
b fui al acuario.
c aprendí a hacer vela.
d visité el Park Güell.

Lo peor fue cuando…

e perdí mi móvil.
f tuve un accidente en la playa.
g vomité en una montaña rusa.
h llegué tarde al aeropuerto.

2 Escucha otra vez. Escribe las opiniones para cada persona. (1–4)

Ejemplo: **1** *Fue flipante, …*

G The preterite tense › Page 212

Use the **preterite tense** to talk about completed actions in the past.

visit**ar** (to visit)	beb**er** (to drink)	sal**ir** (to leave / to go out)	irregular verbs
			ir (to go)
			ser (to be)
visit**é**	beb**í**	sal**í**	fui
visit**aste**	beb**iste**	sal**iste**	fuiste
visit**ó**	beb**ió**	sal**ió**	fue
visit**amos**	beb**imos**	sal**imos**	fuimos
visit**asteis**	beb**isteis**	sal**isteis**	fuisteis
visit**aron**	beb**ieron**	sal**ieron**	fueron

Other irregular verbs in the preterite include:
tener (e.g. **tuve** – I had), **hacer** (e.g. **hice** – I did / made) and **ver** (e.g. **vi** – I saw / watched).

Some verbs have a spelling change in the 'I' form only:
jugar → ju**gu**é   llegar → lle**gu**é   sacar → sa**qu**é

Listen for ways to give opinions about the past:
- (No) Me gust**ó** / Me encant**ó**
- Lo pasé…   bomba / fenomenal / bien
             mal / fatal
- Fue…   inolvidable / increíble
         impresionante / flipante
         horroroso / un desastre

How do you pronounce these words in Spanish? Take extra care with cognates such as *desastre*.

doce

Módulo 1

3 hablar Con tu compañero/a, haz diálogos sobre Barcelona. Inventa los detalles.

- ¿Cuándo visitaste Barcelona?
- ¿Cómo viajaste y con quién fuiste?
- ¿Qué fue lo mejor de tu visita?
- ¿Qué fue lo peor de tu visita?

- *Visité Barcelona hace… Lo pasé…*
- *Viajé… y fui con… Fue…*
- *Lo mejor fue cuando…*
- *Lo peor…*

4 leer Lee el texto de la página web. Escribe <u>cinco</u> ventajas *(advantages)* de visitar Barcelona en Segway.

Ejemplo: It's easy

¡Explora Barcelona en Segway!
con Vamosensegway.com

- Una manera fácil, rápida y diferente de visitar la ciudad.
- Una actividad ideal para toda la familia.
- Recorridos de dos, tres o cuatro horas con guías expertos.
- Cuatro idiomas: español, catalán, inglés y francés.

La opción perfecta para conocer esta ciudad mágica donde puedes…

- disfrutar del Barrio Gótico
- subir al Monumento a Colón
- sacar fotos de la Sagrada Familia
- ver los barcos en el puerto
- descubrir el Museo Picasso
- pasear por las Ramblas

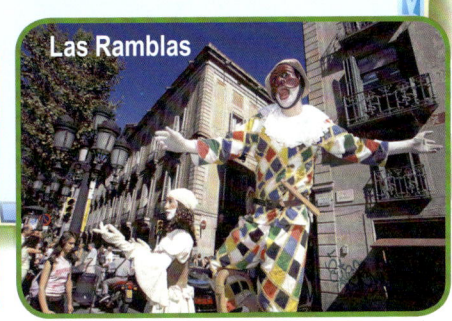

Monumento a Colón

Port Vell

Las Ramblas

5 escuchar Escucha a Daniel. Contesta a las preguntas en inglés.

1. Look at the locations in Barcelona listed on the website. Which place did Daniel visit first?
2. What happened in the gothic quarter?
3. What was his opinion of the Sagrada Familia?
4. Where was he sick?
5. Give <u>two</u> examples of how the website information is incorrect.
6. What was his overall opinion of the experience?

> Listen again to Daniel. Can you spot examples of the following?
> - Sequencers: **primero** (first), **luego** (then), **más tarde** (later), **después** (after that), **finalmente** (finally)
> - Opinion phrases
> - **Lo mejor /Lo peor**
> - Verbs in the 'we' form
>
> Use as many of these things as possible in exercise 6.

6 escribir Imagina que visitaste Barcelona en Segway. Escribe un texto.

> El año pasado exploré Barcelona en Segway con mi… y lo pasé bomba. Primero subí a…, donde perdí mi… Luego fuimos…

trece

4 ¿Cómo era?

- Describing where you stayed
- Using the imperfect tense
- Working out the meaning of new words

1 Escucha y lee el foro. Escribe la letra correcta para cada persona. Sobra una foto.

Me quedé en un albergue juvenil y me gustó mucho. **Estaba** cerca de la playa y **tenía** una cafetería y un aparcamiento. Además, **era** bastante moderno – ¡y muy barato!
Hassan

Me alojé en una pensión pequeña. **Estaba** en el centro de la ciudad, y por eso **era** un poco ruidosa. No **tenía** ni restaurante ni bar. Tampoco **había** piscina, pero **era** acogedora.
Alejandro

Nos alojamos en un camping en las afueras de la ciudad. **Era** muy tranquilo y **había** mucho espacio para mi tienda. También **tenía** una lavandería.
Asun

Fui de crucero por el Mediterráneo. **Era** caro, pero me encantó. En el barco **había** una piscina cubierta y un gimnasio. **Era** como un hotel de cinco estrellas – ¡pero más lujoso!
Yoli

| **Me alojé / Me quedé** | I stayed |
| **Nos alojamos / Nos quedamos** | We stayed |

2 ¿Qué significan las palabras en violeta en los textos del ejercicio 1?

3 Lee los textos del ejercicio 1 otra vez y escribe el nombre correcto.

Who stayed somewhere…
1. with good sports facilities?
2. on the outskirts of the city?
3. with facilities for washing clothes?
4. with a car park?
5. noisy?
6. cheap?
7. expensive?

4 Escribe un texto para el foro con una descripción del hotel.

⭐⭐⭐ hotel
Outskirts of city
Comfortable + cheap
✓ swimming pool, car park
✗ gym, restaurant
Loved it

G The imperfect tense › Page 214

The **imperfect tense** is used for describing things in the past.

El hotel **estaba** en la costa.   The hotel **was** on the coast.
Tenía una piscina antigua.   It **had** an old swimming pool.

	est**ar** (to be)	ten**er** (to have)
(yo)	est**aba**	ten**ía**
(tú)	est**abas**	ten**ías**
(él/ella/usted)	est**aba**	ten**ía**
(nosotros/as)	est**ábamos**	ten**íamos**
(vosotros/as)	est**abais**	ten**íais**
(ellos/ellas/ustedes)	est**aban**	ten**ían**

–er and **–ir verbs** have the same endings.
Only three verbs are irregular in the imperfect, including ser (to be) ➝ **era** (it was).
The verb **había** is the imperfect tense of hay and means 'there was / there were'.

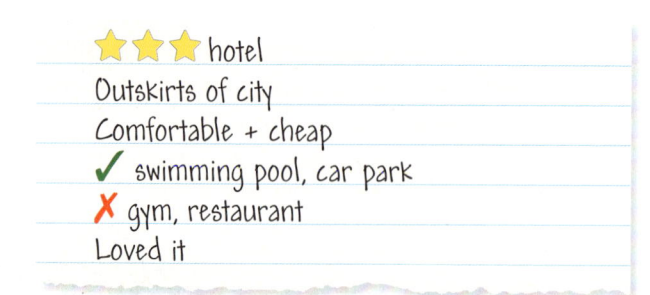

⭐ **Pay attention:**

El hotel **tenía** un bar.   The hotel **had** a bar.
but: En el hotel **había** un bar.   In the hotel **there was** a bar.

No tenía ni un bar ni una sauna.   It **didn't** have a bar **or** a sauna.
Tampoco tenía un gimnasio.   **Nor** did it have a gym.

Módulo 1

5 Lee el texto y elige los verbos correctos. Luego traduce el texto al inglés.

Nos alojamos en un hotel pequeño. **1 Era / Tenía** muy acogedor y **2 era / estaba** en el centro de la ciudad, cerca de la bolera. Lo bueno de la ciudad era que **3 había / era** animada y **4 había / estaba** muchos lugares de interés. Sin embargo, lo malo era que no **5 estaba / tenía** ni tiendas ni cine. Tampoco **6 estaba / había** espacios verdes. Además, **7 había / era** muchos turistas, y por eso **8 era / tenía** demasiado ruidosa.
Blanca

> ⭐ Use **era** (*ser*) for describing what something was like.
> La ciudad **era** ruidosa.
> The city **was** noisy.
>
> Use **estaba** (*estar*) for talking about a location or a temporary state.
> El hotel **estaba** en las afueras.
> The hotel **was** on the outskirts.

6 Escucha. Para cada persona apunta los detalles en inglés. (1–4)

- Accommodation:
- Location:
- Good points:
- Bad points:

el parador state-run luxury hotel, usually in a historic building

Lo bueno / Lo malo (del pueblo / de la ciudad) era que…				
era	demasiado muy bastante	animad**o**/**a** bonit**o**/**a** pintoresc**o**/**a** tranquil**o**/**a**	antigu**o**/**a** histórico**o**/**a** turístic**o**/**a** ruidos**o**/**a**
tenía / había… También tenía / había… no tenía / había… Tampoco tenía / había…		much**o**	ambiente / tráfico que hacer
		much**a**	contaminación gente
		much**os**	espacios verdes lugares de interés monumentos turistas
		much**as**	discotecas tiendas
no tenía ni cine ni bolera			

7 Con tu compañero/a, completa las preguntas.

- ¿Adónde ■ hiciste?
- ¿Cómo ■ viajaste?
- ¿Qué ■ (el hotel) / (la ciudad)?
- ¿Dónde ■ bien?
- ¿Cómo era ■ fuiste de vacaciones?
- ¿Lo pasaste ■ te alojaste?

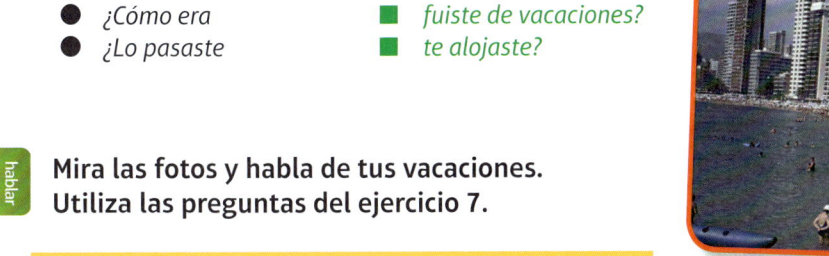

8 Mira las fotos y habla de tus vacaciones. Utiliza las preguntas del ejercicio 7.

> ⭐ • Use your imagination – don't just say what you can see in the photo!
> • Extend your sentences by giving extra details (e.g. when, who with, etc.).
> • Try to add an <u>opinion</u> phrase to <u>every</u> answer.
> • Include negative phrases (e.g. *No… ni… ni…, Tampoco…*).
> • Use the **preterite** for saying what you did (e.g. *Descansé en…, Jugué al…*).
> • Use the **imperfect** for descriptions in the past (e.g. *Era…, Había…, Estaba…*).

quince

5 Quisiera reservar…

- Booking accommodation and dealing with problems
- Using verbs with usted
- Using questions to form answers

1 leer

Lee la página web. Escribe el precio correcto.

Ejemplo: **1** 95 + 14 = 109 euros

1. Single room + full board
2. Double room + breakfast
3. Double room + sea view + half board
4. Wifi access
5. Single room + sea view + half board

Hotel Dos Palomas, Alicante

En pleno centro de Alicante, el hotel Dos Palomas cuenta con piscina climatizada, tienda de recuerdos, restaurante y terraza. Todas las habitaciones disponen de:

- Aire acondicionado
- Wifi gratis
- Televisor de pantalla plana
- Baño con bañera o ducha
- Servicio de limpieza todos los días

Restaurante abierto hasta medianoche.
Recepción abierta 24 horas.
Desayuno entre las 7.00 y las 10.00.
No se admiten mascotas.

Tipo de habitación	con…	Precio por noche
Habitación individual* Opciones • con / sin balcón	desayuno incluido	79 €
	media pensión**	95 €
Habitación doble* Opciones • con dos camas • con cama de matrimonio	desayuno incluido	116 €
	media pensión**	~~145 €~~ **Oferta especial 122 €**

* Vistas al mar – suplemento de 18 €
** Pensión completa – suplemento de 14 €

2 escuchar

**Lee el texto del ejercicio 1 otra vez y escucha la conversación.
Escribe en inglés las <u>ocho</u> diferencias entre el texto y la conversación.**

Ejemplo: It <u>does</u> have a pool.

3 hablar

Con tu compañero/a, haz un diálogo sobre la información del ejercicio 1.

- ¿Hay… en el hotel?
- ¿Hay… en las habitaciones?
- ¿Cuánto cuesta una habitación… con…?
- ¿A qué hora se sirve…?
- ¿Cuándo está abierto/a el/la…?
- ¿Cuánto es el suplemento por…?
- ¿Se admiten…?

> ⭐ **Take care with question words.**
>
> ¿Cuánto(s)…? How much / How many…?
> ¿Cuándo…?   When…?
> ¿A qué hora…? At what time…?
>
> When answering questions in the 'he/she/it' or 'they' form you can usually re-use the same verb in your answer.
>
> ¿Cuánto **cuesta** una habitación doble?
> How much does a double room cost?
>
> Una habitación doble **cuesta** 122 €.
> A double room costs 122 euros.

dieciséis

4 Escucha los dos diálogos. Escribe las palabras que faltan en español. (1–2)

Ejemplo: **a** individual

- Hotel Dos Palomas, ¿dígame?
- Quisiera reservar una habitación **a** ———— con **b** ————.
- ¿Quiere una habitación **c** ———— o **d** ————?
- Pues, **e** ————, por favor.
- ¿Para cuántas noches?
- Para **f** ———— noches, del **g** ———— al **h** ———— de **i** ————.
- ¿Cómo se llama usted?
- Me llamo **j** ————. Se escribe…
- ¿Puede repetir, por favor?
- …
- Muy bien. Son **k** ———— € por noche.
- De acuerdo. ¿Hay **l** ————?
- Por supuesto, señor(a).

G Using usted

Use **usted** (polite form of 'you') in formal situations, such as when booking a room. It uses the same verb endings as the 'he/she/it' form of the verb.

The plural form is **ustedes**, which uses the 'they' form of the verb.

| ¿Cómo se llam**a** usted? | What are you (polite singular) called? |
| ¿De dónde **son** ustedes? | Where are you (polite plural) from? |

Often the word **usted/ustedes** is omitted.

| ¿Puede repetir, por favor? | Can you repeat, please? |
| ¿Puede hablar más despacio? | Can you speak more slowly? |

5 Con tu compañero/a, haz <u>dos</u> diálogos. Utiliza el ejercicio 4 como modelo.

a
Double, inc half board
Sea view
3–6 Feb
140 €
Air con?

b
Single, inc breakfast
Balcony
14–19 Sep
79 €
Pool?

6 Escribe <u>tres</u> frases para cada dibujo.

¿Cuál es el problema?

Quiero	quejarme hablar con el director cambiar de habitación
El ascensor El aire acondicionado La ducha / La luz La habitación	no funciona está estropead**o/a** está suci**o/a**
Hay	ratas en la cama
No hay Necesito	papel higiénico (un) secador / toallas champú / jabón
¡Socorro!	Es inaceptable.
Perdone / Lo siento…	El hotel está completo. Voy a llamar el servicio de limpieza. Tenemos otra habitación libre.

7 Escucha. Copia y completa la tabla en inglés. (1–4)

	room	problems	guest satisfied in the end? (✓/✗)
1	226	no toilet paper, …	

8 Con tu compañero/a, inventa <u>dos</u> diálogos cómicos.

- ¡Socorro! Hay ratas en la ducha y… Estoy en la habitación… Quiero…
- Lo siento,…
- ¡Es inaceptable! Quiero…

diecisiete 17

6 Mis vacaciones desastrosas

- Giving an account of a holiday in the past
- Using three tenses together
- Identifying positive and negative opinions

1 Lee el texto de Álex y pon los párrafos en el orden correcto. Escribe las letras.
Ejemplo: b,…

los Picos de Europa

el teleférico a Fuente Dé

a Sin embargo, este año decidimos **acampar** en Cantabria, en el norte de España. Por un lado lo pasamos muy bien, pero por otro lado tuvimos varios problemas. Primero, en Dover el barco tuvo **un retraso** de tres horas porque hubo tormenta. ¡Qué aburrido!

b Normalmente veraneamos en Grecia todos los años ya que a mis padres les chifla **el paisaje**. Además, hace mucho calor. Siempre nos alojamos en un apartamento en una de las islas donde tomo el sol, leo ¡y como demasiado! No hay mucho que hacer, pero es muy relajante.

c El último día salimos del camping muy temprano y fuimos a Santander para **volver** a Inglaterra en barco. Esta vez no tuvimos ningún problema con el viaje. ¡Menos mal! Estaba muy cansado y dormí durante todo el viaje.

d El primer día mi hermano y yo alquilamos unas bicicletas y visitamos el pueblo medieval de Santillana del Mar. Fue impresionante. **Por desgracia**, mi hermano chocó con un coche aparcado y tuvo que ir al hospital. ¡Qué miedo!

e Continuamos el viaje a Cantabria en coche, pero luego tuvimos **una avería** en **la autopista** y tuvimos que llamar a un mecánico. Cuando llegamos al camping, la recepción ya estaba cerrada, dado que era muy tarde.

f **Al día siguiente** fuimos de excursión a los Picos de Europa. No hicimos **alpinismo**, pero decidimos coger el teleférico a Fuente Dé. ¡Me encantó! No había mucha gente, así que no tuvimos que **esperar** mucho tiempo. Hizo buen tiempo y las vistas eran preciosas.

¡Menos mal! — Just as well!

2 Escucha y comprueba tus respuestas. Luego traduce las palabras en **negrita** al inglés.

3 Lee el texto del ejercicio 1 otra vez. Busca las expresiones en español en el texto. ¿Es presente, pretérito o imperfecto?

Ejemplo: 1 chocó con – preterite

1 (he) crashed into
2 I was very tired
3 (it) was closed
4 we always stay
5 we decided to
6 (they) love
7 we hired
8 the views were
9 There isn't much to do
10 I slept

G Using three tenses together > Pages 208, 212, 214

Use the **present tense** to describe what things are like or to say what usually happens.

Es relajante. — It's relaxing.
Como demasiado. — I eat too much.

Use the **imperfect tense** to describe what something was like.

Las vistas eran preciosas. — The views were beautiful.

Use the **preterite tense** to say what you did / what happened.

Llegamos tarde. — We arrived late.

Remember that irregular verbs do not follow the usual patterns. For example:

	ser (to be)	**tener** (to have)	**haber**
present	es	tiene	hay
imperfect	era	tenía	había
preterite	fue	tuvo	hubo

18 *dieciocho*

Módulo 1

4 Escucha y escribe P (positivo), N (negativo) o P+N (positivo y negativo). (1–6)

Tuve / Tuvimos	un accidente / un pinchazo / un retraso / una avería
Tuve que ir	a la comisaría
Perdí / Perdimos	el equipaje / la cartera / la maleta / las llaves

When listening for positive and negative opinions, don't jump to conclusions! Listen to the end of the sentence, and listen for clues:

Lo bueno / Lo malo — The good thing / The bad thing
Lo mejor / Lo peor — The best thing / The worst thing
Lo que más / menos me gustó — What I liked most / least

Remember that *tampoco* introduces a negative sentence.

For mixed opinions you may hear phrases like *pero* (but), *sin embargo* (however) or *por un lado… por otro lado* (on one hand… on the other hand).

5 Con tu compañero/a, describe las <u>dos</u> vacaciones e inventa más detalles. Luego describe tus propias vacaciones.

Say:
- where you normally go and why
- what you do there
- where you went last year
- what you did and what went wrong
- what the town was like
- what the weather was like.

Usually
Wales
beautiful + hot weather
tennis + relax

2 years ago
Ireland – campsite
sightseeing + photos
puncture
lost suitcase
windy

Usually
Turkey
quiet + sunny
sunbathe + swim

3 months ago
France – apartment
shopping + walks
breakdown
lost keys
stormy

6 Traduce el texto al español. ¡Cuidado con los verbos! (¿Presente, pretérito o imperfecto?)

Look back at Unit 2.

Every year we spend the summer holidays abroad. My Mum likes to rent a house in the south of France, but my Dad prefers to go camping.

However, last year we decided to go to Scotland, where we had a great time. On one hand, the town didn't have a cinema or a swimming pool, but on the other hand, the landscape was beautiful and it was sunny every day.

Which negative expression do you need?

Which tense do you need here? And which verb?

The best thing was when we went sightseeing. My sister bought a camera and took lots of photos. However, unfortunately I lost my wallet, and we had to go to the police station.

Do you need tener or tener que here?

diecinueve 19

Módulo 1 Leer y escuchar

1 leer Ideas para el verano
Tus amigos están considerando diferentes actividades de verano.

¿Cómo pasar las vacaciones?

1 Inscríbete en nuestros cursos de windsurf y vela. También ofrecemos clases de natación y buceo para principiantes.

2 ¡No tienes que pasar el verano jugando a los videojuegos! Apúntate a nuestros talleres de cocina para toda la familia.

3 Excursión al parque temático más visitado de España. ¡Las mejores atracciones para los amantes de la adrenalina!

4 Ofrecemos una variedad de actividades artísticas – dibujo, pintura, manualidades, baile, teatro. Menores de dieciséis años.

5 ¿Te interesa crear una revista para otros adolescentes? ¿Quieres escribir artículos o sacar fotos? Actividad gratis.

6 Actividades deportivas en pleno campo. Disfruta de unas vistas preciosas mientras practicas una variedad de deportes.

¿Cuál es la actividad ideal para cada persona? Escribe el número correcto.

1. No tengo mucho dinero. Quiero hacer una actividad sin coste. **Lorena**
2. No me interesan los deportes acuáticos, pero me gustan mucho los paisajes bonitos. **Enrique**
3. Me encantan las montañas rusas. Son muy divertidas. **Aurora**
4. Quiero aprender a preparar mi comida favorita. **Pablo**

> ⭐ Remember that the texts and questions will usually use different words to express the same thing. Look at the questions and try to predict what clues you might find in the text. For example, the first person says that she hasn't got much money. What information might you look for in the texts?

2 leer Discover Havana
Read this article about Havana. Answer the questions at the top of page 21.

Hace más de tres años que decidí visitar la capital cubana y todavía recuerdo perfectamente el viaje del aeropuerto al hotel en uno de esos curiosos taxis, popularmente conocidos como 'coco-taxi'.

Durante el trayecto, vi parte de lo que ofrece esta ciudad: pintorescas calles con los viejos coches clásicos, una elegante arquitectura colonial y casas pintadas con colores vivos, donde la actividad, la creatividad y la música están siempre presentes.

Decidí conocer el país con unos amigos, combinando la comodidad de un hotel con régimen 'todo incluido' con la libertad que tienes cuando alquilas un coche. Aunque para conocer La Habana Vieja, lo mejor es recorrerla a pie. Así puedes disfrutar de unos de los entornos coloniales mejor conservados de América Latina, con su Catedral, los palacios señoriales… y descubrir lo mejor de este país: los cubanos.

los coco-taxis

1 Which **two** statements are true?
Write the correct letters.

A The writer saw lots of brightly coloured cars.
B She was impressed by the buildings.
C She was surprised by how quiet the city was.
D The hotel only served breakfast.
E The old buildings are still in a good state.

3 leer

A summer camp

Read this extract from *75 consejos para sobrevivir en el campamento,* a novel by María Frisa, and answer the questions which follow in **English**.

> Normalmente los campamentos están alejados de la civilización. Nuestro fantástico 'Happy English' está en medio del monte, a casi dos horas del pueblo más cercano. Por eso nos sorprende cuando una tarde, Nicole nos dice que podemos bajar al pueblo para comprar regalos y recuerdos.
> —Es una actividad voluntaria. Los que quieran venir deben estar aquí a las cinco —nos informa Nicole.
> A las tres y media ya estamos TODOS aquí. Esperando. El sol pega tan fuerte que llevamos gorras y sombreros.

1 Where **exactly** is the Happy English summer camp located?
2 What is the purpose of their trip down to the village?
3 What time were the children told to meet?
4 What are the children wearing when they meet up? Name **one** item.

> ⭐ When reading extracts from novels, plays or poems there will be lots of language that you don't know. Don't panic – you are not expected to understand every word! Use the questions to give you clues about the information you are looking for. Also, use your common sense.

1 escuchar

Travel bulletin

You are listening to a radio travel bulletin. Match the correct summary to each item of travel news. Write the correct letter. (1-4)

A 40 minute delay on motorway
B Wet weather causes traffic jams across the capital
C Snow brings airport to a standstill
D Broken down vehicle causes delays
E Air passengers affected by fog
F Expect congestion ahead of tonight's sports event

> ⭐ Beware of distractors which are there to catch you out! Also, you have to draw conclusions rather than simply spotting the Spanish equivalents of the words used in the summaries.

2 escuchar

Campsite

You are listening to your Spanish friend and his sister talking about what they like and dislike about a campsite they go to each year.

A Internet access
B Leisure facilities
C Staff
D Shopping facilities
E Landscape
F Weather
G Toilet/Wash block
H Meals
I Rules regarding pets
J Other guests

What do they like and dislike about their town?
Write the correct letter for each gap. Answer both parts of each question.

1 Imanol likes ☐ and ☐.
   Imanol dislikes ☐ and ☐.

2 Nerea likes ☐ and ☐.
   Nerea dislikes ☐ and ☐.

> ⭐ This task is testing whether you can **infer** opinions, so don't expect to hear words like *me gusta*! Also, they may talk about what they dislike first.

veintiuno

Módulo 1   Prueba oral

A – Role play

1 *leer* Look at the role play card and prepare what you are going to say.

> Your teacher will play the part of the receptionist and will speak first.
>
> You should address the receptionist as *usted*.
>
> When you see this – **!** – you will have to respond to something you have not prepared.
>
> When you see this – **?** – you will have to ask a question.
>
> Usted está hablando con el / la recepcionista de un hotel en España.
> - Tipo de habitación (**dos** detalles).
> - Problema con el viaje (**un** detalle).
> - Tu opinión sobre esta ciudad (**una** opinión y **una** razón).
> - **!**
> - **?** Piscina.

Start with 'I would like…'. Pay attention to the number of details required.

Remember to use the preterite or imperfect tense here.

There are several possibilities here (e.g. 'Is there…?' 'At what time…?').

In role play tasks you have to give at least one opinion, often with a reason.

The unprepared question may be a two-part question.

2 *escuchar* Practise what you have prepared. Then, using your notes, listen and respond to the teacher.

3 *escuchar* Now listen to Ryan doing the role play task. Note down:
1. what type of room he wants
2. what happened on his journey
3. what he says about the town
4. how he answers the unprepared question(s).

⭐ Role play tasks always require you to ask a question. Decide whether this needs to start with a question word. Can you remember what these question words mean?

¿Qué?   ¿Cuándo?   ¿Cuánto?   ¿Dónde?
¿Quién?   ¿Cómo?   ¿Por qué?   ¿A qué hora?

B – Photo card

Look at the photo and make notes. Your teacher will then ask you questions about the photo and about topics related to **travel and tourism**.

Your teacher will ask you the following **three** questions and then **two** more questions which you have not prepared.
- ¿Qué hay en la foto?
- ¿Te gustan las vacaciones en el extranjero? … ¿Por qué (no)?
- ¿Dónde pasaste tus últimas vacaciones?

veintidós

Módulo 1

1 Look at the photo and read the task. Then listen to Lucy's response to the first question on the task card.
1. Why does she think this is a photo of New York?
2. What do you think *edificios muy grandes* are?
3. Which **three** Spanish weather phrases does she use?
4. What does she say about the people in the photo?

2 Listen to and read Lucy's response to the second question on the task card.
1. Write down the missing word for each gap.
2. Look at the Answer Booster on page 24. Note down **six** examples of language which Lucy uses to give a strong answer.

> Sí, a mí me encanta ir al extranjero porque soy una **1** ———— de la playa. Me encanta tomar el sol, **2** ———— y escuchar música con mi hermana. Además, nos chifla hacer deportes acuáticos, pero en Inglaterra es difícil, puesto que **3** ———— demasiado. Cuando voy de vacaciones siempre hago vela y a veces **4** ———— en el mar también. Normalmente veraneamos en Egipto o Grecia, donde el clima es muy **5** ————. ¡Qué suerte! Sin embargo, lo malo es que es muy **6** ————.

3 Listen to Lucy's response to the third question on the task card.
1. Which negative expressions does she use?
2. In **English**, note down **six** details that she gives.

4 Prepare your own answers to the first **three** questions. Think about which other **two** questions you might be asked. Then listen and take part in the full photo card discussion with the teacher.

> ⭐ The photo card task always includes questions about things in the past and the future.
>
> To talk about what you **are going to do** use the **near future tense**. Use the present tense of the verb *ir* + *a* + **infinitive**.
>
> **Voy a *ir*** a Francia con mi familia.
> I'm going to go to France with my family.
>
> **No vamos a *viajar*** en coche.
> We aren't going to travel by car.

C – General conversation

1 The teacher asks Stephen *'¿Qué haces en verano?'* Read the statements and correct the mistakes.
a. Stephen lives in south Wales.
b. He plays football on the beach.
c. He loves riding his horse.
d. His brother goes sailing.

> ⭐ During the general conversation you must ask your teacher at least one question. What does Stephen ask?

2 The teacher then asks Stephen *'¿Dónde prefieres pasar las vacaciones?'* Note down **three** examples of how Stephen also includes other people's opinions.

3 Listen to Stephen's response to the next question *'¿Adónde fuiste de vacaciones el año pasado?'* Look at the Answer Booster on page 24. Note down **six** examples of language which Stephen uses to give a strong answer.

4 Prepare your own answers to Module 1 questions 1–6 on page 198. Then practise with your partner.

veintitrés

Módulo 1   Prueba escrita

Answer booster	Aiming for a solid answer	Aiming higher	Aiming for the top
Verbs	**Different time frames**: past, present, future	**Different persons** of the verb **Verbs with an infinitive**: tener que, decidir	**Preterite and imperfect to talk about the past**: Cuando llegamos, era… **Phrases with more than one tense**: creo que voy a visitar…
Opinions and reasons	**Opinions**: me chifla, me encanta, me apasiona **Reasons**: porque	**Exclamations**: ¡Qué suerte! **Verbs of opinion for other people**: A mi padre le mola…	**Reasons**: ya que, dado que, puesto que, por eso, así que **Verbs of opinion in the past**: me gustó
Connectives	y, pero, también	además, sin embargo, desafortunadamente, por desgracia	aunque, por un lado… por otro lado…
Other features	**Qualifiers**: muy, un poco, bastante **Sequencers**: primero, luego, después **Adjectives**: pintoresco, agotador	**Sentences with** *cuando, donde*: Cuando llegamos… **Negatives**: no… ni… ni…, tampoco…	**Positive/Negative phrases**: lo bueno/malo, lo mejor/peor, lo que más/menos me gustó, una desventaja es… **Interesting vocabulary**: veranear, un pinchazo

A – Short writing task

1 Look at the task and answer the questions.
- What type of text are you asked to write?
- What is each bullet point asking you to do?
- Which tense(s) will you need to use to answer each one?

2 Read Mohammed's answer on page 25. What do the phrases in **bold** mean?

3 Look at the Answer Booster. Note down **eight** examples of language which Mohammed uses to write a strong answer.

4 Look at the plan of Mohammed's answer. Write down the missing word for each gap.

5 Prepare your own answer to the task.
- Look at the Answer Booster and Mohammed's plan for ideas.
- Think about how you can develop your answer for each bullet point.
- Write a detailed plan. Organise your answer in paragraphs.
- Write your answer and carefully check what you have written.

Tu amigo español quiere saber cómo pasas las vacaciones. Escríbele una carta.

Menciona:
- adónde fuiste de vacaciones el año pasado
- por qué (no) te gustó el pueblo / la ciudad
- las ventajas de diferentes tipos de alojamiento
- dónde vas a pasar las vacaciones este verano.

Escribe aproximadamente **90** palabras en **español**.

Responde a todos los aspectos de la pregunta.

Paragraph 1
- Where I **1** ⎯⎯⎯
- The **2** ⎯⎯⎯ thing about it
- The **3** ⎯⎯⎯ thing about it

Paragraph 2
- Where the **4** ⎯⎯⎯ was located
- What the **5** ⎯⎯⎯ was like

Paragraph 3
- Opinion of staying in a **6** ⎯⎯⎯
- Opinion of staying in a **7** ⎯⎯⎯

Paragraph 4
- **8** ⎯⎯⎯ I'm going to go this year
- Opinion of the **9** ⎯⎯⎯
- What I'm going to **10** ⎯⎯⎯

veinticuatro

Módulo 1

Hola Ricardo

En febrero fui de vacaciones a **una estación de esquí** en Austria con mi insti. Nos alojamos en un albergue juvenil y viajamos en autocar. **¡Qué incómodo!** Lo mejor fue que aprendí a esquiar, pero lo peor fue cuando **me caí en la pista** y tuve que ir al hospital.

El albergue estaba en un pueblo pequeño que tenía vistas bonitas. Era pintoresco, pero **desafortunadamente**, no tenía ni tiendas ni cafeterías. Tampoco había mucho que hacer.

En mi opinión, es mejor alojarse en un hotel dado que hay aire acondicionado. Lo bueno de un camping es que se admiten perros, pero **una desventaja es que es ruidoso**.

Este año creo que vamos a ir a Pakistán ya que mis abuelos viven allí. Me chifla viajar en avión, aunque **el vuelo es agotador**. Voy a **ir de pesca** con mi abuelo porque le encanta.

¡Hasta luego!

Mohammed

Mohammed

⭐ Remember, to talk about what you **are going to do** you need to use the **near future tense**. Use the present tense of the verb *ir* + *a* + **infinitive**.

B – Translation

1 *escribir* Read the English text and Laura's translation of it. Write down the missing word for each gap.

In summer I go out every day because I love being outdoors. When it's nice weather I go sailing. However, when it rains I prefer to chat online with my friends. Yesterday we went to the beach, but we didn't swim in the sea since it was cold. Next week it's my birthday and therefore I'm going to go to the bowling alley.

En **1** ———— salgo todos los **2** ———— porque me encanta estar al **3** ———— libre. Cuando hace buen tiempo **4** ———— vela. Sin embargo, cuando **5** ———— prefiero **6** ———— en la red con mis **7** ————. Ayer **8** ———— a la playa, pero no **9** ———— en el mar dado que hizo **10** ————. La semana que viene es mi cumpleaños y por eso **11** ———— a ir a la **12** ————.

2 *escribir* Translate the following passage into Spanish.

In the holidays I often go to the cinema given that I love watching films. Last summer I went to Fréjus in the south of France, where my best friend has a caravan. It was sunny every day and so we went sightseeing. We took photos and ate lots of ice creams, too. Next year my parents are going to rent a house in the country.

⭐ Look out for phrases which don't translate word for word. For example, which verb do you need to use for 'we <u>went</u> sightseeing'?

veinticinco **25**

Módulo 1 Palabras

¿Dónde vives?	Where do you live?
Vivo en el…	I live in the…
norte/noreste/noroeste…	north/northeast/northwest…
sur/sureste/suroeste…	south/southeast/southwest…
este/oeste/centro…	east/west/centre…
de Inglaterra/Escocia	of England/Scotland
de Gales/Irlanda (del Norte)	of Wales/(Northern) Ireland

¿Qué haces en verano?	What do you do in summer?
En verano/invierno…	In summer/winter…
chateo en la red	I chat online
cocino para mi familia	I cook for my family
descargo canciones	I download songs
escribo correos	I write emails
hago natación/esquí/windsurf	I go swimming/skiing/windsurfing
hago una barbacoa	I have a barbecue
juego al baloncesto/fútbol	I play basketball/football
monto a caballo/en bici	I go horseriding/cycling
nado en el mar	I swim in the sea
salgo con mis amigos/as	I go out with my friends
toco la guitarra	I play the guitar
trabajo como voluntario/a	I work as a volunteer
veo la tele	I watch TV
voy al polideportivo/al parque/	I go to the sports centre/to the park/
a un centro comercial	to a shopping centre
voy de paseo	I go for a walk

¿Con qué frecuencia?	How often?
siempre	always
a menudo	often
todos los días	every day
a veces	sometimes
de vez en cuando	from time to time
una vez a la semana	once a week
dos o tres veces al año	two or three times a year
(casi) nunca	(almost) never

¿Qué tiempo hace?	What's the weather like?
Hace buen/mal tiempo.	It's good/bad weather.
Hace calor/frío/sol/viento.	It's hot/cold/sunny/windy.
Llueve/Nieva.	It's raining/snowing.
El tiempo es variable.	The weather is changeable.
El clima es caluroso/soleado.	The climate is hot/sunny.
Hay niebla/tormenta.	It's foggy/stormy.
Hay chubascos.	There are showers.
Está nublado.	It's cloudy.

¿Qué te gusta hacer?	What do you like doing?
Soy adicto/a a…	I'm addicted to…
Soy un(a) fanático/a de…	I'm a … fan/fanatic.
ya que/dado que/puesto que	given that/since
Prefiero…	I prefer…
Me gusta…	I like…
Me encanta/Me mola/Me chifla/	
Me flipa/Me apasiona…	I love…
No me gusta (nada)…	I don't like… (at all)
Odio…	I hate…
A (mi padre) le gusta…	(My dad) likes…
Nos encanta…	We love…
bucear	diving
estar al aire libre	being outdoors
estar en contacto con los amigos	being in touch with friends
hacer artes marciales	doing martial arts
hacer deportes acuáticos	doing water sports
ir al cine/a la pista de hielo	going to the cinema/ice rink
ir de compras	going shopping
leer (un montón de revistas)	reading (loads of magazines)
usar el ordenador	using the computer
ver películas	watching films
Prefiero veranear…	I prefer to spend the summer…
en el extranjero/en España	abroad/in Spain
en la costa/en el campo	on the coast/in the country
en la montaña/en la ciudad	in the mountains/in the city

¿Adónde fuiste de vacaciones?	Where did you go on holiday?
hace una semana/un mes/un año	a week/month/year ago
hace dos semanas/meses/años	two weeks/months/years ago
fui de vacaciones a…	I went on holiday to…
Francia/Italia/Turquía	France/Italy/Turkey
¿Con quién fuiste?	Who did you go with?
Fui…	I went…
con mi familia/insti	with my family/school
con mi mejor amigo/a	with my best friend
solo/a	alone
¿Cómo viajaste?	How did you travel?
Viajé…	I travelled…
en autocar/avión	by coach/plane
en barco/coche/tren	by boat/car/train

¿Qué hiciste?	What did you do?
primero	first
luego	then
más tarde	later
después	after
finalmente	finally
Lo mejor fue cuando…	The best thing was when…
Lo peor fue cuando…	The worst thing was when…
aprendí a hacer vela	I learned to sail
comí muchos helados	I ate lots of ice creams
compré recuerdos	I bought souvenirs
descansé	I rested
fui al acuario	I went to the aquarium
hice turismo	I went sightseeing
llegué tarde al aeropuerto	I arrived at the airport late
perdí mi móvil	I lost my mobile
saqué fotos	I took photos
tomé el sol	I sunbathed
tuve un accidente en la playa	I had an accident on the beach
vi un partido	I saw/watched a match
visité el Park Güell	I visited Park Güell
vomité en una montaña rusa	I was sick on a roller coaster
Puedes…	You can…
descubrir el Museo Picasso	discover the Picasso Museum
disfrutar del Barrio Gótico	enjoy the gothic quarter
pasear por las Ramblas	walk along Las Ramblas
subir al Monumento a Colón	go up the Columbus Monument
ver los barcos en el puerto	see the boats in the port

¿Qué tal lo pasaste?	How was it?
Me gustó/Me encantó.	I liked it/I loved it.
Lo pasé bomba/fenomenal.	I had a great time.
Lo pasé bien/mal/fatal.	I had a good/bad/awful time.
Fue…	It was…
inolvidable/increíble	unforgettable/incredible
impresionante/flipante	impressive/awesome
horroroso	awful
un desastre	a disaster
¿Qué tiempo hizo?	What was the weather like?
Hizo buen/mal tiempo.	It was good/bad weather.
Hizo calor/frío/sol/viento.	It was hot/cold/sunny/windy.
Hubo niebla/tormenta.	It was foggy/stormy.
Llovió/Nevó.	It rained/snowed.

¿Cómo era el hotel?

Me alojé/Me quedé…	I stayed…
Nos alojamos/Nos quedamos…	We stayed…
en un albergue juvenil	in a youth hostel
en un apartamento	in an apartment
en un camping	on a campsite
en un hotel de cinco estrellas	in a five-star hotel
en un parador	in a state-run luxury hotel
en una casa rural	in a house in the country
en una pensión	in a guest house
Fui de crucero.	I went on a cruise.
Estaba…	It was…
cerca de la playa	near the beach
en el centro de la ciudad	in the city centre
en las afueras	on the outskirts
Era…	It was…
acogedor(a)	welcoming
antiguo/a	old
barato/a	cheap
caro/a	expensive
grande	big
lujoso/a	luxurious
moderno/a	modern
pequeño/a	small
ruidoso/a	noisy
tranquilo/a	quiet
Tenía/Había…	It had/There was/were…
No tenía ni… ni…	It had neither… nor…
No había ni… ni…	There was neither… nor…
Tampoco tenía…	Nor did it have…
(un) aparcamiento	a car park
(un) bar	a bar
(un) gimnasio	a gym
(un) restaurante	a restaurant
(una) cafetería	a café
(una) lavandería	a launderette
(una) piscina cubierta	an indoor pool
mucho espacio para mi tienda	lots of space for my tent

¿Cómo era el pueblo?

Lo bueno/Lo malo…	The good thing/The bad thing…
del pueblo…	about the town/village…
de la ciudad…	about the city…
era que era…	was that it was…
demasiado/muy/bastante…	too/very/quite…
animado/a	lively
bonito/a	pretty
histórico/a	historic
pintoresco/a	picturesque
turístico/a	touristic
Tenía…	It had…
mucho ambiente/tráfico	lots of atmosphere/traffic
mucho que hacer	lots to do
mucha contaminación/gente	lots of pollution/people
muchos espacios verdes	lots of green spaces
muchos lugares de interés	lots of places of interest
muchas discotecas	lots of discos

Quisiera reservar…

¿Hay…	Is/Are there…
wifi gratis…	free wifi…
aire acondicionado…	air conditioning…
en el hotel/las habitaciones?	in the hotel/the rooms?
¿Cuánto cuesta una habitación…?	How much does a… room cost?
¿A qué hora se sirve el desayuno?	What time is breakfast served?
¿Cuándo está abierto/a el/la…?	When is the… open?
¿Cuánto es el suplemento por…?	How much is the supplement for…?
¿Se admiten perros?	Are dogs allowed?
Quisiera reservar…	I would like to book…
una habitación individual/doble	a single/double room
con/sin balcón	with/without balcony
con bañera/ducha	with a bath/shower
con cama de matrimonio	with double bed
con desayuno incluido	with breakfast included
con media pensión	with half board
con pensión completa	with full board
con vistas al mar	with sea view
¿Para cuántas noches?	For how many nights?
Para… noches	For… nights
del… al… de…	from the… to the… of…
¿Puede repetir, por favor?	Can you repeat, please?
¿Puede hablar más despacio?	Can you speak more slowly?

Quiero quejarme

Quiero hablar con el director.	I want to speak to the manager.
Quiero cambiar de habitación.	I want to change rooms.
El aire acondicionado…	The air conditioning…
El ascensor…	The lift…
La ducha…	The shower…
La habitación…	The room…
está sucio/a	is dirty
La luz…	The light…
no funciona	doesn't work
Hay ratas en la cama.	There are rats in the bed.
No hay…	There is no…
Necesito…	I need…
papel higiénico	toilet paper
jabón/champú	soap/shampoo
toallas/(un) secador	towels/a hairdryer
¡Socorro!	Help!
Es inaceptable.	It's unacceptable.
Lo siento/Perdone.	I'm sorry.
El hotel está completo.	The hotel is full.

Mis vacaciones desastrosas / My disastrous holiday

Por desgracia	Unfortunately
Por un lado… por otro lado…	On the one hand… on the other hand…
El primer/último día	(On) the first/last day
Al día siguiente	On the following day
Tuve/Tuvimos…	I had/We had…
un accidente/un pinchazo	an accident/a puncture
un retraso/una avería	a delay/a breakdown
Tuve/Tuvimos que…	I had to/We had to…
esperar mucho tiempo	wait a long time
ir al hospital/a la comisaría	go to the hospital/to the police station
llamar a un mecánico	call a mechanic
Perdí/Perdimos…	I lost/We lost…
el equipaje/la cartera	the luggage/the wallet
la maleta/las llaves	the suitcase/the keys
Cuando llegamos…	When we arrived…
era muy tarde	it was very late
estaba cansado/a	I was tired
la recepción ya estaba cerrada	the reception was already closed
acampar	to camp
decidir	to decide (to)
alquilar bicicletas	to hire bicycles
coger el teleférico	to catch/take the cable car
chocar con	to crash into
hacer alpinismo	to go mountain climbing
volver	to return
el paisaje	the landscape
la autopista	the motorway
precioso/a	beautiful

2 Mi vida en el insti
Punto de partida 1

- Giving opinions about school subjects
- Describing school facilities

1 Escucha y escribe las asignaturas que faltan. (1–5)

Mi horario

hora	lunes	martes	miércoles	jueves	viernes
08.15	biología	c	inglés	inglés	informática
09.00	a	religión	e	g	i
09.45	RECREO				
10.15	lengua	empresariales	lengua	historia	educación física
11.00	b	biología	f	lengua	j
11.45	RECREO				
12.15	química	d	física	arte dramático	matemáticas
13.00	física	inglés	matemáticas	h	tecnología

2 Lee las opiniones y mira el horario del ejercicio 1. ¿Cuál es su día preferido?

lengua	Spanish class

1 Me encantan los idiomas porque son interesantes e importantes.
2 ¡No me gusta escribir! Prefiero las asignaturas prácticas.
3 No me gustan las ciencias porque son aburridas y difíciles. Mi día preferido es el día que no tengo ciencias.
4 Me chifla el arte dramático porque es creativo y me interesa mucho la historia porque es útil.
5 ¿Mi día favorito? Es el día que tengo las materias fáciles: geografía, religión, música y empresariales.
6 No me gusta nada el insti, pero mi día preferido es el día que no tengo inglés. ¡Odio el inglés!

> **G Opinion verbs** — Page 222
>
> *Interesar* works like *gustar* and *encantar*. It uses a pronoun like *me* or *te*.
>
> **Me** *interesa* el dibujo.   Art interests **me**.
> ¿**Te** *interesan* los idiomas?   Do languages interest **you**?
>
> **Odiar** and **preferir** don't need a pronoun.
>
> Remember to use the definite article (*el/la/los/las*) when giving opinions about nouns.

3 Con tu compañero/a, haz diálogos.

● ¿Qué día tienes <u>inglés</u>?
■ Tengo <u>inglés</u> los martes. Me interesa <u>el inglés</u> porque es <u>útil</u>, pero no me gustan <u>las ciencias</u> porque son <u>difíciles</u>.
● ¿Cuál es tu día preferido?
■ Mi día preferido es <u>el jueves</u> porque tengo <u>educación física</u>. Me chifla porque es <u>práctica</u> y <u>divertida</u>.

(no) me gust**a** (no) me encant**a** (no) me interes**a**	**el** francés **la** geografía	porque es	práctic**o/a**, creativ**o/a**, aburrid**o/a** útil, fácil, difícil importante, interesante
(no) me gust**an** (no) me encant**an** (no) me interes**an**	**los** idiomas **las** empresariales	porque son	práctic**os/as**, creativ**os/as**, aburrid**os/as** útil**es**, fácil**es**, difícil**es** importante**s**, interesante**s**

Módulo 2

4 leer Mira el horario del ejercicio 1. Completa las frases.

1 Los lunes a las doce y cuarto tengo _____.
2 Los martes a las diez y cuarto tengo _____.
3 Los miércoles a la una tenemos _____.
4 Los jueves a las _____ tenemos una clase de lengua.
5 Los viernes a las _____ tenemos informática.
6 Todos los días a las _____ y las _____ hay un recreo.

5 escuchar Escucha y mira el horario del ejercicio 1. Corrige las frases. (1–5)

6 leer Lee las frases. ¿Verdadero o Falso? Escribe V o F.

Educación infantil
0–6 años

Educación primaria
6–12 años

Educación Secundaria
Obligatoria (ESO)
12–16 años

Bachillerato o
formación profesional
16–18+ años

1 Los niños españoles empiezan la educación primaria a los seis años.
2 En los institutos normalmente los alumnos tienen que llevar uniforme.
3 Los alumnos empiezan la educación secundaria más tarde en España que en Inglaterra.
4 La Educación Secundaria Obligatoria generalmente dura seis años en España.
5 A los 16 años los alumnos tienen dos opciones.
6 El bachillerato es obligatorio para todos.

7 escuchar Escucha e identifica las <u>tres</u> letras correctas. Sobra una letra. (1–3)

a muchas aulas
b una biblioteca
c un comedor
d un gimnasio
e una piscina
f un laboratorio
g un campo de fútbol
h un salón de actos
i una pista de tenis
j un patio

8 escuchar Escucha otra vez. ¿Las opiniones son positivas o negativas?
Escribe P (positivo), N (negativo) o P+N (positivo y negativo). (1–3)

Lo bueno / malo es que…
Lo mejor / peor es que…
Lo que más me gusta es / son…
Lo que menos me gusta es / son…

Unidad 2

veintinueve 29

Punto de partida 2

- Describing school uniform and the school day
- Using adjectives

1 Mira los uniformes. Escribe los artículos de ropa y los colores en español.

Ejemplo: **a** *una camisa blanca*

el uniforme escolar en Chile

Zona Cultura

En Chile es muy normal llevar uniforme en las escuelas, públicas y privadas. Normalmente es una chaqueta azul oscuro, pantalones grises y camisa blanca para los chicos, y una falda gris, camisa blanca y medias azules para las chicas. Por eso los alumnos chilenos tienen el apodo 'pingüinos'.

(No…) Llevo… Llevamos… Tengo que llevar… Tenemos que llevar…	un jersey (de punto) un vestido una camisa una camiseta una chaqueta (a rayas) una corbata una falda (a cuadros) unos pantalones unos calcetines unos zapatos unos vaqueros unas medias

G Adjectival endings for colours

Remember to make colour adjectives agree with the noun.

ending	singular		plural	
	masculine	feminine	masculine	feminine
–o	blanco	blanca	blancos	blancas
–e	verde	verde	verdes	verdes
consonant	azul	azul	azules	azules

Naranja, *rosa* and *violeta* often do not change, but some people add an –s with plural nouns.

A colour followed by **claro** (light) and **oscuro** (dark) always takes the masculine form:

un**os** calcetines **azul claro**, un**as** medias **azul oscuro**

2 Escucha. Copia y completa la tabla en inglés. (1–4)

	uniform details (2)	opinions (2)
1		

gris   morado / violeta   blanco   negro

amarillo   naranja   azul

marrón   rosa   verde   rojo

cómodo   anticuado   bonito

fácil   feo   incómodo

práctico   elegante

Módulo 2

3 Lee los textos. Busca las expresiones en español en el texto.

¿El uniforme te mola?

En mi insti todos llevamos uniforme y es superfeo. ¡Qué horror! Tengo que llevar una falda verde oscuro a cuadros y una chaqueta de punto del mismo color. Pienso que es aburrido y formal, pero mi madre dice que el uniforme mejora la disciplina y da una imagen positiva de nuestro insti. **Alicia**

Tenemos que llevar uniforme. Llevamos unos pantalones grises, una corbata azul y roja, y una chaqueta negra. Mi amiga dice que limita la individualidad, pero me gusta porque me ahorra tiempo por la mañana. Además, es importante porque así las diferencias económicas no son tan obvias. **Fran**

1 we all wear
2 checked
3 a cardigan of the same colour
4 improves discipline
5 gives a positive image of our school
6 we have to wear
7 it saves me time
8 economic differences are not as apparent

4 Con tu compañero/a, haz un diálogo sobre el uniforme.

- ¿Qué llevas en el insti?
- ¿Qué opinas?

- *Tengo que llevar uniforme. Llevo…*
- *(No) me gusta porque es… y…*

5 Escucha y lee. Traduce las expresiones en **negrita** al inglés.

- Mayra, ¿cómo vas al insti **por la mañana**?
- Voy en taxi. **Salgo de casa** a las siete. ¡**Es demasiado temprano**!
- ¿A qué hora empiezan las clases?
- **Las clases empiezan** a las siete y media y **terminan** a las dos de la tarde.
- ¿Cuántas clases tienes al día?
- Tenemos siete clases al día y **cada clase dura** cincuenta minutos.
- ¿A qué hora es el recreo?
- Hay dos recreos de veinte minutos, pero no hay **hora de comer**.
- ¿Qué días tienes ciencias?
- Tengo ciencias los lunes y los miércoles. **Me fascinan** las ciencias porque me interesa mucho el mundo natural.

Mayra vive en Arequipa en Perú

¿Cómo vas al insti?
a pie / andando   en metro
en bici   en taxi
en autobús   en tren
en coche

6 Habla sobre tu día escolar. Utiliza el diálogo del ejercicio 5 como modelo.

7 Escribe un párrafo sobre tu uniforme y tu día escolar. Incluye opiniones y razones.

⭐ To say you do things on certain days use **los** + the day of the week.
Los viernes tengo matemáticas.
To say 'in the morning / afternoon' use **por**:
Por la mañana tenemos dibujo.
Por la tarde hay tres clases.

Unidad 4

treinta y uno 31

1 ¿Qué tal los estudios?

- Talking about subjects and teachers
- Using comparatives and superlatives
- Justifying opinions using a range of language

1 **leer** Lee y empareja las opiniones con las razones.

¿Qué asignaturas te gustan?

Sergio
1 Una asignatura que me gusta un montón es el inglés porque…
2 Lo que más me gusta es el dibujo porque…

Cristina
3 Me interesa mucho la biología porque…
4 La física me gusta menos porque…
5 La historia me fascina, pero…

Julián
6 Una asignatura muy buena es la educación física porque…
7 Me chiflan las matemáticas porque…

a **es más práctica y relevante que** las demás ciencias. Vemos temas de la naturaleza, como las células, y hacemos experimentos.

b **no es tan difícil como** el inglés. Para mí, **es la mejor asignatura**. El profe me deja trabajar a mi manera, ¡incluso con música! Me dice que pinto y dibujo muy bien.

c me gusta resolver problemas. **Es mejor que** las otras asignaturas porque **es la asignatura más exacta y lógica**.

d no puedo memorizar las fechas. Soy **la peor** de la clase y no saco buenas notas en las pruebas.

e **es menos complicado que** los otros idiomas que estudio. Además, ya sabemos mucha gramática y mucho vocabulario.

f **es más difícil que** la biología.

g **es la asignatura más divertida y activa**

2 **escuchar** Escucha y comprueba tus respuestas.

3 **leer** Traduce las expresiones en **negrita** del ejercicio 1 al inglés.

4 **hablar** Con tu compañero/a, haz un diálogo. Utiliza el texto del ejercicio 1 como modelo. Da opiniones y razones.

- ¿Qué asignaturas te gustan?
- A mí me chifla(n)… porque… Es la asignatura más importante. Otra asignatura que me gusta un montón es… porque…
- ¿Qué asignaturas no te gustan?
- No me gusta mucho la tecnología porque es menos interesante que la informática.

G Comparatives and superlatives

Comparatives
más… que	more… than
menos… que	less… than
mejor que…	better than…
peor que…	worse than…
tan… como…	as… as…

El español es **más fácil que** el mandarín.
La informática es **tan creativa como** la tecnología.

Superlatives
el/la más…	the most…
el/la menos…	the least…
el/la mejor…	the best…
el/la peor…	the worst…

Mi profesora de inglés es **la más divertida**.
El español es la asignatura **más interesante**.

⭐ Giving reasons adds length and interest to what you say. Check that your answers have 12 or more words. Repeat the task with your book closed.

32 treinta y dos

Módulo 2

5 Lee y busca las expresiones en el texto.

¿Qué tal tus profes?

Me llamo Laura y estoy en 3º de ESO. Mi nuevo profesor de matemáticas me cae bien porque es muy listo y divertido. Tiene buen sentido del humor, así que crea un buen ambiente de trabajo. También es muy trabajador. Nos pone muchos deberes y tiene expectativas altas, pero aprendo mucho con él porque me hace pensar. Antes tenía problemas con el cálculo. Lo peor era que mi profesora de 2º de ESO era muy impaciente y no era nada tolerante.

1. creates a good working atmosphere
2. makes me think
3. has a good sense of humour
4. I like my new maths teacher
5. I learn a lot
6. was not at all tolerant
7. has high expectations
8. gives us lots of homework

6 Lee el texto otra vez. Busca el antónimo de los siguientes adjetivos.

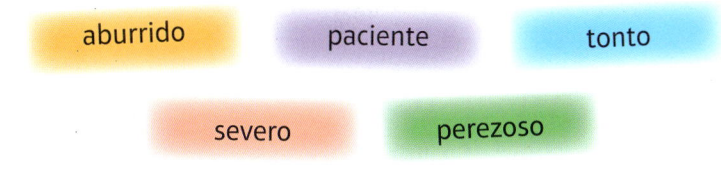

- aburrido
- paciente
- tonto
- severo
- perezoso

Zona Cultura

La **E**ducación **S**ecundaria **O**bligatoria (ESO) tiene cuatro cursos académicos, que se llaman 1º de ESO, 2º de ESO, etc. Generalmente, la ESO se inicia a los 12 años y se acaba con 16 años. Si los alumnos suspenden tres o más asignaturas, tienen que repetir el curso.

| el curso académico | academic year |
| suspender | to fail |

7 Escucha a Andrés. Completa el resumen con las opciones correctas. Luego traduce el texto al inglés.

La nueva profe de **ciencias / inglés** es mucho más **estricta / simpática** que su profe de antes. La señora Martínez **enseña / explica** muy bien y por eso le resulta **menos / más** difícil comprender. También da **consejos / estrategias** para estudiar mejor. Cree que no va a **aprobar / suspender** sus evaluaciones este año.

| evaluaciones | assessments |

8 Escribe dos párrafos sobre tus asignaturas y tus profes.

¿Qué tal tus asignaturas y tus profes?

- A mí me chifla(n)… porque es la asignatura más…
- Otra asignatura que me gusta…
- Me gusta menos… porque no es tan… como…
- Me gusta mi profe de… porque…
- Siempre… así que…
- También…
- Nunca…

Mi profesor(a) / profe…
- enseña bien
- explica bien
- tiene buen sentido del humor
- tiene expectativas muy altas
- me hace pensar
- crea un buen ambiente de trabajo
- nos da consejos / estrategias
- nos pone muchos deberes
- nunca se enfada

treinta y tres **33**

2 ¡Mi nuevo insti!

- *Describing your school*
- *Using negatives*
- *Comparing then and now*

1 Escucha y lee el podcast de Josué. Contesta a las preguntas en inglés.

Josué es de Ecuador, pero ahora vive en España.

¡Hola a todos! ¿Qué hay?

Hoy fue mi primer día de clase en mi nuevo instituto, que se llama IES Martín Galeano. Como ya sabéis, mi mamá tiene un nuevo empleo y ahora vivimos en Gijón.

¿Cómo es mi insti? Pues, es mixto y público. Hay unos quinientos alumnos y setenta profes. El edificio es bastante pequeño y moderno, muy diferente a mi insti de antes en Quito, que era mucho más grande y antiguo.

Tiene muchas aulas, pero no son parecidas a las aulas de Quito. ¡Todos los muebles (las mesas y la sillas) son verdes! Incluso las pizarras son verdes, y no hay ninguna pizarra interactiva. Sin embargo, hay un salón de actos y una biblioteca bien equipada.

Como estamos en el centro de la ciudad, no hay ningún espacio verde para practicar deporte, ni campo de fútbol, ni pista de atletismo. Lo bueno es que estamos a ciento cincuenta metros de la playa, donde tenemos las clases de educación física. ¡Qué guay!

Tampoco hay comedor, pero no es un problema porque las clases terminan a las dos y ¡vamos a casa para comer!

Todavía no conozco a nadie y no tengo nada que hacer esta tarde porque todavía no tengo deberes, por lo tanto voy a ir a la playa. ¡Hasta luego!

Gijón, España

1. Why has Josué moved to Spain?
2. What is different about the classrooms? (two details)
3. What does he say about the library?
4. Explain one advantage and one disadvantage of the sports facilities.
5. Why is the lack of canteen not a problem?
6. Why is Josué going to the beach this afternoon? (two details)

IES Instituto de Educación Secundaria
todavía still

2 Escucha y apunta las preguntas en español. Luego contéstalas como Josué. (1–6)

Ejemplo: **1** ¿Cómo se llama tu instituto? Se llama IES Martín Galeano.

3 Traduce los párrafos 4 y 5 del podcast al inglés.

G Negatives ▶ Page 227

These negatives are often used after the verb as a 'sandwich' with **no** before the verb.

No hago **nada**.	I **don't** do **anything**.
No conozco a **nadie**.	I **don't** know **anyone**.
No tenemos **ni** tabletas **ni** ordenadores.	We **don't** have **either** tablets **or** computers.
No tiene **ningún** laboratorio.	It **doesn't** have a **single** laboratory.
No tiene **ninguna** pista de tenis.	It **doesn't** have a **single** tennis court.

Nunca can go **before** or **after** the verb. When after, use **no** in front of the verb as well.

Nunca estudia.	He/She **never** studies.
No estudia **nunca**.	He/She **never** studies.

Tampoco (not either) usually goes in front of the verb.

Tampoco hay piscina.	There **isn't** a swimming pool **either**.

4 Escribe un párrafo sobre tu instituto. Contesta a las preguntas del ejercicio 2. Utiliza diferentes expresiones negativas.

34 treinta y cuatro

Módulo 2

5 Escucha. Copia y completa la tabla en inglés.

	my primary school	my secondary school
Camilo		
Noa		

mi insti

mi escuela primaria

⭐ **antes** + **imperfect tense**, **ahora** + **present tense**
Antes no **había** donde jugar. Before there wasn't anywhere to play.
Ahora hay un patio cubierto. Now there is a covered playground.

6 Con tu compañero/a, compara tu escuela primaria con tu instituto.

- ¿Cómo era tu escuela primaria?
- Mi escuela primaria era <u>bastante antigua</u> y…
  No había <u>pizarras interactivas</u> ni…
  pero había…
  Tampoco había…
  Antes <u>los recreos</u> eran <u>más largos</u> y
  <u>los profes</u> eran… pero…

- ¿Cómo es tu insti de ahora?
- Mi insti de ahora es <u>muy grande</u> y…
  Tiene <u>buenas instalaciones</u> y…
  Las clases son <u>más duras</u>, pero hay
  <u>más oportunidades</u> para hacer…

En mi escuela primaria En mi insti	(no) había (no) hay	(una) piscina (un) polideportivo (unas) pizarras (interactivas) (unas) aulas de informática exámenes / deberes (un) uniforme espacios verdes más tiempo libre más alumnos / profesores más oportunidades para hacer…
Mi escuela primaria Mi insti	(no) tenía (no) tiene	
El edificio Las instalaciones El día escolar Las asignaturas Las clases	(no) era(n) (no) es (no) son	(in)adecuado / colorido moderno / antiguo más corto / largo más fácil / duro mejor / peor

⭐ Use the correct endings!

7 Lee el texto. Elige las respuestas correctas.

Jatun Kasa – antes y ahora

Jatun Kasa es una comunidad remota de unas 40 familias en los Andes de Bolivia. Hoy hay un nuevo colegio allí, con seis aulas modernas, servicios y un patio cubierto para el recreo.

Sara, una alumna de 15 años, describe cómo era el colegio antes:

'Bueno, la verdad es que las instalaciones no eran apropiadas para aprender. El aula era estrecha y fría. No había ninguna ventana y el techo estaba roto. Tampoco había mesas ni sillas suficientes – ¡estábamos como sardinas en lata!'

Ramón Darío, profesor, vive ahora en una de las nuevas casas para los profesores:

'Antes era muy difícil vivir allí porque yo tenía una sola habitación. Igual que en el colegio, no había electricidad ni agua corriente. Estaba sucia y había ratas, arañas y serpientes. Ahora mi casa es una de las mejores. Tiene dos habitaciones, una cocina y un baño. Mi mujer y yo estamos supercontentos y trabajamos con ganas.'

1 Jatun Kasa es…
   a una ciudad.
   b un colegio.
   c un pueblo.
   d una persona.

2 Antes el colegio tenía…
   a instalaciones inadecuadas.
   b muchos muebles.
   c ventanas sucias.
   d aulas grandes.

3 Antes el profesor tenía…
   a electricidad y agua corriente.
   b dos habitaciones.
   c muy poco espacio.
   d una mascota.

4 Ahora Ramón está…
   a muy feliz.
   b triste.
   c en otro colegio.
   d cansado.

treinta y cinco **35**

3 ¡Está prohibido!

- Talking about school rules and problems
- Using phrases followed by the infinitive
- Tackling harder listening exercises

1 Lee y empareja las fotos con las expresiones. Luego haz una frase para cada foto. Utiliza diferentes expresiones.

Ejemplo: **a** *No se debe usar el móvil en clase.*

¿Cuáles son las normas de tu insti?

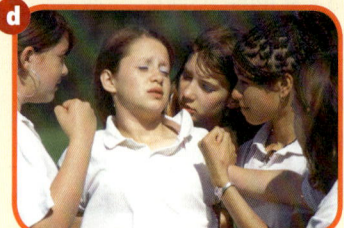

- **mantener** limpio el patio
- **comer** chicle
- **respetar** el turno de palabra
- **correr** en los pasillos
- **ser** puntual
- **usar** el móvil en clase
- **dañar** las instalaciones
- **ser** agresivo o grosero
- **llevar** piercings en el insti

💬 When reading from a text, apply the pronunciation patterns you know. E.g. the **ll** in **ll**evar and pasi**ll**o as in came**ll**o, and the **u** in **u**sar, p**u**nt**u**al and t**u**rno as in b**ú**falo.

G Verbs with an infinitive

To describe rules, use these structures followed by the infinitive:

está prohibido	it is forbidden to
no se permite	you are not allowed to
no se debe	you/one must not
hay que	it is necessary to
tenemos que	we have to

No se permite **ser** *agresivo o grosero.*

2 Escucha y escribe las letras del ejercicio 1. ¿La opinión es positiva (P), negativa (N) o positiva y negativa (P+N)? (1–3)

3 Con tus compañeros, haz un debate sobre las normas de tu instituto.

- ● *Está prohibido llevar piercings en el colegio. Creo que es justo. ¿Qué opinas?*
- ■ *Sí, estoy de acuerdo.*
- ▲ *¡Qué va!*
- ◆ *Yo tampoco estoy de acuerdo. En mi opinión, es injusto. No me gusta esta norma.*

⭐ Speak more expressively by using exclamations.

¡Qué va!	No way!
¡Qué horror!	How awful!
¡Qué bien!	How great!

36 treinta y seis

Módulo 2

4 Escucha a Alejandra y a Román. Apunta sus respuestas.

¿Necesitamos normas?

1 ¿Qué opinas del uniforme escolar en general?
   a es una buena idea
   b es feo
   c es caro

2 ¿Cuáles son las normas más importantes de tu instituto?
   a cuidar el material y las instalaciones
   b respetar a los demás
   c llevar el uniforme correcto

3 ¿Qué piensas de las normas de tu instituto?
   a son necesarias
   b son demasiado severas
   c unas son positivas

4 ¿Por qué tenemos reglas?
   a para fomentar la buena disciplina
   b para limitar la libertad de expresión
   c para fastidiar a los alumnos

5 ¿Hay problemas en tu insti?
   a no hay ningún problema
   b sí, a veces
   c muchos

6 ¿Qué es lo mejor de tu insti?
   a las oportunidades después del colegio
   b los amigos
   c las calificaciones

para	in order to
cuentan	they count
restringir	to restrict

⭐ Listening questions often include <u>distractors</u>. More than one option is mentioned, so listen to the end before jumping to conclusions.

They also require you to listen out for things expressed <u>in different words</u> from the ones you read on the page.

5 Lee los textos y escribe la letra correcta. Sobra una opción. Luego traduce las expresiones en **negrita** al inglés.

exigir	to demand
hacer novillos	to skive
la pandilla	gang

1 Este año es duro porque en el insti nos exigen más que en otros años. Los profes nos dan mucho trabajo. Nos dicen que **debemos aprobar los exámenes**, pero **estoy superestresado** y **tengo miedo de suspender mis pruebas**. *Adrián*

2 Hay alumnos que sufren intimidación en el insti porque hay otros alumnos que siempre **se burlan de ellos** y no los dejan en paz. ¡No es justo! Se refugian en la biblioteca durante los recreos y a la hora de comer, pero la verdad es que tienen mucho miedo. *Mateo*

3 Hay algunos alumnos que son una mala influencia. Hacen novillos y otros compañeros quieren ser amigos de ellos porque quieren ser parte de su pandilla. **Todos tenemos que sacar buenas notas**, pero **los amigos cuentan más**. *Ivanna*

a el acoso escolar   **b** las normas estrictas   **c** la presión del grupo   **d** el estrés de los exámenes

6 Entrevista a tu compañero/a.

- Use the questions from exercise 4.
- Use additional ideas from the texts in exercise 5.
- Answer the questions with whole sentences.

7 Escribe un texto sobre las normas de tu insti.

Include:
- if uniform is compulsory and what you have to wear
- a positive and negative opinion and justification
- any other rules and what you think of them
- one problem that exists in your school
- the best thing about your school

treinta y siete 37

4 ¡Destino Zaragoza!

- Talking about plans for a school exchange
- Using the near future tense
- Asking and answering questions

1 Escucha y lee el vídeo mensaje de Víctor. Escribe las letras en el orden correcto.

Víctor • Colegio M. Mª Rosa Molas

¡Hola! Te quiero dar la bienvenida al Colegio M. Mª Rosa Molas. Ahora **voy a contestar** a tus preguntas sobre la visita de intercambio.

Vas a llegar el martes a las tres al aeropuerto de Zaragoza. Allí **vamos a estar** todos, y nuestras familias también.

El miércoles nos toca ir al colegio. Algunos compañeros **van a ir** en coche, pero nosotros **vamos a ir andando** porque vivimos muy cerca, como la mayoría de los alumnos.

Las clases empiezan a las ocho y para 3º y 4º de ESO terminan a las dos. Por la mañana tenemos tres clases y un recreo a las once menos cinco. Luego hay otras tres clases.

Es obligatorio llevar uniforme (excepto los de bachillerato, que 'van de calle'). Llevamos pantalón o falda gris, polo blanco y jersey azul marino. Pero vosotros **vais a llevar** ropa de calle.

El primer día **vamos a comer** juntos en el comedor, donde comen normalmente los de 1º y 2º de ESO.

Después de la hora de comer, tenemos dos horas de lengua castellana, y luego una hora de inglés, lo que **va a ser** superfácil para vosotros.

El resto de la semana tenemos una programación variada. ¡Seguro que **te va a gustar**!

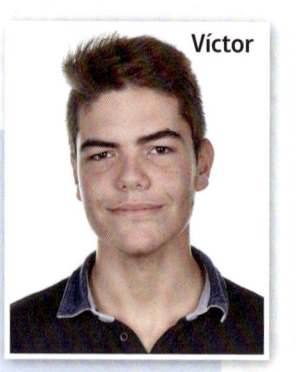

Zona Cultura

Destino:	ZARAGOZA
Ubicación:	Noreste de España, en el interior
Población:	666 mil habitantes (4ª ciudad de España)
Famosa por:	Su fiesta en honor a la Virgen del Pilar

nos toca ir — we have to go
ropa de calle — casual clothes / non-uniform

2 Lee el texto del ejercicio 1 otra vez. Traduce las expresiones en **negrita** al inglés.

3 Escribe la programación para el miércoles en inglés.
Ejemplo: Walk to school. Classes start at…

G The near future — Page 216

Use the **near future tense** to say what you are going to do. Use the present tense of *ir* + *a* + infinitive.

voy		
vas		
va		visitar
vamos	a	comer
vais		salir
van		

Módulo 2

4 leer Lee el mensaje del ejercicio 1 otra vez. ¿A qué preguntas contesta Víctor? Empareja las mitades de las preguntas.

1 ¿Cuándo vamos
2 ¿Qué
3 ¿Cómo
4 ¿A qué hora
5 ¿Qué ropa tenemos
6 ¿Dónde

vamos a hacer el miércoles?
empiezan y terminan las clases?
a llegar a Zaragoza?
que llevar?
vamos a comer?
vamos a ir al instituto?

G Asking questions

To form questions, follow the question word with the verb.

Vamos a llegar a las dos. — We are going to arrive at two.
¿Cuándo **vamos a llegar**? — When are we going to arrive?

Simply start 'Yes/No' questions with the verb.
¿**Llevas** uniforme? — Do you wear a uniform?

Remember to use an inverted question mark at the start, and a 'tilde' on each question word.

5 escuchar Escucha. Copia y completa la tabla en español. (1–3)

Castillo de Loarre

Zaragoza

chocolate con churros

	por la mañana	por la tarde
1 miércoles		
2 jueves		
3 viernes		

los/las demás — the others

voy a	llegar…	salir…
vas a	practicar…	ir a…
vamos a	ir (juntos/as) a…	comer…
vais a	pasar todo el día en…	
	hacer una visita guiada de…	
	ver los edificios…	
	ir de excursión el día entero	
	pasarlo bien	
va a	ser guay	

6 hablar Con tu compañero/a, improvisa un diálogo. Pregunta y contesta.

You and your Spanish exchange partner are talking about a day in your school. Your partner wants to know:

- when lessons start and finish
- what times break and lunch are
- where he/she is going to have lunch
- what he/she is going to wear in school
- how he/she is going to get to school
- what lessons he/she is going to have
- what he/she is going to see and do during his/her stay

7 escribir Escribe un correo a tu estudiante de intercambio. Describe los planes para su próxima visita.

Programación: Intercambio

Primer día: Día en Londres

Mañana
Excursión en barco a Westminster

Tarde
Visita al Palacio de Buckingham

Segundo día: Día en el colegio

Mañana
Asistir a clases

Tarde
Trabajos en grupo
Actividades deportivas

⭐ Vary your writing by including general details about your school routine as well as specific plans for the exchange. Use sequencers and time expressions to give structure:

Primero…, después…, por la mañana…, por la tarde…, después del cole…, a las once…

treinta y nueve 39

5 Mis clubs y mis éxitos

- Talking about activities and achievements
- Using object pronouns
- Saying how long you have been doing something

1 Lee los textos. Completa las frases en inglés.

Amelia
Asisto a mi instituto desde hace tres años y me encanta porque hay muchísimos clubs extraescolares. Voy al club de ajedrez todas las semanas. Juego desde hace cuatro años y se me da muy bien. Me encanta porque te ayuda a pensar estratégicamente. Participamos en torneos nacionales y el año pasado gané un trofeo en mi categoría.

Tomás
Toco la trompeta en el club de jazz de mi insti. Me mola la música Big Band porque te enseña a improvisar y es superdivertida. El verano pasado dimos un concierto para los padres y yo toqué un solo de trompeta. ¡Fue un éxito! Ahora voy a aprender a tocar el saxofón también.

Gael
Me chiflan las artes marciales y soy miembro del club de judo de mi instituto. Practico el judo desde hace nueve años. El trimestre pasado gané el cinturón marrón. ¡Qué guay! Tengo clases particulares para mejorar mi técnica porque quiero conseguir el cinturón negro.

solemos ganar — we usually win

1. In the summer jazz concert, Tomás ———.
2. Now he is going to ———.
3. Gael has been ——— for nine years.
4. He is having lessons to ———.
5. Amelia is very good at ———.
6. Last year, she ———.

G Desde hace

To say how long you've been doing something use **desde hace** and the present tense of the verb.

¿**Desde hace** cuánto tiempo tocas el piano?
How long have you been playing the piano?

Toco el piano **desde hace** seis años.
I have been playing the piano for six years.

2 Escucha y apunta los detalles en inglés. (1–3)

a Activity?
b How long?
c Opinion of the activity?
d Achievements?
e Opinion of clubs more generally?

Para mí / En mi opinión / Creo que… las actividades extraescolares…	
son	algo diferente / muy divertidas
te ayudan a	olvidar las presiones del colegio desarrollar tus talentos hacer nuevos amigos
te dan	una sensación de logro más confianza la oportunidad de ser creativo/a la oportunidad de expresarte

3 Con tu compañero/a, pregunta y contesta.

- ¿Desde hace cuánto tiempo asistes a este instituto?
- ¿Qué actividades extraescolares haces?
- ¿Desde hace cuánto tiempo (tocas / juegas al / haces)…?
- ¿Participaste en algún (concierto / concurso / torneo)?
- ¿Qué opinas de las actividades extraescolares?

40 cuarenta

Módulo 2

4 Escucha y lee. Copia y completa la tabla en inglés.

	past events	present	future plans
José		drama club	
Kiara			

Kiara: ¿Qué actividades extraescolares haces este año, José?
José: Este trimestre voy al club de teatro. **Lo hago** todos los lunes. En marzo fuimos a ver una obra de teatro y en dos meses **la vamos a montar**. Y tú, ¿qué haces?
Kiara: Pues soy miembro del club de periodismo y canto en el coro del colegio. En julio cantamos en un concurso nacional y **lo ganamos**.
José: ¡Qué guay! ¿Vas a seguir con los mismos clubs el próximo trimestre?
Kiara: Sí, por supuesto. **No los voy a dejar** porque me molan. ¿Y tú?
José: Sí, voy a continuar con el club de lectores. El trimestre pasado tuvimos una charla de un escritor que nos leyó una parte de su última novela. ¡Me inspiró mucho!
Kiara: A mí me mola leer novelas. En casa **las leo** todo el tiempo. Voy a ir al club contigo.
José: ¡Genial! También voy a apuntarme al club de Ecoescuela.
Kiara: ¡Qué bien! **Lo hice** el trimestre pasado cuando conseguimos la clasificación como escuela ecológica. ¡Tenemos muchos planes para mejorar el insti!

> ⭐ Time expressions can help you decide if people are talking about the past, present or future:
>
> **Past:** el año pasado, el trimestre pasado
> **Present:** ahora, este trimestre
> **Future:** el próximo trimestre, el año que viene
>
> The preterite tense is used to refer to past achievements and successes.
>
> Gané… I won…
> Participé… I took part…
> Toqué… I played…
> Di… I gave…

5 Lee el diálogo otra vez. Traduce las expresiones en **negrita** al inglés.

6 Traduce el texto al español.

> In my school there are lots of extracurricular activities. I love photography and I've been a member of the photography club for two years. I do it on Tuesdays at lunchtime. Sometimes we take part in exhibitions. Last term I won a prize with my best photo. Last year I did swimming too, but I am going to stop it because it is a bit dull.

- Where do you put the direct object pronoun? Which one do you need?
- Use *desde hace* here.
- Use a dictionary to look up any words you don't know.
- Will you use *lo* or *la* here?
- Use the preterite here.

G Direct object pronouns — Page 228

Direct object pronouns replace the **noun** which has just been mentioned and avoid repetition. The pronoun agrees with the noun it replaces:

	masculine	feminine
singular	lo	la
plural	los	las

It usually goes before the verb:

*Toco **el saxofón**. **Lo** toco.*
I play **the saxophone**. I play **it**.

*Participé en **una competición**. **La** gané.*
I took part in **a competition**. I won **it**.

With the near future tense, the direct object pronoun can go either at the end of the infinitive or before the present tense of *ir*:

*Voy a hacer**los**.* — I am going to do **them**.
***Los** voy a hacer.* — I am going to do **them**.

The pattern is the same for other verb + infinitive structures:

*Puedo hacer**lo**.* — I can do **it**.
***Lo** puedo hacer.* — I can do **it**.

7 Escribe un artículo sobre tus actividades extraescolares.

- ¿Qué actividades extraescolares haces? ¿Desde hace cuánto tiempo?
- ¿Qué opinas de las actividades extraescolares?
- ¿Participaste en algún evento especial como un concurso, torneo o concierto el trimestre pasado?
- ¿Qué actividades quieres hacer el trimestre / año que viene?
- ¿Vas a participar en algún evento en el futuro?

cuarenta y uno 41

Módulo 2 Leer y escuchar

1 leer Life at school

Read this extract from *Amor y pedagogía*, a novel by Miguel de Unamuno, and answer the questions which follow in **English**.

> Y vuelve Apolodoro de la escuela, y hoy le dice a su padre:
> —Papá, ya sé quién es el más inteligente de la escuela…
> —¿Y quién es?
> —Joaquín es el más inteligente de la escuela, el que sabe* más…
> —¿Y crees tú, Apolodoro, que la persona que sabe más es la persona más inteligente?
> —Claro que es la persona más inteligente…
> —Pero uno puede saber menos y ser más inteligente.
> —Entonces, ¿en qué se le conoce?
> Y el pobre padre, confundido por todo esto, dice: "¡Parece imposible que sea hijo mío! ¡Qué niño tan extraño!"
> —Vamos, Apolodoro escribe a tu tía.
>
> ** saber = to know*

1. When exactly does the conversation between Apolodoro and his father take place?
2. According to Apolodoro, who is Joaquín?
3. Apolodoro's father disagrees with Apolodoro. What does he say?
4. What does Apolodoro's father tell him to do?

2 leer A magazine article

You read this article on a Spanish website.

> ⭐ You won't always find exact equivalents or synonyms in the text. In question 2, for example, what evidence are you given to help you deduce the answers?

Clases de refuerzo

Estos centros ofrecen cursos intensivos de refuerzo escolar a aquellos alumnos que lo necesitan.

Clases y estudio dirigido en lugar de playa y piscina sin límite. Cada año durante los meses de verano, un millar de jóvenes españoles se enfrenta a la disciplina exigente de estos internados de verano.

Siete de la mañana: levantarse y desayuno. Ocho de la mañana: clases. Una del mediodía: almuerzo y descanso. Tres de la tarde: estudio. Seis y media de la tarde: deportes. Ocho y media de la tarde: cena… Este es un ejemplo del estricto horario que tienen los estudiantes.

El objetivo principal de estos programas intensivos es ayudar a repetir los exámenes con éxito en septiembre. ¿Y los resultados? En la mayoría de los casos, los resultados finales de sus alumnos son positivos. Pero queremos su opinión: ¿es justo que estos alumnos pasen *todo* el verano estudiando?

1. According to the article, when do the courses take place?
   Write the correct letter.
   A at weekends
   B in the holidays
   C all year round

2. According to the article, what is the daily routine like?
   Write the **two** correct letters.
   A flexible
   B challenging
   C variable
   D busy

Answer the questions in **English**.

3. According to the article, what is the main aim of these courses?
4. What issue is the writer trying to raise at the end of the article?

Módulo 2

3 leer — Extracto de un diario sobre las experiencias en el insituto

Completa el texto usando palabras de la lista. Escribe la letra correcta.

> Mi primer día
>
> Estaba un poco **1** ☐, pero mi profesora era muy paciente. Por la mañana hicimos una **2** ☐ guiada por todos los edificios. En mi horario tengo muchas asignaturas. Mañana voy a tener **3** ☐ con el señor Martínez. ¡Qué guay!

- **A** visita
- **B** estudios
- **C** tranquila
- **D** empresariales
- **E** nerviosa
- **F** recorrido
- **G** presentación

> ⭐ If you can, work out which type of word you need, i.e. verb, adjective, noun etc. The options usually have more than one of each word type, but only one that makes sense in the context.

1 escuchar — Opinions about school uniform

Listen to your Spanish friends, Aurelia y Pedro, talking about school uniform.

What is their opinion of these aspects?

Write **P** for a **positive** opinion.

Write **N** for a **negative** opinion.

Write **P+N** for a **positive** and **negative** opinion.

Aurelia
a achievement
b money

Pedro
a time
b identity

> ⭐ Beware of the occasional distractor in these questions! You are asked to identify **their** opinions so don't pay attention to the opinions of others. For **P+N** listen out for clues that signal a change of opinion, e.g. *por otro lado, sin embargo, pero*.

2 escuchar — Interview with a Spanish chess expert

You are listening to a podcast with the chess expert, Juan Molinero.

Answer all parts of the question in **English**.

- a Why is participation in chess set to increase amongst children in Spain?
- b According to the expert, what are the advantages of playing chess? Give **two** reasons.
- c What do the opponents of the initiative say? Give **two** details.
- d What is another problem with the initiative?

cuarenta y tres

Módulo 2   Prueba oral

A – Role play

1 *leer* Look at the role play card and prepare what you are going to say.

> Use language that you know well to give your reason. Remember that accuracy and correct pronunciation are important.

> The unprepared question is usually a two-part question.

> What question word might you need here?

> Your teacher will play the part of your Spanish friend and will speak first.
> You should address your friend as *tú*.
> When you see this – **!** – you will have to respond to something you have not prepared.
> When you see this – **?** – you will have to ask a question.
>
> Estás hablando con tu amigo español / tu amiga española sobre el instituto.
>
> - Opinión de tu instituto y **una** razón.
> - **!**
> - Instalaciones en tu instituto.
> - Actividad extraescolar el año pasado (**dos** detalles).
> - **?** Actividad en el recreo.

> Use the present tense and use language that you are confident with.

> Remember to use the preterite. Pay attention to the number of details required.

2 *hablar* Practise what you have prepared. Take care with pronunciation and intonation.

3 *escuchar* Using your notes, listen and respond to the teacher.

4 *escuchar* Now listen to Zoah doing the role play task. Note down what she says in Spanish.

B – Photo card

Look at the photo and make notes. Your teacher will then ask you questions about the photo and about topics related to **life at school/college**.

Your teacher will ask you the following **three** questions and then **two** more questions which you have not prepared.

- ¿Qué hay en la foto?
- ¿Te gusta tocar música en el instituto? … ¿Por qué (no)?
- ¿Qué excursiones escolares hiciste el año pasado?

1 *escuchar* Look at the photo and read the task. Then listen to Cameron's response to the first question on the task card.
   1 Why does he think they are in school?
   2 What is his impression of the drummer?
   3 What does he say about the mood of the pupils in the photo?
   4 Which **four** expressions does he use to introduce his impressions?

cuarenta y cuatro

Módulo 2

2 Listen to and read Cameron's response to the second question on the task card.

1. Write down the missing word for each gap.
2. Look at the Answer Booster on page 46. Note down **six** examples of language which Cameron uses to give a strong answer.

> Me encanta la música porque para mí, es la actividad más **1**_____ y más divertida. No toco **2**_____ instrumento, pero canto en el coro desde hace cinco años. Antes en mi escuela primaria **3**_____ un coro muy pequeño, pero **4**_____ en mi insti hay un coro muy grande y muy bueno. El año pasado **5**_____ en un concurso nacional y ganamos. ¡Fue guay! Lo que más me gusta es que te da la oportunidad de **6**_____ tus talentos y de hacer nuevos amigos.

⭐ If you prefer sport to music, say so! Then develop your answer in a similar way to this one, giving details of sporting clubs and activities you do and events and successes you have had.

This question also gives you the ideal opportuniy to use the object pronoun **te** (you). Remember that it usually goes in front of the verb:

Te da la oportunidad de desarrollar tus talentos.
It gives **you** the opportunity to develop your talents.

3 Listen to Cameron's response to the third question on the task card.

1. In **Spanish**, note down **six** verbs that he uses. Which different persons of the verb does he use?
2. How does Cameron say 'you learn a lot on a school trip because it makes the subject more real and relevant'? Transcribe the phrase he uses.

4 Prepare your own answers to the first **three** questions. Think about which other **two** questions you might be asked. Then listen and take part in the full photo card discussion with the teacher.

⭐ The photo card task always includes questions about things in the past and the future. To say what you **want** or **would like** to do in the future, you can use **quiero** or **me gustaría** + the **infinitive**.

Quiero ser miembro del club de baloncesto.
I want to be a member of the basketball club.
Me gustaría participar en el viaje de esquí.
I would like to take part in the ski trip.

C – General conversation

1 The teacher asks Joe '¿Cómo es tu instituto?' Listen to his answer and complete the sentences in **English**.

a. Joe has been going to this school…
b. He likes it because…
c. His primary school was… and had neither…
d. His dad gives him a lift in the car when…
e. The good thing about finishing at quarter to three is that…
f. Today Joe is going to…

2 The teacher then asks Joe '¿Qué asignaturas te gustan y no te gustan?' Look at the Answer Booster on page 46. Note down **six** examples of language which Joe uses to give a strong answer.

⭐ During the general conversation you must ask your teacher at least one question. What does Joe ask?

3 Listen to Joe's response to the next question '¿Qué opinas del uniforme escolar?' Note down in **English** the **three** negative and **three** positive aspects of school uniform that Joe mentions.

⭐ You can produce a more developed answer if you describe both positive and negative points of view. Use *por un lado… por otro lado…* to introduce opposing opinions.

4 Prepare your own answers to Module 2 questions 1–6 on page 198. Then practise with your partner.

cuarenta y cinco **45**

Módulo 2   Prueba escrita

Answer booster	Aiming for a solid answer	Aiming higher	Aiming for the top
Verbs	**Different time frames**: past (preterite or imperfect), present, near future	**Different persons** of the verb: *improvisamos, vamos a escribir* **Verbs with an infinitive**: *hay que, está prohibido*	**More than one tense to talk about the past** (preterite and imperfect) **Unusual verbs**: *parecer, desarrollar, enseñar, suspender*
Opinions and reasons	**Verbs of opinion**: *me interesa, me encanta, me fastidia, pienso que, creo que* **Reasons**: *porque*	**Exclamations**: *¡Qué va! ¡Qué horror!* **Comparatives**: *es más relevante que…*	**Opinions**: *lo que más me gusta es…, lo peor es, para mí* **Reasons**: *así que, ya que* **Comparatives/Superlatives**: *tan…como…, es la asignatura más exigente*
Connectives	*y, pero, también*	*además, sin embargo, no obstante*	**Linking past and present**: *antes…, pero ahora* **Balancing an argument**: *por un lado… por otro lado…, aunque*
Other features	**Qualifiers**: *muy, un poco, bastante* **Time phrases**: *el año que viene, el trimestre pasado*	**Desde hace**: *desde hace tres años* **Negatives**: *no… ni… ni…, tampoco, nunca, ningún/ninguna*	**Object pronouns**: *me/te/lo/la/los/las* **Interesting phrases**: *me permite expresarme, te da la oportunidad de…, recién renovado*

A – Short writing task

1 Look at the task and answer the questions.
- What **type** of text are you asked to write?
- What is each bullet point asking you to do?
- Which tense(s) will you need to use to answer each one?

2 Read Rebekah's answer on page 47. What do the phrases in **bold** mean?

3 Look at the Answer Booster. Note down **eight** examples of language which Rebekah uses to write a strong answer.

4 Look at the plan of Rebekah's answer. Write down the missing word for each gap.

5 Prepare your own answer to the task.
- Look at the Answer Booster and Rebekah's plan for ideas.
- Think about how you can develop your answer for each bullet point.
- Write a detailed plan. Organise your answer in paragraphs.
- Write your answer and carefully check what you have written.

Tu amigo español / Tu amiga española va a visitar tu instituto. Escríbele un correo electrónico.

Menciona:
- cómo es tu instituto
- cómo compara tu instituto con tu escuela primaria
- lo que piensas de las normas y por qué
- lo que vas a hacer con Maya en tu colegio durante su visita.

Escribe aproximadamente **90** palabras en **español**. Responde a todos los aspectos de la pregunta.

Paragraph 1
- What the **1** ———— are like
- The **2** ———— thing about it

Paragraph 2
- What the **3** ———— were like
- Why I **4** ———— my secondary school

Paragraph 3
- Opinion of some **5** ————
- Opinion of the rule on **6** ————
- What I'm going to **7** ———— next year

Paragraph 4
- The plan for the **8** ———— of Maya's visit
- The reason why my science teacher is the **9** ————
- What we will do in the **10** ————

Módulo 2

Hola Maya

Mi instituto es grande, mixto y público. Hay edificios modernos, pero también edificios antiguos y **recién renovados**, aunque no hay ni piscina ni pista de atletismo. Lo peor es que hay bastante **estrés por los exámenes**.

Antes, en mi escuela primaria, las clases eran más fáciles, los profesores eran menos estrictos y **el día escolar era más corto**. No obstante, ahora mi insti **nos ofrece más oportunidades** y lo prefiero.

En mi opinión, algunas normas son justas y necesarias. Sin embargo, está prohibido llevar piercings y creo que esta norma **limita mi libertad de expresión**. El año que viene voy a hacer el bachillerato y voy a llevar **ropa de calle** y muchos piercings. ¡Qué guay!

El miércoles durante tu visita vamos a ir **juntas a clase**. Lo que más me gusta de los miércoles es la clase de ciencias porque mi profe es el mejor. Enseña muy bien porque **relaciona los temas** de la clase **con noticias actuales**. Por la tarde vamos a ir al club de fotografía, donde vamos a sacar y a editar fotos.

¡Hasta pronto!
Rebekah

Rebekah y Maya

⭐ Remember, even when a bullet does not require it, you can improve your answer by including more than one tense. Can you spot an example of this in the third paragraph?

B – Translation

1 Read the English text and Grace's translation of it. Write down the missing word(s) for each gap.

My school is in the centre of the city and **1** ──── walk. It is important to pass the exams and get **2** ──── but the best thing about my school is the **3** ────. I've been learning Spanish for three years so last year I took part in the **4** ────. I had an amazing time! **5** ──── I want **6** ──── with Spanish.

Mi insti **7** ──── en el centro de la ciudad y puedo ir a pie. Es importante **8** ──── los exámenes y sacar buenas notas pero **9** ──── de mi insti son las excursiones. **10** ──── español desde hace tres años, así que el año pasado **11** ──── en el intercambio. ¡Lo pasé bomba! El año que viene **12** ──── continuar con el español.

⭐ Look out for phrases which don't translate word for word. For example, which tense do you need for 'I've been learning'?

2 Translate the following passage into Spanish.

Normally I cycle given that I live quite near to my school. Lessons start at quarter to nine so I leave home early. I like my school because the facilities are good, but the worst thing is the rules, which are too strict. I've been a member of the orchestra for two years and last summer we did a concert in the school hall. It was great!

cuarenta y siete **47**

Módulo 2   Palabras

¿Te interesa(n)…? — Are you interested in…?

el arte dramático	drama
el dibujo	art / drawing
el español	Spanish
el inglés	English
la biología	biology
la educación física	PE
la física	physics
la geografía	geography
la historia	history
la informática	ICT
la lengua	language
la química	chemistry
la religión	RE
la tecnología	technology
los idiomas	languages
las empresariales	business studies
las matemáticas	maths
las ciencias	science
la materia / la asignatura	subject
me encanta(n) / me chifla(n)	I love
me interesa(n) / me fascina(n)	I'm interested in / fascinated by
me gusta(n) / no me gusta(n)	I like / I don't like
odio	I hate
prefiero	I prefer
porque es / son	because it is / they are
Mi día preferido es (el viernes).	My favourite day is (Friday).
mi horario	my timetable
¿Qué día tienes…?	What day do you have…?
Tengo inglés los martes.	I have English on Tuesdays.
¿A qué hora tienes…?	What time do you have…?
a la una / a las dos	at one o'clock / at two o'clock
y / menos cuarto	quarter past / to
y / menos cinco	five past / to
y media	half past
la educación infantil / primaria	pre-school / primary education
la educación secundaria	secondary education
el bachillerato	A levels
la formación profesional	vocational training
el instituto	secondary school

¿Qué tal los estudios? — How are your studies?

La física es más / menos … que…	Physics is more / less … than…
Es mejor / peor que…	It's better / worse than…
tan … como	as … as
fácil / difícil	easy / difficult
divertido/a / aburrido/a	fun / boring
útil / relevante / práctico/a	useful / relevant / practical
creativo/a / relajante	creative / relaxing
exacto/a / lógico/a / exigente	precise / logical / demanding
Mi profesor(a) (de ciencias) es…	My (science) teacher is…
paciente / impaciente	patient / impatient
tolerante / severo/a	tolerant / harsh
listo/a / tonto/a	clever / stupid
trabajador(a) / perezoso/a	hard-working / lazy
simpático/a / estricto/a	nice / strict
Mi profe…	My teacher…
enseña / explica bien	teaches / explains well
tiene buen sentido del humor	has a good sense of humour
tiene expectativas altas	has high expectations
crea un buen ambiente de trabajo	creates a good working atmosphere
nunca se enfada	never gets angry
me hace pensar	makes me think
nos da consejos / estrategias	gives us advice / strategies
nos pone muchos deberes	gives us lots of homework
el curso académico	academic year
las pruebas / las evaluaciones	tests / assessments
suspender / aprobar	to fail / to pass

¿Cómo es tu insti? — What is your school like?

En mi instituto hay… / Mi instituto tiene…	In my school there is… / My school has…
un salón de actos	a hall
un comedor	a canteen
un campo de fútbol	a football pitch
un patio	a playground
un gimnasio	a gym
una piscina	a pool
una biblioteca	a library
una pista de tenis / atletismo	a tennis court / an athletics track
unos laboratorios	some laboratories
muchas aulas	lots of classrooms
Lo bueno / malo es que…	The good / bad thing is that…
Lo mejor / peor es que…	The best / worst thing is that…
Lo que más me gusta es / son …	What I like most is / are…
Lo que menos me gusta es / son …	What I like least is / are…
no…ningún / ninguna	not a single…
ni…ni…	(n)either…(n)or
nada	nothing / anything
nadie	no-one / anyone
tampoco	not either
Mi insti es…	My school is…
mixto / femenino / masculino	mixed / all girls / all boys
público / privado	state / private
pequeño / grande	small / large
moderno / antiguo	modern / old
En mi escuela primaria había… Mi escuela primaria tenía…	In my primary school there was/were… My primary school had…
más / menos…	more / fewer, less
exámenes / deberes / alumnos	exams / homework / pupils
muebles / espacios verdes	furniture / green spaces
tiempo libre	free time
oportunidades / instalaciones	opportunities / facilities
pizarras interactivas / clases	interactive whiteboards / lessons
aulas de informática	ICT rooms
donde jugar	somewhere to play
poco espacio	little space
antes / ahora	before / now
El edificio / El colegio / El día escolar es / era…	The building / The school / The school day is / was…
(in)adecuado/a / corto/a / largo/a	(in)adequate / short / long
Las clases son / eran…	The lessons are / were…
Instituto de Educación Secundaria (IES)	secondary school

Las normas del insti — School rules

Tengo que llevar …	I have to wear …
Tenemos que llevar …	We have to wear …
(No) Llevo …	I (don't) wear …
(No) Llevamos …	We (don't) wear …
Es obligatorio llevar	It's compulsory to wear
un jersey (de punto)	a (knitted) sweater
un vestido	a dress
una camisa	a shirt
una camiseta	a T-shirt
una chaqueta (a rayas)	a (striped) jacket
una chaqueta de punto	a cardigan
una corbata	a tie
una falda (a cuadros)	a (checked) skirt
unos pantalones	trousers
unos calcetines	socks
unos zapatos	shoes
unos vaqueros	jeans
unas medias	tights

cuarenta y ocho

amarillo/a	yellow	llevar piercings	to have piercings
blanco/a	white	Hay que…	It is necessary…
negro/a	black	ser puntual	to be on time
rojo/a	red	respetar el turno de palabra	to wait for your turn to speak
morado/a / violeta	purple	mantener limpio el patio	to keep the playground clean
naranja	orange	La norma más importante es…	The most important rule is…
rosa	pink	respetar a los demás	to respect others
azul	blue	Las normas son…	The rules are…
verde	green	necesarias / demasiado severas	necessary / too strict
gris	grey	para fomentar la buena disciplina	for promoting good discipline
marrón	brown	para limitar la libertad de expresión	for limiting freedom of expression
oscuro / claro	dark / light	para fastidiar a los alumnos	for annoying the pupils
a rayas / a cuadros	striped / checked	sacar buenas / malas notas	to get good / bad grades
bonito / feo	pretty / ugly	Estoy de acuerdo.	I agree
cómodo / incómodo	comfortable / uncomfortable	¡Qué va!	No way!
anticuado / elegante / formal	old-fashioned / smart / formal	¡Qué horror!	How awful!
El uniforme…	Uniform…	¡Qué bien!	How great!
mejora la disciplina	improves discipline	Un problema de mi insti es…	One problem in my school is…
limita la individualidad	limits individuality	el estrés de los exámenes	exam stress
da una imagen positiva del insti	gives a positive image of the school	el acoso escolar	bullying
ahorra tiempo por la mañana	saves time in the morning	las presión del grupo	peer pressure
Está prohibido…	It is forbidden…	Hay (unos) alumnos que…	There are (some) pupils who…
No se permite…	You are not allowed…	se burlan de otros	make fun of others
No se debe…	You / one must not…	sufren intimidación	are victims of intimidation
comer chicle	to chew chewing gum	tienen miedo de…	are afraid of…
usar el móvil en clase	to use your phone in lessons	hacen novillos	skive
dañar las instalaciones	to damage the facilities	quieren ser parte de la pandilla	want to be part of the friendship group
ser agresivo o grosero	to be agressive or rude	son una mala influencia	are a bad influence
correr en los pasillos	to run in the corridors		

¿Cómo es tu día escolar?	***What is your school day like?***	Las clases empiezan / terminan a las…	*Lessons start / finish at …*
normalmente	*usually*	Tenemos … clases al día.	*We have … lessons per day.*
Salgo de casa a las…	*I leave home at…*	Cada clase dura … minutos	*Each lessons lasts … minutes.*
Voy…	*I go…*	El recreo / La hora de comer… es a la(s)…	*Break / Lunch is at…*
a pie / andando	*on foot / walking*		
en bici / en autobús / en coche	*by bike / by bus / by car*		
en metro / en taxi / en tren	*by underground / by taxi / by train*		

¿Qué vas a hacer?	***What are you going to do?***	pasar todo el día en…	*spend the whole day in…*
Voy / Vas / Vamos a…	*I'm going / You're going / We're going to…*	asistir a clases	*attend lessons*
llegar / salir / estar	*arrive / go out / be*	practicar el español	*practise Spanish*
ir en coche / andando	*go by car / walk*	ir de excursión	*go on a trip*
llevar ropa de calle	*wear casual clothes / non-uniform*	tener una programación variada	*have a varied programme*
ir / comer juntos	*go / eat together*	Va a…	*It's going to…*
hacer una visita guiada	*do a guided tour*	ser fácil / guay	*be easy / cool*
ver los edificios	*see the buildings*		

Las actividades extraescolares	***Extra-curricular activities***	El año / trimestre / verano pasado…	*Last year / term / summer…*
Toco la trompeta…	*I play / I've been playing the trumpet…*	participé en un evento especial / un concierto / un concurso / un torneo	*I took part in a special event / a concert / a competition / a tournament*
Canto en el coro…	*I sing / I've been singing in the choir…*	gané un trofeo	*I won a trophy*
Voy al club de…	*I go / I've been going to the … club*	toqué un solo	*I played a solo*
Soy miembro del club de…	*I am / I've been a member of the … club*	conseguimos la clasificación como…	*we achieved the award / designation as…*
ajedrez / judo / teatro / periodismo	*chess / judo / drama / reporters*	tuvimos una charla	*we had a talk / presentation*
lectores / Ecoescuela / fotografía	*reading / eco-schools / photography*	ganamos una competición nacional	*we won a national competition*
desde hace … años / meses	*for … years / months*	dimos un concierto	*we gave a concert*
Para mí…	*For me…*	¡Fue un éxito!	*It was a success!*
Pienso que / Creo que…	*I think that…*	Este trimestre / El próximo trimestre…	*This term / Next term*
las actividades extraescolares son…	*extra-curricular activities are*	voy a	*I'm going to…*
muy divertidas	*a lot of fun*	aprender a …	*learn to …*
algo diferente / un éxito	*something different / an achievement*	continuar con…	*continue with…*
te ayudan a…	*they help you to…*	dejarlo	*stop doing it*
olvidar las presiones del colegio	*forget the pressures of school*	apuntarme al club de…	*sign up for the … club*
desarrollar tus talentos	*develop your talents*	vamos a…	*we are going to…*
hacer nuevos amigos	*make new friends*	montar una obra de teatro	*put on a play*
te dan…	*they give you…*	conseguir…	*achieve…*
una sensación de logro	*a sense of achievement*		
más confianza	*more confidence*		
la oportunidad de ser creativo/a	*the opportunity to be creative*		
la oportunidad de expresarte	*the opportunity to express yourself*		

3 Mi gente
Punto de partida 1

- Talking about socialising and family
- Using verbs in the present tense

1 Escucha. Identifica las <u>dos</u> actividades y la persona del verbo. (1–6)

Ejemplo: **1** *I play on phone, I read texts.*

hablar por Skype
sacar fotos
mandar mensajes
chatear con mis amigos
descargar canciones y aplicaciones
jugar con mi móvil
ver vídeos o películas
leer mis SMS
compartir mis vídeos favoritos

2 Traduce las frases al español.

1. I talk via Skype with my friends.
2. Do you (singular) take photos with your phone?
3. They chat with their friends.
4. We download songs and apps.
5. He watches his favourite videos.
6. She plays on her phone.
7. We read our texts.
8. Do you (plural) share your photos?

G Possessive adjectives

Most possessive adjectives have two forms, singular and plural.

	singular	plural
my	m**i**	mi**s**
your (singular)	t**u**	tu**s**
his/her/its	s**u**	su**s**
our	nuestr**o**/nuestr**a**	nuestr**os**/nuestr**as**
your (plural)	vuestr**o**/vuestr**a**	vuestr**os**/vuestr**as**
their	s**u**	su**s**

Nuestro (our) and *vuestro* (your – plural) also have masculine and feminine forms:
nuestr**os** hermanos — our brothers
nuestr**as** hermanas — our sisters

For *usted* (you – polite, singular) and *ustedes* (you – polite, plural) use *su/sus* to mean 'your'.

3 ¿Qué significan los adjetivos? ¿Cómo se pronuncian?

- animado
- popular
- útil
- práctico
- necesario
- rápido
- peligroso
- fácil
- cómodo

> Words ending in –*n*, –*s* or a vowel are stressed on the penultimate syllable, whereas words ending in any other consonant are stressed on the final syllable. Any exceptions have a tilde (or accent) to indicate the stress. E.g. dif**í**cil, canci**ó**n.

4 Escucha y comprueba.

Módulo 3

5 Escucha y escribe la forma correcta de **querer** o **poder**. Luego tradúcelas al inglés. (1–7)

Ejemplo: **1** podemos = we can

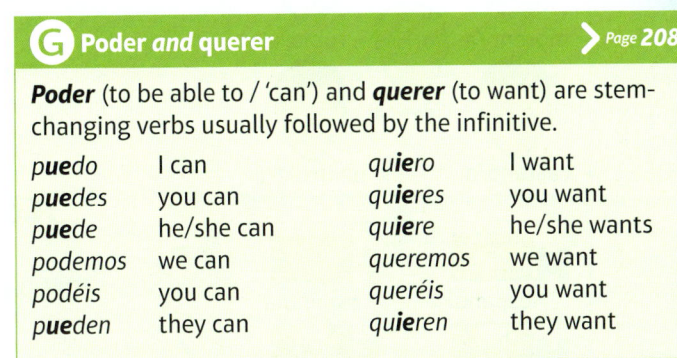

> When identifying the person of the verb, remember that the last letter(s) usually give(s) you a clue.

6 Completa las frases con la forma correcta del presente de **poder** o **querer**. Traduce las frases al inglés.

1. ¿(**querer**) ir de compras con nosotros? (you singular)
2. No (**poder**) ir a la bolera porque tengo que estudiar. (I)
3. ¿Miguel no viene? No, no (**poder**) venir al partido hoy. (he)
4. ¿(**querer**) ir al centro con nosotros? (you plural)
5. ¡Sí, (**poder**) ir! ¡Qué guay! (we)
6. Señor Gómez, ¿(**querer**) usted tomar algo en la cafetería? (you, polite singular)

G Poder and querer > Page 208

Poder (to be able to / 'can') and **querer** (to want) are stem-changing verbs usually followed by the infinitive.

puedo	I can	quiero	I want
puedes	you can	quieres	you want
puede	he/she can	quiere	he/she wants
podemos	we can	queremos	we want
podéis	you can	queréis	you want
pueden	they can	quieren	they want

7 Completa las frases en español con las palabras del recuadro. Usa un diccionario si es necesario. Sobran <u>cuatro</u> opciones. ¿Qué significan?

1. El marido de tu abuela es tu _____.
2. El hermano de tu padre es tu _____.
3. La mujer de tu padre es tu _____.
4. La hija de tus tíos es tu _____.
5. El hijo de tus padres es tu _____.
6. La abuela de tu padre es tu _____.
7. La hermana de tu padre es tu _____.
8. El hijo de tu hermano es tu _____.

hermanastra · hermano · abuelo · bisabuela · marido · tío

hija · madre · sobrino · prima · padrastro · tía

8 Escribe las palabras en español.

1. niece
2. stepbrother / half-brother
3. wife
4. male cousin
5. great-grandfather
6. son

> Adapt the family members from exercise 7 to do exercise 8.
>
> E.g. If *sobrino* = nephew, what is niece?
>
> If *padrastro* = stepfather, what is stepbrother / half-brother?

cincuenta y uno

Punto de partida 2

- Describing people
- Using adjectival agreement

1 Escucha y escribe la letra correcta. (1–6)

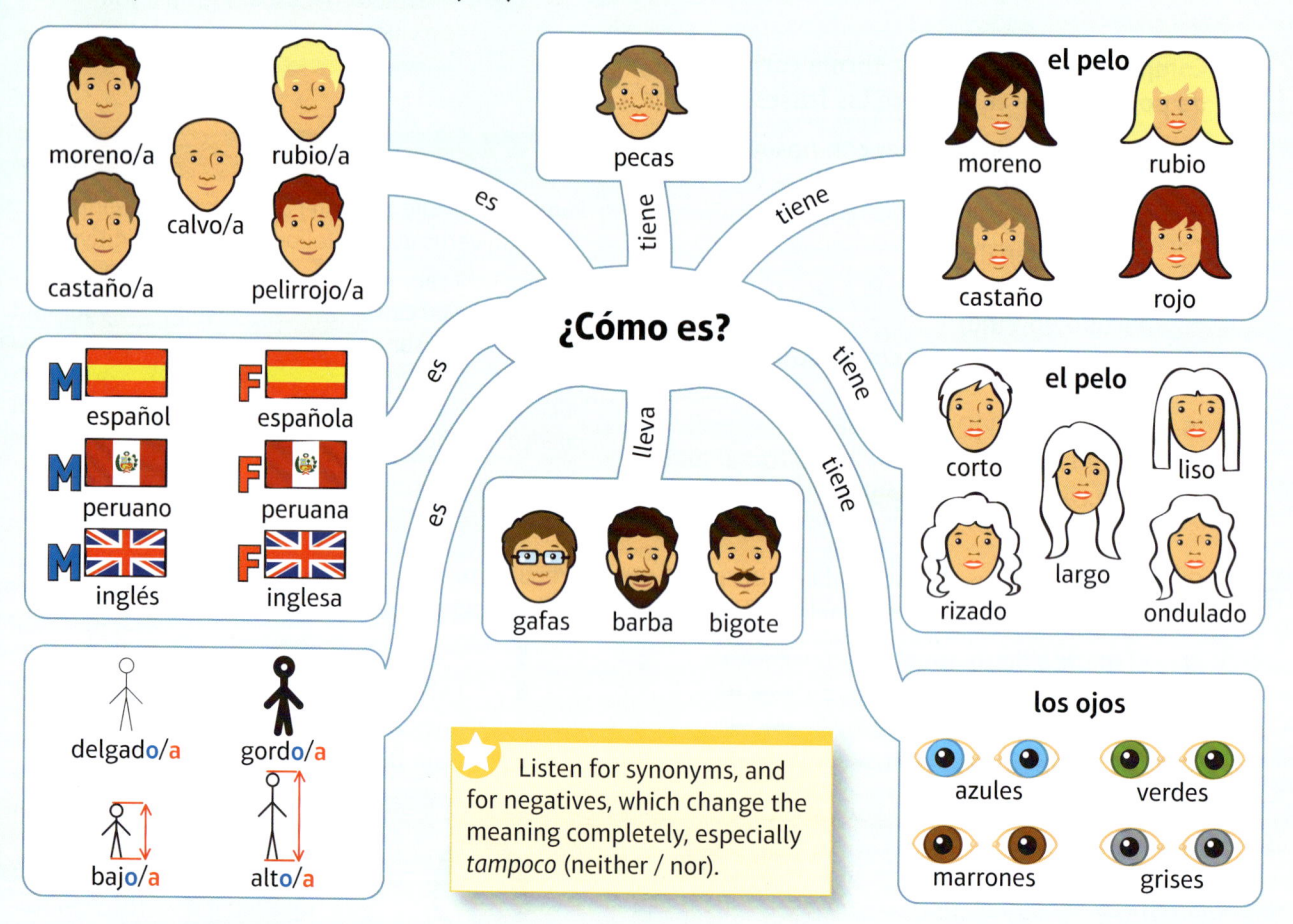

moreno/a   rubio/a
calvo/a
castaño/a   pelirrojo/a

pecas

el pelo
moreno   rubio
castaño   rojo

¿Cómo es?

M español   F española
M peruano   F peruana
M inglés   F inglesa

gafas   barba   bigote

el pelo
corto   liso
rizado   largo   ondulado

delgado/a   gordo/a
bajo/a   alto/a

⭐ Listen for synonyms, and for negatives, which change the meaning completely, especially *tampoco* (neither / nor).

los ojos
azules   verdes
marrones   grises

1 La madre de Lola…
   a) es colombiana.
   b) tiene el pelo castaño.
   c) no es gorda.

2 Su padre…
   a) es bajo.
   b) es delgado.
   c) no tiene pelo.

3 Su hermano menor…
   a) tiene 15 años.
   b) lleva barba.
   c) es más bajo que Lola.

4 Su hermana mayor…
   a) tiene una hija.
   b) tiene el pelo rubio.
   c) tiene los ojos azules.

5 Su abuela…
   a) es peruana.
   b) lleva ropa verde.
   c) tiene 97 años.

6 Lola…
   a) tiene pecas.
   b) tiene el pelo largo.
   c) lleva gafas.

2 Traduce el texto al inglés.

Jesse & Joy es un dúo mexicano de pop latino. Son hermanos. Su padre es mexicano y su madre es estadounidense. Joy es bastante baja y delgada. Tiene el pelo castaño, largo y ondulado, y los ojos marrones. No lleva gafas. En el grupo toca la guitarra y canta. Jesse es más alto que su hermana y tiene los ojos marrones y bigote. Tiene menos pelo que Joy y a veces lleva un sombrero.

Módulo 3

3 hablar — Describe a un(a) cantante de pop. Tu compañero/a adivina la identidad. Usa el texto del ejercicio 2 como modelo.

> ⭐ Use comparatives to give more precision to your description.
> más… que… more… than…
> menos… que… less… than…
> tan… como… as… as…

4 leer — Completa las frases con los adjetivos antónimos. Sobran <u>cuatro</u> adjetivos.

simpático
~~optimista~~
bueno
trabajador
generoso
hablador
divertido
inteligente
fiel

1 Soy bastante pesimista, pero mi hermano es siempre <u>optimista</u>.
2 Mi profesora de español es ———, pero mi profe de historia es muy serio.
3 Un buen amigo es ———; nunca es infiel.
4 Mi perro es muy travieso, pero a veces también puede ser ———.
5 Normalmente mi padre es ———, pero los fines de semana es un poco perezoso.

G Adjectival endings ▶ Page 224

Adjectives in Spanish usually come after the noun and 'agree' with the noun they describe.

You have seen the –o/a, e and consonant endings already. Adjectives ending in –or/ora and –ista follow a slightly different pattern.

adjective ending	masculine singular	feminine singular	masculine plural	feminine plural
–o/a	seri**o**	seri**a**	seri**os**	seri**as**
–e	inteligent**e**	inteligent**e**	inteligent**es**	inteligent**es**
consonant	fiel	fiel	fiel**es**	fiel**es**
–or/ora	hablad**or**	hablad**ora**	hablad**ores**	hablad**oras**
–ista	optim**ista**	optim**ista**	optim**istas**	optim**istas**

5 hablar — Describe tu carácter y el carácter de un(a) amigo/a. ¿Tu compañero/a está de acuerdo?

● ¿Cómo eres? Y tu amigo (David), ¿cómo es?
■ Pienso que soy <u>bastante alto</u>, y tengo… (David) es…
● ¿Cómo eres de carácter?
■ Creo que soy <u>muy hablador</u>. (David) es…

Sí, es verdad.
Sí, estoy de acuerdo.
No, no estoy de acuerdo.
¡Qué va!

6 leer — Lee los textos y contesta a las preguntas.

Who has…
1 an Argentinian aunt?
2 Spanish parents?
3 nephews?

Who is…
4 smaller than one of her parents?
5 taller than her sister?
6 more impatient than her sibling?

Mi madre tiene siete hermanos. ¡Todos tienen niños! Mi hermana y su marido viven en Berlín con sus tres hijos. Lola, mi hermana, es más pequeña que yo, y mucho más paciente y tranquila. **Luna**

De momento vivo con mi tía porque estudio en Buenos Aires. Ella es argentina y trabaja como médica. No es nunca perezosa. Mis padres son de Valencia y viven allí con mi hermano menor. **Isaac**

Mi padrastro es de Argentina y es ambicioso y trabajador. Es más alto que yo. No tenemos mucho en común, pero es más simpático y comprensivo que mi madre. **Alba**

Unidad 3

cincuenta y tres **53**

1 Mis aplicaciones favoritas

- Talking about social networks
- Using **para** with infinitives
- Extending responses by referring to others

1 Escucha y escribe la letra correcta. ¡Ojo! Sobran tres frases. (1–6)
Ejemplo: **1** d

¿Qué aplicaciones usas?

a buscar y descargar música
b controlar mi actividad física
c pasar el tiempo
d compartir fotos
e contactar con mi familia
f conocer a gente nueva
g subir y ver vídeos
h organizar las salidas con mis amigos
i chatear y mandar mensajes

1 Uso Instagram para…
2 Uso WhatsApp para…
3 Uso Skype para…
4 Uso Spotify para…
5 Uso YouTube para …
6 Uso Facebook para…

2 Escucha otra vez.
Escribe **dos** razones para cada aplicación. (1–6)

Es / No es…		
barato/a	popular	necesario/a
divertido/a	útil	rápido/a
práctico/a	gratis	cómodo/a
fácil de usar	peligroso/a	amplio/a

G Para + infinitive

Use **para** to mean 'in order to…' or 'for –ing'. It is followed by the infinitive.

Uso Moves **para controlar** mi actividad física.
I use Moves **in order to record** my physical activity.

Es una aplicación muy buena **para descargar** música.
It is a very good app **for downloading** music.

3 Con tu compañero/a, haz diálogos.

- ¿Qué aplicación usas para <u>compartir fotos</u>?
- Uso <u>Instagram</u>.
- ¿Por qué te gusta?
- Me gusta porque es <u>fácil de usar</u>.

⭐ Extend your responses by referring to others, using different parts of the verb.

E.g. *Mis amigos y yo* **usamos** *WhatsApp para chatear, pero mi madre* **usa** *Twitter.*

Remember to change the pronoun to say what others like:
E.g. *A mi madre* **le** *gusta Twitter porque es práctica y rápida.*

54 cincuenta y cuatro

4 Escucha y lee. Contesta a las preguntas en inglés.

Las redes sociales – lo bueno y lo malo

La red social que más me gusta es WhatsApp. Lo bueno es que todos mis amigos la usan, así que es el canal de comunicación más importante en mi vida. Además, uso Netflix para ver mis series favoritas desde mi móvil. La tengo desde hace seis meses y es muy práctica para pasar el rato en el autobús o en casa. Lo único malo es que te engancha.

Mi hermana Jessica está completamente enganchada. Es un problema porque no puede estar sin su móvil – ¡lo utiliza para todo! Le chiflan las fotos y usa varias apps para editar. Personaliza las fotos con efectos y filtros y luego las sube a Instagram.

Mi padre tiene que viajar a menudo a otros países y por eso mis padres usan Skype para estar en contacto. En cada país mi padre usa Duolingo. Dice que es la mejor app para mejorar sus idiomas. Antes mi madre no tenía un Smartphone, pero ahora lo usa para todo. Usa una app para controlar las calorías. ¡Yo pienso que es una pérdida de tiempo!

Alejandro

pasar el rato	to pass the time	no puede estar sin	(she) can't be without
te engancha	it gets you hooked	una pérdida de tiempo	a waste of time

1. Why is WhatsApp Alejandro's most important means of communication?
2. Why does he think Netflix is so handy?
3. What does Alejandro say about Jessica's relationship with her phone? Give two details.
4. What does Jessica do with her photos? Give two details.
5. What does Alejandro's dad use Duolingo for?
6. What does Alejandro's mum use her phone for, in particular?

5 Lee el texto del ejercicio 4 otra vez. Copia y completa la tabla con frases del texto.

frases positivas	frases negativas
es el canal de comunicación más importante en mi vida	lo único malo es que te engancha

6 Traduce las frases al español. Usa el texto del ejercicio 4 como modelo.

1. I am hooked on my mobile. I use it for everything.
2. Twitter is my favourite social network. I have been using it for six months.
3. My friends use Duolingo to improve their Spanish.
4. Before I didn't have Instagram, but now I use it every day.
5. My parents use Facebook to keep in touch with their friends.
6. My friend Gabriela uses lots of apps to personalise her phone.

7 *Nuestras aplicaciones favoritas de la A a la Z.* En grupos de 4 a 6 personas, prepara un post. Incluye la información siguiente:

- ¿Para qué usas la aplicación?
- ¿Desde hace cuánto tiempo la tienes?
- ¿Por qué te gusta?
- ¿Tiene algún inconveniente?

> ⭐ Improve the flow of your writing. Use direct object pronouns (it/them) to refer to things you have already mentioned. Look back at exercise 4. What do the pronouns refer to?

cincuenta y cinco **55**

2 ¿Qué estás haciendo?

- *Making arrangements*
- *Using the present continuous tense*
- *Improvising dialogues*

1 Lee y busca las expresiones en los mensajes.
Ejemplo: **1** *estoy esperando*

Sara Moya Cortés
¡Holaaaaaaaaaaaa a todoooosss! ¿Qué estáis haciendo ahora mismo?

Carlos Santos Bedoya
Estoy escuchando música, estoy tomando el sol en el balcón y estoy esperando a David, que está en la ducha.

Elena Fernández
Rebecca y yo estamos viendo una peli en casa. Mi madre está preparando algo para merendar.

James Baker
¡Hola Sara! Estoy leyendo porque Mateo está repasando para un examen de matemáticas. Y sé que Bea y Tom están haciendo footing. ¿Y los demás? ¿Qué estáis haciendo?

Alfonso Peresín Rojas
Nada especial. Estoy haciendo el vago porque Phil está durmiendo ¡desde hace dos horas ya! 😊😊

Gabriela Reyes Telmo
Yo estoy escribiendo aquí en Facebook para responderte. ¡Ja ja ja! Y tú, Sara, ¿qué estás haciendo?

Sara Moya Cortés
¿Yo? Estoy pensando en salir para dar una vuelta por la Plaza Mayor. ¿Queréis venir conmigo?

la Plaza Mayor, Salamanca

hacer el vago — to laze around

1. I am waiting
2. He is revising
3. They are jogging
4. We are watching a film
5. She is preparing something for tea
6. What are you doing?

2 Escucha. Apunta los detalles en inglés. (1–4)
- Where are they in Salamanca?
- What are they doing?

charlar — to chat / talk

⭐ When listening or reading you may encounter different forms of familiar verbs. E.g. You know *comer* (to eat) but hear *comiendo*. What does this mean?

3 Improvisa una conversación con tu compañero/a.
● ¿Qué está haciendo *Carlos*?
■ Pues, está…

Rebecca y Elena   James
Mateo   Bea y Tom
Phil   Gabriela

G The present continuous tense › Page 218

Use the **present continuous tense** to say what you are doing at the moment. Take the present tense of the verb *estar* and the **present participle** ('–ing' form) of the action verb.

	estar (to be)	present participle
(yo)	estoy	
(tú)	estás	mir**ando**
(él/ella/usted)	está	beb**iendo**
(nosotros/as)	estamos	escrib**iendo**
(vosotros/as)	estáis	
(ellos/ellas/ustedes)	están	

To form the present participle, take the infinitive, remove the *–ar*, *–er* or *–ir* and add the endings *–ando*, *–iendo*, *–iendo*.
Estoy buscando canciones. — **I am looking** for songs.
No **estamos haciendo** nada. — **We are not doing** anything.
Irregular present participles include: *leer* → *leyendo*, *dormir* → *durmiendo*

56 *cincuenta y seis*

Módulo 3

¿Quieres salir conmigo?

4 Escucha. Copia y completa la tabla en inglés. (1–4)

	activity	excuses
1		

No puedo porque…		
tengo que quiero	salir… terminar… subir… visitar a…	cuidar a… hacer… quedarme en casa… hacer el vago
está lloviendo		
estoy estamos	actualizando… viendo…	editando… descansando

5 Lee la conversación. Rellena los espacios en blanco con el verbo correcto.

Lucas: Hola, Ana. ¿Qué estás **1**_____?
Ana: No mucho. Estoy **2**_____ una serie.
Lucas: ¿**3**_____ salir conmigo? Podemos **4**_____ una vuelta por la ciudad.
Ana: Ahora no **5**_____ porque **6**_____ que visitar a mi tía.
Lucas: ¡Qué rollo! Pues, ¿más tarde, entonces?
Ana: ¡Claro que sí! ¿A qué hora quedamos?
Lucas: A las seis.
Ana: Vale. ¿Dónde **7**_____?
Lucas: En la Plaza Mayor, debajo del reloj. ¡Qué bien! Hasta las seis.

el reloj clock

quedamos
puedo
viendo
tengo
quieres
haciendo
dar

6 Escucha y comprueba tus respuestas.

la Puente Nuevo, Salamanca

Zona Cultura

Salamanca está en la parte central de España, a 212 kilómetros al oeste de Madrid. Su Plaza Mayor es el punto de encuentro más popular. La gente pasa mucho tiempo allí charlando, paseando, tomando el sol o disfrutando de un helado en una de las cafeterías. Es ideal por la tarde, pero es aún más bonita por la noche, cuando la iluminación es impresionante.

7 Organiza un encuentro en la Plaza Mayor de Salamanca con tu estudiante de intercambio. Utiliza el ejercicio 5 como modelo.

- Hola Víctor. ¿Qué estás haciendo?
- No mucho. Estoy escuchando música. ¿Por qué?
- ¿Quieres salir? Podemos…

detrás de	behind
delante de	in front of
debajo de	underneath
enfrente de	opposite
al lado de	next to
en (el/la)	in (the)

cincuenta y siete **57**

3 Leer es un placer

- Talking about reading preferences
- Using a range of connectives
- Recognising similar ideas expressed differently

1 Escucha. Apunta las <u>dos</u> letras correctas para cada persona. (1–5)
Ejemplo: **1** *a, c*

¿Qué te gusta leer?

a los blogs
b los tebeos / los cómics 
c los periódicos 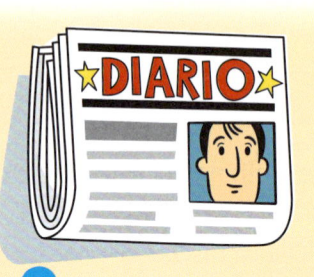
d las revistas 
e las poesías 
f las novelas de ciencia ficción 
g las novelas de amor 
h las historias de vampiros 
i las biografías 

2 Escucha otra vez. Apunta la expresión de frecuencia que se menciona. (1–5)
Ejemplo: **1** *una vez a la semana*

¿Con qué frecuencia lees?
cada día / todos los días
a menudo
generalmente
de vez en cuando
una vez a la semana
dos veces al mes
una vez al año
nunca

3 Habla con tu compañero/a.

- ¿Qué te gusta leer?
- Me gusta leer <u>revistas</u> y <u>biografías</u>.
- ¿Con qué frecuencia lees?
- Leo revistas <u>muy a menudo</u> y biografías <u>de vez en cuando</u>.
  En este momento (no) estoy leyendo…
- ¿Qué no te gusta leer? ¿Por qué no?
- No me gusta leer <u>novelas</u> porque son <u>aburridas</u>.

4 Lee los textos y apunta la información en inglés.

- Who:
- What he/she likes reading:
- How often:
- Preferred format:
- Reason:

Mi tía Salomé es el mayor ratón de biblioteca de mi familia. Lee cada noche y le interesan mucho las biografías y las novelas históricas. Prefiere leer libros en papel porque le gusta pasar las páginas a mano y escribir anotaciones.

A mi primo Rafael le encantan los cómics y es un fan del manga. Lee a través de una aplicación en su móvil, lo cual prefiere porque es más práctico. Lee a veces por la mañana cuando está esperando el autobús.

58 cincuenta y ocho

Módulo 3

5 Lee las opiniones sobre leer en formato digital. Busca <u>tres</u> ventajas y <u>tres</u> desventajas.

Ejemplo: Ventajas: 1, …, …,
Desventajas: …, …, …

Leer en formato digital…

1. protege el planeta, ya que no malgasta papel.
2. cansa la vista más que leer libros en papel.
3. depende de la energía eléctrica.
4. te permite llevar contigo miles de libros.
5. cuesta mucho menos que leer en formato tradicional.
6. fastidia porque no hay numeración de páginas.

| fastidiar | to annoy / be annoying |

6 Escucha y comprueba tus respuestas.

7 Lee el blog. Busca las opiniones en **negrita** que significan lo mismo que las frases del ejercicio 5.

Ejemplo: **1** *los libros digitales son más ecológicos*

E-book o libro en papel, ¿cuál es mejor?

¡Hola, ratones de biblioteca! El tema de hoy es: e-book o libro en papel, ¿cuál es mejor?

Primero, yo personalmente prefiero leer en papel, porque me gusta tocar las páginas. Además, **no leo más que una página en formato digital y ya tengo los ojos cansados**, mientras que con un libro de verdad puedo leer horas y horas.

Sin embargo, sé que leer libros electrónicos tiene muchas ventajas. Una ventaja es que **son mucho más fáciles de transportar**, ya que no ocupan espacio. También **los libros digitales son más ecológicos**. Mis amigos fanáticos de lo digital dicen que **son mucho más baratos que los libros tradicionales**.

Por otro lado, **una desventaja de los ebooks es el uso de batería**. Si se te acaba la batería, tienes que recargarla. Otra desventaja es que así **no se pueden numerar las páginas,** y por lo tanto no es muy práctico.

En resumen, pienso que leer es algo muy personal. Si puedo escoger, prefiero en papel, pero también puedo leer perfectamente en ebook. Y vosotros, ¿qué pensáis?

| recargar | to recharge |

8 Escribe un blog sobre las ventajas y desventajas de **los libros en papel**.

⭐ Adapt language from exercise 7 and use a range of connectives to structure your arguments clearly:
- Introduction: *primero*
- Addition: *además, también*
- Opposition: *sin embargo, por otro lado, mientras que*
- Justification: *porque, ya que*
- Consequence: *por lo tanto, así que*
- Conclusion: *en resumen*

Zona Cultura

'El que lee mucho y anda mucho, ve mucho y sabe mucho.' Miguel de Cervantes

Miguel de Cervantes Saavedra (1547–1616) fue un soldado y autor español. Es el autor de la novela más famosa de la literatura española, **Don Quijote de la Mancha**. Es el libro más editado y traducido de la historia, solo superado por la Biblia.

cincuenta y nueve 59

4 Retratos

- Describing people
- Using ser and estar
- Understanding more detailed descriptions

1 Lee el texto. Apunta los detalles en inglés.

- Name:
- Age:
- From:
- Physical description:
- Character:
- Position:
- Place:
- Activity:
- Emotion:

Ésta es Mafalda. Es una niña de ocho años de Buenos Aires, Argentina. Es morena y baja, con el pelo negro y los ojos marrones. Como persona, es simpática, pensativa y pesimista. En la imagen está sentada en el jardín, con los ojos cerrados. Está escuchando música y sonriendo. Está feliz.

Zona Cultura

Mafalda es un personaje de una tira argentina que se publicó de 1964 a 1973. Su creador fue el humorista gráfico Quino. Mafalda es una niña que está preocupada por la humanidad y la paz mundial, y a menudo está desilusionada por la realidad. Es un cómic muy popular en Latinoamérica, así como en muchos países europeos. Ha sido traducido a más de 30 idiomas.

la tira — comic strip

G Ser and estar > Page 210

Ser is used for:
- **D**escription: **Soy** alto y bastante delgado.
- **O**rigin: ¿**Eres** de Colombia?
- **C**haracter: **Es** muy honesto.
- **T**ime: **Son** las cinco de la tarde.
- **O**ccupation: **Somos** mecánicos.
- **R**elation: ¿**Sois** mis primos, no?

Estar is used for:
- **P**osition: **Estoy** de pie.
- **L**ocation: ¿**Estás** en Madrid?
- **A**ction: **Está** estudiando.
- **C**ondition: **Estamos** cansados. ¿**Estáis** bien?
- **E**motion: **Están** contentos.

2 Escucha y escribe la letra correcta. (1–3) Sobran dos personajes (y Mafalda).

a Miguelito
b Manolito
c Felipe
d Susanita
e Guille

el racimo de plátanos — bunch of bananas

3 Escucha otra vez. ¿Cómo son de carácter? Apunta tres detalles en inglés para cada personaje.

Ejemplo: **1** ambitious, …, …

For exercises 2 and 3, you will hear adjectives you have seen already as well as some new, more descriptive, language for character and appearance:

Es — alegre / ambicioso / cómico / dinámico / egoísta / explosivo / histérico / idealista / modesto / molesto / pensativo / romántico / sincero / tímido / travieso

Tiene — los ojos grandes / pequeños / brillantes
el pelo de punta / ondulado
la cara redonda / alargada
los dientes prominentes / la piel blanca

En la imagen…
Está — de pie / sentado / al lado izquierdo / derecho de…
sonriendo / hablando / mirando
feliz / contento / triste

4 Mira la imagen del ejercicio 2. Describe a los dos personajes que quedan. Usa también los adjetivos de carácter.

- Se llama… Es… En la imagen está…

sesenta

Módulo 3

5 Lee el texto. Busca las expresiones en español.

Mi hermana y yo, ¡qué diferentes somos!

Mientras que yo soy baja y mido 1,60, mi hermana es bastante alta, ya que mide 1,80. No nos parecemos físicamente, pues yo tengo el pelo negro como el carbón y ella es rubia como el sol. Ella tiene los ojos grandes y redondos, mientras que mis ojos son tan pequeños como dos botones.

Por otra parte, yo soy una persona muy enérgica porque no puedo estar sentada y siempre estoy haciendo algo. No obstante, mi hermana es tan tranquila como el agua de un pozo, y no se impacienta nunca con nadie.

Por último, ella es una persona muy ordenada, así que siempre sabe dónde está todo. En cambio, yo paso horas y horas buscando mis cosas porque soy una persona muy caótica.

Sandra y Lorena

el pozo — well

1. I am 1.60 m tall
2. we are not physically alike
3. I can't be sitting / sit still
4. she never gets impatient with anyone
5. she always knows where everything is
6. I spend hours and hours looking for my things

6 Busca ejemplos con **ser** y **estar** en el ejercicio 5. Explica la razón de su uso.

Ejemplo: yo soy baja – ser – description

7 Lee el texto del ejercicio 5 otra vez. Completa los símiles en inglés.

1. My hair is as black as ———.
2. She is as blonde as ———.
3. My eyes are as small as ———.
4. She is as calm as ———.

8 Escucha. Completa la tabla en español. (1–2)

	persona	descripción física	carácter	comparaciones / símiles
1	abuela	pelo – fino, blanco, …	alegre, …	piel blanca como el papel, …

la piel — skin

⭐ Listen out for negatives. They often change the meaning completely. Sometimes the negative is in two parts, sometimes not.

No se pelea **nunca**. — He/She doesn't **ever** argue.
Nunca se pelea. — He/She **never** argues.
No es **ni** gordo **ni** delgado. — He is **neither** fat **nor** thin.
Tampoco tiene pecas. — **Nor** does he/she have freckles.

9 Escribe una descripción de una persona, real o imaginaria. Incluye:

- adjetivos físicos
- adjetivos de carácter
- comparaciones
- símiles

No es ni alto ni bajo. Es moreno con los ojos…
Como persona, es optimista y alegre.
No es tan inteligente como Einstein, pero…
Es tan enérgico como una pila Duracell.

⭐ Including similes adds a literary dimension to description.

Use a photo or drawing if you have one. Add specific details about the person's location, position and mood, and what he/she is doing.

sesenta y uno **61**

5 Relaciones

- Talking about friends and family
- Using a range of relationship verbs
- Referring to the present and past

1 Escucha y lee los textos. ¿Qué significan las expresiones en **violeta** en inglés?

¿Te llevas bien con tu familia y tus amigos?

1 **Me llevo muy bien con** mi madre porque es paciente y simpática. **Me apoya** en todos los momentos difíciles.

2 **Me peleo con** mi hermana a menudo porque es tonta y egoísta.

3 **No me llevo bien con** mis padres porque son muy estrictos. ¡**Me dan demasiados consejos**!

4 **Me divierto con** mi padre porque **tenemos mucho en común**. Siempre es optimista y **nunca me critica**.

5 Mi amigo y yo **nos llevamos superbién** porque es muy divertido y **me hace reír**.

6 Mi amiga y yo **nos divertimos** siempre porque es muy graciosa. Además, **es fiel** y **me acepta como soy**.

2 Lee los textos del ejercicio 1 otra vez. Busca las frases en español.

1 She supports me in hard times.
2 They give me too much advice!
3 We have a lot in common.
4 He never criticises me.
5 He makes me laugh.
6 She is loyal.
7 She accepts me as I am.

3 Con tu compañero/a, haz diálogos.

● ¿Te llevas bien con <u>tu madre</u>?
■ Sí, me llevo bien con <u>mi madre</u> porque es <u>generosa</u> y <u>siempre me apoya</u>. Y tú, ¿te llevas bien con <u>tus padres</u>?

⭐ Increase the interest of your speaking by using a wide variety of adjectives. Can you find all ten in exercise 1?

Remember to use adverbs to add detail: *siempre, a veces, de vez en cuando, nunca…*

G Reflexive verbs for relationships ▶ Page 211

Some verbs for describing relationships are reflexive in Spanish.

llevarse (to get on)

(yo)	me llevo	
(tú)	te llevas	
(él/ella/usted)	se lleva	bien con…
(nosotros/as)	nos llevamos	mal con…
(vosotros/as)	os lleváis	
(ellos/ellas/ustedes)	se llevan	

Me llevo bastante **bien** con mis padres.
I get on quite well with my parents.

Verbs like this include: **pelearse** (to argue) and **divertirse** (to have fun).

Other verbs use reflexive pronouns to mean 'each other'.

conocerse →
Nos conocemos desde hace cinco años.
We have known each other for five years.

apoyarse →
Se apoyan en todo.
They support each other in everything.

🇪🇸 Zona Cultura

'Deben buscarse los amigos como los buenos libros: pocos, buenos y bien conocidos.'

Mateo Alemán (1547–1615), novelista español

Módulo 3

4 Escucha y completa la tabla en inglés. (1–4)

	where they met	what a good friend is like (2 details)
1	at badminton club	

¿Cómo es un buen amigo / una buena amiga?
Un buen amigo / Una buena amiga es alguien que…

te apoya / te ayuda te escucha
te conoce bien te hace reír
te acepta como eres no te critica
te da consejos nunca te juzga

5 Lee los textos. Contesta a las preguntas para cada texto en español.

¿Cómo conociste a tu mejor amigo/a?

Santi y John

Pues, yo conocí a mi amigo John hace cuatro años en Málaga, cuando él estaba de vacaciones. Nos conocimos en la playa, jugando al fútbol. Como tenemos el deporte en común, nos llevamos muy bien. Es muy alto y bastante delgado. Es moreno con los ojos marrones y el pelo corto y rizado. Es una gran persona, siempre animado y optimista. Aunque vive en Inglaterra, estamos en contacto por MSN. Para mí, un buen amigo es alguien que te conoce bien y nunca te juzga.

Tom y Kiara

Mi mejor amiga es Kiara, mi mujer. La conocí en el colegio, cuando tenía 10 años. Nos hicimos amigos un día en clase. A los 15 años nos hicimos novios. Convivimos después de la universidad y luego nos casamos. Kiara es baja y rubia, con los ojos verdes. Como persona, es creativa, tolerante y enérgica. Nos llevamos superbién. Bueno, a veces nos llevamos como el perro y el gato porque tenemos opiniones distintas, pero ella es el amor de mi vida. Nos encantan las películas, y por lo tanto vamos cada semana juntos al cine. Para mí, un buen amigo es alguien que te quiere mucho y te ayuda en todo.

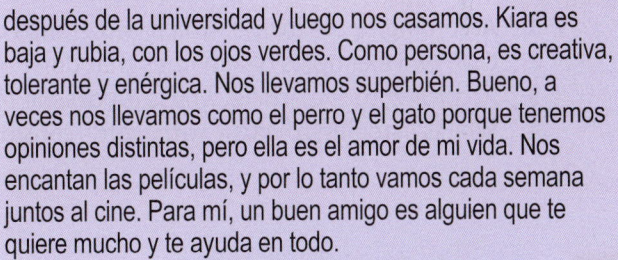

convivir to live together
casarse to get married

1 ¿Cuándo conoció a su mejor amigo/ su mejor amiga?
2 ¿Dónde lo/la conoció?
3 ¿Qué tienen en común?
4 ¿Cómo se llevan?
5 ¿Cómo es su carácter?
6 En su opinión, ¿cómo es un buen amigo/una buena amiga?

G The personal 'a'

When the object of the verb is a specific, known person, use the personal 'a'.
Conocí **a** mi mejor amigo Félix. I met my best friend Félix.

Do not use it when the person is not someone you can picture.
Busco **a** mi amigo. I'm looking for **my** friend.
Busco un amigo. I'm looking for **a** friend.

6 Escribe un texto de 80–90 palabras. Incluye:

- what a good friend does
- how you met a good / your best friend
- what he/she looks like
- what he/she is like as a person
- why you get on well
- what you have in common / do together

Para mí, un buen amigo es alguien que…
Conocí a mi (mejor) amigo/a…
Es bastante alto/a. Tiene el pelo…
Como persona, es divertido/a y fiel.
Nos llevamos bien porque…
Nos gusta… / Tenemos… en común y por eso…

⭐ Remember to use the **preterite tense** for completed actions in the past.
Use the **imperfect tense** for describing in the past.

sesenta y tres

Módulo 3 Leer y escuchar

1 Multi-tasking

You often do your homework whilst listening to music, and you read this article about multi-tasking. Answer the questions in **English**.

¡La multitarea no existe!

Parece que los adolescentes pueden hacer multitarea, y dicen que las mujeres lo hacen: hablamos por el móvil, enviamos un correo y leemos una carta, todo al mismo tiempo..., pero existe un problema: la multitarea no existe.

La multitarea implica participar en dos tareas al mismo tiempo, y eso solo es posible si se cumplen dos condiciones:

1) al menos una de las tareas es automática y no requiere atención para hacerla (por ejemplo, caminar o comer) y,

2) las dos tareas necesitan diferentes tipos de procesamiento cerebral*. Por ejemplo, podemos leer mientras escuchamos música clásica, porque el cerebro* procesa la música y el texto en dos partes diferentes.

Sin embargo, no ocurre lo mismo cuando leemos y escuchamos música *con letra* porque las dos tareas requieren la activación de la misma parte del cerebro.

* *procesamiento cerebral* = mental processing
* *el cerebro* = brain

1 According to the article, which **two** groups of people seem to multi-task?
2 Give **two** examples of activities that don't require conscious attention.
3 According to the article, why is it possible to read and listen to classical music at the same time?
4 Why is listening to music with words considered to be different?

2 Meeting a neighbour

Lee este extracto de *El príncipe de la niebla* de Carlos Ruiz Zafón.
Contesta a las preguntas en **español**.

—¿Qué tal la casa? ¿Os gusta?— preguntó Roland.
—Hay opiniones divididas. A mi padre le encanta. El resto de la familia lo ve diferente— explicó Max.
—Conocí a tu padre hace unos meses, cuando vino al pueblo— dijo Roland—. Me pareció un tipo divertido.
Max asintió.
—Es un tipo divertido— corroboró Max—, a veces.
—¿Por qué habéis venido al pueblo?— preguntó Roland.
—La guerra— contestó Max—. Mi padre piensa que no es un buen momento para vivir en la ciudad. Supongo que tiene razón.

Ejemplo ¿Qué opina el padre de Max sobre la nueva casa? *Le encanta*

1 ¿Cuándo conoció Roland al padre de Max?
2 ¿Cómo describe Max a su padre?
3 ¿Por qué Max y su familia viven ahora en el pueblo?

> Read the questions first to determine the information you need. You do not have to write whole sentences, and should be able to 'lift' the language directly from the text.

Módulo 3

3 leer — Translation into English

Your mother has received this text from her former penfriend in Spain. Her Spanish is rusty and she asks you to translate the text message into **English**.

> Vivo con mis dos hijos en Valencia. Mi hijo va al instituto y saca muy buenas notas. Mi hija está estudiando idiomas en la universidad porque le gustaría trabajar en el extranjero. Mi marido y yo nos separamos hace dos años y no voy a casarme de nuevo. Estoy muy feliz ahora.

1 escuchar — An interview with Manolo Ibáñez, director of a company that produces eReaders

You are listening on the Internet to this interview with Manolo.
What questions does the interviewer ask him?
Answer in **English**. (1–4)

Example When did the new eReader arrive on the market?

2 escuchar — A radio programme about social media

On the Internet you listen to a Spanish radio correspondent reporting on social media. In the first part of his report he focuses on Gabriela and her teacher. He then summarises views about the advantages and dangers of social media.

Write the correct letter.

1 The correspondent says that Gabriela…
   A believes she has a problem.
   B is addicted to her phone.
   C wants to change her lifestyle.

2 She also says that Gabriela's teacher is worried that Gabriela…
   A will fail her exams.
   B is not able to concentrate.
   C does not do her homework.

Write the two correct letters.

3 According to the correspondent, what are said to be **two** advantages of social media?
   A You can chat to friends and family very cheaply.
   B Social media enable family members who live far apart to keep in touch.
   C Your world goes with you wherever you go.
   D Young people are better informed about events in their local area.
   E World news is shared quickly and easily via your mobile.

4 According to the correspondent, what are **two** possible dangers?
   A People become addicted to social media.
   B People only share good news.
   C People become less physically active when using social media.
   D People don't do anything useful on social media.
   E Virtual friendship is not real friendship.

Gabriela

⭐ Multiple choice questions often contain distractors. Don't jump to conclusions, as you will probably hear several of the options mentioned. Be aware that you often won't hear the same words used as in the question, either.

sesenta y cinco 65

Módulo 3   Prueba oral

A – Role play

1 Look at the role play card and prepare what you are going to say.

> Your teacher will play the part of your Spanish friend and will speak first.
>
> You should address your friend as *tú*.
>
> When you see this – **!** – you will have to respond to something you have not prepared.
>
> When you see this – **?** – you will have to ask a question.
>
> Estás hablando con tu amigo español / tu amiga española sobre la tecnología móvil y los amigos.
>
> - Cómo usas tu móvil y **una** razón.
> - Las redes sociales – **una** ventaja.
> - **!**
> - La última vez que saliste con tus amigos (**dos** detalles).
> - **?** Leer.

Use the present tense. Remember that accuracy and correct pronunciation are important.

There are lots of ways to introduce advantages: 'The good thing about…', 'An advantage of…', '…are good because…'.

Remember to use the preterite. Pay attention to the number of details required.

There are several possibilities here: 'What do you..?' 'Do you like..?' 'How often do you…?'

Remember there may be two parts to this question.

2 Practise what you have prepared. Then, using your notes, listen and respond to the teacher.

3 Now listen to Zac doing the role play task. Note down:
1. what he uses his phone for
2. the advantage of social media that he gives
3. how he answers the unprepared question(s)
4. what question he asks.

B – Photo card

Look at the photo and make notes. Your teacher will then ask you questions about the photo and about topics related to **me, my family and friends**.

Your teacher will ask you the following **three** questions and then **two** more questions which you have not prepared.

- ¿Qué hay en la foto?
- En tu opinión, ¿el matrimonio es importante? … ¿Por qué (no)?
- ¿Qué hiciste la última vez que celebraste algo con tu familia?

1 Look at the photo and read the task. Then listen to Anya's response to the first question on the task card.
1. Why does it seem like a special occasion?
2. Why does she think it is a wedding?
3. What makes her think the people in the photo are happy?
4. Can you note down the **Spanish** for the following phrases: well-dressed; champagne; wedding; white dress; wedding cake?

Módulo 3

2 Listen to and read Anya's response to the second question on the task card.
1. Write down the missing word for each gap.
2. Note down the **Spanish** for the expressions below.

> En mi opinión, **1** ——— es importante porque representa un compromiso para **2** ——— con tu pareja. Quiero casarme un día porque me importa la estabilidad. Creo que todo el mundo quiere **3** ——— su pareja ideal. Esta persona te comprende, te quiere y **4** ——— en todos los momentos difíciles. Sin embargo, hay una diferencia entre el matrimonio y una boda. Para mí, **5** ——— son solo un día de fiesta con tu familia y tus amigos, y cuestan demasiado. Por eso no voy a tener una boda grande.

- a commitment
- your partner
- cost too much
- stability matters to me
- loves you
- a big wedding
- I want to get married

> ⭐ Questions like this give you the chance to explain your opinions fully. Give more sophisticated answers by justifying and qualifying your opinions, using a range of phrases such as *porque*, *sin embargo*, *para mí* and *por eso*.

3 Listen to and read Anya's response to the third question on the task card.
1. Note down **five** differences.
2. Look at the Answer Booster on page 68. Note down **six** examples of language which Anya uses to give a strong answer.

> La última vez que celebré algo con mi familia fue el Día del Padre. Mis padres, mi hermano y yo fuimos en tren a Londres para ir a un concierto. Es el tipo de actividad que más le gusta a mi padre porque le chifla la música clásica, pero a mí no me interesa nada, así que fue un poco monótono. Sin embargo, después fuimos a cenar en un restaurante mexicano, donde cenamos faijtas y tacos. ¡Qué rico!

4 Prepare your own answers to the first **three** questions. Think about which other **two** questions you might be asked. Then listen and take part in the full photo card discussion with the teacher.

C – General conversation

1 The teacher asks Jennifer '*Describe a un buen amigo tuyo o una buena amiga tuya.*' Listen to her answer and rewrite the **five** incorrect statements below.

a Ana y Jennifer se conocen desde hace siete años.
b Se llevan superbién, pero no tienen mucho en común.
c Ana y Jennifer se parecen físicamente.
d A Ana y a Jennifer les gusta llevar ropa de diferentes estilos.
e Ana es una buena amiga, pero a veces no le dice la verdad a Jennifer.

2 The teacher then asks Jennifer '*¿Quiénes son más importantes, tus amigos o tus padres?*' Note down **six** examples of how Jennifer justifies and qualifies her opinions.

3 Listen to Jennifer's response to the next question '*¿Crees que los jóvenes están obsesionados con sus móviles?*'
1. Look at the Answer Booster on page 68. Note down **six** examples of language which Jennifer uses to give a strong answer.
2. Note down **three** examples of how Jennifer uses different persons of the verb.

> ⭐ What does Jennifer ask her teacher at the end of her answer to the third question?

4 Prepare your own answers to Module 3 questions 1–6 on page 198. Then practise with your partner.

Módulo 3   Prueba escrita

Answer booster	Aiming for a solid answer	Aiming higher	Aiming for the top
Verbs	**Different time frames**: past, present, near future	**Different persons** of the verb **Verbs with an infinitive**: poder, querer, tener que	**Unusual verbs**: apoyar, escoger, conocerse, llevarse, divertirse **Mixed tenses**: present tense and present continuous
Opinions and reasons	**Verbs of opinion**: me interesa, me chifla, me fastidia, pienso que **Reasons**: porque **Adjectives**: simpático, monótono	**Comparatives**: es más paciente que, es más barato que… **Exclamations**: ¡Qué pesado! ¡Qué rico!	**Opinions**: creo que, lo que más/menos me gusta… **Reasons**: por lo tanto, así que, por eso **Comparatives/Superlatives**: no es tan… como…, la persona más importante…
Connectives	y, pero, también	además, sin embargo, aparte de eso	**Balancing an argument**: una ventaja…, otra ventaja…, una desventaja…, aunque, mientras que
Other features	**Qualifiers**: muy, un poco, bastante **Sequencers**: primero, después **Other time phrases**: la última vez que…, a menudo, siempre	**Sentences with cuando, donde, si**: fuimos a…, donde… **Desde hace** **Negatives**: nunca, no… ni… ni… **Para + infinitive**: para ir a un concierto	**Object pronouns**: me/te/lo/la/los/las **Interesting phrases**: aprovechar, hacer el vago

A – Extended writing task

1 *leer* **Look at the task and answer the questions.**
- What information does each bullet point ask you to give?
- How could you develop your answer to each one?

2 *leer* **Read Martyn's answer on page 69. What do the phrases in bold mean?**

3 *leer* **Look at the Answer Booster. Note down eight examples of language which Martyn uses to write a strong answer.**

4 *leer* **Look at the plan of Martyn's answer. Correct the eight mistakes.**

5 *escribir* **Prepare your own answer to the task.**
- Look at the Answer Booster and Martyn's plan for ideas.
- Write a detailed plan. Organise your answer in paragraphs.
- Write your answer and carefully check what you have written.

Lees un blog sobre las desventajas de las tecnologías móviles y de las redes sociales para los jóvenes. Escribe una respuesta.

Menciona:
- cómo usas las tecnologías móviles todos los días
- algo que hiciste recientemente que confirma los beneficios educativos de las redes sociales.

Escribe aproximadamente **150** palabras en **español**. Responde a los dos aspectos de la pregunta.

Paragraph 1
- Uses his mobile for searching for and downloading music
- Useful when waiting in school

Paragraph 2
- Not really for passing time and communication
- Last week used for sharing photos for a school project
- found an explanation on YouTube

Paragraph 3
- Brings the world into the home
- Allows you to personalise learning
- Next week going to make a film

⭐ When planning and organising your answer, focus on the **two** compulsory bullets. In this answer you need to write about how you use mobile technologies in your daily life, and the educational benefits of social media, including a recent example. It may be useful to sub-divide your ideas for each bullet further, as in Martyn's answer.

sesenta y ocho

Módulo 3

Me mola la tecnología y soy un fanático de mi móvil, sobre todo porque **me ayuda a organizar** y a descargar música. Lo uso todos los días para escuchar música, y es muy práctico cuando **estoy haciendo el vago en casa** o esperando el autobús por la mañana. **Nunca me aburro** si tengo música. Además, lo uso para mandar mensajes a mis amigos y a mi familia.

Además, las redes sociales no son solo útiles para **pasar los ratos libres**, ni para contactar con la familia y los amigos. La semana pasada usé Facebook para buscar y compartir información con mis amigos para un proyecto de historia, así que también **sirven para** ayudarte con los deberes. Después encontré una canción en YouTube que usé para memorizar verbos en el pretérito. Siempre **puedes aprovechar los minutos libres** para aprender algo.

No es posible **imaginarse la vida** en el insti sin las tecnologías móviles. La tecnología **lleva el mundo al aula**, y permite personalizar **el aprendizaje**. La semana que viene vamos a crear nuestra propia página web. ¡Viva la tecnología!

Martyn

B – Translation

1 leer Read the English text and Emily's translation of it. Correct the **five** mistakes in the Spanish translation.

> My mum works in Germany, so we talk via Skype during the week. We get on really well because she is fun and she always supports me. My best friend is from Spain. I met her when we did an exchange. I want to visit her in the holidays, but I can't go now because I have to study for my exams.

> Mi madre trabaja en Austria, así que hablamos por Skype durante el fin de semana. Nos llevamos bastante bien porque es divertida y siempre me ayuda. Mi mejor amiga es de España. La conocí cuando hicimos un examen. Quiero visitarla en las vacaciones, pero no puedo ir ahora porque tengo que estudiar para mis exámenes.

⭐ Translations will always include high-frequency language that is not specific to any one topic. For example, time expressions such as 'during the week', 'in the holidays' and 'now'. Make sure you keep a list of this language and revisit it often.

2 escribir Translate the following passage into Spanish.

> My sister, Tia, and I are quite different. She is talkative and can be annoying, but I get on well with her because we love technology. We are always looking for new apps for editing photos or sending messages. Last year I made an app and won a competition. This year Tia is going to take part in the competition too.

⭐ Always check your Spanish adjectives carefully, as they change their form to match gender and number. Think about how you will spell the Spanish words for 'different', 'talkative' and 'new'.

sesenta y nueve **69**

Módulo 3 Palabras

¿Qué aplicaciones usas?	What apps do you use?		
Uso … para…	I use … (in order) to…	una red social	a social network
ver mis series favoritas	watch my favourite series	amplio/a	extensive
organizar las salidas con mis amigos	organise to go out with my friends	cómodo/a	convenient
controlar mi actividad física /	monitor my physical activity / my	divertido/a	fun
las calorías	calorie intake	necesario/a	necessary
contactar con mi familia	get in touch with my family	peligroso/a	dangerous
chatear con mis amigos	chat with my friends	práctico/a	practical
La tengo desde hace … meses.	I've had it for … months	rápido/a	quick
Es una aplicación buena para…	It's a good app for…	fácil de usar	easy to use
buscar y descargar música	looking for and downloading music	popular	popular
pasar el tiempo / el rato	passing the time	útil	useful
sacar / editar / personalizar fotos	taking / editing / personalising photos	gratis	free
compartir / subir fotos	sharing / uploading photos	un canal de comunicación	a channel / means of communication
estar en contacto	keeping in touch	una pérdida de tiempo	a waste of time
conocer a nueva gente	meeting new people	Soy / Es adicto/a a…	I am / He/She is addicted to…
subir y ver vídeos	uploading and watching videos	Estoy / Está enganchado/a a a…	I am / He/She is hooked on…
chatear y mandar mensajes	chatting and sending messages	Lo único malo es que…	The only bad thing is that …
Es / No es…	It is / It isn't…	te engancha	it gets you hooked

¿Qué estás haciendo?	What are you doing?		
Estoy…	I am…	está lloviendo	it's raining
actualizando mi página de Facebook	updating my Facebook page	tengo que…	I have to…
editando mis fotos	editing my photos	salir	go out
Estás / Está / Están…	You are / He/She is / They are…	visitar a (mi abuela)	visit (my grandmother)
escuchando música	listening to music	cuidar a (mi hermano)	look after (my brother)
esperando a (David)	waiting for (David)	hacer los deberes	do homework
descansando	relaxing	quiero…	I want to…
pensando en salir	thinking about going out	subir mis fotos a…	upload my photos to…
preparando algo para merendar	preparing something for tea	quedarme en casa	stay at home
repasando para un examen	revising for an exam	¡Qué rollo!	What a pain!
tomando el sol	sunbathing	¿A qué hora quedamos?	What time shall we meet?
haciendo footing	jogging	¿Dónde quedamos?	Where shall we meet?
haciendo el vago	lazing about	en la Plaza Mayor	in the main square
leyendo	reading	debajo de	underneath
viendo una peli	watching a film	detrás de	behind
escribiendo	writing	delante de	in front of
¿Quieres salir conmigo?	Do you want to go out with me?	enfrente de	opposite
No puedo porque…	I can't because…	al lado de	next to

¿Qué te gusta leer?	What do you like reading?		
los blogs	blogs	las novelas de ciencia ficción	science fiction novels
los tebeos / los cómics	comics	las novelas de amor	romantic novels
los periódicos	newspapers	las historias de vampiros	vampire stories
las revistas	magazines	las biografías	biographies
las poesías	poems		

¿Con qué frecuencia lees?	How often do you read?		
cada día / todos los días	every day	una vez a la semana	once a week
a menudo	often	dos veces al mes	twice a month
generalmente	generally	una vez al año	once a year
de vez en cuando	from time to time	nunca	never

¿Qué es mejor, leer en papel o en la red?	What is better, reading paper books or online?		
Leer en formato digital…	Reading in digital format…	no ocupan espacio	don't take up space
protege el planeta	protects the planet	Una desventaja es…	One disadvantage is…
no malgasta papel	doesn't waste paper	el uso de batería	the battery use
cansa la vista	tires your eyes	Me gusta / prefiero…	I like / I prefer…
depende de la energía eléctrica	relies on electricity	tocar las páginas	to touch the pages
te permite llevar contigo miles	allows you to take thousands of books	pasar las páginas a mano	to turn the pages by hand
de libros	with you	escribir anotaciones	to write notes
cuesta mucho menos	costs a lot less	leer horas y horas	to read for hours and hours
fastidia porque no hay	is annoying because there is no	un ratón de biblioteca	a bookworm
numeración de páginas	page numbering	un fan del manga	a manga fan
Los libros electrónicos / Los e-books…	Electronic books / E-books…	un libro tradicional	a traditional book
son fáciles de transportar	are easy to transport	un libro de verdad	a real book
son más ecológicos / baratos	are more environmentally-friendly / cheaper		

Módulo 3

La familia / Family

el padre / la madre	father / mother
el padrastro / la madrastra	step-father / step-mother
el hermano / la hermana	brother / sister
el hermanastro / la hermanastra	step-brother / step-sister
el abuelo / la abuela	grandfather / grandmother
el bisabuelo / la bisabuela	great grandfather / great grandmother
el tío / la tía	uncle / aunt
el primo / la prima	male cousin / female cousin
el sobrino / la sobrina	nephew / niece
el marido / la mujer	husband / wife
el hijo / la hija	son / daughter
el nieto / la nieta	grandson / granddaughter
mayor / menor	older / younger

¿Cómo es? / What is he/she like?

Tiene los ojos… / He/She has … eyes
- azules / verdes / marrones / grises — blue / green / brown / grey
- grandes / pequeños / brillantes — big / small / bright

Tiene el pelo… / He/She has … hair
- moreno / rubio / castaño / rojo — dark brown / blond / mid-brown / red
- corto / largo — short / long
- rizado / liso / ondulado — curly / straight / wavy
- fino / de punta — fine / spiky

Tiene… / He/She has…
- la piel blanca / morena — fair / dark skin
- la cara redonda / alargada — a round / oval face
- los dientes prominentes — big teeth
- pecas — freckles

Lleva… / He/She wears / has…
- gafas — glasses
- barba — a beard
- bigote — a moustache

Es… / He/She is…
- alto/a / bajo/a — tall / short
- delgado/a / gordito/a / gordo/a — slim / chubby / fat
- calvo/a — bald
- moreno/a — dark-haired
- rubio/a — fair-haired
- castaño/a — brown-haired
- pelirrojo/a — a redhead
- español / española — Spanish
- inglés / inglesa — English
- peruano / peruana — Peruvian

Mide 1,60. — He/She is 1m60 tall.
No es ni alto ni bajo. — He/She is neither tall nor short.
(No) Nos parecemos físicamente. — We (don't) look like each other.

¿Cómo es de carácter? / What is he/she like as a person?

Como persona, es… / As a person, he/she is…
- optimista / pesimista — optimistic / pessimistic
- simpático/a / antipático/a — nice / nasty
- trabajador(a) / perezoso/a — hard-working / lazy
- generoso/a / tacaño/a — generous / mean
- hablador(a) / callado/a — chatty / quiet
- divertido/a / gracioso/a / serio/a — fun / funny / serious
- fiel / infiel — loyal / disloyal
- feliz / triste — happy / sad
- ordenado/a / caótico/a — tidy / chaotic
- enérgico/a / animado/a / tranquilo/a — energetic / lively / calm
- pensativo/a — thoughtful
- comprensivo/a — understanding
- honesto/a — honest
- alegre — cheerful
- molesto/a — annoying
- ambicioso/a — ambitious
- egoísta — selfish

Está feliz / triste. — He/She is happy / sad.

¿Te llevas bien con tu familia? / Do you get on well with your family?

(No) Me llevo bien con…porque… / I (don't) get on well with… because…
- me apoya — he/she supports me
- me acepta como soy — he/she accepts me as I am
- nunca me critica — he/she never criticises me
- tenemos mucho en común — we have a lot in common

Me divierto con… — I have a good time with…
Me peleo con… — I argue with…
Nos llevamos superbién. — We get on really well.
Nos llevamos como el perro y el gato. — We fight like cat and dog.
Nos divertimos siempre. — We always have a good time.

¿Cómo es un buen amigo / una buena amiga? / What is a good friend like?

Un buen amigo es alguien que… / A good friend is someone who…
- te apoya — supports you
- te escucha — listens to you
- te conoce bien — knows you well
- te acepta como eres — accepts you as you are
- te quiere mucho — likes / loves you a lot
- te da consejos — gives you advice
- te hace reír — makes you laugh
- no te critica — doesn't criticise you
- nunca te juzga — never judges you

Conocí a mi mejor amigo/a… — I met my best friend…
Nos conocimos — We met / got to know each other
Nos hicimos amigos — We became friends
Nos hicimos novios — We started going out
convivimos — we lived together
nos casamos — we got married
Es el amor de mi vida. — He/She is the love of my life.
Tenemos … en común. — We have … in common.
nos gustan (las mismas cosas) — we like (the same things)
nos encantan (las películas) — we love (films)

setenta y uno 71

4 Intereses e influencias
Punto de partida 1

- *Talking about free-time activities*
- *Using stem-changing verbs*

1 Escucha y lee. Rellena los espacios en blanco.

¿Qué haces en tus ratos libres?

Tengo **1** _____ pasatiempos. Después del insti toco la **2** _____ y también juego al futbolín y a los **3** _____. Los fines de semana normalmente **4** _____ con mis amigos. A veces vamos al polideportivo, donde **5** _____ al squash y montamos en **6** _____.
El problema es que no tengo **7** _____ dinero. Mis padres me dan **8** _____ euros a la semana, pero gasto mi paga en saldo para el **9** _____. De vez en cuando compro **10** _____ también.

| quedar con | to meet up with |
| gastar | to spend (money) |

Alex, 16

2 Con tu compañero/a, haz un diálogo.

- ¿Qué haces después del insti?
- ¿Adónde vas los fines de semana?
- ¿Tus padres te dan dinero? ¿Cuánto?
- ¿Qué haces con la paga?

Después del insti Los fines de semana Cuando tengo tiempo,	voy de compras toco la flauta / trompeta monto en bici / monopatín juego al billar / futbolín
Mis padres me dan… Mi madre/padre me da…	a la semana al mes
Gasto mi paga en También compro	saldo para el móvil ropa, joyas y maquillaje zapatillas de marca videojuegos y revistas

3 Escribe un texto. Usa el texto del ejercicio 1 como modelo.

Say:
- what you do in your free time, and when
- how much pocket money you receive
- what you spend it on

Use:
- verbs in the 'I' form and the 'we' form
- connectives and adverbs of frequency

G The verb *jugar* › Page 208

Jugar is a stem-changing verb.

	jug**ar** (to play)
(yo)	j**ue**go
(tú)	j**ue**gas
(él/ella/usted)	j**ue**ga
(nosotros/as)	jugamos
(vosotros/as)	jugáis
(ellos/ellas/ustedes)	j**ue**gan

4 Lee el texto. Escribe un resumen en inglés.

Los padres españoles, entre los más generosos

Según los resultados de una encuesta, los padres españoles son de los más generosos de Europa.
- Los españoles son los terceros de Europa en dar más cantidad de paga a sus hijos, después de los italianos y franceses.
- El 41% de los niños españoles de entre 5 y 15 años reciben de cinco a diez euros por semana.
- Un 13,8% de niños mayores de 15 años reciben más de cincuenta euros a la semana.

72 *setenta y dos*

Módulo 4

Unidad 2

5 leer Empareja el deporte con el dibujo correcto.
Ejemplo: **1** e

Juego / Jugué al…
1 baloncesto
2 fútbol
3 rugby
4 bádminton
5 ping-pong
6 hockey
Hago / Hice…
7 gimnasia
8 atletismo
9 equitación
10 natación
11 ciclismo
12 remo

6 escuchar Escucha y escribe la letra del deporte que mencionan <u>en el pasado</u>. ¡Ojo! Cada persona menciona <u>dos</u> o <u>tres</u> deportes. (1–6)
Ejemplo: **1** g

7 leer Lee y apunta <u>ocho</u> detalles en inglés.
Ejemplo: She's addicted to sport.

Sara, 32

Para mí, el deporte es como una droga – ¡estoy enganchada! Me chifla hacer judo y también juego al pádel desde hace dos años. Tenemos un partido todas las semanas. Sin embargo, nunca juego al golf, puesto que es un poco aburrido.

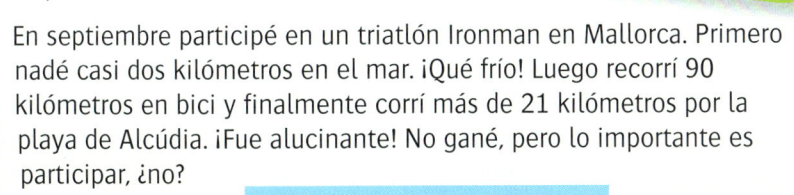

En septiembre participé en un triatlón Ironman en Mallorca. Primero nadé casi dos kilómetros en el mar. ¡Qué frío! Luego recorrí 90 kilómetros en bici y finalmente corrí más de 21 kilómetros por la playa de Alcúdia. ¡Fue alucinante! No gané, pero lo importante es participar, ¿no?

| recorrer | to cover (distance) |
| correr | to run |

Zona Cultura

El pádel es muy popular en España y Latinoamérica. Este deporte de raqueta, que fue inventado en México, se juega con una pala especial y una pelota.

💬 Cognates and near-cognates look like English words, but usually follow Spanish pronunciation rules. Practise saying these words:

crÍquet   tenis   rugby
fútbol   gimnasia   voleibol

However, the words for some sports break these rules.
hockey   judo

8 hablar Con tu compañero/a, habla del deporte.

Say:
- Which sports you do / play
- Which sports you never do
- Which activity you did recently
- How it went

Hago / Juego… ya que es sano / emocionante / fácil… También…
Sin embargo, … porque es…
(En febrero) participé / hice / jugué…
(No)…

setenta y tres **73**

Punto de partida 2

- *Talking about TV programmes and films*
- *Using adjectives of nationality*

1 Escucha. Copia y completa la tabla in inglés. (1–5)

¿Eres teleadicto/a?

Sí, soy teleadicto/a.

No, no soy teleadicto/a.

	telly addict?	likes	dislikes
1	✓	h – informative	…

a un concurso
b un programa de deportes
c un reality
d un documental
e un culebrón / una telenovela
f una comedia
g una serie policíaca
h el telediario / las noticias

2 Con tu compañero/a, haz diálogos.

- ¿Eres teleadicto/a?
- ¿Qué tipo de programas te gustan? ¿Por qué?
- ¿Cuál es tu programa favorito?
- ¿Qué tipo de programas no te gustan? ¿Por qué?

Es	muy	aburrid**o/a/os/as**
Son…	bastante	adictiv**o/a/os/as**
	más… que…	divertid**o/a/os/as**
	menos… que…	entretenid**o/a/os/as**
		tont**o/a/os/as**
		informativ**o/a/os/as**
		mal**o/a/os/as**
		emocionant**e(s)**
		interesant**e(s)**

3 Escribe una entrada para el foro.

¿Eres teleadicto/a?

- En mi opinión, (no) soy…
- Veo la tele…
- Me gusta(n)… porque…
- Creo que los/las… son más/menos… que…
- Mi programa favorito es…
- No me gusta(n)… porque…

When giving your opinion about a type of programme, remember to use the definite article and the plural form of the noun:

un concurso → Me chiflan **los** concurso**s**.
una telenovela → No me gusta ver **las** telenovela**s**.
El telediario is always singular in Spanish.

setenta y cuatro

4 Escucha y apunta la nacionalidad correcta en español. (1–8)

Ejemplo: **1** *italiana*

Premios Festival de Izarra

1. Mejor película de amor.
2. Mejor película de terror.
3. Mejor película de acción / aventuras.
4. Mejor película de animación.
5. Mejor película de ciencia ficción.
6. Mejor película de fantasía.
7. Mejor actor.
8. Mejor director.

Zona Cultura

Cada año los Premios Goya celebran lo mejor del cine español. Los ganadores de los Goya incluyen al actor Javier Bardem y la actriz Penélope Cruz, que se casaron en 2010, y a los directores Guillermo del Toro y Pedro Almodóvar.

G Adjectives of nationality › Page 224

Adjectives of nationality do not start with a capital letter in Spanish.
Like all adjectives, they have to agree with the noun.
Those ending in a **vowel** usually follow the regular pattern:

| italian**o** | italian**a** | italian**os** | Italian**as** |

Adjectives of nationality ending in a **consonant** follow an irregular pattern (the same pattern as adjectives ending in –*or*, like *hablador*).

ending in –*l*	español	español**a**	español**es**	español**as**
ending in –*n*	alemán	aleman**a**	aleman**es**	aleman**as**
ending in –*s*	inglés	ingles**a**	ingles**es**	ingles**as**

americano	alemán
argentino	danés
británico	español
chino	francés
griego	holandés
italiano	inglés
mexicano	irlandés
sueco	japonés

5 Lee el texto y completa las frases.

Soy una fanática de las películas extranjeras y mi actor favorito es el mexicano Gael García Bernal. ¡Qué guapo es! También es muy dinámico e idealista. Me chiflan las pelis de Escandinavia, sobre todo los misterios daneses y suecos. Sin embargo, no me gustan las películas de dibujos animados japoneses porque son un poco infantiles.

Voy al cine todos los sábados por la noche, y la semana pasada vi una película de Bollywood con mi novio, que es chino. Me gustó, pero era un poco larga. Después fuimos a un restaurante italiano. ¡Fue una noche muy cosmopolita!
Paula

extranjero/a foreign

1. Paula is a fan of ———.
2. She thinks that Gael García Bernal is ———.
3. Her favourite Scandinavian films are ———.
4. She doesn't like ——— because ———.
5. Last week she ———.
6. She mentions ——— different nationalities.

6 Escribe un texto sobre el cine. Usa el texto del ejercicio 5 como modelo.

Give details about:
- types of films you like/don't like, and why.
- how often you go to the cinema
- a recent trip to the cinema
- your opinion of the film you saw.

Módulo 4

Unidad 3

setenta y cinco 75

1 ¿Qué sueles hacer?

- *Talking about what you usually do*
- *Using* **soler** *+ infinitive*
- *Identifying correct statements about a text*

1 escuchar
Lee el artículo. Luego escucha y apunta los detalles para cada persona en español. (1–6)
- su nombre
- el número de la actividad
- ¿con qué frecuencia?
- ¿cuándo?

los (lunes)
por la mañana / tarde / noche
después del insti
a la hora de comer
mientras desayuno / como

Los pasatiempos de los jóvenes españoles

Según una encuesta del Instituto de la Juventud, en España los jóvenes suelen tener una media de 32,6 horas de tiempo libre a la semana.

Las diez actividades de ocio más populares son:

1. usar el ordenador
2. salir con amigos
3. escuchar música
4. ver la tele
5. descansar
6. leer periódicos o revistas
7. escuchar la radio
8. leer libros
9. hacer deporte
10. ir al cine

el ocio — leisure

G soler + infinitive ▶ Page 208

To say what you usually do or tend to do, you can use **soler** + infinitive.

Suelo *salir* con amigos.
I usually / I tend to go out with friends.

Soler is a stem-changing verb.

(yo)	s**ue**lo
(tú)	s**ue**les
(él/ella/usted)	s**ue**le
(nosotros/as)	solemos
(vosotros/as)	soléis
(ellos/ellas/ustedes)	s**ue**len

2 hablar
Con tu compañero/a, haz diálogos.

- ¿Cuándo sueles escuchar música?
- *Suelo escucharla por la noche.*
- ¿Con qué frecuencia haces deporte?
- *Lo hago…*

⭐ Remember to avoid repetition by using direct object pronouns: **lo/la/los/las**.
These usually come before the verb, but can be added to the end of an infinitive.

¿Cuando ves la tele?
La veo por la noche.
but Suelo ver**la** por la noche.

3 escuchar
Escucha y apunta en inglés: (a) ¿qué actividades hacen? (b) ¿por qué? (1–5)

Ejemplo: **1** (a) Plays the saxophone…
(b) needs…, ….

4 escribir
Escribe un texto sobre tus pasatiempos.
- Mention four activities you do.
- Say how frequently / when you do them.
- Give reasons.

Es	divertido	informativo
	relajante	sano
Soy	creativo/a	sociable
	perezoso/a	activo/a
	adicto/a a…	
Me ayuda a	relajarme	
	olvidarme de todo	
Me hace	reír	
Me encanta	estar al aire libre	
Necesito	practicar…	
	salir / comunicarme (con otra gente)	
Mi pasión es	la lectura	el deporte
	la música	

setenta y seis

Módulo 4

5 Lee el texto. Identifica las cuatro frases correctas.

Silvano, 15 Puerto Plata

En la República Dominicana hay una gran variedad de pasatiempos. Mi padre juega al dominó desde hace muchos años (es muy popular aquí) y recientemente participó en un torneo. ¡Ahora es el campeón de nuestra región! Mucha gente suele practicar deporte también, sobre todo el béisbol.

Sin embargo, a mí me interesa más la música. Mi madre adora a Juan Luis Guerra, un cantante muy conocido por la bachata y el merengue (dos estilos de música y baile tradicionales), pero yo suelo escuchar el R 'n' B. Mis hermanos y yo tenemos nuestra propia banda – yo toco la batería, José toca el teclado y Félix canta.

Soy fan de Bruno Mars. Su música es una mezcla de muchos estilos distintos y tiene una voz hermosa. Asistí a un concierto suyo cuando visitó Santo Domingo, nuestra capital, durante su gira mundial. El espectáculo fue increíble y cuando entró en el escenario, el público empezó a gritar y a aplaudir. Cantó todas mis canciones favoritas y fue una noche inolvidable.

MAR CARIBE

el merengue

Bruno Mars

1 Su padre es un buen jugador de dominó.
2 El béisbol no es muy popular.
3 Juan Luis Guerra toca un instrumento.
4 Silvano y su madre prefieren diferentes estilos de música.
5 Silvano tiene tres hermanos.
6 La música de Bruno Mars es muy variada.
7 Bruno Mars empezó su gira en la República Dominicana.
8 Los espectadores disfrutaron del concierto.
9 Silvano cantó mucho en el concierto.

⭐ To identify the correct statements, look at each one and decide whether:
1 it gives information that doesn't quite match the text (not correct!)
2 it is talking about something which is simply not mentioned (not correct!)
3 it is true, though it may use different words from those in the text (correct!)

6 Lee el texto otra vez y busca el equivalente de las expresiones.

1 he took part in a tournament
2 a singer very well known for
3 our own band
4 I play the drums
5 he has a beautiful voice
6 I went to a concert of his
7 during his world tour
8 the show
9 when he came on stage

7 Escribe un texto sobre los pasatiempos y la música en tu país.

Use both the present and the preterite tenses, and include language from exercise 5 to write about:

- Which hobbies are popular in your country
- What people in your family do in their free time
- What type of music you like
- A concert you have been to.

⭐ Most types of music in Spanish are cognates or near-cognates. For example:
el soul, el rap, el funk, el dance, el hip-hop, el pop, el rock, el jazz, la música clásica, la música electrónica.
When talking about a concert you have been to, use a variety of preterite tense verbs to:

- say what you did   *Saqué muchas fotos.* (I took lots of photos.)
- talk about other people *El público cantó.* (The audience sang.)
- give your opinion   *Fue inolvidable.* (It was unforgettable.)

setenta y siete 77

2 ¡Fanático del deporte!

- Talking about sports
- Using the imperfect tense to say what you used to do
- Listening for different tenses

1 Escucha y lee. Escribe el nombre correcto.

¿Qué dicen los alumnos de 4º de ESO de sus pasiones deportivas?

Cuando tenía diez años jugaba al balonmano, pero ya no juego. Ahora soy miembro de un club de natación y entrenamos todos los días. ¡Me flipa! También hago tiro con arco de vez en cuando.
Rocío

Cuando era más joven hacía gimnasia e iba a clases de equitación. Ya no hago equitación porque es caro, pero todavía hago gimnasia y soy miembro de un equipo. A veces voy de pesca con mi padre. ¡Es guay!
Diego

Soy muy deportista. Voy al gimnasio todos los días, juego al baloncesto, hago kárate… ¡Soy un fanático del deporte! Antes jugaba al fútbol y era aficionado del Athletic de Bilbao, pero ya no me interesa.
Joaquín

Cuando era más pequeña, iba a clases de judo, pero ahora prefiero deportes como la escalada y el parkour. ¡Soy adicta a la adrenalina! También soy miembro de un club de piragüismo, y en verano hago submarinismo.
Gloria

1 Hago dos deportes acuáticos.
2 Voy a la piscina a menudo.
3 Ya no practico artes marciales.
4 Me molan los deportes de riesgo.
5 ¡El deporte es mi vida!
6 Antes montaba a caballo.

⭐ Use **ya no** to say that you **no longer** do something.
Ya no juego al fútbol.
I **no longer** play football.
Use **todavía** to say that you **still** do something.
Todavía hago judo. I **still** do judo.

2 Lee los textos otra vez. Apunta los deportes mencionados. ¿Presente o imperfecto?

Ejemplo: handball (imperfect), …

3 Con tu compañero/a, haz diálogos.

- ¿Eres muy deportista?
- ¿Qué deportes hacías cuando eras más joven?
- ¿Qué deportes haces ahora?
- ¿Eres miembro de un club / un equipo?
- ¿Cuándo entrenas?
- ¿Eres aficionado/a de un equipo?

Cuando era más joven tenía (ocho) años	Ahora (no) Ya no Todavía	
(no) era	soy	deportista miembro de… aficionado/a de… un(a) fanático/a de…
jugaba	juego	al balonmano
hacía	hago	piragüismo
iba	voy	a clases de…

G The imperfect tense ▶ Page 214

You have seen the **imperfect tense** for describing things in the past. It is also used for saying what you <u>used to</u> do.

Jugaba al baloncesto. **He/She used to play** basketball.

	jug**ar** (to play)	hac**er** (to do/make)	viv**ir** (to live)
(yo)	jug**aba**	hac**ía**	viv**ía**
(tú)	jug**abas**	hac**ías**	viv**ías**
(él/ella/usted)	jug**aba**	hac**ía**	viv**ía**
(nosotros/as)	jug**ábamos**	hac**íamos**	viv**íamos**
(vosotros/as)	jug**abais**	hac**íais**	viv**íais**
(ellos/ellas/ustedes)	jug**aban**	hac**ían**	viv**ían**

Only three verbs are irregular in the imperfect. These are:
ser (to be) → **era, eras,** etc.
ir (to go) → **iba, ibas,** etc.
ver (to see / watch) → **veía, veías,** etc.

Módulo 4

4 Escucha. Copia y completa la tabla en inglés. (1–5)

	sport in past	details	sport now	details
1	basketball	3 times…		

⭐ Listen carefully to work out whether the sports are mentioned in the present or the imperfect.

Remember that 'I' form regular verbs end in *–aba* or *–ía* in the imperfect.

Also, listen out for time markers such as *antes, todavía, ahora*, etc.

5 Lee el texto y escribe los verbos correctos. Luego escucha y comprueba tus respuestas.

Ejemplo: **1** era

Cuando **1** (**ser**) más joven, **2** (**hacer**) gimnasia dos veces a la semana. También **3** (**ir**) a clases de patinaje sobre hielo con mi hermana.

Me chifla la gimnasia y todavía la **4** (**hacer**) cuando tengo tiempo, pero ya no **5** (**patinar**). Ahora mi pasión es el fútbol y **6** (**jugar**) en un equipo de fútbol femenino. **7** (**Ser**) delantera y **8** (**soler**) entrenar cada domingo. Hace dos semanas **9** (**marcar**) mi primer gol de la temporada en un partido contra otro equipo de mi ciudad. ¡Qué ilusión!

Mi hermano y yo **10** (**ser**) hinchas del Barça y nuestro jugador preferido es el argentino Lionel Messi, el mayor goleador de la Liga de Campeones. ¡Es un crack! Messi **11** (**ganar**) el Balón de Oro por primera vez en 2009, aunque para mí, su punto culminante fue cuando **12** (**batir**) el récord de mayor cantidad de goles en un mismo año.

| un(a) hincha | a fan |

Begoña, 15

⭐ Take care to choose the correct **tense** and **person** of the verb.

Use the **imperfect** tense for what you used to do.

Use the **preterite** tense for completed actions in the past.

Remember that some verbs have a spelling change in the 'I' form of the preterite (e.g. *marcar, jugar*).

6 Escribe un texto sobre el deporte. Usa el texto del ejercicio 5 como modelo.

Write about:
- Sports you used to do.
- Sports you do / don't do now.
- Whether you are a member of a club / team.
- Your favourite player / team.
- A highlight of their career.

Cuando era…
Todavía…, pero ya no… Ahora…
(No) soy…
Mi… preferido/a es…
Su punto culminante fue cuando (ganó / batió)…

7 Lee el texto y tradúcelo al inglés.

Estrella del boxeo con orígenes humildes

Ganador de docenas de títulos mundiales, hoy es uno de los boxeadores más ricos del mundo. Pero la vida no era siempre así para Manny Pacquiao, que nació en Filipinas en 1978. Con seis hijos, sus padres eran muy pobres, y a la edad de 14 años Pacquiao decidió escaparse de casa. Fue a Manila, donde vivía en las calles y dormía en una caja de cartón. Vendía pan y donuts en la calle, y de esta manera ganaba bastante dinero para sobrevivir.

| así / de esta manera | like this / in this way |
| la caja | box |

setenta y nueve

3 #Temas del momento

- *Talking about what's trending*
- *Using the perfect tense*
- *Using words which have more than one meaning*

1 **Lee los tuits. Busca las expresiones en español.**

Juana @JMtopbajista
#temasdelmomento ¿**Has leído** la última novela de Ruiz Zafón? Ya **ha vendido** más de un millón de ejemplares y es fenomenal.

Aitor @AitorP-Getxo
#temasdelmomento En mi página de Facebook **he compartido** las fotos del cumpleaños de Joseba. También **he subido** un vídeo. ¡Fiesta brutal!

Daniela @DaniJsevilla
No he visto todavía la nueva peli de Jennifer Lawrence, pero mis padres me **han comprado** el CD de la banda sonora. ¡Me flipa! #temasdelmomento

Marina López @mariluzL
¿Ya **has oído** la nueva canción de Paloma Faith? **La he descargado** y creo que es preciosa. #temasdelmomento

Ignacio Torres @NachoTgamer
¿**Has jugado** al videojuego *Gladiador Valiente 3*? #temasdelmomento Yo **no lo he probado** todavía porque ¡mi hermano me **ha roto** la consola!

temas del momento	trending topics
la banda sonora	sound track

1 I have uploaded
2 I haven't tried it
3 (they) have bought
4 Have you read…?
5 I have downloaded it
6 (he) has broken
7 I haven't seen
8 Have you heard…?
9 I have shared
10 it has sold
11 Have you played…?

2 **Escucha. Copia y completa la tabla en inglés. (1–6)**

	have you…?	✓/✗	extra details
1	bought new edition of…	✗	has spent…

⭐ Listen out for five examples of the perfect tense with verbs that you didn't see in exercise 1. Can you spot them?

3 **Con tu compañero/a, haz diálogos sobre:**
- los últimos videojuegos / libros / diseños de moda / programas
- las últimas películas / canciones / revistas / aplicaciones / noticias

● ¿Ya has (descargado / visto)…?
■ Sí, ya (lo/la) he (descargado / visto) y creo que es…
■ No, no (lo/la) he… **todavía** porque…

G The perfect tense ▶ Page 219

This is used to talk about what you have done.
Use the present tense of the verb **haber** + **past participle**.

(yo)	**he**	
(tú)	**has**	escuch**ado**
(él/ella/usted)	**ha**	vend**ido**
(nosotros/as)	**hemos**	compart**ido**
(vosotros/as)	**habéis**	
(ellos/ellas/ustedes)	**han**	

To form the past participle, remove the –*ar*, –*er* or –*ir* from the infinitive and add:

–ado (–*ar* verbs)
–ido (–*er*/–*ir* verbs)

Some past participles are irregular:

escribir (to write)	→	**escrito**
poner (to put)	→	**puesto**
hacer (to do / make)	→	**hecho**
romper (to break)	→	**roto**
morir (to die)	→	**muerto**
ver (to see / watch)	→	**visto**

⭐ When used with the perfect tense, **ya** and **todavía** have different meanings.

¿**Ya** has visto la nueva peli?	Have you **already** seen the new film?
Sí, **ya** la he visto.	Yes, I've **already** seen it.
No, no la he visto **todavía**.	No, I haven't seen it **yet**.

ochenta

Módulo 4

4 leer Lee la página web y las frases 1–6. Escribe C (cine), V (videojuegos) o T (televisión).

Estrenos de la semana

Cine
Esta semana se ha estrenado la nueva película de aventuras *Dina*, que ya ha ganado varios premios. **Cuenta la historia de** una chica rusa con poderes mágicos. **La mezcla de** comedia y misterio y la banda sonora muy original son aspectos positivos, pero el argumento es **débil** y los efectos especiales son **decepcionantes**.

Videojuegos
El nuevo título multijugador *Gladiador Valiente 3* acaba de **salir al mercado**. Disponible para diferentes plataformas, este juego de acción tiene gráficos **de alta calidad**, aunque también tiene una melodía irritante y los personajes principales son poco plausibles. Sin embargo, tiene un buen argumento, y las animaciones parecen muy naturales.

Televisión
Acaba de estrenarse **la nueva temporada** de la comedia *Big Bang Theory*, la serie americana que ha tenido mucho éxito en todo el mundo. **Sigue las vidas de** los siete **protagonistas**, con situaciones hilarantes, como siempre. Recomendamos que la veas **en versión original**.

estrenarse	to be released
el argumento	plot
tener éxito	to be successful

1 Buen aspecto visual.
2 Es muy popular en diferentes países.
3 No me gustan los personajes.
4 Combina el suspense con el humor.
5 Es mejor verla en inglés.
6 Banda sonora malísima.

⭐ Use the perfect tense to say what you have done. However, to say what you have just done use the present tense of **acabar de** + **infinitive**.

He visto un buen documental.   **I have seen** a good documentary.
but **Acabo de ver** un buen documental.   **I have just seen** a good documentary.

Acabar de is an example of a phrase which cannot be translated word for word.

5 leer Lee la página web otra vez. Escribe las palabras en **negrita** en inglés.

6 escuchar Escucha y apunta los detalles en inglés. (1–5)

Ejemplo: **1** watched new soap – good plot, …

- What have they just done?
- What is their opinion of it?

7 hablar Con tu compañero/a, habla de un videojuego, un programa o una película.

- ¿Qué acabas de hacer?
- ¿Qué tipo de videojuego / programa / película es?
- ¿De qué trata?
- ¿Te gustó? ¿Por qué (no)?

Acabo de ver / jugar a…	
Es un/una…	
Cuenta la historia de…	
Trata de …	
Combina el misterio / la comedia / la acción con…	
El argumento La banda sonora El protagonista	es buen**o**/**a**, fuerte, débil, guapo
Los personajes Los gráficos Los efectos especiales Los actores Las animaciones Las canciones	son buen**os**/**as**, estupend**os**/**as** guap**os**/**as**, guay impresionantes interesantes mal**os**/**as**, originales naturales, repetitiv**os**/**as**

ochenta y uno **81**

4 En directo

- Discussing different types of entertainment
- Using algunos / ciertos / otros / muchos / demasiados / todos
- Adapting a model dialogue to fit different situations

1 Lee los anuncios y contesta a las preguntas en español.

Nuevo espectáculo de baile

La compañía de danza flamenca *Flamencomás* pone en escena su nuevo espectáculo *Alma Ajena* en el teatro Lope de Vega. Una experiencia auténtica de cante, toque y baile flamenco.

Horario: 19.45 y 22.15 (todos los días excepto los lunes)
Duración: 1 hora y media
Entradas: 40 € (bebida incluida)

¡El Circo Mil Sueños ha vuelto!

El Circo Mil Sueños presenta *Viaje a Venús* en la plaza de toros de Santa María. En un espectáculo de dos horas, cincuenta acróbatas, ilusionistas, contorsionistas y bailarines nos llevan a otro planeta. Funciones a las 15.00 y 19.30.

Tarifas: 32 € (20 € menores de 18 años)

Cine de verano

Con la llegada del calor vuelve el festival de cine al aire libre. Disfruta de más de 140 películas de todos los géneros en una pantalla gigante. Algunos de los mejores estrenos del año, incluso *Star Wars Episodio VIII*. A diario a las 20.15 / 22.45 hasta el 12 de septiembre.

Entrada general – **7 €**
Carné de estudiante – **5 €**
Abono 10 sesiones – **60 €**

1. ¿De qué tipo de baile es el espectáculo?
2. ¿Cuántas sesiones hay al día?
3. ¿Dónde tiene lugar el circo?
4. ¿Cuánto cuesta una entrada para niños?
5. ¿Cuándo termina el festival de cine de verano?
6. ¿Cuántas películas distintas ponen?

2 Escucha. Rellena los espacios en blanco. (1–2)

- ¿Qué vamos a hacer a _____ ?
- ¿Tienes ganas de ir b _____ ?
- Depende. ¿Qué ponen?
- c _____ . Es d _____ .
- ¿Cuánto cuesta?
- Son e _____ euros.
- Vale. ¿A qué hora empieza?
- Empieza a las f _____ y termina a las g _____ .
- De acuerdo.

- Dos entradas para h _____ , por favor.
- ¿Para qué sesión?
- Para la sesión de las i _____ .
- Lo siento, no quedan entradas.
- Pues, para la sesión de las j _____ .
- Muy bien.
- ¿Hay un descuento para estudiantes?
- Sí. ¿Tiene su carné de estudiante?
- Aquí tiene.

⭐ To say what you are going to do, remember to use **ir + infinitive** (the near future):

¿Qué **vamos a hacer**?   What **are we going to do**?
Voy a ir al cine.   I'm going to go to the cinema.

To say what you fancy / feel like doing, use **tener ganas de + infinitive**:
Tengo ganas de ver la tele.   I fancy / feel like watching TV.

esta tarde / noche mañana el (viernes)	
ir al	cine / teatro / circo
ir a	un concierto / un festival / un espectáculo
es	un musical una película / obra de…

82 *ochenta y dos*

Módulo 4

3 hablar Con tu compañero/a, inventa diálogos. Usa el ejercicio 2 como modelo. Habla de los anuncios del ejercicio 1 o inventa los detalles.

> ⭐ **¿Qué ponen?** means 'What's on?' when talking about cinema, etc.
> To talk about a concert use **¿Quién canta / toca?** (Who's singing / playing?)
> How would you change the dialogue to talk about a football match?

4 leer Lee las opiniones. ¿Quién habla? Escribe B (Berto) o Y (Yolanda).

Prefiero ver las pelis en casa. **Berto**

Prefiero ir al cine. **Yolanda**

a Las palomitas que venden están ricas.

b El ambiente es mejor con muchas personas.

c Es mejor porque no tienes que hacer cola.

d Hay demasiadas personas y los otros espectadores me molestan.

e Me encanta porque ponen tráilers para todas las nuevas pelis.

f No me gusta, dado que los asientos no son cómodos.

g La imagen es mejor en la gran pantalla.

h Las entradas son muy caras.

i Si vas al baño te pierdes una parte.

hacer cola to queue

5 escuchar Escucha. Copia y completa la tabla. (1–4)

| en directo | live |
| la corrida de toros | bull fight |

	prefers...	opinions from exercise 4	other points
1	watching a band live	b, ...	can buy...

G Useful adjectives ▶ Page 224

These adjectives are useful in lots of different topics:
algunos/as (some)   **ciertos/as** (certain)
otros/as (other)   **muchos/as** (many/lots of)
demasiados/as (too many)   **todos/as** (all/every)

Todos/as is followed by **los/las**:
Me gustan **todas las** películas.   I like **all** films.

6 escuchar Escucha otra vez y mira la gramática. ¿Qué palabras menciona cada persona?

Ejemplo: **1** muchos, ...

7 escribir Traduce el texto al español.

Look back at Unit 3.

I have just seen a new animated film and it was incredible. I tend to go to the cinema every week because I love the big screen. However, some cinemas show too many trailers. I like certain science fiction films because the special effects are brilliant, but others are stupid and the plot is boring.

Look back at Unit 1.

ochenta y tres **83**

5 Modelos a seguir

- Talking about who inspires you
- Using a range of past tenses
- Talking about dates

1 Escucha y elige la respuesta correcta. (1–4)

¿Crees que los famosos son buenos modelos a seguir?

1. La cantante Taylor Swift es un buen modelo a seguir porque…
   a tiene mucho talento.
   b tiene mucho éxito.
   c usa su fama para ayudar a otros.

2. El actor Ryan Gosling es un buen modelo a seguir porque…
   a apoya varias organizaciones benéficas.
   b trabaja en defensa de los animales.
   c recauda fondos para Amnistía Internacional.

3. La actriz Angelina Jolie es un buen modelo a seguir porque…
   a lucha contra la pobreza.
   b lucha contra la homofobia.
   c lucha por los derechos de los refugiados.

4. Muchos futbolistas son malos modelos a seguir porque…
   a se emborrachan.
   b se comportan mal en el campo de fútbol.
   c se meten en problemas con la policía.

2 Has oído estas expresiones en el ejercicio 1. ¿Qué significan?

a organizaciones que ayudan a las víctimas de desastres naturales
b apoya muchos proyectos de educación
c apoya varias campañas para mejorar las condiciones de vida
d hace mucho para combatir la injusticia en el mundo
e un buen modelo a seguir es alguien que ayuda a los demás
f los jóvenes imitan su comportamiento

3 Empareja las fotos con los textos. ¿A quién se refiere el texto que sobra? Escucha y comprueba tus respuestas.

1 Rigoberta Menchú
2 Tom Daley
3 Emma Watson

a Es un joven nadador que ha ganado varias medallas de oro. Además, ha hablado abiertamente de su sexualidad e inspira a muchos jóvenes.

b Tiene mucho talento como cantante. Ha creado la *Fundación Pies Descalzos* para ayudar a los niños pobres de Colombia.

c Lucha por la justicia social en Guatemala. Ha ganado el Premio Nobel de la Paz por su trabajo como activista.

d Lucha por los derechos de la mujer y es embajadora de buena voluntad de la ONU. Ha tenido mucho éxito como actriz.

un(a) embajador(a) de buena voluntad — a goodwill ambassador

4 Con tu compañero/a, habla de los modelos a seguir.

- ¿En qué consiste un buen modelo a seguir?
- Da un ejemplo de un buen modelo a seguir.
- ¿Y un mal modelo a seguir?

- Un buen modelo a seguir es alguien que…
- En mi opinión… es un buen modelo a seguir porque…
- Creo que… es un mal modelo a seguir…

84 ochenta y cuatro

Módulo 4

5 Escucha. Apunta los detalles en inglés.

¿A quién admiras?
Malala Yousafzai

- Qualities: brave, ...
- Fights for: _____
- Childhood: _____
- 2009: _____
- 2012: _____
- 2013: _____
- 2014: _____

> When referring to a year in Spanish, say it as if it is a number. For example, 1995 is said as 'one thousand nine hundred and ninety-five'.
> To make it easier, break it down into its separate elements.
> **1995** mil novecientos noventa y cinco
> **2017** dos mil diecisiete

| valiente | brave |

6 Lee los textos. ¿Qué significan las palabras en **negrita**? Luego contesta a las preguntas en español para las <u>dos</u> personas.

Mi inspiración es el tenista Rafa Nadal, dado que tiene todas las **cualidades** importantes de un buen deportista: talento, dedicación, perseverancia y resistencia física y mental. Nació en Mallorca en 1986 y de niño practicaba varios deportes. Sin embargo, su pasión era el tenis, y a los 15 años **empezó** su carrera profesional.

A pesar de todas las **lesiones** físicas que ha sufrido, Nadal ha batido varios récords, y fue el primer jugador en ganar nueve veces el mismo torneo de Grand Slam. También ha ganado más títulos que **cualquier** otro español, y en 2008 ganó una medalla de oro en los Juegos Olímpicos de Pekín.

Más que nada, admiro a Nadal porque es buena persona, y porque en 2007 estableció la *Fundación Rafa Nadal* para ayudar a los **niños desfavorecidos** en España y en la India.

Bea

Mi ídolo no es ni rico ni famoso, pero es una persona cariñosa, amable y muy fuerte. Y como todos los héroes anónimos, no ha ganado **ningún** premio. Es mi abuela, Conchita Jiménez.

De pequeña vivía en Canarias, donde conoció a mi abuelo cuando tenía diez años. Se casaron ocho años más tarde, pero con solo 25 años se quedó **viuda** con cuatro hijos pequeños cuando mi abuelo murió en un accidente marítimo.

Su vida no ha sido fácil, y ha sufrido varias **enfermedades** graves. Sin embargo, siempre ha superado sus problemas para ayudar a otras personas, y en los últimos 25 años **ha acogido temporalmente** a más de cien niños en casa.

Sobre todo, admiro a mi abuela porque siempre **sonríe** y nunca es egoísta. Solo piensa en los demás.

Enrique

| a pesar de | despite |
| el héroe anónimo | unsung hero |

1. ¿Qué cualidades tiene?
2. ¿Cómo era su infancia?
3. ¿Qué problemas ha tenido?
4. ¿Qué ha hecho a pesar de sus problemas?
5. ¿Qué premios o títulos ha ganado?
6. ¿Por qué es un buen modelo a seguir, sobre todo?

G Using past tenses
> Pages **212, 214, 219**

Use the **imperfect tense** for saying what someone <u>used to do</u>, or for describing things in the past.
Vivía en Pakistán. He/She **used to live** in Pakistan.
No *era* justo. It **wasn't** fair.

Use the **preterite tense** for saying what they <u>did</u>.
Ganó un premio. He/She **won** a prize.

Use the **perfect tense** for saying what they <u>have done</u>.
Ha superado muchos problemas. He/She **has overcome** lots of problems.

7 Lee los textos otra vez. Busca <u>cuatro</u> ejemplos de cada tiempo verbal.
- Imperfect
- Preterite
- Perfect

8 Escribe un texto sobre una persona que admiras. Contesta a las preguntas del ejercicio 6.

ochenta y cinco 85

Módulo 4   Leer y escuchar

1 leer   Planes para mañana

Recibes estos mensajes de tus amigos españoles.

> ¿Has oído la nueva canción de Amaia Montero? Mañana da un concierto en mi ciudad y me gustaría ir. Las entradas son muy caras, aunque lo bueno es que hay descuentos para estudiantes.
> **Merche**

> Tengo ganas de ir al nuevo cine que acaban de abrir. Mi padre dice que hay mucho espacio entre los asientos, pero por desgracia, siempre hay colas muy largas en la taquilla.
> **Jorge**

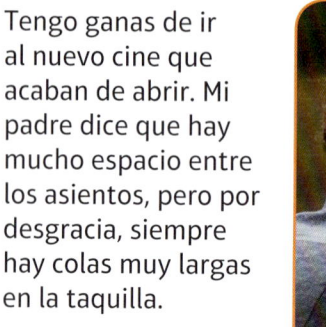

Contesta a las preguntas en español.
1. ¿Adónde quiere ir Merche?
2. ¿Cuál es la ventaja de esta idea?
3. ¿Adónde quiere ir Jorge?
4. ¿Cuál es la desventaja de esta idea?

> ⭐ Start by working out exactly what information you are asked to give. In your answers you should be able to 'lift' words from the text. Make sure you know words like *ventaja/beneficio* and *desventaja/inconveniente*, which are often used in reading exams.

2 leer   A football team

Read this extract from *Sara y las Goleadoras: El último gol*, a novel by Laura Gallego, and answer the questions which follow in **English**.

> Me gusta el fútbol, pero creo que los estudios son más importantes —dijo Dasha.
> —Yo prefiero el fútbol —suspiró Eva— pero mi padre no me deja salir de casa por las tardes porque dice que tengo que estudiar.
> —Tienes que ser razonable, Eva —intervino Mónica. —A todas nos encantaría poder entrenar todos los días y jugar fenomenal en los *play-off*, pero hay que aceptar que no podemos hacerlo todo.
> —Además —añadió Vicky— las jugadoras de los otros equipos también tienen exámenes, así que están en la misma situación que nosotras.
> —No exactamente —murmuró Sara— porque las chicas de los otros equipos ya juegan mejor que nosotras, así que debemos entrenar más que ellas.
> —Bueno, considerando que es nuestro primer año, lo hemos hecho muy bien —razonó Dasha.

1. Why is Eva unhappy?
2. Mónica gives a balanced view. What are the **two** sides to her argument?
3. What is Vicky's opinion?
4. According to Sara, why should they train more than the other teams?
5. Why does Dasha think their team has done well?

> ⭐ Written dialogues often include words like 'she said' or 'he added'. These may include **añadir** (to add), **gritar** (to shout), **suspirar** (to sigh), **decir** (to say), **intervenir** (to intervene), **murmurar** (to murmur) and **razonar** (to reason).

Módulo 4

3 leer — Translation into English

You are looking at a Spanish news website and see this introduction to an article. Translate it into **English**.

> Ver la tele es el pasatiempo favorito de mucha gente. A pesar de la reciente popularidad de los realitys, los españoles todavía prefieren los programas deportivos. Sin embargo, una excepción notable tiene que ser *La Voz*. Este concurso musical ha tenido un éxito enorme en todo el mundo. Además, ha ganado muchos premios en otros países.

1 escuchar — Tiempo libre

Estás con tus amigos, Bea y Nacho, que hablan del tiempo libre.
¿De qué actividades hablan y cuándo las realizan?
Completa la tabla en **español**.

1

En el pasado	Ahora	En el futuro
hacer equitación		

2

En el pasado	Ahora	En el futuro
		ir a clases de baile

⭐ Remember that if an example is given, it's there for a reason! In this question, what do the examples show you about how you must start your answers?

2 escuchar — Who I admire

You are listening online to a tribute programme about the writer and director Sam Simon.
Write the correct letter.

1 The presenter says that Sam Simon died…
   A following a fight.
   B whilst appearing on TV.
   C from an illness.

2 He says that, in the United States, *The Simpsons* is…
   A the longest-running animated series.
   B the oldest TV programme.
   C the most popular comedy show.

Write the **two** correct letters.

3 What **two** things does the presenter admire most about him.
   A He was an award-winning writer and director.
   B He was an incredibly talented and creative person.
   C He was very generous with his money.
   D He supported a charity for homeless dogs.
   E He set up a foundation to help deaf people.

⭐ Remember that there will be lots of distractors in this type of task! Read the options carefully, and try to eliminate them as you are listening. Don't worry if there are words in the questions which you don't know in Spanish (e.g. homeless, deaf) – use the context, and a process of elimination, to help you.

3 escuchar — Interview with a Mexican singer

You are listening to a podcast with the singer, Marisa Escario.

1 Answer all parts of the question in **English**.
   a What has Marisa done recently?
   b Who did she want to help? Give **one** detail.
   c What does performing live enable her to do?

2 Answer both parts of the question in **English**.
   a When **exactly** does her new tour begin?
   b What is different about this tour? Give **two** details.

ochenta y siete 87

Módulo 4   Prueba oral

A – Role play

1 *leer* Look at the role play card and prepare what you are going to say.

> In the role play task you don't need to expand your answers. Just give the number of details stated on the card.

> This question involves inviting someone to do something. Which phrase could you use?

Your teacher will play the part of your Spanish friend and will speak first.

You should address your friend as *tú*.

When you see this – **!** – you will have to respond to something you have not prepared.

When you see this – **?** – you will have to ask a question.

Estás hablando con tu amigo español / tu amiga española sobre la música y los conciertos.
- La música – **una** ventaja.
- **?** Concierto el sábado.
- **!**
- Tu opinión sobre los conciertos – **una** opinión y **una** razón.
- Tus planes para después del concierto (**dos** detalles).

> Remember that this may be a two-part question.

> Which tense do you need here?

2 *hablar* Practise what you have prepared. Take care with pronunciation and intonation.

3 *escuchar* Using your notes, listen and respond to the teacher.

4 *escuchar* Now listen to Megan doing the role play task. In **English**, note down what she says for each bullet point.

> ⭐ Listen carefully to the unprepared questions (!). If you don't understand, ask the teacher (in Spanish!) to repeat the question – *¿Puede(s) repetir, por favor?*
>
> For the other bullet points, don't get distracted by what the teacher says – stick to what you have prepared!

B – Photo card

Look at the photo and make notes. Your teacher will then ask you questions about the photo and about topics related to **free-time activities**.

Your teacher will ask you the following **three** questions and then **two** more questions which you have not prepared.
- ¿Qué hay en la foto?
- Háblame de la última vez que hiciste deporte.
- ¿Crees que los deportistas son buenos modelos a seguir? … ¿Por qué (no)?

88 *ochenta y ocho*

Módulo 4

1 **Look at the photo and read the task. Then listen to Ben's response to the first question on the task card.**

1. Which athlete is he describing?
2. Note down the **two** present continuous verbs that he uses.
3. What do you think the word *carrera* means in this context?

2 **Listen to Ben's response to the second question on the task card.**

1. In **English**, note down **six** details that he gives.
2. Can you work out the meaning of *estilo libre* and *mariposa* from the context?

3 **Listen to and read Ben's response to the third question on the task card.**

1. Write down the missing word for each gap.
2. Look at the Answer Booster on page 90. Note down **six** examples of language which Ben uses to give a strong answer.

> En mi opinión, **1** ——— deportistas son buenos modelos a seguir, pero otros no. Por ejemplo, creo que el futbolista **2** ——— Cristiano Ronaldo es el mejor modelo a seguir porque es dinámico y muy trabajador. Es un **3** ——— rápido que no es ni egoísta ni agresivo. **4** ——— es arrogante. Ha jugado en equipos como el Sporting, el Manchester United y el Real Madrid, y ha batido muchos récords. Por ejemplo, en **5** ——— marcó sesenta y nueve goles. Sobre todo, admiro a Ronaldo **6** ——— que siempre usa su fama para ayudar a otras personas.

4 **Prepare your own answers to the first three questions. Think about which other two questions you might be asked. Then listen and take part in the full photo card discussion with the teacher.**

> ⭐ To talk about sports you **would like** to try, use *me gustaría* + **infinitive**.

C – General conversation

1 **The teacher asks Aisha '¿Qué sueles hacer en tus ratos libres?' In which order does she mention the following?**

a what instrument she plays
b what instrument she used to play
c who her favourite singer is
d where she is going to go
e what she has just done

> ⭐ Remember that you must ask your teacher at least one question. What does Aisha ask?

2 **The teacher then asks Aisha '¿Eres teleadicta?' Listen to how Aisha develops her answer. What hidden questions does she also answer?**

Example *How often do you watch TV?*

> ⭐ A good way of developing your answer is to think about what 'hidden questions' you could also respond to in order to give a full, well-developed answer.

3 **Listen to Aisha's response to the next question '¿Prefieres ver películas en casa o en el cine?' Look at the Answer Booster on page 90. Note down six examples of language which Aisha uses to give a strong answer.**

4 **Prepare your own answers to Module 4 questions 1–6 on page 198. Then practise with your partner.**

ochenta y nueve **89**

Módulo 4   Prueba escrita

Answer booster	Aiming for a solid answer	Aiming higher	Aiming for the top
Verbs	**Different time frames**: past (preterite or imperfect), present, near future	**Different persons** of the verb **Verbs with an infinitive**: tener ganas de, soler, acabar de	**More than one tense to talk about the past** (preterite, imperfect and perfect)
Opinions and reasons	**Verbs of opinion**: me chifla, me interesa **Reasons**: porque	**Exclamations**: ¡Qué horror!, ¡Qué timo! **Comparatives**: más… que, menos… que	**Opinions**: creo que, a mi modo de ver, en mi opinión **Reasons**: dado que, ya que, por eso, por lo tanto, así que, como **Comparatives**: tan… cómo…
Connectives	y, pero, también	sin embargo, por desgracia, por ejemplo, sobre todo	ya no, todavía **Balancing an argument**: aunque, por un lado… por otro lado…
Other features	**Negatives**: no, nunca **Qualifiers**: muy, un poco, bastante **Adjectives**: emocionante, original **Time phrases**: siempre, a menudo, ahora	**Sentences with cuando, donde**: Cuando tenía… **Negatives**: ni… ni…, tampoco… **para + infinitive**: para ayudar	**Object pronouns**: lo/la/los/las **Specialist vocabulary**: la campeona, el argumento **Interesting phrases**: me ayuda a desconectar, la gran pantalla

A – Extended writing task

1 Look at the task and answer the questions.
- What information does each bullet point ask you to give?
- How could you develop your answer to each one?

2 Read Rahma's answer on page 91. What do the phrases in **bold** mean?

3 Look at the Answer Booster. Note down **six** examples of language which Rahma uses to write a strong answer.

4 Look at the plan of Rahma's answer. Write the letters for each paragraph in the correct order.

5 Prepare your own answer to the task.
- Look at the Answer Booster and Rahma's plan for ideas.
- Write a detailed plan. Organise your answer in paragraphs.
- Write your answer and carefully check what you have written.

En un sitio web español hay un concurso sobre 'el deporte y el tiempo libre en diferentes países'. Decides participar.

Escribe al sitio web con esta información:
- la importancia del deporte para ti
- otra actividad que hiciste en tu tiempo libre recientemente.

Escribe aproximadamente **150** palabras en **español**. Responde a los dos aspectos de la pregunta.

Paragraph 1
- a   A recent triumph
- b   Role models in sport
- c   Why I do sport
- d   Team sports
- e   Sports I used to play

Paragraph 2
- f   How often I go to the cinema
- g   What we did afterwards
- h   My last cinema trip
- i   What I didn't like
- j   What I liked about the film
- k   My opinion of the music

Módulo 4

Soy muy deportista porque soy una persona competitiva. En mi opinión, el deporte es sano y **me ayuda a desconectar**. Cuando tenía doce años, jugaba al 'netball' (un deporte que es **parecido al baloncesto**), pero ya no juego. Soy miembro de un club de natación desde hace cinco años y acabamos de ganar un torneo. También me flipan los deportes de equipo, ya que **me permiten hacer nuevos amigos**. Además, **a mi modo de ver**, los deportistas son buenos modelos a seguir. **Admiro a la campeona olímpica** Jessica Ennis-Hill porque tiene mucha perseverancia. Ha ganado muchos títulos por eventos como **el salto de altura**.

Jessica Ennis-Hill

También me chifla ir al cine, puesto que me ayuda a olvidarme de todo. El miércoles pasado vi la nueva comedia de mi actor favorito. Me encantó, dado que tenía un argumento original y **el protagonista era muy gracioso**. Suelo ir al cine dos o tres veces al mes porque el ambiente es mejor cuando hay muchos espectadores. Por desgracia, **tuvimos que hacer cola en la taquilla** y no había descuento para estudiantes. **¡Qué timo!** Sin embargo, **las canciones eran pegadizas**, así que voy a descargar la banda sonora. Después de la película fuimos a una hamburguesería y luego volvimos a casa.

> ⭐ Make sure that what you write is **fully relevant** to the question. Notice how Rahma cleverly shows off that she can use the near future tense, whilst still answering the bullet point about what she did recently.

B – Translation

1 Read the English text and Lauren's translation of it. Write down the missing word(s) for each gap.

> I'm a music fanatic and I used to play the drums. I tend to listen to the radio while I do my homework, since it helps me to relax. Last week I went to a concert with my cousin. We sang lots of our favourite songs. The atmosphere was incredible and I'm going to buy the DVD.

> 1 ──── un fanático de la música y 2 ──── la batería. 3 ──── escuchar la radio mientras 4 ──── mis deberes, dado que me 5 ──── a relajarme. La semana pasada 6 ──── a un concierto con mi primo. 7 ──── muchas de nuestras canciones favoritas. El ambiente 8 ──── increíble y 9 ──── el DVD.

2 Translate the following passage into Spanish.

> I used to be a telly addict, but I no longer watch television because I don't have time. I spend my pocket money on computer games because they're fun. Yesterday I played with my brother, but I lost. He is addicted to the computer and tends to use it every day. Tomorrow we are going to buy a new game.

> ⭐ Examiners test your ability to use different types of verbs in different tenses and to talk about different people (for example, I, he/she,…). Think about which person and tense you need and take extra care with irregular verbs and those with a spelling change.

noventa y uno

Módulo 4 Palabras

La paga / Pocket money
Mis padres me dan…	My parents give me…
Mi madre / padre me da…	My mum / dad gives me…
…euros a la semana / al mes	…euros a week / a month
Gasto mi paga en…	I spend my pocket money on…
También compro…	I also buy…
saldo para el móvil	credit for my phone
ropa / joyas / maquillaje	clothes / jewellery / make-up
zapatillas de marca	designer trainers
videojuegos / revistas	computer games / magazines

Mis ratos libres / My free time
las actividades de ocio	leisure activities
Tengo muchos pasatiempos.	I have lots of hobbies.
A la hora de comer…	At lunchtime…
Cuando tengo tiempo…	When I have time…
Después del insti…	After school…
Los fines de semana…	At weekends…
Mientras desayuno / como…	Whilst I have breakfast / lunch…
juego al billar / futbolín	I play billiards / table football
monto en bici / monopatín	I ride my bike / skateboard
quedo con mis amigos	I meet up with friends
voy de compras	I go shopping
mi pasión es la música / la lectura	my passion is music / reading
Suelo…	I tend to / I usually …
descansar	rest
escuchar música / la radio	listen to music / the radio
hacer deporte	do sport
ir al cine	go to the cinema
leer libros / revistas / periódicos	read books / magazines / newspapers
salir con amigos	go out with friends
usar el ordenador	use the computer
ver la tele	watch TV
Es divertido / relajante / sano	It's fun / relaxing / healthy
Soy creativo/a / perezoso/a / sociable	I'm creative / lazy / sociable
Soy adicto/a a…	I'm addicted to…
me ayuda a relajarme	it helps me to relax
me ayuda a olvidarme de todo	it helps me to forget everything
me hace reír	it makes me laugh
necesito comunicarme / relacionarme con otra gente	I need to have contact with other people

La música / Music
Me gusta el soul / el rap / el dance / el hip-hop / el pop / el rock / el jazz / la música clásica / electrónica	I like soul / rap / dance / hip-hop / pop / rock / jazz / classical / electronic music
asistir a un concierto	to attend a concert
cantar (una canción)	to sing (a song)
tocar el teclado / el piano /	to play the keyboard / the piano /
la batería / la flauta / la guitarra / la trompeta	the drums / the flute / the guitar / the trumpet
mi cantante preferido/a es…	my favourite singer is…
un espectáculo	a show
una gira (mundial)	a (world) tour

El deporte / Sport
Soy / Era…	I am / I used to be…
(bastante / muy) deportista	(quite / very) sporty
miembro de un club / un equipo	a member of a club / a team
aficionado/a / hincha de…	a fan of…
un(a) fanático/a de…	a … fanatic
juego al…	I play…
jugué al…	I played…
jugaba al…	I used to play…
bádminton / baloncesto	badminton / basketball
béisbol / balonmano	baseball / handball
críquet / fútbol	cricket / football
hockey / ping-pong	hockey / table tennis
rugby / tenis / voleibol	rugby / tennis / volleyball
hago…	I do…
hice…	I did…
hacía…	I used to do…
baile / boxeo / ciclismo	dancing / boxing / cycling
deportes acuáticos	water sports
equitación / escalada	horseriding / climbing
gimnasia / judo	gymnastics / judo
kárate / natación	karate / swimming
patinaje sobre hielo	ice skating
piragüismo / remo	canoeing / rowing
submarinismo	diving
tiro con arco	archery
voy…	I go…
fui…	I went…
iba…	I used to go…
a clases de…	to … classes
de pesca	fishing
ya no (juego)…	(I) no longer (play)…
todavía (hago)…	(I) still (do)…
batir un récord	to break a record
correr	to run
entrenar	to train
jugar un partido contra…	to play a match against…
marcar un gol	to score a goal
montar a caballo	to go horseriding
participar en un torneo	to participate in a tournament
patinar	to skate
mi jugador(a) preferido/a es…	my favourite player is…
su punto culminante fue cuando…	the highlight (of his/her career) was when…
el campeón / la campeona	the champion
la temporada	the season

La tele / TV
(No) Soy teleadicto/a.	I'm (not) a TV addict.
Mi programa favorito es…	My favourite programme is…
un concurso	a game / quiz show
un programa de deportes	a sports programme
un reality	a reality TV show
un documental	a documentary
un culebrón / una telenovela	a soap
una comedia	a comedy
una serie policíaca	a crime series
el telediario / las noticias	the news
Me gustan las comedias.	I like comedies.
Es / Son…	It is / They are…
aburrido/a/os/as	boring
adictivo/a/os/as	addictive
divertido/a/os/as	fun
entretenido/a/os/as	entertaining
tonto/a/os/as	silly
informativo/a/os/as	informative
malo/a/os/as	bad
emocionante(s)	exciting
interesante(s)	interesting

Módulo 4

Las películas / Films

un misterio	a mystery
una película de amor	a love film
una película de terror	a horror film
una película de acción	an action film
una película de aventuras	an adventure film
una película de animación	an animated film
una película de ciencia ficción	a sci-fi film
una película de fantasía	a fantasy film
una película extranjera	a foreign film

Nacionalidades / Nationalities

americano/a	American
argentino/a	Argentinian
británico/a	British
chino/a	Chinese
griego/a	Greek
italiano/a	Italian
mexicano/a	Mexican
sueco/a	Swedish
alemán/alemana	German
danés/danesa	Danish
español(a)	Spanish
francés/francesa	French
holandés/holandesa	Dutch
inglés/inglesa	English
irlandés/irlandesa	Irish
japonés/japonesa	Japanese

Temas del momento / Trending topics

he compartido…	I have shared…
he comprado…	I have bought…
he jugado…	I have played…
he leído…	I have read…
he oído…	I have heard…
he roto…	I have broken…
he subido…	I have uploaded…
¿Has probado…?	Have you tried…?
mi hermano ha descargado…	my brother has downloaded…
se ha estrenado…	…has been released.
la nueva canción	the new song
el último libro	the latest book
Ya lo/la/los/las he visto.	I have already seen it/them.
No lo/la/los/las he visto todavía.	I haven't seen it/them yet.
acabo de ver / jugar a…	I have just seen / played…
cuenta la historia de…	it tells the story of…
trata de…	it's about…
combina el misterio con la acción	it combines mystery with action
el argumento es fuerte / débil	the plot is strong / weak
la banda sonora es buena / mala	the soundtrack is good / bad
los actores…	the actors…
los efectos especiales…	the special effects…
los gráficos…	the graphics…
los personajes…	the characters…
las animaciones…	the animations…
las canciones…	the songs…
son guapos/as / guay	are good looking / cool
son estupendos/as / impresionantes	are great / impressive
son originales / repetitivos/as	are original / repetitive

Ir al cine, al teatro, etc. / Going to the cinema, theatre, etc.

¿Qué vamos a hacer…	What are we going to do…
esta tarde?	this afternoon / evening?
esta noche?	tonight?
mañana / el viernes?	tomorrow / on Friday?
¿Tienes ganas de ir…	Do you fancy going…
a un concierto / un festival?	to a concert / a festival?
a un espectáculo de baile?	to a dance show?
al cine / al teatro / al circo?	to the cinema / theatre / circus?
¿Qué ponen?	What's on?
Es una película / obra de…	It's a … film / play
¿A qué hora empieza / termina?	What time does it start / finish?
Empieza / Termina a las…	It starts / finishes at…
Dos entradas para…, por favor.	Two tickets for …, please.
para la sesión de las…	for the … showing / performance
No quedan entradas.	There are no tickets left.
¿Hay un descuento para estudiantes?	Is there a discount for students?
Aquí tiene mi carné de estudiante.	Here is my student card.

¿En el cine o en casa? / At the cinema or at home?

(No) Me gusta ir al cine porque…	I (don't) like going to the cinema because…
Prefiero ver las pelis en casa porque…	I prefer watching films at home because…
el ambiente es mejor	the atmosphere is better
hay demasiadas personas	there are too many people
la imagen es mejor en la gran pantalla	the picture is better on the big screen
las entradas son muy caras	the tickets are very expensive
las palomitas están ricas	the popcorn is tasty
los asientos no son cómodos	the seats aren't comfortable
los otros espectadores me molestan	the other spectators annoy me
ponen tráilers para las nuevas pelis	they show trailers for new films
si vas al baño te pierdes una parte	if you go to the toilet you miss part of it
tienes que hacer cola	you have to queue
una corrida de toros	a bull fight
en directo	live

Los modelos a seguir / Role models

Admiro a…	I admire…
Mi inspiración / ídolo es…	My inspiration / idol is…
…es un buen / mal modelo a seguir	…is a good / bad role model
Un buen modelo a seguir es alguien que…	A good role model is someone who…
apoya a organizaciones benéficas	supports charities
recauda fondos para…	raises money for…
tiene mucho talento / éxito	is very talented / successful
trabaja en defensa de los animales	works in defence of animals
usa su fama para ayudar a los demás	uses his / her fame to help others
se emborrachan	they get drunk
se comportan mal	they behave badly
se meten en problemas con la policía	they get into trouble with the police
es amable / cariñoso/a / fuerte	he/she is nice / affectionate / strong
lucha por / contra…	he/she fights for / against…
la pobreza / la homofobia	poverty / homophobia
los derechos de la mujer	women's rights
los derechos de los refugiados	the rights of refugees
los niños desfavorecidos	underprivileged children
la justicia social	social justice
a pesar de sus problemas…	despite his/her problems…
ha batido varios récords	he/she has broken several records
ha creado…	he/she has created…
ha ganado … medallas / premios	he/she has won … medals / awards
ha sufrido varias enfermedades	he/she has suffered several illnesses
ha superado sus problemas	he/she has overcome his/her problems
ha tenido mucho éxito como…	he/she has had lots of success as…
siempre sonríe	he/she always smiles
solo piensa en los demás	he/she only thinks of other people

noventa y tres

5 Ciudades
Punto de partida 1

- Talking about places in a town
- Asking for and understanding directions

1 Lee los textos. Pon los dibujos en el orden correcto. (NB Not all places mentioned are shown in the pictures!)

1. En mi ciudad hay un cine y una piscina. También hay muchas tiendas y unos museos, pero no hay ni mercado ni biblioteca. Tampoco hay pista de hielo.
2. Vivo en un pueblo tranquilo donde solo hay una iglesia, un parque y Correos. También hay un castillo en ruinas, pero no hay ni bolera ni ayuntamiento.
3. Mi ciudad tiene un centro comercial con muchos restaurantes y bares. Está en la costa, así que hay playas y un puerto también. Desafortunadamente, no hay polideportivo.

2 Escribe una lista en español e inglés de los lugares del ejercicio 1.

3 Escucha y mira los dibujos. ¿Hay uno, unos o muchos? (1–3)
Ejemplo: **1** e ✓✓, …, …

Hay	un / una ✓
	unos / unas ✓✓
	muchos / muchas ✓✓✓
No hay	--- ✗

4 Lee y empareja las preguntas y respuestas.

1. ¿Dónde vives?
2. ¿Dónde está?
3. ¿Cómo es tu ciudad?
4. ¿Qué hay en tu ciudad?
5. ¿Te gusta vivir allí?

a. Está bien porque siempre hay algo que hacer.
b. Hay muchos lugares de interés.
c. Está situada en el sur del país.
d. Vivo en Córdoba.
e. Es una ciudad bastante grande, turística y muy bonita.

5 Con tu compañero/a, pregunta y contesta a las preguntas del ejercicio 4.

> **No** hay **ni** un polideportivo **ni** una plaza mayor.
> **Tampoco** hay un teatro.
>
> There **isn't** a sports centre **or** town square.
> **Nor** is there a theatre.

Vivo en	Manchester, Cardiff,	una ciudad un pueblo	grande pequeño/a	y/e pero	histórico/a moderno/a tranquilo/a ruidoso/a turístico/a industrial bonito/a feo/a
Está situado/a en	el norte / el sur / el este / el oeste	de Inglaterra / Gales / Escocia / Irlanda (del Norte)		cerca de…	
En… hay Mi ciudad tiene	un ayuntamiento una bolera / unos bares unas pistas de tenis	pero no hay	teatro muchos espacios verdes		
(No) me gusta porque	(no) hay mucho que hacer / siempre hay algo que hacer / no hay nada que hacer				

94 noventa y cuatro

Módulo 5

6 Escribe un párrafo sobre tu ciudad o pueblo.

> Use *e* to mean 'and' when the next word begins with *i-* or *hi-*.
> Vivo en una ciudad pequeña **e** histórica.

7 Pon la conversación en el orden correcto. Luego tradúcela al inglés.

a De nada.

b ¿Dónde está?

c Perdón. ¿La Plaza Mayor está lejos de aquí?

d Muchas gracias.

e No, está muy cerca.

f Toma la primera calle a la izquierda. Luego sigue todo recto y está a la derecha.

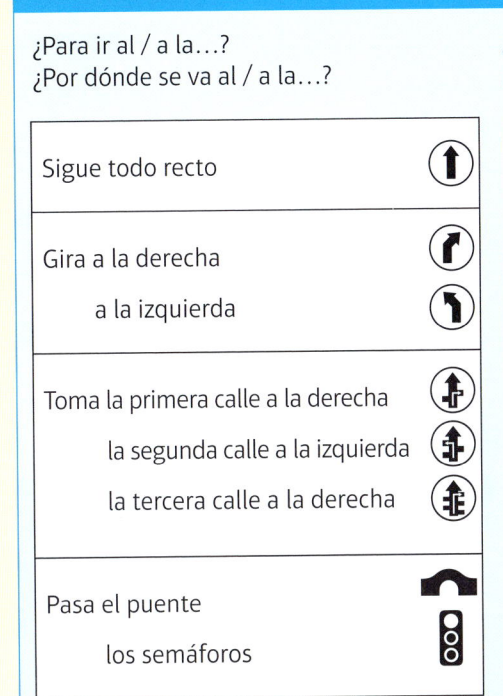

¿Para ir al / a la…?
¿Por dónde se va al / a la…?

Sigue todo recto	↑
Gira a la derecha / a la izquierda	↱ ↰
Toma la primera calle a la derecha / la segunda calle a la izquierda / la tercera calle a la derecha	
Pasa el puente / los semáforos	

¿Dónde está el / la…?
¿El / La … está cerca / lejos?

Cruza la plaza / la calle	
Coge el autobús número 37	🚌
Está cerca / lejos / en la esquina / al final de la calle / al lado del museo / enfrente de la piscina / a la derecha / a la izquierda / a mano derecha / a mano izquierda	

8 Escucha y mira el mapa. Escribe la letra correcta (a–f). (1–6)

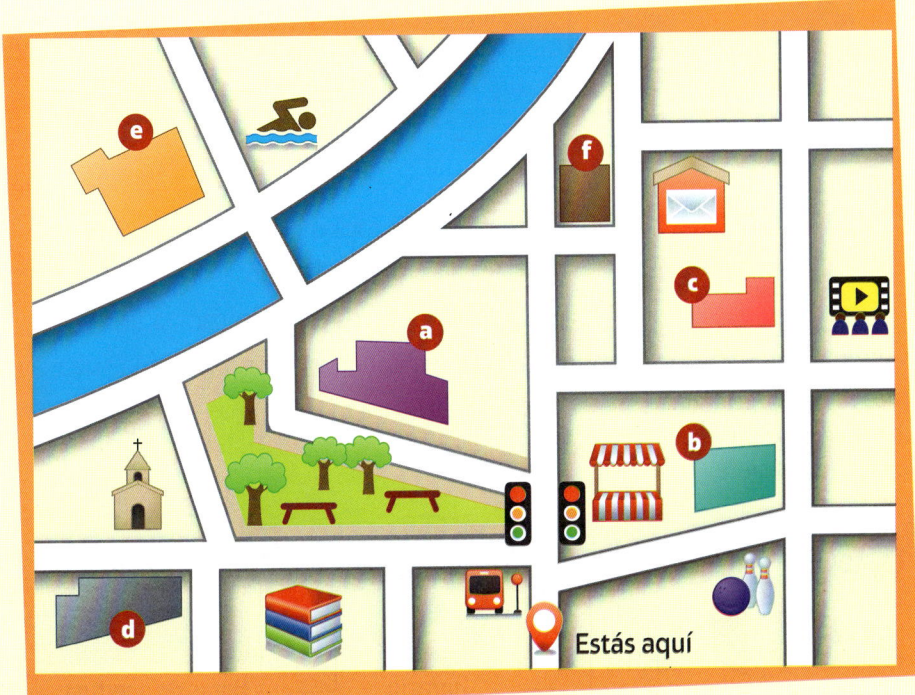

> Remember:
> *a + el = al*
> *de + el = del*

Estás aquí

9 Con tu compañero/a, pregunta y contesta. Utiliza el mapa.
● ¿Dónde está <u>la iglesia / el mercado / la biblioteca / el cine / la bolera</u>?

Unidad 1

noventa y cinco 95

Punto de partida 2

- Talking about shops
- Shopping for souvenirs

1 ¿Qué se compra en estas tiendas? Copia y completa la tabla en español.

tienda	cosa
la panadería	pan
la zapatería	
la frutería	
la papelería	
la cafetería	
la joyería	
la carnicería	
la pastelería	
la pescadería	
la librería	

★ Many shop names contain the word for what they sell. Try to work out what these shops are without a dictionary.

2 Escucha. ¿Adónde van? Escribe la letra correcta. (1–6)

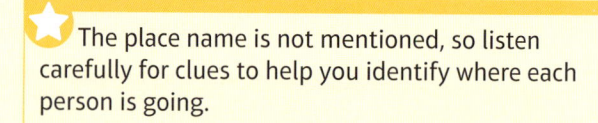

a la estación de trenes
b el banco
c la tienda de ropa
d la peluquería
e la farmacia
f el estanco

★ The place name is not mentioned, so listen carefully for clues to help you identify where each person is going.

3 Lee la lista de Carolina, ¿adónde va? Escribe los lugares en español.

- buscar un regalo para mi madre (¿unos pendientes?)
- comprar carne para la barbacoa
- recoger la tarta de cumpleaños para la fiesta
- devolver la camiseta nueva que compré la semana pasada
- comprar sellos para mandar unas cartas

4 Escribe frases para cada lugar.
Ejemplo: **1** De lunes a viernes la panadería **abre** a las ocho y **cierra** a la una.
Por la tarde **abre** de las dos hasta las siete…

1 Panadería El Faro
Horario comercial:
lunes–viernes
08.00–13.00
14.00–19.00
sábados
09.00–13.00

2 Heladería San Isidro
bar helados bebidas   bar helados bebidas
lunes–viernes 11.00–21.00
sábados y domingos 13.00–23.00
no cierra a mediodía

3 Centro comercial
Horario
lunes–sábado 10.00–22.00
cerrado domingos y festivos

4 Pescadería Cangrejo
Horas de apertura:
abierto todos los días 8.15–14.00
fines de semana 07.30–12.30

noventa y seis

Módulo 5

Unidad 3

5 ¿Cuánto cuesta? Pregunta y contesta.

● *Creo que el llavero cuesta tres euros noventa y cinco (céntimos). ¿Y tú?*
■ *Sí, yo también. En mi opinión, los pendientes cuestan cincuenta y seis euros.*

a. el abanico
b. el chorizo
c. el llavero
d. el oso de peluche
e. la gorra
f. la taza
g. los pendientes
h. las golosinas
i. las pegatinas

23,50 €	56,00 €
3,95 €	4,99 €
15,75 €	9,50 €
12,25 €	1,45 €
2,50 €	

6 Escucha y comprueba tus respuestas. Escribe la letra correcta y el precio. (1–9)

⭐ Prices can be said in different ways:
- ocho euros **y** cincuenta y cinco
- ocho **con** cincuenta y cinco
- ocho euros cincuenta y cinco

7 Escucha y lee. Escribe las palabras que faltan en español. (1–2)

● *Buenos días. ¿Me puede ayudar? Quiero comprar a _____.*
■ *Muy bien. ¿Para quién es?*
● *Es para b _____.*
■ *Vale. ¿De qué color?*
● *c _____, por favor.*
■ *De acuerdo. Aquí tiene.*
● *¿Tiene uno/una/unos/unas d _____, por favor?*
■ *Sí, por supuesto.*
● *Gracias. ¿Cuánto es / son?*
■ *e _____.*
● *Solo tengo un billete de cincuenta / cien euros.*
■ *No pasa nada, tengo cambio.*

G Polite form of address

Use the **usted** (polite) form of the verb with an adult you don't know well.
¿Me **puede** ayudar?   **Can you** help me?
Aquí **tiene**.   Here **you are**.

8 Con tu compañero/a, haz diálogos. Utiliza los siguientes detalles.

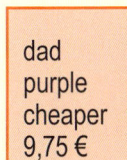

brother	dad	girlfriend	sister
red	purple	blue	white
smaller	cheaper	longer	larger
13,25 €	9,75 €	35,95 €	18,40 €

⭐ *Largo* means 'long', not 'large'!
'Big' or 'large' = *grande*.

noventa y siete **97**

1 ¿Cómo es tu zona?

- *Describing the features of a region*
- *Using se puede and se pueden*
- *Asking and responding to questions*

1 Escucha y lee. Escribe la ciudad correcta para cada frase.

¿Cómo es tu zona?

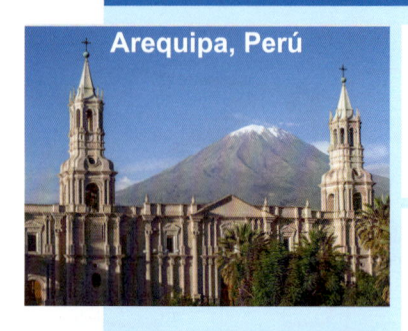

Arequipa, Perú

Arequipa está rodeada de tres volcanes y tiene unos impresionantes paisajes naturales. Es un oasis verde entre el desierto y la sierra. Me encanta el clima soleado. Solo llueve un poco en verano, así que se puede pasar mucho tiempo al aire libre. **Lidia**

Coroico, Bolivia

Vivo en Coroico, un pueblo situado en un valle de la cordillera de los Andes. Es una región muy húmeda con muchas nieblas, pero es un paraíso de selva subtropical, ríos y bosques, perfecto para los que quieren caminar o ir en bici. **Alberto**

Córdoba, España

Córdoba es mi ciudad natal y me gusta mucho. Las varias influencias culturales (árabe, romana y judía) la hacen acogedora y atractiva, y se pueden visitar edificios de estilos muy diferentes. **Vicente**

La verdad es que en Valencia tenemos de todo: el bullicio de una ciudad, pero al lado del mar Mediterráneo. Mi lugar favorito es la Ciudad de las Ciencias, donde se pueden alquilar bolas de agua para pasear por los lagos artificiales. **Mariana**

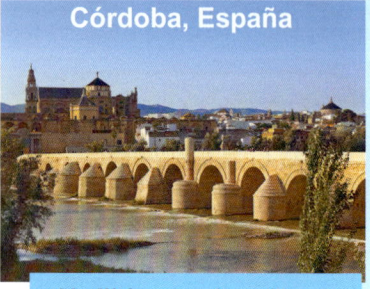

Valencia, España

el bullicio hustle and bustle

1. Aquí se puede apreciar la arquitectura variada.
2. Aquí se pueden practicar senderismo y ciclismo.
3. Aquí se puede disfrutar del ambiente urbano y de la costa al mismo tiempo.
4. El clima es seco en invierno, otoño y primavera.
5. Es una zona muy montañosa y pintoresca, donde llueve a menudo.
6. Aquí se puede aprovechar el buen tiempo.

G se puede / se pueden + *infinitive*

Use these to say 'you can…'.
(Singular noun) *Se puede visitar la galería de arte.*
(Plural noun) *Se pueden probar platos típicos.*

2 Lee los textos de nuevo. Haz **dos** listas en español y luego traduce las palabras al inglés:
- **diez** palabras relacionadas con la geografía física
- **cuatro** palabras relacionadas con el clima

3 Escucha. Copia y completa la tabla en inglés. (1–4)

city	geography	climate	two things you can do there
Rosario			

Está	situado/a en un valle / al lado del río rodeado/a de sierra lleno/a de bosques a… metros sobre el nivel del mar
El clima es	soleado, caluroso, seco, frío, templado
Hay	riesgo de tormentas mucha marcha
Es	famoso/a por (la Alhambra) conocido/a por (sus playas)
Aquí se puede	subir a la torre esquiar en invierno hacer un recorrido en autobús disfrutar de las vistas viajar en el AVE
Aquí se pueden	probar platos típicos practicar deportes acuáticos

4 Busca información y escribe un texto sobre una de estas ciudades.

Sevilla   Palma de Mallorca   La Habana   Santiago de Compostela

noventa y ocho

Módulo 5

5 Estás en la oficina de turismo. Empareja las mitades de las preguntas. Escribe frases completas.

1. ¿Me puede dar más información…
2. ¿Cuándo abre…
3. ¿Cuánto cuesta una…
4. ¿Dónde se pueden…
5. ¿A qué hora…
6. ¿Hay visitas guiadas…
7. ¿Me puede dar…
8. ¿Me puede recomendar…

un plano de la ciudad?
la cueva?
sale el autobús?
entrada?
sacar las entradas?
un restaurante típico?
a caballo o en Segway?
sobre la excursión a la Cueva de los Murciélagos?

6 Escucha el diálogo y comprueba tus respuestas.

7 Estás en la oficina de turismo en Córdoba. Con tu compañero/a, haz diálogos.

- ● Say which excursion you would like more information about.
- ■ *Sí, por supuesto.*
- ● Ask about times. *(¿Cuándo abre / empieza(n)?)*
- ■ *Abre a las / Empieza(n) a las…*
- ● Ask the price.
- ■ *Cuesta…*
- ● Ask where you can buy tickets.
- ■ *Aquí en la oficina de turismo.*
- ● Ask what time the bus leaves.
- ■ *Sale…*
- ● Ask for another item (brochure, map of the city).
- ■ *Aquí tiene (un folleto) / (un plano de la ciudad).*

Excursión	Día / Horario	Tarifa
Cueva de los Murciélagos	ma.–vi. 12.30–17.00	6 €
Castillo de Almodóvar	lu.–do. 10.00–15.00	7 €
Visitas guiadas (a caballo, en bici, en Segway)	todos los días, cada dos horas, a las 10, 12…	40 €
Costa del Sol (Málaga)	cada hora diariamente 9–18	27 €

8 Lee el texto. Contesta a las preguntas utilizando frases completas.

24 horas en Córdoba. ¡Todo es posible!

Por la mañana: ¡Merece la pena madrugar! A primera hora hace menos calor y se puede aprovechar para visitar la Mezquita, que hasta las 9.30 es gratis. Luego puedes bajar al río Guadalquivir y contemplar la ciudad desde el puente romano. Para desayunar, podemos comer unos *jeringos* (o churros) en la churrería de la plaza del Campo Santo de los Mártires. Después es hora de descansar en los baños árabes Hammam Al Ándalus.

Al mediodía: Tenemos el bar Casa Santos y sus tortillas, hechas con cinco kilos de patatas y treinta huevos, quizá las más grandes y las mejores del mundo.

Por la tarde: Conocer el barrio más popular de Córdoba: la Judería, un laberinto de calles estrechas. La más pintoresca es la calleja de las Flores. Está llena de geranios y es un imán para los aficionados a la fotografía.

la Mezquita

Por la noche: El espectáculo ecuestre que se ofrece en las Caballerizas Reales es algo que no te puedes perder.

calleja de las Flores

1. ¿Cuándo se puede visitar la Mezquita sin pagar?
2. ¿Dónde se puede desayunar?
3. ¿Qué se puede hacer en los baños árabes?
4. ¿Qué se puede comer en el bar Casa Santos?
5. ¿Qué se puede hacer en la calleja de las Flores?
6. ¿Qué animales se pueden ver por la noche?

noventa y nueve 99

2 ¿Qué haremos mañana?

- Planning what to do
- Using the future tense
- Understanding the geography of Spain

1 Lee el texto y elige las <u>tres</u> frases correctas. Luego traduce las expresiones en **negrita**.

San Cristóbal de la Laguna, 7 de junio

¡Hola mamá!

Ya estoy muy a gusto en casa de Elena. ¡Su familia es guay! La zona donde viven es muy bonita, pero también es bastante lluviosa. ¡No ha dejado de llover en dos días! Por lo tanto, todavía no he visto mucho de Tenerife, pero mañana **el papá de Elena nos llevará** al Pico del Teide, donde **subiremos en teleférico**. Elena me dice que **pasaremos entre las nubes** para llegar a la cumbre. Aunque es verano, **habrá nieve** en la sierra. ¡**Será genial**! Luego **bajaremos a pie** para disfrutar del paisaje. **Sacaré muchas fotos** y **las subiré** a mi Facebook. **Te enviaré** un comentario mañana por la noche. Hoy, si sale el sol, **iremos a la playa**. ¿Qué tiempo hace allí en Cartagena?

Un beso, Juliana

1. Juliana está muy feliz en casa de Elena.
2. Siempre hace buen tiempo en San Cristóbal de la Laguna.
3. Juliana y Elena irán de excursión en barco.
4. Mañana Juliana y Elena irán a la montaña.
5. Juliana escribirá otro mensaje a su madre.
6. Hoy hará sol.

G The future tense > Page 216

Add these endings to the infinitive stem of regular –ar, –er and –ir verbs.

visitar**é**	I will visit
visitar**ás**	you will visit
visitar**á**	he/she/you (polite) will visit
visitar**emos**	we will visit
visitar**éis**	you (plural) will visit
visitar**án**	they/you (plural, polite) will visit

A few verbs have an **irregular stem** in the future tense:
har**é** (I will do)   podr**ás** (you will be able to)
tendr**é** (I will have)   saldr**ás** (you will leave, go out)
dir**á** (he/she/you will say)   habr**á** (there will be)

2 Escucha. Escribe los detalles en inglés. (1–4)

Ejemplo: **1** *if good weather – go on boat trip, …*

| está despejado | it's fine / cloudless |

⭐ Use 'if' clauses to discuss plans:

Si + **present**, + **future**

Si **hace** calor, **nadaremos** en el mar.
If **it's** hot, **we'll swim** in the sea.

3 Con tu compañero/a, habla de los planes posibles.

- ● ¿Qué haremos el lunes?
- ■ Si hace sol, iremos a la playa.
- ● ¡Qué bien! ¿Y si llueve?
- ■ Jugaremos al tenis de mesa.

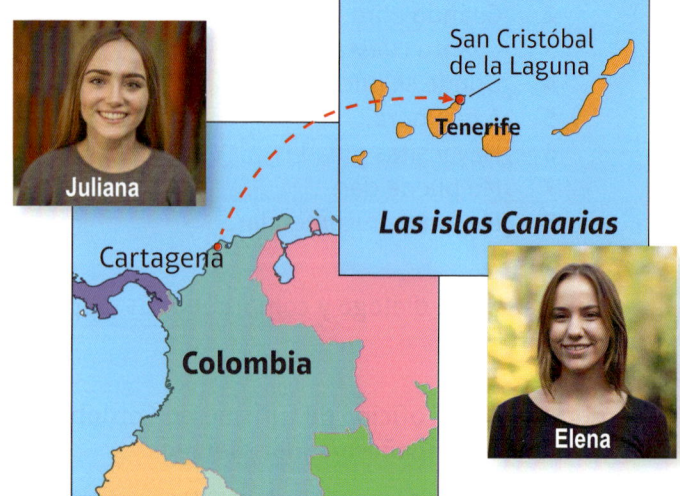

lunes	☀️	jueves	🌡️☀️
martes	🌡️❄️	viernes	🌧️
miércoles	👎☁️		

100 *cien*

Módulo 5

4 Escucha y lee. Contesta a las preguntas en inglés.

E: Bueno, ¿qué haremos el resto de la semana? Ya has visto el Pico del Teide y el parque nacional…
J: Sí, ¡fue genial! También hemos pasado un día en la playa.
E: Pues, mira. Hoy es martes. Según el pronóstico del tiempo, hará viento en la costa, así que será mejor ir al zoo que a la playa. ¿Qué te parece?
J: ¡Qué bien! Quiero ver los monos. Mañana parece que lloverá bastante.
E: ¿Por qué no vamos a la Cueva del Viento? El tiempo no nos importará allí.
J: Buena idea. ¿Y el jueves?
E: Será muy variable, según el pronóstico. Habrá nubes y claros, con chubascos. Bueno, iremos a Santa Cruz. Si no hace viento, podremos hacer paddle surf, y si hace demasiado viento, haremos piragüismo.
J: ¡Qué guay! Me encantan los dos.
E: El viernes será tu último día.
J: ¡Qué triste!
E: Sí, pero iremos al centro comercial y podrás comprar regalos para tu familia.
J: De acuerdo.

Santa Cruz de Tenerife

1 Name three things that Juliana has already done.
2 Why does Elena suggest going to the zoo on Tuesday?
3 Where does Elena think they should go tomorrow and why?
4 What is the weather forecast for Thursday? Give three details.
5 What are the two options for Thursday?
6 Give two details about the plan for Juliana's last day.

5 Estás en España. Escribe un post para el blog de tu clase.

Mention:
- something you have already visited
- something you have not yet seen
- an activity you will do if the weather is good
- an activity you will do if the weather is bad
- what you will do on the last day

Ya he visitado…
Todavía no he visto…
Si hace buen tiempo, …
Si llueve, …
El último día…

6 Escucha el pronóstico meteorológico. Escribe las letras correctas.

¿Qué tiempo hará en…?
1 el sur
2 la costa cantábrica
3 el norte
4 el este
5 las Baleares

Habrá…
a una ola de calor *(heatwave)*
b truenos y relámpagos *(thunder and lightning)*
c temperaturas más altas *(higher temperatures)*
d temperaturas más bajas *(lower temperatures)*
e granizo *(hail)*
f brisas fuertes *(strong breezes)*
g periodos soleados *(sunny spells)*

Las temperaturas…
h subirán *(will rise)*
i bajarán *(will fall)*

El tiempo…
j se despejará *(will clear up)*
k cambiará *(will change)*
l lloverá *(It will rain)*

Spain has 17 *comunidades autónomas*.

ciento uno **101**

3 De compras

- Shopping for clothes and presents
- Using demonstrative adjectives
- Explaining preferences

1 Escucha y lee. Busca las frases en español.

Speech bubbles:
- Aquí tienen de todo. ¿Por dónde quieres empezar?
- Primero quiero devolver algo.
- Perdone, señora. Ayer compré **esta camiseta**, pero tiene un agujero. ¿Puede reembolsarme el dinero, por favor?
- No, lo siento. Pero podemos hacer un cambio.
- Aquí tiene el recibo. No quiero otra camiseta. ¿Qué me recomienda?
- ¿Qué tal **este cinturón** de cuero?
- No, gracias ¿Me puedo probar **esta falda amarilla**?
- Elena, ¿qué te parece?
- Bueno, **esta falda** me la llevo. ¡Y **estas sandalias** también! Ahora necesito regalos para mi familia…
- ¡Qué bonitos!
- Por supuesto. ¿Qué talla tiene? ¿La 36? ¿Y qué tal con **aquellos zapatos negros**?
- La falda te queda muy bien, pero **esos zapatos** te quedan demasiado grandes. Prefiero **estas sandalias**.

1 I want to return something.
2 It has a hole.
3 Can you refund me?
4 We can exchange it.
5 Here is the receipt.
6 Can I try on this yellow skirt?
7 What size are you?
8 The skirt looks very good on you.
9 I'll take it.

2 Lee la historia del ejercicio 1 otra vez. Traduce las palabras en **negrita** al inglés.

G Demonstrative adjectives

	singular		plural	
	masculine	feminine	masculine	feminine
this, these	est**e** bolso	est**a** corbata	est**os** bolsos	est**as** corbatas
that, those	es**e** bolso	es**a** corbata	es**os** bolsos	es**as** corbatas
that, those… over there	aqu**el** bolso	aqu**ella** corbata	aqu**ellos** bolsos	aqu**ellas** corbatas

3 Escucha. Copia y completa la tabla en inglés. (1–4)

| en rebajas | on sale |
| una talla más grande | a bigger size |

	item bought	problem	solution
1			

4 Con tu compañero/a, haz diálogos.

1
– Say what you bought, what the problem is, and ask for a refund
– Say yes, of course, ask for the receipt
– Say here you are
– Say here's the money
– Say thank you and goodbye

2
– Say what you bought, what the problem is, and ask for a refund
– Say no, sorry, but you can change it
– Say OK, ask what he/she recommends
– Say what about this (T-shirt)?
– Say you like it and you'll take it

está	rot**o/a**
es demasiado	estrech**o/a**, larg**o/a**
tiene	una mancha, un agujero
le falta	un botón

102 *ciento dos*

Módulo 5

5 ¿Quién dice las siguientes frases? Escribe el nombre correcto.

¿Te gustan los centros comerciales?

Bruno
A mí me mola ir de tiendas con mis amigos. Solemos ir al nuevo centro comercial. Tiene prácticamente todas las tiendas que necesitas y grandes almacenes donde se puede comprar de todo, incluso artículos de marca en las tiendas de diseño. Prefiero ir allí que al centro porque es un buen sitio para pasar la tarde con mis amigos.

Iker
Odio los centros comerciales porque siempre hay demasiada gente. La última vez que fui de compras en la ciudad hacía mucho calor y tuve que hacer cola en todas las tiendas. Fue una absoluta pérdida de tiempo. Desde entonces compro todo por Internet porque es mucho más cómodo. Hago mis compras sin salir de casa. ¡Es genial!

Fabiana
Me encanta la ropa alternativa y por eso nunca me ha gustado comprar en las cadenas. Tengo un estilo muy diferente, y por eso busco lo que necesito en tiendas de segunda mano. Allí siempre puedes encontrar gangas y ropa con mucha originalidad.

Clara
Prefiero comprar cosas por Internet porque creo que hay más variedad que en las tiendas. Además, los precios son más bajos y hay más ofertas. No obstante, como no se pueden probar las cosas antes de comprar, hay que devolverlas a menudo. ¡Qué rollo!

grandes almacenes	department stores
las cadenas	chain stores
las gangas	bargains

1. Es más económico comprar en la red.
2. Ir de compras con tus amigos es muy divertido.
3. No compro ropa de moda.
4. Me gusta comprar por Internet, pero hay inconvenientes también.
5. Me gustan los centros comerciales.
6. Es mucho más práctico comprar por Internet.

6 Traduce el post de Clara al inglés.

7 Escucha. Apunta en inglés (a) dónde prefiere comprar y (b) por qué. (1–4)

8 Con tu compañero/a, pregunta y contesta.

- ¿Adónde vas de compras normalmente?
- ¿Dónde prefieres comprar? ¿Por qué?
- ¿Te gusta comprar por Internet? ¿Por qué?
- ¿Adónde fuiste de compras la última vez y qué compraste?
- ¿Vas a ir de compras el próximo fin de semana?

Normalmente voy / Suelo ir	a los centros comerciales / al centro de la ciudad		
Prefiero comprar / Me gusta comprar / Odio comprar	en	(las) cadenas / (los) grandes almacenes / (las) tiendas de diseño / (las) tiendas de segunda mano	porque…
	por	Internet	
La última vez que fui de compras	compré… y…		
El próximo fin de semana	voy a… para comprar…		

⭐ Adapt the opinions and reasons from exercise 5 to explain your preferences.

ciento tres 103

4 Los pros y los contras de la ciudad

- Talking about problems in a town
- Using the conditional
- Using synonyms and antonyms

1 Escucha. Escribe las dos letras correctas. (1–4)

Lo mejor de vivir en la ciudad es que…

- a) es tan fácil desplazarse.
- b) hay tantas diversiones.
- c) las tiendas están tan cerca.
- d) hay muchas posibilidades de trabajo.

Lo peor es que…

- e) el centro es tan ruidoso.
- f) se lleva una vida tan frenética.
- g) hay tanto tráfico.
- h) la gente no se conoce.

2 ¿Qué dos cosas cambiaría cada persona? Apunta los datos en inglés.

La vida aquí en la ciudad es bulliciosa, pero a mí me gusta. Tienes todas las tiendas a poca distancia y es imposible aburrirse. También es fácil encontrar empleo. Lo único que cambiaría sería el centro. Introduciría más zonas peatonales y renovaría algunos edificios antiguos. **Julio**

Se dice que en la ciudad no hay un gran sentido de comunidad, pero yo conozco a todos mis vecinos. Por otro lado, opino que la gente siempre tiene prisa. Por mi parte, pondría más áreas de ocio, donde la gente podría descansar. También plantaría más árboles. **Valentina**

Se lleva una vida muy relajada en el campo. ¡Es tan tranquila! No hay tanto que hacer, pero diría que tienes todo lo necesario para vivir bien. Sin embargo, el transporte público no es fiable y por eso hay tantos coches. Mejoraría el sistema de transporte público y sería gratis para todos. **Ariana**

Aunque vivo en el campo, ahora hay una red de transporte público muy buena y no hay tantos atascos como antes. Sin embargo, las tiendas están demasiado lejos y por eso construiría un nuevo centro comercial. Otro problema es que hay bastante desempleo. Invertiría en el turismo rural porque crearía una mejor oferta de empleo. **Hugo**

G The conditional — Page 220

Most verbs in the conditional translate as 'would'. You already know **me gustaría** (I would like). To form the conditional, add the imperfect endings of –er/–ir verbs to the infinitive:

mejoraría	I would improve
mejorarías	you would improve
mejoraría	he/she/you (polite) would improve
mejoraríamos	we would improve
mejoraríais	you (plural) would improve
mejorarían	they/you (plural, polite) would improve

G Irregular verbs in the conditional — Page 220

Verbs which are irregular in the future tense are also irregular in the conditional. Here are the most common:

decir → diría (I would say)
haber → habría (there would be)
hacer → haría (I would do)
poder → podría (I would be able to)
poner → pondría (I would put)
tener → tendría (I would have)

Módulo 5

3 Busca en el texto del ejercicio 2 frases sinónimas a las frases del ejercicio 1.

Ejemplo: **a** *Es tan fácil desplazarse.*
→ *Hay una red de transporte público muy buena.*

> **G** so..., so much..., so many...
>
> | | | |
> |---|---|---|
> | **tan** + adjective | **tan** tranquilo | **so** quiet |
> | **tanto/a** + singular noun | **tanta** contaminación | **so much** pollution |
> | **tantos/as** + plural noun | **tantos** problemas | **so many** problems |

4 Busca en el texto del ejercicio 2 frases antónimas a las frases del ejercicio 1. Tradúcelas al inglés.

Ejemplo: **a** *El transporte público no es fiable.*
→ *Public transport is not reliable.*

5 Escucha y apunta en inglés (a) <u>tres</u> problemas y (b) <u>seis</u> soluciones.

6 Con tu compañero/a, habla de donde vives.

- ¿Qué es lo mejor del lugar donde vives?
- Lo mejor es que las tiendas están tan cerca y…
- ¿Qué es lo peor?
- Lo peor es que hay tanto tráfico y…
- ¿Cómo cambiarías tu zona?
- Mejoraría el sistema de transporte público y…

Ciudad de Panamá

7 Escucha. Copia y completa la tabla en inglés. (1–4)

	past problem	improvement made	improvement needed
1			

⭐ You may hear expressions you have met before but in a different tense. Listen out for both past problems in the **imperfect tense** and the improvements that have already been made in the **perfect tense**.

han mejorado	they have improved
han introducido	they have introduced
han renovado	they have renovated
han construido	they have built
han creado	they have created
han plantado	they have planted
han abierto	they have opened

8 Lee el artículo. Contesta a las preguntas en inglés.

> Mi ciudad se llama Bilbao. Antes era muy industrial, pero ahora es un lugar muy atractivo para vivir. Lo mejor es que hay mucho que ver en la ciudad, como por ejemplo el famoso Museo Guggenheim. Todavía es ruidosa, pero han creado muchas áreas de ocio que son muy tranquilas. Han mejorado la red de transporte e incluso han introducido un sistema de alquiler de bicis. Es tan fácil desplazarse que se puede coger el metro o el tranvía para pasar un día en un pueblo en la costa.

1. How did Bilbao use to be and how is it now?
2. What is the best thing about the city?
3. Name one disadvantage.
4. List three improvements that have been made.
5. What evidence is there that it is easy to get around nowadays?

9 Escribe un artículo sobre el lugar donde vives.

⭐ Use:
- the **present tense** for describing your town/village and saying what the best/worst thing is
- the **imperfect tense** for saying what problems there used to be (*Antes (no) había… / era… / estaba…*)
- the **perfect tense** for saying what improvements have been made (*Han renovado / creado…*)
- the **conditional** for saying what else you would do to improve it (*Mejoraría… / Construiría…*)

ciento cinco **105**

5 ¡Destino Arequipa!

- *Describing a visit in the past*
- *Using different tenses together*
- *Recognising and using idioms*

1 Escucha y lee. Busca las expresiones en español.

Aventura sudamericana

Lucas Walker

El estudiante Lucas Walker nos cuenta cómo va su año sabático, y su visita a Arequipa en el sur del país.

¿Qué tal tu visita a Arequipa, Lucas?
¡Fue fenomenal! Me quedé impresionado con la ciudad. Vimos lugares interesantes como el monasterio de Santa Catalina. Tuvimos un guía que nos hizo un recorrido y nos ayudó a entender toda la historia.

¿Visitaste la ciudad a pie?
Sí, recorrí a pie el centro histórico, donde vi la plaza de Armas y la Catedral Blanca. Y en el Mundo Alpaca compré tantas cosas que ¡casi me quedé sin dinero!

Otro día alquilé una bici de montaña. Subimos en grupo al pie del volcán Misti, donde había unas vistas maravillosas. Luego bajamos en bici de la montaña a la ciudad. ¡Fue una experiencia única, pero al final de cada día estaba muy cansado!

la alpaca

¿Cómo era la ciudad?
Era muy acogedora porque la gente era muy abierta y comunicativa. Aprendí mucho sobre la cultura peruana.

¿Qué tal la comida?
La comida estaba muy buena. Comí de todo: pollo, patatas (o papas, como se llaman en Perú) y rocoto relleno.

¿Qué es lo que más te gustó?
Lo que más me gustó fue el clima porque hizo mucho sol. Lo que menos me gustó fueron los taxis. Eran baratos, pero iban demasiado rápido. ¡Qué miedo!

¿Vas a volver algún día?
Por supuesto que volveré algún día. Primero voy a visitar otras ciudades. Creo que voy a ir a Trujillo, en el norte de Perú, donde aprenderé a hacer surf. Luego quiero viajar a Colombia y a Ecuador. Allí trabajaré unas semanas como voluntario en un orfanato.

la gente peruana

el volcán Misti

rocoto relleno stuffed rocoto pepper

Completed actions
1 We saw…
2 He/She did a tour for us…
3 I went on foot round the historic centre.
4 We went up…
5 What I liked most…

Description in the past
6 There were amazing views.
7 The people were very open.
8 I was very tired.
9 The food was very good.

Future plans
10 I will return…
11 I'm going to visit…
12 I think I'm going to…
13 I will work…

G Using the preterite and the imperfect › Pages 212, 214

Remember, you use the **preterite** for completed actions in the past.
***Comí** de todo.* I **ate** everything.
Use the **imperfect** to describe what something was like, and for repeated actions in the past.
*La ciudad **era** acogedora.* The city **was** welcoming.

Zona Cultura

Arequipa, 'la Ciudad Blanca'

Destino:	AREQUIPA
Ubicación:	Sur de Perú, en el interior
Población:	1,3 millones (2ª ciudad de Perú)
Famosa por:	el volcán Misti
	la arquitectura blanca
	los textiles de alpaca

2 Lee la entrevista otra vez. Luego identifica las <u>cuatro</u> frases correctas.

1 Lucas visitó el monasterio de Santa Catalina con un guía.
2 A Lucas le gustó mucho la ciudad de Arequipa.
3 Cogió un autobús turístico para visitar la ciudad.
4 No comió rocoto relleno porque es vegetariano.
5 No le gustó el clima porque hizo mucho calor.
6 Lucas tiene la intención de regresar a Perú en el futuro.
7 Primero Lucas visitará otra ciudad en Perú.

ciento seis

Módulo 5

3 Escucha y escribe las letras correctas. Sobran <u>tres</u> opciones. (1–3)
Escucha otra vez. ¿La opinión es positiva (P) o negativa (N)?

- **a** museums
- **b** food
- **c** music and culture
- **d** atmosphere
- **e** people
- **f** transport
- **g** language
- **h** architecture
- **i** shopping

la plaza de Armas, Arequipa

> ⭐ **Quedarse** literally means 'to stay' or 'to remain'.
> **Me quedé** en un hotel. **I stayed** in a hotel.
> It is also used idiomatically to mean 'to end up', but we sometimes translate it into English using other verbs.
> **Me quedé** sin dinero. **I ended up** without money / I ran out of money.
> Can you work out what these expressions mean?
> Me quedé sin palabras.
> Me quedé dormido.
> Me quedé jugando al fútbol todo el día.
> Me quedé enamorado de la ciudad.

4 Con tu compañero/a, habla de una visita a una ciudad.

- ¿Adónde fuiste?
- ¿Cuánto tiempo pasaste allí?
- ¿Qué tal tu visita a <u>Londres</u>?
- ¿Visitaste la ciudad a pie?
- ¿Qué tiempo hizo?
- ¿Qué tal la comida?
- ¿Qué es lo que más te gustó?
- ¿Vas a volver?

- *Fui a <u>Londres</u>.*
- *Pasé…*
- *¡Fue <u>genial</u>! Vi… Fui a…*
- *Visité… a pie / Cogí… / Alquilé…*
- *Hizo…*
- *La comida estaba…*
- *Lo que más me gustó fue / fueron… pero lo que menos me gustó…*
- *Sí, volveré… Creo que… Quiero….*

5 Traduce este texto al español.

mucho, mucha, muchos or muchas?

Say 'did a guided tour for us'. Use the preterite of *hacer*, with *nos* (us) in front of it.

Do you need the preterite or the imperfect here?

Last year I visited Santander, a city in the north of Spain, with my school. We saw a lot of interesting places. The teacher took us on a guided tour and I learned a lot. The food was very good, but what I liked most was the windsurfing. It was amazing! I will go back one day, but next year I think I am going to go to Italy.

🇪🇸 Zona Cultura

Aunque se habla español en Perú, hay unas palabras diferentes.

Por ejemplo:

cuy chactado

España	Perú
coche	carro
patata	papa
cobaya	cuy
zumo de naranja	jugo de naranja
ordenador	computadora
móvil	celular
plaza Mayor	plaza de Armas

¿Qué significan en inglés?

ciento siete 107

Módulo 5   Leer y escuchar

1 **A travel article**
Read the article about cities of the world.

> La mejor ciudad del mundo para vivir está en España: es Palma de Mallorca, según el diario británico *The Times*.
>
> 'La capital de las islas Baleares cuenta con playas a las que se puede llegar andando y con un clima excepcional', concluye *The Times*. Palma supera a rivales como Toronto (el mejor destino para los urbanitas), Auckland (la mejor ciudad marítima), Hoi An en Vietnam (el número uno de la gastronomía) y Berlín.
>
> El equipo de periodistas especializados en viajes de *The Times* ha utilizado diversas estadísticas sobre la calidad de vida, las infraestructuras, la gastronomía, el clima, el entorno y la facilidad de 'asimilación' de los británicos. El diario describe Palma como 'una de las ciudades más pintorescas de España', y también la recomienda para unas vacaciones o para vivir.
>
> Los primeros países de la lista son Estados Unidos (con diez ciudades entre las cincuenta elegidas), Francia (con cinco), España, Italia y Australia (con cuatro cada una).

Palma de Mallorca

1 Which **two** statements are true? Write the correct letters.
  A One reason for Palma de Mallorca being the best city is the proximity of its beaches.
  B The annual report lists four reasons why Palma tops the list.
  C Toronto is listed as the best coastal city.
  D The quality of the food was one of the criteria.
  E Palma is described as one of the most popular cities in Spain.

Answer in **English**.
2 For what **two** purposes does the newspaper recommend Palma to its readers?
3 Give **one** detail that the article gives about the United States.

2 Read this extract from *La casa de los espíritus*, a novel by Isabel Allende. Esteban is talking to his sister, Férula, about a house he owns called *Las Tres Marías*.
Answer the questions which follow in **English**.

> —Creo que me iré al campo, a Las Tres Marías.
> —Eso es una ruina, Esteban. Siempre te he dicho que es mejor vender esa tierra, pero tú eres testarudo como una mula.
> —Nunca hay que vender la tierra. Es lo único que queda cuando todo lo demás se acaba*.
> —No estoy de acuerdo. La tierra es una idea romántica, lo que enriquece a* los hombres es el buen ojo para los negocios* —alegó Férula. —Pero tú siempre decías que algún día te ibas a ir a vivir al campo.
> —Ahora ha llegado ese día. Odio esta ciudad.
> —¿Por qué no dices mejor que odias esta casa?
> —También —respondió él brutalmente… […]
> Terminaron de comer en silencio.
>
> * *acabarse* = to finish
> * *lo que enriquece a* = what enriches
> * *los negocios* = business

1 What does Esteban say he is planning to do?
2 What does Férula want him to do with the land?
3 In response, what is Esteban's point of view?
4 What does Férula feel is better for men than owning land?
5 Why did Férula and Esteban finish their meal in silence?

> ⭐ With texts that include dialogue, it's important to be clear who is speaking. In the exam you can write F (Férula) and E (Esteban) next to each line of speech to help you pinpoint the correct information to answer each question.

3 Your area

Your Spanish friend, Marco, has answered this questionnaire about the area where he lives.
You read the questionnaire and look at the answers he has circled.

¿Qué tal es tu zona?

Buscamos la mejor zona de España para vivir o para visitar. Completa este cuestionario y danos tu opinión.

1   La red de transportes públicos…
    - (A) se ha mejorado mucho en los últimos años.
    - B   es la mejor del país.
    - C   es poco fiable y hay muchos retrasos.

2   Las tiendas…
    - A   ¡Ni hablar! Hay que comprar por Internet.
    - (B) quedan bastante lejos, pero la oferta es muy buena.
    - C   están a un paso y tienen todo lo que necesitas.

3   Tu zona atrae a visitantes porque…
    - A   el clima es soleado y se puede estar mucho tiempo al aire libre.
    - B   se puede disfrutar de la gastronomía maravillosa, aunque hace mal tiempo.
    - (C) si llueve, todavía se pueden visitar las galerías de arte y los museos.

4   Tu ciudad merece una visita…
    - (A) aunque todavía hay barrios por renovar.
    - B   porque ya han creado muchas áreas de ocio muy bonitas.
    - C   dado que el entorno es limpio y las vistas son preciosas.

⭐ Read all of the options, not just the circled ones, to help you reach your conclusions.

Answer the questions in English.

1   According to the circled answer, does Marco have a positive view of the public transport network in his area? Write YES or NO. Give a reason for your answer.

2   According to the circled answer, does Marco believe the shopping opportunities are as good as they could be? Write YES or NO. Give a reason for your answer.

3   According to the circled answer, does Marco think it is the weather that attracts visitors to his area? Write YES or NO. Give a reason for your answer.

4   According to the circled answer, is Marco's view of his city as positive as it could be? Write YES or NO. Give a reason for your answer.

1 Conversation in a shopping centre

You overhear a conversation between a mother and her son, David, in a shopping centre in Santander.

1   Answer all parts of the question in **English**.
    a   Why is the mother cross with her son? Give **one** reason.
    b   Why is David late? Give **one** reason.
    c   What does his mother say about their last shopping trip? Give **one** detail.

2   Answer both parts of the question in **English**.
    a   What decision has David made?
    b   Why has he decided this? Give **one** reason.

2 Medellín – ciudad colombiana

Estás escuchando la radio. La periodista habla de la ciudad de Medellín, en Colombia.

1   Escribe las **tres** letras correctas.
    La ciudad colombiana de Medellín…
    - A   ha cambiado mucho.
    - B   tiene un nuevo sistema de transporte público.
    - C   es mucho más segura.
    - D   tiene setenta colegios nuevos.
    - E   tiene unas vistas impresionantes.
    - F   es muy innovadora.

2   Escribe la letra correcta.
    El alcalde reconoce sobre todo los esfuerzos de…
    - A   la policía.
    - B   las autoridades.
    - C   los habitantes.

ciento nueve 109

Módulo 5   Prueba oral

A – Role play

1 leer — Look at the role play card and prepare what you are going to say.

> Your teacher will play the part of the assistant and will speak first.
> You should address the assistant as *usted*.
> When you see this – **!** – you will have to respond to something you have not prepared.
> When you see this – **?** – you will have to ask a question.
> Usted está hablando con el empleado / la empleada de una agencia de viajes en España.
> - Una excursión – adónde y cuándo.
> - **!**
> - Por qué este lugar (**una** razón).
> - **?** Viaje – cuánto tiempo.
> - Una excursión ayer (**dos** detalles).

- Be specific. Name a city or a specific attraction that you want to visit.
- What sort of information might the agent need from you in this situation?
- Which verb do you need in your question? (*¿Cuánto tiempo...?*)
- Stick to what you know here. You only need to give **one** reason.
- Which tense do you need to talk about **ayer**? Remember to give **two** details.

2 hablar — Practise what you have prepared. Take care with pronunciation and intonation.

⭐ In the role play **correct pronunciation** will help you to communicate each message clearly and without ambiguity. As you practise, focus on the pronunciation of each word and make your utterances sound as Spanish as you can.

3 escuchar — Using your notes, listen and respond to the teacher.

4 escuchar — Now listen to Mark doing the role play task.
- Which excursion does he want to book?
- How does he answer the unexpected question?
- What reason does he give for choosing his destination?

B – Photo card

Look at the photo and make notes. Your teacher will then ask you questions about the photo and about topics related to **home, town, neighbourhood and region.**

Your teacher will ask you the following **three** questions and then **two** more questions which you have not prepared.

- ¿Qué hay en la foto?
- ¿Qué es lo positivo y lo negativo de vivir en la ciudad?
- ¿Qué hiciste recientemente en tu ciudad o pueblo?

ciento diez

Módulo 5

1 **Look at the photo and read the task. Then listen to Karolina's response to the first question on the task card.**
1. Note down **two** things she says about the street?
2. What do you think the words for 'pedestrian zone' and 'market stall' are?
3. What season does she think it is, and why?

> ⭐ You hear Karolina use the following positional phrases. What do they mean?
>
> en primer plano   detrás de
> al otro lado   en el fondo
> a la derecha

2 **Listen to and read Karolina's response to the second question on the task card.**
1. Write down the missing word for each gap.
2. Look at the Answer Booster on page 112. Note down **six** examples of language which Karolina uses to give a strong answer.

> ⭐ To give as much detail as you can, use one or more of the following strategies:
> - include the views of others
> - present a balanced view by including opposing opinions
> - say what something is **not,** as well as what it is.

Para mí, **1** ———— de vivir en la ciudad es que hay más diversiones. Además, es mucho **2** ———— desplazarse. Se puede **3** ———— la red de transporte público para ir al cine o a conciertos. Por otro lado, mis padres **4** ———— que prefieren vivir en el campo. En su opinión, la vida en la ciudad es demasiado frenética porque hay tantos coches y tanto ruido. Sin embargo, creo que la vida en la ciudad no es **5** ————. En cambio, es animada y divertida. Estoy segura de que **6** ———— en la ciudad en el futuro.

3 **Listen to Karolina's response to the third question on the task card. Note down answers to the following questions in English.**

- When?
- Where?
- Why?
- What did she buy?
- What was the problem? (**two** details)
- How was it resolved?

4 Prepare your own answers to the first **three** questions. Think about which other **two** questions you might be asked. Then listen and take part in the full photo card discussion with the teacher.

C – General conversation

1 The teacher asks Leigh *'¿Cómo es la ciudad o el pueblo donde vives?'* Listen to her answer and note down which **four** additional hidden questions she answers.

2 The teacher then asks Leigh *'¿Cuál es tu ciudad favorita? y ¿por qué te gusta?'* Listen to Leigh's response and identify the **five** aspects that she mentions.

a weather
b geography
c buildings
d why it is special
e a previous visit
f food
g an annual event
h disadvantages

> ⭐ Develop your answers wherever possible by narrating a specific past event or by mentioning your plans for the future. This helps you to include tenses not explicitly required in the question.

3 Listen to Leigh's response to the next question *'¿Dónde te gusta comprar? ¿Por qué?'* Look at the Answer Booster on page 112. Note down **six** examples of language which Leigh uses to give a strong answer.
What is the question that Leigh asks her teacher?

4 Prepare your own answers to Module 5 questions 1–6 on page 199. Then practise with your partner.

ciento once **111**

Módulo 5   Prueba escrita

Answer booster	Aiming for a solid answer	Aiming higher	Aiming for the top
Verbs	**Different time frames**: past, present, near future **Different types of verbs**: regular, irregular, reflexive, stem-changing	**Different persons** of the verb **Verbs with an infinitive**: se puede(n), querer, soler, acabar de	**A wide range of tenses**: present, preterite, imperfect, perfect, future, conditional **Less common verbs**: disfrutar de, desplazarse, aprovechar
Opinions and reasons	**Verbs of opinion**: me chifla, me encanta, pienso que…, creo que… **Reasons**: porque	**Exclamations**: ¡Qué pena!, ¡Qué rollo! **Comparatives**: más bajo que	**Opinions**: desde mi punto de vista, a mi modo de ver, para mí **Reasons**: ya que, dado que, puesto que, así que, por lo tanto
Connectives	y, pero, también	además, sin embargo, por desgracia, sobre todo, incluso, en cambio, no obstante	todavía **Balancing an argument**: aunque, por un lado… por otro lado, lo bueno es, un inconveniente es, a pesar de…
Other features	**Qualifiers**: muy, un poco, poco, bastante, demasiado **Adjectives**: pintoresco/a, lluvioso/a, conocido/a	**Sentences with cuando, donde, si**: Si hace buen tiempo,… **Tan, Tanto/a/os/as**: es tan tranquilo/a, no hay tantos coches	**Positive/Negative phrases**: lo bueno/malo/mejor/peor **Specialist vocabulary**: zona peatonal, gangas **Idioms**: hay mucha marcha

A – Extended writing task

1 Look at the task and answer the questions.
- What is each bullet point asking you to write about?
- How could you develop your answer to each one?
- Which tenses and structures could you use, as well as those required by the bullets?

2 Read George's answer on page 113. What do the phrases in bold mean?

3 Look at the Answer Booster. Note down eight examples of language which George uses to write a strong answer.

4 Complete the essay plan based on George's answer.

5 Prepare your own answer to the task.
- Look at the Answer Booster and George's plan for ideas.
- Think about how you can develop your answer for each bullet point.
- Write a detailed plan. Organise your answer in paragraphs.
- Write your answer and carefully check what you have written.

Escribes un artículo titulado 'Mi zona' para un concurso de una revista española.

Menciona:
- lo bueno de vivir en tu zona
- cómo ha cambiado tu zona en los últimos años.

Escribe aproximadamente **150** palabras en **español**. Responde a los dos aspectos de la pregunta.

Paragraph 1
- My home town size/location and opinion
- Climate bad but…
- Number of visitors and why

Paragraph 2
- Lots for…

⭐ As you complete your essay plan, write a couple of words or a short phrase for each idea. In the exam, you will not want to spend too long writing your plan but you will need to have a clear sense of how your answer will develop.

112   ciento doce

Módulo 5

Mi ciudad natal es Newcastle, la ciudad más grande del noreste de Inglaterra. Es una ciudad genial, **aunque tiene un clima bastante frío y variable**. A pesar del tiempo, **la ciudad acoge a** más de dos millones de visitantes todos los años, quizás porque la gente es tan alegre y abierta.

Newcastle **ofrece muchas posibilidades para los turistas**. **Se puede salir a la montaña** con solo un corto viaje en coche o en autobús. Además, las familias con niños **pueden disfrutar de un día interesante** en el Centro de Ciencias de la Vida, mi lugar favorito, que está situado en el centro.

En los últimos años han mejorado el sistema de transporte público, así que ahora es una ciudad bien conectada por tren con otras ciudades importantes. Además, han renovado varios edificios antiguos, incluso el centro comercial, donde **acaban de abrir nuevas tiendas de marca**.

Desde mi punto de vista, ahora **se debería introducir todavía más** zonas peatonales y poner más áreas verdes en el centro **para hacerlo todavía más pintoresco y acogedor**.

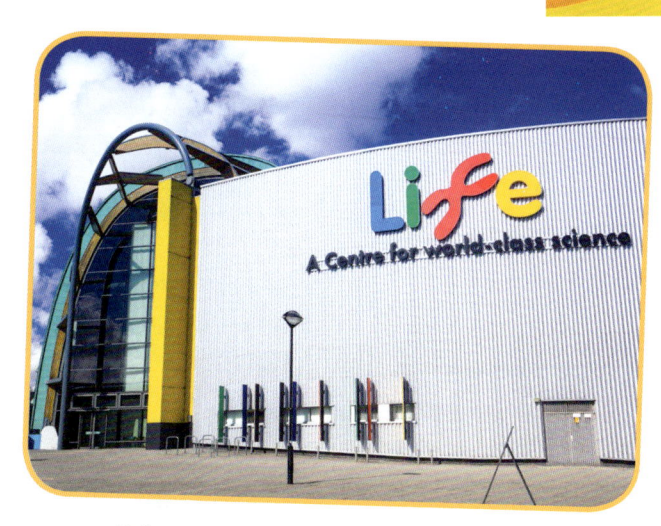

⭐ Focus on making links to join your phrases and sentences. How many different links can you spot in George's answer? What do *a pesar de* and *incluso* mean?

B – Translation

1 Translate the passage into Spanish.

> My town used to be quite horrible because there was so much pollution, but they have introduced a new system and now there are not as many cars. I like living here because there is a lot to do, and all the shops are nearby. However, in the future, I will live in another city as there is a lot of unemployment here.

- Which tense do you need to use to describe things in the past?
- Translate these using the same word in Spanish, but don't forget to use the correct ending.
- Don't translate this phrase word for word. How do you translate 'to'?
- Do you need *ser* or *estar* here? In which person of the verb?
- You have lots of possibilities here. The meaning is 'because' or 'given that'.

2 Now translate the following passage into Spanish. Use your answer to exercise 1 to help you.

> My life in the country used to be too quiet but now I think it is fun because I have so many friends who live nearby. They have introduced more buses so therefore public transport is more reliable. In the future, I will live here if there are more job opportunities.

Módulo 5 Palabras

En mi ciudad / In my town

Hay… / Mi ciudad tiene… — There is/are… / My town has…
- un ayuntamiento — a town hall
- un bar / muchos bares — a bar / lots of bars
- un castillo (en ruinas) — a (ruined) castle
- un cine — a cinema
- un mercado — a market
- un museo / unos museos — a museum / a few museums
- un parque — a park
- un polideportivo — a sports centre
- un puerto — a port
- muchos restaurantes — lots of restaurants
- un teatro — a theatre
- una biblioteca — a library
- una bolera — a bowling alley
- una iglesia — a church
- una piscina — a swimming pool
- una playa / unas playas — a beach / a few beaches
- una Plaza Mayor — a town square
- una pista de hielo — an ice rink
- una oficina de Correos — a post office
- una tienda / muchas tiendas — a shop / lots of shops
- muchos lugares de interés — lots of sights
- algo / mucho que hacer — something / a lot to do
- no hay nada que hacer — there is nothing to do

Vivo en un pueblo… — I live in a … village
- histórico / moderno — historic / modern
- tranquilo / ruidoso — quiet / noisy
- turístico / industrial — touristy / industrial
- bonito / feo — pretty / ugly

Está situado/a en … del país. — It is situated in … of the country.
- el norte / el sur / el este / el oeste — the north / the south / the east / the west

¿Por dónde se va al / a la…? / How do you get to the…?

- ¿Dónde está el / la…? — Where is the…?
- ¿El / La …. está cerca / lejos? — Is the …nearby / far away?
- sigue todo recto — go straight on
- gira a la derecha / izquierda — turn right / left
- toma la primera / segunda / tercera calle a la derecha / a la izquierda — take the first / second / third road on the right / left
- pasa el puente / los semáforos — go over the bridge / the traffic lights
- cruza la plaza / la calle — cross the square / the street
- coge el autobús número 37 — take the number 37 bus
- está… — it is…
- en la esquina / al final de la calle — on the corner / at the end of the street
- al lado del museo / enfrente de… — next to the museum / opposite…

¿Cómo es tu zona? / What is your area like?

- está situado/a en un valle — it is situated in a valley
- entre el desierto y la sierra — between the desert and the mountains
- al lado del río / mar Mediterráneo — by the river / Mediterranean sea

Está… — It is…
- rodeado/a de volcanes / sierra — surrounded by volcanoes / mountains
- lleno/a de bosques / selvas — full of woods / forests
- a … metros sobre el nivel del mar — at … metres above sea level

Tiene… — It has…
- unos impresionantes paisajes naturales — some amazing natural landscapes
- varias influencias culturales — various cultural influences
- el bullicio de una ciudad — the hustle and bustle of a city

El clima es… — The climate is…
- soleado / caluroso / seco / templado / frío — sunny / hot / dry / mild / cold
- llueve (muy) poco / a menudo — it rains (very) little / often
- en primavera / verano / otoño / invierno — in spring / summer / autumn / winter
- hay mucha marcha — there is lots going on

Es… — It is…
- mi ciudad natal / mi lugar favorito — My home town / my favourite place
- acogedor/a / atractivo/a — welcoming / attractive
- famoso/a / conocido/a por — famous for / well-known for
- una región muy húmeda — a very humid region
- una zona muy montañosa / pintoresca — a mountainous / picturesque area
- tan fácil desplazarse — so easy to get around

Se puede… — You / One can…
- estar mucho tiempo al aire libre — spend lots of time in the open air
- subir a la torre — go up the tower
- hacer un recorrido en autobús — do a bus tour
- disfrutar de las vistas / del ambiente — enjoy the views / the atmosphere
- viajar en el AVE — travel on the AVE high-speed train
- pasear por los lagos artificiales — go boating on the artificial lakes
- apreciar la arquitectura variada — appreciate the variety of architecture
- aprovechar el buen tiempo — make the most of the good weather

Se pueden… — You / One can…
- probar platos típicos — try local dishes
- practicar deportes acuáticos — do water sports
- ver edificios de estilos muy diferentes — see buildings with very different styles
- alquilar bolas de agua — hire water balls
- practicar senderismo y ciclismo — go hiking / trekking and cycling

En la oficina de turismo / At the tourist office

¿Me puede dar…? — Can you give me…?
- un plano de la ciudad — a map of the town / city
- más información sobre… — more information about…

- ¿Cuánto cuesta una entrada? — How much is a ticket?
- para adultos / niños — for adults / children
- ¿Dónde se pueden sacar las entradas? — Where can you get tickets?

¿A qué hora…? — What time…?
- sale el autobús? — does the bus leave?
- abre…? — does…open?

- ¿Hay visitas guiadas? — Are there guided tours?
- ¿Me puede recomendar…? — Can you recommend…?
  - un restaurante típico — a typical restaurant
  - un hotel / una excursión — a hotel / a trip

¿Qué haremos mañana? / What will we do tomorrow?

- Sacaré muchas fotos. — I will take lots of photos.
- Subiremos al teleférico. — We will go up on the cable car.
- Bajaremos a pie. — We will go down on foot.
- Pasaremos entre las nubes. — We will go through the clouds.
- Iremos a la playa / a la montaña / de excursión en barco. — We will go to the beach / to the mountains / on a boat trip.
- Haremos piragüismo. — We will go canoeing.
- Podremos hacer paddlesurf. — We will be able to go paddlesurfing.
- Podrás comprar regalos. — You will be able to buy presents.
- será genial / mejor — it will be great / better
- nos llevará — he/she will take us
- Estoy (muy) a gusto. — I am feeling (very much) at home.
- ¡Buena idea! — Good idea!
- de acuerdo — OK
- ¡Qué pena! / ¡Qué mal (rollo)! — What a shame! / What a nightmare!
- ¡Qué triste! — How sad!

¿Qué tiempo hará? / What will the weather be like?

- Hará sol / viento. — It will be sunny / windy.

Habrá… — There will be…
- nubes / claros / chubascos — clouds / clear spells / showers
- una ola de calor — a heat wave
- truenos y relámpagos — thunder and lightning
- temperaturas más altas / bajas — higher / lower temperatures
- granizos / brisas fuertes — hail / strong winds
- periodos soleados — sunny periods

- lloverá (bastante) — it will rain (quite a bit)
- Las temperaturas subirán / bajarán. — The temperatures will rise / fall.

El tiempo… — The weather….
- será variable — will be variable
- se despejará — will clear up
- cambiará — will change
- no nos importará — will not matter to us

Módulo 5

Las tiendas / Shops
el banco	bank
el estanco	tobacconist's
la cafetería	café
la carnicería	butcher's
la estación de trenes	train station
la farmacia	pharmacy / chemist
la frutería	greengrocer's
la joyería	jeweller's
la librería	book shop
la panadería	bakery
la papelería	stationery shop
la pastelería	cake shop
la peluquería	hairdresser's
la pescadería	fish shop
la tienda de ropa	clothes shop
la zapatería	shoe shop
un regalo	a present
sellos	stamps
una carta / unas cartas	a letter / a few letters
recoger	to pick up
mandar	to send
horario comercial / horas de apertura	business hours / opening hours
de lunes a viernes	from Monday to Friday
abre a la(s)… / cierra a la(s)…	it opens at… / it closes at…
no cierra a mediodía	it doesn't close at midday
cerrado domingo y festivos	closed on Sundays and public holidays
abierto todos los días	open every day

Recuerdos y regalos / Souvenirs and presents
el abanico	fan
el chorizo	chorizo (sausage)
el llavero	key ring
el oso de peluche	teddy bear
los pendientes	earrings
la gorra	cap
la taza	mug
las golosinas	sweets
las pegatinas	stickers
¿Me puede ayudar?	Can you help me?
Quiero comprar…	I want to buy…
¿Tiene uno/a/os/as más barato/a/os/as?	Do you have a cheaper one / cheaper ones?
un billete de (cincuenta) euros	a (fifty) euro note
tengo cambio	I have change

Quejas / Complaints
Quiero devolver…	I want to return…
está roto/a	it is broken
es demasiado estrecho/a / largo/a	it is too tight / long
tiene un agujero / una mancha	it has a hole / a stain
falta un botón	it's missing a button
¿Puede reembolsarme (el dinero)?	Can you reimburse me (the money)?
Podemos hacer un cambio.	We can exchange (it).
¿Qué me recomienda?	What do you recommend?
¿Qué tal…? / ¿Qué te parece(n)…?	What about…? / What do you think of…?
Te queda bien.	It suits you.
Te quedan demasiado grandes.	They are too big on you.
una talla más grande / pequeña	a bigger / smaller size
en rebajas	on sale
Me lo/la/los/las llevo.	I'll take it / them.

De compras / Shopping
Normalmente voy… / Suelo ir…	Usually I go… / I tend to go…
a los centros comerciales	to shopping centres
de tiendas con mis amigos	shopping with my friends
Nunca me ha gustado / Prefiero / Odio…	I've never liked / I prefer / I hate…
comprar en…	shopping in…
cadenas / grandes almacenes	chain stores / department stores
tiendas de diseño / segunda mano	designer shops / second-hand shops
comprar por Internet / en la red	shopping on the internet / online
hacer cola	queueing
porque…	because…
es más económico / práctico / cómodo	it's cheaper / more practical / more convenient
es un buen sitio para pasar la tarde	it's a good place for spending the afternoon
hay más variedad / demasiada gente	there is more variety / there are too many people
los precios son más bajos	the prices are lower
hay más ofertas	there are more offers
ropa alternativa / de moda	alternative clothing / fashionable clothing
gangas	bargains
artículos de marca	branded items

Los pros y los contras de la ciudad / The for and against of living in a city
Lo mejor de vivir en la ciudad es que…	The best thing about living in a city is that…
es tan fácil desplazarse	it's so easy to get around
hay una red de transporte público	there is a public transport system
hay tantas diversiones	there are so many things to do
hay muchas posibilidades de trabajo	there are lots of job opportunities
Lo peor es que…	The worst thing is that…
el centro es tan ruidoso	the centre is so noisy
hay tanto tráfico / tantos coches	there is so much traffic / so many cars
se lleva una vida tan frenética	life is so frenetic
la gente no se conoce	people don't know each other
En el campo…	In the countryside…
el transporte público no es fiable	public transport is not reliable
hay bastante desempleo	there is quite a lot of unemployment
no hay tantos atascos como antes	there are not as many traffic jams as before
yo conozco a todos mis vecinos	I know all my neighbours

¿Qué harías? / What would you do?
Introduciría más zonas peatonales.	I would introduce more pedestrian areas.
Renovaría…	I would renovate…
algunos edificios antiguos	some old buildings
las zonas deterioradas en las afueras	the dilapidated areas on the outskirts
Mejoraría el sistema de transporte.	I would improve the transport system.
Pondría / Crearía más áreas de ocio.	I would put in / create more leisure areas.
Construiría un nuevo centro comercial.	I would build a new shopping centre.
Invertiría en el turismo rural.	I would invest in rural tourism.
Controlaría el ruido.	I would limit the noise.

Destino Arequipa / Destination Arequipa
Vi / Vimos lugares interesantes.	I saw / We saw interesting places.
Tuvimos un guía.	We had a guide.
Nos hizo un recorrido.	He/She did a tour for us.
Nos ayudó a entender toda la historia.	He/She helped us to understand all of the history.
Recorrí a pie el centro histórico.	I walked around the historic centre.
Compré tantas cosas.	I bought so many things.
Alquilé una bici de montaña.	I hired a mountain bike.
Cogí un autobús turístico.	I took a tourist bus.
subimos / bajamos	we went up / we went down
Aprendí mucho sobre la cultura.	I learned a lot about the culture.
Me quedé impresionado con la ciudad.	I was really impressed by the city.
Había vistas maravillosas.	There were amazing views.
La comida estaba muy buena.	The food was very good.
La gente era abierta.	The people were open.
Lo que más me gustó fue / fueron…	What I liked most was / were…
¡Fue una experiencia única!	It was a one-off experience!
¡Qué miedo!	What a scare!
Volveré algún día.	I will go back one day.
Aprenderé a hacer surf.	I will learn to surf.
Trabajaré como voluntario/a.	I will work as a volunteer.

ciento quince 115

6 De costumbre
Punto de partida 1

- Describing mealtimes
- Talking about daily routine

1 **escuchar** Escucha y apunta los detalles para Zoe y Ángel. (1–4)

1. el desayuno   *Ejemplo:* Zoe – 7.15, f, …
2. la comida / el almuerzo
3. la merienda
4. la cena

2 **hablar** Con tu compañero/a, haz diálogos.

- ¿A qué hora <u>desayunas</u>?
- Normalmente <u>desayuno</u> a las…
- ¿Qué <u>desayunas</u>?
- Depende. A veces <u>desayuno</u>…, pero…

3 **leer** Empareja las mitades de las frases. ¿Qué significan las palabras en **negrita**?

1. Normalmente desayuno **algo muy rápido**, ya que…
2. Sin embargo, los fines de semana…
3. **Entre semana** almuerzo en casa…
4. **De postre** siempre como **algo dulce**…
5. Por lo general, después del insti…
6. Por la noche no ceno mucho…

a. meriendo **algo ligero, como** fruta o un yogur, por ejemplo.
b. (por ejemplo, un pastel o un helado) porque **soy muy goloso**.
c. dado que no **tengo mucha hambre**.
d. tomo un desayuno **más fuerte** porque tengo más tiempo.
e. **tengo mucha prisa** por la mañana.
f. con mi familia a las dos y media.

¿A qué hora ¿Qué	desayunas? comes / almuerzas? meriendas? cenas?
Desayuno Como / Almuerzo Meriendo Ceno	a las ocho al mediodía
	cereales, churros, tostadas, fruta, galletas, un huevo, un yogur, un pastel, un bocadillo, una hamburguesa, carne, pollo, pescado, marisco, paella, sopa, tortilla, ensalada, verduras, patatas fritas Cola Cao, leche, café, té, zumo de naranja

4 **escribir** Escribe un texto sobre las comidas en tu casa. Usa expresiones del ejercicio 3.

Entre semana, normalmente desayuno a las… Suelo desayunar algo…

⭐ In Spanish there are different verbs for each meal:

Desayunar to have breakfast / to have… for breakfast
Comer / Almorzar to have lunch / to have… for lunch
Merendar to have tea / to have… for tea
Cenar to have dinner / to have… for dinner

You can also use the word **tomar**, which means 'to have' (food / drink).

⭐ To add variety to your language:

- use **soler** + infinitive.
  Suelo almorzar a la una.   I **tend to** have lunch at 1.00.
- use verbs in the 'we' form.
  En mi casa **cenamos** *a las diez.*   In my house **we have dinner** at 10.00.

Take care with stem-changing verbs, e.g. **almorzar** (al*mue*rzo) and **merendar** (mer*ie*ndo).

Módulo 6

5 Lee el texto. Copia y completa la tabla.

activity	time	details
e	6.20	Hates getting up early in winter

Me despierto a las seis y veinte y me levanto enseguida. Odio levantarme temprano en invierno. Primero, a las seis y media, voy a la cocina donde desayuno mientras que mi hermana se ducha. A las siete menos cuarto (¡o cuando mi hermana termina!) me ducho y luego me peino. Solo me afeito una vez a la semana. A las siete me visto en mi dormitorio, y después salgo de casa a las siete y cuarto para coger el autobús escolar.

Por la tarde vuelvo a casa a las cuatro y media, o más tarde si tengo actividades deportivas. Finalmente, después de la cena, me lavo los dientes a las diez y media u once menos cuarto y me acuesto enseguida.

Gabriel

6 Escucha. Contesta a las preguntas en inglés.

1. What is Héctor's job and where does he work?
2. What time does he get up?
3. What does he find difficult about this?
4. What does he do to save time? (give <u>two</u> details)
5. What is the worst thing about his routine?
6. What does he like most about it?

Héctor

G Reflexive verbs › Page 211

Remember, many daily routine verbs are reflexive in Spanish.

me levanto	I get up
te levantas	you get up
se levanta	he/she gets up
nos levantamos	we get up
os levantáis	you (plural) get up
se levantan	they get up

When the verb is used in the infinitive, the correct reflexive pronoun is added to the end.

No me gusta levantar**me** temprano.   I don't like getting up early.

Remember that lots of daily routine verbs are also stem-changing.

Me ac**ue**sto a las once.   I go to bed at 11.00.
Prefiero ac**o**star**me** temprano.   I prefer going to bed early.

⭐ To vary and extend your language:
- use sequencers (**Primero**… **y luego**…)
- use connectives such as **donde**, **cuando** and **para**
- add opinions (*Odio ducharme cuando hace frío*)
- use other persons of the verb (*Mi madre se acuesta más tarde*)

7 Con tu compañero/a, habla de tu rutina diaria durante <u>un minuto</u>.

● Me despierto a las… Prefiero despertarme temprano porque…

ciento diecisiete **117**

Punto de partida 2

- Talking about illnesses and injuries
- Asking for help at the pharmacy

1 Lee los textos y escribe la letra correcta.

1 Tengo catarro y tengo tos. También tengo dolor de garganta y estoy muy cansado. Me siento fatal.

2 No me encuentro bien. Tengo diarrea y tengo náuseas. Además, tengo dolor de cabeza.

3 Tengo quemaduras de sol y creo que tengo una insolación. Tengo mucho sueño. También tengo una picadura.

4 Estoy enfermo. Tengo fiebre – primero tengo calor y luego tengo frío. Creo que tengo gripe.

2 Estás en la farmacia. Escucha y apunta los detalles en español. (1–5)

Ejemplo: **1** *fiebre, dos días*

¿Desde hace cuánto tiempo?	Desde hace un día / mes una hora / semana más de…
¿Desde cuándo?	Desde ayer / anteayer esta mañana / tarde el (martes) pasado

> Remember to use **estar** for temporary states and feelings.
>
> **Estoy** enfermo.   **I am** ill.
>
> Use **tener** to say that that you <u>have</u> something, but also for certain expressions where English uses the verb 'to be'.
>
> **Tengo** gripe.   **I have** flu.
> Mi madre **tiene** sueño.   My mum **is** sleepy.

3 Escribe consejos para las personas del ejercicio 1.

Tiene(s) que Hay que	beber mucha agua descansar tomar este jarabe / estas pastillas tomar aspirinas ir al hospital / médico / dentista usar esta crema

4 Estás en la farmacia. Con tu compañero/a, haz diálogos.

- *Estoy enfermo/a.*
- *¿Qué le pasa?*
- *Estoy / Tengo… Además…*
- *¿Desde hace cuánto tiempo? / ¿Desde cuándo?*
- *Desde hace… / Desde…*
- *No se preocupe. Hay que… También tiene que…*
- *Muchas gracias.*

> When saying new words, apply the pronunciation rules you know.
> How do you pronounce … ?
>   aspirinas   jarabe   pastillas   hospital   crema

Módulo 6

5 Escucha y escribe las letras en el orden correcto. (1–3)

- a la espalda
- b los oídos / las orejas
- c los dientes / las muelas
- d la mano
- e el brazo
- f la nariz
- g los ojos
- h la cabeza
- i la boca
- j la garganta
- k el estómago
- l la pierna
- m la rodilla
- n el tobillo
- o el pie

Zona Cultura

La Tomatina es una fiesta que tiene lugar en Buñol (Valencia) el último miércoles de agosto. Cada año, los 20.000 participantes lanzan más de 150.000 tomates en una hora. Después de la batalla los bomberos limpian las calles, que están cubiertas de jugo de tomate.

6 Escucha. Apunta los detalles en inglés. (1–5)

- What hurts?
- Why?

Me Te Le	duele duelen	la pierna el tobillo los ojos las muelas etc.
Me he Te has Se ha	roto torcido cortado quemado hecho daño en	

Doler (to hurt) is a stem-changing verb. It works like *gustar*.

Me duele la espalda. — My back hurts.
A mi abuela **le** duelen los oídos. — My gran has earache.

To say you have hurt/broken/twisted/cut/burned something, use the **perfect tense**. Put the correct **reflexive pronoun** before the verb, and use the **definite article**.

Me he roto **la** pierna. — I have broken my leg.

7 Tu familia está enferma. El médico no habla inglés. Haz diálogos.

● Mi padre se ha <u>torcido la rodilla</u> y ahora le duele mucho <u>la pierna</u>.
■ ¡Qué mala suerte! / ¡Qué desastre! Tiene que <u>descansar</u> y <u>tomar…</u>

8 Traduce las frases al español.

1 I've had a cold for a week and my stomach aches.
2 I feel awful. I think I have flu because I have a temperature. I also have a sore throat.
3 My sister has hurt her foot. Also, she has a headache.
4 I've broken my leg and I have to rest. What a disaster!

When learning a new verb phrase (e.g. *Me siento mal*), try to learn the infinitive too.
What do you think these infinitives mean?

romperse (el brazo)   torcerse (el tobillo)
sentirse (mal)   hacerse daño (en el pie)

ciento diecinueve

1 Sabores del mundo

- Talking about typical foods
- Using the passive
- Spotting words which indicate an increase/decrease

1 Empareja las fotos con la lista de la compra correcta. Sobra una lista.

Guatemala

Cuba

Dietas del mundo

¿Qué consume una familia típica cada semana?

El fotógrafo Peter Menzel visitó a familias de 24 países.

a
- siete latas de cerveza
- dos botellas de refrescos
- novecientos gramos de queso
- dos barras de pan grandes
- una docena de huevos
- una piña

b
- doce paquetes de patatas fritas
- una caja de cereales
- un paquete de mantequilla
- cien gramos de azúcar
- quinientos gramos de harina
- un bote de mermelada

c
- tres kilos y medio de zanahorias
- veintitrés litros de agua
- una botella grande de aceite
- veintidós kilos de maíz
- dos kilos de judías verdes
- tres coliflores

2 Escucha y comprueba tus respuestas. Apunta en inglés otros <u>dos</u> o <u>tres</u> productos mencionados para cada país.

⭐ Words for quantities or containers are followed by *de*. Find <u>ten</u> examples in exercise 1.

3 ¿Qué comen los españoles? Escucha y escribe las letras correctas.

1 Hoy en día la dieta mediterránea en España es…
  a más popular que antes.
  b menos popular que antes.
  c tan popular como antes.

2 Cada vez más españoles comen…
  a una dieta variada, equilibrada y sana.
  b comida sabrosa.
  c comida rápida y sencilla de preparar.

3 Ahora los españoles consumen cada vez menos…
  a carne, dulces y aceite de oliva.
  b legumbres (judías, guisantes, lentejas).
  c lácteos (leche, yogur, queso).

4 Las frutas más populares son…
  a los plátanos, las manzanas y las naranjas.
  b los melones, las uvas y los pomelos.
  c las fresas, las peras y los albaricoques.

⭐ Try to spot phrases which indicate whether something has **increased**, **decreased** or stayed **the same**. For example:

↑	cada vez más	more and more
	un incremento	an increase
↑↓	mismo	same
	seguir	to carry on
↓	cada vez menos	less and less
	perder	to lose
	ya no	no longer

4 Con tu compañero/a, habla de lo que consume tu familia.

● ¿Qué come tu familia cada semana?
■ Creo que comemos <u>tres kilos de naranjas</u> porque son <u>sanas</u>. Además,…
● ¿Y qué bebe tu familia?
■ Bebemos <u>cinco litros de leche</u> porque es…

ciento veinte

5 Lee el texto. Identifica las cuatro frases correctas.

El sabor latino por Víctor Mediavilla

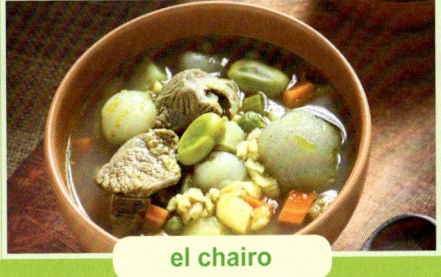

el chairo   el borí borí

¿Has probado la gastronomía latina? Con un sinfín de sabores, la cocina latinoamericana disfruta de gran prestigio mundial. Uno de los platos es **el cebiche**, un plato de pescado que fue inventado en Perú por la población indígena hace dos mil años. Otra joya de la cocina latinoamericana es **el chairo** boliviano, un tipo de guiso que contiene zanahorias, cebolla, carne de ternera y patatas, que fue introducido por el pueblo aimara.

La gastronomía de Venezuela es una mezcla de sabores tropicales y andinos. También incluye **las arepas** (similares a las tortillas mexicanas), preparadas con harina de maíz, que fueron exportadas a las islas Canarias. Si prefieres la cocina caribeña, la República Dominicana lo tiene todo. Por ejemplo, **la bandera dominicana** es un plato suculento que combina el arroz, las judías y la carne.

Sin embargo, mi recomendación personal es **el borí borí** de Paraguay, una sopa muy típica compuesta de harina de maíz, queso fresco y pollo. ¡Está riquísima!

el sinfín	endless number
el sabor	flavour / taste
el guiso	stew

1. La comida latina es muy variada.
2. No es muy conocida internacionalmente.
3. *El cebiche* es un plato bastante nuevo.
4. Su ingrediente principal es el pescado.
5. *El chairo* es el plato nacional de Bolivia.
6. *Las arepas* no fueron inventadas en las islas Canarias.
7. *La bandera* contiene muchas verduras distintas.
8. *El borí borí* no es un plato vegetariano.

6 Escucha las entrevistas. Apunta en inglés: (1–4)

- Name of dish:
- Origin:
- Ingredients:
- Opinion:

> **G** The passive Page 232
>
> The **passive** is used to say what is / was / will be done to something or someone. To form it, use the correct person and tense of **ser** followed by the **past participle**, which must agree.
>
> **Fue inventado** hace mil años. It was invented a thousand years ago.
> **Es conocida** en todo el mundo. It's known throughout the world.
>
> Can you spot the other examples of the passive used in exercise 5?

7 Con tu compañero/a, habla de los platos de los ejercicios 5 y 6.

- ● ¿Has probado el/la/los/las…?
- ■ ✓ Sí, lo/la/los/las he probado y (no) me gustó/gustaron (mucho/nada).
- ■ ✗ No, no lo/la/los/las he probado. ¿En qué consiste(n)?
- ● Es/Son…

8 Escribe un artículo sobre la comida típica de tu país.

¿Has probado la comida (inglesa)?
Tiene una mezcla de…
Uno de los platos más… es…
Es un plato… que fue…
Si prefieres…

¿Has probado…?		el gazpacho, la fabada, la ensaladilla rusa, la paella
Es	un tipo de	bebida, guiso, sopa, postre, pescado
	un plato	caliente / frío típico de…
Contiene(n) Consiste(n) en		carne de cerdo / cordero / ternera, pollo marisco, huevos, chorizo, atún, arroz, ajo, cebolla, pepino, pimientos, judías, zanahorias
Fue	inventado introducido	en (Colombia) por (la población indígena)

ciento veintiuno **121**

2 ¡De fiesta!

- Comparing different festivals
- Avoiding the passive
- Paying attention to question words

1 Escucha y lee. Busca los verbos en español.

Fiestas curiosas
¡Las fiestas más raras de España!

La fiesta de **Els Enfarinats se celebra** el 28 de diciembre en el pueblo pequeño de Ibi. Esta extraña tradición, con más de 200 años de historia, **se caracteriza por** una gran batalla en la que **se lanzan** huevos y harina.

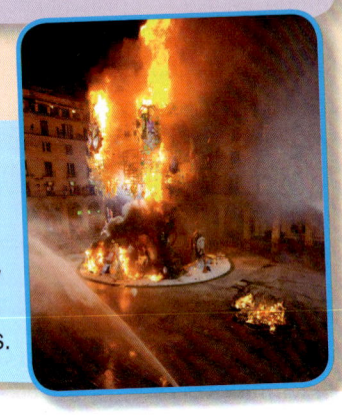

Entre el 7 y el 14 de julio **se celebran los Sanfermines**, una tradición antigua en la que más de un millón de españoles y extranjeros visitan la ciudad de Pamplona. Los más valientes se visten de blanco con un pañuelo rojo y corren delante de los toros en 'el encierro', un evento que **se repite** cada día a las ocho de la mañana.

En junio, Alicante **se llena de** música y desfiles para celebrar la llegada del verano con **las Hogueras de San Juan**. Las 'hogueras', que **se construyen** por toda la ciudad, consisten en espectaculares y gigantescas figuras de madera y cartón que **se queman** el 24 de junio, la noche de San Juan. También **se disparan** fuegos artificiales.

el pañuelo	scarf
el desfile	procession
la hoguera	bonfire

1 is filled with
2 is celebrated
3 is repeated
4 is characterised by
5 are set off
6 are burned
7 are celebrated
8 are built
9 are thrown

2 Lee los textos del ejercicio 1 otra vez. Contesta a las preguntas en español.

1 ¿**Quiénes** son los visitantes de los Sanfermines?
2 ¿**Por qué** son valientes los participantes de los encierros?
3 ¿**A qué hora** empieza el encierro?
4 ¿**Cómo** se celebra la fiesta de Els Enfarinats?
5 ¿**Cuándo** se celebra la llegada del verano en Alicante?
6 ¿**Dónde** se construyen figuras enormes?
7 ¿**Qué** fiesta no se celebra en verano?

Pay special attention to **question words** to make sure you give the correct information. What do the question words in exercise 2 mean?

G Avoiding the passive > Page 232

In Spanish the passive is often avoided by using the reflexive pronoun **se**.

La fiesta se celebra en marzo. — The festival **is celebrated** (literally 'celebrates itself') in March.

Sometimes the subject of the verb comes after the verb.

Se lanzan huevos. — Eggs **are thrown** (literally 'throw themselves').

3 Escucha. Copia y completa la tabla en inglés. (1–3)

	festival	where	when	details
1	Las Fallas	Valencia		

4 Con tu compañero/a, habla de las fiestas de los ejercicios 1 y 3.

- ¿Qué fiesta te interesa más / menos?
- ¿Cuándo / Dónde / Cómo se celebra?
- ¿Por qué (no) te interesa?

Módulo 6

5 Rellena los espacios en blanco. Escribe la forma correcta del verbo.

El Día de Muertos

Esta costumbre mexicana, que coincide con la fiesta católica de Todos los Santos, es popular hoy en muchos países del mundo. Se celebra el 1 y 2 de noviembre cuando, según la leyenda, los muertos **1** <u>vuelven</u> a ver a sus familiares. En México muchas personas **2** ———— los cementerios donde **3** ———— las tumbas y las **4** ———— con velas y flores. En casa, los mexicanos **5** ———— altares en honor de los muertos con calaveritas de azúcar, objetos personales y la comida favorita de sus seres queridos. También **6** ———— 'pan de muerto', un tipo de pan dulce. En muchas ciudades los niños **7** ———— y **8** ———— a la calle con sus padres para ver los desfiles de calaveras.

calaveritas de azúcar

la tumba	grave
la vela	candle
la calavera	skull
la seres queridos	loved ones

comer   visitar   disfrazarse   salir
~~volver~~   limpiar   decorar   preparar

⭐ Use the 'they' form of the verb in each of the blanks. Take extra care with reflexive, stem-changing and irregular verbs.

6 Con tu compañero/a, haz una comparación de las dos fiestas.

● *En mi opinión, son muy similares porque en las dos fiestas los niños…*
■ *Sí, pero también son diferentes porque en Halloween…, pero en el Día de…*

El Día de Muertos
- 1–2 November
- Mexico
- 'bread of the dead'
- altars at home
- decorate graves
- processions

- coincides with All Saints' Day
- celebrated in many countries
- fancy dress
- special food

Halloween
- 31 October
- US, UK, Canada, Ireland
- toffee apples
- pumpkin lanterns
- 'trick or treat'
- horror films

7 Escribe un texto en español sobre la Noche de Guy Fawkes.

- an old English tradition
- more than four hundred years old
- celebrated 5th November every year
- children eat toffee apples
- dummies (muñecos) of Guy Fawkes are burned
- bonfires are built
- fireworks are set off

Halloween / El Día de Muertos	se celebra	en (otoño) / el… de…
Muchas personas / Los jóvenes / Los niños / Los ingleses / Los mexicanos / Los familiares / Las familias	comen	manzanas de caramelo / pan de muerto
	decoran	las tumbas con… / las casas con…
	se disfrazan	de brujas / fantasmas / de calaveras
	ven	desfiles / películas de terror
	preparan	linternas de calabaza / altares
	juegan a 'truco o trato'	

ciento veintitrés **123**

3 Un día especial

- Describing a special day
- Using reflexive verbs in the preterite
- Inferring meaning in literary texts

1 Lee y escribe el número y la letra correctos para cada texto.
Lee los textos otra vez y busca los verbos reflexivos en el presente.

A medianoche comemos doce uvas, una por cada campanada, para tener buena suerte en el nuevo año. Los adultos beben 'cava' (que es parecido al champán) y todos nos acostamos muy tarde. Otra tradición es que ¡llevamos ropa interior roja! **Alba**

Celebramos el final del mes de Ramadán con una rutina especial. Nos levantamos muy temprano, rezamos, nos bañamos, nos lavamos los dientes y nos vestimos con nuestra mejor ropa. Desayunamos algo dulce y luego vamos a la mezquita. Después, mi madre prepara una comida deliciosa y visitamos a los amigos. **Mariam**

Hacemos una cena especial con toda la familia. Cenamos bacalao y pavo, y luego comemos dulces navideños como turrón o mazapanes. Mucha gente va a la iglesia para celebrar la 'Misa del Gallo' y canta villancicos tradicionales. El día siguiente es el Día de Navidad y me despierto temprano para abrir los regalos. **Fer**

1 Nochebuena (24 de diciembre)
2 Eid al-Fitr
3 Domingo de Pascua
4 Nochevieja (31 de diciembre)

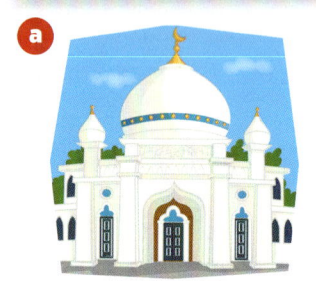

2 Escucha. ¿Qué día especial celebraron ayer? (1–7)
Ejemplo: **1** *Nochebuena*

la campanada	stroke (of a bell)
rezar	to pray
el bacalao	cod

3 Daniel habla de su día especial. Escucha y apunta los detalles en inglés.

- the occasion: *13th birthday and…*
- getting ready / clothes:
- the ceremony:
- the celebration / gifts:

G Preterite tense of reflexive verbs

In the **preterite tense**, reflexive verbs behave in the same way as other verbs but need a reflexive pronoun in front of the verb.

me acosté	**nos** acostamos
te acostaste	**os** acostasteis
se acostó	**se** acostaron

Stem-changing verbs only have a stem change in the present tense, <u>not</u> in the preterite.

infinitive	present	preterite
ac**o**starse	me ac**ue**sto	me ac**o**sté
desp**e**rtarse	me desp**ie**rto	me desp**e**rté

4 Eres Alba, Mariam o Fer. Describe tu día especial de ayer.

- ¿Qué hiciste ayer?
- *Ayer fue… Por la noche cené… Luego comí…*

Módulo 6

5 Traduce el texto al español.

> Proms don't really exist in Spain, so there isn't a word for this. You could use the phrase *el baile de fin de curso* to explain what you mean.

> Last Saturday was a very special day because it was the School Prom. In the afternoon I went to the hairdresser's and then had a shower and did my make up. I wore my new dress, which I received for Christmas. Then I went to the hotel with my friends, where we had dinner, danced and took lots of photos. It was an unforgettable night!

> Which word do you need for 'in' here?

> Don't translate this word for word. Use the reflexive verb *maquillarse*.

> Which verb do you need to use here?

6 Lee los dos extractos de una novela. Escribe las letras correctas.

Una madre de Alejandro Palomas

Sentados a la mesa del comedor, mamá cuenta uvas y yo doblo las servilletas rojas mientras en el horno se enfría la crema de espárragos y un asado de pavo.

Barcelona. Hoy es 31 de diciembre.

–Seremos cinco –dice mamá. Eso sin contar a Olga, claro. – Olga es la novia de Emma.

–Aunque tío Eduardo llegará un poco más tarde, porque su vuelo lleva retraso –aclara.

* * * * *

Olga y Silvia van metiendo platos y copas en el lavavajillas y organizan el cava, las uvas y el turrón.

Instantes después suena un pequeño tintineo en mi móvil. Lo saco del bolsillo y veo un WhatsApp. Es de ella. "Si es niña, se llamará Sara".

Alejandro Palomas

contar	to count
el horno	oven
el bolsillo	pocket

1. For dinner they are going to have…
   a a home-cooked meal.
   b a vegetarian meal.
   c a selection of meats.

2. Including Olga there will be…
   a four people.
   b five people.
   c six people.

3. Emma and Olga are…
   a mother and daughter.
   b sisters.
   c a couple.

4. Uncle Eduardo is travelling…
   a on foot.
   b by plane.
   c by train.

5. The second extract takes place…
   a before dinner.
   b after dinner.
   c after midnight.

6. We suspect that the person who has sent the message…
   a is pregnant.
   b has had a baby girl.
   c knows she is going to have a baby girl.

> ⭐ When reading extracts from novels or plays you often have to 'read between the lines' to infer what is being said.
> For example, what can you deduce from these details?
> *porque su **vuelo** lleva retraso* (question 4)
> ***Si** es niña, se llamará Sara* (question 6)

ciento veinticinco **125**

4 ¡A comer!

- Ordering in a restaurant
- Using absolute superlatives
- Spotting irregular verb patterns in the preterite

1 Escucha y lee los anuncios. ¿Qué restaurante recomiendas? (1–8)

a Restaurante El Faro

En el restaurante El Faro te espera un ambiente acogedor. Con más de cincuenta platos innovadores, variados e imaginativos, es el destino ideal para los amantes del marisco y del pescado. Espectacular terraza al aire libre.

Apto para alérgicos, celiacos e intolerancias alimentarias. Acceso para minusválidos.

b Parrilla Río Plata

En pleno centro de Madrid, la parrilla Río Plata ofrece la posibilidad de probar los filetes de ternera y de buey más suculentos de la ciudad. Con su iluminación suave también es el lugar perfecto para una cena romántica.

Salón privado disponible para eventos familiares, bodas, comuniones, etc.

c Bufé Libre Estrella

Ubicado muy cerca de la estación de Atocha, no hay mejor sitio para comer bien y barato. Disfruta de una amplia selección de pastas, pizzas, ensaladas, carnes y platos vegetarianos en nuestro bufé libre. Algo para todos los gustos.
Menú infantil a mitad de precio.

2 ¿Y tú? ¿Qué restaurante prefieres? ¿Por qué?

- Prefiero… porque me gusta / soy…
- Yo prefiero… porque es / tiene / ofrece…

3 Lee el menú. Luego escucha el diálogo y rellena los espacios en blanco.

- Buenos días. ¿Qué va a tomar?
- De primer plato voy a tomar **1** _____.
- Muy bien. ¿Y de segundo plato?
- ¿Qué me recomienda?
- Le recomiendo la especialidad de la casa, **2** _____. Está riquísimo.
- Bueno, voy a tomar **3** _____, entonces.
- ¿Y para beber?
- **4** _____, por favor.
- Muy bien. ¡Que aproveche!
****
- ¿Qué tal la comida?
- Estaba **5** _____.
- ¿Quiere postre?
- Sí, voy a tomar **6** _____.
- ¿Algo más?
- Nada más, gracias. ¿Me trae la cuenta, por favor?

MENÚ DEL DÍA
14 € (servicio incluido)
* * *
Primer plato
Calamares
Sopa de fideos
Albóndigas
Croquetas caseras (atún)
Jamón serrano
* * *
Segundo plato
Filete de cerdo
Chuletas de cordero asadas
Merluza en salsa verde
Trucha a la plancha
Tortilla de espinacas
* * *
Postre
Flan, natillas, melocotón o piña
* * *
pan, agua y vino o cerveza

G Absolute superlatives

To say **really** (nice), **extremely** (expensive), etc. use the absolute superlative. Add **-ísimo** to the end of the adjective, and make it agree.

Este ejercicio es facilísimo.   This exercise is **really** easy.

If the adjective ends in a vowel, remove it before adding the ending.

Estas gambas están buenísimas.   These prawns are **extremely** good.

4 Con tu compañero/a, haz diálogos. Cambia los detalles del ejercicio 3.

126 *ciento veintiséis*

Módulo 6

5 Escucha. Copia y completa la tabla en inglés. (1–3)

	starter	main course	dessert	drink	problem
1	noodle soup				

Me hace falta	un cuchillo un tenedor una cuchara
No hay	aceite vinagre sal
El plato El vaso El mantel La cuchara	está suci**o**/**a** está rot**o**/**a**
El vino La carne	está mal**o**/**a** está frí**o**/**a**

6 Lee el texto. Escribe P (positivo), N (negativo) o P+N (positivo y negativo).

1 La comida
2 El servicio
3 El precio
4 El ambiente
5 La limpieza

Platosenlinea.com

Almudena Sánchez *(Santander)*
Restaurante Mil Maravillas

Vinimos aquí el sábado pasado para celebrar las bodas de plata de mis padres. Cuando llegamos, había mucha gente y por eso tuvimos que esperar media hora. Sin embargo, el ambiente era animado y acogedor, y todo estaba muy limpio.

El camarero era encantador y nos recomendó la especialidad de la casa, las gambas.

A mi padre le encanta el marisco, así que pidió las gambas, mientras que yo pedí pollo al ajillo. Lo malo fue que el camarero se equivocó y me trajo merluza. ¡Soy alérgica al pescado!

Mi madre se quedó un poco decepcionada con el bistec (estaba frío), pero mi padre dijo que las gambas estaban riquísimas. Desafortunadamente, la cuenta tardó mucho tiempo en llegar, y cuando finalmente la recibimos, era carísima: 185 €. ¡No dejamos propina!

7 Lee el texto del ejercicio 6 otra vez. Busca las expresiones en español.

1 silver wedding anniversary
2 we had to wait
3 (he) made a mistake
4 (she) was a bit disappointed
5 (it) took a long time to arrive
6 we didn't leave a tip

8 Escribe una crítica para el foro. Usa el ejercicio 6 como modelo.

El (lunes) pasado fuimos al restaurante… para celebrar…
El ambiente era… y el camarero era… Pedí…, pero…

⭐ Use the **preterite tense** for completed actions in the past.

Pedí cerdo, pero el camarero trajo pollo. **I ordered** pork but the waiter **brought** chicken.

Use the **imperfect tense** for descriptions in the past.

El plato estaba sucio. The plate **was** dirty.
¡Había una mosca en la sopa! **There was** a fly in the soup!

G *Irregular verbs in the preterite tense* ▶ Page 212

If you know the 'I' form of the preterite you can usually work out the other forms.

E.g. **tener** (to have):
tuve	I had
tuviste	you had
tuvo	he/she had
tuvimos	we had
tuvisteis	you (plural) had
tuvieron	they had

Now work out the other forms of these verbs.

poner (to put) → puse (I put)
poder (to be able to) → pude (I was able to)
venir (to come) → vine (I came)
traer (to bring) → traje (I brought)*
decir (to say) → dije (I said)*

* 'they' form ends in –*jeron*

ciento veintisiete **127**

6 El festival de música

- Talking about a music festival
- Using expressions followed by the infinitive
- Adding interest when narrating a story

1 Escucha y apunta los detalles en inglés. (1–5)

Ejemplo: **1** Likes: *Coldplay – music is original*
Dislikes: …

¿Cuál es tu cantante favorito / tu banda favorita?

🇪🇸 Zona Cultura

El Festival Internacional de Benicàssim (FIB) se celebra cada año a mediados de julio. Durante cuatro días este festival de música pop, rock, indie y electrónica, entre otros estilos, atrae a más de 150.000 personas de todo el mundo a la costa valenciana.

(No) me gusta	su actitud
Me fascina	su comportamiento
Admiro	su determinación
No aguanto	su estilo
No soporto	su forma de vestir
	su talento

Su música	(no) es	atrevida(s)
Su voz		imaginativa(s)
Sus coreografías	(no) son	preciosa(s)
Sus canciones		repetitiva(s)
Sus ideas		original(es)
Sus letras		triste(s)

2 Lee el programa y la página web. Apunta la información en español.

1. La fecha del primer día del festival
2. El precio de las entradas más baratas
3. El nombre del sitio donde se puede acampar
4. Los documentos requeridos para obtener la pulsera
5. La edad mínima para ir al festival solo/a
6. <u>Tres</u> artículos que te hacen falta si hace buen tiempo
7. Una manera de protegerse del ruido
8. Un artículo recomendado en caso de accidente / enfermedad

VIVIENDO EL FESTIVAL

Campfest. Es la zona de acampada gratuita para todos los poseedores de abono de 2, 3 o 4 días.
Cómo moverse. Alquila una bici por 40 € (4 días).
Tu pulsera. Al llegar al festival cambia tu entrada por la pulsera (se necesita pasaporte / DNI).
Menores de 15 años. Siempre deben estar acompañados de un adulto.
Te hace falta… Crema solar, gafas de sol, sombrero/gorra, tapones para los oídos, un minibotiquín (tiritas, aspirinas…).

me/te hace(n) falta	I/you need
DNI	Documento Nacional de Identidad

fib Benicàssim Costa Azahar
Julio 16 | 17 | 18 | 19
ENTRADAS DESDE: 40 €

JUEVES 16 — VIERNES 17 — SÁBADO 18 — DOMINGO 19

LAS PALMAS

FLORENCE + THE MACHINE — THE PRODIGY — BLUR — PORTISHEAD

CRYSTAL FIGHTERS — NOEL GALLAGHER'S HIGH FLYING BIRDS — LOS PLANETAS — BASTILLE

CLEAN BANDIT — JAMIE T — KAISER CHIEFS — VETUSTA MORLA

L.A. — BRODINSKI — TIMO MAAS — MADE ON

SWIM DEEP — MOODOÏD — REVEREND & THE MAKERS — AUGUSTINES

TRAJANO! — NUNATAK — BEACH BEACH — DEBIGOTE

ELYELLA DJ'S

FIBERFIB.COM - radio 3

GODSPEED YOU! BLACK EMPEROR — MARK RONSON — FFS (FRANZ FERDINAND & SPARKS)

PALMA VIOLETS — TIGA (DJ) — PUBLIC ENEMY

LA BIEN QUERIDA — FRANK TURNER & THE SLEEPING SOULS — THE CRIBS

EVAN BAGGS — HINDS — MØ

MONKI — EDU IMBERNON — A-TRAK

HAMSANDWICH — THE ZOMBIE KIDS (ARTISTA DESPERADOS) — BELAKO

HOLÓGRAMA — LA M.O.D.A. — HUDSON TAYLOR

PAPAYA

RED BULL TOUR BUS FIBCLUB

DMA'S — NUDOZURDO — DARWIN DEEZ — JOE CREPÚSCULO

OCELLOT — VESSELS — CURTIS HARDING — CROCODILES

THE LAST DANDIES — POLOCK — LOYLE CARNER — NOVEDADES CARMINHA

MOX NOX — PUBLIC ACCESS T.V. — SIESTA! — THE RIPTIDE MOVEMENT

LUIS LE NUIT — ELSA DE ALFONSO Y LOS PRESTIGIO — THE DEATH OF POP — JONATHAN TOUBIN

MIQUI BRIGHTSIDE — LEY DJ — OPATOV — ALDO LINARES

— DIEGO RJ (RADIO 3) — SUNTA TEMPLETON (XFM) — LITTLE JESUS

— — ORLANDO — CELICA XX

3 Con tu compañero/a, haz diálogos.

- ¿Cuál es tu cantante favorito / tu banda favorita? ¿Por qué?
- ¿Qué bandas / cantantes no aguantas?
- ¿Te gustaría ir al Festival de Benicàssim?
- ¿Qué día del festival te interesa más? ¿Por qué?

Módulo 6

4 Escucha a estas personas que hablan del FIB. (1–6) Apunta:
- Si es **pasado**, **presente** o **futuro**
- Dos detalles más

> Remember the 'we' forms of *-ar* and *-ir* verbs are identical in the present and preterite:
> *Cantamos y bailamos.* We **sing** and **dance** / We **sang** and **danced**.
>
> Time phrases do not always give you a clue. E.g. Do *en julio* and *este año* help you identify the tense?

5 Lee el texto e identifica las <u>cuatro</u> frases correctas.

Siempre he querido ir al Festival de Benicàssim y por fin tuve la oportunidad de asistir la semana pasada. Acabo de cumplir 17 años, así que pude ir con mis amigos (¡y sin padres!). Decidimos acampar porque era la opción más barata – ¡aunque también la menos cómoda!

Al llegar al festival, montamos la tienda. ¡Nunca habíamos visto tantas tiendas! Por desgracia, mi amigo Roberto se hizo daño con el martillo – se rompió la mano. ¡Es muy torpe! Después de ir al hospital, volvimos al festival para ver las primeras actuaciones.

Durante los cuatro días del festival vi muchas de mis bandas favoritas, incluso el grupo indie *Los Planetas*, que salieron al escenario con una canción nueva, antes de tocar una selección de sus mejores canciones. El sonido era increíble y no me quedé nada decepcionado.

Lo que menos me gustó fue el calor. Por eso, cuando me acosté, decidí dormir con los pies fuera de la tienda (aunque, en realidad, el camping era tan ruidoso que pasé cuatro noches sin dormir). Sin embargo, al día siguiente me desperté con las piernas llenas de picaduras. La proxima vez usaré repelente de mosquitos. O mejor todavía, nos alojaremos en un hotel. ¡Seguro que Roberto preferiría esa opción también!

Álvaro

montar una tienda	to put up a tent
torpe	clumsy

1. Álvaro is nearly 17.
2. He didn't find camping very comfortable.
3. He was surprised by how big the tents were.
4. Roberto cut his hand.
5. *Los Planetas* started their set with a new song.
6. Álvaro was impressed by their performance.
7. It was very hot at night.
8. Álvaro didn't sleep much because of the insects.

6 Traduce el primer párrafo del texto del ejercicio 5 al inglés.

7 Has ido a un festival de música. Describe tus experiencias.

Use ideas from exercise 5 and include:
- different tenses
- time phrases
- expressions followed by the infinitive

> **G Expressions followed by the infinitive**
>
> To enhance your writing, use a range of expressions which are followed by the infinitive:
>
> | | |
> |---|---|
> | *para* + infinitive | in order to (do) |
> | *al* + infinitive | on (doing) |
> | *sin* + infinitive | without (doing) |
> | *antes de* + infinitive | before (doing) |
> | *después de* + infinitive | after (doing) |
>
> ***Al** **llegar** al festival…*   **On arriving** at the festival…
> *Pasé cuatro noches **sin dormir**.*   I spent four nights **without sleeping**.

> Narrating a story in Spanish is an important exam skill. To add interest, include anecdotes about things that went wrong (e.g. lost something, got ill, arrived late, bad meal, etc).

ciento veintinueve **129**

Módulo 6 Leer y escuchar

1 **leer** **Accidents at Christmas**
You read this article on a Spanish website.

> ### Accidentes navideños
>
> El 30% de los hogares españoles sufre accidentes domésticos durante la Navidad, según un estudio realizado por Línea Directa. Son frecuentes los accidentes de cocina y las quemaduras por culpa de los fuegos artificiales, aunque el peligro más común son las intoxicaciones alimentarias. Las luces navideñas pueden provocar problemas de electrocución, así que es esencial prestar atención a la calidad del producto a la hora de comprar.
>
> La cocina es el espacio más peligroso para los españoles (80%), y las manos son la parte del cuerpo más afectada en los accidentes domésticos. Uno de cada cinco españoles no tiene botiquín de primeros auxilios en casa. Según Francisco Valencia de Línea Directa, 'Queremos concienciar de los peligros de actividades como cocinar, limpiar o decorar la casa por Navidad'.
>
> El estudio también revela que uno de cada cuatro españoles ha regalado juguetes 'ilegales' a los niños, es decir, juguetes no aprobados por la Comunidad Europea.

1 What does the article say about accidents in Spanish homes?
   Write the **two** correct letters.
   A 30% of accidents occur at Christmas.
   B Burns are often caused by cooking accidents.
   C Food poisoning is the greatest risk at Christmas.
   D Care must be taken when choosing Christmas lights.

2 What does the article suggest about a fifth of Spanish people?
   Write the correct letter.
   A They suffer injuries in the kitchen.
   B They suffer injuries to their hands.
   C They don't have a first aid kit at home.

Answer the questions in English.

3 According to Francisco Valencia, what does his company want to raise awareness of?
4 According to the article, how have some parents put their child in danger?

> ⭐ Use context and clues from the questions to work out the meaning of unfamiliar words. What do you think these words mean?
> un hogar   el peligro
> luces navideñas   peligroso

2 **leer** **Una página web**
Ves este artículo sobre cómo se celebra 'la quinceañera' en Latinoamérica.

> ### Tradiciones y rituales de la quinceañera
>
> En Latinoamérica, la celebración de los quince años marca la transición de niña a mujer. La fiesta empieza con la llegada de la 'quinceañera'. Una tradición importante es 'lanzar la muñeca' a las otras niñas invitadas. Este juguete (normalmente una Barbie o alguna muñeca similar) simboliza la última muñeca de la niñez de la joven.
>
> En Uruguay, 'la ceremonia de las 15 velas y 15 rosas' es una de las más frecuentes. Antes de bailar con su padre, la quinceañera baja una escalera mientras se escucha una canción que ella ha escogido. Al pie de la escalera 15 chicos la esperan con rosas, mientras que 15 chicas la esperan con velas. La quinceañera coge las rosas y apaga las velas.

Contesta a las preguntas en español.

Ejemplo ¿Qué indica el comienzo de la fiesta de los quince años?

la llegada de la quinceañera

1 ¿Qué representa la muñeca que se lanza?
2 En Uruguay, ¿cuál es la primera cosa que hace la niña?
3 ¿Quién selecciona la música para esta ceremonia?
4 ¿Qué 'regalo' acepta la quinceañera después de bajar la escalera?

3 leer Un foro sobre restaurantes

Completa el texto usando palabras de la lista. Escribe la letra correcta.

La Gaviota Loca

Cené en La Gaviota Loca **1** ☐ celebrar mi cumpleaños. Una ventaja era el precio, y también que tenía **2** ☐ ambiente. Sin embargo, tuve que quejarme, ya que las chuletas que pedí **3** ☐ frías. Además, el servicio era muy **4** ☐. Por eso no volvería.

A rápido
B cuando
C estaban
D decepcionante
E para
F eran
G buen

⭐ To find the missing words you have to think about what is **grammatically correct**, as well as what is **logical**. Pay attention to connectives and the sentences which come before/after.

1 escuchar Anuncios

Escuchas estos anuncios en un supermercado en España. Indica el tipo de comida para cada anuncio.
Contesta en español. (1–3)

Ejemplo dulces

2 escuchar Radio discussion about music festivals

You are listening to a radio programme about issues to consider when going to a music festival.
For each speaker, choose the issue and write the correct letter.

A Communication
B Staying healthy
C Lost property
D Noise
E Drunken behaviour

Answer all parts of the question.
a Sofía
b Moisés
c Nicolás

⭐ When you see 'Answer all parts of the question' in a Listening exam, this tells you that the recording is **not** split up into separate extracts.

3 escuchar A festival in Argentina

You are listening to a travel report about the *Fiesta de la Vendimia*, which celebrates the end of the grape harvest. What does the presenter say?

Answer both parts of the question in English.

a Why did the presenter enjoy the festival? Give **two** reasons.
b What is the main reason for her feeling so tired?

Módulo 6 Prueba oral

A – Role play

1 leer Look at the role play card and prepare what you are going to say.

Your teacher will play the part of your Spanish friend and will speak first.

You should address your friend as *tú*.

When you see this – **!** – you will have to respond to something you have not prepared.

When you see this – **?** – you will have to ask a question.

Estás hablando con tu amigo español / tu amiga española sobre la comida.
- Tu plato preferido – descripción (**dos** detalles).
- Tu opinión sobre la comida española – **una** opinión y **una** razón.
- **!**
- Tu última vez en un restaurante (**dos** detalles).
- **?** Recomendación – plato típico.

You could say what type of dish it is, what the ingredients are, etc.

If you use an adjective in your answer, don't forget to make it agree.

Remember to use the preterite tense to say where you went, what you ate, etc., but the imperfect tense if you want to describe the meal or the restaurant.

How could you turn this into a question? (¿Qué …?)

2 hablar Practise what you have prepared. Take care with pronunciation and intonation.

3 escuchar Using your notes, listen and respond to the teacher.

4 escuchar Now listen to Freja doing the role play task.

1 How does she describe her favourite dish?
2 How does she answer the unprepared question(s)?
3 Do you think she liked the restaurant? Why (not)?

⭐ In the photo card discussion and general conversation you have to develop your answers fully. However, for the role play you only need to give the information you are asked to give. Focus on the **accuracy** of what you are saying.

B – Photo card

Look at the photo and make notes. Your teacher will then ask you questions about the photo and about topics related to **customs and festivals in Spanish-speaking countries/communities**.

Your teacher will ask you the following **three** questions and then **two** more questions which you have not prepared.
- ¿Qué hay en la foto?
- ¿Crees que la Navidad es importante? … ¿Por qué (no)?
- Háblame de lo que hiciste en un día especial reciente.

ciento treinta y dos

Módulo 6

1 Look at the photo and read the task. Then listen to Natalie's response to the first question on the task card.

1 What **two** things does she say about the boy in the photo?
2 What do you think the following phrases mean: *en el fondo, árbol de Navidad, día de los Reyes Magos*?
3 Why does she think this may **not** be the 25th December?
4 What is her opinion of the children? Why?

2 Listen to and read Natalie's response to the second question on the task card.

1 Write down the missing word for each gap.
2 Look at the Answer Booster on page 134. Note down **six** examples of language which Natalie uses to give a strong answer.

En mi opinión la Navidad es una fiesta importantísima porque es muy especial y **1** ———— para toda la familia. Siempre decoramos la casa con luces y en el salón ponemos un árbol de Navidad con una **2** ———— enorme. También solemos poner un belén para recordar la importancia **3** ———— de esta fiesta. Es una buena oportunidad para pasar tiempo con la familia y descansar. Además, es importante porque se **4** ———— tarjetas a los amigos y a los familiares, y se dan **5** ———— a los seres queridos. Sin embargo, lo malo de las fiestas navideñas es que comemos demasiados **6** ————.

3 Listen to Natalie's response to the third question on the task card. In **English** note down **six** details that she gives.

4 Prepare your own answers to the first **three** questions. Think about which other **two** questions you might be asked. Then listen and take part in the full photo card discussion with the teacher.

⭐ To answer the second unprepared question, you could give a specific example of a festival in each country, and say which one you prefer and why.

C – General conversation

1 The teacher asks Lucas '*¿Qué te gusta comer?*' Listen to his answer and complete the sentences in **English**.

a Lucas eats lots of…
b He has a quick breakfast because…
c He drinks hot chocolate…
d He never eats…
e After school he has…
f The meal that his brother cooked wasn't…
g Lucas asks his teacher if…

2 The teacher then asks Lucas '*¿Has probado la comida española?*' Note down the **seven** adjectives that he uses. What do they mean?

asqueroso/a   riquísimo/a   sabroso/a   buenísimo/a   frío/a
salado/a   dulce   picante   refrescante   típico/a

⭐ To add variety to your language try to use a wide range of adjectives, including examples of the absolute superlative (e.g. *Estaba buenísimo* – It was extremely nice).

3 Listen to Lucas' response to the next question '*¿Prefieres cenar en casa o en un restaurante?*' Look at the Answer Booster on page 134. Note down **six** examples of language which Lucas uses to give a strong answer.

4 Prepare your own answers to Module 6 questions 1–6 on page 199. Then practise with your partner.

ciento treinta y tres **133**

Módulo 6   Prueba escrita

Answer booster	Aiming for a solid answer	Aiming higher	Aiming for the top
Verbs	**Different time frames**: past, present, near future **Different types of verbs**: regular, irregular, reflexive, stem-changing	**Different persons** of the verb **Verbs with an infinitive**: *tener que, soler, acabar de* **Phrases followed by the infinitive**: *para, sin, antes de, después de, al*	**A wide range of tenses**: present, preterite, imperfect, perfect, future **Passive**: *fue fundado* **Avoiding the passive**: *se celebra, se construyen*
Opinions and reasons	**Verbs of opinion**: *me chifla, me encanta, no aguanto* **Reasons**: *porque*	**Exclamations**: *¡Qué miedo! ¡Ni hablar!* **Absolute superlatives**: *carísimo, importantísimo*	**Opinions**: *desde mi punto de vista, a mi modo de ver, para mí* **Reasons**: *ya que, por eso, así que, por lo tanto*
Connectives	*y, pero, también*	*además, sin embargo, por desgracia, sobre todo*	*primero…, segundo…, como* **Balancing an argument**: *aunque, por un lado… por otro lado…*
Other features	**Qualifiers**: *muy, un poco, bastante, demasiado* **Adjectives**: *sabroso/a, rico/a, emocionante* **Adverbs of frequency**: *siempre, a veces*	**Sentences with *cuando, donde, si***: *Si es un día especial…* **Phrases with *tener***: *tener suerte/sueño/hambre/sed/prisa*	**Positive/Negative phrases**: *lo bueno/malo/mejor/peor* **Specialist vocabulary**: *navideño/a, un belén, los seres queridos, los fuegos artificiales*

A – Extended writing task

1 Look at the task and answer the questions.
- What information does each bullet point ask you to give?
- How could you develop your answer to each one?

> Escribes un artículo para una revista española sobre 'las fiestas y las tradiciones'.
>
> Menciona:
> - la importancia de las fiestas y las tradiciones para ti
> - una fiesta a la que has asistido
>
> Escribe aproximadamente **150** palabras en **español**.
> Responde a los dos aspectos de la pregunta.

2 The first bullet point asks you why festivals and traditions are important. Match the sentence halves to give you some ideas. What do the sentences mean in **English**?

1 Las tradiciones son una parte…
2 Enseñan a los niños a…
3 Las fiestas te hacen sentir más…
4 Te dan la oportunidad de divertirte…
5 Muchas fiestas y tradiciones tienen…
6 Son populares entre los turistas, y…

a con tus amigos y tu familia.
b orgulloso de tu cultura.
c importante de nuestra cultura.
d una importancia religiosa o histórica.
e por eso ayudan a la economía.
f valorar la historia del país.

3 Read Matthew's answer on page 135. What do the phrases in **bold** mean?

4 Look at the Answer Booster. Note down **eight** examples of language which Matthew uses to write a strong answer.

5 Prepare your own answer to the task.
- Look at the Answer Booster and Matthew's text for ideas.
- Write a detailed plan. Organise your answer in paragraphs.
- Write your answer and carefully check what you have written.

ciento treinta y cuatro

Desde mi punto de vista, las fiestas y tradiciones son importantísimas **por muchas razones**. Primero, enseñan a los niños a apreciar la historia del país. Por ejemplo, una tradición importante en Inglaterra es cuando se queman muñecos en una hoguera el 5 de noviembre (la Noche de Guy Fawkes) para conmemorar **el fracaso de la conspiración de la pólvora**. Comemos **delicias culinarias** como las manzanas de caramelo y lo pasamos fenomenal. Segundo, las fiestas y tradiciones te hacen sentir más orgulloso de tu cultura. También, **en algunos casos**, ayudan a la economía, ya que atraen a muchos turistas extranjeros que **suelen gastar mucho dinero**.

El verano pasado fui a Vilafranca del Penedès en España para ver la Fiesta Mayor que se celebra **a finales de agosto**. Durante tres días las calles se llenan de desfiles, bailes y música. Es **una festividad religiosa en honor de** Sant Fèlix, pero también hay conciertos, procesiones y fuegos artificiales. Lo mejor de la fiesta fue cuando vimos a los Castellers de Vilafranca, un grupo **que fue fundado en 1948**. En esta tradición antigua **se construyen torres humanas muy altas**. ¡Qué miedo! Fue muy impresionante, aunque hizo demasiado calor y mi madre tuvo una insolación. Creo que los Castellers son muy valientes. ¿Me gustaría probarlo? **¡Ni hablar!**

> ⭐ Matthew talks about Bonfire Night to help him answer the first bullet point. Giving a specific example like this can help you to explain why something is important.

los Castellers de Vilafranca

B – Translation

1 Read the English text and Jamie's translation of it. Correct the **eight** mistakes in the Spanish translation.

> Usually I get up early, have a shower and then have toast with apple juice for breakfast. However, this morning I woke up late. I had to leave the house without eating and so now I'm hungry. I'm going to have fish and chips for lunch. I love seafood and my favourite dish is paella.

> Normalmente me despierto temprano, me baño y luego desayuno tostadas con zumo de piña. Sin embargo, esta noche me acosté tarde. Tuve que salir de casa sin comer así que ahora tengo prisa. Voy a almorzar carne con patatas fritas. Me encantan las verduras y mi plato favorito es la paella.

2 Translate the following passage into Spanish.

> Usually we have dinner at eight o'clock and then I go to bed at ten. However, today I am very sleepy. I have just been to a music festival where I spent two nights without sleeping. It was incredible and I saw many of my favourite bands. Next time I'm not going to camp.

> ⭐ Remember that some phrases do not translate word for word. Take extra care with 'I am very sleepy' and 'I have just been'.

ciento treinta y cinco **135**

Módulo 6   Palabras

Las comidas	**Meals**	(el) Cola Cao	Cola Cao (Spanish chocolate drink)
el desayuno	breakfast	(el) marisco	seafood
la comida / el almuerzo	lunch	(el) pescado	fish
la merienda	tea (meal)	(el) pollo	chicken
la cena	dinner / evening meal	(el) zumo de naranja	orange juice
desayunar	to have breakfast / to have … for breakfast	(la) carne	meat
comer / almorzar	to have lunch / to have … for lunch	(la) ensalada	salad
merendar	to have tea / to have … for tea	(la) fruta	fruit
cenar	to have dinner / to have … for dinner	(la) leche	milk
tomar	to have (food / drink)	(la) sopa	soup
beber	to drink	(la) tortilla	omelette
entre semana…	during the week…	(los) cereales	cereals
los fines de semana…	at weekends…	(los) churros	fried doughnut sticks
Desayuno a las ocho.	I have breakfast at eight o'clock.	(las) galletas	biscuits
Desayuno / Como / Meriendo / Ceno…	For breakfast / lunch / tea / dinner I have…	(las) patatas fritas	chips
		(las) tostadas	toast
un huevo	an egg	(las) verduras	vegetables
un yogur	a yogurt	algo dulce / ligero / rápido	something sweet / light / quick
un pastel	a cake	ser goloso/a	to have a sweet tooth
un bocadillo	a sandwich	tener hambre	to be hungry
una hamburguesa	a hamburger	tener prisa	to be in a hurry
(el) café / (el) té	coffee / tea	tomar un desayuno fuerte	to have a big (lit. strong) breakfast

Las expresiones de cantidad	**Expressions of quantity**	una barra de…	a loaf of…
cien / quinientos gramos de…	100 / 500 grammes of…	una botella de…	a bottle of…
un bote de…	a jar of…	una caja de…	a box of…
un kilo de…	a kilo of…	una docena de…	a dozen…
un litro de…	a litre of…	una lata de…	a tin / can of…
un paquete de…	a packet of…		

Los alimentos	**Food products**	los pimientos	peppers
el aceite de oliva	olive oil	los plátanos	bananas
el agua	water	los pomelos	grapefruits
el ajo	garlic	los refrescos	fizzy drinks
el arroz	rice	las cebollas	onions
el atún	tuna	las fresas	strawberries
el azúcar	sugar	las judías (verdes)	(green) beans
el chorizo	spicy sausage	las legumbres	pulses
el maíz	corn	las lentejas	lentils
el pan	bread	las manzanas	apples
el queso	cheese	las naranjas	oranges
la cerveza	beer	las peras	pears
la carne de cerdo / cordero / ternera	pork / lamb / beef	las piñas	pineapples
la coliflor	cauliflower	las uvas	grapes
la harina	flour	las zanahorias	carrots
la mantequilla	butter	¿Has probado…?	Have you tried…?
la mermelada	jam	el gazpacho	gazpacho (chilled soup)
los albaricoques	apricots	la ensaladilla rusa	Russian salad
los guisantes	peas	la fabada	stew of beans and pork
los lácteos	dairy products	Es un tipo de bebida / postre.	It's a type of drink / dessert.
los melocotones	peaches	Es un plato caliente / frío.	It's a hot / cold dish.
los melones	melons	Contiene(n)…	It contains / They contain…
los pepinos	cucumbers	Fue inventado/a / introducido/a…	It was invented / introduced…

Mi rutina diaria	**My daily routine**	me acuesto	I go to bed
me despierto	I wake up	salgo de casa	I leave home
me levanto	I get up	vuelvo a casa	I return home
me ducho	I have a shower	temprano / tarde	early / late
me peino	I brush my hair	enseguida	straight away
me afeito	I have a shave	odio levantarme	I hate getting up
me visto	I get dressed		
me lavo los dientes	I clean my teeth		

¿Qué le pasa?	**What's the matter?**	Tengo dolor de cabeza.	I have a headache.
No me encuentro bien.	I don't feel well.	Tengo fiebre.	I have a fever / temperature.
Me siento fatal.	I feel awful.	Tengo gripe.	I have flu.
Estoy enfermo/a / cansado/a.	I am ill / tired.	Tengo mucho sueño.	I am very sleepy.
Tengo calor / frío.	I am hot / cold.	Tengo náuseas.	I feel sick.
Tengo catarro.	I have a cold.	Tengo quemaduras de sol.	I have sunburn.
Tengo diarrea.	I have diarrhoea.		

Módulo 6

Tengo tos.	I have a cough.
Tengo una insolación.	I have sunstroke.
Tengo una picadura.	I've been stung.
Me duele(n)…	My … hurt(s)
Me he cortado el/la…	I've cut my…
Me he hecho daño en…	I've hurt my…
Me he quemado…	I've burnt my…
Me he roto…	I've broken my…
Me he torcido…	I've twisted my…
el brazo / el estómago	arm / stomach
el pie / el tobillo	foot / ankle
la boca / la cabeza	mouth / head
la espalda / la garganta	back / throat
la mano / la nariz	hand / nose
la pierna / la rodilla	leg / knee
los dientes / las muelas	teeth
los oídos / las orejas	ears
los ojos	eyes
¿Desde hace cuánto tiempo?	How long for?
desde hace…	for…
un día / un mes	a day / a month
una hora / una semana	an hour / a week
¿Desde cuándo?	Since when?
desde ayer	since yesterday
desde anteayer	since the day before yesterday
no se preocupe	don't worry
¡Qué mala suerte!	What bad luck!
Tiene(s) que / Hay que…	You have to…
beber mucha agua	drink lots of water
descansar	rest
ir al hospital / médico / dentista	go to the hospital / doctor / dentist
tomar aspirinas	take aspirins
tomar este jarabe / estas pastillas	take this syrup / these tablets
usar esta crema	use this cream

Las fiestas / Festivals

la fiesta de…	the festival of…
esta tradición antigua…	this old tradition…
se caracteriza por…	is characterised by…
se celebra en…	is celebrated in…
se repite…	is repeated…
se queman figuras de madera	wooden figures are burnt
se construyen hogueras	bonfires are built
se disparan fuegos artificiales	fireworks are set off
se lanzan huevos	eggs are thrown
las calles se llenan de…	the streets are filled with…
los niños / los jóvenes…	children / young people…
los familiares / las familias…	relations / families…
comen manzanas de caramelo	eat toffee apples
decoran las casas / las tumbas con flores / velas	decorate houses / graves with flowers / candles
preparan linternas / altares	prepare lanterns / altars
se disfrazan de brujas / fantasmas	dress up as witches / ghosts
ven desfiles	(they) watch processions

Un día especial / A special day

Abrimos los regalos.	We open presents.
Buscamos huevos de chocolate.	We look for chocolate eggs.
Cantamos villancicos.	We sing Christmas carols.
Cenamos bacalao.	We have cod for dinner.
Comemos dulces navideños / doce uvas / pavo.	We eat Christmas sweets / twelve grapes / turkey.
Nos acostamos muy tarde.	We go to bed very late.
Nos levantamos muy temprano.	We get up very early.
Rezamos.	We pray.
Vamos a la mezquita / iglesia.	We go to the mosque / church.
Ayer fue…	Yesterday was…
el baile de fin de curso	the school prom
el Día de Navidad	Christmas Day
(el) Domingo de Pascua	Easter Sunday
(la) Nochebuena	Christmas Eve
(la) Nochevieja	New Year's Eve
Me bañé y luego me maquillé.	I had a bath and then did my make up.

¿Qué va a tomar? / What are you going to have?

de primer / segundo plato…	for starter / main course…
de postre…	for dessert…
Voy a tomar…	I'm going to have…
(el) bistec	steak
(el) filete de cerdo	pork fillet
(el) flan	crème caramel
(el) jamón serrano	Serrano ham
(la) merluza en salsa verde	hake in parsley and wine sauce
(la) sopa de fideos	noodle soup
(la) tortilla de espinacas	spinach omelette
(la) trucha a la plancha	grilled trout
(los) calamares	squid
(las) albóndigas	meatballs
(las) chuletas de cordero asadas	roast lamb chops
(las) croquetas caseras	homemade croquettes
(las) gambas	prawns
(las) natillas	custard
¿Qué me recomienda?	What do you recommend?
el menú del día	the set menu
la especialidad de la casa	the house speciality
está buenísimo/a / riquísimo/a	it's extremely good / tasty
¡Que aproveche!	Enjoy your meal!
¿Algo más?	Anything else?
Nada más, gracias.	Nothing else, thank you.
¿Me trae la cuenta, por favor?	Can you bring me the bill, please?
No tengo cuchillo / tenedor / cuchara.	I haven't got a knife / fork / spoon.
No hay aceite / sal / vinagre.	There's no oil / salt / vinegar.
El plato / vaso / mantel está sucio.	The plate / glass / table cloth is dirty.
El vino está malo.	The wine is bad / off.
La carne está fría.	The meat is cold.
dejar una propina	to leave a tip
equivocarse	to make a mistake
pedir	to order / ask for
ser alérgico/a…	to be allergic to…
ser vegetariano/a	to be a vegetarian

Un festival de música / A music festival

Me fascina(n)…	…fascinate(s) me.
Admiro…	I admire…
No aguanto / soporto…	I can't stand…
su actitud / talento	his/her attitude / talent
su comportamiento	his/her behaviour
su determinación / estilo	his/her determination / style
su forma de vestir	his/her way of dressing
su música / voz	his/her music / voice
sus canciones / coreografías	his/her songs / choreography
sus ideas / letras	his/her ideas / lyrics
atrevido/a(s)	daring
imaginativo/a(s)	imaginative
precioso/a(s)	beautiful
repetitivo/a(s)	repetitive
original(es)	original
triste(s)	sad
Me/Te hace(n) falta…	I/You need…
crema solar	sun cream
el pasaporte / DNI	your passport / national ID card
un sombrero / una gorra	a hat / cap

ciento treinta y siete

7 ¡A currar!
Punto de partida

- *Talking about different jobs*
- *Discussing job preferences*

1 Escucha. Copia y completa la tabla. (1–5)

	trabajo	¿le gusta? (✓/✗)	¿por qué (no)?
1	camarera	✗	repetitivo, …

peluquero/a   camarero/a   veterinario/a   jardinero/a   profesor(a)   dependiente/a

ayudar
contestar
cuidar
enseñar
hacer
preparar
reparar
servir
trabajar
vender
viajar

entrevistas con famosos
coches
llamadas telefónicas
platos distintos
ropa de marca
comida y bebida
las plantas y las flores
a los clientes / pacientes / pasajeros / niños
en un taller / un hospital / un hotel / una tienda
a bordo de un avión
por todo el mundo

⭐ When saying what job someone does, you don't use the indefinite article.
Soy periodista.   I am **a** journalist.
However, you do use it if giving more specific details.
Es **una** cantante muy conocida.   She's **a** very well known singer.

G Masculine and feminine nouns ▶ Page **222**

Some nouns have different masculine and feminine forms.
camarer**o** → camarer**a**
diseñad**or** → diseñad**ora**

Those ending in **-e** or **-ista** are usually invariable.
cantant**e** → cantant**e**
recepcion**ista** → recepcion**ista**

2 Escribe tres frases para cada persona. Inventa los otros detalles.

Ejemplo: **1** *Soy cocinera y trabajo en un restaurante italiano. Todos los días preparo… Me gusta mi trabajo porque…*

¿En qué trabajas?

1 Soy cocinera.    2 Soy enfermero.    3 Soy azafata.    4 Soy periodista.    5 Soy recepcionista.    6 Soy mecánico.

3 Lee los textos. ¿En qué trabajan? Utiliza un diccionario si es necesario.

1 Trabajo para una revista de moda, pero no escribo artículos. Tampoco soy modelo ni diseñador gráfico. Nunca salgo sin llevar mi cámara.

2 No soy ni recepcionista ni camarera, pero trabajo en un hotel de lujo. Nunca cocino ni cuido los jardines. Todos los días corto el pelo a los clientes.

3 En mi trabajo viajo por todo el mundo en un crucero enorme. No sirvo comida ni hago manicuras. Tampoco limpio las cabinas. Cada noche canto en un espectáculo.

4 Trabajo en una clínica, pero no soy ni médica ni enfermera. Tampoco trabajo con animales. Ayudo a mis pacientes a cuidar los dientes.

138 ciento treinta y ocho

Módulo 7

4 Con tu compañero/a, juega a '¿Cuál es mi profesión?'

Ejemplo:
- ¿Trabajas en un hotel?
- ¿Sirves comida y bebida?
- Sí, trabajo en un hotel.
- No, no sirvo…

5 Mira las cuatro listas. Escribe el título correcto. (A–D)

1
bombero/a
médico/a
policía
soldado

2
abogado/a
contable
funcionario/a
guía turístico/a

3
albañil
electricista
fontanero/a
ingeniero/a

4
bailarín/bailarina
diseñador(a)
escritor(a)
músico/a

A Seguridad / Sanidad
B Actividades artísticas
C Construcción / Ingeniería
D Sector servicios

6 Escucha. ¿Qué trabajos les gustaría hacer? ¿Por qué? (1–5)

Ejemplo: **1** c – quite serious, …

(No) Soy	ambicioso/a	paciente
	comprensivo/a	práctico/a
	creativo/a	responsable
	extrovertido/a	serio/a
	fuerte	trabajador(a)
	inteligente	valiente
	organizado/a	

Es un trabajo	artístico	exigente
	manual	variado
	para personas sociables	
	con responsabilidad	
	con buenas perspectivas	
	con un buen sueldo	

7 Con tu compañero/a, haz <u>cuatro</u> diálogos. Inventa los detalles.
- ¿Qué tipo de persona eres?
- Creo que soy… y…, pero no…
- Pues, creo que serías un buen… / una buena… porque es un trabajo…

⭐ Remember that you use the conditional to say what you **would** do.

Me gusta**ría** ser fontanero.   I **would** like to be a plumber.
Se**rías** un buen… / una buena…   You **would** be a good…

8 Traduce las frases al español.

1. I love my job because it's quite varied.
2. My dad is a receptionist. He works in a clinic.
3. I serve food and drink to passengers on board a plane.
4. I would like to be a civil servant because it's a job with good prospects.
5. You are patient and understanding, and so I think you would make a good nurse.

ciento treinta y nueve **139**

1 ¿Qué haces para ganar dinero?

- Talking about how you earn money
- Using **soler** in the imperfect tense
- Using verbs in different forms

1 Escucha. Apunta los detalles en inglés. (1–5)

Ejemplo: **1** b – when they need me – 4 € per hour

¿Tienes un trabajo a tiempo parcial?

Sí, tengo un trabajo.

No, no tengo trabajo, pero ayudo en casa.

a Reparto periódicos.

b Hago de canguro.

c Trabajo de cajero.

d Cocino y lavo los platos.

e Paso la aspiradora y plancho la ropa.

f Pongo y quito la mesa.

g Paseo al perro y corto el césped.

¿Cuándo trabajas? / ¿Cuándo lo haces?	
Trabajo Lo hago	los (sábados) todos los días en verano antes / después del insti cuando necesito dinero cuando mi madre está trabajando cuando me necesitan cada mañana una vez / dos veces a la semana
¿Cuánto ganas?	
Gano	… euros / libras (a la hora / al día / a la semana)
¡No gano nada!	

2 Lee el texto. Busca las expresiones en español.

Soy estudiante, pero también trabajo como socorrista en un parque acuático en Benidorm. Lo hago desde hace seis meses y me encanta. Suelo trabajar dos veces a la semana. Tengo que vigilar a los niños que nadan en la piscina de olas. Me llevo bien con mis compañeros y mi jefe es muy amable. Aunque no gano mucho, es un trabajo divertido y el horario es flexible.

En casa siempre ayudo a mis padres con las tareas domésticas. Arreglo mi habitación y de vez en cuando preparo la cena. Cuando era más joven, solía hacer de canguro para mi hermano, pero ya es mayor. Antes mi hermana y yo solíamos lavar los platos, pero ahora es más fácil – ¡ponemos los platos en el lavavajillas!

1 I've been doing it for six months
2 I have to supervise the children
3 I get on well with my colleagues
4 My boss is very nice
5 I help my parents with the housework
6 I tidy my room
7 but now he's older
8 we used to wash the dishes

> **G** Soler *in the imperfect tense*
>
> In the present tense you use **soler** + infinitive to talk about what you usually / tend to do.
>
> **Suelo** lavar el coche.   **I tend to** wash the car.
>
> You can also use it in the imperfect tense to talk about things you used to do regularly. Alternatively, simply use the imperfect tense of the verb.
>
> **Solía** cortar el césped.   **I used to** cut the lawn.
> **Cortaba** el césped.   **I used to cut** the lawn.

ciento cuarenta

Módulo 7

3 hablar Imagina que tienes un trabajo a tiempo parcial. Con tu compañero/a, haz diálogos.

- ¿Tienes un trabajo a tiempo parcial?
- ¿Qué haces?
- ¿Cuándo lo haces?
- ¿Cuánto ganas?
- ¿Te gusta tu trabajo?
- ¿Ayudas con las tareas en casa?

4 escuchar Escucha a Guillermo. Elige la opción correcta.

a **Cocina / Lava los platos / Sirve** en un restaurante.
b Trabaja cada **mañana / tarde / fin de semana**.
c Opina que el salario es **bajo / justo / alto**.
d Se lleva bien con **su jefe / sus compañeros / los clientes**.
e Antes **cocinaba / ponía la mesa / quitaba la mesa**.
f Ya no **pasea al perro / plancha la ropa / pasa la aspiradora**.

Guillermo

5 escribir Escribe un texto sobre lo que haces en tu trabajo y en casa.

Give details of:
- your part-time job (or invent one!)
  - what you do / when you work
  - how much you earn
  - your opinion of it
- how you help out at home
  - what you do / how often
  - what you used to do
  - what other people in your family do

⭐ You often learn new verbs in the 'I' form of the present tense (e.g. *plancho, reparto*). Make sure you also know the **infinitive** so that you can use them:

- with expressions followed by the **infinitive**

  *Tengo que **pasar** la aspiradora.* I have **to do** the vacuuming.
  *Solía **preparar** la cena.* I used **to prepare** dinner.

- in different tenses / persons of the verb.

  Ayer planché mi uniforme. Yesterday I ironed my uniform.
  Mi padre pone la mesa. My dad sets the table.
  Preparaba la cena. I used to prepare dinner.

6 leer Lee el texto y contesta a las preguntas en inglés.

Buscar empleo para jóvenes de 16 años

Como adolescente, es probable que tengas una buena cantidad de tiempo libre y el deseo de ganar dinero. Los trabajos típicos para los adolescentes incluyen:
- Trabajo en un restaurante de comida rápida
- Dependiente en una tienda
- Repartidor de periódicos

Si tienes 16 años, también existen otras posibilidades de ganar tu propio dinero sin descuidar el colegio:
- Cuidado de niños: Es ideal si haces el curso de la Cruz Roja de primeros auxilios.
- Arreglo de jardines: Los jardines dan trabajo todo el año: en primavera y verano cortar el césped, en otoño barrer las hojas y en invierno quitar la nieve.
- Lavado de coches de los vecinos.
- Enseñar a las personas mayores a usar los ordenadores o Internet.

Si tienes 14 o 15 años, solo puedes trabajar tres horas al día y un máximo de 18 horas a la semana.

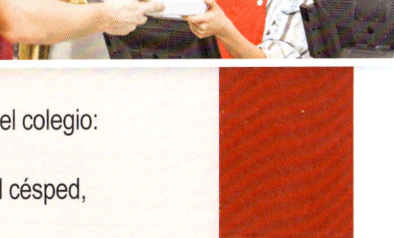

descuidar	to neglect
las hojas	leaves

1 Which two things are you likely to have as a teenager?
2 What are you advised to do if you want to look after children?
3 How do gardening tasks vary according to the time of year? (Give <u>three</u> details.)
4 Which job could you do for your neighbours?
5 What is the last idea suggested for earning money?
6 What restrictions apply to younger teenagers?

ciento cuarenta y uno **141**

2 Mis prácticas laborales

- Talking about work experience
- Using the preterite and imperfect together
- Using alternatives to 'and'

1 Lee y escribe C (Carolina), E (Eduardo), o C+E (Carolina y Eduardo).

Las prácticas laborales, ¿merecen la pena?

Carolina
Hice mis prácticas en una emisora de radio local. Por desgracia, estaba lejos de mi casa, así que tenía que ir en metro y en tren cada mañana. La primera semana trabajé en el departamento de ventas y marketing. Todos los días sacaba fotocopias y archivaba documentos. Luego, la segunda semana trabajé con el equipo de producción. ¡Qué ilusión! Ayudaba al ingeniero de sonido y me llevaba muy bien con mi jefe. Fue una experiencia tanto divertida como educativa, y aprendí muchísimas cosas.

Eduardo
En mayo pasé quince días trabajando en una granja. Cada día me levantaba a las seis de la mañana para coger el autobús. Empezaba a las siete y terminaba a las cinco, sin tener ni un momento para comer. ¡Me trataban como un esclavo! Tenía que hacer todos los trabajos sucios. No solo tenía que ordeñar las vacas, sino también dar de comer a los cerdos. Fue una pérdida de tiempo y solo aprendí una cosa útil en toda la semana – ¡no quiero ser granjero!

| merecer / valer la pena | to be worthwhile |
| ordeñar | to milk |

1. No vale la pena hacer prácticas laborales.
2. Aprendí muchas habilidades nuevas.
3. Pasé dos semanas haciendo prácticas.
4. Trabajé al aire libre.
5. Iba en transporte público.
6. No tenía descanso.
7. Hacía varias tareas administrativas.
8. El horario era muy duro.

2 Lee los textos otra vez. Busca <u>cuatro</u> verbos en el pretérito y <u>ocho</u> verbos en el imperfecto.

> Try using phrases such as these to provide interesting alternatives to **y** (and):
> no solo…, sino también…   not only…, but also…
> tanto… como…   both… and…

3 Escucha a Antonio. ¿A qué pregunta está contestando? (1–7)
Ejemplo: **1** c

a ¿Dónde hiciste tus prácticas?
b ¿Qué tal fue tu primer día?
c ¿Cómo era tu rutina?
d ¿Qué ropa llevabas?
e ¿Qué tareas hacías cada día?
f ¿Cómo era tu jefe?
g ¿Qué cosas aprendiste?

| la reunión | meeting |
| los estantes | shelves |

G Using the preterite and the imperfect tense   > Pages 212, 214

The **preterite** tense is used for completed actions in the past.
   El primer día **llegué** *temprano.*   On the first day **I arrived** early.
It is also often used for opinions in the past.
   Me gustó *trabajar allí.*   **I liked** working there.
The **imperfect** tense is used for repeated actions in the past, and for descriptions.
   Cada mañana **cogía** *el autobús.*   Each morning **I caught** the bus.
   Mis colegas **eran** *muy agradables.*   My colleagues **were** very pleasant.

4 Escucha otra vez. Apunta <u>dos</u> detalles en inglés para cada pregunta. (1–7)
Ejemplo: **1** left home at 7.00, …

5 Con tu compañero/a, haz diálogos. Usa las preguntas del ejercicio 3.

Hice mis prácticas laborales en… Pasé (quince días) trabajando en…		Mi jefe/a era Mis compañeros eran Los clientes eran	alegre(s) (des)agradable(s) (mal)educado/a(s)
El primer / último día	llegué… conocí a… fui…	(No) aprendí	a trabajar en equipo a usar… nada nuevo
Cada día Todos los días	empezaba / terminaba a las… llevaba… trabajaba… ayudaba… escribía… cogía… iba…		

6 Escucha. Copia y completa la tabla. Sobra una opción. (1–5)

	cuándo	dónde	opinión
1	hace tres meses	c	experiencia muy positiva

a una agencia de viajes
b un polideportivo
c una escuela
d la empresa de mi madre
e una tienda benéfica / solidaria
f una fábrica de juguetes

7 Lee el texto y elige los verbos correctos. Luego traduce el <u>primer</u> párrafo al inglés.

Cada año mi insti organiza prácticas laborales para los alumnos. **1 Decidí / Decidía** ir a trabajar a una empresa cerca de donde vivo. Cada día **2 salí / salía** de casa a las ocho y cuarto y luego **3 fui / iba** a la oficina a pie. **4 Llevé / Llevaba** un traje azul oscuro que **5 recibí / recibía** por Navidad. Todos los días **6 hice / hacía** muchas tareas diferentes.

Mis compañeros de trabajo **7 fueron / eran** amables y siempre **8 pasé / pasaba** la hora de comer con ellos. Lo mejor fue el último día, cuando mi jefe **9 organizó / organizaba** una pequeña fiesta de despedida para mí. Mis prácticas fueron una experiencia muy positiva y **10 aprendí / aprendía** muchas habilidades nuevas.

8 Escribe un texto sobre tus prácticas laborales.

Use the **preterite** to give details about:
- When / where you did your placement
- Your first / last day
- What you learned + your opinion

Use the **imperfect** to give details about:
- How you travelled each day
- What time you started / finished
- What you wore
- Your daily tasks
- The people you worked with

> Try to include some other tenses, such as the **present**, the **perfect**, the **future** or the **conditional**. For example:
>
> Creo que las prácticas laborales (no) **merecen** la pena.
>
> **He decidido** que (no) **voy a ser**… en el futuro.
>
> (No) **recomendaría** estas prácticas a otro alumno.

Módulo 7

ciento cuarenta y tres 143

3 ¿Por qué aprender idiomas?

- Talking about the importance of learning languages
- Using the present and the present continuous
- Using *saber* and *conocer*

1 Escucha. ¿Cuál es la ventaja <u>más importante</u> para cada persona? (1–4)

el cerebro — brain

a Te abre la mente.
b Aumenta tu confianza.
c Te hace parecer más atractivo.
d Mejora tus perspectivas laborales.
e Te ayuda a conocer nuevos sitios.
f Te permite hacer nuevos amigos.
g Te permite trabajar o estudiar en el extranjero.
h Estimula el cerebro.
i Te permite descubrir nuevas culturas.
j Te ayuda a mejorar tu lengua materna.

Diez ventajas de aprender un idioma

2 Lee y apunta las opiniones del ejercicio 1 que mencionan.

Ejemplo: **Paulina:** d, …

⭐ In exercise 1 you have to identify the **most important** reason for each person. Beware of distractors and listen out for clue words such as *más*, *sobre todo*, *principal*, *más que nada*.

> No domino el inglés, pero lo hablo bastante bien. También hablo un poco de ruso. Creo que es más fácil encontrar trabajo si sabes hablar otro idioma, y a veces aun ganas un salario más alto. Además, te permite viajar a lugares más exóticos, conocer a mucha gente distinta y establecer nuevas amistades. Finalmente, mejora la memoria y te ayuda a solucionar problemas.
>
> **Paulina**

> Saber hablar otro idioma te da la oportunidad de buscar un empleo o ir a la universidad en otro país. Por ejemplo, yo pasé un año estudiando en Estados Unidos. También te ayuda a apreciar la vida cultural de otros países – el cine, la literatura, la música e incluso el humor. Reduce los prejuicios y el racismo porque te hace una persona más abierta a las diferencias. Además, te permite aprender cosas sobre tu propio idioma que no sabías.
>
> **Íñigo**

dominar — to master / be fluent in
aun / incluso — even

3 Lee los textos del ejercicio 2 otra vez. Traduce al inglés las <u>cuatro</u> frases donde se usa 'saber' o 'conocer'.

⭐ The verbs **saber** and **conocer** both mean 'to know'.

saber – to know (facts / information), to know how to (do something)

No sé la respuesta. — **I don't know** the answer.
¿**Sabes** conducir? — Do **you know how** to drive?

conocer – to know / be acquainted with (person / place / thing), to get to know / meet

¿**Conoces** a Eva? — Do **you know** Eva?
Conocí a mucha gente. — **I got to know / met** lots of people.

4 Traduce el texto al español. Utiliza frases de los ejercicios 1 y 2 como modelo.

I'm not fluent in Spanish, but I speak it quite well. I also speak a bit of French. In my opinion, if you know how to speak another language it allows you to meet lots of different people. Furthermore, it improves your job prospects. Above all, it increases your confidence and opens your mind.

5 Escucha y lee el texto. Luego apunta la información en inglés.

Trabajo como corresponsal de guerra para un canal de televisión. Es el trabajo de mis sueños porque me permite hacer todas las cosas que me interesan: viajar, conocer a gente nueva y, sobre todo, compartir historias importantes con el resto del mundo. Aunque es un trabajo emocionante, también puede ser peligroso, y siempre hay que recordar que esto no es ninguna película de Hollywood. La realidad de la guerra es muy triste y afecta a la vida de tanta gente inocente.

Para hacer bien mi trabajo me hace falta hablar idiomas extranjeros. Pasé diez años aprendiendo inglés cuando era más joven, y antes de venir aquí hice un curso de árabe. Esto me permite hacer entrevistas, leer documentos y escuchar las noticias locales para preparar mis reportajes. Más que nada, me ayuda a establecer buenas relaciones con la gente – algo esencial para un buen periodista.

Susana

recordar to remember
compartir to share

Ejemplo: **1** *Her job: war correspondent for a…*

1 Her job:
2 Why it's her dream job:
3 How she describes the job:
4 Why it's not like a film:
5 Her language studies:
6 How languages help her:

6 Mira las fotos. Con tu compañero/a, haz diálogos.

- ¿Qué está haciendo <u>este hombre / esta mujer</u>?
- Está <u>trabajando como…</u> y está…
- En tu opinión, ¿cómo usa los idiomas en su trabajo?
- Creo que <u>organiza…</u> También…
- ¿Y tú? ¿Qué idiomas hablas?
- Domino… y hablo…
- ¿Por qué es importante aprender idiomas?
- En mi opinión, es importante porque… Además,…

is working in a hotel
is helping people

organises excursions
answers phone calls
solves problems

guía turístico

is visiting a company
is buying clothes

travels a lot
meets lots of people
writes emails

compradora de moda

G Present and present continuous ▶ Page 218

Use the **present continuous** to talk about what he/she <u>is doing</u> in the photo.
Use the **present tense** to talk about what he/she <u>does</u> more generally.

Está escogiendo ropa. **She is choosing** clothes.
Todos los días soluciona problemas. Every day **he solves** problems.

Remember, the present continuous uses the present tense of *estar* + present participle (*–ando / –iendo*).

4 Solicitando un trabajo

- *Applying for a summer job*
- *Using indirect object pronouns*
- *Writing a formal letter*

1 **leer** Lee los anuncios y contesta a las preguntas.

A Animadores
¿Has terminado los exámenes? ¿Te apetece pasar el verano trabajando en Menorca? ¿Eres un(a) fanático/a del deporte? Se buscan animadores con buen nivel de inglés y español para campamento de verano. Precioso entorno rural. No hace falta experiencia.

B Au pair
Estamos buscando a un(a) joven británico/a agradable y cariñoso/a para compartir nuestro hogar en Ibiza y cuidar de nuestros dos hijos encantadores. No se requiere experiencia. Flexibilidad horaria necesaria. Salario a convenir.

C Varios puestos
¿Quieres trabajar en un parque de atracciones en Mallorca? Se requieren operarios de atracciones, camareros, ayudantes de cocina y dependientes. Experiencia deseable. Buenas capacidades de comunicación esenciales.

Zona Cultura

Destino: ISLAS BALEARES
Ubicación: Mar Mediterráneo, a 100 km de la costa valenciana.
Población: 1,1 millones (¡y más de 13 millones de turistas cada año!)
Famosas por: Sus playas, su paisaje hermoso y su vida nocturna.

¿Te apetece…?	*Do you fancy…? / Does… appeal to you?*
cariñoso/a	*affectionate*
el hogar	*home*

¿Qué anuncio/trabajo…

1. te permite negociar el sueldo?
2. requiere buenas habilidades lingüísticas?
3. te ofrece alojamiento?
4. prefiere una persona con experiencia?
5. te permite disfrutar del campo?
6. te da la oportunidad de trabajar en una tienda?
7. no tiene horario fijo?

2 **escuchar** Escucha a Rafa. Copia y completa la tabla.

anuncio	ventaja	inconveniente
A	trabajar al aire libre	

3 **hablar** Con tu compañero/a, haz diálogos.

- ¿Te apetece ser <u>animador(a)</u>?
- Sí / No, (no) me apetece ser… porque…
- ¿Te apetece trabajar en…?

(No) soy una persona…
(No) he trabajado en…
(No) me interesa (+ *infinitive*)
(No) tengo experiencia trabajando en/como…
Me da la oportunidad de (+ *infinitive*)

G Indirect object pronouns ▶ Page 228

me	(to) me	**nos**	(to) us
te	(to) you	**os**	(to) you
le	(to) him/her/you (formal, singular)	**les**	(to) them/you (formal, plural)

The indirect object pronoun usually comes before the verb.

Me apetece trabajar en España. Working in Spain appeals **to me**.

With verbs followed by the infinitive it can come before or after.

Le voy a escribir / Voy a escribir**le**. I am going to write **to you**.

In English we often miss out the word 'to'.

Nos da la oportunidad de… It gives **us** the opportunity to…

146 *ciento cuarenta y seis*

Módulo 7

4 **leer** Lee y completa la carta de presentación con las palabras del recuadro.

> Muy Señor mío:
>
> En referencia a su **1** _____ publicado en la página web www.empleosdeverano.es, le escribo para solicitar el **2** _____ de animador.
>
> Aunque no tengo **3** _____ previa en un campamento de verano, he **4** _____ con niños pequeños en el polideportivo local y también he hecho de canguro para mis **5** _____. Soy responsable y **6** _____, practico muchos deportes en mi tiempo libre y me gusta trabajar en **7** _____.
>
> Le adjunto mi currículum vitae. Como podrá ver, además del inglés (mi lengua materna) hablo bien el español y tengo **8** _____ de alemán.
>
> Le agradezco su amable atención y quedo a la espera de su respuesta.
>
> Atentamente,
>
> Tom Hughes

vecinos	anuncio
equipo	puesto
experiencia	trabajado
trabajador	conocimientos

⭐ Just like in English, you have to follow special conventions when writing a formal letter. Can you spot these phrases in Spanish?
- Dear Sir
- I'm enclosing my CV
- Thank you for your kind attention
- Yours sincerely

Remember to use the **usted** (formal singular) form of the verb.

5 **escribir** Escribe una carta de presentación para uno de los puestos del ejercicio 1.

Mention:
- the job you are applying for and where you saw it advertised
- your previous experience
- your personal qualities and interests
- your language skills / other skills

6 **leer** Lee la entrevista. Empareja las preguntas con las respuestas.

1. ¿Por qué quiere ser (ayudante de cocina)?
2. ¿Qué asignaturas ha estudiado?
3. ¿Qué experiencia laboral tiene?
4. ¿Ha trabajado (en equipo) antes?
5. ¿Qué cualidades tiene usted?
6. ¿Qué otras habilidades tiene?

a He estudiado todas las asignaturas típicas, tales como las matemáticas, las ciencias y la informática, pero también he hecho un curso optativo de pastelería.

b Soy una persona honrada, amable y sincera. También tengo buen sentido del humor y me llevo bien con la gente.

c Sí, estoy haciendo un programa especial que se llama el 'Duke of Edinburgh Award'. Tenemos que trabajar en grupos para hacer una expedición.

d Me interesa este trabajo porque me encanta cocinar y quiero aprender más. En el futuro me gustaría ser cocinero.

e Domino el español y entiendo el francés escrito. También tengo buenas capacidades de comunicación y de resolución de problemas.

f El año pasado hice mis prácticas laborales en una carnicería, donde aprendí mucho. También tengo un trabajo a tiempo parcial en una cafetería.

7 **escuchar** Escucha y comprueba tus respuestas.

tales como — such as

8 **hablar** Con tu compañero/a, haz una entrevista para un trabajo. Utiliza las preguntas del ejercicio 6.

ciento cuarenta y siete **147**

5 Un año sabático

- Discussing gap years
- Revising the conditional
- Using the 24-hour clock

1 Escucha y elige la respuesta correcta. (1–4)

¿Cómo pasarías un año sabático?

1 Marc iría a España, donde…
- a enseñaría inglés.
- b mejoraría su nivel de español.
- c ganaría mucho dinero.

2 Fernanda pasaría un año en Honduras, donde…
- a apoyaría un proyecto medioambiental.
- b trabajaría en un orfanato.
- c ayudaría a construir un colegio.

3 Ramón buscaría un trabajo para tres meses y luego…
- a viajaría como mochilero por el mundo.
- b visitaría Latinoamérica.
- c haría un viaje en Interrail por Europa.

4 Pilar dice que trabajaría en una estación de esquí, donde…
- a aprendería a esquiar.
- b el alojamiento sería muy caro.
- c nunca olvidaría la experiencia.

el orfanato	orphanage
viajar como mochilero/a	to go backpacking

G The conditional — Page 220

Remember to use the **conditional** to say what you would do.

Enseñaría inglés. — **I would teach** English.
Trabajaríamos en un orfanato. — **We would work** in an orphanage.

To form the conditional, add the imperfect endings of –er/–ir verbs to the infinitive.

Some verbs have an irregular stem. They include:
- hacer → haría (I would do)
- poder → podría (I would be able to)
- tener → tendría (I would have)

2 Con tu compañero/a, haz diálogos.

- ¿Cómo pasarías un año sabático?
- Primero…, donde… Luego…

1 job (4 months) + earn money
2 Interrail (Europe)
3 Colombia + help build orphanage
= never forget

1 Argentina + improve Spanish
2 backpack (Latin America)
3 job (hotel) + earn money
= learn a lot

3 Lee el texto y tradúcelo al inglés.

Si pudiera tomarme un año sabático, lo aprovecharía para trabajar como voluntaria porque, en mi opinión, es importantísimo ayudar a los demás. Sin embargo, no me gustaría trabajar como profesora – ¡estoy harta de los colegios! Iría a Costa Rica, donde trabajaría en un proyecto medioambiental para salvar las tortugas marinas. Creo que el voluntariado aumenta tu confianza y te permite mejorar tus habilidades sociales. Después, viajaría como mochilera por los países de Centroamérica (¡si tuviera bastante dinero!).

⭐ These phrases use a form of the verb called the **imperfect subjunctive**.

Si **pudiera** tomarme un año sabático… — If **I could** take a gap year…
Si **tuviera** bastante dinero… — If **I had** enough money…
Si **fuera** más ambicioso/a… — If **I were** more ambitious…

aprovechar	to make the most of
estar harto/a	to be fed up
el voluntariado	volunteering

148 ciento cuarenta y ocho

4 Lee la página web. ¿Quién habla? Escribe el nombre correcto.

Tu año sabático.com

¿Cómo viajarías?

💬 Cogería el tren, ya que es más cómodo y puedes ver vídeos en tu tableta mientras viajas. También puedes dejar la maleta en la consigna mientras visitas una ciudad. No viajaría en autobús porque no me gusta nada esperar en la parada de autobús. **Óscar (Bilbao)**

💬 Para viajar entre diferentes ciudades cogería el autocar dado que es rápido – normalmente hay pocos atascos en las autopistas. No iría en tren porque los conductores siempre están en huelga. Y lo peor es que los billetes son carísimos. **Conchita (Vigo)**

💬 No viajaría en autobús, pues las carreteras están en muy mal estado en muchos sitios. También tengo miedo a volar, y suele haber muchos retrasos en los aeropuertos. Creo que iría en tren. Por lo menos los trenes tienen aire acondicionado y no contaminan el medio ambiente. **Lourdes (Jaén)**

1 I'm scared of flying.
2 Train drivers are always on strike.
3 I can't stand waiting at bus stops.
4 Motorways are congestion-free.
5 You can store your luggage.
6 I can do other things while travelling.
7 The roads are poor.
8 Tickets are really expensive.

5 ¿Cómo pasarías un año sabático? ¿Cómo viajarías? Escribe un texto.

Give details of:
- Where you would go
- What you would do
- How you would travel, and why

6 Escucha y mira la información. Corrige los errores. (1–5)

Ejemplo: **1** *Retraso – 10 min*

Destino	Salida	Llegada	Vía	Observaciones
Gijón	09:39	15:32	5	Retraso – 12 min
Málaga	09:41	12:47	8	
Zaragoza	09:46	11:25	11	Cancelado
Coruña	09:53	15:20	4	Tren AVE
Toledo	09:58	10:29	7	

⭐ Train stations and airports often use the 24-hour clock. When listening to announcements be prepared to hear the hour (0–23) followed by the minutes (up to 59).

las catorce — 14:00
las quince cero dos — 15:02
las dieciséis cuarenta y siete — 16:47

7 Escucha y rellena los espacios en blanco. (1–3)

En la taquilla

● Buenos días. ¿Qué desea?
■ Quisiera **a** ———— billete(s) de **b** ———— a **c** ————, por favor.
● ¿A qué hora?
■ A las **d** ———— ¿De qué andén sale?
● Sale del andén **e** ————.
■ ¿Y a qué hora llega?
● Llega a las **f** ————.
■ ¿Es directo o hay que cambiar?
● **g** ————.

el tren con destino a	the train to
efectuará su salida	will leave / depart
de la vía / del andén (dos)	from platform (two)
un billete de ida	a single ticket
un billete de ida y vuelta	a return ticket

8 Con tu compañero/a, haz diálogos. Utiliza la información del ejercicio 6 e inventa los otros detalles.

6 El futuro

- *Discussing plans for the future*
- *Using the subjunctive with cuando*
- *Using different ways to express future plans*

1 Escucha y escribe las <u>dos</u> letras correctas. (1–5)

¿Qué planes tienes para el futuro?

a Quiero montar mi propio negocio.
b Espero aprobar mis exámenes. 
c Tengo la intención de casarme. 
d Pienso trabajar como voluntario/a en… 
e Voy a aprender a conducir. 
f Me gustaría tener hijos. 
g Espero ser feliz. 
h ¡Seré famoso/a! 

2 Escucha otra vez. Apunta las <u>dos</u> razones que mencionan. (1–5)

Ejemplo: **1** *success is important to him, …*

(No)	el desempleo / paro
Me gusta(n)	el dinero
Me interesa(n)	el éxito
Me importa(n)	el matrimonio
Me preocupa(n)	la responsabilidad
	la independencia
	la pobreza
	los niños
	las notas

Zona Cultura

En España casi la mitad de los adultos menores de 30 años (el 49%) todavía vive con sus padres, comparado con el 26% en el Reino Unido. Es menos común irse de casa para compartir piso con amigos o una pareja. Por un lado, es una consecuencia del problema del paro juvenil, pero por otro lado, muestra la importancia tradicional de la familia.

3 Con tu compañero/a, haz diálogos.

- ¿Vas a <u>aprender a conducir</u>?
- Sí, voy a <u>aprender a conducir</u> porque me importa el/la…
- ¿Tienes la intención de…?
- No, no tengo la intención de… ya que…

G Talking about future plans ▶ Page 216

You can express future plans with a variety of phrases followed by the **infinitive**:

quiero	I want to
tengo la intención de	I intend to
espero	I hope to
pienso	I plan to / intend to
voy a	I am going to
me gustaría	I would like to

Espero *ir a la universidad*. — I hope to go to university.
Tengo la intención de *casarme*. — I intend to get married.

You can also use the simple future tense.

Buscaré un trabajo. — **I will look for** a job.

> ⭐ When asking questions don't forget to use the **tú** form of the verb. For reflexive verbs the pronoun also has to change.
>
> Quier**o** casar**me** → ¿Quier**es** casar**te**?

150 ciento cincuenta

4 Lee los textos. Busca el equivalente de las expresiones en español.

Tomás
Me interesan las asignaturas prácticas, así que el próximo año pienso ir a otro instituto para hacer un ciclo de formación profesional. Espero obtener el título de Técnico en Cocina y Gastronomía. La formación profesional es una buena opción si quieres un oficio en sectores como la gestión administrativa o la hostelería. Cuando termine el curso buscaré un trabajo como cocinero. Más tarde cuando me enamore me casaré, ya que me importa el matrimonio.

Lina
Estoy en cuarto de ESO y espero sacar buenas notas en los exámenes porque me preocupa el paro y hay que tener éxito en los estudios para conseguir un buen empleo. Cuando termine los exámenes seguiré estudiando en mi insti, donde haré el bachillerato. Luego tengo la intención de ir a Londres para hacer una carrera universitaria. Cuando gane bastante dinero voy a aprender a conducir.

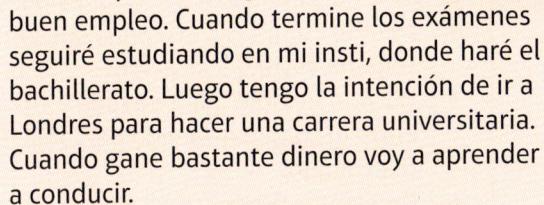

el oficio — trade / profession

1. to do a vocational training course
2. I hope to qualify as
3. such as business management
4. when I fall in love
5. I'm in Year 11
6. to get a good job
7. where I will do A Levels
8. a university degree

5 Lee los textos del ejercicio 4 otra vez. Escribe <u>cinco</u> detalles en inglés para cada persona.

6 Escucha. Copia y completa la tabla. (1–6)

	when…	I will…
1	I go to university	buy…

⭐ If your plans aren't certain, use words like **quizás** or **tal vez** (maybe/perhaps).

G Cuando + *present subjunctive* ▶ Page 234

When using the word **cuando** to talk about future plans you have to use a form of the verb called the **subjunctive**.

To form the present subjunctive, start with the 'I' form of the present tense, remove the –*o* and add these endings:

	gan**ar** (to earn / win)	vend**er** (to sell)	viv**ir** (to live)
(yo)	gan**e**	vend**a**	viv**a**
(tú)	gan**es**	vend**as**	viv**as**
(él/ella/usted)	gan**e**	vend**a**	viv**a**
(nosotros/as)	gan**emos**	vend**amos**	viv**amos**
(vosotros/as)	gan**éis**	vend**áis**	viv**áis**
(ellos/ellas/ustedes)	gan**en**	vend**an**	viv**an**

Verbs which are irregular in the present subjunctive include:

ser (to be) → **sea**   **ir** (to go) → **vaya**

el amo/a de casa — househusband / housewife

7 Escribe un texto sobre tus planes para el futuro.

Include:
- Details of your plans for study and work
- Personal ambitions (learning to drive, relationships, etc.)
- A range of verbs for talking about future plans
- Phrases such as *me interesa(n)*
- *Cuando* + subjunctive

Cuando…	buscaré un trabajo
sea mayor	compartiré piso con…
me enamore	me compraré un coche / una casa
gane bastante dinero	seguiré estudiando en mi insti
vaya a la universidad	iré a otro insti / a la universidad
tenga… años	me casaré
Cuando termine…	me iré de casa
este curso	me tomaré un año sabático
el bachillerato	trabajaré como…
la formación profesional	
la licenciatura	

Módulo 7   Leer y escuchar

1 Oportunidades laborales

Ves este anuncio sobre oportunidades laborales en una empresa internacional.

Seis ventajas de trabajar con nosotros

1. Buen paquete de beneficios para los empleados: restaurante subvencionado, plan de seguro médico e inscripción en el gimnasio gratuita.
2. Días adicionales de vacaciones por antigüedad – cuando cumplas cinco años en la empresa, tendrás una semana extra de vacaciones.
3. Horario flexible que te ayuda a mantener el equilibrio entre el trabajo y la vida personal. Posibilidad de teletrabajo.
4. Excelentes perspectivas con un innovador programa de cursos de formación.
5. Oportunidades para trabajar en diferentes tipos de proyectos y con diversos equipos.
6. Experiencias internacionales para los que tienen habilidades lingüísticas avanzadas.

¿Qué parte del anuncio le interesa más a cada persona? Escribe el número correcto.

1. Me interesa mucho la variedad. Me aburro si siempre trabajo con la misma gente. **Diego**
2. Prefiero poder empezar más tarde por la mañana, o incluso trabajar desde casa de vez en cuando. **Lidia**
3. Quiero seguir estudiando mientras trabajo para conseguir un mejor puesto en el futuro. **Teresa**
4. Me gustaría tener asistencia sanitaria privada en caso de enfermedad. **Gorka**

2 Work and future plans

You read this post about Samuel's job and plans for the future.

Estaba contentísimo trabajando en el departamento de ventas. Aunque ganaba menos, tenía un jefe muy comprensivo. Por desgracia, he cambiado de puesto recientemente y no soporto a mi nueva jefa. Es demasiado exigente – si pudiera conseguir otro empleo, lo haría. El problema es que, con la crisis económica, no será nada fácil encontrar un trabajo con un sueldo tan alto como el que gano ahora.

Estoy ahorrando porque, cuando pueda, pienso comprar una casa con mi novia y no será nada barata. Lo bueno de donde trabajo es que hay buenas perspectivas para los que quieren progresar en la empresa, como yo. Estoy haciendo una licenciatura a distancia a tiempo parcial que me ayudará en el futuro.

Which stages of Samuel's life do the following statements apply to?
Write **P** for something that happened in the **past**.
Write **N** for something that is happening **now**.
Write **F** for something that is going to happen in the **future**.

1. A new house
2. A good salary
3. A university course
4. A nice boss

> ⭐ Pay attention to tenses, time markers and phrases which refer to future plans. Beware of distractors, though. For example, don't be fooled by *el futuro* in the last sentence!

3 leer — Waiting for a job interview

Read this extract from *El método Grönholm*, a play by Jordi Galcerán.

> Enrique: ¿Has venido en coche?
> Fernando: Sí.
> Enrique: Yo también. Mucho tráfico, ¿no?
> Fernando: Como cada día.
> Enrique: Yo ya he hecho tres entrevistas. No sé qué más quieren saber de mí. Y tú, ¿cuántas llevas?
> Fernando: Tres.
> Enrique: Vengo de una empresa pequeña, y no he trabajado nunca en una multinacional. ¿Y tú?
> Fernando: Yo he trabajado en muchos sitios.
> Enrique: Y las condiciones son increíbles. El sueldo es… Bueno, no sé qué ganas tú, pero yo ganaría casi el doble… Tenía miedo de llegar tarde. Estaba en la avenida Diagonal, atascado, y pensaba, 'ahora llegarás tarde'. Estas cosas son importantes. A veces los pequeños detalles son los que hacen tomar una decisión. La manera de vestir, el coche…

1 Which **two** statements are true? Write the correct letters.
   A Today there was more traffic than normal.
   B This is Enrique's fourth interview.
   C If successful, this would be Enrique's first job.
   D Fernando has worked in several different places.

Answer the questions in **English**.
2 Why do you think Enrique is interested in this job?
3 How did Enrique feel on his way to the interview?
4 Why did he feel like this?

1 escuchar — Taking a gap year

You are listening to an interview with Begoña, a careers adviser, who is talking about gap years.

1 Answer all parts of the question in **English**.
   a Where do many people decide to travel to?
   b Why is this easier for young people?
   c Which skill will you develop in particular?

2 Answer both parts of the question in **English**.
   a What does Begoña think is a waste of time?
   b What advice does she give? Give **two** details.

> ⭐ In tasks like this, try to avoid writing down the answer as soon as you hear it. Otherwise, you may miss the answer to the next question. Trust your short-term memory and write down the answers when you hear the 'beep'.

2 escuchar — El jefe de Sara

Una amiga española, Sara, está hablando de su jefe con su marido. Escuchas su conversación.

1 Escribe las **tres** letras correctas.
   Según Sara, su jefe…
   A siempre es impaciente.
   B no valora su trabajo.
   C no es amable con nadie.
   D es perezoso.
   E le acusa de ser habladora.
   F no le ha enseñado nada.

2 Escribe la letra correcta.
   Según su marido, normalmente Sara es…
   A valiente.
   B sensible.
   C tímida.

> ⭐ Remember that you won't necessarily hear the actual words used on the page. Also, for question 1, you may hear the correct statements in a different order.

Módulo 7   Prueba oral

A – Role play

1 Look at the role play card and prepare what you are going to say.

How do you say 'I would like…'? Make sure you give both details.

What might the assistant ask you here?

Remember, in Spanish you say 'From which…?'.

Your teacher will play the part of the assistant and will speak first.
You should address the assistant as *usted*.
When you see this – **!** – you will have to respond to something you have not prepared.
When you see this – **?** – you will have to ask a question.

Usted está hablando con el empleado / la empleada de la taquilla de una estación de trenes en España.
- Billetes – cuántos y adónde.
- **!**
- **?** Andén.
- Viajar en tren – **dos** ventajas.
- Tu último viaje en tren – **un** problema.

Make sure that you only say positive things!

Use your imagination. What type of problem could you have encountered?

2 Practise what you have prepared. Take care with pronunciation and intonation.

3 Using your notes, listen and respond to the teacher.

4 Now listen to Bethany doing the role play task.
   1. What does she ask for?
   2. How does she answer the unprepared question(s)?
   3. What does she say for the last **two** bullets?

B – Photo card

Look at the photo and make notes. Your teacher will then ask you questions about the photo and about topics related to **jobs, career choices and ambitions**.

Your teacher will ask you the following **three** questions and then **two** more questions which you have not prepared.
- ¿Qué hay en la foto?
- ¿Crees que es una buena idea tomarse un año sabático? … ¿Por qué (no)?
- ¿En qué te gustaría trabajar?

1 Look at the photo and read the task. Then listen to Oliver's response to the first question on the task card.
   1. How does he describe the adult in the middle?
   2. Write down the **four** verbs he uses in the present continuous.

ciento cincuenta y cuatro

Módulo 7

2 Listen to and read Oliver's response to the second question on the task card.

1. Write down the missing word for each gap.
2. Look at the Answer Booster on page 156. Note down **six** examples of language which Oliver uses to give a strong answer.

> ¡Claro que sí! Desde un punto de vista **1** ———, un año sabático te da la oportunidad de viajar, descubrir culturas distintas y **2** ——— a gente nueva. Además, no solo te permite aumentar tu **3** ———, sino también mejorar tus habilidades sociales, ya que haces muchísimos amigos nuevos. Sin embargo, a mi modo de ver, no **4** ——— la pena tomarse un año sabático si no **5** ——— el tiempo para ayudar a los demás también. Para mí, esto es importantísimo, y si tuviera bastante dinero iría a Latinoamérica, donde **6** ——— a los niños que viven en la calle.

3 Listen to Oliver's response to the third question on the task card. In **Spanish**, note down **four** different expressions which he uses to refer to his future plans.

Example: Me gustaría continuar…

> ⭐ Remember that phrases for referring to future plans usually include the **infinitive**, unless the verb is in the simple future tense:
> *Quiero **ir** a la universidad.*
> *Iré a otro insti.*

4 Prepare your own answers to the first **three** questions. Think about which other **two** questions you might be asked. Then listen and take part in the full photo card discussion with the teacher.

C – General conversation

1 The teacher asks Mark *'¿Tienes un trabajo a tiempo parcial?'* In **English**, make notes about his <u>current</u> job, under these headings:

Job   Opinion   When   Tasks   Pay

2 Listen to Mark's response to the next question *'¿Qué planes tienes para seguir estudiando en el futuro?'* Look at the Answer Booster on page 156. Note down **six** examples of language which Mark uses to give a strong answer.

3 The teacher then asks Mark *'¿Qué opinas de ir a la universidad?'* Look at the following statements and decide if they are **for** or **against**. Then listen to Mark's answer and note down which ones he mentions.

a Las personas con títulos universitarios ganan más.
b Abre muchas puertas en el mundo laboral.
c Es muy caro – terminas la licenciatura con deudas.
d Pasar tres años estudiando es una pérdida de tiempo.
e Aprendes a ser más independiente.
f Para muchos trabajos no es necesario.
g Haces amigos para toda la vida.

> ⭐ What does Mark ask his teacher? Note down the question.

4 Prepare your own answers to Module 7 questions 1–6 on page 199. Then practise with your partner.

ciento cincuenta y cinco **155**

Módulo 7   Prueba escrita

Answer booster	Aiming for a solid answer	Aiming higher	Aiming for the top
Verbs	**Different time frames**: past, present, near future **Different types of verbs**: regular, irregular, reflexive, stem-changing	**Verbs with an infinitive**: *tener que, soler, acabar de* **Phrases with an infinitive**: *para, sin, antes de, después de, al* **Phrases to refer to future plans**: *espero, pienso, quiero, tengo la intención de* + infinitive	**A wide range of tenses**: present, present continuous, preterite, imperfect, perfect, future, conditional ***Cuando* + subjunctive**: *cuando sea mayor, cuando termine*
Opinions and reasons	**Verbs of opinion**: *me chifla(n), me encanta(n), me interesa(n)* **Reasons**: *porque*	**Verbs of opinion**: *me importa(n), me preocupa(n), me apetece* + infinitive, *no aguanto* **Absolute superlatives**: *muchísimo, importantísimo*	**Opinions**: *desde mi punto de vista, a mi modo de ver, a mi juicio* **Reasons**: *ya que, dado que, por lo tanto, por eso, así que*
Connectives	*y, pero, también*	*además, sin embargo, sobre todo*	*aunque, a pesar de, ya no, todavía* **Alternatives to 'and'**: *no solo… sino también, tanto… como…*
Other features	**Qualifiers**: *muy, un poco, bastante, demasiado* **Negatives**: *no, nunca* **Sequencers**: *luego, después, más tarde*	**Different uses of** *saber/conocer* **Indirect object pronouns**: *te da la oportunidad de, te permite*	**Complex sentences with *si***: *si tuviera bastante* **More complex vocabulary**: *valer/merecer la pena, aprovechar, alistarse, estoy harto/a de* **Other complex structures**: *por si eso fuera poco, ¡Ojalá no fuera…!*

A – Extended writing task

1 *leer* **Look at the task and answer the questions.**
- What information does each bullet point ask you to give?
- How could you develop your answer to each one?

> Una revista española para jóvenes está preparando un artículo sobre 'el trabajo y los planes para el futuro'. Decides contribuir con tus ideas.
>
> Escribe a la revista incluyendo esta información:
> - qué hiciste para tus prácticas laborales
> - qué planes tienes para el futuro.
>
> Escribe aproximadamente **150** palabras en **español**. Responde a los dos aspectos de la pregunta.

2 *leer* **Read Polly's answer on page 157. What do the phrases in bold mean?**

3 *leer* **Look at the Answer Booster. Note down eight examples of language which Polly uses to write a strong answer.**

Paragraph 1
- Importance of work experience
- Two advantages

4 *leer* **Complete the essay plan based on Polly's answer.**

Paragraph 2
- Where I…

5 *escribir* **Prepare your own answer to the task.**
- Look at the Answer Booster and Polly's plan for ideas.
- Think about how you can develop your answer for each bullet point.
- Write a detailed plan. Organise your answer in paragraphs.
- Write your answer and carefully check what you have written.

Módulo 7

Como todo el mundo sabe, es muy útil tener experiencia laboral si quieres **solicitar un trabajo**. Te da la oportunidad no solo de mejorar tus perspectivas laborales, sino también de aumentar tu confianza.

Acabo de pasar dos semanas haciendo prácticas en una escuela de equitación, donde aprendí mucho (**¡a pesar del olor!**). Cada día ayudaba a los niños y limpiaba los establos. Mis colegas eran muy amables y el último día organizaron una fiesta de despedida para mí. **Por si eso fuera poco**, mi jefe me ha ofrecido un trabajo a tiempo parcial. ¡Qué guay!

Todavía no estoy segura de lo que quiero hacer en el futuro. Cuando era más joven, quería ser bombera, pero ya no me interesa. **Tal vez me alistaré en el ejército**. Me apetece la idea de ser soldado y creo que mis padres **estarían orgullosos de mí**. Sobre todo, te permite viajar por el mundo. **¡Ojalá no fuera tan peligroso!**

Cuando termine los exámenes de 'A Level' (equivalentes al bachillerato), espero tomarme un año sabático **antes de empezar la carrera universitaria**. Me gustaría trabajar en un proyecto medioambiental en Latinoamérica. Después, si tuviera bastante dinero, viajaría como mochilera por Perú (¡y **cumpliría mi sueño de** subir a Machu Picchu!).

Polly

> ⭐ If you haven't done any work experience or you don't know what you want to do in the future, use your imagination! The important thing is to show off your Spanish.

B – Translation

1 *escribir* — Translate the passage into Spanish.

- Which words do you **not** need to translate here?
- Which person of the verb do you need?
- Do you need *ser* or *estar* here? In which tense?

My mum used to be a hairdresser but now she is a chef. Usually she does all the household chores. However, yesterday my brother and I cooked because she was tired. In the future I hope to be a nurse because I am very understanding. When I earn enough money I will leave home because independence is important to me.

- Remember to use *cuando* + present subjunctive.
- Do not translate this word for word. Start with *Me importa…*

2 *escribir* — Now translate the following passage into Spanish. Use your answer to exercise 1 to help you.

I don't like my part time job because I don't earn much money. Usually I deliver newspapers but yesterday I also helped in the shop because my boss was ill. When I am older I would like to be a journalist. It's a varied job with a good salary. Unemployment worries me so I hope to pass my exams.

> ⭐ Take care with words which are similar but mean different things.
>
> un(a) enfermero/a (a nurse) — enfermo/a (ill)
> un(a) cocinero/a (a cook/chef) — cocinar (to cook)
> un(a) periodista (a journalist) — un periódico (a newspaper)

ciento cincuenta y siete

Módulo 7 Palabras

¿En qué trabajas?	What is your job?		
Soy… / Es…	I am… / He/She is…	profesor(a)	teacher
Me gustaría ser…	I would like to be…	recepcionista	receptionist
abogado/a	lawyer	socorrista	lifeguard
albañil	bricklayer / builder	soldado	soldier
amo/a de casa	housewife / househusband	veterinario/a	vet
azafato/a	flight attendant	Es un trabajo…	It's a … job
bailarín(a)	dancer	artístico / emocionante	artistic / exciting
bombero/a	firefighter	exigente / importante	demanding / important
camarero/a	waiter / waitress	fácil / difícil	easy / difficult
cantante	singer	manual / monótono	manual / monotonous
cocinero/a	cook	variado / repetitivo	varied / repetitive
contable	accountant	con responsabilidad	with responsibility
dependiente/a	shop assistant	con buenas perspectivas	with good prospects
diseñador(a)	designer	con un buen sueldo	with a good salary
electricista	electrician	Tengo que… / Suelo…	I have to… / I tend to…
enfermero/a	nurse	cuidar a los clientes / pacientes / pasajeros	look after the customers / patients / passengers
escritor(a)	writer	contestar llamadas telefónicas	answer telephone calls
fontanero/a	plumber	cuidar las plantas y las flores	look after the plants and flowers
fotógrafo/a	photographer	enseñar / vigilar a los niños	teach / supervise the children
funcionario/a	civil servant	hacer entrevistas	do interviews
guía turístico/a	tour guide	preparar platos distintos	prepare different dishes
ingeniero/a	engineer	reparar coches	repair cars
jardinero/a	gardener	servir comida y bebida	serve food and drink
mecánico/a	mechanic	trabajar en un taller / en un hospital / en una tienda / a bordo de un avión	work in a workshop / in a hospital / in a shop / aboard a plane
médico/a	doctor	vender ropa de marca	sell designer clothing
músico/a	musician	viajar por todo el mundo	travel the world
peluquero/a	hairdresser		
periodista	journalist		
policía	police officer		

¿Qué tipo de persona eres?	What type of person are you?		
Creo que soy…	I think I'm…	organizado/a	organised
ambicioso/a	ambitious	paciente	patient
comprensivo/a	understanding	práctico/a	practical
creativo/a	creative	serio/a	serious
extrovertido/a	extroverted / outgoing	trabajador(a)	hardworking
fuerte	strong	valiente	brave
inteligente	intelligent		

¿Qué haces para ganar dinero?	What do you do to earn money?		
¿Tienes un trabajo a tiempo parcial?	Do you have a part-time job?	los sábados	on Saturdays
Reparto periódicos.	I deliver newspapers.	antes / después del insti	before / after school
Hago de canguro.	I babysit.	cuando necesito dinero	when I need money
Trabajo de cajero/a.	I work as a cashier.	cuando mi madre está trabajando	when my mum is working
Ayudo con las tareas domésticas.	I help with the housework.	cuando me necesitan	when they need me
Cocino.	I cook.	cada mañana	each / every morning
Lavo los platos.	I wash the dishes.	una vez / dos veces a la semana	once / twice a week
Paso la aspiradora.	I do the vacuuming.	Gano … euros / libras a la hora / al día / a la semana.	I earn … euros / pounds per hour / day / week.
Plancho la ropa.	I iron the clothes.	Me llevo bien con mis compañeros.	I get on well with my colleagues.
Pongo y quito la mesa.	I lay and clear the table.	Mi jefe/a es amable.	My boss is nice.
Paseo al perro.	I walk the dog.	El horario es flexible.	The hours are flexible.
Corto el césped.	I cut the lawn.		
Lo hago…	I do it…		

Mis prácticas laborales	Work experience		
Hice mis prácticas laborales en…	I did my work experience in…	iba en transporte público	I went by public transport
Pasé quince días trabajando en…	I spent a fortnight working in…	llevaba ropa elegante	I wore smart clothes
un polideportivo	a sports centre	ponía folletos en los estantes	I put brochures on the shelves
una agencia de viajes / una granja	a travel agency / a farm	sacaba fotocopias	I did photocopying
una escuela / una oficina	a school / an office	Mi jefe/a era…	My boss was…
una fábrica de juguetes	a toy factory	Mis compañeros eran…	My colleagues were…
una tienda benéfica / solidaria	a charity shop	Los clientes eran…	The customers were …
la empresa de mi madre	my mum's company	alegre(s)	cheerful
El primer / último día conocí a / llegué…	On the first / last day I met / I arrived…	(des)agradable(s)	(un)pleasant
Cada día / Todos los días…	Each / Every day…	(mal) educado/a(s)	polite (rude)
archivaba documentos	I filed documents	El trabajo era duro.	The job was hard.
ayudaba…	I helped…	Aprendí…	I learned
cogía el autobús / el metro	I caught the bus / underground	muchas nuevas habilidades	lots of new skills
empezaba / terminaba a las …	I started / finished at…	a trabajar en equipo	to work in a team
hacía una variedad de tareas	I did a variety of tasks	a usar…	to use…
		No aprendí nada nuevo.	I didn't learn anything new.

Módulo 7

¿Por qué aprender idiomas? / Why learn languages?

Aumenta tu confianza.	It increases your confidence.
Estimula el cerebro.	It stimulates the brain.
Mejora tus perspectivas laborales.	It improves your job prospects.
Te abre la mente.	It opens your mind.
Te hace parecer más atractivo.	It makes you appear more attractive.
Te ayuda a…	It helps you to…
Te permite…	It allows you to…
apreciar la vida cultural de otros países	appreciate the cultural life of other countries
conocer a mucha gente distinta	meet lots of different people
conocer nuevos sitios	get to know new places
encontrar un trabajo	find a job
descubrir nuevas culturas	discover new cultures
establecer buenas relaciones	establish good relationships
hacer nuevos amigos	make new friends
mejorar tu lengua materna	improve your first language
solucionar problemas	solve problems
trabajar o estudiar en el extranjero	work or study abroad
Me hace falta saber hablar idiomas extranjeros.	I need to know how to speak foreign languages.
(No) Domino el inglés.	I (don't) speak English fluently.
Hablo un poco de ruso.	I speak a bit of Russian.

Solicitando un trabajo / Applying for a job

Se busca / Se requiere…	… required.
(No) Hace falta experiencia.	Experience (not) needed.
Muy señor mío	Dear Sir
Le escribo para solicitar el puesto de…	I'm writing to apply for the post of…
Le adjunto mi currículum vitae.	I'm enclosing my CV.
Le agradezco su amable atención.	Thank you for your kind attention.
Atentamente	Yours sincerely/faithfully
Me apetece trabajar en…	Working in… appeals to me.
(No) Tengo experiencia previa.	I (don't) have previous experience.
He estudiado / trabajado…	I've studied / worked…
He hecho un curso de…	I've done a course in…
Tengo…	I have…
buen sentido del humor	a good sense of humour
buenas capacidades de comunicación / resolución de problemas	good communication / problem-solving skills
buenas habilidades lingüísticas	good language skills

Un año sabático / A gap year

Si pudiera tomarme un año sabático…	If I could take a gap year…
Si tuviera bastante dinero…	If I had enough money…
apoyaría un proyecto medioambiental	I would support an environmental project
aprendería a esquiar	I would learn to ski
ayudaría a construir un colegio	I would help to build a school
buscaría un trabajo	I would look for a job
enseñaría inglés	I would teach English
ganaría mucho dinero	I would earn a lot of money
haría un viaje en Interrail	I would go Interrailing
iría a España, donde…	I would go to Spain, where…
mejoraría mi nivel de español	I would improve my level of Spanish
nunca olvidaría la experiencia	I would never forget the experience
pasaría un año en…	I would spend a year in…
trabajaría en un orfanato	I would work in an orphanage
viajaría con mochila por el mundo	I would go backpacking around the world

¿Cómo viajarías? / How would you travel?

Cogería el / Viajaría en autobús / autocar / avión / tren.	I would catch the / travel by bus / coach / plane / train.
Es más barato / cómodo / rápido.	It's cheaper / more comfortable / quicker.
Puedes…	You can…
ver vídeos mientras viajas	watch videos whilst you travel
dejar tu maleta en la consigna	leave your suitcase in the left-luggage office
Hay muchos / pocos atascos / retrasos…	There are lots of / few traffic jams / delays…
en las autopistas / las carreteras	on the motorways / roads
Los billetes son carísimos.	The tickets are extremely expensive.
Los conductores están en huelga.	The drivers are on strike.
Odio esperar en la parada de autobús.	I hate waiting at the bus stop.
Tengo miedo a volar.	I'm scared of flying.

Viajando en tren / Travelling by train

El tren con destino a…	The train to…
efectuará su salida…	will leave / depart…
de la vía / del andén dos	from platform two
el (tren) AVE	high-speed train
la taquilla	the ticket office
Quisiera un billete de ida a…	I would like a single ticket to…
Quisiera un billete de ida y vuelta a…	I would like a return ticket to…
¿De qué andén sale?	From which platform does it leave?
¿A qué hora sale / llega?	What time does it leave / arrive?
¿Es directo o hay que cambiar?	Is it direct or do I have to change?

El futuro / The future

Me interesa(n)…	…interest(s) me.
Me importa(n)…	…matter(s) to me.
Me preocupa(n)…	…worry/worries me.
el desempleo / el paro	unemployment
el dinero / el éxito	money / success
el fracaso / el matrimonio	failure / marriage
la responsabilidad	responsibility
la independencia / la pobreza	independence / poverty
los niños / las notas	children / marks
Espero…	I hope to…
Me gustaría…	I would like to…
Pienso…	I plan to/intend to…
Quiero…	I want to…
Tengo la intención de…	I intend to…
Voy a…	I am going to…
aprender a conducir	learn to drive
aprobar mis exámenes	pass my exams
casarme	get married
conseguir un buen empleo/trabajo	get a good job
estudiar una carrera universitaria	study a university course
montar mi propio negocio	set up my own business
sacar buenas notas	get good marks
ser feliz	be happy
tener hijos	have children
trabajar como voluntario/a	work as a volunteer
Cuando…	When…
gane bastante dinero…	I earn enough money…
me enamore…	I fall in love…
sea mayor…	I'm older…
tenga … años…	I'm … years old…
vaya a la universidad…	I go to university…
termine este curso / el bachillerato / la formación profesional / la licenciatura…	I finish this course / my A Levels / my vocational course / my degree
buscaré un trabajo	I will look for a job
compartiré piso con…	I will share a flat with…
compraré un coche / una casa	I will buy a car / house
iré a otro insti / a la universidad	I will go to another school / to university
me casaré	I will get married
me iré de casa	I will leave home
seguiré estudiando en mi insti	I will carry on studying at my school
seré famoso/a	I will be famous
me tomaré un año sabático	I will take a gap year
trabajaré como…	I will work as…

ciento cincuenta y nueve

8 Hacia un mundo mejor
Punto de partida 1

- *Describing types of houses*
- *Talking about the environment*

1 Escucha y escribe la letra correcta. (1–4)

¿Dónde vives?

Hogar, dulce hogar

Vivo en…
　un bloque de pisos
　una casa individual
　una casa adosada
　una residencia de ancianos
　una finca / granja

Está en…
　un barrio de la ciudad
　las afueras
　el campo
　la costa
　la montaña / sierra

2 Escucha otra vez. Escribe <u>dos</u> detalles en inglés.

| el entorno | surrounding area |

3 Lee los textos. Apunta los detalles en inglés para cada texto.

Rooms mentioned:　　Would change:
Positive(s):　　　　　Ideal house would be/have:
Negative(s):

Vivimos en el cuarto piso de un edificio antiguo. El apartamento tiene tres dormitorios, dos cuartos de baño y una cocina amplia y bien equipada, que me encanta. Pintaría el salón de otro color porque es demasiado oscuro. Mi casa ideal sería una finca en el campo, que tendría una piscina climatizada y mi propio cine en casa.
Verena

Alquilamos esta casa amueblada. La habitación que más me gusta es el comedor porque está recién renovado y tiene una mesa y unas sillas nuevas. Además, el estudio es útil para estudiar. Sin embargo, el aseo necesita una reforma, y cambiaría los demás muebles porque son muy anticuados. Mi casa ideal tendría una gran sala de fiestas en el sótano.
Eduardo

| amueblado/a | furnished |

Zona Cultura

casa cueva en Granada

Las casas cueva eran típicas de la región de Andalucía. Hay gente que vive todavía en estas viviendas subterráneas y son una opción popular entre los turistas.

4 Con tu compañero/a, haz un diálogo.
- ¿Dónde vives?
- ¿Cómo es tu casa?
- ¿Te gusta dónde vives? ¿Qué cambiarías?
- ¿Cómo sería tu casa ideal? ¿Qué tendría?

⭐ 'First' and 'third' drop the -o in front of masculine singular nouns:
Está en el primer / tercer piso.
It is on the 1st/3rd floor.
Piso can mean 'flat' or 'floor'.

quinto 5°
cuarto 4°
tercero 3°
segundo 2°
primero 1°
planta baja
sótano

160　ciento sesenta

Módulo 8

5 Empareja las frases con los dibujos.

¿Cómo se debería cuidar el medio ambiente en casa?

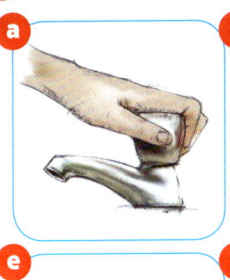

a b c d
e f g h

Para cuidar el medio ambiente, se debería…
1 apagar la luz.
2 ducharse en vez de bañarse.
3 separar la basura.
4 reciclar el plástico y el vidrio.
5 cerrar el grifo.
6 desenchufar los aparatos eléctricos.

No se debería…
7 malgastar el agua.
8 usar bolsas de plástico.

6 Escucha. Apunta las <u>dos</u> letras correctas del ejercicio 5. (1–4)

G Se debería > Page 220

Se debería + infinitive means 'you/we should'. It is the conditional form of **se debe**.

Se debería ahorrar energía. **You/We should** save energy.
No se debería tirar basura al suelo. **You/We shouldn't** throw rubbish on the ground.

7 Escucha y lee la entrevista. Busca las expresiones en español.

– ¿Qué se debería hacer para cuidar el medio ambiente, Marta?
– ¡Mucho! Se debería ahorrar energía y no malgastar el agua.
– Y, ¿qué hacéis en casa?
– Ya hacemos bastantes cosas. Todos desenchufamos los aparatos eléctricos, y nos duchamos en vez de bañarnos. Mi hermana menor tiene la mala costumbre de no cerrar el grifo cuando se lava los dientes, pero me ayuda a separar la basura. Cuando vamos al colegio, siempre vamos en bici o a pie. Así hacemos todo lo posible para ser verdes.

Marta

1 save energy
2 we already do quite a few things
3 we all unplug the electrical appliances
4 bad habit
5 she helps me to
6 to be green

8 Traduce el texto al español.

Use para + infinitive here.

Ayudar means 'to help'. Don't forget to change the ending for 'we help'.

This is we/one in general.

There is a lot that we should do in order to save energy. At home we all help. I turn the lights off and my dad separates the rubbish. When we go shopping we never use plastic bags. They are small things, but we should do everything possible to look after the environment.

What two things do you have to remember about adjectives in Spanish?

Change the verb ending to match the subjects 'I' and 'my dad'.

Use para + infinitive here.

Unidad 3

ciento sesenta y uno 161

Punto de partida 2

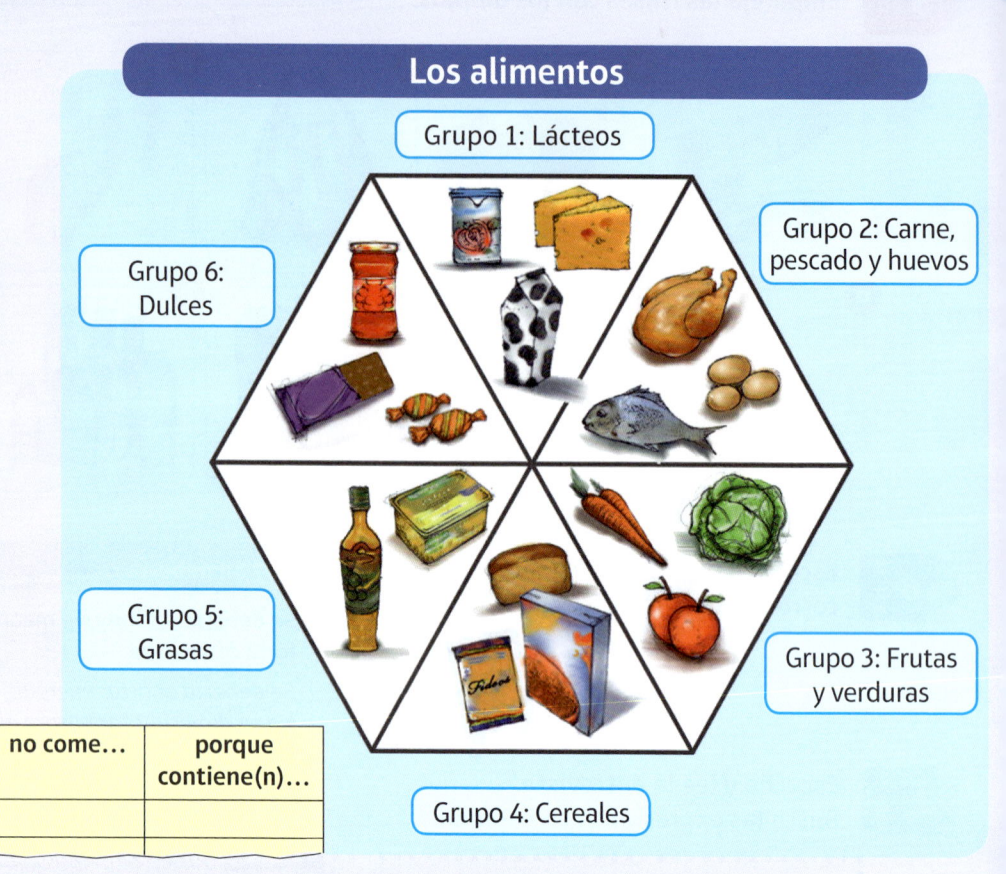

- Talking about healthy eating
- Discussing diet-related problems

1 Escucha y mira el diagrama. Completa la tabla. (1–4)

Los nutrientes

a proteínas
b minerales
c grasa
d sal
e vitaminas
f azúcar
g gluten

Los alimentos

Grupo 1: Lácteos
Grupo 2: Carne, pescado y huevos
Grupo 3: Frutas y verduras
Grupo 4: Cereales
Grupo 5: Grasas
Grupo 6: Dulces

	come… (grupo)	porque / aunque contiene(n)…	no come…	porque contiene(n)…
1	3	e		

2 Lee los textos. Completa las frases con las palabras de abajo. Sobran dos palabras.

Como zanahorias y ensalada a menudo porque es importante comer verduras, ya que contienen muchas vitaminas, aunque no me gusta mucho el sabor. La fibra de la fruta y la verdura también es importante porque protege contra el cáncer y combate la obesidad. **Timo**

Soy vegana, así que no como carne de ningún tipo. Tampoco consumo huevos, lácteos ni miel. A mi madre le preocupa porque piensa que mi dieta tiene pocas proteínas, pero suelo comer una variedad de frutos secos, legumbres y cereales. **Soraya**

Suelo saltarme el desayuno porque nunca tengo hambre por la mañana. En el recreo me compro un trozo de pizza. Sé que no es saludable porque tiene demasiada grasa y sal, pero está rica. **Isabel**

1 A Timo no le gustan mucho las _____.
2 La fibra _____ el riesgo de ciertas enfermedades.
3 Soraya no _____ alimentos de origen animal.
4 Su madre cree que Soraya necesita comer más _____.
5 Soraya opina que lleva una dieta _____.
6 Isabel no _____ nada por la mañana.
7 La pizza no es sana, pero está _____.
8 Isabel lleva una _____ bastante malsana.

las legumbres — pulses

come | deliciosa | energía | malsana | equilibrada
verduras | come | dieta | reduce | proteínas

3 Con tu compañero/a, haz un diálogo.
- ¿Qué comes / no comes? ¿Por qué?
- ¿Qué se debe comer todos los días para estar en forma?
- ¿Crees que llevas una dieta sana? ¿Por qué (no)?

Suelo Intento	comer beber	much**o/a/os/as**… demasiad**o/a/os/as**…
(No) Se debe Es importante Es necesario Es esencial Hay que	evitar	tant**o/a/os/as**…
porque / aunque contiene(n)	much**o/a** poc**o/a** demasiad**o/a**	azúcar fibra grasa sal
	much**os/as** poc**os/as** demasiad**os/as**	minerales proteínas vitaminas

4 Escucha. Apunta los detalles en inglés para cada persona. (1–3)
- the problems
- how they want to change their lifestyle

Ahora
suelo comer / beber…
como / bebo…
  galletas
  refrescos
  agua
  comida rápida
(no) desayuno
(no) tengo tiempo para cocinar
(no) tengo energía
(no) tengo hambre / sed
me causa sueño

En el futuro
(No) Voy a…
  evitar comer / beber…
  comer / beber más…
  cambiar mi dieta
  preparar comida con
    ingredientes frescos
(No) Quiero…
  engordar
  saltarme el desayuno
  praticar más deporte

5 Escribe un párrafo sobre tu dieta.
Include:
- whether you have / don't have a healthy diet
- one problem with your diet
- what people must do to keep in shape generally
- what you are going to do to lead a healthier life (diet, exercise, etc.)

6 Lee el artículo. Contesta a las preguntas en inglés.

Solo un 7,5% de los niños en España toma un desayuno adecuado compuesto por hidratos de carbono, lácteos y fruta. El 8% de los niños se salta completamente el desayuno, mientras que el 59,5% de los niños dedica menos de 10 minutos a su desayuno. Uno de los efectos de saltar el desayuno es la disminución de la atención en las primeras horas de clase. También se ha demostrado que el fenómeno de la obesidad es más alto en las personas que no toman un desayuno equilibrado.

1. According to the article, what should a balanced breakfast consist of?
2. What percentage of children skip breakfast altogether?
3. What do 59.5% of Spanish children do?
4. What can happen in school as a result of not eating a good breakfast?
5. What is the connection between obesity and breakfast?

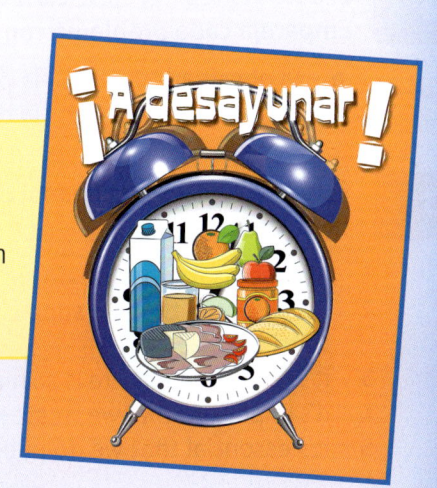

1 ¡Piensa globalmente…!

- Considering global issues
- Using the present subjunctive
- Listening for high numbers

1 Escucha y lee. Escribe la letra correcta.

Ejemplo: **1** c

Parlamento de la Juventud

¿Cuáles son los problemas globales más serios hoy en día?

1 Lo que más me preocupa es la diferencia entre ricos y pobres en el mundo. No es justo que haya tanta desigualdad social y que muchos no tengan para comer. Es esencial que apoyemos proyectos de ayuda en el tercer mundo y que compremos productos de comercio justo.
Silvio, Guatemala

2 Me preocupan sobre todo los problemas del medio ambiente. Por ejemplo, en mi país destruyen la selva, y por consecuencia amenazan la supervivencia de muchas especies de fauna. Es muy importante que cuidemos el planeta. Es necesario que hagamos proyectos de conservación y que usemos productos verdes.
Óscar, Bolivia

3 A mi parecer, el mayor problema es la crisis económica. Es terrible que haya tanta gente sin trabajo y sin techo. Es importante que creemos oportunidades de trabajo y que recaudemos dinero para organizaciones de caridad.
Maya, España

4 En mi país lo más preocupante son los problemas de la salud. Hay tanta gente obesa y tantos drogadictos. Es esencial que hagamos campañas publicitarias sobre los riesgos de estas enfermedades y que ayudemos a evitar el consumo de sustancias perjudiciales.
Eduardo, Estados Unidos

a  el paro / desempleo
b  los animales en peligro de extinción
c  el hambre
d 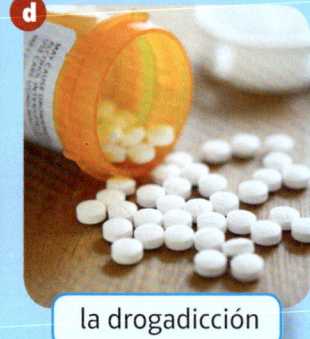 la drogadicción

amenazar to threaten
sin techo homeless

2 Lee los textos del ejercicio 1 otra vez. Empareja cada problema con uno de los textos.

a la obesidad   c la pobreza
b los sin hogar d la deforestación

3 Busca las frases en español en los textos del ejercicio 1.

1 it's necessary that we do conservation projects
2 it's essential that we support aid projects in the third world
3 it's not fair that there is so much social inequality
4 it's important that we create job opportunities
5 it's essential that we do publicity campaigns

G The present subjunctive › *Page 234*

You have already learned to use the subjunctive with *cuando*.
The subjunctive is also used to express points of view, using the structure **Es** + adjective + **que**:

Es importante **que**…   No **es** justo **que**…
Es esencial **que**…   **Es** terrible **que**…
Es necesario **que**…

ahorr**ar** →
*Es esencial que ahorr**emos** energía.*
It is essential that we save energy.

aprend**er** →
*Es importante que aprend**amos** más sobre el medio ambiente.*
It is important that we learn more about the environment.

permit**ir** →
*No es justo que permit**amos** la deforestación.*
It is not right that we allow deforestation.

Verbs which are irregular in the present subjunctive include:
ser (to be) → **sea**   **ir** (to go) → **vaya**
dar (to give) → **dé**   **haber** (there is/are) → **haya**

164 ciento sesenta y cuatro

Módulo 8

4 Escucha. Apunta el problema en inglés. (1–5)

| la ley | the law |
| la sociedad de usar y tirar | throwaway society |

> As you listen, you will hear these verbs in the subjunctive. See if you can pick them out in order to write the phrases in Spanish.
>
> **ahorrar** (to save), **construir** (to build), **recaudar** (to collect), **cambiar** (to change), **consumir** (to consume)

5 Escucha otra vez y apunta las soluciones en español.

- Es importante / esencial que…
- we build more houses
- we consume less
- we save water
- we collect money for aid projects
- we change the law

6 Con tu compañero/a, haz diálogos.

- ● ¿Cuál es el problema global más serio hoy en día?
- ■ Para mí, el mayor problema <u>es la crisis económica</u>.
- ■ Lo que más me preocupa <u>son los problemas del medio ambiente</u>.
- ● ¿Cuál es la solución?
- ■ Es <u>esencial</u> que <u>actuemos rápidamente</u>.
- ■ Es <u>terrible</u> que haya…

7 Escucha y escribe la cifra correcta. (1–5)

La crisis del agua

1. Al menos ——— millones de personas en todo el mundo beben agua que está contaminada.
2. Unos ——— millones de personas no tienen servicios sanitarios.
3. Cada ——— horas mueren ——— niños por falta de agua y saneamiento.
4. Para producir un kilo de arroz hacen falta unos ——— litros de agua, mientras que para un kilo de carne son necesarios unos ——— litros.
5. La demanda mundial de agua para la fabricación se incrementará en un ——— entre los años ——— y ———.

> 95% = el noventa y cinco por ciento
> 1.000 = mil
> 3.574 = tres mil quinientos setenta y cuatro
> 1.000.000 = un millón
> Use a **full stop** to separate thousands and a **comma** for decimals.

8 Lee el artículo y completa las frases en inglés.

¿Es posible una guerra mundial del agua?

En 2000 hubo una 'guerra del agua' en Cochabamba, Bolivia. La empresa multinacional Aguas del Tunari triplicó los precios del servicio del agua, lo que provocó una revuelta masiva. Hubo manifestaciones, luchas y al menos una muerte, pero finalmente los ciudadanos ganaron. La acción colectiva consiguió defender el agua como un bien común y frenar la privatización.

Actualmente existen conflictos por la escasez de agua entre varios países, incluso hay una disputa entre México y Estados Unidos sobre el río Bravo.

La Asociación Mundial del Agua (GWP) ya ha advertido sobre una crisis en el planeta hacia el 2025, afirmando que la falta de agua podría llevar a una guerra mundial. Es importante que cuidemos este elemento esencial.

la escasez	shortage / scarcity
consiguió	managed to
frenar	to stop

1. In 2000 there was…
2. The multinational company Aguas del Tunari…
3. This provoked…
4. The people's action managed to…
5. Currently there are…
6. The Global Water Partnership has already warned of…
7. The lack of water could…
8. It is important…

ciento sesenta y cinco **165**

2 ¡Actúa localmente!

- Talking about local actions
- Using the subjunctive in commands
- Presenting a written argument

1 leer Lee los comentarios. Empareja el problema 1–6 con el consejo apropiado a–f.

1 La destrucción de los bosques es un problema muy serio.
2 El aire está contaminado.
3 Hay demasiada basura en las calles.
4 La polución de los mares y ríos me preocupa mucho.
5 Hay demasiada gente sin espacio para vivir.
6 Los combustibles fósiles se acaban.

a No corte tantos árboles. 
b No tire basura al suelo. 
c No construya tantas casas grandes. 
d No vaya en coche si es posible ir a pie. 
e No malgaste energía. 
f No eche tantos desechos químicos en los mares.

2 escuchar Escucha y comprueba tus respuestas. (1–6)

3 escuchar Escucha otra vez. Apunta otro consejo en español e inglés. (1–6)

Ejemplo: **1** *Plante más bosques y selvas.*
Plant more woods and forests.

G The subjunctive in commands — Page 233

The present subjunctive is also used:

For **all negative** commands.
us**ar** (to use)
¡No us**es** tanta agua! (tú)
¡No us**e** tanta agua! (usted)

For **formal positive** commands.
¡Us**e** menos agua!

There are a few spelling changes to keep the same pronunciation:

apag**ar** (to switch off) → apag**ue**
proteg**er** (to protect) → prote**ja**
utiliz**ar** (to use) → utili**ce**

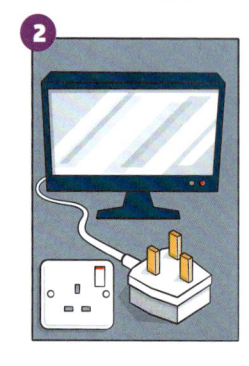

4 escribir Escribe un slogan para cada póster. Usa la forma *usted*.

desenchufar	el plástico y el papel
no utilizar	el agua
reciclar	las luces
apagar	bolsas de plástico
no malgastar	los aparatos eléctricos

166 *ciento sesenta y seis*

5 Lee el blog. ¿Es la casa A, la casa B, las casas A + B?

estuverde.com

Creo que es posible llevar una vida más verde y salvar el planeta. ¿Soy demasiado optimista? Aquí tenéis unos pequeños ejemplos de cómo la gente intenta reducir la huella de carbono con sus casas.

A Casas de plástico
Desde hace más de ocho años un chileno, Santi Morales, lleva un proyecto de construcción de casas de botellas de plástico recicladas. Las botellas se llenan de arena o tierra y así forman 'eco-ladrillos'. Santi Morales comentó: 'Es esencial que busquemos soluciones nuevas. Con este proyecto reciclamos la basura de cada día en una casa económica para muchos años.'

B Casas prefabricadas
Sencilla, cálida, ecológica y más barata. Así definen a Cas4, una casa prefabricada de Argentina que utiliza recursos naturales. Es ecológica porque utiliza paneles solares para generar energía. El techo de la casa recoge el agua de lluvia que sirve incluso para el consumo. Las casas se hacen en una fábrica, lo que acelera el proceso de construcción (90 días) y de montaje (una semana). Otro aspecto positivo es que son móviles. Si la persona se muda, puede llevarse su casa al nuevo domicilio.

1. Se usan materiales reciclados.
2. Las casas se construyen en Chile.
3. El proceso de construcción es rápido.
4. Las casas cuestan menos que las casas tradicionales.
5. Las casas son transportables.
6. Las casas usan energía renovable.

> Remember that in Spanish *se* is often used to avoid the passive.
> Las botellas **se llenan** de arena.
> The bottles **are filled** with sand.

6 Lee el blog otra vez. Contesta a las preguntas en inglés.

1. What are people trying to reduce with their houses?
2. In text A, how are the eco-bricks made?
3. According to Santi Morales, what are the <u>two</u> advantages of his houses?
4. Apart from the cost, list <u>three</u> further characteristics of the Cas4 houses.
5. What does the roof of the Cas4 do?
6. Where exactly are these Argentinian houses made?

7 Escribe una redacción *en contra* del argumento 'No se puede salvar el planeta'.

- Say it is true there are a lot of problems
- Say which problems most concern you

Es verdad que…
Para mí, el mayor problema es (la contaminación del aire). Otro problema que me preocupa es (la pobreza).

- Say you believe it is possible to solve the problems
- Say what it is important to do globally
- Say what you should do locally

Es posible solucionar…
Es importante que (cambiemos la ley) para…
Localmente se debería (reciclar)…

8 Presenta tu redacción en clase.

> When saying what we need to do, e.g. to protect the environment, we usually use structures such as **Se debería**, **Hay que**, etc. + infinitive, whereas in a poster we use commands for giving instructions.

3 ¡Vivir a tope!

- Discussing healthy lifestyles
- Understanding different tenses
- Giving extended reasons

1 escuchar Escucha y lee. Empareja los textos con los dibujos a–d.

1 Por un lado, **no me parece un problema serio** porque todos mis amigos lo hacen. Por otro lado, **daña los pulmones** y el corazón, **provoca mal aliento** y **mancha los dientes de amarillo**. ¡Qué asco!

3 En mi opinión, **es muy perjudicial para la salud**. También **afecta tu capacidad para tomar decisiones**. Sin embargo, tomar una copa con tus amigos también **te hace sentir bien**.

2 Aunque no es tan peligroso como tomar heroína o cocaína, tiene muchos riesgos y **es un vicio muy caro**. Algunos dicen que fumar porros **te hace sentir más adulto**, pero en realidad **causa el fracaso escolar**.

4 **Produce una fuerte dependencia física**, y por eso **es ilegal y peligroso**. Además, **es fácil engancharse** y la rehabilitación es larga y dura.

a beber alcohol
b tomar drogas blandas
c fumar cigarrillos
d tomar drogas duras

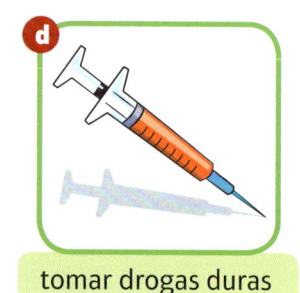

2 leer Lee los textos otra vez. Completa la tabla con las frases en **negrita**.

	en contra	a favor
fumar	daña los pulmones	no me parece un problema serio

3 escuchar Escucha. Apunta los detalles en inglés. (1–4)
Ejemplo: **1** *boyfriend smokes spliffs, …*
- bad habit
- opinion
- reason (two details)

| me emborracho (emborracharse) | I get drunk |
| parar | to stop |

4 hablar Con tu compañero/a, haz un diálogo.
- ¿Tienes algún vicio?
- Sí / No. A veces <u>bebo / fumo</u>.
- ¿Qué opinas de beber alcohol / fumar / tomar drogas duras / blandas?
- Creo que <u>beber alcohol</u> es una tontería porque…

⭐ Use the language from exercise 2 to give extended reasons.
E.g. … *porque el alcohol afecta a tu capacidad para tomar decisiones. Por otro lado, …*

Creo que…	Por un lado, … por otro lado, …
En mi opinión…	Desde mi punto de vista…
Sin embargo…	

| beber alcohol / emborracharse fumar (cigarrillos / porros) tomar drogas blandas / duras | no es tan malo es una tontería es (muy) perjudicial |
| porque ya que dado que | te relaja te quita el estrés / sueño / control causa la depresión es un malgasto de dinero te engancha |

ciento sesenta y ocho

Módulo 8

5 Lee el blog de Lorenzo. Elige las respuestas correctas.

> Antes llevaba una vida sana en todos los aspectos: comía y bebía bien, hacía ejercicio todos los días y cuidaba mi cuerpo. Pero hace un año cedí ante la presión de grupo y probé un cigarrillo en una fiesta, y luego caí en el hábito de fumar cuando salía con mis amigos.
>
> Después de unos meses me di cuenta de que era adicto a la nicotina. Ya no tenía ganas de entrenar y lo pasaba muy mal. Un día, cuando veía la tele en casa, vi un maratón y decidí cambiar mi estilo de vida. Todavía me queda mucho por hacer, porque no estoy en forma y todavía no he dejado de fumar, pero creo que en seis meses tendré el mismo nivel de estado físico que antes. Luego espero participar en una carrera patrocinada de 20 km.

Lorenzo

1 Lorenzo **has / had** a healthy lifestyle.
2 He **looks / used to look** after his body.
3 Smoking **is / was** a regular habit when he **goes / went** out with friends.
4 He **still smokes / has quit smoking**.
5 He **has / will have** the same level of fitness as before.
6 He **hoped / hopes** to do a 20k sponsored run.

6 Lee el texto del ejercicio 5 otra vez. Busca las frases en español.

1 I fell into the habit of
2 I realised that
3 I was having a really bad time
4 I decided to change
5 There is still a lot for me to do
6 I still haven't stopped

> ⭐ Look carefully at the verb endings to help you work out the tense.
> The **imperfect** (–*aba*, –*ía* endings) describes a scene, what you used to do, or repeated actions in the past.
> The **preterite** (–*é*, –*í* endings) refers to finished actions in the past.
> The **future** (infinitive + –*é*) expresses what you 'will / shall' do.
> Remember that there are several ways to express future meaning: future tense, near future tense, *esperar* + infinitive, *querer* + infinitive.

7 Escucha. Completa la tabla con los detalles en inglés. (1–2)

	in the past (2)	now (2)	in the future (3)
1			

8 Escribe un post para el blog *Estilo de vida*. Usa tu imaginación.

Incluye:
- un vicio que tenías
- por qué era un problema
- cómo es la situación ahora
- tus planes para el futuro
- tus recomendaciones para una vida sana

Antes	Ahora	A partir de ahora
tenía (mucho estrés / la mala costumbre de…)	no puedo parar	voy a mejorar…
fumaba, comía, bebía, hacía, llevaba, lo pasaba…	estoy un poco obsesionado/a	dejar de…
	ya no bebo / fumo…	entrenar…
cedí ante la presión de grupo	ya he empezado a…	cambiar…
empecé a (saltarme el desayuno)	todavía no he dejado de…	hacer…
probé…		llevar…
caí en el hábito de…		También debo…
decidí…		Intentaré…
perdí peso		Luego espero…

ciento sesenta y nueve **169**

4 ¡El deporte nos une!

- Talking about international sporting events
- Using the pluperfect tense
- Explaining your point of view

1 Escucha. Apunta la letra y los <u>dos</u> beneficios correctos. (1–3)
Ejemplo: **1** *b 3, …*

¿Para qué sirven los eventos deportivos internacionales?

a la Copa Mundial de Fútbol
b los Juegos Olímpicos
c la Vuelta a España

Sirven para…
1 promover la participación en el deporte.
2 regenerar los centros urbanos.
3 elevar el orgullo nacional.
4 transmitir los valores de respeto y disciplina.
5 unir a la gente.
6 animar el turismo.

2 Escucha otra vez. Apunta otros detalles en inglés.
Ejemplo: **1** *raise national pride, …*

⭐ We often rephrase what we say in order to explain our ideas or give more detail. Listen out for clue words such as **en otras palabras** (in other words), **o sea** (I mean) and **es decir** (that is to say).

3 Lee los posts. Apunta <u>dos</u> opiniones del ejercicio 1 y las desventajas que se mencionan.

💬 **Natalia**
Soy una fan de los grandes acontecimientos deportivos, sobre todo de los Juegos Paralímpicos. Me inspiran a ser una buena persona, es decir, a respetar a los demás. Siempre estoy muy orgullosa de ser española cuando gana uno de mis compatriotas. No obstante, no se puede hablar de los eventos deportivos sin mencionar la batalla contra el dopaje. Otro inconveniente es el tráfico que producen estos eventos.

💬 **Lorena**
Por una parte, los eventos deportivos dan un impulso económico, sobre todo a los sectores de la construcción y la hostelería. Además, fomentan el espíritu de solidaridad. Por otra parte, los costes de organización son muy altos, y a menudo resultan en deudas para la ciudad anfitriona. Otra desventaja es el riesgo de ataques terroristas durante la temporada del evento.

la ciudad anfitriona host city

Una / Otra desventaja es…	
el riesgo de ataques terroristas	el dopaje
el coste de la organización / de la seguridad	la deuda
	el tráfico

⭐ The opinions are not given in the same words as in exercise 1, so pay attention to the overall meaning and look for expressions that mean the same thing.

4 Con tu compañero/a, haz un diálogo.
- ¿Qué evento deportivo internacional es el más interesante para ti?
- ¿Qué piensas de los eventos deportivos internacionales?
- ¿Hay otros beneficios?
- ¿Hay desventajas?

■ El evento que me interesa más es… porque…
■ <u>Desde mi punto de vista</u>, sirven para…
■ Sí, también <u>unen a la gente</u>.
■ Sí, una desventaja es <u>el dopaje</u>.

ciento setenta

Módulo 8

5 Escucha y lee el comentario. ¿Las frases se refieren a Maribel (M), a Pedro (P), o a los dos (M+P)?

Voluntarios olímpicos comparten sus experiencias

Mi abuela Maribel y yo conseguimos puestos de voluntariado en los JJ. OO. Decidí solicitarlo porque **nunca había trabajado como voluntario**. Mi abuela estaba disponible porque **había dejado de trabajar dos meses antes**. Además, **ya había hecho un voluntariado** en los JJ. OO. de 1992 en Barcelona. Ella **siempre había dicho** que fue una experiencia inolvidable.

La primera semana, fui embajador de los valores olímpicos: la amistad, la armonía y la solidaridad. Tuve que saludar a los visitantes y guiarlos a los eventos, lo que fue muy gratificante. Hice muchos amigos durante esta semana y me gustó mucho trabajar en equipo. La segunda semana trabajé en la piscina olímpica. Yo soy estudiante y un fanático de la natación, pero **nunca había visto de cerca a mis modelos**. Asistí a los nadadores y trabajé de socorrista en la piscina. ¡Qué ilusión!

Mi abuela era asistente del equipo colombiano y lo pasó fenomenal. Los ayudó a organizar sus visitas turísticas. Aprovechó su experiencia porque **antes había sido guía turística en la ciudad**. A mi parecer, el voluntariado es una experiencia muy buena porque te permite desarrollar tus habilidades comunicativas. Se la recomendaría a todos, ¡jóvenes y jubilados! **Pedro**

JJ. OO. Juegos Olímpicos
desarrollar to develop

1. Hizo el trabajo voluntario con otro miembro de su familia.
2. Trabajó en la piscina olímpica.
3. Le gustó trabajar con otras personas.
4. Aprovechó su experiencia previa de voluntario.
5. Vio a sus ídolos.

6 Lee los textos otra vez. Traduce las expresiones en **negrita** al inglés.

7 Escucha *Voluntarios: ¡Inspiración en acción!* Apunta los detalles en inglés. (1–2)

Opinion of volunteering:
Event:
Reason for applying:
Tasks (two details):
Opinion:
Future plans:

me ocupé de — I was in charge of

G The pluperfect tense ▸ Page 231

The **pluperfect** is used to talk about what someone <u>had</u> done, referring to a past action which happened earlier than another action.

	haber	past participle
(yo)	había	
(tú)	habías	
(él/ella/usted)	había	trabaj**ado**
(nosotros/nosotras)	habíamos	quer**ido**
(vosotros/vosotras)	habíais	viv**ido**
(ellos/ellas/ustedes)	habían	

Remember that some past participles are irregular:
hacer → **hecho** (done)   **ver** → **visto** (seen)
poner → **puesto** (put)   **decir** → **dicho** (said)

8 Escribe un artículo sobre tus experiencias como voluntario/a en un evento deportivo. Usa tu imaginación. Incluye:

- lo que opinas del voluntariado
  A mi parecer, el voluntariado es una buena experiencia porque…
- por qué solicitaste un trabajo voluntario
  Solicité un trabajo voluntario porque…
  (Nunca) había sido…
  Antes ya había trabajado como…
- qué hiciste
  Tuve que… Ayudé a… Trabajé con…
  La gente / El trabajo era…
- tus planes para el voluntariado
  En el futuro, pienso trabajar como voluntario/a en…

ciento setenta y uno **171**

5 ¡Apúntate!

- Talking about natural disasters
- Using the imperfect continuous
- Using grammar knowledge in translation

1 Escucha y lee. Empareja los tuits con las fotos. Sobra una foto. (1–5)

¿Qué **estabas haciendo**?

1 **Estaba durmiendo** y de repente me desperté. ¡El edificio **se estaba moviendo**!

2 **Estábamos ensayando** para un concierto en el colegio, pero **estaba nevando** tanto que nos tuvimos que ir a casa.

3 Me asomé por la ventana y ¡la calle **se estaba convirtiendo** en un río! El agua **estaba entrando** en la casa.

4 Los niños **estaban leyendo** en la biblioteca cuando se sintió el seísmo. Tenían miedo porque los libros se **estaban cayendo**.

5 **Estaba conduciendo** por la ciudad. ¡A mi alrededor había coches que **estaban volando** por el aire!

a un temblor, Colombia
b unas inundaciones, Bolivia
c una tormenta de nieve, Estados Unidos
d un incendio forestal, Mallorca, España
e un huracán, Estados Unidos
f un tornado, México

2 Lee los tuits otra vez. Busca el equivalente de estas frases.

1. it was snowing
2. the children were reading
3. we were rehearsing
4. I was sleeping
5. the building was moving
6. the books were falling
7. the street was turning into a river
8. What were you doing?

me asomé por la ventana — I looked out of the window
se sintió el seísmo — the earthquake was felt

G Imperfect continuous > Page 230

The **imperfect continuous** translates as 'was / were …ing'.
Estaba cenando cuando la tormenta azotó al pueblo.
I was having dinner when the storm hit the town.

	estar (to be)	gerund
(yo)	estaba	
(tú)	estabas	
(él/ella/usted)	estaba	trabaj**ando**
(nosotros/as)	estábamos	beb**iendo**
(vosotros/as)	estabais	escrib**iendo**
(ellos/ellas/ustedes)	estaban	

To form the gerund, take the infinitive, remove the *–ar*, *–er* or *–ir* and add the endings *–ando*, *–iendo*, *–iendo*.

3 Escucha y completa la tabla. (1–6)

	desastre natural	¿qué estabas haciendo?	¿cómo te enteraste?
Santi			

172 *ciento setenta y dos*

Módulo 8

4 Con tu compañero/a, pregunta y contesta. Cierra el libro. Utiliza tus respuestas al ejercicio 3.
- ¿Cómo te enteraste <u>del temblor / de las inundaciones</u>?
- ■ <u>Estaba viendo las noticias</u> cuando <u>encontré un reportaje</u>.

5 Escucha y lee. Traduce las frases en **negrita** al inglés.

una Shelterbox

Alba

¿Cómo te enteraste de la acción humanitaria para Nepal, Alba?
Estaba buscando información en Internet para mis deberes de geografía y encontré un artículo sobre *Interact*.

¿Y eso qué es?
Es una organización internacional de servicio voluntario para los jóvenes. El artículo contaba la historia de una chica en Nepal que no tenía ni siquiera cepillo de dientes. **Su casa fue destruida por el terremoto que dejó a miles de personas sin hogar**.

¿*Interact* hacía una campaña para las víctimas?
Sí. Mi club local estaba preparando una caja de supervivencia, una *Shelterbox*, para mandar a Nepal. Tiene todo lo esencial para vivir seis meses.

¿Qué hiciste tú?
Decidí apuntarme. Tuvimos que recaudar fondos, así que organizamos algunos eventos en el instituto y en la ciudad.

¿Qué tipo de eventos?
Hicimos un concierto y un espectáculo de baile. **Otros miembros del grupo participaron en una carrera de bici apadrinada**. Yo organicé una venta de pasteles cada viernes en el insti. También **escribimos cartas a tiendas de la ciudad para solicitar donativos**. Ya tenemos la caja completa y **la mandaremos a Nepal** la semana que viene.

Otros jóvenes se podrían apuntar, ¿cómo les convencerías?
Diría que es importante ser solidario porque te hace sentir más conectado con los demás. ¡Apúntate!

- This is the passive. What does *por* mean here?
- *que* refers back to the earthquake.
- Which tense is this?
- Remember the group is raising money. What sort of activity is this?
- Use the context again here. Why might you write letters to local shops?
- Is there a time phrase to help you decide which tense this is?
- We can't translate word for word here. What captures the idea of solidarity?

ni siquiera — not even

6 Escucha y contesta a las preguntas en inglés.
1. How did Manolo find out about the campaign being run by Ciudades Refugio?
2. Who are they trying to help?
3. What is being done to raise awareness of the issues?
4. What sort of aid is being offered by the organisation?
5. Why did Manolo decide to sign up to work with them?
6. What are the benefits of being involved with aid work, according to Manolo?

los refugiados — refugees

7 Escribe un post sobre tus actividades benéficas.

Me enteré de… cuando estaba… Es un grupo / una organización que… La organización hacía una campaña para (las víctimas de…) Decidí apuntarme porque… Tuvimos que recaudar fondos, así que organicé… Diría que es importante ser solidario porque… El mes que viene vamos a…

ciento setenta y tres **173**

Módulo 8 Leer y escuchar

1 A family falls on hard times
Read the extract from the novel 'Las luces de septiembre' by Carlos Ruiz Zafón.

> Tras seis meses de sufrimiento, una enfermedad había quitado la vida a Armand Sauvelle. Armand Sauvelle se llevó a la tumba su magia y su risa contagiosa, pero sus numerosas deudas no lo acompañaron en el último viaje.
>
> Colegios de prestigio y ropa impecable fueron sustituidos por empleos a tiempo parcial y ropa más modesta para Irene y Dorian. Lo peor, sin embargo, cayó sobre Simone, su madre. Retomar su empleo como profesora no era suficiente para hacer frente al torrente de deudas de Armand.
>
> Semanas más tarde, apareció la promesa de un buen empleo para su madre en un pequeño pueblo de la costa. Lazarus Jann, inventor y fabricante de juguetes, necesitaba una ama de llaves para cuidar su residencia en el bosque de Cravenmoore.
>
> La paga era generosa y, además, Lazarus Jann les ofrecía la posibilidad de instalarse en la Casa del Cabo, una modesta residencia construida al otro lado del bosque de Cravenmoore.
>
> *risa = laugh*

1 According to the text, how did Armand Sauvelle die?
Write the correct letter.
  A from a unknown tropical illness
  B after seeing a ghost
  C after several months of suffering

2 According to the text, what sort of man was he?
Write the correct letter.
  A funny
  B lonely
  C hard-working

3 According to the text, which **two** statements are true?
Write the correct letters.
After the death of Armand Sauvelle...
  A his children wore more expensive clothes.
  B his children had to get part-time jobs.
  C his wife re-married.
  D the family was poor.
  E his wife was unable to work.

4 What were the **two** advantages of Lazarus Jann's job offer?
Answer the question in **English**.

2 La Fiesta de la Bici
Lee este artículo sobre un evento deportivo en Madrid.

> Vuelve la **Fiesta de la Bici**. Un evento sano, deportivo, colorido, festivo… Un evento familiar. El recorrido será igual al de años anteriores.
>
> Durante el recorrido encontrarás zonas de animación con música, actividades y disfraces, así que la Fiesta de la Bici es una gran experiencia para los más pequeños. Si vas con los niños, tu objetivo principal debe ser su vigilancia e integridad. Hay que darles instrucciones en caso de pérdida.
>
> Antes de la fiesta es aconsejable hacer una revisión básica de la bicicleta. Asegúrate de que las ruedas llevan la presión necesaria, y sobre todo, debes revisar la tensión de los frenos*.
>
> La Fiesta de la Bici es una marcha no competitiva de carácter popular. Si vas de carreras, puedes provocar accidentes y molestias a otros participantes.
>
> *los frenos = brakes*

la Puerta de Alcalá, Madrid

174 *ciento setenta y cuatro*

Contesta a las preguntas en español.

1. ¿Cómo sabemos que no es el primer año que se celebra este recorrido?
2. ¿Por qué esta fiesta es una gran experiencia para los niños?
3. ¿Qué deben hacer los padres si van con sus niños?
4. Antes de la fiesta, ¿qué es lo más importante que tienen que hacer los participantes?
5. ¿Qué puede pasar si los ciclistas son competitivos?

⭐ Work out what the question means and identify the relevant detail(s). To answer you can usually lift the words directly from the text.

3 leer

Translation into English

Your friend, who has bought a magazine in Spain, has asked you to translate this short article for him. Translate it into **English**.

> Marco está en ruta hacia Bolivia. Solicitó un trabajo como voluntario en un orfanato, donde va a pasar seis meses. ¡Tiene muchas ganas de empezar a trabajar con los niños! Piensa que el voluntariado ofrece muchos beneficios, sobre todo la oportunidad de ayudar a los demás. Ganará mucha experiencia, y después todavía tendrá tiempo suficiente para explorar Sudamérica.

1 escuchar

News report

You are listening to a news report about Mexico on Spanish radio. Answer all parts of the question in **English**.

a Mexico is the world's greatest consumer of which product?
b According to the report, what are the consequences of this? Give **two** details.
c What has been the response by the *Alianza por la Salud Alimentaria*?
d Why has the organisation done this? Give **two** reasons.

⭐ Use the questions to give you clues about the information you are looking for. For example, what could the *Alianza por la Salud Alimentaria* be? How does this help you predict which sort of product you are listening out for in question a?

2 escuchar

Interview with a Spanish meteorologist

You are listening to a podcast with a Spanish meteorologist.

1 Answer all parts of the question in **English**.
   a What does the meteorologist say about heat waves?
   b When do the conditions qualify as a heat wave in Spain?
   c What has happened in India as a result of the lack of early warning systems?

2 Answer both parts of the question in **English**.
   a According to the meteorologist, what is the most important thing to do in a heat wave?
   b Where could future disasters occur, in the view of the meteorologist?

Módulo 8   Prueba oral

A – Role play

1 leer   Look at the role play card and prepare what you are going to say.

> Your teacher will play the part of the interviewer and will speak first.
>
> You should address the interviewer as *usted*.
>
> When you see this – **!** – you will have to respond to something you have not prepared.
>
> When you see this – **?** – you will have to ask a question.
>
> Usted está en una entrevista. Está solicitando un trabajo voluntario.
> - Tu motivo para ser voluntario/a (**dos** detalles).
> - **!**
> - Tu experiencia laboral (**un** detalle).
> - Tu preferencia – hospital o tienda (**una** razón).
> - **?** El horario de trabajo.

- Imagine how the examiner may ask this question to help you start your answer.
- What information might you be asked to give? Think about typical interview scenarios.
- You are asked to give a reason for your preference here. When planning your answer, focus first and foremost on what you know how to say.
- What can you add to turn this into a question?
- Use either the **perfect tense** to say what you **have done**, or the **preterite tense** to say what you **did at a specific time** (e.g. last year).

2 hablar   Practise what you have prepared. Take care with pronunciation and intonation.

3 escuchar   Using your notes, listen and respond to the teacher.

4 escuchar   Now listen to Arthur doing the role play task. Note down how he answers the unprepared question(s).

B – Photo card

Look at the photo and make notes. Your teacher will then ask you questions about the photo and about topics related to **global issues**.

Your teacher will ask you the following **three** questions and then **two** more questions which you have not prepared.

- ¿Qué hay en la foto?
- ¿Crees que hay más gente sin techo en España hoy en día? … ¿Por qué (no)?
- ¿Qué debería hacer el gobierno para mejorar esta situación?

ciento setenta y seis

Módulo 8

1 escuchar **Look at the photo and read the task. Then listen to Ed's response to the first question on the task card.**

1 How does he describe the man?
2 Where does he suggest the man lives, and why does he think this? Give **two** reasons.
3 Why does he suggest the man is playing the guitar?
4 What does he think the weather is like, and why does he think this?

2 escuchar **Listen to and read Ed's response to the second question on the task card.**

1 Write down the missing word for each gap.
2 Look at the Answer Booster on page 178. Note down **six** examples of language which Ed uses to give a strong answer.

> Sí, creo que ahora hay muchísimas personas **1** ———— en España a causa de la crisis económica. Hay mucho **2** ————, y por eso la gente pierde su casa. Luego es un círculo vicioso. Los sin techo **3** ———— muchos problemas, como la depresión, **4** ———— e incluso la adicción. Pero desde mi punto de vista, lo peor es la exclusión social y **5** ———— porque les baja la autoestima y no ven ninguna **6** ———— a su situación. La vida es realmente horrible cuando no tienes donde dormir.

3 escuchar **Listen to Ed's answer to the third question on the task card. Match the infinitive verbs to the noun phrases. Then translate them into English.**

crear	proporcionar
ofrecer	participar
mejorar	apoyar
comprar	

en proyectos locales
las casas vacías
formación profesional gratis
más viviendas sociales

su confianza en sí mismos
los bancos de alimentos
más oportunidades de trabajo

4 hablar **Prepare your own answers to the first three questions. Think about which other two questions you might be asked. Then listen and take part in the full photo card discussion with the teacher.**

C – General conversation

1 escuchar **The teacher asks Alison '¿Cómo te puedes mantener en forma hoy en día?' Listen to her answer and complete the statements.**

a She believes that…
b She tries to… and usually…
c She used to… but unfortunately…
d She knows that…
e She is going to try to…
f She has heard that…

2 escuchar **Listen to Alison's response to the next question '¿Qué opinas de fumar?' Note down five examples of the preterite tense.**

3 escuchar **The teacher then asks Alison '¿Cómo se debería cuidar el medio ambiente?'**

1 Look at the Answer Booster on page 178. Note down **six** examples of language which Alison uses to give a strong answer.
2 Note down **four** different uses of the subjunctive, and match them to the correct infinitives below. ¡Ojo! Not all of these infinitives are used in the subjunctive.
3 Note down the question that Alison asks her teacher.

> ⭐ Improve the complexity of your answers by including more than one tense, even when the question itself does not require it. Which of these strategies does Alison use?
> • refers to future plans
> • contrasts then and now
> • narrates a past event
> • states what should or would happen
> • mentions something already/not yet done

trasmitir   consumir   apoyar   haber   mejorar   insistir   regenerar   cambiar   hacer   tomar

4 hablar **Prepare your own answers to Module 8 questions 1–6 on page 199. Then practise with your partner.**

ciento setenta y siete **177**

Módulo 8   Prueba escrita

Answer booster	Aiming for a solid answer	Aiming higher	Aiming for the top
Verbs	**Different time frames**: past, present, near future **Different types of verbs**: regular, irregular, reflexive, stem-changing	**Verbs/Expressions with an infinitive**: poder, intentar, se debería, servir para **Phrases with an infinitive**: antes de, después de **Phrases to refer to future plans**: espero, pienso, tengo la intención de + infinitive	**A wide range of tenses**: present, present continuous, conditional, preterite, perfect, pluperfect, future *Si* + present + future *Es... que* + subjunctive: es esencial que usemos...
Opinions and reasons	**Verbs of opinion**: me chifla(n), me encanta(n), me interesa(n) **Reasons**: porque	**Opinions**: me apasiona(n), me preocupa(n), me importa(n) **Absolute superlatives**: muchísimo, importantísimo	**Opinions**: desde mi punto de vista, a mi juicio, en mi opinión, creo que **Reasons**: a causa de, ya que, por lo tanto, por eso, así que **Opinions in the preterite**: me encantó
Connectives	y, pero, también	además, sin embargo, sobre todo, no obstante, por ejemplo	gracias a **Alternatives to 'and'**: no solo..., sino también... **Balancing an argument**: un/otro beneficio, un inconveniente, a pesar de, aunque
Other features	**Qualifiers**: muy, realmente, bastante, un poco, poco, demasiado **Sequencers**: luego, después, más tarde	**Sentences with *cuando, donde, si*** ***Para* + infinitive**: Para ayudar ***Tan, Tanto/a/os/as***: tan grande **Indirect object pronouns**: te da la oportunidad de..., te permite...	**Complex sentences with *si***: si tuviera bastante... **Specialist vocabulary**: una caminata patrocinada, una sociedad de usar y tirar, un círculo vicioso

A – Extended writing task

1 leer Look at the task and answer the questions.
- What is each bullet point asking you to write about?
- How could you develop your answer to each one?
- Which tenses and structures could you use, as well as those required by the bullets?

2 leer Read Alexandra's answer on page 179. What do the phrases in **bold** mean?

3 leer Look at the Answer Booster. Note down **eight** examples of language which Alexandra uses to write a strong answer.

4 leer Complete the essay plan based on Alexandra's answer.

5 escribir Prepare your own answer to the task.
- Look at the Answer Booster and Alexandra's plan for ideas.
- Think about how you can develop your answer for each bullet point.
- Write a detailed plan. Organise your answer in paragraphs.
- Write your answer and carefully check what you have written.

Escribe un artículo para una revista sobre la importancia de ser solidario/a.

Escribe incluyendo esta información:
- los problemas más serios en el mundo de hoy
- qué hiciste recientemente para ser solidario/a.

Escribe aproximadamente **150** palabras en **español**. Responde a los dos aspectos de la pregunta.

Paragraph 1
- Social inequality
-

Paragraph 2
-
-

Módulo 8

Me preocupa sobre todo la desigualdad social. **No es justo que haya** gente que muera por falta de comida y de agua potable. Además, la pobreza **no solo afecta a los países en desarrollo**, sino que también **amenaza a muchos niños** en mi país. Sin embargo, si todos ayudamos **podremos crear** un mundo mejor para todos.

Hay muchas cosas que podemos hacer para mejorar la situación, y es esencial que actuemos pronto. Por ejemplo, cuando compramos productos de comercio justo, **estamos apoyando** a familias en el tercer mundo. Además, podemos colaborar en eventos patrocinados* para recaudar fondos para organizaciones caritativas **o globales o locales**.

El año pasado decidí participar en **una caminata patrocinada de 20 km**. Fue organizada por UNICEF **para crear conciencia sobre** la crisis de los refugiados en zonas de conflicto. Luego hicimos un día de silencio organizado en mi instituto **para la misma campaña**. Fue la primera vez que **colaboré** en un evento solidario tan grande, pero me encantó.

Desde mi punto de vista, es muy importante ser solidario porque te da la oportunidad de hacer algo concreto para ayudar a los demás. **Ya me he afiliado al** club de Amnistía Internacional en mi insti y escribimos cartas cada semana. **Si tuviera más tiempo**, **participaría** en todavía más eventos. Después de hacer el bachillerato, solicitaré un trabajo voluntario en una escuela primaria en África porque pienso ser profesora un día.

* *patrocinado = sponsored (for events, e.g. a sponsored walk)*
apadrinado = sponsored (for people, e.g. a sponsored child in Africa)

> ⭐ Use your imagination to help you produce a longer, more interesting answer. Remember that in an exam you don't have to tell the truth, as long as what you write is plausible!

B – Translation

1 Read the English text and Gillian's translation of it. Write down the missing word(s) for each gap.

> ⭐ Think carefully about which person and tense you need. Take extra care with verbs that do not translate word for word, for example 'it's cold', or where you need to choose between verbs, for example *ser* or *estar* for 'would be in the country'.

I used to live in a flat in the city, but my family and I now have an old house on the outskirts. Two months ago I decorated my bedroom. For that reason it's my favourite room. I tend to eat in the kitchen because it's cold in the dining room. My ideal house would be in the country.

1 _____ en un apartamento en la ciudad, pero ahora mi familia y yo **2** _____ una casa antigua en las afueras. Hace dos meses **3** _____ mi dormitorio. Por eso **4** _____ mi habitación favorita. **5** _____ en la cocina porque **6** _____ frío en el comedor. Mi casa ideal **7** _____ en el campo.

2 Translate the following passage into Spanish.

My house in the country was old, but very comfortable. However, for six months we've been living in a large, modern flat. The only bad thing is the small garden. I would like to have a bigger space to plant flowers. Last week my dad bought a farm in Wales. In two months we will go to live there.

ciento setenta y nueve **179**

Módulo 8 Palabras

¿Cómo es tu casa?
Vivo en…
  un bloque de pisos
  una casa individual
  una casa adosada
  una residencia de ancianos
  una finca / granja
Alquilamos una casa amueblada.
Está en…
  un barrio de la ciudad
  las afueras
  el campo
  la costa
  la montaña / sierra
  el cuarto piso de un edificio antiguo
Mi apartamento / piso tiene…
  tres dormitorios

What is your house like?
I live in…
  a block of flats
  a detached house
  a semi-detached / terraced house
  an old people's home
  a farmhouse
We rent a furnished house.
It is in / on…
  a district / suburb of the city / town
  the outskirts
  the country
  the coast
  the mountains
  the fourth floor of an old building
My apartment / flat has…
  three bedrooms

dos cuartos de baño
una cocina amplia y bien equipada
un comedor recién renovado
un estudio
un aseo
un sótano
un salón
una mesa
unas sillas
Mi casa ideal sería…
Tendría…
  una piscina climatizada
  mi propio cine en casa
  una sala de fiestas
Cambiaría los muebles.
Pintaría … de otro color.

two bathrooms
a spacious, well-equipped kitchen
a recently refurbished dining room
a study
a toilet
a basement / cellar
a living room
a table
some chairs
My ideal house would be…
It would have…
  a heated swimming pool
  my own home cinema
  a party room
I would change the furniture.
I would paint … another colour.

¿Cómo se debería cuidar el medio ambiente en casa?
Para cuidar el medio ambiente se debería…
  apagar la luz
  ducharse en vez de bañarse
  separar la basura
  reciclar el plástico y el vidrio

How should you look after the environment at home?
To care for the environment you / one should…
  turn off the light
  have a shower instead of taking a bath
  separate the rubbish
  recycle plastic and glass

desenchufar los aparatos eléctricos
ahorrar energía
cerrar el grifo
hacer todo lo posible
no se debería…
  malgastar el agua
  usar bolsas de plástico

unplug electric appliances
save energy
turn off the tap
do everything possible
you / one should not…
  waste water
  use plastic bags

¿Cuáles son los problemas globales más serios hoy en día?
Me preocupa(n)…
  el paro / desempleo
  el hambre / la pobreza
  la deforestación
  la diferencia entre ricos y pobres
  la drogadicción / la salud / la obesidad
  la crisis económica
  los problemas del medio ambiente
  los sin hogar / techo
  los animales en peligro de extinción
Es necesario / esencial que…
  cuidemos el planeta
  hagamos proyectos de conservación
  compremos / usemos
    productos verdes / de comercio justo
  apoyemos proyectos de ayuda

What are the most serious global issues today?
I am worried about…
  unemployment
  hunger / poverty
  deforestation
  the difference between rich and poor
  drug addiction / health / obesity
  the economic crisis
  environmental problems
  the homeless
  animals in danger of extinction
It's necessary / essential that (we)…
  look after the planet
  do conservation projects
  buy / use
    green / fairtrade products
  support aid projects

creemos oportunidades de trabajo
ayudemos a evitar el consumo
  de sustancias perjudiciales
ahorremos agua
construyamos más casas
cambiemos la ley
consumamos menos
hagamos campañas publicitarias
recaudemos dinero
  para organizaciones de caridad
  en el tercer mundo
No es justo / Es terrible que haya…
  tanta desigualdad social / contaminación
  tanta gente sin trabajo y sin techo
  tanta gente obesa y tantos drogadictos

create job opportunities
help to avoid the consumption
  of harmful substances
save water
build more houses
change the law
consume less
carry out publicity campaigns
raise money
  for charities in the third world
It's not fair / terrible that there is…
  so much social inequality / pollution
  so many people out of work and homeless
  so many obese people and so many drug addicts

¡Actúa localmente!
Hay demasiada…
  basura en las calles
  gente sin espacio para vivir
  destrucción de los bosques
  polución de los mares y ríos
El aire está contaminado.
Los combustibles fósiles se acaban.
No corte tantos árboles.
No vaya en coche si es posible ir a pie.
No tire basura al suelo.
No malgaste energía.
No construya tantas casas grandes.
No eche tantos desechos químicos.
Plante más bosques y selvas.
Reduzca las emisiones de los vehículos.
Recicle el papel, el vidrio y el plástico.

Act locally!
There is / are too much / many…
  rubbish on the streets
  people with nowhere to live
  destruction of woodland / forest
  pollution of seas and rivers
The air is polluted.
Fossil fuels are running out.
Don't cut down so many trees.
Don't go by car if it's possible to walk.
Don't throw rubbish onto the ground.
Don't waste energy.
Don't build so many large houses.
Don't release so much chemical waste.
Plant more woods and forests.
Reduce vehicle emissions.
Recycle papel, glass and plastic.

Use energías renovables.
Diseñe casas más pequeñas.
Introduzca leyes más estrictas.
llevar una vida más verde
salvar el planeta
reducir la huella de carbono
ecológico/a
el techo
el agua de lluvia
el domicilio
los recursos naturales
los paneles solares
la arena
los (eco-)ladrillos
una fábrica
mudarse (de casa)

Use renewable energy.
Design smaller houses.
Introduce stricter laws.
(to) live a greener life
(to) save the planet
(to) reduce your carbon footprint
environmentally-friendly
roof
rain water
home
natural resources
solar panels
sand
(eco-)bricks
a factory
(to) move house

Una dieta sana
los alimentos
lácteos
carne, pescados y huevos
frutas y verduras
cereales
fideos

A healthy diet
foods
milk products
meat, fish and eggs
fruit and vegetables
cereals
noodles

grasas
dulces
legumbres
frutos secos
los nutrientes
proteínas

fats
sugars / sweet things
pulses
nuts and dried fruit
nutrients
proteins

minerales	minerals	La fibra…	Fibre…
grasa	fat	protege contra el cáncer	protects against cancer
sal	salt	combate la obesidad	combats obesity
vitaminas	vitamins	reduce el riesgo de enfermedades	reduces the risk of diseases
azúcar	sugar	evitar comer / beber…	avoid eating / drinking…
gluten	gluten	cambiar mi dieta	change my diet
el sabor	taste	llevar una dieta equilibrada	have a balanced diet
vegetariano / vegano	vegetarian / vegan	preparar con ingredientes frescos	prepare with fresh ingredients
saludable / sano / malsano	healthy / healthy / unhealthy	engordar	to put on weight
(No) Tengo hambre / sed / sueño.	I am (not) hungry / thirsty / tired.	saltarse el desayuno	to skip breakfast
tiempo para cocinar	time to cook	practicar más deporte	to do more sport
contiene / contienen	it contains / they contain		

¡Vivir a tope! / Live life to the full

Beber alcohol…	To drink / Drinking alcohol…	tiene muchos riesgos	has many risks
Fumar cigarrillos / porros…	To smoke / Smoking cigarettes / joints…	afecta a tu capacidad para tomar decisiones	affects your capacity to make decisions
Tomar drogas blandas / duras…	To take / Taking soft / hard drugs…	te relaja / te quita el estrés	relaxes you / relieves stress
Es / No es…	It is / isn't…	te quita el sueño / control	robs you of sleep / self-control
ilegal / peligroso	illegal / dangerous	te hace sentir bien / más adulto	makes you feel good / more adult
un malgasto de dinero	a waste of money	Es fácil engancharse.	It is easy to get hooked.
una tontería / un problema serio	stupid / a serious problem	¡Qué asco!	How disgusting!.
un vicio muy caro	an expensive habit	Cedí ante la presión de grupo .	I gave in to peer pressure.
muy perjudicial para la salud	very damaging to your health	Caí en el hábito de…	I fell into the habit of…
tan malo	as bad	Empecé a…	I started to…
provoca mal aliento	causes bad breath	Perdí peso.	I lost weight.
daña los pulmones	damages the lungs	No puedo parar.	I can't stop.
mancha los dientes de amarillo	stains your teeth yellow	Ya he empezado a…	I've already started to…
causa el fracaso escolar / depresión	causes failure at school / depression	Todavía no he dejado de…	I still haven't given up…
produce una fuerte dependencia física	produces a strong, physical dependence	A partir de ahora intentaré…	From now on I will try to…

¡El deporte nos une! / Sport unites us!

¿Para qué sirven…?	What are…for?	dar un impulso económico	give a boost to the economy
los eventos deportivos internacionales	international sporting events	inspirar a la gente	inspire people
los grandes acontecimientos deportivos	big sporting events	Una / Otra desventaja es…	A / Another disadvantage is…
		el riesgo de ataques terroristas	the risk of terrorist attacks
los Juegos Paralímpicos / Olímpicos	the Paralympics / Olympics	el tráfico	the traffic
la Copa Mundial del Fútbol	the Football World Cup	el dopaje	doping
Sirven para…	They serve to…	la deuda	the debt
promover…	promote / foster / encourage…	el coste de organización de la seguridad	the cost of organising the security
la participación en el deporte	participation in sport	la ciudad anfitriona	the host city
el espíritu de solidaridad	team spirit	el voluntariado	volunteering
regenerar los centros urbanos	regenerate city centres	Solicité un trabajo voluntario porque…	I applied for a volunteering job because…
elevar el orgullo nacional	increase national pride	(Nunca) Había sido…	I had (never) been…
transmitir los valores de respeto y disciplina	convey / instil the values of respect and discipline	Antes ya había trabajado como…	Previously I had already worked as…
unir a la gente	unite people		

¡Apúntate! / Sign up!

¿Qué estabas haciendo?	What were you doing?	Estaba…	I / He/She was…
Estaba / Estábamos / Estaban…	I/He/She/It was / We were / They were…	mirando/viendo las noticias / la tele	watching the news / the TV
ensayando	rehearsing	buscando informaciones en línea	looking for information online
nevando	snowing	charlando con un amigo / una amiga	chatting with a friend
entrando en casa	coming into the house	leyendo un post en Facebook	reading a Facebook post
durmiendo	sleeping	cuando…	when…
conduciendo por la ciudad	driving through the city	encontré un reportaje / un artículo	I found a report / an article
leyendo	reading	recibí un SMS	I received a text message
volando por el aire	flying through the air	(lo) vi en las noticias	I saw (it) on the news
Se estaba convirtiendo en un río.	It was turning into a river.	mi novio me llamó / me contó la historia	my boyfriend called me / told me the story
Se estaba moviendo.	It was moving.	una organización de servicio voluntario	a voluntary organisation
a mi alrededor	around me	una campaña para las víctimas	a campaign for the victims
Se estaban cayendo.	They were falling.	una caja de supervivencia	a survival box
¿Cómo te enteraste del/de la/ de las…?	How did you find out about the…?	Decidí apuntarme.	I decided to sign up.
temblor	tremor	recaudar fondos / solicitar donativos	to raise funds / ask for donations
incendio forestal	forest fire	organizamos algunos eventos	we organised some events
huracán	hurricane	un concierto / un espectáculo de baile	a concert / a dance show
tornado	tornado	una carrera de bici apadrinada	a sponsored bike race
terremoto	earthquake	una venta de pasteles	a cake sale
tormenta de nieve	snow storm	ser solidario	showing solidarity / supporting…
acción humanitaria	humanitaria campaign	Te hace sentir más conectado con los demás.	Makes you feed more connected to others.
inundaciones	floods		

Módulo 1 ¡A repasar!

1 *Refresh your memory!* Translate these adjectives into **Spanish**. Write a sentence about a past holiday using each one.

Ejemplo 1 *picturesque – pintoresco/a*

El verano pasado fuimos a Barcelona y vi unos monumentos **pintorescos**.

1. picturesque
2. amazing
3. luxurious
4. cosy
5. unforgettable
6. lively
7. noisy

> Remember to make adjectives agree. Is the noun masculine or feminine and is it singular or plural?

2 *Refresh your memory!* Rewrite these sentences in the past tense. Do you need the preterite or the imperfect for each verb?

Ejemplo 1 *Saqué fotos cuando estaba en la montaña.*

1. Saco fotos cuando estoy en la montaña.
2. La pensión está cerca de la costa, pero no tiene piscina.
3. Vamos a la playa y hacemos una barbacoa cuando hace calor.
4. Voy solo y me quedo en un parador pequeño que tiene mucho ambiente.
5. El hotel tiene vistas al mar y además, es muy cómodo.
6. Lo paso muy bien porque hago el vago y leo mis libros.

3 *Refresh your memory!* Listen to these people talking about their holidays. (1–4)

Note down in **English**:
- where they stayed
- what was good about the holiday
- what was bad about it.

4 **Opinions about a hotel in Costa Rica.**

Listen to your Spanish friends, Maribel and Luis, talking about a new hotel.

What is their opinion of these aspects?
Write **P** for a **positive** opinion.
Write **N** for a **negative** opinion.
Write **P+N** for a **positive** and **negative** opinion.

Maribel
a location ☐   b restaurant ☐

Luis
a rooms ☐   b sports' facilities ☐

Costa Rica

> Listen to the whole sentence before choosing your answers. Concentrate on identifying any positive or negative adjectives as well as any opinions. Pay attention to any connectives that could indicate a positive and negative view such as *aunque*.

Módulo 1

5 leer

Holidays

You receive this email from your Spanish friend, Carmen, while she is on holiday.

> ¿Qué tal? Estoy fenomenal aquí en Portugal. Llegamos hace tres días y el camping está muy limpio y hay un montón de actividades de las que se puede disfrutar. El año pasado pasamos cuatro días aquí, pero esta vez vamos a estar una semana entera.
>
> Me encanta este camping y ahora es mucho mejor porque lo han renovado completamente. Antes no había tienda y los baños estaban muy sucios, pero han construido una tienda que tiene mucha variedad de productos. Ayer compramos dos bañadores y mucha fruta deliciosa. Tampoco te daban toallas para usarlas en la piscina, pero ahora sí te las dan y no hay que pagar nada. También es fantástico que ahora se puedan alquilar equipos deportivos como cañas de pescar. Sin embargo, lo que más me gusta es la nueva piscina. Es increíble y cuenta con dos toboganes.
>
> Ayer mi hermano menor y yo nos lanzamos por el tobogán más grande y aterrizamos en la piscina riéndonos a carcajadas. ¡Fue muy divertido!
>
> Tengo muchas ganas de verte muy pronto.
>
> Un abrazo,
> Carmen

Answer the questions in English.

1. How long is Carmen staying at the campsite?
2. How has the campsite changed recently? Mention **three** things.
3. What does she like best about the campsite?
4. How did her brother and her feel yesterday?

6 leer

Translate the first paragraph from exercise 5 into English.

7 escribir

Look at the task card and do this extended writing task.

> Has hecho un intercambio con un colegio español en Madrid. Escribe un artículo para una revista española para interesar a otros estudiantes en hacer un intercambio.
> Menciona:
> - lo que hiciste en el intercambio
> - por qué los intercambios son importantes.
>
> Escribe aproximadamente **150** palabras en **español**. Responde a los dos aspectos de la pregunta.

⭐ To answer the second bullet point, look back at page 144 about why languages are important. Could you adapt any ideas from there to use here?

8 escribir

Translate the following passage into Spanish.

> Often people go on holiday to the mountains and, if the weather is good, it is fun to be outside. The views are beautiful. According to a survey, last winter many families stayed in apartments instead of luxury hotels. However, I am going to stay at home because last year I had a skiing accident.

ciento ochenta y tres **183**

Módulo 2 ¡A repasar!

1 *escribir*

Refresh your memory! Look back at Module 2 and find examples of the following. Then close the book and write them down from memory.

- **five** items of school uniform, e.g. *una chaqueta*
- **five** opinion verbs/phrases to say what you think of your school, e.g. *me interesa…*
- **five** reasons for liking or disliking teachers, e.g. *explica bien*
- **five** phrases about your primary school (in the imperfect), e.g. *no había laboratorios*

2 *escuchar*

Refresh your memory! Listen to a girl talking about school rules. Note down in **English** the **four** things you are <u>not</u> allowed to do in her school.

3 *escuchar*

An interview with María Luisa, a volunteer at a nursery in Ecuador

You are listening on the Internet to this interview with María Luisa.

What **four** questions does the interviewer ask her? Write the questions in **English**.

4 *escuchar*

El instituto

Estás con tus amigos, Jorge y Gabriela, que hablan de sus actividades extraescolares.

¿De qué actividades hablan y cuándo las realizan? Completa la tabla en **español**.

1

En el pasado	Ahora	En el futuro
volver a casa		

2

En el pasado	Ahora	En el futuro
		cantar en el coro

⭐ You need to make sure that you complete the grid in Spanish with the **complete phrase** that describes the activity. For example, if the activity mentioned were *prefiero aprender francés* you could not just write *francés*, nor could you write just the word *aprender*. The correct phrase to write would be *aprender francés*.

184 *ciento ochenta y cuatro*

5 leer

My life as a girl in Chile

Read this extract from *Mi país inventado*, a memoir by Isabel Allende, and answer the questions which follow in **English**.

> Algunas familias [...] mandaban a sus hijas a la universidad, pero no era el caso de la mía. [...] Se esperaba que mis hermanos fueran profesionales – en lo posible abogados, médicos o ingenieros. [...] En esos años las mujeres profesionales provenían en su mayoría de la clase media. [...] Eso ha cambiado y hoy el nivel de educación de las mujeres es incluso superior al de los hombres. Yo no era mala estudiante, pero como ya tenía novio, a nadie se le ocurrió que podía obtener una profesión. [...] Terminé la secundaria a los dieciséis años confundida e inmadura, [...] pero siempre tuve claro que debía trabajar.

Isabel Allende

1. Whom did some families send to university?
2. What jobs did her family want her brothers to do? Give **two** examples.
3. Why did her family think she would not need a job?
4. How old was she when she left school?

⭐ When faced with a complex text, read the questions first to give you an idea on what the text is about and what information you will need to find. Try not to worry if the first few sentences contain unfamiliar words or difficult grammar. Keep going and focus on the answers you have to find!

6 hablar

Prepare and perform this role play.

Your teacher will play the part of your Spanish friend and will speak first.
You should address your friend as *tú*.
When you see this – **!** – you will have to respond to something you have not prepared.
When you see this – **?** – you will have to ask a question.

Estás hablando con tu amigo español / tu amiga española sobre el intercambio.
- Club de informática – cuándo.
- Tus planes para después del colegio.
- **!**
- **?** Preferencias – comida.
- Tu opinión sobre el intercambio.

7 escribir

Translate the following passage into Spanish.

> My friend is addicted to her mobile. At school she takes photos of everyone and downloads music at break time. She never wants to talk with us and she does not have time to read or do anything else. Last week she lost it on the bus and we had to go to the police station. She is going to have to buy another one.

ciento ochenta y cinco **185**

Módulo 3   ¡A repasar!

1 *Refresh your memory!* Complete the sentences with an appropriate word or phrase. Look back through Module 3 for ideas.

1. Siempre uso aplicaciones para ———.
2. Mi móvil es útil para ———.
3. En este momento estoy ——— en casa.
4. No puedo ir al concierto porque tengo que ———.
5. Quiero ——— porque está lloviendo.
6. Creo que leer en formato digital ———.

⭐ Think carefully about which of the phrases in exercise 1 require a verb in the infinitive and which require a different verb form.

2 *Refresh your memory!* Listen to Ángel and Cristina talking about reading.

1. What does Ángel like and dislike reading?
2. Why does Cristina like reading?
3. What do they each think about e-books and why?

Ángel   Cristina

3 *Refresh your memory!* Choose **four** family members or friends. Note down **two** physical characteristics and **two** character traits for each of them. Then write out a full description of **one** of them.

Example *Mi hermano – pelo corto, bajo, tonto, travieso*
Mi hermano es bastante bajo y tiene el pelo corto. Creo que es muy tonto y es travieso.

4 A radio announcement

You are listening to this public announcement on Spanish radio.
Answer the question in **English**.

What does the public announcement urge people to do?

5 A science and technology fair

You are listening to a programme about a science and technology fair.
The presenter is giving information about the fair.

What does he say?

Answer both parts of the question in **English**.

a. Why is this fair aimed at students in particular? Give **two** reasons.
b. What does he advise doing before purchasing tickets online?

⭐ Prepare by thinking about key vocabulary you may hear to answer the questions. You would expect to hear *estudiantes* or *alumnos* for students and *entradas* and/or the verb *comprar* for purchasing tickets.

ciento ochenta y seis

Módulo 3

6 A magazine article

You read this article on a Spanish website.

> **Las redes sociales. ¿Diversión o peligro?**
>
> Los adolescentes dedican gran parte de su tiempo libre a las redes sociales. Millones de usuarios chatean y mandan mensajes a través de Twitter, Snapchat y muchas otras redes. Las ventajas son muchas, sin embargo, muchos adolescentes no conocen los peligros existentes.
>
> Un gran problema es la privacidad. Por ejemplo, se pueden recibir y aceptar solicitudes de amistad de extraños. También las fotos que sube un adolescente pueden ser vistas por personas desconocidas. Esto puede representar un peligro para la seguridad de los adolescentes.
>
> Un experimento reciente intenta alertar de los peligros que pueden suponer las redes sociales. Un hombre contactó con tres niñas adolescentes, y aunque ellas conocían los peligros de contactar con extraños, accedieron a tener una cita con el desconocido.
>
> No todo es negativo, pero los padres deberían dar más consejos a los jóvenes y apoyarlos en cualquier problema. Es importante aceptar que las redes también están para divertirse.

1 According to the article, what do lots of social media users do? Write the correct letter.
- **A** Use the networks safely
- **B** Spend too much time on the networks
- **C** Communicate in different ways on the sites

2 According to the article, what risks do social media sites pose? Write the **two** correct letters.
- **A** Users' age is not always verified correctly.
- **B** On some sites strangers can contact teenagers easily.
- **C** Inappropriate photos can be seen online.
- **D** Photos are never truly private.

Answer the questions in **English.**

3 Who was involved in a recent social media experiment?

4 According to the writer of the article, what should parents or teachers do to help young people? Give **one** detail.

7 Prepare and perform this photo card discussion.

Look at the photo and make notes. Your teacher will then ask you questions about the photo and about topics related to **free-time activities**.

Your teacher will ask you the following **three** questions and then **two** more questions which you have not prepared:
- ¿Qué hay en la foto?
- ¿Es importante leer libros?
- ¿Qué hiciste con tus amigos la semana pasada?

⭐ Use part of the preparation time to think about what the two unprepared questions might be. What else could you be asked about? Brainstorm some ideas in Spanish on a separate sheet.

8 Translate the following passage into **Spanish.**

I am quite tall and I have long curly hair. My friends tell me that I am a little lazy, but it's not true. I met my best friend three years ago at school. We get on very well. For me, a good friend is someone who never judges you. I hope to be his friend forever.

ciento ochenta y siete **187**

Módulo 4 ¡A repasar!

1 *Refresh your memory!* Listen to Mónica talking about her leisure activities and note down the following:

- what hobbies she does regularly
- what she likes to do most and why
- how her taste in films has changed
- what she does to relax
- something she has done recently.

2 *Refresh your memory!* Complete the following sentences with an appropriate phrase. Look back through Module 4 for ideas.
1 Gasto mi paga en ———.
2 Acabo de ———.
3 Suelo ver ———.
4 ¿Has leído ———?

3 *Refresh your memory!* Make a list of **ten** adjectives that you could use to describe a book, film or leisure activity. Avoid the obvious ones like *interesante*, *aburrido* and *divertido*!

> ⭐ Having a bank of interesting and less common adjectives at your fingertips will raise the level of your Spanish. Create your own top ten!

4 **Christmas celebrations**

You are listening to your Spanish friends, Antonio and Cristina, who are talking about what they like and dislike about celebrating Christmas.

What do they like and dislike about the celebrations?

A Traditional food
B Being with family
C Videogames
D Television
E Going out with friends
F Church
G Board games
H Fireworks
I Night life
J Relaxing

Write the correct letter for each gap.
Answer both parts of each question.

1 Antonio likes ☐ and ☐.
   Antonio dislikes ☐ and ☐.

2 Cristina likes ☐ and ☐.
   Cristina dislikes ☐ and ☐.

ciento ochenta y ocho

5 Una página web

Vas de vacaciones a Madrid con tu familia y buscas información en Internet sobre lo que podréis hacer allí.

El festival nacional de lectura

En mayo va a tener lugar la Feria del Libro de Madrid, que se celebra una vez al año. Fanáticos de la lectura van a asistir y habrá un ambiente perfecto para encontrar los últimos libros. Hay más de trescientas casetas* dedicadas a libros, revistas y tebeos. Es uno de los eventos de ocio más importantes de la capital.

A finales de la primavera en la ciudad hace sol aunque hizo mal tiempo cuando la feria reunió a miles de visitantes el año pasado. Éstos aprovecharon para hablar de sus libros favoritos y participaron en muchos de los eventos. En el pabellón infantil, los niños suelen hacer actividades como escuchar cuentos emocionantes.

*las casetas = stalls / stands

Contesta a las preguntas en español.

Ejemplo ¿Cuándo va a tener lugar la feria? En mayo.

1. ¿Qué tipo de personas suelen visitar el evento?
2. ¿Qué tiempo hizo durante la feria del año pasado?
3. ¿Qué suelen hacer los visitantes más pequeños?

> Don't try to translate every word as you read. It will take too long and you may get stuck on certain phrases. Read through quickly to get the gist, then look at the questions, to see what information you need to find.

6 Translate the first paragraph from exercise 5 into English.

7 Look at the task card and do this shorter writing task.

Acabas de ver una película. Escribe un artículo para una revista española para adolescentes sobre la película.

Menciona:
- cuándo fuiste y con quién
- el tema de la película
- tu opinión de la película
- tus planes para el sábado que viene

Escribe aproximadamente **90** palabras en **español**. Responde a todos los aspectos de la pregunta.

8 Translate the following passage into Spanish.

In my free time, I love to use the computer at home. I have just played a new videogame, which has amazing graphics. I am already a fan! Sometimes my friends and I go to the cinema. On Saturday we are going to see a foreign film. Last month we went to the circus and I would love to see another similar show.

Módulo 5   ¡A repasar!

1 escribir — *Refresh your memory!* Look back at Module 5 and write down:
- **four** phrases which use *estar* to describe the location of a town or village, e.g. *Está al lado de las montañas.*
- **five** adjectives to describe a city, e.g. *famosa*
- **five** phrases which use verbs in the future tense, e.g. *Iremos a la playa.*
- exclamations to enhance your speaking or writing, e.g. *¡Qué bien!*

2 escuchar — *Refresh your memory!* Listen to these conversations in different shops. Note down in **English** the problem and the outcome in each case. (1–3)

3 hablar — *Refresh your memory!* In pairs, take five minutes to look at the pros and cons of living in a city on page 104, then close the book. Who can remember the most statements?
- Lo mejor es…
- Lo peor es…

4 escuchar — **Interview with a Spanish company director**
You are listening to a podcast with the company director, Pilar Gutiérrez.

1 Answer all parts of the question in **English**.
 a What does her company sell?
 b How does she describe the products?
 c According to Pilar, why is the company successful?

2 Answer both parts of the question in **English**.
 d What will the company do before purchasing more shops in other countries?
 e Why should you work in the clothing industry?

> ★ Remember, you will need to be able to **deduce meaning** from what you hear by extracting the correct information and drawing conclusions. When you are listening to interviews, the questions asked are key for being able to do this. Do not ignore them!

190 *ciento noventa*

5 leer

Mateo's day in Barcelona

Read the extract from *El día de mañana,* a novel by Ignacio Martínez de Pisón, and answer the questions which follow in **English**.

> Lo que más me gustaba era subir la torre de la iglesia, que era el punto más alto de la ciudad, y observarlo todo desde allí arriba: los campos, las carreteras cercanas, las calles, el mar. Para mí, el día más feliz de todos fue el de la gran Navidad del 1962. Durante toda la Nochebuena no paró de nevar y, cuando nos despertamos por la mañana, había casi un metro de nieve por todas partes.
>
> Salimos al jardín e hicimos una guerra de bolas de nieve y cuando subí las escaleras de la iglesia me sentí feliz al ver Barcelona. Las calles, los coches y hasta* los barcos del Puerto estaban cubiertos de nieve. Eso fue para mí un momento de felicidad absoluta, mirando en silencio aquella Barcelona tan blanca y tan hermosa…
>
> *hasta = even*

Example *What did Mateo like most?* climbing the church tower

1. What happened on Christmas Eve?
2. What was he surprised to see covered in snow?
3. How does he describe the moment when he viewed Barcelona from the tower?

6 hablar

Prepare and perform this role play.

Your teacher will play the part of the assistant and will speak first.
You should address the assistant as *usted*.
When you see this – **!** – you will have to respond to something you have not prepared.
When you see this – **?** – you will have to ask a question.

Usted está hablando con el empleado/la empleada de una tienda de recuerdos.
- Regalo comprado – cuál, cuándo.
- Problema con el regalo (**dos** detalles).
- **?** Solución – cambiar.
- **!**
- Tu opinión sobre el pueblo.

7 escribir

Translate the following passage into Spanish.

My area is located in a valley which has beautiful landscapes. The best thing is that there are incredible views and lots of great shops to visit in the city centre. Last summer, my Spanish friend and I took a tourist bus to see all the old buildings. If the weather is good tomorrow, we will go to the beach.

Módulo 6 ¡A repasar!

1 **Refresh your memory!** Put the food and drink from the box into **four** lists using the headings below. Then translate each item into **English**.

- Lácteos
- Carnes y pescados
- Frutas y verduras
- Bebidas

una lata de cerveza	unas chuletas de cerdo	queso de cabra
un kilo de zanahorias	un filete	un yogur de frambuesa
medio kilo de albaricoques	dos cebollas	un zumo de pomelo
un litro de leche semidesnatada		

2 **Refresh your memory!** Listen to people describing music festivals. (1–3)

Note down in **English**:
- the type of music mentioned
- whether the festival is in the past or the future
- whether the description is positive (P), negative (N) or positive and negative (P+N).

> ⭐ Time expressions do not always tell you whether something is in the past or the future, so listen for the tense of the verb used. E.g.
>
> El jueves **fuimos** a un concierto. — On Thursday **we went** to a concert.
>
> El jueves **vamos a ir** a un concierto. — On Thursday **we are going to go** to a concert.

3 **San Sebastián**

Un amigo español, Rubén, está hablando de los 'pinchos' de San Sebastián. Escuchas su conversación.

1 Escribe las **tres** letras correctas.
Según Rubén, los 'pinchos'…
- A no son caros.
- B no son famosos en el extranjero.
- C se comen sentados.
- D no son platos grandes.
- E pueden contener pescado.
- F no pueden contener huevos.

2 Escribe la letra correcta.
En San Sebastián, la amiga de Rubén prefiere…
- A los museos.
- B las fiestas.
- C los parques.

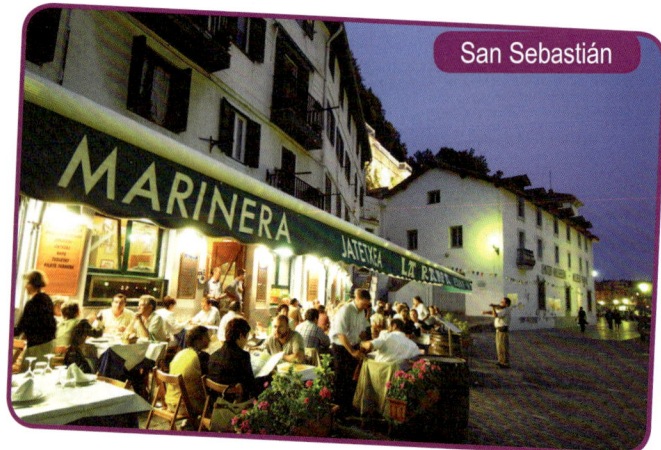

4 Trabajos de verano para estudiantes

Unos estudiantes españoles buscan trabajo este verano.

Trabajos de verano

Ejemplos de los trabajos de verano que se ofrecen este año:

1. Una cafetería en la costa está buscando gente con energía, buen humor y lenguas extranjeras para trabajar en su establecimiento.
2. Una escuela de idiomas necesita jóvenes que quieran enseñar inglés como lengua extranjera.
3. Tendrás la oportunidad de aprender a cocinar platos típicos como mariscos, arroces y paellas.
4. ¿Te interesa saber más de la cultura Japonesa? Ven a servir comida en un nuevo restaurante.
5. Una experiencia inolvidable: ser voluntario en los Sanfermines y ayudar a miles de personas a participar en la fiesta.
6. El campo te necesita. Buscamos jóvenes para la recogida de albaricoques, aguacates y ciruelas.
7. Un centro de deportes acuáticos busca gente para ayudar en su tienda los sábados.

Tus amigos te envían un mensaje mencionando los trabajos que les interesan.
¿Qué trabajos van a escoger?

Escribe el número correcto.

Ejemplo *Quiero saber más de la cocina española.* **Paula** 3

1. Hago windsurf o piragüismo en mi tiempo libre y ya he trabajado en un supermercado. **Félix**
2. Hablo francés y alemán y soy muy divertida. **Nuria**
3. Ya tengo experiencia de trabajar en eventos grandes. **Óscar**
4. Estoy estudiando en la universidad y quiero trabajar por las tardes. Me apasiona la cultura asiática. **Ainhoa**
5. Trato de llevar una vida muy sana y la fruta es mi pasión. **Darío**

5 Translate into **English** the first **three** job descriptions in exercise 4.

6 Look at the task card and do this extended writing task.

Lees un blog sobre eventos benéficos y se lo mandas a tu amigo español. Escríbele un mensaje.

Menciona:
- lo que hiciste cuando fuiste a un festival musical benéfico
- qué vas a hacer por una organización benéfica.

Escribe aproximadamente **150** palabras en **español**. Responde a los dos aspectos de la pregunta.

⭐ Remember to use the correct tense(s) when responding directly to both bullet points. For this question, you need to write, in detail, about a past event and what you are going to do in the future to support a charity. To score highly, you need to make sure you also **express** and **justify opinions**.

7 Translate the following passage into **Spanish**.

I am very interested in Spanish culture and therefore last year I went to a very exciting festival in the north of Spain with my parents. They let off lots of fireworks. We loved the processions and the music. Next year I hope to go back again as I would like to take more photos.

Módulo 7 ¡A repasar!

1 **Refresh your memory!** In pairs, look at pages 158–159 and memorise as many jobs and adjectives as you can in two minutes. Then take it in turns to say a sentence about a job.

- Me gustaría ser jardinero/a porque es un trabajo variado.
- Quiero ser profesor/a porque es un trabajo importante.

2 **Refresh your memory!** Copy and complete the grid with the first person singular and plural forms of the verbs.

infinitive	present	preterite	imperfect	conditional
ganar (to earn)	gano ganamos	gané ganamos	ganaba ganábamos	ganaría ganaríamos
ayudar (to help)		ayudamos		
tener (to have)		tuvimos		tendría
hacer (to do)	hago			haríamos
ir (to go)	voy		iba	

⭐ Try to use the *nosotros* (we) form in your spoken and written work. It will add variety to your work.

3 **Refresh your memory!** Listen and answer the questions.

1. What job does Lucía do?
2. What are the good and bad points?
3. What has helped her career?
4. What does she want to do next?

4 **Opinions on jobs**

Listen to your Spanish friends, Laura and Tomás, talking about their jobs.

What are their opinions of these aspects?
Write **P** for a **positive** opinion.
Write **N** for a **negative** opinion.
Write **P+N** for a **positive** and **negative** opinion.

Laura
a salary   b colleagues

Tomás
a hours   b place of work

5 **Working in a bank**

You are listening to a radio programme about working for international companies.
Listen to Javier Fernández talking about his experiences.

Answer both parts of the question in **English**.

a Why does Javier think it is important to speak different languages? Give **two** reasons.
b What is the main advantage at work?

Módulo 7

6 Los primeros trabajos
Ves esta página en una revista sobre los primeros trabajos de estos jóvenes.

Recuerdo perfectamente mi primer trabajo. Fue en una empresa de marketing. Sacaba muchas fotocopias y me encargaba de repartir el correo. No era un trabajo muy interesante, pero mis colegas eran muy amables. **Rafael**

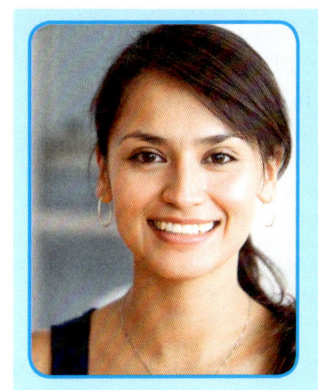

Mi primera experiencia tuvo lugar en la biblioteca de la universidad. El sueldo no era muy bueno, sin embargo, el horario me permitía asistir a clase. Organizaba los libros y muchas veces ayudaba en la sala de ordenadores. **Elena**

Contesta a las preguntas en español.
1. ¿Dónde trabajó Rafael por primera vez?
2. ¿Cuál fue la ventaja del trabajo?
3. ¿Dónde trabajó Elena por primera vez?
4. ¿Cuál fue la desventaja del trabajo?

> ⭐ When reading or listening for opinions, such as advantages and disadvantages, watch out for connectives which can change a negative statement into a positive one, or vice versa. E.g.
>
> *Mi trabajo no era muy interesante, **sin embargo**, el sueldo era excelente.*

7 Translate Rafael's text into English.

8 Prepare and perform this photo card discussion.

Look at the photo and make notes. Your teacher will then ask you questions about the photo and about topics related to **jobs, career choices and ambitions**.

Your teacher will ask you the following **three** questions and then **two** more questions which you have not prepared.
- ¿Qué hay en la foto?
- ¿Qué piensas de las prácticas laborales?
- ¿Qué te gustaría hacer cuando termines el colegio?

> ⭐ Use every opportunity possible to show you can use different tenses. E.g.
>
> *Para ganar dinero, normalmente **ayudo** a mis padres con algunas tareas en casa, pero antes **lavaba** el coche de mi madre.*

9 Translate the following passage into Spanish.

I love my job now because I work outside. Tomorrow, I am going to buy a car. I used to work in a hospital, but the salary was very bad. I had to answer telephone calls. I used to get on well with my boss because he was very understanding and I learned lots of new things.

ciento noventa y cinco

Módulo 8   ¡A repasar!

1 *Refresh your memory!* Read and unjumble these sentences about the importance of international sporting events. Then translate them into **English**.

1. para a eventos la Los sirven internacionales gente deportivos unir
2. de el Fomentan solidaridad espíritu
3. valores y Sirven los transmitir respeto para de disciplina
4. costes desventaja altos son una Los

2 *Refresh your memory!* In pairs, choose **three** of the following headings and create a mind map for each. Write at least **three** phrases for each one.

Example

- el desempleo
- las drogas
- la contaminación ambiental
- la pobreza mundial
- la violencia

el alcohol

Afecta a tu capacidad para tomar decisiones.

⭐ Make sure you have a good supply of opinion phrases to discuss complex issues. E.g.
Me parece muy importante el tema de…
Para mí, el problema más… es…
Look back through Module 8 and write down at least **six** other opinion phrases.

3 *Refresh your memory!* Listen to the conversation about environmental issues and note down which of the following are **not** mentioned:

- Floods
- Pollution of rivers and seas
- Too much rubbish
- Air pollution
- Fossil fuels running out
- Deforestation

4 **Radio forum about young people in Mexico**

You are listening to a radio programme. People are talking about problems facing young people in Mexico. For each speaker, choose the problem and write the correct letter.

A   Unemployment
B   Violence
C   Poverty
D   Obesity
E   Drugs

Answer all parts of the question.
a   Andrea
b   Sergio
c   Alba

⭐ It's a good idea to make notes in Spanish as you listen the first time, then choose the correct letter during or just after the second time the recording is played.

ciento noventa y seis

5 · The Galapagos Islands

You are doing some research on the Galapagos Islands and you find this interview with a Galapagos naturalist in a Spanish magazine.

– ¿Cuáles son los problemas a los que se enfrentan las islas Galápagos?
– Desafortunadamente, algunas de las especies de plantas y varios animales están en peligro de extinción. Además, existen otros problemas como la sobrepoblación, la contaminación y el exceso de turismo.

– ¿Algo en particular ha dañado estas islas?
– En enero de 2001, un barco petrolero derramó trescientas toneladas de petróleo, y el agua estuvo contaminada durante años. Este accidente se considera uno de los mayores desastres naturales. Para limitar el daño, el gobierno de Ecuador tomó medidas para la conservación del espacio ecológico de las islas: reguló el número de turistas y la navegación. A partir de ahora, el énfasis de las soluciones estará en la educación de la población para cuidar el medio ambiente.

las islas Galápagos

When do these headings apply to the Galapagos Islands? Write the correct letter.

Write **P** for something that happened in the **past**.
Write **N** for something that is happening **now**.
Write **F** for something that is going to happen in the **future**.

1. Oil spillages
2. Pollution
3. Public information
4. Lower number of tourists

6 · Look at the task card and do this extended writing task.

En un sitio web hay un concurso sobre '¿Por qué ser voluntario/a?'. El premio es la publicación del artículo en una famosa revista española. Decides participar.

Escribe un artículo con esta información:

- qué viste e hiciste cuando trabajaste como voluntario/a
- por qué te gustaría ser voluntario/a otra vez.

Escribe aproximadamente **150** palabras en **español**. Responde a los dos aspectos de la pregunta.

⭐ To impress in your writing, try to use a variety of verb endings, avoiding too many *yo* (I) endings.

e.g. La última vez que trabajé como voluntario **fue** cuando ayudé en un centro para animales abandonados y enfermos cerca de mi casa. Mi amiga también **trabajó** conmigo allí los fines de semana y **había** mucho que hacer. Muchos animales **sobrevivieron** y **encontraron** un nuevo hogar, pero otros no. **Fue** bastante triste, pero mi amiga y yo **aprendimos** mucho.

7 · Translate the following passage into **Spanish**.

In my opinion, smoking is dangerous and also a waste of money. In my school, some young people think that it is fun to drink alcohol, but from my point of view it causes violence and can cause depression too. Last week my older sister stopped smoking and now she is going to take part in a 10 km run.

General conversation questions

⭐ Your course is made up of several topics which are grouped into three **Themes**:
- Theme 1 – Identity and culture
- Theme 2 – Local, national, international and global areas of interest
- Theme 3 – Current and future study and employment

For the **General Conversation** in the speaking exam, you will be required to answer questions on **two** Themes. You can choose one of the Themes in advance. Your teacher may ask you to prepare answers to the questions below (on your chosen Theme and the other Themes) in order to get ready for this.

Module 1
(From Theme 2) Travel and tourism
1. ¿Qué haces en verano?
2. ¿Dónde prefieres pasar las vacaciones? ¿Por qué?
3. ¿Adónde fuiste de vacaciones el año pasado?
4. ¿Dónde te alojaste?
5. ¿Cómo era el pueblo/la ciudad?
6. ¿Qué fue lo mejor de tus vacaciones?
7. ¿Qué planes tienes para el próximo verano?
8. ¿Por qué son importantes las vacaciones?
9. ¿Por qué veranea tanta gente en el extranjero?
10. ¿Adónde irías si tuvieras mucho dinero? ¿Por qué?

Module 2
(From Theme 3) My studies; Life at school/college
1. ¿Cómo es tu instituto? ¿Qué instalaciones tiene/no tiene?
2. ¿Qué asignaturas te gustan y no te gustan? ¿Por qué?
3. ¿Qué opinas del uniforme escolar?
4. ¿Qué piensas de las normas de tu insti?
5. ¿Qué actividades extraescolares haces?
6. ¿Qué planes tienes para este trimestre?
7. ¿Qué es lo bueno/malo de tu insti?
8. Compara tu escuela primaria con tu instituto.
9. ¿Hay diferencias entre los institutos españoles y tu instituto?
10. ¿Puedes describir un intercambio o un viaje escolar que hiciste en el pasado?

Module 3
(From Theme 1) Me, my family and friends; Technology in everyday life
1. Describe a un buen amigo tuyo/una buena amiga tuya.
2. ¿Quiénes son más importantes, tus amigos o tus padres? ¿Por qué?
3. ¿Crees que los jóvenes están obsesionados con sus móviles? ¿Por qué (no)?
4. ¿Qué aplicaciones usas para estar en contacto con tus amigos y con tu familia?
5. ¿Qué piensas de las redes sociales?
6. ¿Qué te gusta leer? ¿Por qué?
7. ¿Te llevas bien con tu familia? ¿Por qué (no)?
8. Describe a una persona de tu familia.
9. ¿Por qué es importante pasar tiempo en familia?
10. ¿Qué planes tienes con tus amigos o con tu familia este fin de semana?

Module 4
(From Theme 1) Free-time activities (music, cinema and TV, sport)
1. ¿Qué sueles hacer en tus ratos libres?
2. ¿Eres teleadicto/a? ¿Por qué (no)?
3. ¿Prefieres ver películas en casa o en el cine? ¿Por qué?
4. ¿Te gusta la música? ¿Por qué (no)?
5. ¿Tus padres te dan dinero? ¿Qué haces con la paga?
6. ¿Qué planes tienes para este fin de semana?
7. ¿Eres muy deportista? ¿Por qué (no)?
8. Háblame de la última vez que participaste en un deporte.
9. ¿En qué consiste un buen modelo a seguir?
10. ¿Quién es tu modelo a seguir?

⭐ As well as answering questions, you must also ask your teacher a question at some point during the General Conversation.

Module 5
(From Theme 2) Home, town, neighbourhood and region

1. ¿Cómo es la ciudad o el pueblo donde vives?
2. ¿Cuál es tu ciudad favorita? ¿Por qué te gusta?
3. ¿Dónde te gusta comprar? ¿Por qué?
4. ¿Qué es mejor, vivir en la ciudad o en el campo? ¿Por qué?
5. ¿Qué hay para turistas en tu zona? ¿Qué se puede hacer?
6. ¿Qué hiciste recientemente en tu zona?
7. ¿Cómo cambiarías tu zona?
8. ¿Qué harás en tu ciudad este fin de semana, si hace buen tiempo? Y ¿si hace mal tiempo?
9. ¿Adónde fuiste de compras la última vez y qué compraste? ¿Qué hiciste?
10. Describe una visita que hiciste a una ciudad (en Gran Bretaña o en otro país).

Module 6
(From Theme 1) Customs and festivals in Spanish-speaking countries/communities; Free-time activities (food and eating out)

1. ¿Qué te gusta comer? ¿Por qué?
2. ¿Has probado la comida española? ¿Te gusta? ¿Por qué (no)?
3. ¿Prefieres cenar en casa o en un restaurante? ¿Por qué?
4. Háblame de lo que hiciste en un día especial reciente con tus amigos o tu familia.
5. ¿Cómo vas a celebrar tu próximo cumpleaños?
6. ¿Has asistido a un festival de música? ¿Puedes describirlo?
7. Háblame de lo que hiciste por Navidad el año pasado.
8. ¿Cuál es la fiesta más importante, en tu opinión?
9. ¿Crees que las fiestas tradicionales son importantes? ¿Por qué (no)?
10. Háblame de una fiesta a la que te gustaría asistir.

Module 7
(From Theme 3) Education post-16; Jobs, career choices and ambitions

1. ¿Tienes un trabajo a tiempo parcial? ¿Qué haces?
2. ¿Qué planes tienes para seguir estudiando en el futuro?
3. ¿Qué opinas de ir a la universidad? ¿Por qué?
4. ¿Cómo ayudas con las tareas domésticas?
5. ¿Dónde hiciste tus prácticas laborales?
6. ¿En qué te gustaría trabajar? ¿Por qué?
7. ¿Crees que es importante aprender otras lenguas? ¿Por qué (no)?
8. ¿Cómo pasarías un año sabático? ¿Por qué?
9. ¿Qué otras ambiciones tienes?
10. ¿Qué cosas te importan más en la vida? ¿Por qué?

Module 8
(From Theme 2) Home; Social issues; Global issues

1. ¿Cómo te puedes mantener en forma?
2. ¿Qué opinas de fumar?
3. ¿Cómo se debería cuidar el medio ambiente?
4. Si fueras millonario, ¿cómo sería tu casa ideal? ¿Qué tendría?
5. ¿Qué haces en casa para proteger el medio ambiente?
6. ¿Cuáles son los problemas globales más serios hoy en día?
7. ¿Cómo se pueden solucionar los problemas?
8. ¿Para qué sirven los eventos deportivos internacionales?
9. ¿Es importante ser solidario? ¿Por qué (no)?
10. ¿Si tuvieras mucho dinero, cómo ayudarías a los demás?

ciento noventa y nueve

Te toca a ti: Módulo 1

1 Match the sentence halves and copy them out in a logical order. Then translate them.

1 El último día fuimos a Terra Mítica, un parque de…
2 Mis vacaciones fueron inolvidables, pero lo…
3 Hace dos años fui de vacaciones a Benidorm…
4 Luego, por la tarde fui al centro de la…
5 Al día siguiente por la mañana hice…
6 El primer día hizo mucho calor. Cuando…

a ciudad y compré recuerdos para mis amigos.
b llegamos al hotel, decidimos ir a la playa.
c mejor fue cuando aprendí a bucear en el mar. ¡Qué guay!
d turismo. Subí a la Torre Morales y saqué muchas fotos.
e con mi familia. Viajamos en avión y en autocar.
f atracciones, donde vomité en una montaña rusa. ¡Qué horror!

2 Write a paragraph about your holidays, using exercise 1 as an example.

3 Read the texts and questions. Write I (Isabel), T (Tomás) or I+T (Isabel and Tomás).

Isabel-98
La Palma

¡Hotel horroroso!
Pasé un finde en este hotel y no era nada barato – 150 € por noche. ¡Qué timo! Las habitaciones estaban muy sucias, la ducha estaba estropeada y no había toallas. También había basura en la piscina. Cuando fuimos a cenar, la comida estaba fría y había un insecto en mi sopa. Pero lo peor fue que el recepcionista tenía muy mala actitud.

TomásFG
Bilbao

Experiencia malísima
No recomiendo este hotel. No tenía ni wifi ni aire acondicionado en las habitaciones. Tampoco tenía aparcamiento. El gimnasio no estaba abierto y el ascensor estaba estropeado. Había una discoteca que tenía la música muy alta, y por eso era imposible dormir. Además, el camarero en el restaurante era muy maleducado. Pero lo peor fue que había una serpiente en el balcón. ¡Qué miedo!

Who mentions…
1 the rooms?
2 the staff?
3 the food?
4 the noise?
5 the sports facilities?
6 the price?
7 the bathroom?
8 a scary reptile?

el finde el fin de semana (slang)
¡Qué timo! What a con!

4 Write about a holiday from hell, using the pictures. Add extra details.

Te toca a ti: Módulo 2

1 Read Lina's text and join the English sentence halves correctly.

> Mi instituto es grande, mixto y tiene muy buena fama, dado que los alumnos siempre sacan buenas notas. Además, no hay ni mucho acoso escolar ni falta de disciplina. El año pasado mi insti ocupó el primer lugar en el ranking oficial de colegios en Madrid.
>
> A mi parecer, mi instituto ofrece muy buenas oportunidades extraescolares, sobre todo si eres músico. En junio mis amigos y yo participamos en un concurso de bandas jóvenes, y los profesores de música nos ayudaron con la grabación y el vídeo. ¡Fue genial!
>
> Otra cosa buena es que no tenemos que llevar uniforme porque es mucho más cómodo llevar ropa de calle. Sin embargo, el nuevo director introduce muchas normas más estrictas. ¡Qué pesado! Por ejemplo, por desgracia ahora está prohibido llevar maquillaje.
>
> No todo es malo porque el nuevo director tiene planes para mejorar las instalaciones deportivas. Vamos a tener un polideportivo, un taller de baile y un gimnasio amplio con un muro de escalada. Va a ser el insti mejor equipado de todo el país. A todos los alumnos nos encanta la posibilidad de tener más clubs y actividades.

Lina

1 My school is large, mixed and has…
2 Last year my school…
3 In my view, my school offers…
4 The music teachers…
5 The new headteacher is…
6 The new headteacher has…
7 It is…
8 All the pupils love the prospect of…

a more clubs and activities.
b very good extracurricular opportunities.
c helped with the competition recording and video.
d a very good reputation.
e going to be the best equipped school in the country.
f plans to improve the sports facilities.
g took first place in the official ranking of schools in Madrid.
h introducing lots of stricter rules.

2 Re-read the text from exercise 1 and find the <u>three</u> correct statements. Correct the false statements.

1 La disciplina en el insti no es buena.
2 El instituto de Lina es el mejor colegio de Madrid.
3 A Lina le gusta mucho la música.
4 El nuevo director va a introducir un uniforme escolar.
5 Lina está de acuerdo con las nuevas normas.
6 El director también tiene propósitos positivos para el insti.
7 El instituto no tiene ningún club.

3 Write a text about your school. Use exercise 1 as a model.

Include:
- a description of your school
- extracurricular opportunities
- past achievements
- uniform and rules
- future plans for your school

Try to link sentences and paragraphs together. Look at how Lina uses the following:

a mi parecer   dado que   otra cosa buena es que

sin embargo   por desgracia

doscientos uno **201**

Te toca a ti: Módulo 3

1 Match the web profiles to the statements below. There is one extra statement.

www.amorcitos.es

| mi media naranja | my other half |
| mi alma gemela | my soulmate |

Tu gran historia de amor te espera

1 Busco a mi media naranja. Mi pareja ideal es alguien trabajador, responsable, romántico, pero también deportista.

2 Quiero casarme porque me importa la estabilidad, pero no quiero tener niños porque mi carrera es más importante.

3 Mi alma gemela es una persona inteligente, con un buen sentido del humor. Me interesa la política, así como la cultura popular.

4 Soy bastante solitaria, pero busco alguien con quien compartir mi amor a la literatura y a las ideas.

a Busco una relación amorosa, aunque me comprometo con mi trabajo.
b Soy extrovertida, y me interesa viajar y hablar de muchos temas diferentes.
c Soy un verdadero ratón de biblioteca.
d Mi profesión me ocupa bastante tiempo, pero me gusta mantenerme en forma.
e Soy graduado en historia, pero también me encanta la música pop.

2 Read the article and complete the sentences in English.

la boda — wedding

Casarse ya no está de moda

En España se casan menos personas, y mucho más tarde. La edad media para casarse es de 34, 5 años. El motivo es, sobre todo, económico. Debido a la crisis económica todavía hay mucho desempleo y el coste medio de una boda se sitúa entre 11.000 y 21.000 euros. Otro factor son las tasas elevadas de divorcio. El año pasado, siete de cada diez matrimonios en España acabaron en separación o divorcio. Además, antes la mayoría de gente se casaba por la iglesia, mientras que ahora prefieren una ceremonia civil.

1 In Spain fewer people ———.
2 The average age for ——— is ———.
3 The economic crisis means that ———.
4 Another factor is the ———.
5 Last year ———.
6 When people marry now, the majority ———.

3 Match the sentence halves. Then translate the views about marriage into English.

1 El matrimonio es una promesa de vivir…
2 Para mí, casarse…
3 Después del matrimonio…
4 Se dice que los casados son…
5 No me gusta la idea de una boda tradicional,…
6 Si quieres formar una familia,…

a es un rito anticuado y mi amor a mi pareja no depende de un papel.
b más felices que los solteros.
c así que prefiero la opción de entrar en una unión civil.
d juntos para siempre. Te da mucha seguridad.
e creo que el matrimonio es la opción más estable para los niños.
f viene el divorcio, así que en mi opinión, no vale la pena.

4 Use the exercises above to help you answer the following questions.

- ¿Cómo es tu pareja ideal?
- Creo que el matrimonio todavía es relevante. Y tú, ¿qué opinas?
- ¿Quieres casarte algún día? ¿Por qué (no)?
- ¿Quieres formar una familia? ¿Por qué (no)?

Te toca a ti: Módulo 4

1 *leer* Write out these jumbled sentences correctly. Then match each one to the correct question.

a fanático Soy las policíacas de series un.
b ambiente al porque mejor ir Prefiero cine el es.
c hinchas y mi Chelsea hermana del yo somos Sí.
d me porque relajarme ayuda chifla a Me.
e monto y monopatín Juego en al futbolín.
f iba e balonmano Jugaba pesca de al.

1 ¿Qué sueles hacer en tu tiempo libre?
2 ¿Eres aficionado/a de un equipo?
3 ¿Qué deportes hacías cuando eras más joven?
4 ¿Dónde prefieres ver las películas?
5 ¿Qué tipo de programas te gusta ver?
6 ¿Por qué te gusta escuchar música?

2 *escribir* Write your own answers to the questions above. Try to give extra details.

3 *leer* Read the news article and answer the questions in English.

Los gustos deportivos del español medio

Según una encuesta reciente, el Real Madrid no es solo el club más premiado de España y de Europa, también es el club con más aficionados en nuestro país (37,9% de los encuestados). Una de cada cuatro personas (25,4%) tiene como su equipo favorito al Barça.

Deportes más seguidos
– Fútbol. Casi la mitad de los encuestados (48%) lo consideran como el deporte que les interesa más.
– Tenis. Los éxitos de Rafa Nadal lo hacen el segundo deporte en interés (21,4%).
– Baloncesto. En el pasado, el deporte de Pau Gasol, Ricky Rubio, etc., ha sido considerado el segundo de España, pero de momento solo ocupa el tercer lugar (17,1%).

Deportes más practicados
– El ciclismo. Montar en bici es el deporte más practicado, con un 18,6%.
– Carrera a pie. El 17,1% de los españoles salen a correr habitualmente.
– Natación. Un 16,1% de los españoles están enganchados a esta práctica sana.
– Fútbol. Aunque verlo es muy popular, solo un 14,7% lo practica.
– Montañismo / Senderismo. Las rutas a pie por el campo son la quinta preferencia para hacer deporte.

1 How do we know that Real Madrid is a successful club?
2 Which is the second most popular football team?
3 What has happened to the popularity of basketball?
4 Which sport is described as healthy?
5 How does the popularity of playing football compare with watching it?
6 Which is the fifth most popular sport?

> To work out the meaning of a new word ask yourself whether it is similar to one you already know. E.g.
> *un premio* = a prize   *el club más premiado* = ?
> *una encuesta* = a survey   *los encuestados* = ?

Te toca a ti: Módulo 5

1 **Translate the clues into English. Which city is it? Do some research, if necessary.**

1. Se habla español allí.
2. Está al oeste del país.
3. No está en la costa.
4. Está cerca de un lago enorme.
5. Está rodeada de montañas.
6. Perú está a su izquierda.
7. No es la capital oficial del país.
8. Es una de las ciudades más altas del mundo.
9. Su nombre significa lo contrario de 'guerra'.

2 **Write in Spanish about a city of your choice. Ask your partner to guess the city.**

3 **In the following extract, the writer describes arriving in a new place. Read the text and answer the questions in English.**

Donde aprenden a volar las gaviotas by Ana Alcolea (abridged and amended)

> Un tren y tres aviones tuve que coger desde Zaragoza hasta Trondheim, que está en el centro de Noruega y es la tercera ciudad del país. Llegué después de pasear todo el día entre nubes y aeropuertos. Me esperaba toda la familia: el padre, que se llamaba Ivar; Inger, la madre, de larga melena rubia, que parecía sacada de un cómic; y Erik, el hijo, que me llevó las maletas hasta el coche. La primera impresión que tuve de Noruega fue que a finales de junio hacía frío, y la segunda que había mucha luz: a pesar de haber llegado a las once y media de la noche, los rayos del sol aún se veían sobre el fiordo.

1. What <u>two</u> details does the writer give about Trondheim?
2. How long did the writer spend travelling?
3. What <u>two</u> pieces of information are we given about Erik?
4. What was the writer's first impression of Norway?
5. Why does the writer comment on the fact that the sun was shining?

⭐ Focus on the details you need to answer the questions and don't get distracted by unfamiliar words in the text.

4 **Write a text about arriving in a new city. Use your imagination, and use exercise 3 as an example.**

- Say how you got there — *Tuve que coger… desde… hasta…*
- Say where the city is — *que está en…*
- Say how long you spent travelling — *Llegué después de…*
- Say who met you on arrival — *Me esperaba(n)…*
- Give one detail about each person — *El padre, que se llamaba…*
- Give your first impression of the city — *La primera impresión que tuve de… fue…*

el AVE

Zona Cultura

AVE (Alta Velocidad Española) es el nombre para los trenes superrápidos españoles que circulan a una velocidad máxima de 310 km/h. El AVE conecta muchas ciudades en España, por ejemplo: Madrid, Barcelona, Sevilla, Málaga, Valencia y Zaragoza.

doscientos cuatro

Te toca a ti: Módulo 6

1 Read the texts and choose the correct title for each one. There is one title too many.

- el Día de la Madre
- Nochebuena
- Diwali
- el Día de San Valentín
- el Día de Reyes

un roscón de Reyes

1 Ayer decoramos la casa con lámparas de colores y cocinamos platos riquísimos. Fue un día importante porque celebramos el nuevo año hindú.

2 Anoche salí con mi novia y fuimos a un restaurante, donde le regalé un ramo de rosas rojas. Fue muy romántico, pero me costaron 40 euros. ¡Qué timo!

3 Me desperté temprano para abrir mis regalos. Más tarde comimos el roscón de Reyes, un bollo dulce especial que se come el 6 de enero.

4 Me levanté temprano porque quería preparar el desayuno para mi mamá. También le di una tarjeta y un regalo.

2 Write two or three sentences for the title you did not use in exercise 1. Use your imagination to describe what you did on that day.

3 Read the text. Complete each sentence with details from the text.

> El 8 de mayo voy a cumplir dieciséis años y no puedo esperar. Cuando era más pequeña, mis padres siempre organizaban una fiesta de disfraces para mi cumpleaños y a veces poníamos un castillo hinchable en el jardín. Generalmente me compraban juguetes o videojuegos. Sin embargo, el año pasado fuimos a la bolera y luego fuimos a un restaurante chino. Mis abuelos me regalaron un reloj, y recibí un montón de tarjetas. Lo pasé fenomenal.
>
> He decidido que este año me gustaría ir de compras por la mañana para gastar el dinero que me regalan. Luego, por la tarde haremos una barbacoa (¡si no llueve, claro!). Pero lo mejor es que mis tíos me van a comprar una entrada para un festival de música. ¡Qué suerte!
>
> **Margarita**

| regalar | to give (a present) |

1 When she was younger…
2 Last year she…
3 This year she…

4 Write a text about your birthday. Use exercise 3 as a model.

Describe:
- how you **used to celebrate** it when you were younger (imperfect)
- how you **celebrated** last year (preterite)
- how you **are going to celebrate** this year (future)

doscientos cinco **205**

Te toca a ti: Módulo 7

1 **leer** Read the adverts and match each one with the requirements below.

BuscamosEmpleo.com

a) LIMPIO Y PLANCHO
Se ofrece chica para limpieza de casas. Soy trabajadora y responsable. También sé cocinar. He trabajado en varios lugares y tengo carné de conducir y coche propio. Horarios flexibles.

c) CLASES PARTICULARES
Doy clases individuales de francés e inglés (ESO / Bachillerato) adaptadas a las necesidades de cada alumno. He terminado la carrera universitaria y soy profesional y paciente.

b) BUEN NIVEL DE INGLÉS
Busco trabajo como recepcionista o secretaria. Tengo diez años de experiencia y he pasado un año trabajando en Inglaterra. Soy seria, puntual y educada, con muchas ganas de trabajar.

d) DOS CHICOS BUSCAN TRABAJO
Tenemos experiencia en albañilería, pintura, carpintería y fontanería. Hemos hecho un ciclo formativo de grado medio en Construcción y somos trabajadores, dinámicos y honestos.

1. Queremos ampliar la cocina y construir una nueva terraza.
2. Los idiomas son dificilísimos. Siempre saco malas notas.
3. Buscamos chico/a para ayudar con las tareas domésticas.
4. Empresa británica busca administrativo/a con buenas habilidades lingüísticas.

⭐ Don't jump to conclusions. Read each text carefully and beware of distractors!

2 **escribir** Write adverts for these people who are looking for work.

- Almudena: waitress – 3 years' experience – has spent year working in Italy – sociable, honest, organised – has driving licence
- Iván: lifeguard – lots of experience – has spent 6 months working in sports centre – punctual, practical, hardworking – has own car

3 **leer** Read the text and answer the questions in English.

¿Qué es Sabática?
Sabática es un consultor educativo que promueve programas de trabajo, voluntariado y formación en todo el mundo.

¿Quién puede inscribirse en un proyecto de Sabática?
Para inscribirte en Sabática debes:
- tener entre 18 y 70 años (algunos proyectos requieren una edad mínima de 21–23 años)
- estar en forma y gozar de buena salud
- tener la capacidad de adaptarte e integrarte
- tener nivel intermedio del idioma del destino

¿Qué tipo de gente participa en los programas de voluntariado?
Hay gente de diversas edades con objetivos comunes: ganas de aventura, de hacer un cambio en su vida, de descansar, de aprender, de ayudar a los demás o de conocer nuevas culturas.

¿Es esencial tener experiencia?
Puedes inscribirte en muchos proyectos sin experiencia previa, pero si quieres hacer un voluntariado en sectores específicos como salud, veterinaria, etc., sí es necesario tener títulos o experiencia en el sector.

estar en forma — to be in shape

1. What three types of programme does Sabática offer?
2. Where do they take place?
3. What are the age requirements?
4. Which two things must you be able to do?
5. Give four reasons why people join these projects.
6. What is required for health or vet's services?

Te toca a ti: Módulo 8

1 Read the text and note down <u>five</u> details in English. Then complete each recommendation with the correct verb.

El Día de la Tierra
La celebración del Día de la Tierra es el 22 de abril y comenzó en 1970. Hoy es un evento a nivel mundial reconocido en más de 192 países. Nos invita a considerar la situación actual de nuestro hogar, las pequeñas acciones que dañan el medio ambiente y nuestros hábitos de consumo. Todos tenemos en nuestras manos la llave del cambio. Aquí tienes algunas propuestas para celebrar la Tierra y cuidarla.

1 ——— el coche y usa otras formas de movilidad.
2 ——— algún deporte al aire libre.
3 ——— algo en tu casa que ibas a tirar.
4 ——— una recogida de basura en tu pueblo.
5 ——— tu ropa usada a una organización caritativa.
6 ——— vegetariano/a por un día.
7 ——— una comida con alimentos de cultivo local.
8 ——— todos los aparatos eléctricos antes de salir de tu casa.

| reutiliza | sé | evita | dona |
| practica | organiza | desenchufa | prepara |

2 Read the text and find the Spanish for the words below.

Cómo ser un ciudadano del mundo
El ciudadano del mundo…
- **valora** la diversidad y **defiende** la multiculturalidad.
- **habla** otros idiomas y **aprecia** el acto de viajar para conocer otras culturas.
- **contribuye** a la comunidad, desde lo local a lo global.
- **cuida** los recursos a nivel local y **protege** el medio ambiente.
- **combate** los estereotipos y **reacciona** contra la xenofobia y la intolerancia.
- **aprende** sobre otros países y **se interesa** por las noticias internacionales.
- **apoya** la justicia social.
- **es** una persona con iniciativa propia que **actúa** con independencia de las modas.

1 world citizen
2 at a local level
3 other countries
4 the news
5 own initiative
6 whatever the fashion

3 Read the text again. Translate the verbs in **bold** into English.

4 Write a declaration about being a world citizen, using verbs in the subjunctive. Rank the statements in order of importance to you.

> Es importante que valoremos la diversidad y defendamos la multiculturalidad.
> Es esencial que…
> Es necesario que…

★ Look back at p.151 to remind yourself how to form the subjunctive of regular verbs.
Remember that **ser** is irregular in the subjunctive → **sea**.

doscientos siete **207**

Gramática Hay que saber bien

The present tense – regular verbs

What is it and when do I use it?
The present tense is used to talk about the present. You use it to talk about:
- What usually happens — *Normalmente* **como** *fruta.* — I normally **eat** fruit.
- What things are like — *La ciudad* **es** *grande.* — The city **is** big.
- What is happening now — **Vivimos** *en Liverpool.* — **We live** in Liverpool.

Why is it important?
Verbs are the building blocks of a language. Using the correct tense helps Spanish people to understand what you want to say. For GCSE, you need to be able to use all the different persons of the verb correctly.

Things to watch out for
The verb ending! This tells you who is speaking. You do not need to include *yo* (I) or *tú* (you), etc. before the verb unless you need to add extra emphasis.

How does it work?
To form the present tense you replace the infinitive ending (*–ar*, *–er* or *–ir*) with the present tense endings like this:

	escuch**ar** (to listen)	com**er** (to eat)	viv**ir** (to live)
(yo)	escuch**o**	com**o**	viv**o**
(tú)	escuch**as**	com**es**	viv**es**
(él/ella/usted)	escuch**a**	com**e**	viv**e**
(nosotros/as)	escuch**amos**	com**emos**	viv**imos**
(vosotros/as)	escuch**áis**	com**éis**	viv**ís**
(ellos/ellas/ustedes)	escuch**an**	com**en**	viv**en**

Stem-changing verbs
Stem-changing verbs are formed in the same way as regular present tense verbs. However, a vowel change occurs in the stem in some of their forms (I, you (singular), he/she/it/you polite (singular), they/you polite (plural)). They are usually regular in their endings.

There are three common groups.

	o → ue p**o**der (to be able to)	e → ie qu**e**rer (to want)	e → i p**e**dir (to ask for)
(yo)	p**ue**do	qu**ie**ro	p**i**do
(tú)	p**ue**des	qu**ie**res	p**i**des
(él/ella/usted)	p**ue**de	qu**ie**re	p**i**de
(nosotros/as)	podemos	queremos	pedimos
(vosotros/as)	podéis	queréis	pedís
(ellos/ellas/ustedes)	p**ue**den	qu**ie**ren	p**i**den

Other examples of stem-changing verbs:

u/o → ue
jugar → j**ue**go — I play
costar → c**ue**sta — it costs
acostarse → me ac**ue**sto — I go to bed
dormir → d**ue**rmen — they sleep
encontrar → enc**ue**ntras — you find
llover → ll**ue**ve — it rains
volver → v**ue**lvo — I return

e → ie
despertarse → se desp**ie**rta — she wakes up
empezar → emp**ie**zan — they begin
entender → ent**ie**ndo — I understand
nevar → n**ie**va — it snows
pensar → usted p**ie**nsa — you think
perder → p**ie**rde — he loses
preferir → pref**ie**ro — I prefer
recomendar → recom**ie**ndas — you recommend

e → i
repetir → rep**i**to — I repeat
servir → s**i**rven — they serve
vestir(se) → me v**i**sto — I get dressed

208 *doscientos ocho*

Gramática

Preparados

1 Choose the correct form of the verb to complete each sentence.

1 Cuando estoy de vacaciones **come / como / comemos** muchos helados.
2 En verano mis amigos y yo **nadamos / nadan / nadas** en el mar.
3 A veces mi hermano **leo / lees / lee** novelas o manda correos.
4 ¿Vosotros nunca **descargas / descargan / descargáis** música?
5 Todos los días, me relajo y **tocamos / tocáis / toco** la guitarra.
6 Mi familia **vivís / vive / viven** en el noroeste de Inglaterra.
7 Mi amigo **prefiere / prefieren / preferimos** ir a la playa.
8 ¿Y tú? ¿Qué deportes **practica / practicas / practicamos** en el colegio?
9 ¿Cuánto **cuestan / cuesto / cuesta** una habitación individual con desayuno incluido?

Listos

2 Complete the sentence with the correct form of the verb. Then translate each sentence into English.

1 En el instituto ___ estudiar varias asignaturas y no tienes que llevar uniforme. (*poder*)
2 Muchas personas ___ unos vaqueros y una camiseta. (*llevar*)
3 Las clases ___ a las nueve y ___ a las tres y media. (*empezar / terminar*)
4 Me gustan las ciencias, pero ___ las matemáticas. (*preferir*)
5 Mi amigo estudia historia porque ___ aprender más del pasado. (*querer*)
6 La profesora de inglés ___ muy bien y ___ un buen ambiente de trabajo. (*enseñar / crear*)
7 Los alumnos de mi colegio ___ mucho durante las vacaciones. (*estudiar*)
8 Mis amigos y yo ___ en varias actividades extraescolares. (*participar*)
9 Desafortunadamente, hay alumnos que ___ intimidación en mi insti. (*sufrir*)

¡Ya!

3 Translate these sentences into Spanish.

1 Every year we spend the summer holidays in Spain.
2 I read a lot and I sometimes download videos.
3 We do sport every day and sometimes we listen to music.
4 How much does a double room cost?
5 I would like to change rooms because the shower does not work.
6 We need three towels and a hairdryer.
7 Juan plays an instrument at school but his brother prefers to play football.
8 Classes last forty minutes and break lasts fifteen minutes.
9 My friends wear grey trousers, a white shirt and a black jacket at school.

doscientos nueve

The present tense – irregular verbs

What are they and when do I use them?
Irregular verbs do not follow the normal patterns of regular –ar, –er and –ir verbs. Many of the most common and most useful verbs in Spanish are irregular.

Why are they important?
You can't speak a language without knowing a wide range of verbs, and some of the most important verbs like 'to be', 'to have', 'to do' and 'to go' are irregular. For your GCSE, you need to use all parts of these verbs accurately.

Things to watch out for
You must learn irregular verbs by heart. Sometimes, just the *yo* form is irregular.

How does it work?
These verbs are only irregular in the 'I' form (the first person)

conducir → *conduzco*	I drive	*hacer* → *hago*	I make/do	*salir* → *salgo*	I go out
conocer → *conozco*	I know	*poner* → *pongo*	I put	*traer* → *traigo*	I bring
dar → *doy*	I give	*saber* → *sé*	I know		

Other verbs are more irregular.

	ser (to be)	**estar** (to be)	**tener** (to have)	**ir** (to go)
(yo)	soy	estoy	tengo	voy
(tú)	eres	estás	tienes	vas
(él/ella/usted)	es	está	tiene	va
(nosotros/as)	somos	estamos	tenemos	vamos
(vosotros/as)	sois	estáis	tenéis	vais
(ellos/ellas/ustedes)	son	están	tienen	van

Look at the verb tables on page 237 for more irregular present tense verbs.

Preparados

1 Complete these sentences with the *yo* (I) form of the verb.

1 Normalmente ___ a las ocho. (*salir*)
2 ___ a toda la clase. (*conocer*)
3 Siempre ___ que llevar uniforme. (*tener*)
4 ___ mucho de los edificios de mi colegio. (*saber*)
5 A veces ___ deportes acuáticos con mi familia. (*hacer*)
6 De vez en cuando ___ un paseo. (*dar*)

Listos

2 Complete these sentences with the correct form of *ser*, *estar*, *tener* or *ir*. Then translate each sentence into English.

1 Mi amiga ___ adicta a la tele y por lo tanto no practica mucho deporte.
2 El clima ___ muy soleado en verano pero a veces ___ nublado.
3 Durante las vacaciones mis amigos y yo ___ al cine.
4 ___ que llevar uniforme pero no nos gusta.
5 El colegio ___ un biblioteca grande y tres pistas de tenis.
6 Salgo de casa a las ocho y ___ al colegio andando.

¡Ya!

3 Translate the text into Spanish.

In my school we all have to wear uniform. The worse thing it that I have to wear a brown skirt. I think it is really ugly. Every day my brother and I go to school on the bus. The journey is easy and we normally leave the house at eight o'clock. We have six classes a day and, for me, the best subject is Spanish as my teacher is fun. The rules in my school are too strict and some pupils are a bad influence.

The present tense – reflexive verbs

What are they and when do I use them?
Reflexive verbs are verbs that include a reflexive pronoun. They describe actions that we do to ourselves.

Why are they important?
They are useful verbs when describing your relationships with others and your daily routine.

Things to watch out for
Check you are using the correct reflexive pronoun as well as the correct ending.

How does it work?
Reflexive verbs are formed in the same way as regular present tense verbs but they include a reflexive pronoun. In the infinitive the pronoun is shown at the end of the verb, *levantar**se***. In the present tense the pronoun precedes the verb and changes according to the person (**me** levant**o**).

	levantarse (to get up)	**divertirse** (to enjoy oneself)	**llevarse con** (to get on with)
(yo)	**me** levanto	**me** div**ie**rto	**me** llevo
(tú)	**te** levantas	**te** div**ie**rtes	**te** llevas
(él/ella/usted)	**se** levanta	**se** div**ie**rte	**se** lleva
(nosotros/as)	**nos** levantamos	**nos** divertimos	**nos** llevamos
(vosotros/as)	**os** levantáis	**os** divertís	**os** lleváis
(ellos/ellas/ustedes)	**se** levantan	**se** div**ie**rten	**se** llevan

Preparados

1 Complete these sentences with the correct form of the verb.

1 ____ a las siete y media. (*ducharse, yo*)
2 Normalmente ____ bien con mi padre. (*llevarse, yo*)
3 Mi hermano y yo ____ mucho en casa. (*divertirse, nosotros*)
4 ¿____ con tus hermanos o con tus padres? (*pelearse, tú*)
5 Mis padres ____ bien y se apoyan en todo. (*llevarse, ellos*)

Listos

2 Complete the second and third rows of the table with the 'you' form and the 'he/she' form of the underlined verbs.

yo	<u>Me levanto</u> todos los días y me digo que mi vida va a cambiar. <u>Pienso</u> que <u>soy</u> una persona simpática. <u>Me llevo</u> muy bien con mucha gente y <u>me divierto</u> cuando <u>puedo</u>.
tú	____ todos los días y te dices que tu vida va a cambiar. ____ que ____ una persona simpática. ____ muy bien con mucha gente y ____ cuando ____.
él/ella	____ todos los días y se dice que su vida va a cambiar. ____ que ____ una persona simpática. ____ muy bien con mucha gente y ____ cuando ____.

¡Ya!

3 Complete these sentences with the correct form of the verb.

1 Mi amigo y yo ____ fenomenal porque ____ mucho en común. (*llevarse / tener*)
2 Siempre ____ con mi padre porque nos interesan los deportes. (*divertirse*)
3 Mis hermanos ____ en casa todos los días, pero siempre ____ en el instituto. (*pelearse / apoyarse*)
4 ____ mal con mi profesor de religión porque él no ____ buen sentido de humor. (*llevarse / tener*)
5 Siempre ____ muy tarde los fines de semana porque no tengo sueño. (*acostarse*)
6 Normalmente mi hermana ____ primero y ____ en la cocina mientras yo ____. (*ducharse / desayunar / vestirse*)

Gramática Hay que saber bien
The preterite tense

What is it and when do I use it?
The preterite tense is sometimes known as the 'simple past'. It is used to talk about completed actions in the past.
   Fui a la playa.   **I went** to the beach.
   Viajó en coche.   **He travelled** by car.

Why is it important?
You often want to say what you or someone else did. Without the preterite tense you could not tell a story in Spanish. It is a key tense to learn and understand for GCSE.

Things to watch out for
- Some forms of regular verbs in the preterite take an accent. Be careful that you use accents correctly as using them incorrectly can change the meaning of a word.
  escucho (I listen), but *escuchó* (he listened)
- Irregular verbs don't take accents in the preterite.
- The verbs *ir* and *ser* are the same in the preterite.

How does it work?
Regular preterite verbs
The preterite tense is formed by taking the infinitive of a verb, removing the infinitive endings (*–ar*, *–er* or *–ir*), and then adding the following preterite endings. Note that *–er* and *–ir* verbs take the same endings in the preterite.

	visitar (to visit)	**comer** (to eat)	**salir** (to go out)
(yo)	visit**é**	com**í**	sal**í**
(tú)	visit**aste**	com**iste**	sal**iste**
(él/ella/usted)	visit**ó**	com**ió**	sal**ió**
(nosotros/as)	visit**amos**	com**imos**	sal**imos**
(vosotros/as)	visit**asteis**	com**isteis**	sal**isteis**
(ellos/ellas/ustedes)	visit**aron**	com**ieron**	sal**ieron**

- When you are using stem-changing verbs make sure you have the correct infinitive:
  encuentro (I find) → *encontrar* (to find) → *encontré* (I found)

Irregular preterite verbs
- The most common irregular verbs are:

	ser/ir (to be/to go)	**ver** (to see)	**hacer** (to do/make)	**tener** (to have)
(yo)	fui	vi	hice	tuve
(tú)	fuiste	viste	hiciste	tuviste
(él/ella/usted)	fue	vio	hizo	tuvo
(nosotros/as)	fuimos	vimos	hicimos	tuvimos
(vosotros/as)	fuisteis	visteis	hicisteis	tuvisteis
(ellos/ellas/ustedes)	fueron	vieron	hicieron	tuvieron

- Other irregular preterite verbs include:

andar	to walk	poner	to put
dar	to give	querer	to want
decir	to say	saber	to know
estar	to be	traer	to bring
poder	to be able to	venir	to come

Look at the verb tables on page 237 for more irregular preterite tense verbs.

Gramática

- Some preterite verbs have **irregular spellings** just in the first person singular (*yo*). For example:

sacar	→	sa**qu**é	I got/took	empezar	→	empe**c**é	I started
tocar	→	to**qu**é	I played	jugar	→	ju**gu**é	I played
cruzar	→	cru**c**é	I crossed	llegar	→	lle**gu**é	I arrived

- Some preterite verbs have irregular spellings in the third person singular (*él/ella/usted*) and third person plural (*ellos/ellas/ustedes*):

  caer → ca**y**ó, ca**y**eron   he/she fell, they fell   leer → le**y**ó, le**y**eron   he/she read, they read

Preparados

1 Look at the list of phrases and decide if the verbs are in the present or the preterite tense. Then translate each sentence into English.

1 Desayuno a las diez.
2 Fuimos al museo antes de comer.
3 Hace mucho sol aquí.
4 Mi amigo decidió comprar unos recuerdos.
5 Practiqué natación en el mar cerca de mi casa.
6 Nunca hacéis vuestros deberes.
7 Observé a la gente en el restaurante.
8 En el colegio comemos a las doce y media.
9 Anoche mis amigos fueron al cine.
10 Silvia jugó al fútbol el sábado.

Listos

2 Write the correct form of the verb in brackets in the preterite. Then translate each sentence into English.

1 La semana pasada yo ____ un libro muy bueno. *(leer)*
2 Ayer yo ____ un reloj y luego fui al cine. *(comprar)*
3 La semana pasada mi amiga ____ paella. *(comer)*
4 Mis amigos ____ una fiesta para celebrar sus cumpleaños. *(hacer)*
5 ¿Cuándo ____ a la piscina? Ayer no te vi. *(ir)*
6 Mis vacaciones ____ increíbles. *(ser)*
7 Ayer mis amigos y yo no ____ nada que hacer. *(tener)*
8 Anteayer fui en metro al centro y ____ una obra de teatro. *(ver)*
9 Mi hermano ____ ocho asignaturas en el colegio. *(estudiar)*
10 Mi madre ____ a Inglaterra en avión. *(volver)*

¡Ya!

3 Write the following story in the past. Change all the present tense verbs into the preterite tense. Then translate the text into English.

¡Un buen día!

Por la mañana **1** *voy* a la bolera y **2** *juego* a los bolos con mi familia. **3** *Bebemos* refrescos pero no **4** *comemos* nada. Mis padres me **5** *dan* cuatro euros para gastar el fin de semana y **6** *es* suficiente para salir por la tarde. **7** *Llamo* a mi amiga y **8** *vamos* al centro comercial para ir de compras. En la tienda de ropa no **9** *veo* nada bonito pero mi amiga **10** *compra* una gorra. **11** *Volvemos* a casa para escuchar música y **12** *descansamos* un poco. Por la noche, **13** *salgo* y **14** *voy* al cine con mi novio pero no **15** *nos gusta* la película. Después yo **16** *vuelvo* a casa para cenar. Mis hermanos **17** *juegan* con el ordenador, pero yo **18** *hago* mis deberes. Finalmente, **19** *leo* un poco y **20** *mando* mensajes a mi novio.

doscientos trece **213**

Gramática Hay que saber bien

The imperfect tense

What is it and when do I use it?
The imperfect tense is another way of talking about the past. It is used in Spanish for:
- Descriptions in the past (what someone or something was like or was doing):
  En mi escuela primaria, las instalaciones **eran** mejores.
  In my primary school, the facilities **were** better.
- Repeated actions in the past:
  Tenía clases de gimnasia cada semana.   **I had** gymnastics classes every week.
- What people used to do and what things used to be like:
  Antes **jugábamos** al fútbol, pero ahora preferimos hacer kárate.
  Before **we used to** play football, but now we prefer to do karate.

Why is it important?
To tell a story in the past successfully you need to be able to use the imperfect for descriptions and repeated actions. The imperfect tense is important for GCSE because you need to describe different types of past events to be successful. If you can combine the imperfect with the preterite tense correctly, you will create more complex and detailed phrases.

Things to watch out for
You use the **preterite tense** for single events in the past and the **imperfect tense** for repeated actions and things you used to do in the past.

How does it work?
- The imperfect tense is formed by taking the infinitive of a verb, removing the infinitive endings (–ar, –er, –ir) and then adding the following endings. Note that –er and –ir verbs take the same endings in the imperfect.

	jugar (to play)	**hac**er (to do/make)	**viv**ir (to live)
(yo)	jug**aba**	hac**ía**	viv**ía**
(tú)	jug**abas**	hac**ías**	viv**ías**
(él/ella/usted)	jug**aba**	hac**ía**	viv**ía**
(nosotros/as)	jug**ábamos**	hac**íamos**	viv**íamos**
(vosotros/as)	jug**abais**	hac**íais**	viv**íais**
(ellos/ellas/ustedes)	jug**aban**	hac**ían**	viv**ían**

- There are three verbs that are irregular in the imperfect tense.

	ir (to go)	**ser** (to be)	**ver** (to see)
(yo)	**iba**	**era**	**veía**
(tú)	**ibas**	**eras**	**veías**
(él/ella/usted)	**iba**	**era**	**veía**
(nosotros/as)	**íbamos**	**éramos**	**veíamos**
(vosotros/as)	**ibais**	**erais**	**veíais**
(ellos/ellas/ustedes)	**iban**	**eran**	**veían**

- The imperfect tense of **hay** (there is) is **había** (there was/were) and the preterite is **hubo** (there was/were). Había is very useful for describing things and saying what things used to be like and hubo is used for completed actions and specific past events.

  En el hotel **había** una piscina cubierta.   In the hotel **there was** an indoor pool.
  El fin de semana pasado **hubo** un accidente   Last weekend **there was** an accident
  y llegué tarde al aeropuerto.   and I arrived at the airport late.

Gramática

Preparados

1 Translate the sentences into English. Write the correct letters next to each sentence to explain why the imperfect is required – D (descriptions in the past), RA (repeated action in the past) or UT ('used to' phrase).

1 La pensión estaba en las afueras de la ciudad.
2 Cada sábado montaba a caballo con mis amigos.
3 Mi escuela primaria era muy pequeña y no había aulas de informática.
4 Cuando tenía doce años, era aficionado de Real Madrid.
5 Antes mi hermano no era muy deportista y nunca jugaba al baloncesto.
6 Cuando era más pequeña hacía deportes acuáticos con mi familia.
7 El albergue juvenil estaba cerca del centro de la ciudad pero no tenía piscina.
8 En el verano íbamos a la playa todos los días.
9 Lo bueno del pueblo era que tenía muchos espacios verdes y era muy tranquilo.
10 La gente era muy simpática y la comida estaba muy buena.

Listos

2 Complete the sentences with the correct form of the imperfect tense. Translate each sentence into English.

1 Antes mi colegio no **teníamos / tenía / tener** un patio grande y no **había / hay / hubo** un teatro pero ahora las instalaciones son muy buenas.
2 Cuando mi padre **tenías / tenía / tenían** quince años **iba / íbamos / ir** al colegio en moto y **jugaba / juega / jugaban** al fútbol todos los días.
3 El hotel **es / era / había** muy grande y **tiene / teníais / tenía** una piscina bonita, pero no **hay / había / era** ni restaurante ni cafetería.
4 El año pasado mis amigos y yo **usábamos / usamos / usaban** nuestros móviles demasiado y siempre **chateábamos / chateo / chateamos** durante muchas horas.
5 ¿Qué **hacías / hacía / hacían** usted cuando **tuviste / tenía / tiene** nueve años?
6 En mi escuela primaria lo malo **eran / éramos / era** que **hay / había / habíamos** poco espacio pero las clases **eran / era / erais** más cortas.
7 Antes yo **era / soy / fui** aficionado del Atlético de Bilbao y mis amigos y yo **iba / íbamos / vamos** a casi todos los partidos pero ahora no me gusta nada el fútbol.
8 Antes mi madre **fuma / fumaba / fumaban** mucho para quitar el estrés, pero ya no fuma nunca.
9 Durante mis prácticas laborales yo **cogía / cogías / cogían** el tren cada día y **llevábamos / llevabais / llevaba** ropa elegante.
10 Los clientes **éramos / era / eran** bastante maleducados pero mi jefe **éramos / era / eran** muy simpático.

¡Ya!

3 Complete the sentences with either the preterite or imperfect tense.

1 Fui de vacaciones a España y el hotel donde nos quedamos ____ bastante lujoso. *(ser)*
2 Ayer mi madre ____ recuerdos pero yo ____ en el hotel. *(comprar, descansar)*
3 Antes Juan ____ en una cafetería todos los sábados, pero ahora quiere ser peluquero. *(trabajar)*
4 Mis padres y yo ____ al parque para jugar al tenis, pero ____ mucho y por lo tanto ____ un desastre. *(ir, llover, ser)*
5 Mi amiga ____ a Francia de vacaciones. El camping ____ cerca de la playa y ____ muy barato y bastante acogedor. *(ir, estar, ser)*
6 Siempre ____ mucha gente en la playa porque era agosto. *(haber)*
7 Me dijeron que mi abuelo era muy alto y ____ el pelo negro como yo. *(tener)*
8 Hicimos nuestros deberes el domingo y después ____ juntas. *(salir)*
9 Mi hermano ____ al rugby cada semana pero ahora tiene que estudiar mucho. *(jugar)*
10 Ya no hago mucho deporte, pero antes ____ baile, gimnasia y equitación cada semana. *(hacer)*

doscientos quince

Gramática Hay que saber bien
The future tense

The near future tense

What is it and when do I use it?
The near future is used to describe what **is going to happen** (for example, tonight, tomorrow, next week, etc.). It is the most common tense in Spanish for describing future plans.

Voy a practicar el español.   **I am going to practise** Spanish.
Vamos a ir de excursión.   **We are going to go** on a trip.

Why is it important?
You often want to say what you or someone else is going to do. You also need to be able to understand and refer to future events for your GCSE.

Things to watch out for
Don't forget to use the preposition *a* when using the near future.

How does it work?
To form the near future, you need:
ir (in the present tense) + *a* + **infinitive**

(yo)	voy		comer
(tú)	vas		jugar
(él/ella/usted)	va	a	tener
(nosotros/as)	vamos		salir
(vosotros/as)	vais		comprar
(ellos/ellas/ustedes)	van		hacer

The future tense

What is it and when do I use it?
The future tense is used to describe what **will happen** in the future.
   Mañana **iremos** al centro comercial.   Tomorrow **we will go** to the shopping centre.

Why is it important?
You often want to say what you or someone else will do. Using two types of future tense will add variety and complexity to your texts.

Things to watch out for
Don't forget to include the accents on future tense verb endings.

How does it work?
To form the future tense of most verbs, you take the infinitive of the verb and add the following endings (these are the same for –ar, –er and –ir verbs):

(yo)	ser**é**
(tú)	ser**ás**
(él/ella/usted)	ser**á**
(nosotros/as)	ser**emos**
(vosotros/as)	ser**éis**
(ellos/ellas/ustedes)	ser**án**

- The following verbs have irregular stems in the future tense. You need to use these stems instead of the infinitive, but the endings stay the same as for regular verbs.

decir	to say	→ **dir**é, **dir**ás, …
hacer	to do/make	→ **har**é, **har**ás, …
poder	to be able to	→ **podr**é, **podr**ás, …
poner	to put	→ **pondr**é, **pondr**ás, …
querer	to want	→ **querr**é, **querr**ás, …
saber	to know	→ **sabr**é, **sabr**ás, …
salir	to leave/go out	→ **saldr**é, **saldr**ás, …
tener	to have	→ **tendr**é, **tendr**ás, …
venir	to come	→ **vendr**é, **vendr**ás, …

- The future tense of *haber* is **habrá** (there will be).

doscientos dieciséis

Gramática

Preparados

1 Rewrite the Spanish sentence to include the missing part of the near future tense.

1. I am going to attend lessons. – Voy asistir a clases.
2. We are going to wear casual clothes. – Vamos a ropa de calle.
3. What are you going to do? – ¿Qué a hacer?
4. She is going to arrive on Thursday. – Va llegar el jueves.
5. My family is going to travel by car. – Mi familia va a en coche.
6. In the morning they are going to do a guided tour. – Por la mañana a hacer una visita guiada.
7. My brother is going to participate in a tournament. – Mi hermano a participar en un torneo.
8. Tomorrow they are going to do ice skating. – Mañana van a patinaje sobre hielo.
9. I'm going to go to France. – Voy ir a Francia.
10. Are you going to work as a volunteer? – ¿Vas a como voluntario?
11. My friends are going to visit other cities. – Mis amigos a visitar otras ciudades.
12. Today you are all going to play football. – Hoy vosotros a jugar al fútbol.

Listos

2 Find all of the near future verbs in this blog and change them into the future tense. Watch out for the irregular ones! Then translate the text into English.

¿Qué vas a hacer mañana? Yo voy a hacer muchas cosas porque mis primos van a venir a visitarnos. Por la mañana mis primos y yo vamos a ir al centro de la ciudad. Mis primos van a comprar unas camisetas y yo voy a comprar unos zapatos. Luego mis padres nos van a llevar a la playa en coche. Mi prima María no va a nadar porque odia el mar, pero mi primo José va a hacer windsurf conmigo. Mis padres van a tomar el sol y van a descansar. Después vamos a pasear por el casco viejo de la ciudad y vamos a ir a un restaurante barato donde se puede comer una gran variedad de marisco.

¡Ya!

3 Complete the conversation with the correct future tense of one of the verbs in the box:

A: ¿Qué haremos mañana?
B: Pues, primero tú y yo **1** _____ al teleférico porque desde allí las vistas son increíbles.
A: ¡Qué guay? ¿Y nosotros qué **2** _____ después?
B: Depende del tiempo. Si hace sol y no llueve, tú **3** _____ fotos de Barcelona y luego nosotros **4** _____ un café en la terraza.
A: ¿A qué hora nosotros **5** _____ otra vez en teleférico?
B: A las once, más o menos. Después yo **6** _____ que ir a mi clase de tenis pero tú **7** _____ visitar unos monumentos.
A: De acuerdo, ¿Y nosotros dónde **8** _____? ¿En un restaurante o en tu casa?
B: Pues si no estamos demasiado cansados, nosotros **9** _____ a mi restaurante favorito para comer tapas, pero está un poco lejos del centro, y por eso **10** _____ en metro. Finalmente, a las cinco mis amigos **11** _____ a mi casa para jugar a los videojuegos.
A: ¡Buena idea! ¡El día **12** _____ fantástico!

sacar
ir
poder
almorzar
bajar
hacer
tener
venir
ser
tomar
viajar
subir

doscientos diecisiete **217**

Gramática Hay que saber bien
The present continuous tense

What is it and when do I use it?
The present continuous is used to say what you are doing at the moment. It is made up of two parts: the present tense of **estar** and the present participle.
- ¿Qué **estás haciendo**? — What **are you doing**?
- **Estoy pensando** en salir. — **I am thinking** about going out.

Why is it important?
For GCSE, it is important to be able to use this form of the present tense to help give your writing or speaking more grammatical variety. You also need to recognise and understand this tense in listening or reading texts.

Things to watch out for
Sometimes in English, we use the present participle when in Spanish you need to use an infinitive.
- **Cantar** es divertido. — **Singing** is fun.
- Le gusta **nadar**. — She likes **swimming**.

How does it work?
Take the present tense of **estar** and add the present participle (the '–ing' form). To form the present participle, take the infinitive of the verb, remove the –ar, –er or –ir and add the endings: **–ando, –iendo, –iendo**.

Estamos viendo la tele. — **We are watching** TV.

(yo)	estoy	
(tú)	estás	hablando
(él/ella/usted)	está	+ comiendo
(nosotros/as)	estamos	saliendo
(vosotros/as)	estáis	
(ellos/ellas/ustedes)	están	

- Stem changing –ir verbs (but not –ar or –er verbs) change their spellings for the present participle:
  - o → u *do*rmir   to sleep → *du*rmiendo   sleeping
  - e → i *pe*dir   to ask   → *pi*diendo   asking

- Some **irregular present participles** include:

  | leer | to read | → leyendo | reading | poder | to be able to | → pudiendo | being able to |
  | oír | to hear | → oyendo | hearing | reír | to laugh | → riendo | laughing |

Preparados

1 Write the present continuous for each of these verbs.

1 (yo) jugar
2 (vosotros) repasar
3 (ustedes) beber
4 (tú) hacer
5 (nosotras) escribir
6 (él) dormir

Listos

2 Use your imagination and a verb from the box to create an answer in the present continuous for each of the questions.

| comer | dormir | jugar | andar | navegar | leer |

1 ¿Qué está haciendo la chica?
2 ¿Qué está haciendo Lucía?
3 ¿Qué están haciendo Pepe y Paco?
4 ¿Qué estás haciendo?
5 ¿Qué estamos haciendo?
6 ¿Qué está haciendo Juan?

¡Ya!

3 Translate the sentences into Spanish.

1 What are you doing right now?
2 I am listening to music and my friend is watching a film.
3 We are not doing anything special.
4 They are reading some comics on the bus.
5 He is writing an email and having a coffee in a café.
6 Are you all revising for the exams?

doscientos dieciocho

The perfect tense

What is it and when do I use it?
The perfect tense is used to talk about what you **have done**.

   He descargado unas canciones nuevas.   **I have downloaded** some new songs.

Things to watch out for
When you want to say that someone has **just** done something you do not use the perfect tense. You use the present tense of the verb *acabar* (a regular *–ar* verb) followed by the preposition *de*.

   Acabamos de comer pizza.   **We have just** eaten pizza.

How does it work?
The perfect tense is formed by using the verb **haber** in the present tense and the past participle of the verb. The past participle is formed by taking the infinitive, removing the *–ar*, *–er* or *–ir* and adding the endings: **–ado**, **–ido**, **–ido**.

(yo)	he		
(tú)	has		hablado
(él/ella/usted)	ha	+	comido
(nosotros/as)	hemos		salido
(vosotros/as)	habéis		
(ellos/ellas/ustedes)	han		

Some common **irregular past participles** are:

abrir	to open	→	*abierto*	opened		*poner*	to put	→	*puesto*	put
decir	to say	→	*dicho*	said		*romper*	to break	→	*roto*	broken
escribir	to write	→	*escrito*	written		*ver*	to see	→	*visto*	seen
hacer	to do/make	→	*hecho*	done/made		*volver*	to return	→	*vuelto*	returned
morir	to die	→	*muerto*	died						

Preparados

1 Put the words in the correct order for each sentence.

1 Delia / el / descargado / ha / videojuego
2 el / he / iPad / roto
3 ha / Pablo / comedia / estupenda / visto / una
4 hemos / palomitas / comido / muchas
5 en / mi / cine / perdido / he / móvil / el
6 emocionantes / leído / han / libros / muchos

Listos

2 Write about what you have done and what you have never done.

| descargar música | montar a caballo | hacer remo | romperse el brazo | leer periódicos |
| ver un buen culebrón | gastar mi paga en unas zapatillas de marca | | asistir a un espectáculo de baile | |

1 …frecuentemente.
2 …recientemente.
3 …muchas veces.
4 …pocas veces.
5 …una vez.
6 No…nunca.

¡Ya!

3 Write about what Pedro and Maite have done today. Change the verbs in brackets into the perfect tense.

Me llamo Pedro y hoy mi amiga Maite y yo **1** *(hacer)* muchas cosas. Primero, Maite **2** *(compartir)* muchas fotos en Instagram y yo **3** *(descargar)* varias canciones nuevas. Luego Maite y yo **4** *(comprar)* por Internet dos entradas para ver la última peli de Robert Pattinson esta noche. También yo **5** *(ver)* un reality mientras Maite **6** *(escribir)* su blog. Mis hermanos **7** *(jugar)* al ping-pong y **8** *(hacer)* ciclismo.

doscientos diecinueve

Gramática Hay que saber bien
The conditional

What is it and when do I use it?
The conditional tense is used to describe what you **would** do in the future.
   En mi ciudad **mejoraría** el sistema de transporte.   In my city **I would improve** the transport system.

Why is it important?
You need the conditional to talk successfully about your future plans and ideas.

Things to watch out for
Don't confuse conditional verbs with imperfect verbs. The conditional is formed by using the future stem and adding the imperfect endings for –er/–ir verbs.

How does it work?
The conditional tense is formed in the same way as the future tense. You take the infinitive of the verb and add the following endings (these are the same for –ar, –er and –ir verbs):

	ser (to be)
(yo)	ser**ía**
(tú)	ser**ías**
(él/ella/usted)	ser**ía**
(nosotros/as)	ser**íamos**
(vosotros/as)	ser**íais**
(ellos/ellas/ustedes)	ser**ían**

- The verbs which have irregular stems in the future also have irregular stems in the conditional tense. For example:

    hacer   (to do/make)   → **har**ía, **har**ías, …   (would do/make)
    poder   (to be able to) → **podr**ía, **podr**ías, …   (would be able to)
    tener   (to have)   → **tendr**ía, **tendr**ías, …   (would have)

    Other verbs which have irregular stems in the future are listed on page 237.

- The conditional tense of *haber* is **habría** (there would be).

- The conditional tense can be used to express future ideas by using the verb *gustar* followed by an infinitive:
    En el futuro, **me gustaría** hablar más idiomas.   In the future, **I would like** to speak more languages.

- The conditional tense of *poder* is used to express the notion of something that you could do.
    Podríamos ir al cine.   **We could** go to the cinema.

- The conditional tense of *deber* is used to express the notion of something that you should do.
    Deberíamos reciclar el plástico y el vidrio.   **We should** recycle plastic and glass.

Gramática

Preparados

1 Read these sentences about making an ideal city. Complete with the correct conditional tense.

1 ¿Qué es lo que ____ de tu ciudad? *(cambiar)*
2 Lo único que yo ____ ____ las afueras. *(cambiar, ser)*
3 Mis padres ____ algunos edificios porque creen que son muy feos. *(renovar)*
4 En un mundo ideal, mi ciudad no ____ tanta contaminación. *(tener)*
5 Mis amigos y yo ____ más áreas de ocio en nuestra zona. *(poner)*
6 Yo sé que mi abuelo ____ más el ruido y le ____ reducir el tráfico. *(controlar, gustar)*
7 ¿Qué ____ tú para mejorar la ciudad? *(hacer)*
8 Yo ____ más árboles en el centro e ____ más zonas peatonales. *(plantar, introducir)*
9 ¡Mis hermanos ____ una pista de monopatín cerca de nuestra casa! *(construir)*
10 Mi profesor de geografía ____ en el turismo rural y ____ las zonas deterioradas. *(invertir, renovar)*

Listos

2 What would you do if you had the time? Translate these examples into Spanish.

1 My brother would play football a lot more.
2 My friends would swim in the sea every day.
3 I would look for and I would download more music.
4 Manuel would go to the cinema every Sunday.
5 Rosa would watch television every evening.
6 My brother would go to a concert every weekend.
7 Would you do water sports?
8 You would all chat more and send more messages.
9 I would visit a museum every month.
10 My friends would read more books.

¡Ya!

3 Give advice to your friends. What would you do in their position? Use as many of the verbs in the box as you can.

estudiar   practicar   comprar   descansar   hacer   jugar   salir   dejar

1 Maite fuma demasiado.
2 Juan no asiste a ningún club.
3 Mohamed juega demasiados videojuegos.
4 Alfonso nunca hace ningún deporte.
5 Alina lleva una vida frenética.
6 Marisol nunca lee.
7 Elena usa las redes sociales demasiado.
8 Iker es teleadicto.
9 Belén no habla con sus padres.
10 Roberto no tiene novia.

doscientos veintiuno

Gramática Hay que saber bien
Nouns and articles

Nouns

What are they and when do I use them?
Nouns are words that name things, people and ideas. You use them all the time!

How do they work?
In Spanish each noun has a gender: masculine or feminine.
Generally, nouns ending in *–o* are masculine (*el libro*) and those ending in *–a* are feminine (*la casa*). However, there are exceptions which you need to learn, for example: *el día, el problema, la mano, la foto*, etc.

- There are some other endings that are generally either masculine or feminine.

  Masculine: nouns ending in: *–or* (actor, pintor), *–ón* (peatón, salchichón) and *–és* (escocés, estrés).

  Feminine: nouns ending in: *–ción* (tradición, educación), *–dad* and *–tad* (ciudad, libertad).

- To form the plural of nouns you normally add:
  –s to words ending in a vowel   *–es* to words ending in a consonant
  bolígrafo pen → *bolígrafos* pens   *actor* actor → *actores* actors

- Nouns which end in *–z* in the singular, end in *–ces* in the plural.
  vez time → *veces* times

Articles

What are they and when do I use them?
Articles are used with nouns. There are definite articles **el / la / los / las** (the) and indefinite articles **un / una** (a, an) and **unos / unas** (some).

How do they work?
In Spanish the **definite article** changes according to whether the noun is masculine or feminine, singular or plural.
el piso → **los** pisos   **la** casa → **las** casas

- The definite article is sometimes used in Spanish where we don't use it in English. You need to use it to:

  Talk about languages (except when the language comes straight after a verb):
  El inglés es fácil.   English is easy.   *Ella habla francés.*   She can speak French.

  Refer to school subjects (except when the subject comes straight after a verb):
  La geografía es genial.   Geography is great.   *Estudio religión.*   I study religion.

  Express an opinion, for example, *me gusta* or *me encanta*:
  Me gusta el pescado.   I like fish.   *Las telenovelas son aburridas.*   Soap operas are boring.

  Refer to days of the week and mean 'on...'
  Voy al cine el sábado.   I am going to the cinema on Saturday.

The **indefinite article** also changes according to whether the noun is masculine or feminine, singular or plural.
un piso   a flat   → *unos pisos*   some flats
una casa   a house → *unas casas*   some houses

- The indefinite article is sometimes not used in Spanish where we do use it in English. You do **not** need to use it when:

  You talk about jobs:
  Soy médico.   I am a doctor.

  It comes after the verb **tener** in negative sentences:
  No tengo coche.   I don't have a car.

  It comes after **sin** or **con**:
  Salí con gorra.   I went out with a cap on.
  Sin duda.   Without a doubt.

Gramática

Preparados

1 Write the plural form for each of the nouns and the correct article.

1. película (some)
2. ordenador (the)
3. montaña (the)
4. ciudad (some)
5. móvil (the)
6. recuerdo (some)
7. habitación (the)
8. secador (the)
9. lugar (some)
10. noche (the)

Listos

2 Complete these sentences with the correct article.

1. Vivo en ____ norte de Gales.
2. Veo ____ tele los sábados.
3. Nos encanta usar ____ ordenador.
4. ____ piscinas del hotel son estupendas.
5. ¿Cuánto cuesta ____ habitación doble?
6. El parador tiene ____ gimnasio pequeño y ____ cafetería bonita.
7. ____ aire acondicionado no funciona y necesito ____ secador.
8. Me interesan ____ dibujo, ____ matemáticas y ____ religión.
9. En mi insti hay ____ salón de actos, ____ laboratorios y ____ biblioteca.
10. Nos quedamos en ____ pensión en ____ centro de ____ ciudad.

¡Ya!

3 Complete these sentences with the correct article. Be careful, you may not need to use one. Then translate each sentence into English.

1. Prefiero veranear en ____ extranjero.
2. Mi madre no habla ____ francés ni ____ alemán.
3. Viajé en ____ autocar y en ____ barco.
4. Creo que ____ inglés es muy difícil.
5. Quisiera reservar ____ habitación con ____ baño.
6. Estudio ____ matemáticas, ____ español y ____ geografía.
7. ____ química es más difícil que ____ informática.
8. En mi insti no hay ____ pistas de tenis ni ____ campos de fútbol.
9. Mi novia va a ____ concierto ____ viernes.
10. ____ uniforme limita ____ individualidad, pero es ____ regla más importante del insti.

doscientos veintitrés **223**

Gramática Hay que saber bien
Adjectives

What are they and when do I use them?
Adjectives are describing words. You use them to describe a noun, a person or thing.

Why are they important?
Adjectives are important to describe things you are talking or writing about. They make your work more interesting and personal. Make sure you can use a variety of adjectives accurately.

Things to watch out for
- In Spanish adjectives have to agree with the person or thing they describe. They may have different endings in the masculine, feminine, singular and plural.
- Most Spanish adjectives come after the noun.

How do they work?
These are the common patterns of adjective endings.

adjective ending	masculine singular	feminine singular	masculine plural	feminine plural
–o	bonito	bonita	bonitos	bonitas
–e	elegante	elegante	elegantes	elegantes
–ista	pesimista	pesimista	pesimistas	pesimistas
–or	acogedor	acogedora	acogedores	acogedoras
other consonants	azul	azul	azules	azules

- Some adjectives of nationality which do not end in –o follow the same pattern as –or above.

adjective ending	masculine singular	feminine singular	masculine plural	feminine plural
–s	inglés	inglesa	ingleses	inglesas
–l	español	española	españoles	españolas
–n	alemán	alemana	alemanes	alemanas

- Some adjectives don't change and always take the masculine singular form. They are mostly colours made up of two words (*azul claro, rojo oscuro*, etc.)

- The majority of adjectives will come after the noun that they are describing.

    una chaqueta anticuada   an old-fashioned jacket
    un vestido gris   a grey dress

    When two adjectives are used to describe a noun, they can come after the noun separated by *y*.
    *Es una persona **generosa y amable.***

- However, there are a few adjectives that often come before the noun.

    mucho, bueno, malo
    primero, segundo, tercero…
    alguno, ninguno

    *No tengo **mucho** tiempo.*   I don't have a lot of time.

- Some adjectives are shortened when they come before a masculine singular noun.

bueno	good	→	buen	Hace buen tiempo.
malo	bad	→	mal	Hace mal tiempo.
primero	first	→	primer	Vivo en el primer piso.
tercero	third	→	tercer	Es el tercer hijo.
alguno	some, any	→	algún	¿Has leído algún libro interesante últimamente?
ninguno	none	→	ningún	No, no tengo ningún bolígrafo.

- ***Grande*** is shortened when it comes before both a masculine and a feminine noun.

    Es un/a gran actor/actriz.   He/She is a great actor/actress.

Gramática

Preparados

1 Choose the correct adjective.

1. Era un hotel **pequeñas / pequeña / pequeño**.
2. Nos alojamos en una pensión **caras / cara / caros**.
3. El pueblo era demasiado **turístico / turísticos / turística**.
4. Tenemos que llevar una chaqueta **negro / negra / negras**.
5. Tengo que llevar una corbata a rayas **rojos / roja / rojas**.
6. Mi profesora de empresariales es muy **severas / severos / severa**.
7. Asistimos a un **gran / grande / grandes** instituto en el centro.
8. Mi novio es **española / español / españolas**, pero vive en Inglaterra.
9. Hay unos alumnos que son muy **divertido / divertidas / divertidos**.
10. En mi insti hay una pista de tenis **nuevo / nueva / nuevas**.

Listos

2 Look at the picture and the description of this family. Put an appropriate adjective, and one that agrees with the noun, in each space.

| marrones | alto | castaña | liso | alargada | corto |
| azul | moreno | gordo | colombiana | simpáticos | |

Me llamo María, soy **1** _____ y tengo siete años. En mi familia todos tenemos el pelo **2** _____ y somos muy enérgicos. En la foto, mi madre lleva una camisa **3** _____ y mi padre tiene bigote. Mi madre tiene el pelo **4** _____ y corto, y tiene los ojos **5** _____. Mi padre no es ni **6** _____ ni bajo, y es un poco **7** _____. Mis tíos son muy **8** _____, y mi tío tiene la cara **9** _____ y el pelo **10** _____ como mi hermano. Me gusta mucho mi familia.

¡Ya!

3 Rewrite these sentences using the adjective provided. Make sure that the ending and the position of the adjective is correct.

1. Mi novio se llamaba Juan. *(primero)*
2. Me gusta leer libros. *(español)*
3. Mi prima es una persona. *(hablador)*
4. Las niñas son. *(español)*
5. Me llevo bien con mis hermanas porque son. *(fiel)*
6. Para mí, es un problema impresionante. *(serio)*
7. Me gusta mi trabajo porque tengo un jefe. *(bueno)*
8. La clase no tiene idea. *(ninguno)*
9. Vivimos en una casa. *(grande)*

doscientos veinticinco **225**

Gramática Hay que saber bien
Adverbs

What are they and when do I use them?
Adverbs are words that describe how **an action** is done (slowly, quickly, regularly, suddenly, badly, well, very…).

Why are they important?
Adverbs are important because they help you give useful information and are an easy way to extend your sentences. Using several adverbs accurately will add interest and complexity to your texts.

Things to watch out for
- Adverbs often end in **–mente** (like '**–ly**' in English).
- Some of the most useful adverbs are irregular!

How do they work?
To form a regular adverb, you add **–mente** to the feminine form of the adjective.
  lento/a   slow   →   *lent**a**mente*   slowly

- The adverbs from **bueno** (good) and **malo** (bad) are irregular and you just have to learn them.
  bien   well   *mal*   badly
- You can learn some adverbs in pairs of opposites.
  mucho   a lot   –   *poco*   a little
  aquí   here   –   *allí*   there
- Other irregular adverbs are used to describe **when** you do something (adverbs of frequency).
  siempre   always   *de vez en cuando*   from time to time
  a menudo   often   *ahora*   now
  a veces   sometimes   *ya*   already
- Adverbs usually follow the verbs they describe. However, they can come before a verb 'for emphasis'.
  *Hablamos **rápidamente**.*   We speak **quickly**.
  ***Siempre** habla en inglés.*   He **always** talks English.

Preparados

1 Change these adjectives into adverbs and translate them into English.
1. general
2. rápido
3. tranquilo
4. amable
5. sincero
6. final
7. fácil
8. feliz
9. constante
10. frecuente

Listos

2 Rewrite the sentences with the correct adverb in the correct position.
1. Ana usa el móvil en clase. *(always)*
2. Nadamos en el mar. *(slowly)*
3. Mis amigos estudian para los exámenes. *(constantly)*
4. Toco la guitarra. *(well)*
5. Mi profe siempre habla. *(calmly)*
6. Viajas en avión. *(a little)*
7. Mi padre habla francés. *(badly)*
8. Montas a caballo. *(easily)*
9. Tuvimos un pinchazo. *(unfortunately)*
10. Fueron a la comisaría. *(quickly)*

¡Ya!

3 Translate these sentences into Spanish.
1. We sometimes have a barbecue if it's sunny.
2. I quickly learned to sail.
3. Often you can see lots of boats in the port.
4. My teacher teaches well.
5. They usually leave home at eight o'clock.
6. Do you sing in the choir now?
7. I am editing my photos perfectly.
8. We look for and download music frequently.
9. I use an app to monitor my physical activity easily.
10. My friends suffer from bullying frequently.

Negatives

Which ones do I need to know?

no…	not	no … ni … ni…	neither … nor…
no … nada	nothing / not anything	no … ningún / ninguna	no / not any
no … nunca	never	no … nadie	nobody / not anybody
no … jamás	never (stronger than nunca)	tampoco	not either

How do they work?

In Spanish the simple negative is **no** and it goes immediately **before** a verb (or before a reflexive pronoun or object pronoun).

No como.	I **don't** eat.
No me levanto temprano.	I **don't** get up early.
No me dan mucho dinero.	They **don't** give me much money.

- Negative expressions go either side of the verb, forming a sandwich around it.

No compro **nada**.	I **don't** buy **anything**.
No hacemos **nunca** deporte.	We **never** do sport.
No fumo **jamás**.	I **never** smoke.
No soy **ni** alto **ni** bajo.	I **am neither** tall **nor** short.
Ella **no** tiene **ningún** libro.	She **doesn't** have **any** books.
No hablamos con **nadie**.	We **don't** speak to **anybody**.

- Sometimes, for emphasis, the negative expression can be placed before the verb and in this case *no* is not used.

Nunca vamos a ir allí.	We are **never** going to go there.
El hotel **tampoco** tenía lavandería.	The hotel **didn't** have a launderette **either**.

- **Sino** means 'but' (with the meaning 'rather' or 'instead'). **Sino** is used to connect a negative first statement with a second statement that is expressing a different opinion.

No bebo agua, **sino** zumo de naranja.	I don't drink water but orange juice.

Preparados

1 Make each statement negative and then translate it into English.

1. Mis abuelos viven en el norte del país.
2. Quiero cambiar de habitación.
3. Perdimos el equipaje en el aeropuerto.
4. Los profesores nos dan buenas estrategias.
5. Jaime se levanta a las ocho y media.
6. Mi madre me compró saldo para el móvil.

Listos

2 Put the words in the correct order to form a negative phrase.

1. a / Elena / caballo / nunca / monta
2. toco / jamás / la / no / trompeta
3. asistimos / no / a / sábados / clase / nunca / los
4. no / cubierta / el / ninguna / parador / tenía / piscina
5. compartir / no / enganchada / está / a / fotos / todavía
6. come / no / examen / un / Juan / de / nada / antes

¡Ya!

3 Match up the sentence halves and translate each sentence into English.

1. Juan no lleva…
2. La escuela primaria no tenía…
3. Ana no aprende…
4. Miguel tampoco…
5. Gabriela no escribe…
6. Antonia no hace…

a …nunca cartas, sino correos electrónicos.
b …ni laboratorios ni biblioteca ni pista de tenis.
c …ni alemán ni francés.
d …uniforme.
e …nada porque siempre está escuchando música.
f …tiene ganas de ir a un festival.

doscientos veintisiete **227**

Gramática Para sacar buena nota

Pronouns

What are they and when do I use them?
Pronouns are used in place of a noun, to avoid repeating it. Make sure the pronoun agrees with the noun it replaces!

How do they work?
- **Subject pronouns** are often only used for emphasis in Spanish, because the verb ending usually indicates who is doing the action: *yo, tú, él, ella, usted, nosotros/as, vosotros/as, ellos, ellas, ustedes*
- **Object pronouns** can be direct or indirect. They replace something or someone that has already been mentioned (e.g. Did you buy **the car**? Yes I bought **it**.)

English	direct	indirect
me	me	me
you	te	te
him/her/it	lo/la	le
us	nos	nos
you	os	os
them	los/las	les

Direct: **Lo** compré. — I bought **it**.
         Los veo allí. — I see **them** over there.

Indirect object pronouns usually have the meaning of 'to' or 'for someone' in Spanish where we wouldn't necessarily say that in English.

Indirect: **Le** compré un regalo. — I bought **him** a present. = I bought a present **for him**.
          Te voy a escribir. — I am going to write **to you**.

- Object pronouns normally go:
Before the verb:

Lo tenemos. We have **it**.   **Lo** has hecho. You have done **it**.

After the negative word:

No **lo** quiero. I don't want **it**.   Nadie **lo** estudia. Nobody studies **it**.

Attached to the end of the infinitive, gerund or imperative:

Van a hacer**lo**. They are going to do **it**.   Estoy haciéndo**lo**. I am doing **it**.
Haz**lo**. Do **it**.

Listos

1 Rewrite these sentences using direct or indirect object pronouns.

1 El profesor da el libro a Pablo.
2 Hacemos los deberes.
3 Voy a preparar la cena esta noche.
4 Mandó un correo electrónico a su jefe.
5 Reparten periódicos antes de ir al instituto.
6 Compré una gorra para mi tía.
7 Va a enseñar inglés a niños pequeños.
8 Todos los días cortamos el pelo a los clientes.
9 Nadie lava el coche en mi familia.
10 Nunca sacaba fotocopias.

¡Ya!

2 Translate these sentences into Spanish.

1 I like newspapers and I read them every day.
2 He writes to her every day.
3 I am going to send messages to you (plural).
4 My grandmother is going to give us money.
5 I told them everything.
6 It gives us the opportunity to work in Spain.
7 You are going to look after them.
8 We met him last year.
9 Do you know how to use it?

doscientos veintiocho

Connectives

Which ones do I need to know?

a pesar de	despite / in spite of	ya que	since	que	that/which
así que	so / therefore	por eso / por lo tanto	therefore	sin embargo	however
aún / aún (si)	even / even if	cuando	when	para	in order to
aunque	although	donde	where	si	if
mientras (que)	while / whilst	como	like/as		

Why are they important?
Using connectives to make extended sentences makes your speaking and writing sound more natural and adds complexity. Try to avoid just using **pero, y** and **o**.

How do they work?
- Connectives link different sentences or phrases together.

  *A las ocho voy a la cocina **donde** preparo el desayuno **mientras que** mi madre se viste.*
  At eight o'clock I go to the kitchen **where** I make breakfast **whilst** my mother gets dressed.

- Remember that **y** changes to **e** if it comes before words beginning with 'i' or 'hi' and **o** changes to **u** if it comes before words beginning with o– or ho–.

  *Estudio matemáticas **e** inglés.* I study Maths **and** English.
  *Puede ser un problema para mujeres **u** hombres.* It can be a problem for women **or** men.

Preparados

1 Complete each sentence with a different connective from the box.

o	ya que	aunque	como	cuando
si	sin embargo	por eso	mientras que	donde

1 Mi hermano puede estudiar inglés, matemáticas ___ geografía.
2 A mi amigo le encanta jugar con su ordenador ___ es divertido.
3 Vuelven a casa tarde ___ tienen actividades deportivas ___ el tenis.
4 Suelo almorzar a las doce y media ___ a veces no puedo.
5 Practican varios deportes en el instituto y ___ prefieren descansar en casa.
6 Fuimos a un restaurante peruano ___ probamos varios platos típicos.

Listos

2 Match up the sentence halves and translate each sentence into English.

1 Mi amigo nunca va al parque,…
2 Estoy en el supermercado,…
3 José juega al baloncesto…
4 Muchos extranjeros visitan España…
5 Viajábamos en coche,…
6 Iré al campo el sábado…

a …aunque tiene dos perros.
b …a pesar de ser muy bajo.
c …para disfrutar de las fiestas.
d …cuando tuvimos un pinchazo.
e …si hace buen tiempo.
f …donde voy a comprar el pescado.

¡Ya!

3 Complete the sentence with the correct connective.

1 Tengo una prima ___ habla italiano perfectamente.
2 Había mucha gente en el restaurante ___ llegamos para celebrar el cumpleaños.
3 A menudo vamos de paseo ___ hace buen tiempo.
4 Se debería usar el transporte público, ___ los autobuses o el metro.
5 Estaban en el supermercado, ___ vieron a Manuel.
6 Mi profesor de inglés es paciente, ___ se enfada a veces ___ no escuchamos.

doscientos veintinueve **229**

Gramática Para sacar buena nota

The imperfect continuous tense

What is it and when do I use it?
It describes something that **was happening** at a particular moment in the past.

Estaba trabajando en el centro cuando la tormenta de nieve azotó el pueblo.
I was working in the town centre when the snow storm hit.

Why is it important?
You need to be able to understand texts that may use this tense. In addition, using this tense in your own writing or speaking will show that you can use an excellent variety of past tenses.

Things to watch out for
In English, we do not distinguish between the imperfect and the imperfect continuous when we translate it.

Alicia **estaba leyendo / leía** un libro cuando su amigo llegó.
Alicia **was reading** a book when her friend arrived.

How does it work?
Use the imperfect tense form of the verb *estar* together with the present participle (the '–ing' form). To form the present participle, take the infinitive of the verb, remove the –*ar*, –*er* or –*ir* and add the endings: **–ando, –iendo, –iendo**.

(yo)	estaba		
(tú)	estabas		hablando
(él/ella/usted)	estaba	+	comiendo
(nosotros/as)	estábamos		saliendo
(vosotros/as)	estabais		
(ellos/ellas/ustedes)	estaban		

Estaba haciendo mis deberes cuando leí el correo.   **I was doing** my homework when I read the email.

- Remember that there are some irregular present participles to watch out for:

  dormir → durmiendo   sleeping   poder → pudiendo   being able to
  leer   → leyendo   reading   reír → riendo   laughing

Listos

1 Complete the sentences. Use the verbs in the box in the correct form of the imperfect continuous tense.

descargar	conducir	correr	dormir	enseñar
buscar	jugar	leer	trabajar	tomar

1 Mi padre ▭ por la ciudad cuando escuchó la noticia del huracán.
2 Mi madre ▭ el periódico cuando recibió un SMS de su amiga.
3 Nosotros ▭ una película cuando hubo un problema con el ordenador.
4 Mi primo ▭ información por Internet cuando le llamé.
5 José ▭ cuando se cayó en la calle y se rompió la pierna.
6 Yo ▭ como voluntario cuando decidí apuntarme a la campaña.

¡Ya!

2 Translate the sentences into Spanish.

1 I was working as a volunteer in the hospital, my brother was playing football and my sister was travelling on the bus when the storm hit.
2 We were reading and looking for information online in the school library when we heard about the earthquake in the south of the country.
3 Carla was watching the news and José was listening to music when the earthquake was felt but they were not scared.

The pluperfect tense

What is it and when do I use it?
The pluperfect tense describes what someone **had done** or what **had happened** at a particular moment in the past.

*Antes ya **había trabajado** como voluntario/a.*   **I had already worked** as a volunteer before.

Why is it important?
Using the pluperfect tense means that you can talk about events in the past in more detail. Using this tense correctly will add variety and complexity to your speaking and writing.

How does it work?
The pluperfect tense is formed using the imperfect tense of the verb **haber** followed by the past participle of a verb.
Remember that the past participle is formed by taking the infinitive, removing the –ar, –er or –ir and adding **–ado** for –ar verbs (hablado, comprado, etc.) and **–ido** for –er and –ir verbs (bebido, vivido, etc.).

(yo)	había		
(tú)	habías		hablado
(él/ella/usted)	había	+	comido
(nosotros/as)	habíamos		salido
(vosotros/as)	habíais		
(ellos/ellas/ustedes)	habían		

*Marta **había conocido** a mucha gente durante el evento deportivo.*
Marta **had made** many friends during the sporting event.

See page 219 for irregular past participles.

- Remember that nothing comes between the part of the verb **haber** and the past participle. All negatives and pronouns (reflexive, object, etc.) come before **haber**.

*No **me habían dado** el uniforme correcto.*   **They hadn't given me** the correct uniform.

Listos

1 Insert the correct form of the verb to make these sentences pluperfect.

1. Mi abuela ya ▭ en el sector de la hostelería. *(trabajar)*
2. Mi amigo y yo nunca ▭ un proyecto de conservación. *(hacer)*
3. La empresa multinacional ▭ demasiada agua. *(malgastar)*
4. Mi instituto ya ▭ dinero para organizaciones de caridad. *(recaudar)*
5. El gobierno no ▭ suficientes casas en los últimos años. *(construir)*
6. Nunca ▭ tan fácil encontrar oportunidades para cuidar el medio ambiente. *(ser)*

¡Ya!

2 Translate these sentences into Spanish.

1. I had already visited many cities in Spain.
2. They had already worked as volunteers during the Olympics in London.
3. Sara had wanted to be a tourist guide but she did not speak English or French.
4. My grandparents had spoken about the floods that left thousands of people homeless.
5. I had already read the book about the dangerous tornado in Mexico but I had not seen the film.
6. We had already been to the restaurant to eat meatballs when we arrived at the cinema.

doscientos treinta y uno

Gramática Hay que saber bien
The passive

What is it and when do I use it?
The passive is used to describe something that is/was/will be done to something or someone. The object becomes the subject of the sentence:

my teacher wrote the text → the text was written by my teacher.
subject   object

*El texto **fue escrito** por mi profesor(a).*   The text **was written** by my teacher.
*La comida italiana **es conocida** en todo el mundo.*   Italian food **is known** throughout the world.

Why is it important?
You may want to use the passive when describing events and you need to be able to understand it in spoken and written texts.

Things to watch out for
English uses the passive more often than Spanish. In Spanish, when you don't know who or what has done the action, the passive is often avoided. For example, you can use the passive to translate this sentence:

English **is spoken** by lots of people. → *El inglés **es hablado** por mucha gente.*

However, if you do not know who has done the action, then you can avoid the passive. You do this by using the pronoun *se*:

English **is spoken**. → ***Se habla** inglés.*

How does it work?
To form the passive, you use the correct tense of the verb ***ser***, followed by the past participle (see page 219). Note that the past participle must agree in number and gender with the object.

*Los tomates **serán lanzados** por muchísimos turistas.*   **The tomatoes will be thrown** by many tourists.

Listos

1 Avoid the passive! Use the reflexive pronoun *se* with the correct form of a suitable verb from the box.

| celebrar | repetir | lanzar | hablar | desenchufar | disparar |

1 The event is celebrated in the Summer. – ▢ el evento en verano.
2 Fireworks are set off. – ▢ fuegos artificiales.
3 Eggs are thrown. – ▢ huevos.
4 The procession is repeated every year. – Cada año ▢ el desfile.
5 Spanish is spoken in Bolivia. – En Bolivia ▢ español.
6 Electrical devices are unplugged. – ▢ los aparatos eléctricos.

¡Ya!

2 Make a list of all the passive phrases or phrases that avoid using the passive, and their meanings. Then translate the whole text into English.

El Carnaval de Cádiz es conocido mundialmente por ser una fiesta 'de la calle'. Son muchos días de baile, música, teatro y, sobre todo, participación popular. La ciudad entera se llena de gente que sale a reír, a cantar y, en definitiva, a pasarlo bien. Se realizan dos cabalgatas y el público se convierte en un desfile multicolor. Las canciones se oyen por toda la ciudad durante las celebraciones. También se disparan muchos fuegos artificiales y hay muchísimas actividades que contribuyen a la diversión de la gente. Toda la ciudad se transforma en una fiesta increíble.

Gramática Para sacar buena nota
The imperative

What is it and when do I use it?
The imperative is a form of the verb that is used to give commands and instructions ('Go to sleep!', 'Don't do that!').

How does it work?
The imperative has a different form depending on whether the command is positive ('Sit down!') or negative ('Don't sit down!') and who is receiving it.

Positive imperatives
- The positive imperative for one person (*tú*) is formed by removing the **–s** from the *tú* form of the verb.
  girar → (tú) giras → ¡Gira!   Turn! (you)   coger → (tú) coges → ¡Coge!   Catch! (you)
- These verbs have irregular imperatives in the *tú* form:
  decir → di   say   salir → sal   go / get out
  hacer → haz   do   tener → ten   have
  ir → ve   go   venir → ven   come
  poner → pon   put
- The positive imperative for more than one person (*vosotros/as*) is formed by taking the infinitive and changing the **–r** to a **–d**.
  tomar → ¡Tomad!   Take! (you plural)
- A formal command is given using the present subjunctive. (See page 234)
  tomar → ¡Tome!   Take! (you polite)   comer → ¡Coman!   Eat! (you polite plural)

Negative imperatives
- You use the present subjunctive form for all negative commands. (See page 234 on the present subjunctive for more information on how to form this tense.)
  pasar → ¡No pas**es**!   Don't pass! (you)   seguir → ¡No sig**áis**!   Don't follow! (you plural)
  coger → ¡No coj**as**!   Don't take! (you)   girar → ¡No gir**en**!   Don't turn! (you polite plural)
  cruzar → ¡No cruc**e**!   Don't cross! (you polite)

Preparados

1 Make these statements into *tú* commands.

1 ___ la segunda calle a la derecha. *(tomar)*
2 ___ el buen tiempo. *(aprovechar)*
3 ___ más despacio. *(comer)*
4 ___ los semáforos. *(pasar)*
5 ___ español, por favor. *(hablar)*
6 ___ algo. *(decir)*

Listos

2 Make these statements into *vosotros/as* commands. Then translate each one into English.

1 ___ la primera calle a la derecha. *(tomar)*
2 ___ a la izquierda. *(girar)*
3 ___ el puente. *(pasar)*
4 ___ a la torre. *(subir)*
5 ¡___ cuidado! *(tener)*
6 ___ la calle. *(cruzar)*

¡Ya!

Use the present subjunctive to make formal commands and negative commands. Then translate each one into English.

1 ___ los semáforos. *(pasa, usted)*
2 No ___ el autobús número 39. *(coger, tú)*
3 ___ más bosques y selvas. *(plantar, usted)*
4 No ___ tantos árboles. *(cortar, vosotros/as)*
5 No ___ la selva. *(destruir, ustedes)*
6 No ___ basura al suelo. *(tirar, tú)*

doscientos treinta y tres

Gramática Para sacar buena nota

The present subjunctive

What is it and when do I use it?
The present subjunctive is a form of the verb which we do not really use anymore in English but which is used a lot in Spanish. The subjunctive has to be used:

- After the word **cuando** when talking about the future.
  *Cuando **sea** mayor, me tomaré un año sabático.*   When **I am** older, I will take a gap year.
- With negative commands and formal commands (*usted/ustedes*). See page 233 for more information.
- After feelings which use the structure *es* + adjective + *que*:
  Es esencial que… / Es importante que… / Es necesario que… / No es justo que…
  *Es importante que no **malgastemos** la energía.*   It's important that **we** do not **waste** energy.
- After verbs of wishing, command, request and emotion and to express purpose, e.g. *querer, pedir*, etc.
  *Quiero que **escuches**.*   I want **you** to **listen**.
  *Piden que no **hagamos** tanto ruido.*   They ask that **we** don't **make** so much noise.
  *Me alegro que **estés** aquí.*   I'm glad **you're** here.
- After the expression *ojalá*.
  *Ojalá **haga** sol.*   Let's hope **it is** sunny.

Why is it important?
Knowing some of the situations in which you use the subjunctive will allow you to be more accurate in your communication in Spanish. If you can use it correctly in your GCSE, it will impress your examiner and add complexity to your speaking and writing.

Things to watch out for
As English no longer uses the subjunctive, it won't come naturally to you. If you want to use it successfully you must learn by heart the situations when you will need it.

How does it work?
To form the present subjunctive, take the first person singular (*yo*) of the present tense, remove the final *–o* and add these endings.

	hablar (to talk)	**comer** (to eat)	**vivir** (to live)
(yo)	hable	coma	viva
(tú)	hables	comas	vivas
(él/ella/usted)	hable	coma	viva
(nosotros/as)	hablemos	comamos	vivamos
(vosotros/as)	habléis	comáis	viváis
(ellos/ellas/ustedes)	hablen	coman	vivan

If the first person singular (*yo*) is irregular, the subjunctive will take the same form, for example, *hago – haga*. There are some irregular present subjunctive verbs:

ir → vaya, vayas, vaya, …   *ser* → sea, seas, sea, …   *hay* → haya

doscientos treinta y cuatro

The present subjunctive

Preparados

1 Complete these sentences with the correct present subjunctive form of a suitable verb from the box.

| trabajar | tener | aprobar | ser | terminar | ganar | enamorarse |

1. Cuando yo ____ este curso, iré a otro insti.
2. Cuando mi mejor amigo ____ mayor, trabajará como médico.
3. Cuando nosotros ____ bastante dinero, compraremos un piso.
4. Cuando yo ____, me casaré.
5. Cuando mi hermano ____ dieciocho años, hará formación profesional.
6. Cuando los alumnos ____ los exámenes, podrán apuntarse a los cursos.

Listos

2 Complete each of the sentences with the correct present subjunctive verb. Then translate them into English.

1. Es importante que mis amigos no ____. *(fumar)*
2. Cuando ____ a España, compraré un abanico bonito. *(ir)*
3. No quiero que mis profesores ____ antipáticos. *(ser)*
4. Ojalá tú ____ venir conmigo a la disco. *(poder)*
5. Pedimos que nuestro barrio ____ un polideportivo nuevo. *(tener)*
6. No es justo que Juan no ____ trabajo como voluntario. *(encontrar)*

¡Ya!

3 Translate this text into Spanish. Watch out for the underlined verbs that need to be in the present subjunctive!

When I finish my exams, I am going to learn to drive and then I will look for a job. I don't think that it is easy to find work at the moment but let's see. Let's hope I am successful! I also want to share a flat with some friends when I earn enough money. It is important that the flat has a big kitchen because I love cooking.

Gramática Para sacar buena nota

The imperfect subjunctive

What is it and when do I use it?
The imperfect subjunctive is a past form of the verb which is not really used anymore in English but which is used a lot in Spanish.

You use the imperfect subjunctive as the past tense equivalent of the present subjunctive (see page 234). You also need to use it when you use an **'if' clause** in the past tense that also requires the conditional tense.

Si **tuviera** dinero, visitaría Latinoamérica.   If **I had** money, I would visit Latin America.
  ↑   ↑
  imperfect subjunctive   conditional tense

Si **pudiera** tomarme un año sabático, trabajaría en un orfanato.

If **I could** take a gap year, I would work in an orphanage.

Si **fuéramos** ricos, compraríamos una casa grande en el centro de la ciudad.

If **we were** rich, we would buy a big house in the city centre.

Why is it important?
Learning and using some phrases in the imperfect subjunctive in your writing or speaking will add complexity and grammatical variety to your work. You may also need to recognise it to fully understand a spoken or written text.

Things to watch out for
You will need to know the preterite tense thoroughly to form this correctly!

How does it work?
To form the imperfect subjunctive, take the third person plural of the preterite tense (*ellos/ellas*), remove the final *–ron* and add these endings:

	hablar (to talk)	**comer** (to eat)	**vivir** (to live)
(yo)	habla**ra**	comie**ra**	vivie**ra**
(tú)	habla**ras**	comie**ras**	vivie**ras**
(él/ella/usted)	habla**ra**	comie**ra**	vivie**ra**
(nosotros/as)	hablá**ramos**	comié**ramos**	vivié**ramos**
(vosotros/as)	habla**rais**	comie**rais**	vivie**rais**
(ellos/ellas/ustedes)	habla**ran**	comie**ran**	vivie**ran**

- If the third person plural of the preterite tense (*ellos/ellas*) is irregular, the subjunctive will take the same form, for example:

  hicieron → hiciera   fueron → fuera

Listos

1 Change these verbs from the infinitive to the 'I' (*yo*) form of the imperfect subjunctive (using the third person plural of the preterite tense).

1 ser   **2** poder   **3** tener   **4** ir   **5** estudiar   **6** hacer

¡Ya!

2 Translate these sentences into English.

1 Si yo pudiera tomarme un año sabático, trabajaría como voluntario.
2 Si tuviéramos bastante dinero, viajaríamos con mochila por el mundo.
3 Si pudieran viajar a Colombia, ayudarían a construir un colegio nuevo.
4 Si tuvieras más tiempo, ¿qué te gustaría hacer?
5 Si Carlota ganara más dinero, viviría más cerca de sus padres.
6 ¡Si yo estudiara cada día, aprobaría todos mis exámenes!

Verb tables

> ⭐ These verbs are continued overleaf. →

infinitive		pronouns (only include for emphasis)	present	future	conditional	preterite
hablar – to speak (regular –ar verb)	I you he/she/you (polite) we you (plural) they/you (polite plural)	yo tú él/ella/usted nosotros/as vosotros/as ellos/ellas/ustedes	hablo hablas habla hablamos habláis hablan	hablaré hablarás hablará hablaremos hablaréis hablarán	hablaría hablarías hablaría hablaríamos hablaríais hablarían	hablé hablaste habló hablamos hablasteis hablaron
comer – to eat (regular –er verb)	I you he/she/you (polite) we you (plural) they/you (polite plural)	yo tú él/ella/usted nosotros/as vosotros/as ellos/ellas/ustedes	como comes come comemos coméis comen	comeré comerás comerá comeremos comeréis comerán	comería comerías comería comeríamos comeríais comerían	comí comiste comió comimos comisteis comieron
vivir – to live (regular –ir verb)	I you he/she/you (polite) we you (plural) they/you (polite plural)	yo tú él/ella/usted nosotros/as vosotros/as ellos/ellas/ustedes	vivo vives vive vivimos vivís viven	viviré vivirás vivirá viviremos viviréis vivirán	viviría vivirías viviría viviríamos viviríais vivirían	viví viviste vivió vivimos vivisteis vivieron
dar – to give	I you he/she/you (polite) we you (plural) they/you (polite plural)	yo tú él/ella/usted nosotros/as vosotros/as ellos/ellas/ustedes	**doy** das da damos **dais** dan	daré darás dará daremos daréis darán	daría darías daría daríamos daríais darían	**di** **diste** **dio** **dimos** **disteis** **dieron**
decir – to say	I you he/she/you (polite) we you (plural) they/you (polite plural)	yo tú él/ella/usted nosotros/as vosotros/as ellos/ellas/ustedes	**digo** **dices** **dice** decimos decís **dicen**	**diré** **dirás** **dirá** **diremos** **diréis** **dirán**	**diría** **dirías** **diría** **diríamos** **diríais** **dirían**	**dije** **dijiste** **dijo** **dijimos** **dijisteis** **dijeron**
estar – to be	I you he/she/you (polite) we you (plural) they/you (polite plural)	yo tú él/ella/usted nosotros/as vosotros/as ellos/ellas/ustedes	**estoy** **estás** **está** estamos estáis **están**	estaré estarás estará estaremos estaréis estarán	estaría estarías estaría estaríamos estaríais estarían	**estuve** **estuviste** **estuvo** **estuvimos** **estuvisteis** **estuvieron**
hacer – to do / make	I you he/she/you (polite) we you (plural) they/you (polite plural)	yo tú él/ella/usted nosotros/as vosotros/as ellos/ellas/ustedes	**hago** haces hace hacemos hacéis hacen	**haré** **harás** **hará** **haremos** **haréis** **harán**	**haría** **harías** **haría** **haríamos** **haríais** **harían**	**hice** **hiciste** **hizo** **hicimos** **hicisteis** **hicieron**
ir – to go	I you he/she/you (polite) we you (plural) they/you (polite plural)	yo tú él/ella/usted nosotros/as vosotros/as ellos/ellas/ustedes	**voy** **vas** **va** **vamos** **vais** **van**	iré irás irá iremos iréis irán	iría irías iría iríamos iríais irían	**fui** **fuiste** **fue** **fuimos** **fuisteis** **fueron**

doscientos treinta y siete

Verb tables

	pronouns (only include for emphasis)	imperfect	gerund (for present and imperfect continuous tenses)	past participle	present subjunctive	imperative
hablar (continued)	yo tú él/ella/usted nosotros/as vosotros/as ellos/ellas /ustedes	hablaba hablabas hablaba hablábamos hablabais hablaban	hablando	hablado	hable hables hable hablemos habléis hablen	habla (tú) hablad (vosotros/as)
comer (continued)	yo tú él/ella/usted nosotros/as vosotros/as ellos/ellas/ustedes	comía comías comía comíamos comíais comían	comiendo	comido	coma comas coma comamos comáis coman	come (tú) comed (vosotros/as)
vivir (continued)	yo tú él/ella/usted nosotros/as vosotros/as ellos/ellas/ustedes	vivía vivías vivía vivíamos vivíais vivían	viviendo	vivido	viva vivas viva vivamos viváis vivan	vive (tú) vivid (vosotros/as)
dar (continued)	yo tú él/ella/usted nosotros/as vosotros/as ellos/ellas/ustedes	daba dabas daba dábamos dabais daban	dando	dado	dé des dé demos deis den	da (tú) dad (vosotros/as)
decir (continued)	yo tú él/ella/usted nosotros/as vosotros/as ellos/ellas/ustedes	decía decías decía decíamos decíais decían	**diciendo**	**dicho**	**diga digas diga digamos digáis digan**	**di** (tú) decid (vosotros/as)
estar (continued)	yo tú él/ella/usted nosotros/as vosotros/as ellos/ellas/ustedes	estaba estabas estaba estábamos estabais estaban	estando	estado	**esté estés esté** estemos estéis **estén**	**está** (tú) estad (vosotros/as)
hacer (continued)	yo tú él/ella/usted nosotros/as vosotros/as ellos/ellas/ustedes	hacía hacías hacía hacíamos hacíais hacían	haciendo	**hecho**	**haga hagas haga hagamos hagáis hagan**	**haz** (tú) haced (vosotros/as)
ir (continued)	yo tú él/ella/usted nosotros/as vosotros/as ellos/ellas/ustedes	**iba ibas iba íbamos ibais iban**	yendo	ido	**vaya vayas vaya vayamos vayáis vayan**	**ve** (tú) id (vosotros/as)

Verb tables

> ⭐ These verbs are continued overleaf. →

infinitive		pronouns (only include for emphasis)	present	future	conditional	preterite
poder – to be able to	I you he/she/you (polite) we you (plural) they/you (polite plural)	yo tú él/ella/usted nosotros/as vosotros/as ellos/ellas/ustedes	**puedo** **puedes** **puede** podemos podéis **pueden**	**podré** **podrás** **podrá** **podremos** **podréis** **podrán**	**podría** **podrías** **podría** **podríamos** **podríais** **podrían**	**pude** **pudiste** **pudo** **pudimos** **pudisteis** **pudieron**
poner – to put	I you he/she/you (polite) we you (plural) they/you (polite plural)	yo tú él/ella/usted nosotros/as vosotros/as ellos/ellas/ustedes	**pongo** pones pone ponemos ponéis ponen	**pondré** **pondrás** **pondrá** **pondremos** **pondréis** **pondrán**	**pondría** **pondrías** **pondría** **pondríamos** **pondríais** **pondrían**	**puse** **pusiste** **puso** **pusimos** **pusisteis** **pusieron**
querer – to want / love	I you he/she/you (polite) we you (plural) they/you (polite plural)	yo tú él/ella/usted nosotros/as vosotros/as ellos/ellas/ustedes	**quiero** **quieres** **quiere** queremos queréis **quieren**	**querré** **querrás** **querrá** **querremos** **querréis** **querrán**	**querría** **querrías** **querría** **querríamos** **querríais** **querrían**	**quise** **quisiste** **quiso** **quisimos** **quisisteis** **quisieron**
salir – to go out	I you he/she/you (polite) we you (plural) they/you (polite plural)	yo tú él/ella/usted nosotros/as vosotros/as ellos/ellas/ustedes	**salgo** sales sale salimos salís salen	**saldré** **saldrás** **saldrá** **saldremos** **saldréis** **saldrán**	**saldría** **saldrías** **saldría** **saldríamos** **saldríais** **saldrían**	salí saliste salió salimos salisteis salieron
ser – to be	I you he/she/you (polite) we you (plural) they/you (polite plural)	yo tú él/ella/usted nosotros/as vosotros/as ellos/ellas/ustedes	**soy** **eres** **es** **somos** **sois** **son**	seré serás será seremos seréis serán	sería serías sería seríamos seríais serían	**fui** **fuiste** **fue** **fuimos** **fuisteis** **fueron**
tener – to have	I you he/she/you (polite) we you (plural) they/you (polite plural)	yo tú él/ella/usted nosotros/as vosotros/as ellos/ellas/ustedes	**tengo** **tienes** **tiene** tenemos tenéis **tienen**	**tendré** **tendrás** **tendrá** **tendremos** **tendréis** **tendrán**	**tendría** **tendrías** **tendría** **tendríamos** **tendríais** **tendrían**	**tuve** **tuviste** **tuvo** **tuvimos** **tuvisteis** **tuvieron**
venir – to come	I you he/she/you (polite) we you (plural) they/you (polite plural)	yo tú él/ella/usted nosotros/as vosotros/as ellos/ellas/ustedes	**vengo** **vienes** **viene** venimos venís **vienen**	**vendré** **vendrás** **vendrá** **vendremos** **vendréis** **vendrán**	**vendría** **vendrías** **vendría** **vendríamos** **vendríais** **vendrían**	**vine** **viniste** **vino** **vinimos** **vinisteis** **vinieron**
ver – to see	I you he/she/you (polite) we you (plural) they/you (polite plural)	yo tú él/ella/usted nosotros/as vosotros/as ellos/ellas/ustedes	**veo** ves ve vemos **veis** ven	veré verás verá veremos veréis verán	vería verías vería veríamos veríais verían	**vi** viste **vio** vimos visteis vieron

doscientos treinta y nueve

Verb tables

	pronouns (only include for emphasis)	imperfect	gerund (for present and imperfect continuous tenses)	past participle	present subjunctive	imperative
poder (continued)	yo tú él/ella/usted nosotros/as vosotros/as ellos/ellas/ustedes	podía podías podía podíamos podíais podían	**pudiendo**	podido	**pueda puedas pueda** podamos podáis **puedan**	**puede** (tú) poded (vosotros/as)
poner (continued)	yo tú él/ella/usted nosotros/as vosotros/as ellos/ellas/ustedes	ponía ponías ponía poníamos poníais ponían	poniendo	**puesto**	**ponga pongas ponga pongamos pongáis pongan**	**pon** (tú) poned (vosotros/as)
querer (continued)	yo tú él/ella/usted nosotros/as vosotros/as ellos/ellas/ustedes	quería querías quería queríamos queríais querían	queriendo	querido	**quiera quieras quiera** queramos queráis **quieran**	**quiere** (tú) quered (vosotros)
salir (continued)	yo tú él/ella/usted nosotros/as vosotros/as ellos/ellas/ustedes	salía salías salía salíamos salíais salían	saliendo	salido	**salga salgas salga salgamos salgáis salgan**	**sal** (tú) salid (vosotros/as)
ser (continued)	yo tú él/ella/usted nosotros/as vosotros/as ellos/ellas/ustedes	**era eras era éramos erais eran**	siendo	sido	**sea seas sea seamos seáis sean**	**sé** (tú) sed (vosotros/as)
tener (continued)	yo tú él/ella/usted nosotros/as vosotros/as ellos/ellas/ustedes	tenía tenías tenía teníamos teníais tenían	teniendo	tenido	**tenga tengas tenga tengamos tengáis tengan**	**ten** (tú) tened (vosotros/as)
venir (continued)	yo tú él/ella/usted nosotros/as vosotros/as ellos/ellas/ustedes	venía venías venía veníamos veníais venían	**viniendo**	venido	**venga vengas venga vengamos vengáis vengan**	**ven** (tú) venid (vosotros/as)
ver (continued)	yo tú él/ella/usted nosotros/as vosotros/as ellos/ellas/ustedes	**veía veías veía veíamos veíais veían**	viendo	**visto**	**vea veas vea veamos veáis vean**	ve (tú) ved (vosotros/as)